A Reader's Guide to the Novels of *Louise Erdrich*

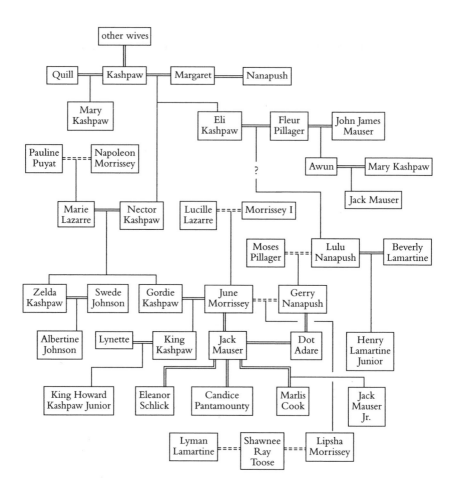

The relationships of some of the central characters in Louise Erdrich's interconnected novels. This chart is designed to give a broad overview of the family connections among important characters in Erdrich's novels that are set mostly in North Dakota. Some relationships are not shown because to do so would greatly complicate the chart. For example, this chart does not show that Lyman Lamartine is the child of Lulu Nanapush and Nector Kashpaw or that Margaret, Marie, and Lulu all have children other than those indicated. For such details, see the thirty individual family charts in Part I. Also because of the complexity of these genealogies, the names of Mary Kashpaw and Jack Mauser appear twice. Unbroken double lines (═══) indicate either Indian or Western marriages; broken double lines (════) indicate nonmarital sexual liaisons; and single lines (───) indicate children resulting from these unions.

A Reader's Guide

to the Novels of

Louise Erdrich

Revised and Expanded Edition

Peter G. Beidler

AND

Gay Barton

University of Missouri Press   *Columbia and London*

Copyright © 2006 by
The Curators of the University of Missouri
University of Missouri Press, Columbia, Missouri 65201
Printed and bound in the United States of America
All rights reserved
5 4 3 2 1   10 09 08 07 06

Library of Congress Cataloging-in-Publication Data

Beidler, Peter G.
    A reader's guide to the novels of Louise Erdrich / Peter G. Beidler
and Gay Barton. — Rev. and expanded ed.
        p.   cm.
    Summary: "A revised and expanded, comprehensive guide to the
novels of Native American author Louise Erdrich from Love Medicine to
The Painted Drum. Includes chronologies, genealogical charts, complete
dictionary of characters, map and geographical details about settings, and
a glossary of all the Ojibwe words and phrases used in the novels"
—Provided by publisher.
    Includes bibliographical references and index.
    ISBN-13: 978-0-8262-1670-0 (alk. paper)
    ISBN-13: 978-0-8262-1671-7 (pbk : alk. paper)
    ISBN-10: 0-8262-1670-6 (alk. paper)
    ISBN-10: 0-8262-1671-4 (pbk : alk. paper)
    1. Erdrich, Louise—Characters—Handbooks, manuals, etc.
2. Erdrich, Louise—Stories, plots, etc.—Handbooks, manuals, etc.
3. Indians in literature—Handbooks, manuals, etc. I. Barton, Gay, 1946–
II. Title.
    PS3555.R42Z59   2006
    813'.54—dc22
                                                            2006010717

♾ ™ This paper meets the requirements of the
American National Standard for Permanence of Paper
for Printed Library Materials, Z39.48, 1984.

Text Design: Elizabeth K. Young
Jacket Design: Susan Ferber
Typesetter: Bookcomp, Inc.
Printer and binder: The Maple-Vail Book Manufacturing Group
Typefaces: Bembo, Helvetica

Once again for Louise,
who drew us into her worlds
and who continues to astonish us
with each new novel

Contents

Preface to the Revised and Expanded Edition

This second edition of *A Reader's Guide to the Novels of Louise Erdrich* is called for on two accounts. First, the original edition, in both cloth and paper, has sold out, indicating that it has served a need for the growing number of Erdrich aficionados. Second and more important, in just seven years the first edition has become out of date because during that period Louise Erdrich has published four more novels, and the scholarship on her work has become even more voluminous.

This new edition continues and updates the features that made the first edition so helpful to its users: the section on the geography of the novels, the genealogical charts that help readers grasp complicated family relationships in each novel, the chronological summaries of the main events in each novel, the comprehensive dictionary of characters that summarizes the lives and doings of the many men, women, and even dogs that populate Erdrich's novels, and the bibliography of scholarship.

New to this edition is information on the four new novels published since the first edition was released: *The Last Report on the Miracles at Little No Horse* (2001), *The Master Butchers Singing Club* (2003), *Four Souls* (2004), and *The Painted Drum* (2005). Also new is a listing of the tables of contents for all ten novels, including page numbers, for easy reference. Half of these are newly constructed since in her most recent novels Erdrich does not provide tables of contents. An important all-new addition to this second edition is the glossary translating into English all of the Ojibwe words, phrases, and sentences that Erdrich has used in the ten novels.

Acknowledgments

We are grateful to four graduate students at Baylor University for bringing together the initial information for the dictionary entries on several of the characters as they appeared in Louise Erdrich's first four novels: Jennifer Alston, Alan C. Jones, Katerina Prajznerová, and Alisan Stevenson. We subsequently revised and expanded these entries to fit the style and scope of this book. L. Tamara Kendig, William A. Meiers, and Harry J. Brown also helped. We are grateful to Trent Duffy, copyeditor for Louise Erdrich at HarperCollins, who kindly offered to check an early draft of the manuscript for the first edition. He called to our attention a number of large and small matters that we had missed or misunderstood.

We are also happy to acknowledge help with this revised edition. Particularly deserving of mention are two present or former graduate students at Lehigh University: Patricia M. Engle, who drafted much of the material on the *Master Butchers Singing Club,* and Robert A. Wilson, who helped to expand the bibliography section. We also express our thanks to Kathy Bennett, who created the index. We want also to thank Clair Willcox of the University of Missouri Press for his enthusiasm about our doing an updated edition and Julie Schroeder for her careful copyediting of both the first and this second edition. Finally, we want to acknowledge the help that Louise Erdrich herself gave on early versions of the glossary of Ojibwe words, phrases, and sentences, which is an entirely new feature of this second edition.

PGB and GB

Abbreviations

Throughout this book, we use the following abbreviations in our parenthetical citations from Erdrich's novels. Full references to the novels are located in our bibliography. Thus far, all editions match the pagination of the editions cited there.

AW	*The Antelope Wife*
BP	*The Bingo Palace*
BQ	*The Beet Queen*
FS	*Four Souls*
LM	*Love Medicine* (we cite the new and expanded edition of 1993)
LR	*The Last Report on the Miracles at Little No Horse*
MBSC	*The Master Butchers Singing Club*
PD	*The Painted Drum*
TBL	*Tales of Burning Love*
Tr	*Tracks*

A Reader's Guide to the Novels of *Louise Erdrich*

Introduction

Louise Erdrich is one of the most important Native American writers of the past twenty years and one of the most accomplished and promising novelists of any heritage now working in the United States. Her fiction has won many awards and has attracted a devoted readership among lay as well as academic readers.

The daughter of Chippewa (Ojibwe) and German parents, Erdrich was born on June 7, 1954, in Minnesota.[1] She is related through her Chippewa/French mother to Kaishpau Gourneau, who in 1882 became the head of the Turtle Mountain Band of Chippewa. An enrolled member of the North Dakota Turtle Mountain Chippewas, Erdrich spent much of her youth in Wahpeton, North Dakota, where her parents taught at a Bureau of Indian Affairs school. Her mother and father encouraged her, even as a small child, to write stories.

In 1972 Erdrich entered Dartmouth College, where she met Michael Dorris, a mixed-blood of Modoc descent, who had just become an assistant

---

1. The terms *Chippewa* and *Ojibwe* (also spelled *Ojibway* and *Ojibwa*) are virtually interchangeable. Both are European renderings of a native word, sometimes transcribed as *Otchipwe*, about whose meaning scholars disagree (see Gerald Vizenor, *The People Named the Chippewa* [Minneapolis: University of Minnesota Press, 1984], 17–19). In his *A Dictionary of the Otchipwe Language* (Cincinnati: Hemann, 1853; facsimile, 1970), the nineteenth-century missionary and lexicographer Frederic Baraga rendered the word as "Chippewa." Twentieth-century anthropologists have preferred some form of "Ojibwa" (see Victoria Brehm, "The Metamorphoses of an Ojibwa *Manido*," 699n1). The term by which this people has traditionally referred to itself is *Anishinabe* (or *Anishinaabe*, "person"; plural, *Anishinaabeg*). (This and subsequent Ojibwe definitions are from either John D. Nichols and Earl Nyholm, *A Concise Dictionary of Minnesota Ojibwe* [Minneapolis: University of Minnesota Press, 1995], or Basil Johnston, *Ojibway Language Lexicon for Beginners* [Ottawa: Indian and Northern Affairs Canada, 1978].)

In modern times, different bands of the Anishinaabeg have often adopted either the name Chippewa or Ojibwa. In her interviews, Erdrich uses both words but tends to refer to her own family heritage as Chippewa. This is also the term used most often in her first five novels. The narrators of *The Antelope Wife*, set primarily in Minneapolis, favor the word Ojibwa. In more recent novels, however, Erdrich fairly consistently uses the spelling Ojibwe, and in doing so follows the majority of contemporary writers and linguists. We have in this volume used the latter spelling except where we are citing a title or quotation that gives a different spelling.

professor of anthropology. Eventually they fell in love and married. Dorris had already adopted three Indian children, and together they had three more children. Erdrich and Dorris encouraged and helped each other with their writing, coauthored two books (*The Crown of Columbus* and *Route Two* [both 1991]), and dedicated several of their works to one another. They seemed, for a time, an ideal Native American couple. They gave a large number of interviews, many of which were published. Their marriage eventually disintegrated, however, and Dorris committed suicide in April 1997. Since then Erdrich has had another child.

Erdrich is an unusually prolific and versatile writer. She writes essays, poetry, personal reflections and narratives, and children's books, some of which she illustrates herself. (A complete list of her books appears in the bibliography at the end of this volume.) Erdrich is best known, however, for her stories and novels. Her stories appear frequently in distinguished magazines like the *New Yorker,* and her novels follow one another with the regularity of a summer sunrise. These stories and novels have earned for her a steadily growing readership, and her reputation as a fiction writer is now more firmly established than ever. By 2005 she had published ten novels set in North Dakota or Minnesota: *Love Medicine* (1984, 1993), *The Beet Queen* (1986), *Tracks* (1988), *The Bingo Palace* (1994), *Tales of Burning Love* (1996), *The Antelope Wife* (1998), *The Last Report on the Miracles at Little No Horse* (2001), *The Master Butchers Singing Club* (2003), *Four Souls* (2004), and *The Painted Drum* (2005).

Erdrich's skill in creating and developing fictional characters is a central aspect of her success as a writer. She can fruitfully be compared with William Faulkner, who peopled the imaginary Yoknapatawpha County in Mississippi with a rich variety of men and women of several races and generations. Like Faulkner, Erdrich has created imaginary landscapes. Her most famous landscape is centered in a fictional North Dakota Ojibwe reservation that, in her seventh novel, she names Little No Horse. Some of her fiction is set in the city of Minneapolis. She peoples these landscapes with a varied, multigenerational group of men and women of white, Indian, and mixed-blood heritage.

Erdrich's narrative technique is equally skillful. She handles multiple points of view, intertextual allusion, and temporal dislocation with skill rivaling that of the best of modern and postmodern writers of the Western tradition. At the same time, she weaves these techniques seamlessly with narrative elements from the Ojibwe oral tradition.

Reviewers are typically enthusiastic, if not downright ecstatic, about

Erdrich's fiction. They hail her as a bright new light—a courageous writer willing to break new narratological ground, a stunningly effective stylist, and a woman who courageously confronts the realities of Native American life in the twentieth century. Yet the depth of characterization and narrative scope that critics praise sometimes render her fiction bewildering. The bewilderment is especially troubling for readers who pick up her books out of sequence, or who, if they have read earlier works, do not remember who the characters are or what they did in previous novels. Even reviewers, who are typically careful and informed readers, at times find themselves perplexed by Erdrich's characters and story lines. The following quotations from reviews and articles illustrate that perplexity:

> I found *Love Medicine* a hard book to penetrate. The episodes, most of them dramatic monologues, are loosely strung together and the relationships of the various narrators and characters are so confusing that one must constantly flip back to earlier sections in an effort to get one's bearings. —Robert Towers[2]

> *The Bingo Palace* is thick with characters from Erdrich's previous books and loaded with background. . . . The string of begats and the tangled skeins of relationships are so complex that they make the reader wish that instead of giving us a first chapter that is less drama than summary, Erdrich had simply provided a genealogical chart. —Kit Reed[3]

> At first, the structure of *Tales of Burning Love* seems as shaggy and chaotic as something from Chaucer. The stories pop up seemingly at random, overlapping, circling back and forth through time and crossing one another in ways that are often ingenious and occasionally confusing. —Mark Childress[4]

> In *The Antelope Wife*, Erdrich has written her most cryptic and unfathomable book thus far. . . . If in the earlier books you needed a genealogical chart to keep track of characters, in *The Antelope Wife* you need a computer program to stay on top of them all. —Mark Shechner[5]

Erdrich has never been a novelist who goes directly from A to B. The shortest road, for her, is neither the most truthful nor the most interesting; there is always

2. "Uprooted," *New York Review of Books*, April 11, 1985, 36.
3. "A Continuing Tangle of History and Myth," *Philadelphia Enquirer*, February 6, 1994, sec. K, p. 2.
4. "A Gathering of Widows," *New York Times*, May 12, 1996, sec. 7, p. 10.
5. "*The Antelope Wife*, Erdrich's Indian 'X-Files,'" *Buffalo News*, May 24, 1998.

another point of view, another story. She is a writer of splendid complications and digressions. —Margot Livesey[6]

The only downfall of Bernard's story [in *The Painted Drum*] is that it's difficult to keep the characters straight, and it takes concentration to remember whether he's talking about his grandfather or father and to make the connections between the various Ojibwe families. —Ashley Simpson Shires[7]

"Confusing." "Thick with characters." "Complex relationships." "Difficult to keep the characters straight." "Always another point of view." "Circling back and forth through time." "Overlapping stories." "Shaggy." "Chaotic." "Cryptic." "Tangled." If these are the comments offered by professional readers, we can imagine how students and lay readers might feel as they try to make their way through an Erdrich novel. Who are all these characters? How are they related? What do they do? When do they do it? Such basic questions are troubling enough when we read one novel, but they become even more bewildering when we encounter other novels in which some of these same characters and incidents appear, often altered and always mixed with new ones.

The purpose of this book is to offer a guide to Louise Erdrich's world, bringing information from her first ten novels together in one place. (Our book deals only with Erdrich's single-author novels, not works she coauthored with Dorris nor her children's books.) This guide is intended primarily for first-time readers of Erdrich's fiction. It will also be of interest to more advanced readers who wish to compare its geographical notes, genealogies, chronologies, dictionary entries, and glossary with their own interpretations. There have been earlier attempts to chart the characters and events of Erdrich's novels, but they have been limited in scope and are often too compressed for clarity.[8]

6. "To Catch a Thief," *Boston Globe,* June 20, 2004, D6.

7. "Life Delicately Resounds in 'Drum,'" *Rocky Mountain News,* September 1, 2005. Spotlight: Books <http://www.rockymountainnews.com/drmn/books/article/0,2792,DRMN;63 ;4047936,00.html>.

8. See, for example, Figure 1, "Central Biological Relationships in *Love Medicine, The Beet Queen,* and *Tracks,*" in Hertha D. Wong's "Adoptive Mothers and Thrown-Away Children in the Novels of Louise Erdrich," 178; Peter G. Beidler's "Three Student Guides to Louise Erdrich's *Love Medicine*"; the chart called "Family Trees in *Love Medicine,*" in Kenneth Lincoln's *Indi'n Humor: Bicultural Play in Native America,* 225; Margie Towery's "Continuity and Connection: Characters in Louise Erdrich's fiction"; and Nancy L. Chick's "Genealogical Charts" in Appendix A of *Approaches to Teaching the Works of Louise Erdrich.* These last two are especially helpful, though

This book grows out of our own conviction that beneath the seeming chaos of story and character in Erdrich's novels lies a series of interlocking patterns, a carefully crafted web of more-than-Faulknerian complexity—as mazelike as life itself, yet ordered by Erdrich's genius. Our attempt to trace patterns through this complexity seems warranted by certain images within the novels themselves, images that invite the reader to look for connections and order within apparent chaos. In *The Bingo Palace,* for example, Gerry Nanapush recognizes that the seeming randomness of chance events actually reveals a pattern when seen from the right perspective:

> He knew from sitting in the still eye of chance that fate was not random. Chance was full of runs and soft noise, pardons and betrayals and double-backs. Chance was patterns of a stranger complexity than we could name, but predictable. There was no such thing as a complete lack of order, only a design so vast it seemed unrepetitive up close, that is, until you sat doing nothing for so long that your brain ached and, one day, just maybe, you caught a wider glimpse. (*BP,* 226)

Faye Travers, one of the narrators in *The Painted Drum,* reiterates Gerry's notion that careful observation reveals the order and pattern in seeming randomness. Her metaphor compares people's stories with the apparent chaos of Revival Road:

> From the air, our road must look like a ball of rope flung down haphazardly, a thing of inscrutable loops and half-finished question marks. But there is order in it to reward the patient watcher. . . . [T]here is order, but the pattern is continually complicated by the wilds of occurrence. The story surfaces here, snarls there, as people live their disorder to its completion. . . . As for the living, we're trapped in scene after scene. We haven't the overview that the dead have attained. Still, I try to at least record connections. (*PD,* 4–5)

For Nanapush in *Tracks,* all the stories are connected, like a snake swallowing its own tail:

---

they conflate the characters from the various novels into single charts. In the present book, except for our frontispiece chart, which integrates genealogical information from several of the novels, we have operated on the assumption that it is more useful to have the information on each novel kept separate. It is interesting to note that Erdrich's publisher has for the most recent novels and for reprintings of some of the older novels been providing sketchy but generally accurate charts inside the cover. Some readers, however, have graciously reported that they find ours easier to follow.

I shouldn't have been caused to live so long, shown so much of death, had to squeeze so many stories in the corners of my brain. They're all attached, and once I start there is no end to telling because they're hooked from one side to the other, mouth to tail. (*Tr,* 46)

In *Four Souls,* Nanapush alludes to the chaotic movement of stories, as they branch off and loop back. But he sees such movement as creating a narrative pattern like the design of the flowering vine used by Ojibwe beaders:

I let myself dream, as I do so often now, of the old days and old people. The women gambling beside the lake. The summer gatherings when we picked berries and made our babies. The winter fires and the aadizokaanag, the stories that branched off and looped back and continued in a narrative made to imitate the flowers on a vine. (*FS,* 114–15)

In the closing paragraph of *The Antelope Wife,* the narrator seeks to understand whether there is a pattern in the seemingly random beadwork of human existence:

Did these occurrences have a paradigm in the settlement of the old scores and pains and betrayals that went back in time? Or are we working out the minor details of a strictly random pattern? Who is beading us? Who is setting flower upon flower and cut-glass vine? Who are you and who am I, the beader or the bit of colored glass sewn onto the fabric of this earth? (*AW,* 240)

That Erdrich gives us no definite answers to such questions suggests that the confusion her readers sometimes experience results as much from the disarray of the human condition as from the complexity of style of the writer seeking meaning within it.

This guide is designed to help readers trace the patterns and connections in the seemingly chaotic vista of Erdrich's world. A book such as this, however, should never be allowed to tame the rich complexity of human experience that Erdrich provides for us. We have no desire to strip her fiction of its beauty or to deprive readers of the fun of figuring out for themselves what is going on in her narratives. We would thus urge our readers to use this guide only after reading, enjoying, and puzzling out the novels for themselves. We do hope, however, that those who, after their own encounter with Erdrich's texts, still have questions about her story lines and characters will find in these pages some sense of direction.

As the group-narrator in the first chapter of *The Bingo Palace* tells us, "no one gets wise enough to really understand the heart of another, though it is the task of our life to try" (*BP,* 6). Our primary purpose in creating the charts and summaries, the dictionary and glossary, the bibliography and index in this guide is to provide assistance to those readers who are trying to understand the hearts of Louise Erdrich's characters.

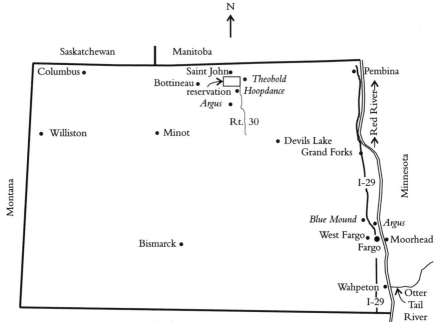

Map of Erdrich's North Dakota. *This map shows in regular type the names of the real towns and cities Erdrich mentions in her novels. The names of fictional towns are given in italics.*

Geography, Genealogy, and Chronology

The following geographical notes, genealogical charts, and chronologies of central events are intended to help readers find their way through the often mazelike narratives of Louise Erdrich's novels. This section traces the overarching patterns in the relationship of place to place, character to character, and event to event. To fill in these broad outlines, our readers should refer to the entries for individuals and families in the dictionary of characters.

In the first part of this section we first offer a map of Erdrich's North Dakota, along with an account of our decisions about where to locate some of its fictional places, particularly the reservation that figures so prominently in *Love Medicine* (1984, 1993), *Tracks* (1988), and *The Last Report on the Miracles at Little No Horse* (2001), and which is named Little No Horse in the last of those novels.[1] We place on the map the two approximate locations of the fictional town of Argus, which figures significantly in *The Beet Queen* (1986), *Tracks* (1988), and *The Master Butchers Singing Club* (2003). We also show Fargo, where many of the events of *The Bingo Palace* (1994) and *Tales of Burning Love* (1996) take place. The map does not show Minneapolis, Minnesota, which is more than 200 miles to the east (and a little south) of Fargo, and which is the location of many of the events in *The Antelope Wife* (1998) and *Four Souls* (2004). In the remainder of this section, which is subdivided by novel, we give a brief overview of each novel, present a series of genealogical charts of its most prominent families, and attempt to unscramble and put into chronological order its central events.

---

1. In her notes at the end of *The Last Report on the Miracles at Little No Horse,* Erdrich asserts the fictional nature of this reservation: "the reservation depicted in this and in all of my novels is an imagined place consisting of landscapes and features similar to many Ojibwe reservations. It is an emotional collection of places dear to me, as is the town called Argus. It is not the Turtle Mountain Reservation, of course, although that is where I am proud to be enrolled" (*LR*, 357).

GEOGRAPHY

Readers will find the map at the beginning of this section helpful as they make their way through Erdrich's novels, particularly those set primarily in North Dakota. This map shows the outline of that state and indicates the principal places in it—along with a few just over the Minnesota line—that are mentioned in the novels.

Several of the towns and cities are real places known to anyone familiar with the geography of North Dakota: Williston, Minot, Devils Lake, Grand Forks, and Fargo (embracing West Fargo and, across the Red River in Minnesota, Moorhead). We also show on the map smaller towns mentioned in the novels, like St. John (where Nanapush gets a Jesuit education), Columbus and Bottineau (through which Lyman Lamartine and Henry Lamartine Junior travel on their way home from Alaska), and Pembina (where Henry Junior drowns in the Red River; also the region of origin of the woman wearing blue beads seen by young Zosie [II] Shawano).

We have put on the map only the highways specifically mentioned in the novels, Route 30 and I-29. The state's other major interstate highway, I-94, which runs west from Fargo through Bismarck and into Montana, is not mentioned in the novels and thus does not appear on the map. The map also does not show towns and cities that Erdrich names but which are located in neighboring states and provinces: Aberdeen, South Dakota; Minneapolis–St. Paul ("the Twin Cities" or just "the Cities"); Silver Bay, Minnesota, on the northern shore of Lake Superior; and Winnipeg, Manitoba, in Canada.

The reservation itself is shown on our map as a small rectangle in the north-central part of the state (the location of Erdrich's own Turtle Mountain Indian Reservation). Although the fictional reservation site is ambiguous from novel to novel, its location in *Love Medicine* is rather precise. Lyman reports that he and Henry Junior drive "across Idaho then Montana and very soon we were racing the weather right along under the Canadian border through Columbus, Des Lacs, and then we were in Bottineau County and soon home" (*LM,* 184–85). The site of the reservation in *The Bingo Palace* is apparently the same. It is clearly not far from Canada, since Lipsha Morrissey and Shawnee Ray Toose drive up to the Canadian border for their supper date. In both novels, it seems to be a long way from Fargo. In *Love Medicine,* Albertine is said to go "all the way down to Fargo on the Jackrabbit bus" (*LM,* 167). In *The Bingo Palace,* as Lipsha and his father, Gerry Nanapush, flee Fargo and head back toward the reservation, Lipsha plans to "check the oil in Devils Lake" (*BP,* 252), suggesting that the reservation is farther in the same direction. We have thus placed the fictional reservation on the map in approximately the same location as the Turtle Mountain Indian Reservation.

This location is complicated, however, in *Tales of Burning Love.* In that novel, Jack Mauser describes the route of Gerry and Lipsha's escape from Fargo differently. Jack speculates that they would drive "toward the home reservation and beyond, to Canada. *Due north*" (*TBL*, 377, emphasis added). In an attempt to catch up with them, Jack himself then heads out of town north on "the interstate" (*TBL*, 380). The Turtle Mountain Reservation is northwest of Fargo rather than due north and is not close to an interstate. Thus, though the "home reservation" referred to in *Tales of Burning Love* is the same as the one in *Love Medicine* and *The Bingo Palace,* in the later novel, Erdrich seems to have moved it east.

Two fictional towns are mentioned as being near the reservation, but their exact location is not revealed. One near-reservation town is Hoop-dance. In the opening chapter of *The Bingo Palace,* Erdrich's reader might take Hoopdance to be the name of the on-reservation town, since immediately after visiting the post office at "the heart of the reservation" (*BP,* 1), Lulu Lamartine buys a picture frame from "the fanciest gift shop in Hoopdance" (*BP,* 4). In other references to the town in both this novel and *Tracks,* however, Hoopdance appears to be off-reservation, a few miles away. *The Bingo Palace* places it "straight south" (*BP,* 67). In *The Painted Drum,* as well, part 2, which describes events that take place on the reservation, is named "North of Hoopdance." *Tracks* also mentions the fictional town of Theobold as being near the reservation, although we are not told the direction. We have placed it somewhat north of Hoopdance. The settlement on the reservation—site of the Sacred Heart Convent, the Senior Citizens, the Indian agent's office, and the Coin-Op laundry where Lipsha picks up Shawnee Ray—is never named.

The town whose location is most ambiguous is Argus. It is always depicted as being fairly close to the reservation, but like the site of the reservation itself, its location shifts. In *Tracks,* Argus is "a few miles south" of the reservation (*Tr,* 12). It is close enough that Bernadette and Napoleon Morrissey can come "down" from the reservation to Argus "one day" in a wagon to get supplies (*Tr,* 63), and when Fleur Pillager returns home from Argus, she walks (*Tr,* 34). In *The Beet Queen,* as well, the distance between town and reservation is not great. When Celestine James, Mary Adare, and Dot Adare leave the reservation and return to Argus, Mary says, "We drove twenty miles in silence . . . until around the turnoff to Argus" (*BQ,* 203).

Two references to Argus in *The Beet Queen* also locate the town up north, near the site of the Turtle Mountain Reservation. When Sita Kozka Bohl is kidnapped from her Argus wedding and taken to the reservation, the kidnappers' route is "north on Highway 30" (*BQ,* 98), and when Karl Adare leaves Argus, Celestine assumes that he takes a bus or hitchhikes "down Highway 30 south" (*BQ,* 139). Highway 30 runs due south from the eastern side of the Turtle Mountain Reservation. It comes nowhere near Fargo.

Throughout most of *The Beet Queen,* however, Argus is near Fargo. In the opening pages of the novel, the town is said to be "in eastern North Dakota" (*BQ,* 1). It is apparently not too far north of Fargo, since Jimmy Bohl, while he is courting Sita Kozka, drives "down from Argus" (*BQ,* 83) to Fargo whenever Sita is modeling in a style show. This would be a regular occurrence, since modeling for DeLendrecies is Sita's job, and he would be unlikely to make such frequent trips if Argus was up near the Canadian border. The novel also refers to a new bypass "that connected the town with the interstate" (*BQ,* 312), and as mentioned, the north-central reservation site is not near an interstate. The interstate referred to is presumably I-29, running north and south through Fargo along the eastern border of the state. The proximity of Argus to Fargo is also suggested by the route of Father Jude Miller as he comes to town by train from Minneapolis. After the train crosses the border into North Dakota, it turns "upward in a long curve that brought him to Argus" (*BQ,* 312). The primary train lines from Minneapolis into North Dakota cross the state line at Moorhead-Fargo. One of these lines veers to the north at the western edge of Fargo and runs parallel to I-29. Father Miller's route thus also suggests a location for Argus to the north of Fargo along I-29.

The association of Argus with I-29 is made more explicit in *Tales of Burning Love.* In 1992 Jack Mauser's construction company is about to begin "an overpass and access road down near Argus" (*TBL,* 151; see also 12). Two years later, Jack's name is mentioned specifically in connection with I-29 (*TBL,* 126). Moreover, the Argus in *Tales of Burning Love,* like that of *The Beet Queen,* is not a great distance from Fargo. When Jack and Dot Mauser drive up from Fargo to Argus to pick up Eleanor Schlick Mauser, they go and return in the same day (see *TBL,* 70–78). In both *The Beet Queen* and *Tales of Burning Love,* the fictional town of Argus may be modeled roughly after the real town of Argusville, just fifteen miles or so due north of Fargo. Like the fictional Argus, Argusville is on a railway line and is connected by a short link with I-29.

Because the reservation is consistently depicted as being just a short distance north of Argus (about twenty miles, according to Mary Adare's account), this second location for Argus reinforces the idea of an alternate location for the reservation. Thus, while *Love Medicine, Tracks,* and *The Bingo Palace* appear to place the reservation in the area of the real Turtle Mountain Reservation, *The Beet Queen* (with two exceptions) and *Tales of Burning Love* suggest that it is close to the eastern border of North Dakota, not far north of Fargo. On our map, however, we have shown only one reservation. We have indicated the ambiguity of its location by showing two fictional towns of Argus. We placed the fictional town of Blue Mound near the southeasterly Argus, since it is mentioned in *The Beet Queen* as being "the next town over" from Argus (*BQ,* 126) and "thirteen miles" away (*BQ,* 266). The other fictional near-reservation towns we placed near the north-central reservation site.

Readers should not be upset by the indeterminate location of the reservation and Argus. Erdrich did not want us to identify the reservation in her novels with the Turtle Mountain Indian Reservation and thus, apparently purposefully, included some inconsistencies. The world she creates is, after all, a fictional world. Like Garrison Keillor's Lake Wobegon, it need not be expected to coincide exactly with real locations in real states.

We do show on the map one real town that Erdrich does not mention in her novels, the town of Wahpeton, on the eastern border of the state. Because her parents taught in a Bureau of Indian Affairs school in Wahpeton, Erdrich spent much of her youth there. It is worth mentioning that just across the river from Wahpeton, Minnesota's Otter Tail River empties into the Red River. In *The Antelope Wife,* the dog carrying the baby who is later named Matilda Roy runs off onto "the vast carcass of the world west of the Otter Tail River." Scranton Roy, the cavalry soldier, "followed and did not return" (*AW,* 3). Thus it would seem that some of the key events even of her sixth novel take place not in Minnesota but in what is now North Dakota, close to the border country that Erdrich knew well from her youth.

The later novels build on and sometimes refine slightly the fictional landscape Erdrich has painted in her earlier novels. As we have seen, *The Last Report on the Miracles at Little No Horse* finally gives the reservation a name, placing it somewhere to the north of Fargo. Fargo, the location of the novel's opening chapters when Agnes becomes the common-law wife of Berndt Vogel, is also mentioned several times later in the novel. Its cathedral is apparently the parent church of the convent and satellite church on the reservation. In this novel the reservation appears to be a good distance from

Fargo, however, since Agnes DeWitt, now impersonating Father Damien, after being swept north in the flood, then speaks of traveling on a "train heading north . . . traveling through a waste of open land in which only rarely could she pick out the slightest human feature. . . . And then the train stopped at a small board shack hardly bigger than an outhouse" (*LR*, 60–61).

That desolate location may be the nucleus of the town that becomes Hoopdance, since there is reference later in the novel to the snow plows opening a roadway "down to the train station at Hoopdance" (*LR*, 196). Argus also appears in the novel, especially as the home of the convent where Sister Leopolda lives for a time before returning to Little No Horse. In any case, from that outhouse-sized train station, Father Damien has to go even farther north by wagon to reach the reservation. Except for these "north" references, we are not told more precisely where the reservation is, except that it is in North Dakota.

The Master Butchers Singing Club is set primarily in Argus. In this novel, Erdrich positions the town only in relation to two large coastal cities. Fidelis Waldvogel, just emigrating from Germany after World War I,[2] boards a train in New York headed for Seattle, but his on-board sale of sausages earns him only enough money to get to Argus. He passes "through Minneapolis and rolling prairie country into the sudden sweep of plains, vast sky, into North Dakota" (*MBSC*, 12). Argus itself is described as "the creation of the railroad" (*MBSC*, 29) in that its location near the railroad makes it accessible to people coming to live, farm, and do business. When Fidelis disembarks at Argus in 1922, he is struck with the "defenseless" and "temporary" nature of the little town, "with its back against a river" (*MBSC*, 12). Eventually, though, Argus becomes the county seat, and at some point, the main highway is rerouted to come right past the shop Fidelis opens on the end of town opposite from Pete Kozka's butcher shop, thus helping Fidelis's business.

Curiously, Argus may be south of Fargo in *The Master Butchers Singing Club*. Argus mortician assistant Clarisse Strub pronounces her preparation of a drowning victim far superior to the shoddy job done by the mortician

---

2. *The Master Butchers Singing Club* is the only Erdrich novel containing action in Europe. It opens in the fictional town of Ludwigsruhe, Germany, Fidelis's hometown, which he revisits near the end of his life in chapter 15. Erdrich may have named Ludwigsruhe after her grandfather Ludwig Erdrich, who fought on the German side in World War I and whose picture appears on the cover of the novel (see *MBSC*, 389).

of a previous drowning "up in Fargo" (*MBSC,* 90)—though of course "up" may refer to elevation rather than direction. While most of the action in this novel takes place in Argus, isolated scenes occur in other northern Midwest locales. Cyprian and Delphine perform their vaudeville act in an unnamed town in northern Minnesota and in the fictional towns of Shotwell, North Dakota, and Gorefield, Manitoba. Partway through the novel, Delphine takes the sick Eva from Argus "down" to the Mayo Clinic which is "south of the Cities" (*MBSC,* 105). Two other stateside locations are mentioned, as well. Delphine and the boys spend two days sightseeing in Chicago while Fidelis and Tante make travel arrangements from there to Germany, and some years later Erich, who fights on the German side in World War II, is captured and brought back to a prison camp in northern Minnesota.

Erdrich brings us back to Minnesota in *Four Souls,* whose central action is divided between the Mauser mansion in a ritzy part of Minneapolis and the North Dakota reservation. In this novel, Erdrich seems to confuse directions purposefully so that readers will not try to associate her fictional reservation with a real place. In the first chapter, for example, Fleur Pillager leaves the reservation with her cart "always bearing east" (*FS,* 1). After weeks or months of travel, "still she travel[s] east" (*FS,* 2) until she gets to Minneapolis. Near the end of the novel, Fleur goes back to the reservation, and Polly Elizabeth Gheen and her new husband, Fantan, plan to follow her there. Instead of going west, however, as we might have expected, she says that "we are heading north to live in a town just outside the reservation boundary" (*FS,* 160). This is clearly Fleur's reservation, since Polly Elizabeth and Fantan plan to pay regular visits to Fleur and her son there. This may simply represent the characters' casual representation of northwest-southeast relationship between the two locales, or Erdrich may be trying to prevent our too-precise location of her imaginary reservation. In *Four Souls,* the reservation is never called Little No Horse.

In *The Painted Drum,* her tenth novel, Erdrich splits the setting between her fictional Ojibwe reservation in North Dakota and semirural western New Hampshire. She mentions several actual locations in New Hampshire, such as the capital, Concord, the town of Claremont, and Jackson Road (there is such a road in Cornish County). She also mentions two Vermont towns, Rutland and Windsor. Windsor, just across the Connecticut River from Cornish, plays a small role in the plot and, as the narrator accurately states, is connected to New Hampshire by the longest covered bridge in the world. Several of the New Hampshire place names that Erdrich mentions, however, seem to be fictional, such as the town of Stokes, Revival and

Tatro roads, and Goodie Hill. It is possible that Revival Road is a fictional renaming of South Parsonage Road, which intersects Jackson Road. In the present time of the story, Faye Travers, one of the narrators, still lives in or near the small town of Stokes, in a house her parents bought when they were first married and from which her father "commuted thirty miles to the college town" where he taught (*PD*, 81). The college town is apparently Hanover, home to Dartmouth College, which would put Faye's place not far from the town of South Cornish, just a short hop north of the end of Jackson Road.

The North Dakota reservation is not named in *The Painted Drum,* but it is clearly the one familiar to us from earlier novels. It is, for example, the reservation where Jewett Parker Tatro is an Indian agent and where Fleur Pillager is born. Faye's mother, Elsie, a half-blood Ojibwe descended from Fleur's Pillager father, refers to this place as "our home reservation" (*PD*, 67), and the house to which she and Faye return the drum sits on the very hill where old Nanapush's cabin once lay. Thus, the lake near which much of the action in part 2 takes place is undoubtedly Matchimanito, though it is not named in this novel.

GENEALOGY AND CHRONOLOGY

Just as the above map and geographical notes are meant to help readers negotiate Erdrich's spaces, so the following genealogical charts and chronologies are "maps" to help them untangle the knots of her intertwined family relationships and interwoven strands of time and event. Because any attempt to create an all-encompassing chronology or set of genealogical charts for the ten novels might create a product more bewildering than the novels themselves and because of variation among the novels, we base the charts and chronologies for each novel only on information in that novel. Where the information for a given family is inconsistent from novel to novel, the genealogical charts reflect those inconsistencies. Also, information about a character's family not available in one novel is omitted from the charts for that novel, but it may be revealed in the charts for another novel—Lulu's possible paternity, for example, or Marie's real parents (compare Charts 2 and 3 with Charts 7 and 8).

In a similar effort to avoid confusion, the genealogical charts group characters into separate families, even though some of these characters appear in more than one chart. In the *Love Medicine* charts, for example, Chart 1 shows where Nector and Marie Kashpaw fit into the Kashpaw family, while Chart 2 shows their relationship with the Lazarre clan. Not all family members appear in a given genealogy. Of Lulu's nine children and many liaisons, for example, only those specifically referred to in *Love Medicine* appear in Chart 3. Henry and Beverly Lamartine's older brother, Slick, is also omitted from that chart, because he does not figure significantly in the novel.

In all genealogical charts, double lines between two boxes (===) indicate either Indian or Western marriage, broken double lines (====) indicate nonmarital sexual liaisons, and single lines (——) indicate children resulting from these unions. Thus, for example, the broken and unbroken double lines emanating from Lulu in Chart 3 indicate that she had six unions that we know of, some of which were marriages and some nonmarital relationships, and the single lines issuing from those double lines indicate the five children who are specifically mentioned in *Love Medicine:* her first son by Moses Pillager, Gerry, Henry Junior, Lyman, and Bonita.

When exact relationships are unclear, we have indicated those uncertainties with question marks. Thus the question marks on Charts 7 and 9 indicate the uncertainty of Lulu's paternity.

LOVE MEDICINE

Love Medicine is a series of stories, many of which had been previously published, that first appeared as a novel in 1984. Erdrich revised and expanded it in 1993. The various stories fit together into a narrative about several interconnected families that live on and near Erdrich's fictional Indian reservation in northern North Dakota. To understand *Love Medicine,* we need to understand the complex interrelationship of three families: the Kashpaws, the Lazarres, and Lulu Nanapush's extended family. Although she freezes to death in the early pages of the first story, June Morrissey is in some ways the central character in the novel, since she is connected in important ways to all three families.

One of the central plots of the novel is the rivalry between Lulu Nanapush and Marie Lazarre for the affections of Nector Kashpaw. Marie marries him and has five of his children, but Lulu has an affair with him and has one child by him. Several subplots enrich the novel: Gerry Nanapush's relationships with June and, later, Dot Adare; Beverly Lamartine's love for Lulu resulting in the birth of Henry Junior; Gordie Kashpaw's grief at June's death; Albertine Johnson's difficulties in adjusting to her family after June's death; Lyman Lamartine's early efforts as an entrepreneur; and Lipsha Morrissey's surreal efforts to administer love medicine to Nector and to discover who his parents are.

The order of events in *Love Medicine* may be confusing. Although Erdrich often gives dates along with the titles to the various stories, and although after the first one, these stories are presented in chronological order, many of them include references to earlier incidents whose dates are unspecified. Thus, in the following summary we have rearranged the novel's most important events and presented them in chronological order. The dates are taken either from the chapter heads or from internal evidence. Where we have guessed at a date we include a parenthetical indicator (?) of the uncertainty. Dates that are uncertain in *Love Medicine* but are revealed in another novel (without contradicting *Love Medicine*) are supplied in square brackets—[1919]. Readers may also be confused by the fact that in the expanded (1993) edition of *Love Medicine* Erdrich has not only added new material but also changed some of the old. In the first edition, for example, Eli and Nector are twins, while in the expanded edition Eli is said to be Rushes Bear's "youngest son" (*LM*, 101). That fact is in turn contradicted by information in *Tracks,* where Nector, born about 1908, is said to be the "younger brother" (*Tr*, 39) of Eli, who is born around 1898. There is no question that Erdrich intended the revised and expanded 1993 edition of *Love Medicine* to be definitive, and our guide accordingly uses this version as its standard text. To indicate where large blocks of new material are added in the expanded 1993 edition, we put those events in italics.

Chronology of Events in *Love Medicine:*

1898–1908(?)—Nector and Eli Kashpaw are born to the original Kashpaw and Margaret.

[1919]—Young Lulu Nanapush finds the body of a dead man in the woods.

c. 1920—Marie Lazarre is born.

[1924]—*Lulu returns from an off-reservation boarding school as a result of letters written by Nanapush.*

1934—Marie goes to stay at the convent, where Sister Leopolda scalds her back and stabs her in the hand. On her way down the hill not long afterward, Marie is accosted by Nector Kashpaw.

1934–1935—Marie and Nector marry. Lulu goes to Moses Pillager's island, where she becomes pregnant. Before her baby is born, Lulu leaves Moses and returns to town. Marie and Nector's first child, Gordie, is born.

1935–1936—Lulu's first son by Moses Pillager is born (we do not know his first name, but his last is Nanapush).

1936–1939(?)—Son and daughter born to Marie and Nector. (Both die of a fever sometime before 1948.)

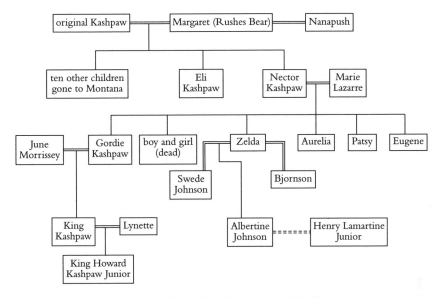

Chart 1. Kashpaw family in Love Medicine.

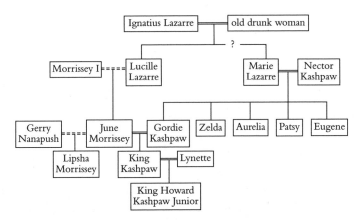

Chart 2. Lazarre family in Love Medicine.

c. 1939—June Morrissey is born to Lucille Lazarre and Morrissey (I).

1941—Zelda Kashpaw is born to Marie and Nector.

c. 1945—Gerry Nanapush is born to Lulu and Moses.

1948—Lucille Lazarre dies, leaving her nine-year-old daughter, June, age nine, to survive on tree sap. Lucille's mother and Morrissey (I) bring June to Marie to rear. Gordie and Aurelia Kashpaw try to hang June.

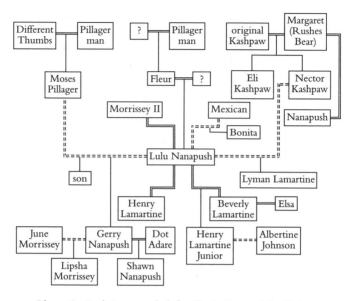

Chart 3. Lulu's extended family in Love Medicine.

June goes to live with Eli. *Rushes Bear moves in with Marie and helps her give birth to her last child, a son (Eugene).*

1950—Henry Lamartine is killed by a train. His brother Beverly comes to the funeral and makes love to Henry's widow, Lulu, after the wake. A boy named Henry Lamartine Junior is born to Lulu nine months later.

1952—Lulu and Nector begin an affair.

c. 1953—Lyman Lamartine is born to Lulu and Nector.

195_(?)—*Gordie and June honeymoon at Johnson's resort.*

1957—The Lulu-Nector affair ends, and Lulu marries Beverly, who has come to take Henry Junior home with him. Lulu discovers that Beverly is already married and sends him back to the Twin Cities to get a divorce. Marie takes Zelda to visit Sister Leopolda. Nector burns Lulu's house, and Lulu is made bald as she rescues their son, Lyman, from the fire.

c. 1958—Albertine Johnson is born to Zelda and Swede Johnson.

196_(?)—King Kashpaw is born to June and Gordie.

c. 1963—Bonita is born to Lulu and a Mexican man.

1965(?)—Gerry kicks a cowboy in the groin and starts the first of many jail terms.

c. 1965—Lipsha Morrissey is born to Gerry and June, then taken to Marie and Nector to rear.

1969(?)—Henry Junior and Lyman buy a red convertible.

1970—Henry Junior goes to Vietnam.

1973—Henry Junior returns from Vietnam. He and Albertine chance to meet in Fargo, where Albertine loses her virginity to him.

1974—Henry Junior drowns himself in the Red River, watched by Lyman, who is unable to save him. *Lyman goes on a one-year drinking binge before becoming involved in tribal politics and business.*

1979–1980(?)—King Howard Kashpaw Junior is born to Lynette and King Kashpaw.

1980—Shawn Nanapush is born to Gerry and Dot (Adare) Nanapush. Gerry kills(?) a state trooper.

1981—June is picked up in Williston by a mud engineer who says his name is Andy. June tries to walk home, but freezes to death. King buys a new car with her insurance money. The Kashpaw family assembles at the old Kashpaw place. Gordie gets drunk, hits a deer with his car, and believes that he has killed June.

1982—Lulu, Marie, and Nector all live at the Senior Citizens. Nector chokes to death on a raw turkey heart brought by Lipsha as love medicine. Marie moves back into the Kashpaw house for a time. *Gordie comes home drunk, drinks Lysol, and dies.* Marie helps Lulu after Lulu's eye surgery.

1983—*Lyman's tomahawk factory venture ends in an interfamily brawl. Lyman makes plans for a bingo hall on the reservation.*

1984—Lipsha learns from Lulu that Gerry and June are his parents and that Lulu is his grandmother. Lipsha visits his half brother, King, in Minneapolis, wins King's insurance-money car in a poker game, helps Gerry escape to Canada in the car, and then brings "her" (June's car) home.

THE BEET QUEEN

The Beet Queen is a loosely structured episodic novel. Like *Love Medicine*, it is a compilation of stories or chapters, some of which had been previously published as separate stories. Some of the cameo characters—Fleur Pillager, and Eli and Russell Kashpaw—are reservation Indians, but they play only a small role in the novel. Key characters, such as the Adares, the Kozkas, and Wallace Pfef, are white, primarily Polish. Celestine James, the mixed-blood daughter of an Ojibwe woman and a white man, is the mother of the "Beet Queen," Dot Adare (the same Dot who is married to Gerry Nanapush in *Love Medicine* and, in the later *Tales of Burning Love*, to Jack Mauser). Karl Adare is Dot's father. Thus Dot is part Ojibwe, but she has almost no on-reservation experiences. Nevertheless, even though *The Beet Queen* is mostly about white characters in a white setting, it is in some ways informed by an Indian consciousness and an awareness of Indian history in a community now dominated by white values. The novel is set in the forty-year period from 1932 to 1972, mostly in the fictional town of Argus.

Although we find a characteristic Erdrichian humor in *The Beet Queen* (particularly in the tales of Chez Sita, the naughty box, the Christmas pageant, and Dot's birthday party), there is also a pervasive note of loneliness and dislocation. Its characters and families are separated and do not much love one another. Letters are written but not sent, sent but delivered to the wrong people, or delivered too late. The three Adare children in particular—Karl, Mary, and Jude—are in a state of perpetual dislocation. After being abandoned first by their father and then by their mother, they are separated and spend the rest of the novel not quite getting back together again.

The dislocation of the characters is offset, however, by the growing love that Celestine feels for her daughter. That love is expressed, with an image characteristic of Erdrich, as a web. As Celestine feeds her newborn baby she notices a spider in Dot's hair: "It was a delicate thing, close to transparent, with long sheer legs. It moved so quickly that it seemed to vibrate, throwing out invisible strings and catching them, weaving its own tensile strand. Celestine watched as it began to happen. A web was forming, a complicated house, that Celestine could not bring herself to destroy" (*BQ*, 176). Sixteen years later, the developing web of love that had joined Celestine with her infant daughter now draws Dot to her mother. "In her eyes I see the force of her love," Dot tells us. "It is bulky and hard to carry, like a package that keeps untying. . . . I walk to her, drawn by her, unable to help myself" (*BQ*, 337). Love ultimately triumphs in this novel, if not for the white family that never finds its way back together, then for the part-Indian characters, who discover the medicine that joins them.

Chronology of Events in *The Beet Queen:*

c. 1918—Karl Adare is born.

c. 1920—Sita Kozka is born.

c. 1921—Mary Adare is born.

1932—Mr. Ober dies, possibly by suicide. Adelaide Adare, pregnant with her third child by Ober, moves with Karl and Mary to Minneapolis. At the Orphans' Picnic, she flies away with stunt pilot Omar, abandoning

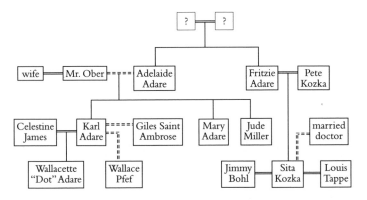

Chart 4. Adare family in The Beet Queen.

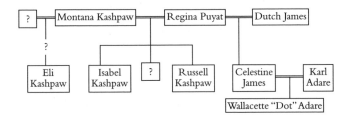

Chart 5. Kashpaw-James family in The Beet Queen.

her three children. Martin and Catherine Miller steal the baby and name him Jude. Karl and Mary take a train to Argus, where Mary stays with Pete, Fritzie, and Sita Kozka. Karl leaps from the boxcar and breaks his feet. Fleur Pillager cares for him and takes him to the nuns on the reservation. They send him to Minneapolis to Saint Jerome's orphanage. Later that year, Mary causes a "miracle" image of Christ to appear in the ice at the school playground in Argus.

19__(?)—Russell Kashpaw returns "from a war," wounded. Mary is infatuated with him, feelings he does not return. [For chronological problems, see Russell's dictionary entry.]

1941—Pete and Fritzie Kozka move south because of Fritzie's health, leaving their butcher shop to Mary. Sita moves to Fargo and starts a modeling career.

1948—Karl sees his brother, Jude Miller, in Minneapolis, for the first time since 1932.

1950—Sita ends a three-year affair with a married doctor. After reading a letter addressed to her parents from Catherine Miller, Sita goes to Jude's ordination as a deacon (later to become a priest). Sita writes Catherine Miller a letter but never mails it.

1950(?)—Sita marries Jimmy Bohl, a restaurant owner.

1952—Wallace Pfef meets Karl Adare in Minneapolis, and they make love in Karl's hotel room. Karl injures his back in a fall.

1953—Russell Kashpaw, even more wounded from military service in Korea, is released from the VA hospital. Karl Adare comes to Argus to look for Mary but meets Celestine James instead. He and Celestine have a brief affair, and she becomes pregnant. Russell goes to live with Eli Kashpaw on the reservation. Divorced from Jimmy Bohl, Sita opens Chez Sita. Sita marries Louis Tappe.

Winter 1953–1954—Russell has a stroke.

January 1954—Wallacette ("Dot") Adare is born to Celestine, who marries Dot's father, Karl, as a formality and returns to Argus without him.

1960—Dot is in first grade. She attacks another schoolchild, is put in the teacher's "naughty box," and is avenged by her aunt, Mary.

Summer 1961—Karl sends Dot a wheelchair, which her mother gives to Russell.

1964—Dot plays the role of Joseph in an ill-fated school Christmas play. Adelaide bloodies her feet in a glass-breaking rage in Florida.

19__(?)—Sita loses her voice but is "cured" in the mental hospital.

1965—Wallace Pfef has a birthday party for the eleven-year-old Dot.

1968—Karl comes to Argus and has breakfast with Celestine and the fourteen-year-old Dot.

1972—Celestine dreams that Sita is sick, and she and Mary go to Blue Mound to help her. Celestine finds and mails Sita's 1950 letter to Catherine Miller. On the day of the Beet Parade (July), Sita takes an overdose of pain pills and dies. Celestine and Mary go to the Beet Festival, with Sita's body propped in the front seat of the delivery truck. Father Jude Miller and Karl Adare come to town and attend the festival, where Karl is reunited with his former lover Wallace. Dot is crowned Beet Queen.

TRACKS

Tracks takes us back to a time before the events of either *The Beet Queen* or *Love Medicine*. It reveals such background material as the origins of Marie Lazarre and Lulu Nanapush, two of the dominant women in *Love Medicine;* the early activities of Nector as he learns the politics of dealing with the dominant white society; Sister Leopolda's early life under a different name;

and the loss of a large portion of reservation land to the lumber companies. The alternating narrators of the story are Nanapush, a pureblood Ojibwe survivor of the consumption epidemic of 1912, and Pauline Puyat, a mixed white-Indian girl who wants to be a white.

Nanapush is a generally truthful narrator who is telling Lulu, now a young woman, the story of her family background. His motives are to convince her that she should not hate her mother, Fleur Pillager, for apparently abandoning her and that she should not marry the Morrissey man she is planning to wed. Pauline's motives in narrating her chapters are not so clear, but she seems to want to justify or cover up her own fanatical, even murderous, actions. She seems more eager to distort the truth than to reveal it. Both narrators focus on Fleur, who has an uncanny ability to survive death herself while luring others to their own.

Tracks is set in the twelve-year period from 1912 to 1924, mostly on the reservation but partly in fictional Argus. Some of the relationships among its main characters are ambiguous. Nanapush describes his own heritage in these terms: "I was a vine of a wild grape that twined the timbers and drew them close. Or maybe I was a branch, coming from the Kashpaws, that lived long enough to touch the next tree over, which was Pillagers" (*Tr*, 33). The primary relationships between Nanapush and the Pillager family are in name rather than blood, as indicated in the first two charts below. Nanapush names Fleur's daughter after himself, although he is not her father, and after the nickname of his own daughter, "Lulu," who had died in 1912. Three of Lulu's sons, in turn, carry the Nanapush name, even though they are Pillagers.

Chronology of Events in *Tracks:*

c. 1862—Nanapush is born.
c. 1895—Fleur Pillager is born.
c. 1898—Pauline Puyat is born.
c. 1898—Eli Kashpaw is born to Kashpaw and Margaret.
Early 1900s—Fleur nearly drowns the first time. Russell Kashpaw is born to Regina Puyat and a Montana Kashpaw.
c. 1908—Nector Kashpaw is born to Kashpaw and Margaret.
c. 1910—Fleur nearly drowns the second time.
Spring 1912—Pauline goes to Argus and works in Pete and Fritzie Kozka's butcher shop.
Winter 1912–1913—Consumption ravages the reservation, wiping out

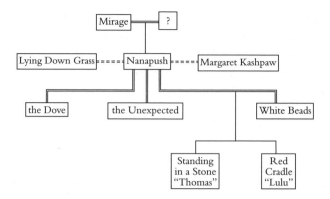

Chart 6. Nanapush's extended family in Tracks.

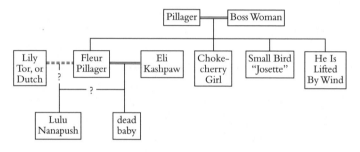

Chart 7. Fleur's family in Tracks.

Nanapush's and Fleur's families. Nanapush rescues the nearly dead Fleur and nurses her back to life.

Spring 1913—Father Damien visits Nanapush and Fleur.

Summer 1913—Fleur goes to Argus, works at Kozka's, and in off-hours plays poker with Kozka's workers. After weeks of her winning, the men get drunk and attack her. When a tornado strikes the next day, the three men seek shelter in the freezer, where two of them freeze to death. Dutch James survives but loses parts of his arms and legs.

Fall–Winter 1913—Fleur returns to Matchimanito Lake. Eli Kashpaw falls in love with Fleur and goes to Nanapush for love advice. Eli and Fleur's relationship begins. In December, Pauline returns to the reservation, where she lives with Bernadette Morrissey's family.

1913–1914—Pauline begins to accompany Bernadette Morrissey on her mission to care for the dying.

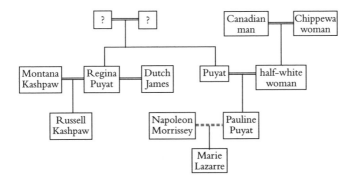

Chart 8. Puyat family in Tracks.

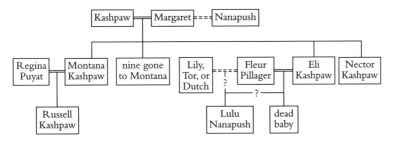

Chart 9. Kashpaw family in Tracks.

Spring 1914—Lulu is born to Fleur.

Autumn 1917—Pauline bewitches Sophie Morrissey and Eli Kashpaw into making love. Sophie goes into a trance in front of Fleur's house, and Fleur banishes Eli, who goes to live with Nanapush.

Winter 1917–1918—In this famine winter, Nanapush sends Eli off to hunt moose guided by Nanapush's spirit. Pauline begins a sexual relationship with Napoleon Morrissey. Boy Lazarre and Clarence Morrissey capture Margaret Kashpaw and Nanapush and shave Margaret's head. Margaret bites Lazarre's hand, and he later dies of blood poisoning. Nanapush snares Clarence with a piano wire. By Ash Wednesday, Nanapush and Margaret are keeping company.

November 1918—Pauline gives birth to Marie. She leaves the baby with Bernadette and enters the convent.

Winter 1918–1919—Pauline believes she hears a message from Jesus. She mortifies her flesh in a variety of ways. Fleur gives birth prematurely, and her baby dies. Going for help, Lulu suffers frostbite. In this second

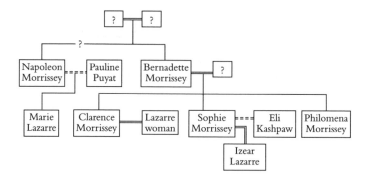

Chart 10. Morrissey family in Tracks.

famine winter, the Kashpaw–Pillager families are saved by government commodities. They work together to collect money for fee payments on their land allotments.

Spring 1919—Margaret and Nector take Kashpaw–Pillager land fee money to town, but they pay the fees only on Kashpaw land. Pauline goes out onto Matchimanito Lake to confront the devil. Ashore, she kills the drunken Napoleon.

Late summer 1919—Lulu finds Napoleon's body in the woods, but keeps it a secret. Surveyors eventually find the corpse.

Fall 1919—The lumber company begins cutting timber on Pillager land, and Nanapush learns that Nector and Margaret did not pay Fleur's land fees. Fleur tries to drown herself (her third near-drowning), but Eli rescues her. Margaret sends Nector and Fleur sends Lulu away to government school. Fleur sabotages the lumber company's equipment and leaves the reservation.

1924—Nanapush, who has become tribal chairman, uses his influence to bring Lulu back from the off-reservation school.

[1940s(?)]—Lulu is about to marry a Morrissey man, and Nanapush tells her the story of her family.

THE BINGO PALACE

The Bingo Palace appears to begin a few years after the final events of the expanded *Love Medicine*. Gerry Nanapush, who has been at large, is recaptured; Lipsha Morrissey, who is drifting aimlessly through life, returns to the reservation at the summons of his grandmother Lulu Lamartine; Zelda Kashpaw has become the family tyrant; and Lyman Lamartine continues his ambitions to get rich regardless of the cost. To these familiar faces Erdrich adds some memorable new characters, particularly Shawnee Ray Toose and her small son, Redford.

The dominant plot of *The Bingo Palace* is Lipsha's Quixotic love for Shawnee Ray, a love complicated by the rivalry of Lipsha's kinsman and employer, Lyman, and by Shawnee Ray's own uncertainty. Several important subplots enrich the novel, such as Xavier Toose's unrequited burning love for Zelda and Lipsha's continued resentment of his dead mother, June Morrissey. The latter subplot culminates in a sometimes comic winter chase in which Gerry and Lipsha follow June's ghostly lead across the snow-engulfed plains—an incident that recalls June's death in the opening sequence of *Love Medicine.*

The Bingo Palace takes place in the course of about a year. Abandoning her usual practice of dating the chapters, however, in this novel Erdrich does not specify the time of the action. At one point, Zelda remembers watching Lulu's house burn thirty years earlier, an event that happened, as we know from *Love Medicine,* in 1957. Thus, in relation to the events in *Love Medicine, The Bingo Palace* seems to be set in the late 1980s. In relation to the events in the next novel, *Tales of Burning Love,* however, the events in *The Bingo Palace* take place in 1994–1995. There is no way to bring the events of all three novels into perfect sequence, nor should we try to do so. The manipulation of time is just one manifestation of Erdrich's trickster-like storytelling.

In addition to the "present-time" events in *The Bingo Palace,* which take place between one midwinter and the next, earlier events are also recounted as memories or flashbacks. Even though the exact times of the events in this novel are uncertain, the sequence of its present-time events is more straightforward and unambiguous than in any of Erdrich's previous novels.

Summary of Events before the Present-Time of *The Bingo Palace:*

[1930s(?)]—Fleur Pillager returns to the reservation with a fancy white car and a white boy and, in a poker game with the retired Indian agent, wins back her land.

[1940s]—As a child, June Morrissey is raped by Leonard, her mother's boyfriend.

[Late 1950s]—Xavier Albert Toose woos Zelda Kashpaw, but she spurns him. In his final effort to win her one snowy winter night, several of Xavier's fingers freeze.

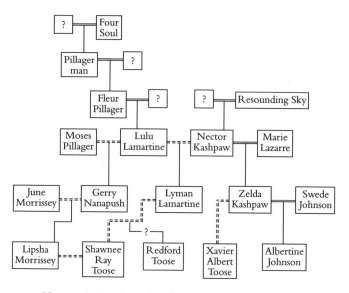

Chart 11. Lipsha's family in The Bingo Palace.

[c. 1965]—According to one story (Zelda's), Lipsha Morrissey's mother, June, tries to drown him as a baby, and Zelda rescues him.

19__(?)—As a teenager, Shawnee Ray Toose becomes pregnant while dating four different men. The presumed father is Lyman Lamartine.

19__(?)—As the novel opens, Shawnee Ray's father is dead, her mother has remarried and moved to Minot, and Shawnee Ray and her son, Redford, are living with Lyman's half sister Zelda. Shawnee Ray is attending junior college.

Sequence of Present-Time Events in *The Bingo Palace:*

Lulu Lamartine sends a copy of Gerry's Wanted poster to Lipsha in Fargo. Lipsha returns to the reservation on the night of the winter powwow, where he falls in love with Shawnee Ray.

Marie Kashpaw gives Lipsha the ceremonial pipe of his adoptive grandfather, Nector. On his first date with Shawnee Ray, Lipsha is held at the Canadian border, suspected of transporting hashish. Lyman rescues him and gives him a job at the bingo parlor.

Zelda tells Lipsha her "tale of burning love" about the courtship of Xavier Toose and her story of rescuing Lipsha from the slough. That night, the ghost of Lipsha's mother, June, shows up and gives Lipsha bingo tickets in trade for "her" car.

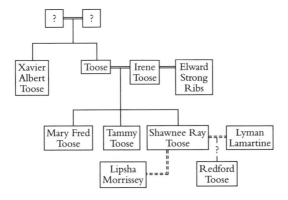

Chart 12. Shawnee Ray's family in The Bingo Palace.

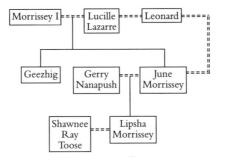

Chart 13. June's family in The Bingo Palace.

Lipsha angers the gas-station clerk, Marty, and makes love to Shawnee Ray in a motel room. Playing with June's bingo tickets the next night, Lipsha wins the bingo van, which Marty and his friends vandalize. Lyman gambles away a large amount of tribal money at a Nevada casino and cheats Lipsha out of his bingo winnings. Lipsha goes to see Shawnee Ray at Zelda's house, where they make love again.

Shawnee Ray leaves Redford with her sisters while she goes to dance in a powwow competition. Lyman and Zelda get a court order giving them custody and have Redford forcibly removed from the Toose sisters.

Lipsha asks Fleur for a love medicine. Instead, Fleur—in the form of a bear—instructs him about love and the sacred value of land.

Shawnee Ray returns home and stays again with Redford at Zelda's house. Lipsha and Lyman go on a vision quest, but Lipsha's "vision" is a skunk. Shawnee Ray takes Redford, leaves Zelda, and enrolls in the university.

The following January, Gerry Nanapush escapes again and calls Lipsha. In Fargo, Lipsha and Gerry steal a car for a getaway vehicle, then discover a baby in the back seat. They evade the police, and in a blizzard the ghost of June shows up in "her" car. Gerry abandons the stolen car and goes off with June. Lipsha zips the baby inside his jacket.

Zelda has a heart attack—or at least a change of heart—and goes to see Xavier Toose. Shawnee Ray, now at the university, acknowledges her love for Lipsha.

In the last chapter, just before men come to seize her land, Fleur takes her death-walk across the frozen lake to the Pillager's island. The ending is ambiguous. Fleur takes the place of "the boy out there" (*BP*, 272) on death's road, and Shawnee Ray hears a radio announcement that a "hostage" is found "in good condition" (*BP*, 268), but the reader does not know if this "boy"/"hostage" is Lipsha or the baby. Like Shawnee Ray, readers have to stay tuned.

TALES OF BURNING LOVE

Erdrich's fifth novel, *Tales of Burning Love,* resolves some of the action left hanging at the close of *The Bingo Palace,* which had ended with Lipsha Morrissey and an unidentified baby about to freeze to death in a snowbound car stolen by Gerry Nanapush, who has fled into the blizzard with the ghost of his former lover, June Morrissey. We discover in the course of *Tales of Burning Love* that the protagonists of this novel—Jack Mauser and his five wives—are connected to Gerry, Lipsha, and the baby in a variety of surprising ways. In fact, connections between this and Erdrich's previous novels abound: the opening chapter recapitulates from a different point of view the opening of *Love Medicine;* a character who was near death in *Love Medicine* reappears here, ancient but alive; one of Jack's wives is the protagonist of *The Beet Queen;* and so on.

Yet despite this interweaving, the chronology of the events in *Tales of Burning Love* cannot be completely coordinated with the events of the previous novels. For example, we learn in *Love Medicine* that Lipsha was born in about 1965, which would make him close to thirty in January 1995, the date of the blizzard in *Tales of Burning Love.* When Jack Mauser rescues him, however, he notices that Lipsha's face is "young, just past twenty maybe" (*TBL,* 386). There is a similar problem with the age of Sister Leopolda. She is said to be 108 when she dies in 1994 in *Tales of Burning Love,* which would put her birth around 1886. By that chronology, she would have been around twenty-seven in 1913 when, as Pauline Puyat, she went to Argus to work in the Kozkas' butcher shop. Yet we remember from *Tracks* that in 1913 "I was fifteen, alone, and so poor-looking I was invisible to most customers" (*Tr*, 15). (Also note the chronological discrepancy cited in the overview of *The Bingo Palace,* above.)

Some of these inconsistencies might be explained as the misperceptions of characters or as the falsifications of unreliable narrators. Some may reflect the dislocations and misunderstandings that naturally result from the oral transmission of tales from character to character. And some, no doubt, reflect authorial changes of mind or rethinking of certain characters and events. We get the sense that Erdrich herself, working close to an oral tradition, is discovering more about her own characters as she hears tales about them in her own mind and writes their stories. In addition, the indeterminacy of time in *The Bingo Palace* may be seen as something of a transition between the chronology of *Love Medicine, The Beet Queen,* and *Tracks* and the rather different chronology of *Tales of Burning Love.* We point out the discrepancies only to warn readers that they exist and to encourage confused readers not to worry overmuch about them. Erdrich herself has larger truths to tell as she allows her story and its characters to develop.

Tales of Burning Love is set mostly in Fargo, North Dakota, where Jack Mauser, the focal character, has his construction business. Some key scenes, however, take place in fictional Argus, and minor scenes take place on the reservation. Although Jack's father is of German ancestry, his mother is from the reservation, and Jack himself is an enrolled member of the reservation tribe.

Much of the narrative concerns Jack's various loves, told largely from the point of view of his four surviving wives in a narrative setting vaguely reminiscent of Chaucer's *Canterbury Tales.* Because of his experience with five wives, Jack emerges as a kind of modern-day, male Wife of Bath. *Tales of Burning Love* is a broadly comic novel with an unrealistically cheerful set of ending sequences. No one freezes to death; characters find or regain true love; even our old friend Sister Leopolda, after dying in the course of the novel, seems at the end headed for beatification. In a later novel, *The Last Report on the Miracles at Little No Horse,* we learn that the Vatican does indeed launch an investigation into Sister Leopolda's life. In that investigation, Jude Miller of *The Beet Queen* and Father Damien of *Tracks* both play central roles.

Many narrative threads interweave in *Tales of Burning Love.* Listed below are some of the events that stand out as keys to an understanding of the development of the narrative. The present-time events of the novel generally take place between the summer of 1994 and the following summer, many of them in the first week of January 1995, but much is revealed along the way about various events from the past.

Chronology of Events in *Tales of Burning Love:*

c. 1962—Eleanor Schlick is born.

c. 1968—Six-year-old Eleanor is rescued from her burning home by her mother.

c. 1970—Jack Mauser studies engineering at North Dakota State University. In November he nearly freezes to death fighting a fire. Anna Schlick saves his life. Assuming Anna's unfaithfulness, Lawrence Schlick casts out both Anna and their daughter, Eleanor.

1970s—Jack leaves school to make money in the construction business.

Late 1970s—The teenage Eleanor stomps Jack's hand into broken glass in a store. Later they have a date and make love in his pickup truck. Eleanor and Jack begin an on-and-off relationship.

1980–1981—During one of his absences from Eleanor, Jack works for a year in western North Dakota, doing construction work in the oil fields.

Easter 1981—On Holy Saturday, Jack meets June Morrissey Kashpaw in Williston. They get married in a bar. June freezes to death attempting to walk home to the reservation. The next day, Jack helps the police find her body.

Fall 1981—Jack returns to Fargo. When Eleanor pretends to be pregnant with his child, her parents reunite. Jack and Eleanor get married in Florida.

1981–198_(?)—Jack and Eleanor's marriage is rocky from the start. They fight continually until Eleanor leaves for London.

1983—On a winter night, Lawrence Schlick sneaks home early from a trade show in Minneapolis, suspicious that his wife may be having an affair with Jack.

Early(?) 1980s—Jack begins his own construction company, Mauser and Mauser. Shortly thereafter, Jack encounters Candice Pantamounty at the city dump, and a few months later they marry.

Mid-late(?) 1980s—Jack buys Chuck Mauser's land west of Fargo and begins trying to get funding to build a housing development.

Summer 1992—Jack and Candice divorce. Jack performs mouth-to-mouth resuscitation on Marlis Cook after she is electrocuted in an accident. She sues him for not doing it correctly.

August 1992—Jack gets the first check of his housing development loan. He runs into Marlis at a local bar, and they drink together. That night

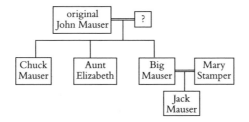

Chart 14. Jack's family of origin in Tales of Burning Love.

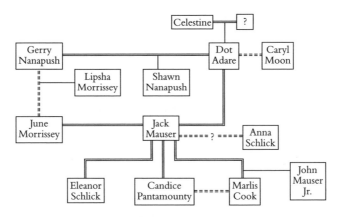

Chart 15. Jack's wives in Tales of Burning Love.

at a motel she steals his loan check. They drive to South Dakota to get married. The next day Marlis deposits Jack's check in her own account. They hide out for a month in Eugene.

September 1992—Jack returns to Fargo. Candice is in his car, drives him to work, and takes his car keys. Jack bulldozes Chuck Mauser's sunflowers.

Fall 1992–early 1994—Jack and Marlis travel to various cities as a musical duo. At the same time, Jack continues to oversee his highway construction and housing development projects near Fargo.

Fall 1993—Eleanor Schlick Mauser, now a college professor, seduces one of her undergraduate students and loses her job. Sometime later, she goes to the Our Lady of the Wheat Priory in Argus to study the aged nun Sister Leopolda.

Near Christmas 1993—In Detroit, Marlis realizes that she is pregnant.

Early 1994 (still winter)—Marlis tells Jack about her pregnancy. He reacts

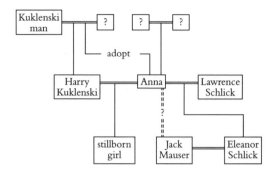

Chart 16. *Eleanor's family in* Tales of Burning Love.

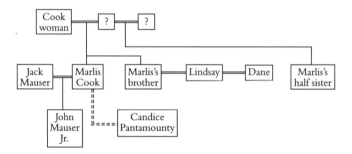

Chart 17. *Marlis's family in* Tales of Burning Love.

to the announcement abusively, and in Billings, Montana, she humiliates him and leaves him.

Early spring 1994—Candice and Marlis take a trip to northern Minnesota, on which Candice says that she wants to adopt the baby Marlis is carrying.

May 1994—Dot Adare Nanapush goes to work for Jack. Dot and Jack have their first date.

Spring–summer 1994—John Mauser Jr. is born to Marlis sometime before June. Marlis and Candice become lovers.

June 1994—Dot marries Jack and brings him to Argus to meet her mother. One June night, about a week after his marriage to Dot, Jack visits Eleanor at the Argus convent, where they make love. Sister Leopolda dies and, in the lightning storm that night, disappears. Two or three weeks later, Eleanor collapses and is hospitalized in Argus.

August 1994—Six weeks after Jack and Dot's wedding, they drive from Fargo to Argus to bring Eleanor back from the hospital. On this trip Dot learns that she herself is Jack's fifth wife and that he has a child by an earlier wife.

December 31, 1994—Jack's house burns down. Jack escapes, naked, out a basement window, after leaving clues to suggest that he burns to death.

January 1, 1995—The freezing Jack is rescued and then beaten by Caryl Moon. Jack manages to walk to his company's garage, where he slowly recovers.

January 4, 1995—Jack's banker, Hegelstead, visits him in the garage. They agree that Jack should work with Lyman Lamartine on his reservation casino project.

January 5, 1995—Three of Jack's wives attend his funeral at Schlick's Funeral Home. A radio bulletin announces a small aircraft crash and the escape of Gerry Nanapush. During his funeral, Jack steals Candice's car and drives off with his son, John Jr. At the railway station, Gerry and his son, Lipsha Morrissey, steal the car, with the baby inside, just as a blizzard breaks. Jack pursues them in a snowplow, heading north on the interstate.

After the funeral, Eleanor, Candice, and Dot drive to the B & B in West Fargo, where they find Marlis. Dot buys pizza for a large Indian woman. Jack's four wives start back to Fargo in the blizzard, pick up a hitchhiker, and about midnight, become stuck in a snowdrift.

January 6, 1995—In the small hours of the morning, the four wives keep each other awake and alive by telling scorching stories. Eleanor blows away into the storm, arrives at the airport, and reports the plight of the women in the car. Snowmobilers rescue Dot, Marlis, Candice, and the hitchhiker, but the hitchhiker (Gerry Nanapush) "falls off" on the way to the hospital. Gerry visits his daughter, Shawn, and escapes again on a neighbor's snowmobile. Just before dawn, guided by June's ghost, Jack rescues his son, John Jr., and June's son, Lipsha Morrissey, from Candice's snowbound car. They drive north to the reservation.

January 7, 1995—Jack and Lyman agree to work together on the casino project.

February 1995—Jack calls Dot, but she refuses to see him.

March 1995—One Saturday morning, Jack visits his son, and he and Marlis make love. The same afternoon Jack visits Candice in her dental office.

April 1995—Jack is nearly crushed by a stone statue of the Virgin being delivered to the Argus convent, but he receives only minor injuries.

July 6, 1995—Father Jude Miller writes to the bishop announcing a miracle connected with the Argus stone Virgin.

August 1995—Anna Schlick dies, and her husband cremates himself along with her body. Eleanor continues her investigations into the life of Sister Leopolda. Jack visits Eleanor at her house near the reservation, where they make love.

THE ANTELOPE WIFE

Erdrich's sixth novel, *The Antelope Wife,* takes us away from the characters and settings that have become familiar to us in her five earlier novels. The novel is set primarily in present-day Minneapolis; in a nineteenth-century Ojibwe village, probably just west of the Red River; and on a reservation somewhere "up north" of Minneapolis. A vague reference to "a Pillager woman" (*AW,* 35) is its one potential connection with the characters from earlier novels. In *The Antelope Wife,* Erdrich gives us a whole new set of intertwined characters and families. Three families dominate: the Roy family, starting with former Quaker Scranton Roy, who joins a U.S. Cavalry unit that raids the Ojibwe village; the Shawano family, descended from Everlasting and his daughter, Magid; and the Whiteheart Beads family, starting when the grandson of Scranton Roy trades red whiteheart beads for a wife.

The central consciousness of *The Antelope Wife* begins the narration with the account of the cavalry soldier who, following a dog with a baby strapped to its back, disappears onto the western prairie: "What happened to him lives on, though fading in the larger memory, and I relate it here in order that it not be lost" (*AW,* 3). The "I," though not identified here, is probably Cally Roy, the great-great-granddaughter of that cavalry soldier. Cally later reports that "I am a Roy, a Whiteheart Beads, a Shawano by way of the Roy and Shawano proximity—all in all, we make a huge old family lumped together like a can of those mixed party nuts" (*AW,* 110). Cally believes that "I was sent here to understand and to report" (*AW,* 220) these families' intermingled histories. She appears at the bottom of each of the charts below, though the family relationships that explain her being there are sometimes vague and tangled.

Although the "mixed party nuts" that Cally tells about in this novel are new, many of the approaches, themes, and ambiguities are familiar. We have seen multiple levels of narration in the earlier novels; here we have episodes recounted by dogs. We have seen humanlike animals; here we find people who have deer and antelope for ancestors. We have seen gender-crossing in previous novels; here we have a soldier who suckles two babies. We have seen confused chronology before; here we find only a single reference to a specific year (1945) to help anchor us. We have seen confusing family relationships before; here we have some eight generations of entangled families, including different characters with the same names. We have also seen Erdrich's use of the Ojibwe language in her earlier fiction; this novel seems to presuppose that the reader has an Ojibwe-English dictionary. We have seen Erdrich's humor; here it takes on new shades and flavors, all sprouting from the conviction that a sense of humor is "an Indian's seventh sense" (*AW,* 115). We have seen her use of extended metaphors; here we follow from first page to last the metaphor of DNA-like bead-stitching, making and remaking the patterns of people's lives.

The genealogical charts for the families in *The Antelope Wife* are more problematical than those in earlier novels, partly because of the number of generations involved and partly because Erdrich leaves out many connections and explanations. For more detail and possible alternate relationships between characters and families, see their entries in the dictionary of characters.

Although the sequence of some specific events is unclear, it is not difficult to follow the general order of events in *The Antelope Wife.* We are assisted by the occasional reference to the age of a character and by allusions to either history or technology, which suggest general time periods. When we read, for example, about the electronic bar-code scanner at a grocery store or the screen saver on a computer monitor, we assume that the surrounding events are contemporary with the writing of the novel.

Erdrich also seems to drop some clues about the undated cavalry raid that begins the action. We are told, for example, that Scranton Roy enlists in the U.S. Cavalry at a fort "on the banks of the Mississippi in St. Paul, Minnesota" (*AW,* 4), that the raided village is "due west" of there, that Scranton wears a "dark blue uniform" (*AW,* 4), and that the raid takes place "during the scare over the starving Sioux" (*AW,* 3). Erdrich may be referring obliquely to the time of the U.S. Civil War, specifically to what is sometimes called Little Crow's War in 1862 and its aftermath in 1863. The Santee Sioux, deprived of rations and money promised them in treaties, tried under the leadership of Little Crow to mitigate their plight by attacking towns (especially New Ulm) and forts (especially Ft. Ridgely) in Minnesota. Colonel Henry H. Sibley led troops west from Ft. Snelling in St. Paul in 1862 (the fort is renamed "Ft. Sibley" in the novel). He defeated the Sioux and took many prisoners, thirty-eight of whom were subsequently executed.[3]

That early date and the events of Little Crow's War, however, do not fit precisely with other information in the novel. For one thing, the historical events took place somewhat farther south than the likely site of the cavalry raid in *The Antelope Wife*, during which dog, baby, and Scranton flee the village into the open prairie "west of the Otter Tail River" (*AW*, 3). Furthermore, counting back from the 1990s through the generations referred to suggests that the raid took place a good deal later, in the 1880s or 1890s, although we know of no specific historical events so late that match those referred to in the novel. For the purposes of this chronology, we assume the later date for the fictional raid in order to maintain consistency within the chronology.

Rather than attempting to assign specific dates to actions, we have listed them in estimated groupings of decades.

Chronology of Events in *The Antelope Wife:*

1880–1890s(?):

In the woods, Apijigo Bakaday meets and marries a stag. Her brothers shoot the stag and bring her back to her people, who name her Blue Prairie Woman.

Scranton Roy is part of a U.S. Cavalry company that attacks Blue Prairie Woman's village (probably in autumn). He kills two children and a grandmother. When a dog runs west into the open prairie with Blue Prairie Woman's infant daughter tied to its back, Scranton follows the dog.

After continuing west for several days, Scranton settles on the Great Plains. He nurses the baby, whom he names Matilda, at his own breast.

Blue Prairie Woman suckles a puppy of the bitch who had carried off her baby. The next spring or summer she gives birth to twin girls, Mary (I) and Josephette (Zosie I). She leaves the babies with her mother, Midass, and sets out to retrieve her first daughter.

Matilda Roy, now six years old, meets the schoolteacher Peace McKnight.

---

3. These events are summarized in chapter 3, "Little Crow's War," in Dee Brown's widely accessible *Bury My Heart at Wounded Knee: An Indian History of the American West* (New York: Holt, Rinehart, and Winston, 1971; also available in Bantam and other editions).

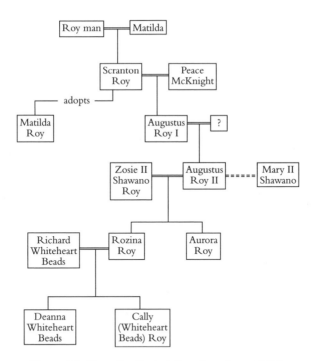

Chart 18. Roy family in The Antelope Wife.

Scranton and Peace marry. Peace becomes pregnant and later falls ill
with a fever.
Blue Prairie Woman finds Matilda, and the girl leaves with her. Matilda
falls ill with the fever. Then Blue Prairie Woman becomes ill and dies
the same day. Matilda recovers and follows a small herd of antelope.
After a difficult labor, Peace gives birth during a blizzard to a boy named
Augustus (I). She dies, and Scranton nurses his son.

1940–1950s(?):
Scranton Roy, now an old man, receives a dream summons from the old
woman he had killed. He sets out to find the remnants of her village, now
confined to a reservation, taking along his grandson Augustus Roy (II).
Augustus (II) falls in love with Zosie (II), granddaughter of Blue Prairie
Woman. In exchange for Zosie, he gives old Midass red whiteheart
beads.
Augustus marries Zosie, but he also has an ongoing affair with her twin,
Mary (II). Zosie becomes pregnant, and Augustus disappears mysteri-

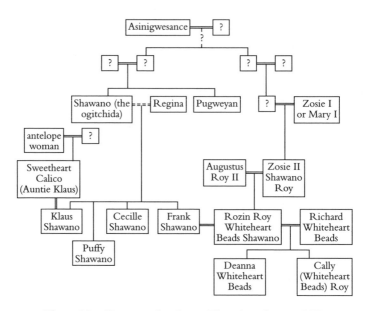

Chart 19. Shawano family in The Antelope Wife.

ously. While pregnant, Zosie sees a vision of Blue Prairie Woman and
her blue beads. Zosie gives birth to twins, Rozina (Rozin) and Aurora.
1945—Shawano the ogitchida comes home from the war. To avenge the
death of his cousin, he captures the German prisoner of war Klaus, who
bakes the "blitzkuchen."
When Rozin is five, her twin sister, Aurora, dies.

1970–1980s(?):

Rozin marries Richard Whiteheart Beads. They have twins, Deanna and
Cally.
Klaus Shawano sees an antelope woman and her three daughters at a
powwow in Elmo, Montana. He falls in love with the mother, kidnaps
her, and takes her back to Minneapolis, where she is called Sweetheart
Calico.
When Deanna and Cally are five, Rozin and Richard move to Minneapolis.
Rozin begins an affair with Frank Shawano. In the park, Richard and
the twins see Frank and Rozin together. Richard eventually confronts
Rozin, and the affair ends.
Richard and Klaus begin a waste disposal company that engages in illegal
dumping practices. Richard gives Klaus and Sweetheart Calico a free trip

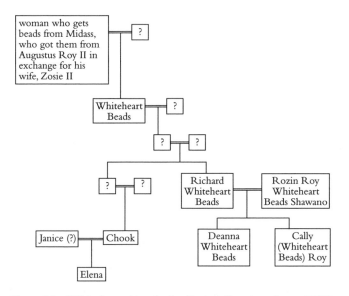

Chart 20. Whiteheart Beads family in The Antelope Wife.

to Hawaii, but on the trip, government agents arrest Klaus, mistaking him for Richard.

Klaus and Sweetheart Calico both disappear for several years, then Klaus for several more, leaving Sweetheart Calico in his family's care in Minneapolis. An explosion throws Sweetheart Calico through a window.

The puppy Almost Soup is born in Bwaanakeeng (Dakota-land), and Cally Roy saves him from being cooked.

When Deanna and Cally are eleven, Frank Shawano is diagnosed with terminal cancer. In March, Rozin tells Richard that she is taking the girls and moving in with Frank. Richard's unsuccessful suicide attempt results in Deanna's death.

Rozin moves back to the reservation. The following February, Cally becomes ill. Her mother, grandmothers, and dog help keep her alive until an ambulance can come.

Richard and Klaus become street drunks. Frank takes radiation treatments and recovers from his cancer.

1990s(?):

Zosie and Mary move to Minneapolis. At age eighteen, Cally also moves to the city. She works in Frank's bakery, lives above the store, and hunts

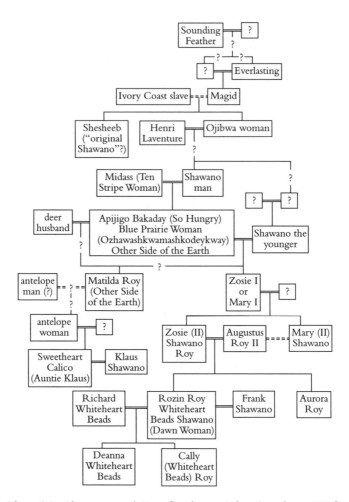

Chart 21. Shawano and Roy families in The Antelope Wife.

for her grandmothers. One day Zosie comes to the bakery, followed by Richard and Klaus, both drunk.

When Cally is twenty, Rozin moves to Minneapolis. She lives with her "mothers," works in a food co-op, and goes to night school. Frank comes to the co-op, then calls Rozin until she agrees to go to the state fair with him. They become lovers again.

Continuing to drink, Klaus is visited by Windigo Dog.

Richard and Klaus check into a recovery lodge. Klaus stops drinking and gets a job, but Richard does not.

In autumn (Cally is probably twenty-one), Frank and Rozin marry. Richard interrupts the ceremony and reception and finally kills himself outside Frank and Rozin's hotel room. Rozin stays alone in her mothers' apartment, where she talks to ghosts and sees dream visions. Frank is eventually able to come care for her.

That Christmas the family gathers at Frank and Rozin's apartment. After dinner Cally talks with Zosie, who reveals that she is Rozin's mother and tells the story of the blue beads. Sweetheart Calico takes beads out of her mouth and speaks her first words in the novel. Cally accompanies Sweetheart Calico to the outskirts of the city.

A lawn mower runs over Klaus's head, and he decides to change his life. He takes Sweetheart Calico to the open spaces west of the city and releases her.

The next autumn, Frank plans a surprise first-anniversary party for Rozin, while Rozin plans an intimate surprise for him. The result is a surprise for everyone.

THE LAST REPORT ON THE MIRACLES AT LITTLE NO HORSE

After the excursion to Minneapolis in *The Antelope Wife,* Erdrich's seventh novel takes us back to North Dakota and the characters she had made famous in her early novels. It revisits some of the events of *Tracks:* Father Damien's arrival at the reservation; the consumption epidemic in which the families of Nanapush and Fleur perish; the continuing feuds of the Kashpaw and Pillager clans with the mixed-blood Morrisseys and Lazarres; the shenanigans of Nanapush and his romance with Margaret Kashpaw; and the evil doings of Pauline Puyat before and after her becoming a nun.

Although several new characters appear in *The Last Report on the Miracles at Little No Horse,* most are of little importance to Erdrich's larger North Dakota story. The most significant new character is Mary Kashpaw, the daughter of Kashpaw and his wife Quill. After her parents are killed in an accident, Mary becomes housekeeper and caretaker for Father Damien. She serves him with singular devotion and faithfully keeps his secrets.

But Mary Kashpaw is not entirely new. It turns out that she is the same person as Mary Stamper, the mother of Jack Mauser in *Tales of Burning Love.* Mary has a brief marriage to a character known in *Last Report* only as Awun (the Mist), the son of land magnate John James Mauser and Fleur Pillager. (Awun is called "the Big Mauser" in *Tales of Burning Love.*) The new information about Mary in *Last Report* thus reveals that Jack Mauser is the descendant of two old-time families, the Kashpaws and the Pillagers. (He is thus a cousin to Lipsha Morrissey, who both kidnaps and saves Jack's baby in *The Bingo Palace* and *Tales of Burning Love.*)

Last Report's most significant connections, however, are with *Tracks.* The key figure in these connections is Father Damien, a minor character in *Tracks* but the protagonist of *Last Report.* The novel begins with his early history as Agnes DeWitt, first as a novice named Sister Cecilia and then as the common-law wife of German immigrant farmer Berndt Vogel. After she is widowed by a bank robber and swept away by a flood, she assumes the robes and character of the "real" Father Damien Modeste, who drowns in the same flood. This decision controls the physical and moral action of the rest of the novel. As Father Damien, Agnes goes north to become a priest to the Ojibwe, from her arrival in March of 1912 until her (his) death eighty-four years later. Father Damien's age at death is not specified, but he is apparently well over 100, probably close to 105.

Throughout his years at Little No Horse, Father Damien writes letters to a half-dozen popes, none of whom reply. The present time of the novel consists of the events of the last three months of Damien's life. During that period, Father Damien writes a final letter to the current pope, including his confession that his life has been fraudulent. Writing this letter, which looks back on his past, causes him to recall afresh some of the earlier events in his life. These recollections are further prompted by his conversations with Father Jude Miller, familiar to readers of *The Beet Queen* and *Tales of Burning Love.* Church hierarchy has sent Jude to investigate the possible beatification of Sister Leopolda, who died in 1994.

The Last Report on the Miracles at Little No Horse builds on the events of the earlier novels and ties up loose ends they left dangling. We learn here who Jack Mauser's parents are; whether Marie Kashpaw learns her mother's identity; where Fleur goes when she sends Lulu off to boarding school; and who that "white boy" is who returns to the reservation with her.

There are a few significant contradictions with earlier novels. For example, in *Tracks,* Father Damien is clearly a man, not a woman. One winter, "[t]o shield himself from the cold he had tried to grow a beard but it was too sparse for warmth" (*Tr,* 174). In the new novel, as a woman, Father Damien can grow no beard at all. Indeed, one of Mary Kashpaw's tasks when he is in a month-long, deathlike trance is to protect his secret by pretending to shave him each morning. The events in Pauline Puyat's life in the spring of 1919 also change considerably from *Tracks* to *Last Report,* as Erdrich rethinks and strengthens Pauline's stigmata story. There are also differences between *Tracks* and *Last Report* in the story of the discovery of Napoleon Morrissey's body. (See these characters' dictionary entries for details.)

As the chronology below shows, the events of the novel cover an eighty-seven-year period from 1910 to 1997. This chronology does not include the earliest incidents referred to, such as Berndt Vogel's experiences in a European war, Nanapush's early marriages, Pauline's mother's history, and so on—all events not associated with any specific dates. The story proper begins with Agnes DeWitt's leaving the convent and joining Berndt Vogel.

Chronology of Past Events in *The Last Report on the Miracles at Little No Horse* (Before 1996):

1910—Sister Cecilia (Agnes DeWitt) plays Chopin, leaves the Fargo convent, and appears at Berndt Vogel's nearby farm. They buy the Caramacchione piano. Agnes, naked, plays Chopin.

Fall–winter 1910–1911—Agnes and Berndt live together as lovers.

Spring 1911—Bank robber "the Actor" wounds Agnes and kills Berndt. Agnes keeps and deposits some of the stolen money.

1911–1912—Agnes teaches piano and tries to manage Berndt's farm.

Spring 1912—The original Father Damien Modeste visits Agnes. The flooding Red River sweeps the Caramacchione and Agnes away to the north. Agnes finds the drowned Father Damien beside the river and takes on his identity and mission.

March 1912—Agnes/Father Damien arrives at Little No Horse. He visits Nanapush and Fleur Pillager, and then Kashpaw's household.

Spring–summer 1912—Kashpaw is baptized and gives up three wives.

Late summer or autumn 1912—Kashpaw and Quill are killed in an accident at the Feast of the Virgin.

Winter 1912–1913—The orphaned Mary Kashpaw is abused by Napoleon Morrissey and falls into madness.

Spring 1913—Mary digs ditch "graves." Father Damien brings her to the convent.

1913—A battered piano is given to the reservation church. Father Damien, having forgotten that he once played, is frightened by the instrument.

Spring 1914—Fleur Pillager's daughter, Lulu, is born.

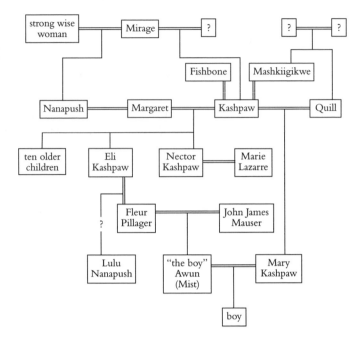

Chart 22. Kashpaw and Mauser families in The Last
Report on the Miracles at Little No Horse.

Winter 1918–1919—The Spanish influenza strikes Little No Horse, and
more than two hundred die. Father Damien, Mary Kashpaw, and Pauline
Puyat care for the ill and dying.

Spring 1919—Pauline confesses to Father Damien having had a child. A
few days later, one cold night she is found in the church, naked and
raving. She falls into a long, rigid trance.

Late summer 1919—The body of Napoleon Morrissey is found in the
woods, and Father Damien investigates. There is a riot at Napoleon's
funeral.

Late summer 1919—Fleur and Nanapush lose their land. Fleur decides to
leave the reservation to destroy her enemy John James Mauser and get
her land back.

September 1919—Fleur puts Lulu on a bus to the government boarding
school.

1919–192_(?)—At first Lulu tries to run away, then decides to hate her
mother and stay. When Fleur attempts to fetch her, Lulu refuses to go
with her.

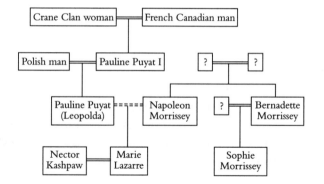

Chart 23. Puyat family in The Last Report
on the Miracles at Little No Horse.

1919–1920—Newly returned from school, Nector Kashpaw helps Bernadette in the tribal land office and takes control of the land documents.

1920—On a joyride in a Model T Ford, Nector and his cousins encounter
a band of young Lazarres, who try to drown them.

Autumn 1920—The devil as a black dog visits Father Damien. The dog
sends Damien a temptation, the young priest Father Gregory Wekkle.

Winter 1920–summer 1921—Father Damien and Father Gregory carry on
an intense affair.

Spring 1921—Bernadette Morrissey confesses to Father Damien her
knowledge of her brother Napoleon's sexual abuse of Mary Kashpaw.

Autumn 1921—After Father Gregory leaves, Damien goes into a sleepless
depression. He takes narcotics and falls into a month-long sleep. Mary
Kashpaw cares for him and follows him in his dream travels.

October 1921—Father Damien begins planning the new church building.

November 1921—Father Damien writes the Minneapolis bishop inquiring
about Fleur and learns that she has married John James Mauser.

Spring 1922(?)—Father Damien, still depressed, goes into the woods with
strychnine. Nanapush guides a sweat lodge ceremony to heal the priest.

April–June 1922—Father Damien oversees the building of the new church.

June 1922—The old piano is moved into the new church building. To his
surprise, Father Damien begins to play it—to an audience of snakes.
When he remembers the stash of robbery money in the Fargo bank, he
buys a new piano and vestments and commissions a new statue of the
Virgin.

Fall 1922—The new statue arrives. Father Damien preaches to the snakes.

1923—In a chess game, Nanapush reveals to Damien that he knows Damien's gender.

192_(?)—Lulu returns to the reservation. [*Tracks* gives the date as spring 1924.]

Spring 1933(?)—Fleur returns to Little No Horse with an unnamed white boy—her son with John James Mauser. Lulu refuses to see her. Pauline (now Sister Leopolda) returns from Argus. She confesses to Father Damien that she had killed Napoleon Morrissey and reveals that she knows that Damien is a woman.

July 1940—Awun (Fleur and Mauser's son) sees Mary Kashpaw chopping wood and is smitten. He abducts her that night, and she chooses to follow him.

1941—Awun and Mary's baby boy is born.

1941—Nanapush has his ill-fated encounter with a moose.

Winter 1941–1942—Margaret punishes Nanapush for the moose fiasco by feeding him undercooked beans. Nanapush dies, but rises twice at his funeral.

1945—Father Damien goes to Lulu's house and sees her laughing baby Gerry.

194_(?)–1950—Mary Kashpaw is confined in a mental institution. [*Tales of Burning Love* indicates that she is taken in for treatment when her son is six.]

1950—Mary is released and returns to Father Damien at Little No Horse.

1962—Father Gregory Wekkle, dying of cancer, returns to the reservation in July. After Gregory dies, Damien sees Mashkiigikwe in a Fargo park.

Chronology of Present-Time Events in *The Last Report on the Miracles at Little No Horse* (1996 and After):

1996

March 19–20—Father Damien begins his "last report" to the pope.

March, Eve of St. Dismas—Father Jude Miller comes to interview Father Damien about Sister Leopolda.

Over the next several days—Father Jude tells Father Damien of miracles attributed to Sister Leopolda, and Damien counters with examples of her evil deeds and twisted family.

About a week later—Father Jude meets Lulu and immediately falls in love with her. Jude visits her culture class the following day and several days later goes with her to the Sweetheart Bingo Bash.

Another day—Father Jude interviews Lulu.

One night—Father Damien wakes, plays the piano, and then wakes again to another encounter with the demonic black dog, which he finally vanquishes.

Next day—Father Damien tells Jude about the black dog.

Later that day(?)—Father Jude interviews Marie Kashpaw, who tells him that Leopolda was her mother.

Next morning—Father Damien finally tells Jude about Pauline's murder of Napoleon and subsequent tetanus.

(?)—Alone in his room, Jude wrestles with what he has learned about Leopolda and finally realizes that Father Damien, not Leopolda, is the potential saint.

June 1996—Father Damien goes to Spirit Island to die. Mary Kashpaw follows a few days later and buries his body in the lake.

1997—Father Jude moves to Little No Horse. The convent receives a fax to Father Damien from the pope. Damien's cabin is a shrine cared for by Mary Kashpaw.

THE MASTER BUTCHERS SINGING CLUB

In its concentration on non-Indian characters residing in the fictional town of Argus, Erdrich's eighth novel represents a significant shift from *Last Report*. It focuses particularly on German émigré Fidelis Waldvogel; his two wives, Eva Kalb Waldvogel and, after her death, Delphine Watzka Waldvogel; and the sons they rear. The majority of the Argus residents who pass through Fidelis's shop, home, and singing club are of German or Polish descent. Butcher-shop owners Pete and Fritzie Kozka are the only characters brought over from previous novels. Cyprian Lazarre comes from the mixed-blood Lazarre family encountered in earlier novels, but references to his background are too vague to connect him with particular Lazarres we have previously met.

Erdrich situates the majority of the novel between the end of World War I and the end of World War II. Thus, the framework for much of the plot lies in German-American relations. Fidelis, who was a sniper in the German infantry during World War I, develops a tense relationship with Cyprian, who served as a U.S. Marine in the war. The interwar years create conflicts in loyalties, and Fidelis's sons fight on opposite sides in the Second World War. Into this primary plot shaped by conflicting cultures, Erdrich weaves numerous subplots. One of these follows the local sheriff's investigation of the bodies found in the basement of the town drunk, an investigation complicated by the sheriff's unrequited love for a lovely young mortician. As in other Erdrich novels, some of these subplots reveal surprising relationships among the characters.

One of the novel's themes is the destructiveness of frustrated love. Sheriff Hock loves Clarisse Strub, but she rejects him and ultimately murders him. Roy Watzka loves Step-and-a-Half, but she rejects him, and he mutates her story into that of the imaginary deceased Minnie, the supposed cause of his alcoholism. Cyprian and Delphine love one another, but because she understands that Cyprian's deepest desires are homosexual, Delphine rejects his offers of marriage, and misunderstanding destroys what relationship they do have. Even when Delphine marries the butcher Fidelis, it may be his children that she loves more than the butcher himself. That love, in turn, is frustrated as personal and international events break the family apart.

Although *The Master Butchers Singing Club,* with its paucity of Native characters, seems less Indian than many of Erdrich's novels, it has a powerful undercurrent of Native perspective. Twice we hear a personal account of the slaughter at Wounded Knee. We hear of the vision and death of Louis Riel from a métis point of view. The retrospective provided in the final chapter reveals just how much one Ojibwe character has shaped the story and influenced its protagonists. The novel also weaves together the stories of the German and the North American struggles. In chapter 9 Fidelis realizes that Cyprian is an Indian and that he, Fidelis, may have offended him. Later, in chapter 12, Fidelis muses on the trajectory of his own journey. It has taken him from European battlefields "onto the wideness of the plains of America where the wars were not between the same old enemies he was used to, but were over before he'd got there, the great dying finished, and the blood already soaked into the ground" (*MBSC,* 290).

The ground is itself a powerful force in this novel. The dead fill the ground; the living are drawn into it, or try to escape it. The earth lures Markus—almost to his death—yet his burial produces a renewed and deepened life. In Eva's garden, the ground represents the chaotic cycling and recycling of life and death, a theme that links many pieces of the novel. Recycling distinguishes Fidelis's butchering philosophy from that of Pete Kozka and characterizes Step-and-a-Half's scrap-picking business. The novel closes with the idea that it is through the constant fluidity of cycling that our stories and our songs endure: "Our songs travel the earth. We sing to one another. Not a single note is ever lost and no song is original. They all come from the same place and go back to a time when only the stones howled" (*MBSC,* 388).

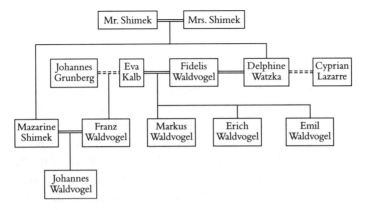

Chart 24. The Waldvogel family in The Master Butchers Singing Club.

Chronology of Events in *The Master Butchers Singing Club:*

October, c. 1907—Delphine is born and is rescued by Step-and-a-Half, who takes her to Roy Watzka to rear.

1915–1918—Fidelis Waldvogel is a sniper in the German trenches of World War I. When his best friend, Johannes Grunberg, is dying, Fidelis promises to marry Johannes's fiancée, Eva Kalb.

[c. same period]—Cyprian Lazarre, an Ojibwe, serves in the U.S. Marines during the war.

November 1918—Fidelis walks home to Ludwigsruhe. He tells the pregnant Eva about Johannes's death, and they later marry.

1919—Eva's baby, Franz, is born.

1922—Fidelis immigrates to the U.S., carrying his butcher's knives and his father's sausages. His money takes him only as far west as Argus, where he finds work as a butcher.

1910s-1920s—Delphine Watzka grows up in Argus with no mother and an alcoholic father. Though a bright student, Delphine quits high school early and goes to work.

Mid-1920s to early 1930s—Fidelis opens his own butcher shop. He saves his earnings until he is able to bring Eva and Franz, and later his sister, Tante, to join him. Three boys are born to Fidelis and Eva: Markus (1925) and twins Emil and Erich (1929). Fidelis and Pete Kozka's rivalry turns sour when a joke over a dog gets out of hand. In the early 1930s, Fidelis's knee is injured by a sow he is slaughtering. He begins a men's singing club.

Early 1934, late winter—Clarisse's father, Cornelius Strub, dies. At the wake, Sheriff Hock tries to tear off Clarisse's beaded dress, and the Chavers family is trapped in Roy Watzka's cellar, where they die.

Spring 1934—Delphine and thirty-two-year-old Cyprian Lazarre, who meet working with the Argus town theater, travel with their balancing act. While in Manitoba, Delphine sees Cyprian with a male lover.

Summer 1934—Delphine and Cyprian return to Argus. They find three bodies in the cellar of Roy Watzka's house and report the finding to Sheriff Hock. Delphine meets Eva and begins working at the Waldvogel butcher shop. Cyprian begins making whiskey runs to Canada.

Eva reveals that she is ill, Doctor Heech determines that she has advanced cancer, and Delphine takes her to the Mayo Clinic in Minnesota. Fidelis joins them while Cyprian runs the shop.

Between summer 1934 and summer 1935—After surgery, Eva undergoes radium treatments at the clinic, but the cancer spreads.

June 1935—A year later, Eva is near death. Franz arranges for Pouty Mannheim to take Eva up for a flight in his plane.

July 4, 1935—Delphine discovers that Eva's morphine is missing, stolen by Tante. Roy helps Eva by stealing morphine from the drugstore.

Late summer 1935—Markus sees Fidelis sing to Eva in the night. Eva buys chinchillas for the boys to raise and soon after dies. Roy begins a long period of sobriety. Delphine leaves the butcher shop and enjoys a brief period of "normal" home life, until Markus runs away to her house. Fidelis begs Delphine to come back to the shop, but she will only do so if Tante leaves.

Autumn 1935—Wild dogs kill the boys' chinchillas, and Fidelis lures and shoots the dogs. Tante buys a metallic suit and looks for work. Franz is courting Mazarine Shimek. Sheriff Hock arrests Roy, and Fidelis pays his bail.

Summer 1936—A year after Eva's death, Markus discovers the mound of earth he and four other boys decide to excavate. Step-and-a-Half vaguely warns Delphine about the boys' digging. One night Cyprian and Fidelis become hostile with each other, largely because of their feelings about Delphine.

November 1936—After days of heavy rain, one night the boys' hill collapses, trapping Markus inside. The others run for help, and Cyprian is able to rescue Markus. Franz's guilt at being with Mazarine during this incident induces him to abandon her and start seeing Betty Zumbrugge. Markus falls into a protracted illness, but a misunderstanding causes him to rouse himself back to health.

December 1936—Tante begins working in Step-and-a-Half's new shop. After a disastrous date, Franz leaves Betty Zumbrugge, but Mazarine will not take him back.

Two days before Christmas, Sheriff Hock searches Clarisse's house. When he tries to blackmail her, she eviscerates him with a carving knife. On Christmas Eve, Delphine's exhausted indifference to Cyprian's efforts causes a crisis. Cyprian drives to Clarisse's house and leaves with her the next day. Christmas morning, Delphine finds the car at Clarisse's. She later learns about Sheriff Hock's murder and Clarisse's disappearance.

February 1937, 1938, or 1939—Fidelis and Delphine drive Tante and the three youngest boys to Chicago in preparation for their trip to Germany. Markus falls ill and cannot make the trip.

March same year—Roy begins drinking again, and Delphine cares for him. One night Fidelis comes to her house and proposes.

Next several months—Delphine begins working again for the Waldvogels. She and Fidelis set a wedding date and give the news to Franz and Markus.

Autumn same year(?)—Fidelis and Delphine marry, and Franz enlists in the air corps. Cyprian returns briefly to Argus with his new performance partner, Vilhus Gast. Near death, Roy tells Delphine Minnie's story of Wounded Knee and reveals that he had in fact locked the Chavers family into his cellar.

1939 or 1940(?)—Early in the war, Emil is killed by a land mine.

1942—When Delphine is 35, Markus joins the U.S. Army.

1942–1943(?)—After horrible experiences in the German infantry, Erich is captured by American GIs. In early summer, he is taken to a POW camp in northeastern Minnesota.

1943–1944—In the autumn of 1943, Mazarine returns to Argus from teacher training college. The next spring, Franz comes home on leave. He and Mazarine become lovers, and she becomes pregnant. Markus and Fidelis go to see Erich in the POW camp, but Erich refuses to acknowledge them.

Autumn 1945—The atom bomb ends the war. Franz suffers a debilitating head injury at a U.S. military airfield. Mazarine goes to see him in the hospital.

1954—Fidelis and Delphine travel to Germany to see his family, including Erich, and to attend a memorial ceremony. But Fidelis is ill, and on the return trip, he collapses and dies in the New York customs area.

Mid-1950s—Delphine is in her forties and operates a plant nursery with Mazarine. Step-and-a-Half is an old woman recalling her experiences at Wounded Knee and her saving of the newborn Delphine from the Shimek outhouse.

FOUR SOULS

Erdrich's original plan had been to expand and reissue *Tracks* at double its original length. The revision would involve following Fleur Pillager from the reservation, which she leaves at the end of *Tracks,* to Minneapolis, where, as readers learned from *The Bingo Palace,* she acquired fine clothes, a white Pierce-Arrow automobile, and a pale boy. Erdrich was eventually persuaded to leave the original *Tracks* as it was and to issue the new material as a fresh and complete novel. Although *Four Souls* is unquestionably dependent on *Tracks* for much of its logic, it nevertheless works well as a stand-alone novel.

There are a few inconsistencies with earlier novels. In *The Beet Queen,* Fleur is making her living as a peddler in 1932. In the version of Fleur's story recorded in *The Last Report on the Miracles at Little No Horse* and *Four Souls,* however, in 1932 Fleur is living with her husband and son in Minneapolis and will return to the reservation the following year—in a Pierce-Arrow, not pulling a peddler's cart. Another variation appears between *The Bingo Palace* and *Four Souls.* Whereas in *Four Souls* the character Four Souls is Fleur's mother, in *The Bingo Palace* she is Fleur's grandmother, and her name is singular, Four Soul. Details about such variations appear in these characters' entries in the dictionary of characters.

The primary narrative in *Four Souls* involves Fleur's adventures and misadventures in Minneapolis, where she marries John James Mauser and bears his child. But like so much of Erdrich's writing, this novel weaves together multiple narrative threads. Subnarratives include Polly Elizabeth Gheen's inner struggle with her subordinate status; the comic strife that marks Nanapush and Margaret's love; Nanapush's attempts at revenge against his old enemy Shesheeb; and Margaret's vision and the making of her great-grandmother's medicine dress. These and other stories are intertwined, especially by their common movement from strife to peace—peace for the warring lovers Nanapush and Margaret; for Polly Elizabeth in her newfound love for Fantan; and especially for Fleur, who after more than a decade of pursuing power and revenge, finally reestablishes a connection with the spirits of her ancestors.

As in *Tracks,* we are never taken into Fleur's mind in this novel but learn about her indirectly. Nanapush narrates all of the odd-numbered chapters, as he does in *Tracks.* Also as in *Tracks,* women narrate the even-numbered chapters. Mauser's sister-in-law, Polly Elizabeth Gheen, tells what happens to Fleur in Minneapolis in the early even-numbered chapters, while Margaret tells of Fleur's return and potential healing in the last two of these chapters.

No dates are given in *Four Souls,* but its opening and closing events are dated in other novels. *Four Souls* clearly begins in the autumn of 1919, shortly after the trees around Fleur's cabin crush the Turcot logging equipment at the end of *Tracks.* After this climactic incident, Nanapush narrates Fleur's departure:

> From behind the cabin, Fleur wheeled a small cart, a wagon that one person could pull, constructed of the green wood of Matchimanito oaks. . . . The wheels groaned as she threw her weight against the yoke. She looked at me, her face alight, and then she set out. (*Tr,* 224)

Four Souls picks up the story at this point and tells us where Fleur, pulling the same cart (though this time holding her ancestors' bones), goes. Again Nanapush narrates:

> Fleur took the small roads, the rutted paths, through the woods traversing slough edge and heavy underbrush, trackless, unmapped, unknown and always bearing east. . . . [She] pulled her cart over farmland and pasture, heard the small clock and shift of her ancestors' bones when she halted, spent of all but the core of her spirit. (*FS,* 1)

Four Souls closes with Fleur's return to the reservation, which, according to chapter 16 of *Last Report,* occurs in the spring of 1933. In addition to this date's appearance in that chapter heading, we are told that Fleur returns during the Depression and that Leopolda returns from Argus about the same time. (See Pauline's dictionary of characters entry for details about the time of her return.) Thus, dating from Erdrich's other novels sets the action of *Four Souls* in the period from 1919 to 1933.

Determining dates within the novel is more difficult. We know some time intervals based on the age of Fleur's son, but we cannot be certain when he is born. The fundamental difficulty is in determining when Fleur arrives in Minneapolis. She leaves the reservation in September 1919; her journey as described in *Four Souls* seems an uninterrupted pursuit of Mauser along the train tracks that had carried away her stolen timber; and a fresh snow falls on unfrozen ground the night before she reaches Minneapolis. Thus, a reader's first impression is that Fleur arrives in the city within a few months after leaving the reservation, late fall or early winter of 1919.

There are possible problems with this reading of the chronology, however. When Fleur arrives, Mauser's house is completely finished and furnished. Yet the oak used in its construction was cut from her property in the late summer of 1919. It is questionable whether so large and grand a house could be completed and occupied by the beginning of winter that same year. These details suggest that Fleur's arrival may occur in the spring or late fall of 1920. Certain details in *The Last Report on the Miracles at Little No Horse* seem to support the later date. In chapter 16 of *Last Report*, Father Damien writes to the bishop of Minneapolis in November 1921, asking if he knows the whereabouts of Fleur. The bishop answers that Fleur is married to John James Mauser. There is nothing said about a child, and Fleur is likely not even pregnant yet, since the bishop describes her social life, and *Four Souls* tells us that she is confined to bed for much of her pregnancy. If Fleur reaches Minneapolis in 1920, then her marriage to Mauser, which Polly Elizabeth says occurs a year later, takes place in 1921. Her son, apparently conceived shortly after the marriage, would then probably be born in 1922.

On the other hand, another circumstance seems to favor the earlier year for the birth of Fleur's son, and thus, for her arrival and marriage. *Four Souls* chapter 8 indicates that when the boy is two, Fleur begins visiting Lulu's school to try to fetch her. We know from *Last Report* chapter 15 that Fleur comes six times, but *Tracks* chapter 9 tells us that Lulu leaves school and returns to the reservation in the spring of 1924. These details suggest that Fleur begins going to the school earlier than 1924, and thus an earlier birth date for the boy.

Either way, this 1921 or 1922 birth date jibes well enough with the ages of Fleur's boy in *Bingo Palace* and *Last Report*. (See the entry for John James Mauser II in the dictionary of characters for details about his age at certain points in these novels.)

The chronology below reflects the uncertainty about exact dates in *Four Souls*.

Chronology of Events in *Four Souls*:

Winter, 1860s or early 1870s—Nanapush's healer uncle tends the child Anaquot, who is ill with a fever. Her mother, Under the Ground, saves the girl by throwing out one of her souls.

1910s (before or during World War I)—John James Mauser marries Placide Gheen.

1914–1918(?)—Sometime during World War I, Mauser serves a year in the

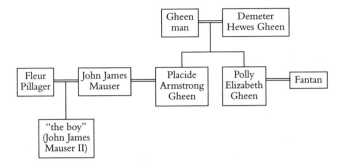

Chart 25. *Mauser and Gheen families in* Four Souls.

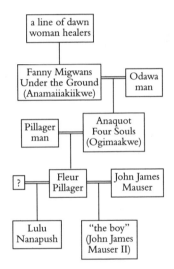

Chart 26. *Fleur's family in* Four Souls.

trenches and meets Fantan. Fantan is wounded, and Mauser, now ill, brings him back to Minneapolis.

Fall 1919—Fleur's land is taken, and she begins her journey east.

Minneapolis, 1919–1933:

1919(?) (or before) to 1920(?)—Mauser builds his mansion on the hill, using fine oak from Fleur's land.

1919 or 1920(?)—Fleur arrives at Mauser's house, and Polly Elizabeth Gheen hires her as the laundry woman. When Mauser has a seizure, Fleur revives him.

The following months—Fleur takes over Mauser's care and learns the house and its inhabitants. One night, she goes to sleep outside Mauser's door, and Mauser sees her there. Dr. Fulmer visits and diagnoses Mauser.

Fleur decides it is time to kill Mauser, but spares him when he promises to marry her and give her everything he owns.

One year after Fleur's arrival: 1920 or 1921(?)—Mauser divorces Placide and marries Fleur.

The following months—Fleur becomes pregnant with Mauser's child and is confined to bed. Polly Elizabeth begins to care for Fleur, giving her whiskey to stop premature labor.

1921 or 1922(?)—Mauser and Fleur's child, a boy, is born. Polly Elizabeth moves back into the house.

1922–early 1930s—The Mauser boy grows, but does not develop normally. At age two he still does not speak. Fleur begins visiting Lulu's boarding school, but Lulu refuses to go with her. The boy has his first spell of mental vacancy. Doctors initially say that he is bright, but eventually declare him retarded. Yet he becomes an expert poker player.

Early 1930s—Mauser's investments begin to fail, and he is troubled by the boy's affliction. He tells Polly Elizabeth about Fantan's being wounded in his place. Fleur, Polly Elizabeth, and the boy encounter Mauser's architect and his fiancée at the lake.

1933—Mauser flees his creditors, Fleur leaves with his automobile and the boy, and Polly Elizabeth and Fantan, now married, prepare Mauser's belongings for auction.

The reservation, 1920s–early 1930s:

(Nanapush is living with Margaret on her land.)

1920s—Margaret sells some of Nector's allotted land to buy linoleum for her house.

Early 1930s—Nanapush's old enemy Shesheeb moves nearby. Nanapush tries to kill Shesheeb with a snare but accidentally snares Margaret. She survives but has a near-death vision of her great-grandmother, Medicine Dress. As Margaret copies the vision dress, she recalls her childhood.

Nanapush steals wine from the convent. He dons Margaret's dress, goes to Shesheeb's house, and tries to steal more wine. Still wearing the dress, the next day he speaks at a council meeting. The following day, Nanapush cuts a hole in Margaret's linoleum and fabricates a story about a falling star.

The reservation, 1933:

Spring 1933—Fleur returns with a white car, white suit, and white boy. She learns that the present owner of her land is Jewett Parker Tatro. Fleur joins the ongoing poker game at Tatro's bar. One night, she wagers her car against Tatro's land and has the boy take her place in the game. He wins every hand and regains the land. The next morning at Margaret's cabin, Margaret bathes Fleur and tells her what she must do to heal.

Over the next months—Nanapush muses about Fleur's story, change, and mortality.

THE PAINTED DRUM

Erdrich's tenth novel opens in the early twenty-first century with Faye Travers relating the series of events that leads to her discovery of a mysterious painted drum in the estate of John Jewett Tatro, a grandson of Jewett Parker Tatro. The latter name is familiar to readers of such earlier novels as *The Bingo Palace* and *Four Souls,* where Jewett Parker Tatro is the Indian agent who helps swindle Fleur out of her land but then loses it back to her in a poker game. There can be little question that as she wrote the end of *Four Souls,* Erdrich anticipated the next novel, as we see from Nanapush's description of the artifacts that adorn the walls of Tatro's bar in chapter 15 of *Four Souls:*

> [B]y now our most beautiful and even sacred objects hung upon the walls of his bar. . . . There were cradle boards, tight beaded on velvet, that once held the drunks beneath them. There were gun belts and shoulder bags that only our head men used to carry. . . . There was even a drum. (*FS,* 190–91)

That drum turns up in an attic in New Hampshire at the start of *The Painted Drum.* Sometime after the poker game in which Fleur regains her land, Jewett Parker Tatro returns to his ancestral home with his ill-gotten loot, which he stows in his closets and attic. As she inventories the Tatro estate, Faye hears the drum sound, drawing her to steal it and return it to its home in North Dakota.

Although the chapters of *The Painted Drum* are undated, we can guess at several of its dates. We know from other novels that the poker game Tatro loses to Fleur occurs in about 1933. Thus it is sometime after this that Tatro returns to New England. We also know from *Tracks* that Fleur is born in

1895, so we can date the beginning action of *Painted Drum* part 2.2 (that is, part 2, chapter 2) in that year. In *The Painted Drum* itself, a gone-wild dog is said to eat a veal calf at the one working farm "that had survived the nineties" (*PD*, 22). This tells us that the novel's present time is the early twenty-first century, a dating corroborated by the reference to "old Mr. Bush" sending Morris String to Desert Storm (*PD*, 105). If there was an "old Mr. Bush," then by implication there is a new one, and George W. Bush was elected in 2000. We learn that in this present time Faye Travers is a little more than fifty, which means that she would have been born in the early 1950s. Faye's younger sister, Netta, steps from the apple tree and dies probably around 1960, since Faye is at least nine at the time.

One feature of the chronological sequence that may puzzle readers is the reference in part 2.5 to a forty-year hiatus in the use of the drum between Simon Jack's death and the drum's return to service in the early twenty-first century (part 3.7). If that hiatus was exactly forty years, the reference would imply that Simon Jack died in the later 1950s, which is far too late. In *The Painted Drum*, Fleur's father dies before her mother, whose death, according to *Tracks* chapter 1, occurs in the winter of 1912–1913. Thus when Bernard Shaawano says in *The Painted Drum* that "the forty years my grandfather spoke of are past" (*PD*, 186), rather than implying that only forty years have elapsed since his grandfather's retirement of the drum, he may mean simply that this forty-year period of waiting lies in the past.

For a discussion of differences between the *Tracks* and *Painted Drum* versions of Fleur's family, see the Pillager family entry in the dictionary of characters.

Four interwoven narrative threads constitute *The Painted Drum*. The first is the story of the drum itself—how the wood is cured, how the drum is made, how it gets to Tatro's bar and then to New Hampshire, and how it is brought back to the Ojibwe reservation. The second is the story of Simon Jack's infidelity and the effect it has on two women and their children, and the connection of this story to the making of the drum. The third is the story of the Pillager woman Faye Travers, a descendant of Simon Jack and Ziigwan'aage, who finds the drum in an attic in New Hampshire and returns it to North Dakota. The fourth is the story of a man who talked to wolves and his daughter, Ira, whose young children survive fire and cold with the help of the painted drum.

In the chronology below, we arrange the novel's events by centuries and parts of centuries, relying on inference and instinct for some of the ordering of events.

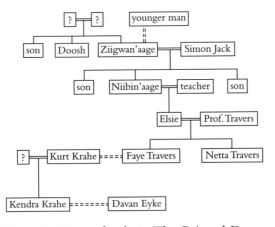

Chart 27. *Travers family in* The Painted Drum.

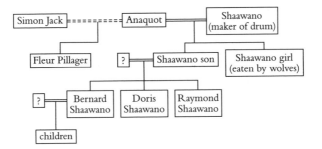

Chart 28. *Shaawano family in* The Painted Drum.

Chronology of Past Events in *The Painted Drum:*

Before 1900—reservation

Great cedar trees are struck by lightning. In each generation, chosen
individuals watch over the wood.

Near 1900—reservation

Anaquot marries Shaawano. They have two children. She has a love affair
with the Pillager Simon Jack and gives birth to his daughter Fleur.

That winter, when Anaquot and her two daughters set out for the Pillager
camp, wolves attack the sled. They kill the Shaawano girl, but the others
escape. Shaawano finds the girl's bones.

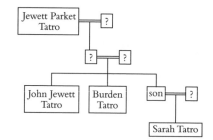

Chart 29. Tatro family in The Painted Drum.

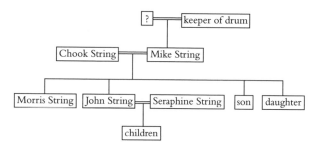

Chart 30. String family in The Painted Drum.

At Simon Jack's cabin, Anaquot meets his wife, Ziigwan'aage. The two
    women form an unlikely bond and turn against Simon Jack.
When Ziigwan'aage's daughter, Niibin'aage, is ten, she goes to Carlisle
    Indian School.

Early 1900s (Shaawano and the drum)—reservation

Shaawano begins wandering, leaving his son for weeks at a time. One
    summer the spirit of his daughter appears to Shaawano in a dream and
    tells him to make the drum. Shaawano visits Kakageeshikok (Geeshik).
The following spring, Albert Ruse gives Shaawano an old canoe. Albert
    and his son Chickie accompany Shaawano across the lake to find the
    drum wood.
Camped beside the wood, Shaawano makes the body of the drum. Going
    home, spirit signs reveal how he should ornament it. Before he stretches
    the drumheads, Shaawano's daughter tells him to put her bones inside.
Though the drum is a powerful healer, when Simon Jack enters the drum

circle, the little girl drum makes him dance to his death. Shaawano puts the drum away to rest for forty years.

Anaquot and Ziigwan'aage die in an epidemic. Of the Pillager family, only Fleur and Niibin'aage survive.

1900s (the next generation)—reservation and New Hampshire

Niibin'aage marries the Carlisle teacher who recruited her. Their daughter, Elsie, is born on the reservation, but they move back to his home in Stokes, New Hampshire.

Shaawano's son marries and has three children: Bernard, and twins Doris and Raymond.

Bernard's Shaawano grandfather tells him the story of the drum. When old Shaawano dies, the drum is given to Bernard's father, who sells it to Indian agent Jewett Parker Tatro. Tatro returns home to New Hampshire, taking his Ojibwe heirlooms with him.

When Bernard is ten and the twins six, their mother dies and their father begins to drink heavily and beat them. When Bernard is thirteen, he fights his father, and his father subsequently tells Bernard of his dead sister. Later, however, Bernard provides a new interpretation of his sister's death.

A despairing young man goes out to talk to the wolves and learns from them.

Near midcentury, Niibin'aage's daughter, Elsie, begins an estate business and marries Professor Travers. In the 1950s, their daughters, Faye and Netta, are born. One summer evening, Netta steps from a high branch and falls to her death. Their father dies six months later.

Bernard marries and has a family. When the children are grown, they and Bernard's wife move to Fargo.

The man who talked to wolves has a daughter, Ira.

Faye Travers joins her mother in the estate business.

Late 1900s—New Hampshire

Kurt Krahe's second wife is killed in a car accident. Their daughter, Kendra, is in junior high school.

Kurt begins a long-term affair with Faye Travers.

Early 2000s (the recent past)—reservation and New Hampshire

Faye gives herself a lawn mower for her fiftieth birthday.

Ira and her children live in the Cities. When her husband leaves them, her father brings them to the reservation. When the old man is in the hospital, he tells Bernard Shaawano about talking to the wolves.

One mid-winter day, Davan Eyke wrecks his father's new car. He leaves home, takes a job with Kurt Krahe, and kills a raven. Angry, Krahe shoots at Davan.

Davan acquires a red Toyota and returns to his parents' house.

The Eyke dog escapes, dragging its chain.

Kendra Krahe is enrolled at Sarah Lawrence College. When she is home visiting her father, Davan begins seeing her.

Chronology of Present-Time Events in *The Painted Drum* (A Two-Year Period in the Early 2000s):

Year 1, late winter—**New Hampshire**

Faye leaves the children's cemetery where her sister, Netta, is buried.

Krahe is upset about Davan's attentions to Kendra and threatens the boy.

The Eyke dog begins killing animals. When it threatens children, the state police are called in. One of the officers recognizes Davan's Toyota as stolen. In the ensuing chase, Davan's out-of-control car kills John Jewett Tatro and goes off a bridge. Both Davan and Kendra die.

Year 1, March—**New Hampshire**

Faye inventories the Ojibwe artifacts in the house of the late John Jewett Tatro. She steals the painted drum.

Kurt mows Elsie and Faye's yard and volunteers to prune their apple orchard, but Faye tells him to leave the orchard alone.

When Elsie finds the stolen drum, she confronts Faye about it, but she eventually agrees that it should be returned to its rightful owners.

Despite Faye's objection, Kurt prunes the orchard.

Year 1, May—**New Hampshire**

The orchard, now in blossom, reminds Faye of Netta's death. She changes the back door lock to turn Kurt away.

Year 1, late summer—**New Hampshire**

Faye sells the Tatro estate items but still has the drum. One August day, Faye gathers blackberries, police officer Lonnie Germaine comes to the house, and details about Netta's death flood Faye's thoughts.

Year 1, early autumn—reservation

Elsie and Faye take the drum back to the reservation. The women meet with a small group at Judge and Geraldine Nanapush's house, where Bernard Shaawano tells them the story of their Pillager forebears and the history of the drum.

Deep winter (probably early Year 2)—reservation

Ira goes to town for food and heating oil, leaving her three children home alone. She meets John String in a bar. He buys groceries for her family, and his brother Morris drives her home.

At the house, Ira's children are hungry and freezing. Shawnee, the eldest, builds a fire in a makeshift stove. But after the house burns down, the children set out through the snow to neighbor Bernard Shaawano's house. The sound of the drum guides Shawnee to Bernard's.

The children spend several days in the Indian Health Service hospital, Apitchi with pneumonia. Bernard uses the drum for the first time in decades in a healing ceremony for Apitchi.

Year 2, September—New Hampshire

Faye and Elsie talk openly about Netta's death. They receive a letter from Bernard telling them about the good the drum has done. Faye and Kurt become lovers again.

Faye visits Netta's grave.

This chapter contains three sections: (1) a brief discussion of how to use the dictionary of characters and the principles that guided us in preparing it, (2) the tables of contents for each of Erdrich's ten novels published through 2005, and (3) the detailed dictionary of characters itself.

This dictionary is designed to help readers of Louise Erdrich's first ten novels find their way through her always interesting but sometimes confusing cast of characters. It is a large cast. In *Love Medicine* alone there are some seventy-five different characters. In all ten novels there are many hundreds. In the main part of this dictionary we have described more than five hundred characters. In the separate section at the end, "Miscellaneous Minor Characters," our readers will find several hundred more characters or groups of characters. All of these characters, major and minor, blend to make up a rich and varied cast in complex dramas involving men and women of different races, ages, and generations.

In many cases, the snatches of narrative and allusion through which readers come to know these characters are scattered unchronologically through several novels. Sorting the people and events of Erdrich's world is further complicated by the fact that different narrative points of view may provide contradictory pictures, and also the fact that Erdrich's own conception of her characters has changed and developed over time.

HOW TO USE THIS DICTIONARY

This dictionary identifies each major character and most minor ones, tells briefly what they do, and gives every chapter in Erdrich's first ten novels where they appear. It will be particularly helpful when used with the map, charts, and chronologies in Part I of this guide. Issues of place, relationships, and time sketched broadly there are addressed in more detail in this section.

Characters are listed under the name by which they are most frequently known—most often the *first* name. Our decision to list characters alphabetically by their first names was carefully considered. Readers will recognize names such as Marie, Nector, Lulu, or Gerry, but they might not always remember last names, especially those of female characters whose names change. It seemed best, for example, to list Lulu Nanapush Morrissey Lamartine under the name **Lulu** rather than under one of her surnames. She is not, after all, a Nanapush by blood, and her marriages to Morrissey and the two Lamartine brothers are brief. In addition, Erdrich almost always uses only Lulu's first name. Characters for whom Erdrich has not given first names we have identified by last names. When there is more than one character with the same name, we use Roman numerals, such as **Morrissey I** and **Morrissey II.** But when one of the characters who share a name is much more important than the other, we add a numeral only to the name of the lesser character. For example, the mother of major character Pauline Puyat is also named Pauline Puyat. The mother is called **Pauline Puyat I,** but the Pauline who becomes Leopolda is simply **Pauline Puyat.** We have generally listed characters under their English rather than their Indian names, unless the Indian name is the primary one used in the novels. Thus, for example, the entry for the mother of Moses Pillager appears under **Different Thumbs** rather than Nanakawepenesick, whereas the woman who has a deer husband is listed as **Apijigo Bakaday** rather than So Hungry. Wherever we thought confusion might result, we have cross-listed characters' alternate names, with references back to the main-entry names. Thus, **Boss Woman**'s Indian name, **Ogimaakwe,** is cross-listed, since on two occasions it is the only form given. Asasaweminikwesens, however, the Indian name of Fleur's sister **Chokecherry Girl,** is not cross-listed, since it never appears apart from its English translation.

For help in determining family relationships, members of the major family groups are also cross-referenced under family names. For example, **Marie Lazarre** is cross-listed under both **Lazarre family** and **Kashpaw family. Lulu Nanapush Morrissey Lamartine** is cross-listed under **Nanapush family, Morrissey family,** and **Lamartine family,** as well as **Pillager family,** since she is a Pillager by blood. There are also family entries for the Adare, Bijiu, Bizhieu, Destroismaisons, Hat, Kuklenski, Mauser, Onesides, Pukwan, Puyat, Roy, Shaawano, Shawano, String, Tatro, Toose, Waldvogel, and Whiteheart Beads families.

The family connections of several of the characters are ambiguous. **Nanapush,** for example, is a confusing case. He is referred to as the grandfather, father, and uncle of various other living characters, some of whom carry his name, but in fact, he is the sole Little No Horse survivor of the consumption epidemic that carried off the rest of his family in about

1912. The ancestry of **Marie Lazarre Kashpaw** is also confusing because she appears to have one set of parents in *Love Medicine,* but we learn in *Tracks* who her true parents are. The paternity of some characters—most notably **Lulu Nanapush** and **Redford Toose**—remains uncertain.

Where a character has no name, we use a descriptive designator, such as **Cowboy, Massive Indian woman, Old drunk woman.** We do not list the names of radio, television, and movie personages, such as Jimi Hendrix and Patti Page, or of other real people mentioned in passing. We do not normally list animals unless they have specifically human traits or play a significant role in the narrative. Thus, we created an entry for the **Antelope and deer people** who intermarry with humans in *The Antelope Wife,* but not for those that Eli stalks in *Tracks.* The speaking dogs **Almost Soup** and **Windigo Dog** have entries, as does **Pepperboy,** whose life and death play an important role in the marriage of Jack and Candice Mauser, but Lily Veddar's dog, Fatso, does not. We do list humanlike spiritual or mythical personages—such as **Misshepeshu, Christ, Satan,** the **Black dog,** and various statues of the Virgin—who, having humanlike qualities, act more or less as people in the minds of some characters.

With only a few exceptions, the various references to each character are gathered into one entry, with alternate names for the same person cross-referenced. Exceptions include characters (such as **Andy, Father Damien Modeste, Father of Fargo baby,** and **Sister Leopolda**) whose alternate names and identities Erdrich does not at first reveal. In order to avoid giving away Erdrich's secrets prematurely, we have created separate entries for each of these characters' identities. When readers look up all of the chapter references in these entries, however, the double identities will become clear. (Readers using this guide who want to avoid uncovering Erdrich's surprises prematurely can limit their tracing of references to those novels that they have already read.)

In addition to the leading players and their family members, lovers, and associates, a multitude of unnamed "extras" brush through Erdrich's pages. We find clerks and customers, photographers and reporters, factory workers and construction workers, drivers of various vehicles, and people just out walking their dogs. To list each of these personages separately would be tedious, and yet calling attention to them makes us realize more fully the vastness of Erdrich's canvas, the breadth as well as the depth of her characterization. Even an anonymous white doctor, for example, who appears only briefly in chapter 7 of *Tracks,* gives readers a sharp glimpse into the racial prejudices present in Erdrich's North Dakota. Most of these bit-part players we have grouped together at the end of the dictionary in a potpourri section, "Miscellaneous Minor Characters," subdivided by novel.

Some such minor characters, however, fall within categories that appear often enough to be significant as types. Group entries for **Doctors** and **Nurses,** for example, highlight the frequency with which medical personnel appear in the novels. Smaller groupings such as **Bartenders** and **Jewelers** call attention to types of characters that a first-time reader would normally overlook. Some small groupings are connected with certain central characters, such as **Dot Adare's classmates** and **Fleur Pillager's customers.** All such groupings are alphabetized into the main dictionary. Perhaps the most significant of these group entries are those for persons who have taken orders within the Catholic Church, which figures so prominently in Erdrich's fiction. These individuals are grouped into entries for **Bishops, Priests and Preachers,** and **Nuns.** The last category is divided by convent to help readers get a sense of what goes on over a period of time at individual locations, such as Sacred Heart on the reservation or Our Lady of the Wheat in Argus.

Entry titles and references to entry titles are in **boldface roman** type. Characters who have no separate entry but are introduced within a group entry are given in *boldface italics.* In addition to these group entries, some minor characters are introduced in individual-character entries, whenever this placement seems most efficient and logical. The entry for **Stan Mahng,** for example, also includes *Stan's baby* and his *girlfriend,* and the entry for the **Gravitron operator** includes the *Gravitron riders* whom he endangers and the *woman* and *people watching* who respond to his dangerous behavior.

We have generally listed the activities of the various characters chronologically within each entry rather than in the order in which those incidents appear in the novels. When the characters appear as ghosts, we discuss their spirit-presences, logically enough, after they have died. Because little in Erdrich's fiction does not break out of its own mold, when in doubt we have followed where her shifting currents seemed to lead us.

We have designed this dictionary to serve as an index for the characters, a guide to the stories and chapters that contain significant references to them. We do not give page number references. Instead, we use story titles or chapter numbers to refer readers to the chapters in which portions of a character's story appear. Our use of story or chapter references is somewhat complicated, however, by the fact that Erdrich designates sections differently in her various novels.

In this section we reproduce or construct tables of contents for all ten of Erdrich's novels. Whereas in her earlier novels Erdrich herself provided tables of contents to guide her readers to the parts and the overall structure of the novels, in her later ones she has tended not to do that. Serious students of Erdrich's work will find it useful to have ready access to tables of contents for all of the novels. These will be particularly helpful to readers wanting to see, at a glance, the structure of a novel, or for finding chapters that we refer to by number or name in the dictionary of characters that follows.

CHAPTERS IN LOVE MEDICINE *(1984, 1993)*

Erdrich does not number the stories in *Love Medicine,* perhaps because she thought of the book less as a novel than a collection of interrelated stories. Nor do we number them here. We do provide in parentheses the dates that Erdrich gives at the start of each story. We use story titles from the expanded 1993 edition, which has eighteen chapters, rather than the earlier 1984 edition, which has four and a half fewer chapters. Erdrich presents the stories in generally chronological order, except that the opening story, set in 1981, jumps ahead in the sequence. Many of the chapters are in the first person, while others are in the third. Erdrich gives the names of first-person narrators, usually at the beginning of the chapter. In the table below, the narrator's name follows the story title.

CHAPTERS IN THE BEET QUEEN *(1986)*

The sixteen chapters in *The Beet Queen* are gathered into four larger units identified only by number. Most of the chapters are subdivided into two or more short narratives, representing shifting points of view. The name of the narrator of each part serves as the subdivision title, each new name signaling a new first-person narrator. At the end of most of the chapters is a more conventional "story" title in italics, and those stories are told from the third-person point of view. *The Beet Queen* is thus a kind of experiment or showcase demonstrating a variety of possible voices and narrative points of view. The chapters are generally chronological from 1932 to 1972.

CHAPTERS IN TRACKS (1988)

Compared to *The Beet Queen*, *Tracks* is a more controlled experiment in point of view. For Fleur Pillager's story, which is the central story of the novel, Erdrich never takes us into Fleur's own mind. Rather, she tells Fleur's story from the alternating points of view of two other characters, who understand her in quite different ways. The five odd-numbered chapters are narrated in the first person by the garrulous Nanapush, who purports to tell Fleur's daughter, Lulu, about her mother. The four even-numbered chapters are first-person narrated by Pauline Puyat, a half-crazed young woman who is somewhat awed by the beautiful and powerful Fleur but who is also jealous of her, especially of her attractiveness to men. The sequence of chapters is roughly chronological, from 1912 through 1924.

1. Little Spirit Sun (Winter 1912)	Nanapush	1
2. Raspberry Sun (Summer 1913)	Pauline	10
3. Crust on the Snow Sun (Fall 1913–Spring 1914)	Nanapush	32
4. Blueberry Sun (Winter 1914–Summer 1917)	Pauline	62
5. Strong Spirit Sun (Fall 1917–Spring 1918)	Nanapush	96
6. Wood Louse Sun (Spring 1918–Winter 1919)	Pauline	131
7. Skeleton Winter (Winter 1918–Spring 1919)	Nanapush	165
8. Patches of Earth Sun (Spring 1919)	Pauline	192
9. Wild Rice Sun (Fall 1919–Spring 1924)	Nanapush	206

CHAPTERS IN THE BINGO PALACE (1994)

Most of the chapters in *The Bingo Palace* are told from the third-person point of view, but in ten of the twenty-seven chapters, Lipsha Morrissey is the first-person narrator. No other single character narrates any of the chapters. A collective "we" of reservation gossips narrates chapter 1, as well as parts of other chapters. The arrangement of the chapters is generally chronological, although no dates are given.

1. The Message	1
2. Lipsha Morrissey (Lipsha)	11
3. Solitary	23
4. Lipsha's Luck	27
5. Transportation (Lipsha)	37
6. June's Luck	57
7. The Bingo Van (Lipsha)	61
8. Lyman's Luck	85
9. Insulation (Lipsha)	95
10. Shawnee's Luck	115
11. Mindemoya (Lipsha)	123
12. Fleur's Luck	139
13. Lyman's Dream	147
14. Religious Wars (Lipsha)	151

CHAPTERS IN TALES OF BURNING LOVE (1996)

Erdrich gathers the forty-six chapters in *Tales of Burning Love* into four large sections, each with its own title. She also gives a title to each chapter but does not number the chapters. To help readers locate chapters, we have inserted chapter numbers in square brackets. We refer to these numbers, along with the chapter titles, in the dictionary of characters. The narration is a combination of third person and first person. Usually, the first-person narrator, if there is one, is indicated on the chapter's title page. Sometimes, however, the name after the title indicates not a first-person narrator but the character on whose perspective the third-person narrative is based or simply the subject of that chapter. Curiously, of the ten novels, this one has the greatest number of chapters, but its primary present-time action covers one of the shortest time spans—barely over a year, from June 1994 through August 1995. (A significant exception is the first chapter, which is a retelling of the Easter 1981 opening sequence of "The World's Greatest Fishermen" from *Love Medicine.*) Despite the brevity of the period covered by the present-time narrative, however, because of Erdrich's intricate interweaving of backstory, this is one of her most chronologically complex novels.

Part One: Jack of Sunflowers

CHAPTERS IN THE ANTELOPE WIFE (1998)

The twenty-three chapters of *The Antelope Wife* are arranged in a mostly chronological sequence, though virtually no dates are given, and some of the characters' memories are of events earlier than the novel's present time. The earliest events in the story appear to take place in the 1880s, while the last seem to take place more than a century later, in the 1990s. Some of the novel is in third-person narration, but much of it is told in the first person by two key narrators, Klaus Shawano and Cally Roy. A few other chapters are told from the first-person points of view of other characters, among them a dog. And some are in third-person limited. The chapters are placed into four large groupings, each with a number from one to four, written in English and Ojibwe.

CHAPTERS IN THE LAST REPORT ON THE MIRACLES AT LITTLE NO HORSE (2001)

The narration of *The Last Report on the Miracles at Little No Horse* is mostly in the third person. Its chronology is divided into two basic time periods, the present (primarily March 1996), when Father Damien is a very old man, and the past, consisting of memories, mostly Damien's, dating from 1910 to 1962 (also including Marie Kashpaw's memories from 1934 and Lulu Nanapush's from 1919 to 1924). Although Damien's memories begin in 1910 and at first move forward chronologically, parts of this past narrative jump backward and forward in time, given in the order in which Damien remembers the events. Although Erdrich heads each chapter with dates, several chapters narrate separate events from different times (especially chapters 7 and 10), and the movement from chapter to chapter is not entirely chronological. The chapters are divided into four large topical groupings, each with its own title.

CHAPTERS IN THE MASTER BUTCHERS SINGING CLUB *(2003)*

The sixteen chapters of *The Master Butchers Singing Club* are all told as third-person narration and are generally organized in chronological order. Although Erdrich is often vague about the dates, it is clear that most of the action runs from the end of World War I to the end of World War II, with brief reference in the final chapters to events in the mid-1950s.

CHAPTERS IN FOUR SOULS *(2004)*

The seventeen chapters of *Four Souls,* which begin in 1919 where *Tracks* ended, have three different narrators, each announced on the chapter's title page. As in *Tracks,* the central character is Fleur, but also as in *Tracks,* Erdrich does not let her narrate any of the chapters. The odd-numbered chapters are again in the first person, narrated by Nanapush, although this time, for the most part he does not seem to be speaking directly to Lulu (there is one apparent exception in chapter 11). The first-person narrator of the first six even-numbered chapters is Polly Elizabeth Gheen, the sister of Fleur's husband's first wife. The last two even-numbered chapters are narrated by Nanapush's wife, Margaret. The action of the novel appears to end in the early-to-middle 1930s as the country is still reeling from the Depression.

CHAPTERS IN THE PAINTED DRUM (2005)

The seventeen chapters of *The Painted Drum* are divided into four unequal parts, with the chapters in each part numbered separately. In the first two parts, the chapters are numbered and given titles; in the third part, the chapters are numbered but not given titles; and the fourth part has a single chapter, not numbered but labeled "Last Chapter: The Chain." References to *The Painted Drum* in the dictionary of characters give the part and chapter numbers. Thus, "part 3.2" refers to the second chapter of part 3. Part 1 is narrated in the first person by Faye Travers, at home in New Hampshire. Part 2 is narrated in the first person by Bernard Shaawano. Some of this second part has much of the character of third-person narration when Bernard relates events that occur before his birth. Yet he includes references to himself and consistently refers to the Shaawano drum maker as "my grandfather." Much of part 2.3 is, strangely, Fleur Pillager's remembrance of her mother's arrival at the home of Simon Jack and Ziigwan'aage, which took place when Fleur was a newborn. Part 3, which focuses on the adventures of a young mother named Ira and her three children, is told in the third person, primarily from the points of view of Ira, her older daughter, Shawnee, Morris String, and Bernard. Part 4 returns to the first person of Faye Travers, now back home in New Hampshire.

Actor. See **Arnold "the Actor" Anderson.**

Adare family. See **Adelaide Adare, Dot Adare Nanapush Mauser, Jude Miller, Karl Adare, Mary Adare,** and **Shawn Nanapush.**

Adelaide Adare. Mother of Karl and Mary Adare, and an unnamed infant later named Jude Miller, in *The Beet Queen*. Adelaide is probably Polish. (See Erdrich's interview in Allan Chavkin and Nancy Feyl Chavkin, eds., *Conversations with Louise Erdrich and Michael Dorris,* 237.)

In chapter 1, Adelaide lives in Prairie Lake, near Minneapolis, with the fourteen-year-old Karl and eleven-year-old Mary, her children by her lover, Mr. Ober. Mr. Ober visits them regularly and provides for them financially, but when he dies in 1932, Adelaide and her children are destitute and homeless. They move to Minneapolis, where Adelaide discovers that she is pregnant. She pawns her jewelry and steals a dozen silver spoons from *her landlady.* When Adelaide gives birth, the landlady discovers the theft and gives her a four-week notice to move. Near the end of that time, she and the children wander into the Saint Jerome's Orphans' Picnic, where she flies away with a stunt pilot, The Great Omar, abandoning her three children. The baby is kidnapped at the Orphans' Picnic, Karl lives at Saint Jerome's, and Mary moves in with Adelaide's sister, Fritzie Kozka, in Argus.

Adelaide never returns to see her children. References to her in the remainder of the novel present her as either admirably free-spirited or selfishly irresponsible, depending on the point of view. Fritzie's daughter, Sita Kozka, admires her as a woman with style (chapter 2), and Karl justifies his mother's actions (chapter 3). Her sister Fritzie and daughter Mary, however, are disgusted with her. In chapter 3, Adelaide sends a postcard to Fritzie from Jacksonville, Florida, inquiring about her children. Pretending to be Fritzie, Mary replies that all three children have starved to death. By the time Mary's postcard reaches them, both Adelaide and Omar have been injured in an airplane crash.

Some twenty years later (1953, chapter 7), Adelaide sends her daughter a sewing machine, which Mary gives to Sita. About eleven years later (chapter 11), Adelaide, still in Florida with Omar, throws a glass-breaking tantrum. Adelaide's spirit lives on in her garnet necklace, which Sita redeems from a pawnshop, and in the stories Sita tells to Karl's daughter, Dot Adare (see chapters 5, 13, 14, 15, and 16).

Adelaide Adare's baby. See **Jude Miller.**

Adelphine, Sister. Nun at the Argus convent where Leopolda is living in 1994. "Night Prayer" [6] in *Tales of Burning Love* identifies this convent as the Our Lady of

Adelphine, Sister

the Wheat Priory. In chapter 3 of *The Last Report on the Miracles at Little No Horse*, we learn that Sister Adelphine is Leopolda's primary caregiver and sees the old nun in the convent garden just before her death. In the epilogue of *Last Report*, when Father Jude moves from Argus to the reservation in 1997, Sister Adelphine moves with him. She sets up the reservation convent's new fax machine and receives the surprise fax from the pope.

Adrian. Boy who works at the Kozka butchery in Argus in *The Beet Queen*. He is a cousin of Celestine James (chapter 7) and watches the shop when Celestine and Mary Adare take a wheelchair to Russell Kashpaw (chapter 10). He is mentioned again twice in chapter 13.

Agent. Indian agent to the Ojibwe in *Tracks*. Different men may hold this position in different chapters, but the Agent is generally depicted as a tool of the government for seizing Indian land. Some of the Indians, such as the Morrissey, Pukwan, Hat, and Lazarre families, cooperate with him; others, including the Pillagers and Nanapush, oppose him. When the Agent tries to collect allotment fees from Fleur Pillager in chapter 1, he gets lost and follows elusive lights. After his second attempt, he is found in the woods, eating roots and gambling with ghosts. When the Agent attempts to make up a tribal roll in chapter 3, Nanapush refuses to give his name. Nevertheless, because Nanapush can read, the Agent designates him in chapter 5 to receive letters from the land court, and in chapter 7, Father Damien urges Nanapush to deal with the Agent in order to help protect the tribe. In chapter 4, Bernadette Morrissey uses the Agent as the conduit for a letter, and in chapter 7, she goes to work for him as housekeeper, secretary, and accountant.

We learn in chapter 7 that the Agent has made a map of fees owed and foreclosure notices on reservation allotments. He receives the fee money collected by the Pillager and Kashpaw families, but in chapter 9, he tells Nanapush that only the fees on Kashpaw land have been paid and that the government has sold the Pillager land. See also **Jewett Parker Tatro.**

Agnes DeWitt. Young woman in *The Last Report on the Miracles at Little No Horse* who is briefly a nun and then the common-law wife to Berndt Vogel, before becoming Father Damien Modeste, reservation priest at Little No Horse. The earliest recorded incidents of her life appear in chapter 1. Agnes is of Swabian descent. She recalls a childhood in a tar-roofed homestead in rural Wisconsin, along with **her mother**'s "cruel visions" and **her father**'s "terrifying gestures of love" (*LR*, 30). As a young woman, she becomes the nun Sister Cecilia in a convent in Fargo. (See **Cecilia, Sister.**) Agnes leaves the convent in 1910. Wearing only a shift, she shows up a few days later at the barn of Berndt Vogel on his farm near Fargo. She refuses to marry Berndt but becomes his housekeeper. Berndt eventually buys her a fine piano, a Caramacchione. After Agnes plays Chopin nude in Berndt's house, the two become lovers. The following spring (1911), the bank robber Arnold "the Actor" abducts and wounds Agnes and kills Berndt. Agnes gathers much of the stolen money and deposits it in the Fargo bank. After Berndt's death, the grieving Agnes teaches piano and tries to take care of the farm. In the spring of 1912, she is visited by Father Damien Modeste on his way north to an Ojibwe reservation. A few days later, the flooded Red River sweeps away Agnes and her piano. She washes up on the river's bank, far north of Fargo, exhausted and famished.

In chapter 2, a man Agnes takes to be Christ ministers to her. As she walks on north, she comes across the body of the drowned Father Damien and takes his clothes and identity. On the Eve of St. Dismas in March 1912 (chapter 4), Agnes arrives at Little No Horse to become the reservation priest. Most of the events of her long life as Father Damien are recorded in the entry **Damien Modeste, Father,** but we record here certain of those incidents that relate particularly to the woman Agnes.

Several people on the reservation recognize that Damien is a woman: Kashpaw, when he gives the priest a ride from the train station to Little No Horse in 1912 (chapter 4); Damien's caretaker, Mary Kashpaw, during Damien's month-long sleep in 1921 (chapter 11); and Nanapush, in a chess game in 1923 (chapter 13). Damien assumes that Fleur also knows his secret (chapter 16). In Sister Leopolda's 1933 confession to Father Damien, she reveals her knowledge that the priest is a woman and uses this knowledge to blackmail him. Even Father Jude Miller, when he is interviewing the hundred-plus-year-old Damien in 1996, twice has the sense that he is seeing a woman (chapter 8).

Damien's affair with Father Gregory Wekkle in 1920–1921 (chapter 11) is, of course, an Agnes incident, reflecting not only her gender but also her passionate history with Chopin and Berndt. After 1922, Father Damien also inherits from the young Agnes her passion for the piano (chapter 12; see also chapter 20).

Agnes frequently struggles with her dual identity, but especially notable are two passages in which Damien and Agnes become one. In chapter 7, in the procession at the Feast of the Virgin in 1912, as "he" walks behind the cart and "he" prays, the text reads: "These days, Agnes and Father Damien became one indivisible person in prayer. That poor, divided, human priest enlarged and smoothed into the person of Father Damien" (*LR,* 109). Then "he" trips, and Agnes later thinks how odd that "she" should stumble in the midst of this full experience of grace (110). A similar passage appears in chapter 10: "Four times a day . . . Agnes and Father Damien became that one person who addressed the unknown" (182).

Agnes's gender also plays a pivotal role in Damien's decision in 1996 to go

Agnes DeWitt

out to Spirit Island to die (chapter 22). Only by drowning himself, Damien feels, can he avoid the harm a discovery of his gender would do to the people he had absolved, married, and baptized.

Albert Hock, Sheriff. Argus sheriff in *The Master Butchers Singing Club,* usually identified simply as "Sheriff Hock." (Once, in chapter 8, he is called "Albert.") Chapters 4 and 5 depict Albert Hock as an incongruous combination of delicacy with a bulky, fleshy body, fed by persistent greed. His face is framed with fat, but he has the "exquisite budded lips of a courtesan" (*MBSC,* 98). For years, Hock has pursued Clarisse Strub. Both his passion and the fact that Clarisse despises him are well known, but Hock is oblivious to the people's mockery and the level of Clarisse's contempt. Before becoming sheriff, he is active in town theater, successfully playing the parts of Henry VIII and Falstaff. When Fidelis Waldvogel establishes his men's singing club in the early 1930s (chapter 3), Sheriff Hock joins, adding his "heartrending falsetto" to the other voices (*MBSC,* 42).

When Clarisse's father dies in the winter of early 1934 (see p. 100), his wake is held at Roy Watzka's house (chapters 7 and 11). Under her coat, Clarisse wears her fanciest dress—a shimmery costume covered with red glass beads. When Sheriff Hock assaults Clarisse in the pantry, ripping the dress and scattering its beads, Clarisse slugs him. Neither of them forgets the incident.

That summer, Delphine Watzka discovers three rotting bodies (the Porky Chavers family) in her father, Roy's cellar and reports the finding to Sheriff Hock (chapter 4). As he investigates, Hock notices that the cellar door is sealed with spilled peach juice and red glass beads (see chapter 5). He sends his **gangly boy-deputy** to oversee the morticians' removal of the bodies (chapter 5).

Late one night (chapter 5), Hock comes to Clarisse's house, and when she shuts the door in his face, he whispers through it, *"I'll huff and puff and blow your house down"* (*MBSC,* 91). Later that summer, Hock comes to the Waldvogel butcher shop to ask Delphine more questions about the Chaverses' deaths, specifically about the glass beads.

The following summer, 1935 (in chapter 6), Sheriff Hock attends the Waldvogels' July 4 gathering. As the men sing patriotic songs, Hock hits the high notes in "The Star-Spangled Banner." When they compare bellies, Hock's is the biggest. He also participates in a puerile stunt: Using a loop attached to Hock's belt, Fidelis picks up the big man with his teeth. Later that summer, Hock, still puzzling over the red glass beads on the cellar door, asks Delphine about costumes—especially hers and Clarisse's. When he asks about Clarisse personally, Delphine calls him a mental wreck and says that he should leave Clarisse alone. Hock broods for months over the insult.

That autumn (chapter 8), Sheriff Hock is working late one night, fretting about the unsolved mystery of the deaths, particularly obsessed with Clarisse and the red beads. He decides to try a trick to uncover some facts. The following afternoon he arrests Roy Watzka for his theft of morphine the previous July 4. Hock tells Delphine about the arrest but not its reason, purposefully leading her to believe it is connected to the Chaverses. He hopes that under pressure, she will let slip details about the possible murders. He then follows Delphine and sees that she goes to visit Clarisse. As he recalls Clarisse and the wake where he assaulted her, his thoughts turn predatory.

A year later, two days before Christmas 1936 (chapter 11), Hock is so obsessed with Clarisse that he is willing to blackmail her into accepting him. He obtains a warrant to search her house for samples of the red beads and is waiting on her porch when she comes home that night. He roots through her underclothes, unaware as always of her loathing and rage. When Clarisse leaves the room briefly, Hock finds a single red bead, which he shows her when she returns, calling it "State's evidence" (*MBSC,* 248). When Hock lunges for her, her hand, now holding a sharpened carving knife, reaches forward. In his shock, Sheriff Hock is uncomprehending as Clarisse's knife eviscerates him. He lies dying among her shoes. When Sheriff Hock's body is found, Clarisse, who has left town, is under suspicion. But the gossip essentially excuses her because, as Roy tells Delphine, it seems clear to everyone that Hock had intended to violate her. After all, he was found with his pants around his ankles.

In chapter 14, we learn that Hock had picked out a tombstone for himself before he died—another example of his now-ironic obsession with control.

Albert Ruse. Helps Shaawano in his preparations for making the drum in *The Painted Drum.* In part 2.4, Albert is a fisherman on Matchimanito Lake who has a *wife* and several *children,* including the fifteen-year-old Chickie. Albert's heritage prepares him to help with the drum. His ***grandfather*** was a keeper of the drum wood, maker of a birchbark canoe used to visit the wood, and holder of a sacred pipe smoked with the wood. As a boy, Albert had accompanied his grandfather across the lake to visit the wood. After Albert gives Shaawano the canoe (in need of repair), Shaawano's deceased daughter speaks to Albert to thank him. He helps Shaawano find the wood, crossing the lake and smoking the pipe with him. In part 2.5, Albert's son Chickie shoots the moose Shaawano will use for drumheads, and Albert helps prepare the hide. As an old man, Albert tells Shaawano's grandson Bernard stories about the drum.

Albertine Johnson. Only child of Zelda Kashpaw, born about 1958. She is named after Zelda's first suitor, Xavier Albert Toose. We learn in "The World's Greatest

Albertine Johnson

Fishermen" in *Love Medicine* that Albertine is born less than nine months after Zelda's marriage to Swede Johnson and that Zelda blames Albertine for Zelda's not being able to become a nun as she had wished. Albertine knows her father only from pictures. As Albertine grows up, she and her mother live in a trailer near her Grandma Marie Kashpaw, who helps take care of her. At age fifteen (1973), in "A Bridge," Albertine runs away by bus to Fargo. There she is picked up by a young Chippewa soldier from her own reservation, Henry Lamartine Junior, who has just returned from Vietnam. That night in a hotel, the frightened Albertine has sexual relations with him.

Seven years later, in "Scales," in the summer of 1980, Albertine falls in with prison-escapee Gerry Nanapush and Dot Adare, who is pregnant with Gerry's child. Albertine and Dot work together in a truck weigh-station at a construction site. When Dot goes into labor in October, Albertine joins Gerry in the hospital waiting room.

Albertine is a nursing student in 1981 ("The World's Greatest Fishermen") when she receives word of her aunt June Morrissey's death. Albertine is bitter that Zelda did not notify her before the funeral, because she had been fond of Aunt June. She drives home two months later. During a gathering of the Kashpaw clan, Albertine tries unsuccessfully to tell Lipsha Morrissey that June is his mother, and she keeps King Kashpaw from drowning his wife, Lynette. The following year, in "Love Medicine," Albertine sits with Lipsha at her Grandpa Nector Kashpaw's funeral. She has decided to continue beyond her nurse's training and become a doctor. In "Crossing the Water," Lipsha says that Albertine is like a sister, the only girl he has ever trusted, and in chapter 9 of *The Bingo Palace,* he recalls that she once loaned him money from her own school loan.

In chapter 1 of *The Bingo Palace,* Albertine is pushing herself hard at her medical studies, but she also dances at the powwows on the reservation (see also chapter 2). At a naming ceremony in chapter 3 conducted by her namesake, Xavier Albert Toose, Albertine receives the traditional name of Four Soul, who was a Pillager healer four generations earlier.

Zelda complains in chapter 10 that Albertine never comes home to stay, but Albertine's friend Shawnee Ray Toose says that it is Zelda's fault. Albertine, in turn, comes to her friend's defense when Zelda tries to control Shawnee Ray (chapter 19). Albertine also confronts her mother with the truth that Zelda has never gotten over her love for her rejected suitor, Xavier Toose. In chapter 20, Albertine advises Lipsha to leave Shawnee Ray alone until he gets himself together, advice he recalls in chapter 22.

Alice. Younger daughter of Ira in *The Painted Drum.* Alice is named for her maternal grandmother. In part 3.1, six-year-old Alice and her siblings are home alone and hungry on a bitterly cold winter day. When the heating oil runs out, Alice helps her older sister, Shawnee, rig a makeshift stove. When they wake in part 3.3, the house is on fire. With Apitchi on her back, Shawnee drags Alice three miles through the woods to their neighbor Bernard Shaawano's house. Alice become unconscious in the cold and wakes only with the warmth of Bernard's house and an ambulance I.V. (3.5 and 3.6).

In part 3.7, the children spend the next several days in the IHS hospital. A woman with a scar on her lip (social worker Seraphine String) comes to interview the girls, and Alice asks how she got her scar. When the children are released, the family stays with Bernard, but the following summer the tribal government rebuilds their house so they can go home (part 4).

Almost Soup. Cally Roy's white dog, who narrates chapters 8 and 9 of *The Antelope Wife*. Almost Soup claims some coyote and Dakota blood mixed with his Ojibwe reservation dog blood. He is born on the prairie, "out in Bwaanakeeng" (Dakota-land). His birthplace may be in the same general area as the Ojibwe village attacked by Scranton Roy in chapter 1, a portion of open Dakota prairie "west of the Otter Tail River." One of his ancestors is Blue Prairie Woman's dog, Sorrow.

Almost Soup acquires his name (Bungeenaboop in Ojibwe) in chapter 8, when he barely escapes being cooked. He is saved by his wits, the advice of **his mother,** and the love of the girl child Cally. Shortly thereafter, he is taken to the Ojibwe reservation where Cally's grandmothers live. Later, Cally also saves him from castration. Much of chapter 8 is Almost Soup's survival advice to younger dogs, whom he calls **his puppies.**

In chapter 9, Almost Soup recounts the incidents following the death of Cally's twin sister, Deanna. About a year after Deanna's death, Cally falls gravely ill. On the second night of her fever, the black dog (death) draws near (chapter 8). Almost Soup calls upon **his ancestors** for help, and he takes Cally's life for safekeeping until her body revives. After Cally moves to Minneapolis in chapter 11, she misses her dog, who would sometimes sleep with her. See also **Windigo Dog.**

Anaquot. Daughter of Under the Ground; wife of Shaawano and mother of his two children; lover of the Pillager man Simon Jack and mother of his daughter Fleur in *Four Souls* and *The Painted Drum*. For variations in the structure of Fleur's family, see **Pillager family.** Anaquot's name means "cloud" (*Four Souls* chapters 5 and 10, *The Painted Drum* part 2.2).

The winter Anaquot is eleven (*Four Souls* chapter 5), she falls ill but recovers. The following winter she falls ill again, and the old healer (Nanapush's uncle) cannot help her. Under the Ground brings her back by throwing out one of the girl's souls. Thereafter, Anaquot's spirit name is Four Souls. (For ambiguity about this name, see **Four Souls.**)

Anaquot

The only comments in *Four Souls* about Anaquot's adult life are that she has a daughter named Red Cradle and a son, apparently by her Shaawano husband, then runs off with a Pillager man and becomes Fleur's mother. *The Painted Drum* gives us more details. In part 2.4, when Anaquot and Shaawano fall in love, they run away to an island in Matchimanito Lake, where they begin their firstborn, a daughter. (This is likely the Red Cradle mentioned in *Four Souls.*) Within ten years, however, in part 2.2 Anaquot takes the Pillager man Simon Jack as a lover, and the autumn her Shaawano daughter is nine, she gives birth to Pillager's child Fleur. That winter, Anaquot becomes so lovesick that Shaawano sends her to her lover's camp. A Pillager man comes to fetch Anaquot, her Shaawano daughter, and the baby Fleur, but on the way wolves attack the sled. The Shaawano girl is killed, but the others escape. The reader is not told whether Anaquot throws her daughter to the wolves or whether the girl sacrifices herself for her family.

When Anaquot arrives at the Pillager cabin in part 2.3, a woman with three children greets her. Aided by the spirit of her dead daughter, Anaquot realizes that this woman, Ziigwan'aage, is Simon Jack's wife and that she is planning to kill Anaquot and the baby. But when Anaquot points out that Simon Jack is the only reason for the women's enmity, they begin to form an alliance against the man who has betrayed them. After Simon Jack returns, Anaquot's situation again becomes dangerous, but her rejection of his advances one night secures the women's friendship, and they begin beading his dance costume. By spring, Anaquot and Ziigwan'aage have become virtual sisters. Anaquot still worries about Ziigwan'aage's daughter Niibin'aage, with her cold, venomous eyes. So when a young teacher and recruiter from the Carlisle Indian School comes to the reservation, Anaquot hints that Niibin'aage should go to the school.

Although Simon Jack boasts in part 2.5 that he is a two-woman man, in fact, Anaquot and Ziigwan'aage bully him, barring him from his own cabin. Once Simon Jack puts on the flamboyant dance costume the women have beaded over several winters, he never takes it off, and the people mock his filth and stench. One summer afternoon, when Simon Jack enters the dance circle, the spirit of Anaquot's dead Shaawano daughter, who lives inside the drum, causes him to dance to his death. When other women prepare his body, they discover that Anaquot and Ziigwan'aage have made the beads in his costume stitch themselves to his flesh. He is buried on the path to the Pillager camp, so Anaquot and Ziigwan'aage walk over him as they come and go.

Sometime later, Anaquot dies in an epidemic, along with all the others in the Pillager camp except Fleur and Niibin'aage, who has gone to Carlisle (part 2.5). Years later, in the 1930s, Margaret Kashpaw remembers Anaquot as a childhood friend (*Four Souls* chapter 16).

Andy. Mud engineer in "The World's Greatest Fishermen" in *Love Medicine.* Andy beckons June Morrissey into a bar in Williston and gives her an egg. Later, they drive out from town, and he seems to fall asleep while attempting to have sex with her in his pickup. In "Easter Snow," the opening chapter in *Tales of Burning Love,* it is revealed that "Andy" is not his true name.

Anna Kuklenski Schlick. Wife of Lawrence Schlick and mother of Eleanor Schlick Mauser. In "White Musk" [4] in *Tales of Burning Love,* Eleanor recalls Anna as a doting mother, and in "The Meadowlark" [7] she mentions their too-close relationship.

The story of Anna's life is told primarily in "Eleanor's Tale" [20]. A young barrel rider in Montana, Anna runs away with a small circus and is taken in by the Flying Kuklenski family, who train her as a trapeze artist. She and young Harry Kuklenski marry, but when Anna is seven months pregnant, she and Harry are involved in a terrible accident in which Harry dies. Anna survives, but her baby, a girl, is born dead six weeks later.

Lawrence Schlick visits Anna in the hospital and falls in love with her. When they marry, Anna grows into her role as the superwife of Fargo's most successful businessman. When their house burns down, Anna rescues the six-year-old Eleanor by leaping from the house with her. One bitterly cold November night, Anna helps to thaw out a nearly frozen young part-time fireman named Jack Mauser by crawling, naked, into bed with him. The next morning her husband finds them asleep in bed together and disowns both Anna and Eleanor. Despite their subsequent poverty, Anna feels liberated, and she recovers her original flamboyant personality.

After many years of separation, Anna and Lawrence are reconciled when Eleanor becomes engaged to Jack Mauser ("The Red Slip" [21]). In "The Box" [22], Anna concentrates on her church work, feeding the ***cast-off elements of society,*** but Lawrence's jealous suspicions linger. One night in late winter 1983 he sneaks home early from a funerary trade show to see if Anna is still seeing Jack. She is not.

Anna sends her daughter a worried note in "Night Prayer" [6] when Eleanor's health declines. When Anna comes to Jack's funeral in "Memoria" [10], although she is suffering from a heart condition, she retains her flair. Just before she dies the following August, in "A Light from the West" [43], Anna remembers ***her parents.*** When she dies, she is cremated by and with her husband.

Anne, Sister Saint. Nun at the Sacred Heart Convent in *Tracks.* She is keeping a vigil in chapter 4 when Clarence Morrissey rushes into the church and steals the statue of the Virgin Mary. She chases him back to Fleur's cabin, where she finds

Anne, Sister Saint

Clarence's sister Sophie in a catatonic stupor. Sister Saint Anne is the one who tells Pauline in chapter 6 that no Indian girls may be accepted into the order at the convent. She feeds Pauline soup in chapter 8 when Pauline's hands are burned. For thanks, Pauline tells the sister that she stinks.

Antelope and deer people. In *The Antelope Wife,* these people include actual antelope and deer who marry or adopt humans, their animal–human descendants, and humans with deer and antelope characteristics. In chapter 6, the *deer people* who are family to Apijigo Bakaday's *deer husband* love her and come when she calls them, even after her deer husband dies. One of them, a *slender doe,* warns the woman (now called Blue Prairie Woman) of an impending cavalry attack. Later, a *band of antelope* adopts Blue Prairie Woman's seven-year-old-daughter, Matilda (chapter 1). Chapters 1 and 2 mention the curiosity of antelope people, and chapter 2 tells of the ease with which they can be confined by fences. See also **Apijigo Bakaday, Cally Whiteheart Beads Roy, Deanna Whiteheart Beads, Frank Shawano, Girl who lived with the antelope, Matilda Roy,** and **Sweetheart Calico.**

In addition to the deer and antelope people of *The Antelope Wife,* the *doe* hit by Gordie Kashpaw's car in "Crown of Thorns" in *Love Medicine* also takes on human qualities, at least in Gordie's intoxicated mind.

Apijigo Bakaday. Daughter of Midass; possibly windigo. Her name means So Hungry. In chapter 6 of *The Antelope Wife,* she marries a *deer husband,* who cures her insatiable hunger but whom her brothers later shoot. See also **Blue Prairie Woman.**

Apitchi. Toddler son of Ira in *The Painted Drum.* He is named for the robin (part 3.7). In part 3.1, Apitchi and his two sisters are home alone one bitterly cold winter day. He is ravenously hungry and tries to eat a crayon. When the house burns down, Shawnee straps Apitchi to her back and, dragging Alice, barely makes it to their neighbor Bernard Shaawano's house, three miles through the snowy woods. Apitchi is nearly frozen.

An ambulance takes the children to the hospital in parts 3.6 and 3.7, but Apitchi develops pneumonia, and his fever brings on a seizure. Bernard uses his grandfather's drum in a healing ceremony for the boy. When he gets well, Apitchi stays with his family at Bernard's house until that next summer when the tribal government builds them a new house (part 4).

Architect. Architect for John James Mauser's opulent Minneapolis house in *Four Souls.* In chapter 1, the finest of the oak from Indian land is processed at the edge of the city to the architect's specifications. Obsessive with detail, as the grain emerges he plans the movements of the entrance, stairwell, high windows, and doorways. Polly Elizabeth Gheen, Mauser's sister-in-law, works with him in the decorating. He notices that she tries to attract him sexually but is not interested. Some years later, in chapter 10, he is at the lake one afternoon with *his fiancée* when he spots Miss Gheen. He and his lady have previously laughed about this woman's sexual advances, so the fiancée speaks to her mockingly. But when the architect learns that the Indian woman with Polly Elizabeth is Mauser's wife, he and his fiancée leave in embarrassment.

Arnold "the Actor" Anderson. Bank robber and murderer who wears various disguises in his robberies in *The Last Report on the Miracles at Little No Horse*. One muddy spring day in 1911 (chapter 1), the Actor, disguised as a priest, and his *two accomplices* rob the Fargo bank. The Actor kills one uncooperative teller, and when another activates an alarm, he kidnaps Agnes DeWitt. Once out of town, the speeding car slips from the road and becomes bogged down in mud. A man on a large horse (Berndt Vogel) comes along and offers to help. Just as the Actor perceives a connection between his hostage and this man, the sheriff arrives. The Actor fires his gun, creasing Agnes's head, then takes Berndt's horse and sets out across the gumbo fields, followed by Berndt. When the horse becomes bogged down, the Actor shoots it and fatally injures Berndt. But Berndt overtakes him and pushes him into the mire, where he smothers.

In chapter 22, more than eighty years later and near her death, Agnes remembers the Actor bitterly, recalling that just before he shot her, she warned him that he would bear the weight of her soul.

Augustus Roy I. Son of Scranton Roy and Peace McKnight in chapters 1 and 23 of *The Antelope Wife*. After a difficult labor, Peace dies in childbirth, and baby Augustus almost succumbs, too. His father nurses him at his own breast. Augustus later has a son, also named Augustus.

Augustus Roy II. Grandson of Scranton Roy; husband of Zosie (II) Shawano Roy in *The Antelope Wife*.

Reared alone by his grandfather somewhere on the Great Plains, Augustus is bookish and shy. As a very young man, in chapter 23 he accompanies his grandfather east to find the remnants of an Ojibwe village Scranton had once raided. The survivors now live on a reservation, where Augustus falls in love with Zosie Shawano, great-great-granddaughter of a woman Scranton had killed. In exchange for Zosie, Augustus offers her great-grandmother, Midass, red whiteheart beads and agrees to take care of Zosie's twin sister, Mary. Chapter 18 tells the story of their ill-fated marriage, which ends when Augustus disappears without a trace.

Augustus Roy II

Rumor has it that the windigo (cannibalistic) Shawano twins have eaten him. Before he disappears, he impregnates Zosie with twins.

Aunt Elizabeth. Jack Mauser's aunt on his German father's side, mentioned in "The Owl" [17] in *Tales of Burning Love.* This aunt, whom Jack refers to as *Tante,* takes in the six-year-old Jack when his mother goes to the hospital for cold-water shock treatments. Aunt Elizabeth is strict and thinks Jack's Ojibwe mother has spoiled him. As a young man, Jack squanders money she apparently has given him. According to "Best Western" [28], Jack feels that she has stolen him away from his mother, and he eventually runs away to his uncle, her brother, Chuck Mauser.

Aurelia Kashpaw. Daughter of Nector and Marie Kashpaw, younger sister to Gordie and Zelda. While they are children, in "The Beads" in *Love Medicine,* Gordie and Aurelia try to hang their cousin June Morrissey. In "The Plunge of the Brave," Aurelia and Zelda share a rollaway cot in the crowded Kashpaw cabin. In "Flesh and Blood," Aurelia takes care of her two youngest siblings (Patsy and Eugene) and the neighbor woman's baby when Marie and Zelda visit Sister Leopolda in 1957. She would prefer to be hunting with June, Gordie, and Gordie's friend, whom Aurelia "likes."

When Nector and Marie move into the Senior Citizens in town, Aurelia moves back into the old family house, which remains a kind of communal Kashpaw property. In about 1979, Aurelia has an addition tacked onto the house containing a toilet, laundry, and kitchen sink. In "The World's Greatest Fishermen" (1981), Aurelia and Zelda are in Aurelia's kitchen, preparing food for a Kashpaw family gathering. As the two sisters visit, the narrator, Albertine, observes their differences. In contrast to the critical Zelda, Aurelia defends both Albertine and the dead June. Aurelia is a "looker"—plump with high, round cheeks, permed hair, tight jeans, and a fancy shirt. She works nights managing a bar, and her wink at Albertine as she leaves to go "see a friend" that evening suggests an interest in men.

When the scattered family members come for Nector's funeral in "Love Medicine," some stay with Aurelia. Afterward, in "Resurrection," Marie returns to the house and Aurelia moves out.

Aurelius Strub. Mortician and owner of Strub's Funerary in Argus; uncle of Clarisse Strub in *The Master Butchers Singing Club.* We learn from chapters 5 and 7 that Aurelius has the first embalmer's diploma awarded in the Midwest between Minneapolis and Spokane. He continues to make his own technical improvements, so that even people at a distance from Argus use his services. His temperament is also well-suited to his business. He is serious and matter-of-fact in his sympathy, and thus reassuring to families of his clients.

Until his brother Cornelius's death in 1934, the two brothers and Aurelius's wife, Benta, work together in the business and teach the trade to Cornelius's daughter, Clarisse. When Clarisse graduates from high school, the men bring her into the business. Aurelius twice helps Clarisse's friend Delphine Watzka—when she discovers three rotting bodies in her father's cellar in 1934 and when her friend Eva dies in 1935. After Clarisse leaves town the next year (chapter 11), Delphine visits Aurelius and Benta.

Aurora Roy. Daughter of Zosie (II) Shawano Roy and Augustus Roy II; twin sister of Rozina Roy in *The Antelope Wife*. According to chapter 3, Aurora dies of diphtheria at age five and must be pried from her sister's arms. The effect of her death on Rozin is alluded to in chapter 18.

Awun. Name meaning "the Mist," which others give to the strange son of Fleur Pillager and John James Mauser in chapter 17 of *The Last Report on the Miracles at Little No Horse*. See **John James Mauser II.**

B

Baby Kuklenski girl. Stillborn daughter of Anna and Harry Kuklenski in "Eleanor's Tale" [20] in *Tales of Burning Love*. In a trapeze accident, her father is killed, and her mother, seven months pregnant with her, is injured. She is born dead six weeks after the accident and is buried in Fargo. She would have been the half sister of Eleanor Schlick Mauser, who recalls seeing her grave.

Baby Pillager. Fleur's baby who is born prematurely and then dies in chapter 6 of *Tracks*. Pauline apparently could have prevented the miscarriage but does not do so. The baby's father, Eli Kashpaw, places its body in a shoebox high in a tree. Fleur mourns the baby's death in chapter 7 and shelters its resting place with her black umbrella. In chapter 9, she is rumored to have assigned the dead child to guard Matchimanito Lake. On her own death walk in chapter 24 of *The Bingo Palace*, Fleur once again sees the child, along with the other dead of her family.

Baby stolen in Fargo. Baby in the car that Gerry Nanapush and Lipsha Morrissey steal in front of the Fargo train station in chapter 24 of *The Bingo Palace*. Later, snowbound in the car, Lipsha zips the baby into his own jacket in an effort to protect it from the cold. In chapter 26, a radio broadcast the next morning announces that a "hostage" has been found in good condition, which may or may not refer to the baby. The baby's identity is revealed in "Funeral Day" [23] and "Blizzard Night" [35] in *Tales of Burning Love*.

Bartenders

Bartenders. The *bartender at the Rigger Bar* in Williston serves June Morrissey and Jack Mauser (alias "Andy") in "The World's Greatest Fishermen" in *Love Medicine* and "Easter Snow" [1] in *Tales of Burning Love.* Two other bartenders appear in *Tales.* The *bartender at the Library bar* (Jack and Candice Pantamounty's favorite bar) serves Jack and Marlis Cook in "The First Draw" [14] and "Marlis's Tale" [27]; and the *bartender at the B & B* is surprised when Dot orders a pizza for the large Indian woman in "The B & B" [16].

Benta Strub. Mortician; wife of Aurelius Strub and aunt of Clarisse Strub in *The Master Butchers Singing Club.* As a mortician, she helps Delphine Watzka in chapters 5 and 7. Benta plays a large part in Clarisse's training, allowing the girl even in high school to help her with the embalming. She praises Clarisse's natural aptitude for embalming (chapter 5) and her comforting presence with families of the deceased (chapter 7). Chapter 7 also depicts Benta as frugal, using leftover visitation calling cards in the embalming process. After Clarisse leaves town in chapter 11, Delphine goes to visit Benta and Aurelius.

Bernadette Morrissey. Mother of Clarence, Sophie, and Philomena Morrissey; sister of Napoleon Morrissey; secretary at the Indian agency office at Little No Horse. Chapter 9 of *The Last Report on the Miracles at Little No Horse* tells us that Bernadette is a half-blood who is contemptuous of full-blood Ojibwe traditionals. In *Tracks* chapter 4, we learn that she is educated by French nuns in Quebec and passes on her French ways to her daughters. At some point, Bernadette and her children move in with her alcoholic brother Napoleon, whose homestead thrives under her supervision. After the death of her cousin Quill Kashpaw in the fall of 1912 (*Last Report* chapter 7), Bernadette asks that Quill's daughter Mary live with her—feigning charity as her motive (she actually wants farm help). But after Napoleon abuses Mary, the following spring she takes the child to the convent to live.

In December 1913 (*Tracks* chapter 4), Bernadette and Napoleon bring the teenage Pauline Puyat back from Argus to live with them. Over the next several years, Bernadette takes Pauline as an assistant in caring for the dying (chapters 3 and 4). In the late summer of 1917 Bernadette whips her daughter Sophie for engaging in sex with Eli Kashpaw and tries to send her away to a strict aunt off-reservation. The following year, Bernadette discovers that Pauline is pregnant by Napoleon. In *Tracks* chapter 6, Bernadette stops Pauline's abortion attempts, delivers baby Marie in November 1918, and, when Pauline leaves, keeps the child.

The winter of 1919 (*Tracks* chapter 7), when Clarence and Sophie marry Lazarres, Bernadette moves to town with Philomena and baby Marie. Although according to *Tracks* she is already showing the first signs of consumption, in town

Bernadette keeps house for the Indian agent and becomes his secretary, handling property records and land fees. There are intimations in chapters 7 and 9 of *Tracks* that, in this position of influence, Bernadette is complicit with the agent's efforts to seize Indian land. By the spring of 1919 (chapter 8) Bernadette is weakened from her consumption, and Sophie often cares for baby Marie. Thus, implicit in this novel is the assumption that Bernadette is dying.

The later novels *The Last Report on the Miracles at Little No Horse* and *Four Souls,* however, give a different version of Bernadette's fate. Although chapter 7 of *Last Report* relates that Bernadette falls ill with influenza in the epidemic of 1918–1919, she survives, and chapters 9, 10, and 11 give no hint of Bernadette's having consumption. Chapter 9 gives a different reason than illness for her sending Marie to the Lazarres—she wants to avoid a repeat of the sexual aggression Napoleon had manifested toward Mary and Pauline.

Napoleon disappears in the spring of 1919, and late that summer his body is found in the woods behind Fleur's house. (See *Tracks* chapters 8 and 9; *Last Report* chapters 7 and 9.) At his funeral, an interfamily brawl begins with an exchange of insults between Bernadette and Margaret Kashpaw (*Last Report* chapter 9). But the reason for Bernadette's agitation is quite different from what her family assumes. Margaret's slurs about Napoleon's morality reminds her of what she herself knows about his evil. She is glad that he is dead. After the funeral, however, she apparently has a change of heart and decides to use her power as handler of land documents to punish her enemies.

But Bernadette does not retain power forever. She hires young Nector Kashpaw as a helper in the agency office, not realizing that he is far cleverer than she and is quietly changing documents in his family's favor. Even so, Bernadette continues to be associated with her neighbors' loss of land. In *Four Souls* chapter 7, when Margaret sells some of Nector's land for cash, she goes to Bernadette for the sale.

In the spring of 1921 (*Last Report* chapter 11), Bernadette confesses to Father Damien that she knew that Napoleon forced himself on Mary Kashpaw in 1912–1913 but did nothing.

Bernadette is still a hindrance to her neighbors' land rights in the spring of 1933. When Fleur returns to the reservation to regain her land (chapter 15 of *Four Souls*), for several days Bernadette refuses to reveal the identity of the present owner until she is worn down by Fleur's persistence.

Bernard Shaawano. Grandson of old Shaawano in *The Painted Drum.* Bernard is born many years after the making of the drum (part 2.5), yet he knows its history intimately because from early childhood he listens to the old people. Among Bernard's earliest memories are those in part 2.4 of listening to the stories told by

Bernard Shaawano

his grandfather and the **old men** and **old ladies** who are his grandfather's friends. Bernard's father and Albert Ruse also tell him stories about his family and the drum (2.1, 2.5).

When Bernard is ten and his twin siblings Doris and Raymond are six, in part 2.2 **their mother** dies and their father descends into drunkenness. He abandons them for days and is violent when he returns, so the children learn to evade him. When Bernard is thirteen, he stands up to his father and fights him with a destructive joy. Then, touched with compassion, he wipes the blood from his father's face with an old shawl, and his father tells the story of his own dead sister. In later years, Bernard suggests another interpretation of this sister's death—that she had willingly sacrificed her life for her family.

After Bernard and his siblings marry, Doris and Raymond move to the Cities, but Bernard stays on the reservation where he works at the Indian Health Service (IHS) hospital. When **his children** are grown, they move to Fargo, and **his wife** follows. Although he misses them and regrets not being with **his grandchildren,** Bernard stays (see parts 2.1, 2.2, and 3.7) and continues to be a receptacle of tribal history. He hears the story of Anaquot and Ziigwan'aage from old Fleur Pillager (part 2.3), and an old friend (Ira's father) talks to him in the hospital shortly before the old man's death, telling of his going out one midwinter long ago to talk to the wolves (see parts 2.3, 3.6, and 3.7).

One autumn sometime after 2000, when Bernard is in his late sixties (see p. 250), Chook String phones him in part 2.1 with an unusual request. She wants Bernard to help her dig up her husband, Mike's grave because it contains song scrolls for old Shaawano's drum. The lost drum, she explains, has returned. Bernard attends a meeting at Judge and Geraldine Nanapush's house with the Strings, the drum, and the two New Hampshire women who have brought the drum home, Pillager descendants Elsie and Faye Travers. Bernard tells the assembly the stories found in parts 2.2, 2.3, and 2.4.

Although Bernard knows the dangers of the drum (see 2.1) and respects his grandfather's decision not to use it, the following winter the drum calls itself into action. One bitterly cold night in part 3.6, Bernard wakes to the sound of a window breaking. Ira's three children—grandchildren of Bernard's old friend who had talked to wolves—have walked three miles through the woods after their house has burned down. Nine-year-old Shawnee tells Bernard that they had given up and almost died, but the sound of a drum led her to his house (see parts 3.5, 3.6, and 3.7). Since Bernard was asleep at the time, he realizes that the drum called to Shawnee on its own.

The following evening, Bernard comes to Apitchi's hospital room in part 3.7. He agrees to take Ira and the children in, and he explains that it is time to put the drum to use. Apitchi is sick and needs its power. The next morning, Bernard prepares for the drum's first ceremony in decades.

After this ceremony, Bernard puts the drum back into regular use. The following September (part 4) he writes a letter to Faye and Elsie, telling about the drum's saving of Ira's children and its subsequent use, thanking them for returning it and inviting them to come back and participate in its ceremonies.

Berndt Vogel. German immigrant farmer near Fargo and common-law spouse of Agnes Dewitt in *The Last Report on the Miracles at Little No Horse*. Berndt's story is recorded in chapter 1 of the novel. After escaping the latest European war, Berndt buys a ravaged but elegant old farm. One morning in 1910, a barefoot, starving woman appears in the doorway of his barn, and Berndt falls passionately in love. The following morning, he asks Agnes to marry him. She refuses, but they agree for her to keep house for him, for which he overpays her. When Agnes wants a piano, Berndt tries again to bargain—as her husband he could buy her a fine piano. But when she balks, he gives in, buying her a Caramacchione grand from Minneapolis. The first night it is in the house, Agnes, nude, plays Chopin, and so begins their love affair.

One muddy morning the following spring, Agnes leaves the house to go to the bank. The next Berndt sees her, she is being held on the running board of a car with three men inside (bank robbers), and there is blood on her leg. Berndt follows on his giant Percheron.

Berndt catches up with the robbers, whose car is stuck in mud, and pretends to help. But in fact he has his horse mire them even more deeply. The sheriff and his deputy show up, and in the exchange that follows, the Actor shoots Agnes, the bullet creasing her skull, and takes Berndt's horse. Thinking that Agnes is dead, Berndt follows the gunman on foot. When the horse becomes hopelessly mired, the Actor shoots it and then shoots Berndt twice. Berndt grabs him and pushes him into the liquid mire, which swallows him. Berndt dies, but Agnes survives.

Even a decade later (as in chapter 16), the old grief overwhelms Agnes at times. In 1996, when she is very old and the demonic black dog visits her in chapter 20, the dog gloats that it enjoyed "tickling" Berndt with bullets and stopping his heart. As she is dying in chapter 22, Agnes wrestles with bitterness at the thought of children she and Berndt might have had and recalls his murder afresh.

Betty Zumbrugge. Daughter of Argus banker Chester Zumbrugge in *The Master Butchers Singing Club*. Betty has at least two sisters and plans to go to nursing school. She is arrogant and shallow, making a display of her family's wealth. Unnaturally blond and sporting bright red lipstick, she is also showy in her appearance. In the fall of 1936 (chapter 9), Betty focuses her attentions on Franz Waldvogel. At first

Betty Zumbrugge

he ignores her advances, but later that fall (chapter 10), he begins accepting Betty's offers of rides. When they pass Mazarine Shimek, Franz's one-time sweetheart, on the road one day, Betty speaks contemptuously of Mazarine's poverty. That December (chapter 11), Betty picks Franz up for a date. They have drinks at a roadhouse, then Betty drives them out to a country road. But when they kiss, Franz is repulsed by her, gets out of the car, and walks away into the bitter cold. They are never together again. We learn in chapter 14 that Delphine Watzka, who helped rear the Waldvogel boys, does not like Betty.

Beverly "Hat" Lamartine. Brother of Henry Lamartine, third husband of Lulu Lamartine, and father of Henry Lamartine Junior in *Love Medicine*. Nector says that Beverly is mixed-blood Cree ("The Plunge of the Brave"). He has an **older brother, Slick,** who dies in boot camp, but Beverly and Henry remain close, serving in the military together and getting similar tattoos ("Lulu's Boys"). They also fall in love with the same woman, Lulu Nanapush Morrissey. After the three play a game of strip poker, Lulu chooses to marry Henry instead of Beverly. Henry, however, dies in a wreck in 1950. After his wake, Beverly and Lulu go outside for some air and end up making love in a shed. When Henry Junior is born nine months later, Beverly is sure that the boy is his.

Beverly lives in the Twin Cities, where he sells children's after-school work-books door-to-door, using Henry Junior's school pictures in his sales pitch. He is married to a natural blond, Elsa, who does not like children and who hides from her family the fact that Beverly is an Indian. A hidden ache in Beverly induces him in 1957 to visit the reservation and try to bring Henry Junior back to the city. His plans change, however, when he finds himself once again attracted to Lulu. While he is staying with her, in "The Good Tears," she becomes angry with her present lover and marries Beverly. When Beverly tells her about his other wife, however, Lulu sends him back to the city to divorce Elsa, accompanied by her twelve-year-old son, Gerry. While there, Gerry is thrown into detention, and Lulu thinks it is Beverly who has turned him in. There is no indication that Beverly ever returns to the reservation. Lulu's brief marriage to "Hat" Lamartine is mentioned again in "The Tomahawk Factory."

Big Mauser. See **Jack Mauser's father.**

Bijiu family. The Bijius sell gooseberries to the Morrisseys in chapter 4 of *Tracks*. **Mrs. Bijiu,** along with her children, is attacked by the devil in the form of a black dog made of smoke in chapter 3 of *Tracks*. See also **Black dog** and **Bizhieu family.**

Bishops. In *Tales of Burning Love,* Jude Miller sends **Bishop Retzlaff** a letter concerning some seemingly miraculous events at the convent in Argus, hinting that Sister Leopolda may be eligible for sainthood ("A Letter to the Bishop" [45]).

Two bishops are mentioned in *The Last Report on the Miracles at Little No Horse.* In the autumn of 1920 (chapter 11), Father Damien receives a letter from **Bishop DuPre** of Fargo saying that he is sending an assistant to stay with Father Damien. He sends Father Gregory Wekkle. The following autumn, Damien writes the bishop asking him to reassign Wekkle to a new post as soon as possible, and several weeks later DuPre replies. In November 1921 Father Damien writes to the **bishop of Minneapolis** to inquire about Fleur Pillager (chapter 16). This bishop replies that he himself had married Fleur to a prominent member of the community, John James Mauser.

Bizhieu family. Family whose members, with different spellings of the name, randomly appear in several novels. When "saint" Pauline Puyat is in her trance in the spring of 1919, the Bizhieu family brings a gift of smoked fish in chapter 7 of *The Last Report on the Miracles at Little No Horse.* In chapter 9, the whip Father Damien uses to drive the rioters out of the church at Napoleon's funeral belongs to **Mr. Bizhieu,** who admires Damien's forcefulness. Nanapush sees **George Bizhiew** (different spelling) pass by as he waits for Margaret to return from church in chapter 9 of *Four Souls.* After the death of **Josette Bizhieu's mother and niece** in 1933 (*The Bingo Palace* chapter 12), a black dog stands in the road "guarding air" (*BP,* 141). More than one generation of women in this family are reservation gossips. See **Josette Bizhieu** and **Zozed Bizhieu.** See also **Bijiu family** and **Black dog.**

Bjornson. Second husband of Zelda Kashpaw. In 1981, in "The World's Greatest Fishermen" in *Love Medicine,* Zelda has been living with him on his wheat farm on the edge of the reservation for about a year. When Zelda reappears some time later in *The Bingo Palace,* she is apparently not living with him. He is never mentioned in this novel, she is again wearing the Kashpaw name, and, according to chapters 4 and 9, she is living in the old Kashpaw house.

Black dog. Manifestation of death and the devil. There are brief references to the black dog in *Tracks, The Bingo Palace,* and *The Antelope Wife.* In each case, its appearance is associated with death. In the fall of 1913, when Fleur's return from Argus stirs up the ghosts that haunt her land, in chapter 3 of *Tracks* Mrs. Bijiu sees a black dog who is "the form of the devil" and leaves behind "the stinking odor of singed fur" (*Tr,* 35). When Fleur returns to the reservation a final time in 1933, in

Black dog

The Bingo Palace chapter 12, after the death of **Josette Bizhieu's mother and niece,** the black dog stands in the road "guarding air" (*BP,* 141). When Cally Roy almost dies in chapter 8 of *The Antelope Wife,* her dog Almost Soup senses the presence of the great black dog, who he says is "death" (*AW,* 82). In chapter 16 of *The Last Report on the Miracles at Little No Horse,* during a time of numerous sightings of the devil in the 1930s, **Mrs. Pentecost and her daughter** see the black dog on their way to Holy Mass.

Readers get a clearer picture of the black dog when Father Damien sees the dog three times in *The Last Report on the Miracles at Little No Horse.* The first is in chapter 7 (1912), when Kashpaw prophesies that two hundred Anishinaabeg will die in the epidemic approaching from the east. Looking to the east, Father Damien sees a tall, gaunt figure with a dog at his side. In chapter 11, in the autumn of 1920, this dog pays Damien a personal visit when the priest is ill. The huge animal walks in the open window and puts a paw in Damien's soup. In this incident, the dog clearly represents the devil as well as death. When the nuns drink the soup that has been touched by "the devil's foot," their dreams are "lurid" and "voluptuous" (*LR,* 192), and the temptation the dog promises does come to afflict Damien. In chapter 13, Damien questions Nanapush about the black dog, and in chapter 16, the damning pact he has made with this devil figure makes Damien resent Lulu's careless lifestyle.

More than seventy-five years later, in March 1996, Damien's conversations with Father Jude cause him to recall his past years at Little No Horse. In this context, the black dog revisits Damien one night. As it lies on Damien's body, the creature's smell is foul, and it emanates fleas. It tries to seduce Damien into coming with it (that is, dying), but the priest resists and finally vanquishes the dog by squeezing its testicles between his knees. The next day, Damien tells Father Jude about the visit, but Jude does not believe him. Damien says of the dog both that it is "Death. That was its name" and that it is "the devil himself" (*LR,* 311, 313).

That summer, when Father Damien goes out to Spirit Island to die, in chapter 22 of *Last Report* he is hopeful that in this place of Ojibwe spirits, he will be protected from the black dog.

Blue Prairie Woman. Daughter of Midass; mother of Matilda Roy and twins Mary (I) and Josephette (Zosie I) Shawano; great-grandmother of Rozina Roy in *The Antelope Wife.*

As a girl in chapter 6, Blue Prairie Woman is known as Apijigo Bakaday (So Hungry) because of her insatiable appetite. While staying in the woods, she falls in love with a deer man. She travels with him and is loved by his people until her **brothers** shoot him and bring her back. She is now renamed Ozhawashkwamashkodeykway, Blue Prairie Woman, an old name that has belonged to *many powerful women,* and she marries Shawano the younger.

The remainder of Blue Prairie Woman's story appears in chapters 1 and 6. Soon after her first daughter is born, a doe warns her to flee. She ties her baby's cradleboard to the back of a female dog and starts to leave but is too late. Bluecoats descend on the village, killing and burning. Blue Prairie Woman sees one of the men murder her grandmother and then run after the dog, which is fleeing onto the prairie with her baby, a necklace of blue beads swaying from the cradleboard. To ease Blue Prairie Woman's impacted breasts, an *old midwife* gives her a puppy to nurse, a female named Sorrow, whose mother is the bitch carrying the cradleboard. The raid occurs in autumn (Shawano the younger is away gathering wild rice at the time, an autumn activity).

In her grief, Blue Prairie Woman eats nothing but dirt for six months. When her husband returns, the two become obsessive lovers, and she conceives twins. Yet Blue Prairie Woman's grief deepens, and by spring, the old ones know they must give her a new name if she is to survive. The *androgynous namer* chooses as her name the place where Blue Prairie Woman's spirit has gone to fetch her child—Other Side of the Earth.

Other Side of the Earth gives birth to twin daughters, Mary and Josephette, leaves them with her mother, Midass, and goes in search of her firstborn, followed by the dog Sorrow. (These incidents are also mentioned in chapter 3.) She walks for years, guided by stories of a man and a young girl with blue beads. When she finds their place, she senses sickness inside, but that night she taps at the house, and her daughter (Matilda Roy) follows her. Matilda falls into a fever as they travel, and the mother gives her child her own life-restoring name, Other Side of the Earth. As she herself succumbs to the same illness, Blue Prairie Woman kills and cooks the dog Sorrow. Blue Prairie Woman dies within the day, but the meat she leaves behind nourishes her child. Matilda follows the antelope people, still wearing the blue beads.

Years later, in chapter 18, the spirit of Blue Prairie Woman, wearing the blue beads, appears to her pregnant granddaughter Zosie Shawano Roy. They gamble and Zosie wins the beads and the spirit woman's names. Zosie will later give these names to her own granddaughters, Cally and Deanna. In *Four Souls* chapter 16, Margaret Kashpaw alludes to this long-ago woman (without mentioning her name), saying that she was Fleur Pillager's aunt.

Blue Prairie Woman's grandmother I (killed). Old woman bayoneted by young Scranton Roy in chapter 1 of *The Antelope Wife.* When Scranton's cavalry unit attacks her village, the old woman charges him with a stone to protect the

Blue Prairie Woman's grandmother I (killed)

children (chapter 23). She dies uttering the word *daashkikaa*. (Six generations later, in chapter 18, her descendant Cally Roy will hear that word and learn its meaning—"cracked apart.") She is identified as Blue Prairie Woman's grandmother in chapter 6.

Years later, Scranton falls ill and the old woman's spirit visits him in his fever (chapter 23). After a hundred nights, he offers to find the remnant of her village, taking with him supplies and his grandson, Augustus II. The old woman accepts this offering, and Scranton's fever abates.

Blue Prairie Woman's grandmother II (living). Woman in chapter 1 of *The Antelope Wife* who says that the dirt Blue Prairie Woman is eating must be rich dirt.

Bonita. Last child and only daughter of Lulu Lamartine. We learn from "The Good Tears" in *Love Medicine* that Bonita is fathered by an unnamed Mexican migrant farmworker, and that she is born when Lulu is almost fifty. In "The Red Convertible" (1974), the eleven-year-old Bonita takes a picture of her half brothers, Lyman Lamartine and Henry Lamartine Junior, shortly before Henry Junior dies. Two decades later, when Lulu comes to visit Father Damien in chapter 8 of *The Last Report on the Miracles at Little No Horse,* he asks about Bonita.

Boss Woman. Wife of Pillager and mother of Fleur Pillager; her Ojibwe name is Ogimaakwe. True to her name, we learn in chapter 3 of *Tracks* that she raises her daughters to be their own bosses. In *Tracks,* she dies of consumption in chapter 1, and Nanapush sees her spirit in chapter 9. In *The Bingo Palace,* she is mentioned in chapter 3 as being listed in the old Pillager records, and in chapter 27 she is one of the Pillagers who welcome Fleur on her death walk to the island in Matchimanito Lake. Chapter 16 of *Four Souls* says that Ogimaakwe is one of the names for Four Souls. See **Four Souls.**

Boy Lazarre. Member of one of the two families who become enemies of the Kashpaws and Pillagers. Boy Lazarre is hired by Margaret Kashpaw in chapter 3 of *Tracks* to spy on her son Eli and Fleur Pillager. For this action, Fleur is said to have cut Lazarre's tongue out and sewn it in backwards. In chapter 5, Lazarre and Clarence Morrissey abduct Nanapush and Margaret, tie them up in a barn, and shave Margaret's head. Margaret, however, manages to bite Lazarre's hand. The wound leads to blood poisoning, which eventually kills him. Before his death, Fleur takes pieces of his hair and nails to make a curse. He seems to die of heart failure the next time he encounters Fleur. His death is referred to again in chapter 7. In Pauline's death vision in chapter 6, Lazarre is among the group of men whose deaths Fleur is presumed to have caused. Many years later, in chapter 14 of *The*

Last Report on the Miracles at Little No Horse, Margaret remembers Clarence and Boy Lazarre's shaving her head, referring to them not quite accurately as "those Lazarres" (*LR,* 179).

Boy Lazarre II. A "second" Boy Lazarre who sends a message in a baking powder can to "saint" Pauline Puyat when she is in her tetanus trance in chapter 7 of *The Last Report on the Miracles at Little No Horse.*

Burden Tatro. See **John Jewett Tatro** entry.

C

Cally Whiteheart Beads Roy. Daughter of Rozina Roy and Richard Whiteheart Beads; twin sister of Deanna Whiteheart Beads in *The Antelope Wife.* Cally's spirit name is Ozhawashkwamashkodeykway, Blue Prairie Woman (chapters 11 and 18). She narrates chapters 6, 11, 14, and 18. Cally may also be the story's central consciousness, the "I" that opens and closes the novel. (See the introduction to *The Antelope Wife* in the "Geography, Genealogy, and Chronology" section of this book.)

Judging from Cally's age at the novel's end, Cally and Deanna are likely born in the mid-1970s. When Rozin discovers that she is pregnant with the twins, she is separating from Richard, but in her joy about the pregnancy she chooses to stay with him (chapter 7). Cally is born minutes after Deanna and tends always to follow the lead of her "maternal" sibling. Cally has a special attachment to animals, whether toy or real (see chapter 3, 7, 8, 9, and 11).

The twins grow up on their parents' reservation. They have twin maternal grandmothers, since Zosie Roy and Mary Shawano refuse to reveal which of them is Rozin's mother (chapters 9 and 11). Their father, Richard, is a young tribal leader (chapter 16). When the girls are five, the family moves to Minneapolis (chapter 3).

One summer afternoon when Cally and Deanna are still small, their father takes them to the city park (chapter 6). There they see a woman who looks like their mother walking with a man Cally describes as a "deer man." Cally's narration includes a description of the couple's lovemaking, an account that fuses what she intuits about her mother with the story of Apijigo Bakaday and the deer husband. On one occasion when the grandmothers are staying with Cally and Deanna, they explain the girls' dancing outside naked by the assertion that they are "part deer." After Richard forces Rozin to end her affair with Frank Shawano, Cally holds her weeping "deer mother."

Cally Whiteheart Beads Roy

While visiting relatives in Bwaanakeeng, in chapter 8 Cally rescues a white puppy from being cooked. Shortly thereafter, the puppy, now called Almost Soup, is taken to Cally's home reservation, where he stays with her grandmothers (chapter 9).

One snowy March day when Cally and Deanna are eleven (chapter 7), the girls come home from school to find their parents fighting. That night, Richard's botched suicide attempt causes Deanna's death. In chapter 9, Rozin and Cally move back to the reservation to stay with the grandmothers. Almost a year later, on a sunny but freezing February day, as Cally plays outside with Almost Soup, she loses her bead-wrapped indis, the birth cord that connects her to her long line of grandmothers (see also chapters 11 and 18). That night Cally develops a high fever that lasts for three days, cut off from medical help by a blizzard. Cally has a seizure and almost dies, but her mother calls her back. An ambulance finally arrives, and Cally recovers at the Indian Health Service hospital. Almost Soup keeps her life until her body is able to hold it.

When Cally is eighteen, she begins to wander from home in chapter 11, a disconnectedness that she attributes to the loss of her indis. Cally stays with Frank Shawano in Minneapolis, working in his bakery and living with the family in the rooms above. Frank is kind to Cally, and she is intrigued by his sister, Cecille, but she finds the silent, jagged-toothed "Auntie Klaus" (Sweetheart Calico) disturbing.

In the city, Cally looks unsuccessfully for her grandmothers, managing only one brief phone visit with them. Finally, Grandma Zosie walks into the bakery announcing that Cally's dad is out on the street. Cally, who is bitter about her sister's death and who has changed her name to Roy, says that she never wants to see him again. As soon as she says this, Richard, sick and hungover, walks in. He mistakes Cally for Deanna and flees in terror.

When Cally is twenty, in chapter 14 her mother moves to the city to go to night school. One August evening when Cally picks her mother up from work, Frank is there, asking Rozin out. Cally's emotions are mixed. She feels possessive of her mother but wants her to be happy. When Rozin finally agrees to go with Frank to the state fair, Cally accompanies them and observes their near-catastrophic Gravitron ride.

Frank and Rozin's wedding is in the autumn, apparently the following year. In chapter 16, Cally is in Frank's kitchen on the wedding day, making preparations with other family members. She recalls with shame her father's phone call the night before, asking why he had not been invited to the wedding. To Cally's horror, Richard shows up at the cliffside ceremony. His suicide attempt at the wedding is unsuccessful, but that night, outside the door of Rozin and Frank's hotel room, he fatally shoots himself. Having already lost her twin and now faced with her father's suicide and her mother's acute depression (chapter 17), Cally is in danger of losing her entire family. Frank, however, is able to bring Rozin back into connection with life.

The following December, the family gathers at Frank and Rozin's apartment for Christmas dinner. As they arrive, Cally slips on the ice and begins to hear the Ojibwe word *daashkikaa,* not knowing its meaning. (See **Blue Prairie Woman's grandmother I.**) At dinner, Cally watches her family and recalls old family stories.

Later, in the kitchen, Cally asks Grandma Zosie about the word *daashkikaa* (an Ojibwe word meaning "cracked apart") and about her own spirit name. In response, Zosie relates her long-ago dream of Blue Prairie Woman and the blue beads, thereby revealing that she, not Mary, is Rozin's mother. Cally longs for the beads, and Sweetheart Calico draws them from her mouth. In exchange for the beads, Sweetheart Calico wants her freedom, so Cally walks with her all night until they reach the outskirts of the city. In the morning, Sweetheart Calico is gone. As Cally hears the chatter of the Hmong grandmas, she thinks of the loss of her indis, which had connected her to her own grandmothers and the earth.

Cally's own story falls silent at the end of chapter 18, but her voice may close the novel in chapter 23.

Candice Pantamounty Mauser. Third wife of Jack Mauser in *Tales of Burning Love.* Descriptions of Candice's supercilious, perfectionist, controlling personality appear in "Jack's House" [9] from Jack's point of view and in "Memoria" [10] in the narrator's voice. In "Candice's Tale" [25], we learn that Jack and Candice date in high school. Candice later recalls having shared him with girlfriends.

In college, Candice dates constantly and in the mid-seventies is fitted with a Dalkon shield, which leads to a perforated uterus and hysterectomy. She goes to dental school and joins a class-action lawsuit against the manufacturer of the shield. She uses her settlement money as down payment on a house and office space. Depressed that she will never be able to bear a child, she copes by overbooking herself at work and getting a dog, Pepperboy. She finds the dog at the dump, where Jack Mauser is about to shoot it. Candice makes a deal with Jack—in return for the dog, she will fix Jack's rotten teeth.

After several months of Jack's visiting Candice's dental office, the two go out for a lunch date and Jack proposes marriage. They marry, but Pepperboy comes between them from the start. In "The Wandering Room" [26], on their way home from a deer hunt, they accidentally drag Pepperboy to his death. (Jack recalls the incident in "Blizzard Night" [35].)

Shortly after Candice and Jack divorce, in August 1992 Jack marries Marlis Cook and takes off with her for a month-long fling. Candice seems to keep track

Candice Pantamounty Mauser

of him, since when he returns to Fargo in September ("The First Draw" [14]), he finds Candice sitting in his car. Trying to make him act responsibly, she drives him to his construction yard and takes his car keys away.

Early in 1994, Candice contacts Marlis, who is separated from Jack and pregnant with his child. Candice wants the baby. In "Baptism River" [29], she invites Marlis to take a trip with her, on which she offers to help Marlis through the birth and then adopt the baby. On this trip, Candice begins to feel an emotional bond with Marlis, and in "Candice" [30], she realizes its lesbian implications.

Although Marlis tells her to stay away, in "The Waiting Room" [31] Candice shows up at Marlis's late-term checkup, attends Lamaze classes with her, visits in her apartment, and helps her through labor. Weeks after the birth of John Jr., Marlis is still suffering severe postpartum depression. Candice moves into the apartment to take care of Marlis and the baby, and the women become lovers. For weeks Candice and Marlis fight over custody of the baby ("The B & B" [16]), and Candice hires a nanny to take care of John Jr.

"Memoria" [10] and "Satin Heart" [12] show Candice at Jack's funeral in January 1995. She has brought Jack's baby, chiefly to attract attention to herself. After the funeral, Candice, Eleanor, and Dot Adare Mauser go to the B & B where Marlis is working and where Candice gets tipsy and loses money at the blackjack table. In "The Hitchhiker" [18], just as a blizzard is striking, she and the other women leave in Jack's red Explorer to ride back to Fargo. Not dressed warmly, Candice argues that they should stay at the B & B rather than risk the roads. As they try to drive beneath an overpass, the Explorer becomes stuck in a snowdrift.

In "Secrets and Sugar Babies" [19], the stranded women begin to argue about Jack, with Candice tending to belittle him. After listening to Eleanor's tale, Candice launches her own storytelling in "Candice's Tale" [25] and "The Wandering Room" [26]. Marlis takes the next turn, and Candice again picks up the thread of the tale in "Baptism River" [29] and "Candice" [30], relating the development of her and Marlis's relationship. Candice and Marlis's memories in "The Waiting Room" [31] appear not to be told to the other women. Overcome with fatigue and cold, in "The Tale of the Unknown Passenger" [34] Candice and Marlis sleep in each other's arms. Eventually a snowmobile rescue squad finds the wives and transports them to the hospital ("The Disappearance" [36] and "Two Front-Page Articles" [37]).

After they are rescued, Candice and Marlis discover that while they were at Jack's funeral, Jack stole Candice's car—with baby John inside (see "Funeral Day" [23]). Jack eventually telephones the hysterical Candice in "Mauser and Mauser" [39].

Candice and Marlis buy one of the houses in Jack's housing development

("Spring Morning" [41]). In March (1995) Candice repairs Jack's latest decayed tooth ("Spring Afternoon" [42]). Marlis calls her before Jack comes to the office, and Candice seems to know that Jack made love to Marlis earlier that day.

Carlisle teacher from Stokes. Man who recruits and later marries Niibin'aage in *The Painted Drum.* A few months after Anaquot comes to the Pillager cabin, she and Ziigwan'aage meet this man at the reservation store (part 2.3). We learn in part 1.2 that he is a twenty-year-old from Stokes, New Hampshire, that he stays with Indian agent Jewett Parker Tatro on the reservation while he is recruiting, that he is the one who induces Niibin'aage to come to the Carlisle Indian School, and that while she is there, he marries her. At first they stay in the east, then live for a time on the reservation, where their daughter, Elsie, is born. They then return to Stokes, where he manages a private game park for the rest of his life.

Caryl Moon. Truck driver at Mauser and Mauser in *Tales of Burning Love,* hired only because Jack Mauser owes some sort of debt to Caryl's lawyer father, Maynard Moon. Caryl is first mentioned in "The Meadowlark" [7], where Dot Adare Nanapush recalls that she met Jack, her second husband, when he tried to kill her boyfriend, Caryl. Dot tells the story in "Caryl Moon" [8]. Jack eventually fires Caryl.

In the second chapter titled "Caryl Moon" [13], shortly after midnight, January 1, 1995, Caryl rescues Jack, who has escaped naked from his burning house, but then beats him into unconsciousness and leaves him in the bitter cold. Moon is mentioned briefly in "February Thaw" [40] as being once again Jack's employee— another payoff to his lawyer father. Caryl is the operator of the crane that drops a statue of the Virgin on Jack in "The Stone Virgin" [44].

Catherine Miller. Woman in *The Beet Queen* who raises the Adare infant, now named Jude Miller. *Her own infant* has just died when her husband, Martin, steals the baby from Mary Adare at the Orphans' Picnic in Minneapolis in 1932 (chapter 1). In chapter 2, Catherine sees in the newspaper an inquiry placed by Pete and Fritzie Kozka concerning the whereabouts of the missing Adare baby, but she merely cuts out the notice and saves it, along with the baby's clothes. We learn in chapter 5 that Martin dies in 1944, and in 1950 Catherine writes the Kozkas to tell them what has happened to the missing baby and that he is about to be ordained as a deacon (on his way to the priesthood). The letter is forwarded to Sita Kozka in Fargo. Sita writes a reply but never mails it. Many years later, in 1972 (chapter 13), Celestine James finds and mails Sita's letter. In chapter 14, ill and weak, Catherine shows Sita's letter to Jude, revealing that he has family in Argus. Catherine's revelation prompts Jude to visit Argus on the day of the Beet Festival.

Cecilia, Sister. The youngest nun at the convent in Fargo in chapter 1 of *The Last Report on the Miracles at Little No Horse,* a musician and teacher; born Agnes DeWitt. Cecilia's two passions are for God and for music, especially the piano music of Frederic Chopin. Discovering that the convent bricks are imprinted with the word *Fleisch,* Cecilia is aware of being surrounded by the repetition of that word. One day Cecilia has a sexual climax while playing Chopin. The passion of her playing disturbs the other sisters, so the Mother Superior hides all the music except Bach. While this measure brings temporary peace, a few weeks later Cecilia begins playing Chopin from memory. When the Mother Superior tries to drag her from the piano, Cecilia resists, strips down to her shift, and leaves the convent. She feels that in her passion for Chopin, she has been unfaithful as a bride of Christ. When she shows up at the farm of Berndt Vogel a few days later, exhausted and starving, Cecilia has taken again the name Agnes DeWitt.

Cecilia's name appears again in chapter 12 when Agnes (now Father Damien) remembers money deposited in a Fargo bank under the name Cecilia Fleisch. See **Agnes DeWitt** and **Damien Modeste, Father.**

Cecille Shawano. Younger sister of Frank Shawano in *The Antelope Wife.* In chapters 11 and 16, Cecille is living above Frank's bakery. She is a thoroughly urbanized Ojibwe who operates a kung fu studio and is studying to be a radio commentator. Cally attributes Cecille's jolting personality to her uneasy mix of Irish and Ojibwe blood. Cecille is an obsessive talker and a creative liar.

On the day of Frank's marriage to Rozina Roy (chapter 16), as the family is busy preparing, Cecille keeps trying to tell the story of *her neighbor* and the missing dishes, although everyone ignores her. When she reports that Rozin's former husband, Richard Whiteheart Beads, is coming to the wedding, no one believes her.

According to chapter 18, Cecille stays with Frank and Rozin occasionally even after their wedding. At the family dinner the following Christmas, Cecille is her usual confrontational self, reminding the family of Richard's suicide and questioning Grandmas Zosie and Mary about the rumor that they ate Zosie's husband.

Celestine James. Daughter of Regina Puyat Kashpaw and Dutch James; mother of Dot Adare. Celestine's story is told primarily in *The Beet Queen.* In chapter 2, we learn that Celestine is Regina's youngest child, born only a month after her marriage to Dutch. She has two half siblings. Celestine's parents both die when she is young, and her older half sister, Isabel Kashpaw, takes care of her. They live together with Isabel's brother, Russell Kashpaw, on Dutch's homestead on the outskirts of Argus. As a seventh grader in 1932, Celestine is best friends with Sita

Kozka until Sita's younger cousin, Mary Adare, arrives and comes between them. Over time Celestine becomes Mary's best friend.

Celestine receives word in chapter 4 that Russell has been wounded in the war. In chapter 7 (1953), Celestine is in her early thirties and works with Mary at the Argus butcher shop. Russell returns home "from his latest war, Korea," with even more wounds, and their sister, Isabel, now married, dies in South Dakota. That year, Celestine, Mary, and Russell attend the near-disastrous grand opening of Sita's new restaurant. Soon after, Karl Adare visits the butcher shop looking for his sister, Mary, and has sex with Celestine on Mary's kitchen floor. Two weeks later, Karl is selling knives door-to-door when he comes to Celestine's house by accident. Celestine invites him in, and when he stays for several months, Russell moves out. Celestine finally forces Karl to leave, even though she is pregnant with his child.

That winter, Celestine finds Russell in his ice-fishing hut, collapsed from a stroke (chapter 8). Celestine goes into labor in the middle of a January blizzard (1954) in chapter 9. Unable to get to town, she goes to Wallace Pfef's house, where Wallace helps deliver her baby girl. Insisting on naming the baby after him, Celestine calls her Wallacette Darlene. The baby's Aunt Mary, however, nicknames her Dot. We learn from chapter 15 that Celestine goes to Rapid City to marry Karl shortly after Dot's birth, but only as a formality. She returns home without him.

In chapter 10, a rivalry for Dot's affections develops between Mary and Celestine. Mary's interference makes it more difficult for Celestine to discipline her willful, spoiled child. Relationships are further strained in chapter 11 (1964) when Mary moves in with them for several weeks while the butcher shop is being repaired after a fire. Chapters 11 and 12 reveal Dot's heartbreaking experiences during and after her school's Christmas play. Later that night, as Celestine holds her sobbing daughter, they are, for a moment, closer than they have been since Dot's infancy.

In chapter 12, Celestine attends the party Wallace throws for Dot's eleventh birthday (1965). Three years later, Karl stops briefly in Argus, and Celestine and the fourteen-year-old Dot have breakfast with him, though the meeting is strained.

In chapter 13 (1972), Celestine has a disturbing dream about Sita, and she and Mary drive to Blue Mound to check on her. They find her ill and stay with her for several weeks. While there, Celestine finds and mails a letter Sita had written to Catherine Miller more than twenty years earlier. During this time, Celestine is also helping Dot prepare for her part in the Beet Festival. In chapter 15, Celestine sends a newspaper clipping to Karl showing Dot as a Beet Queen candidate, and in chapter 14, she receives a postcard from him in reply, saying that he is on his way.

Celestine James

In chapter 16, Celestine insists that Dot must wear to the coronation ceremony the loud green dress Mary has bought for her.

On the day of the Beet Festival (July 1972), in chapter 13 Celestine and Mary find Sita outside her house, dead from an overdose of medication. Because the whole town, even the undertaker, has gone to the festival, they put Sita in the passenger seat of the delivery truck and take her with them to the fairground. In chapter 15, Celestine and Mary watch Dot's coronation from the grandstand. When Dot jumps into the skywriting plane and it disappears from sight, Celestine is terrified. Celestine is still waiting in the grandstand an hour later when Dot returns (chapter 16). That evening, Celestine and Dot fall into the familiar routines of their life together.

In 1994, Celestine is still living in Argus. On a sweltering June day in "A Wedge of Shade" [3] in *Tales of Burning Love,* Dot comes to Argus to tell her mother of her sudden marriage to Jack Mauser (without divorcing her previous husband). Celestine is dubious, but when she discovers that the family of Jack's mother are her distant relatives, she accepts him. (She refers to herself as a Kashpaw in this chapter, though we know from *The Beet Queen* that she is a Puyat. Her half siblings are Kashpaw.) Dot comments in "The Meadowlark" [7] that her mother likes Jack.

The following January, after Dot is stranded for a time in a snowbound car during a blizzard, Celestine and Mary take turns staying with her in the hospital while she recovers ("February Thaw" [40]). There, Celestine and Dot express their love for each other. Celestine goes along with Dot's ruse that the car's missing passenger is Celestine herself. (The missing person is actually Dot's other husband, Gerry Nanapush.)

Center of the Sky. See **Margaret Kashpaw.**

Chester Zumbrugge. Argus banker in *The Master Butchers Singing Club.* When Fidelis Waldvogel forms his men's singing club in the early 1930s (chapter 3), Chester is one of its charter members. Chapters 5 and 8 depict Chester as one the few wealthy customers at Fidelis's butcher shop. He lives in a mansion on a bluff overlooking the river and eats a perfectly cooked steak every night. At the butcher shop, Delphine Watzka makes certain to get as much money as possible from men like Zumbrugge.

Zumbrugge apparently has no feeling for those suffering during the Depression. In chapter 8, although the governor has forbidden it, he still forecloses on one or two farms a year. Also, though money is tight for Fidelis, Chester runs up a large bill at the butcher shop before paying (chapter 9). Chester rears his daughter Betty to be much like himself. She is arrogant, puts on rich-girl airs, and is contemptuous of the poor (see chapter 10).

When the singing club meets (chapter 13), shortly after the beginning of World War II, Chester, concerned about his standing in town, fears the singers will appear treasonous if they sing German songs.

Chickie Ruse. Son of Albert Ruse in *The Painted Drum.* Although he is sent to the mission school, Chickie continually runs away, so in part 2.4 his father is teaching him traditional ways. Chickie is fifteen when he goes with his father to smoke the pipe with Shaawano, future maker of the drum. He also accompanies the men across the lake to find the drum wood. In part 2.5, Chickie is berry-picking with *his sister* when big flies tip him off that moose are near. He kills the bull that appears, helps his father tan the hide, and gives it to Shaawano for his drumheads.

Children who die in fire. Victims in Richard Whiteheart Beads's apocryphal story of his past in chapter 15 of *The Antelope Wife.* Since Richard's invented pasts are concocted from stories he has heard, this tale may allude to Sweetheart Calico's experience recorded in chapter 5.

Chokecherry Girl. Sister of Fleur Pillager; her Indian name is Asasaweminikwesens. She dies of consumption in chapter 1 of *Tracks.* She is also referred to in chapter 3 of *The Bingo Palace.*

Chook. *(The Antelope Wife).* Nephew of Richard Whiteheart Beads. In preparation for the wedding of Frank Shawano and Richard's ex-wife, Rozina Roy (chapter 16), Chook cooks buffalo and moose meat and runs errands for the women. When Richard shows up at the reception with a letter for Rozin, Chook delivers it.

According to chapter 18, Richard is Chook's favorite uncle, and he is so upset by Richard's suicide that he speeds in a motorboat until it runs out of gas. Although he is apparently still married that autumn, by the time he shows up at the family Christmas, Chook has gone through a difficult divorce. He brings his daughter, Elena, with him. At dinner, he is pained when Cecille Shawano insists on talking about Richard, but he still jokes with the others and pretends to have a seizure.

Chook's wife. *(The Antelope Wife).* Watches Chook's escapade in the motorboat after the suicide of Richard Whiteheart Beads in chapter 18. By that Christmas, she and Chook have divorced. Chook's wife may be the "Janice" of chapter 16, since Janice is mentioned in conjunction with Chook at Frank Shawano and Rozina Roy's wedding.

Chook String. Widow of Mike String; mother of John and Morris String in *The Painted Drum.* Chook also has two younger children, a *boy* and a *girl,* and helps rear her *grandchildren.* Faye Travers recalls Mrs. String as a vivid, lumpy-bodied woman

Chook String

who wears bright, flowery clothes and whose English has a musical Ojibwe accent (1.3). Bernard Shaawano describes in part 2.1 her infamously persistent requests for help from reservation people.

Chook has deep roots on the reservation, since her **mother** knew the original signers of the treaty that created it (1.3). She also has several family connections with the painted drum. She is kin to the Shaawano man who made the drum (1.3), her husband, Mike, was a keeper of the drum's property (2.1), and her son Morris knows many of its songs (3.7). Thus, when Elsie Travers discovers the drum her daughter Faye found in the Tatro estate, she thinks of Chook (1.3).

When the Travers women return the drum to the reservation in part 2.1, Chook is one of the first to be notified. She phones Bernard Shaawano asking him to help her dig up Mike's grave to recover the drum song scrolls, and she is part of the small gathering with the drum at the Nanapush house. When she tells the Travers women, "You cannot buy the drum. You cannot steal the drum" (*PD*, 106), Faye will not make eye contact.

Chopin. Composer whose piano music Agnes DeWitt plays with great passion in *The Last Report on the Miracles at Little No Horse.* As Sister Cecelia in the Fargo convent in chapter 1 (1910), Agnes's playing of Chopin disturbs the peace of the other nuns, even the Mother Superior. As she is playing one day, Cecelia has a sexual climax. Agnes ultimately leaves the convent, feeling that she has been unfaithful to her rightful husband, Christ, with her lover, Chopin. When Berndt Vogel buys her a Caramacchione grand, Agnes plays Chopin nude, precipitating the beginning of her and Berndt's love affair. Because of several traumas, Agnes forgets for a time her ability to play the piano. But when the Little No Horse piano is moved into the new church in 1922 (chapter 12), she remembers, and Chopin is among the composers whose music she plays that day. Years later, in 1996 when Agnes is over a hundred, she is still able to play Chopin's easier preludes. One night (chapter 20), as she wrestles with the black dog, she thinks of Chopin for strength.

Christ. Seems to appear to two of Erdrich's characters. In chapter 6 of *Tracks,* Pauline Puyat tells us that she sees Christ sitting on the convent stove one cold night in 1919, and he tells her that she must hunt down the devil to save the Indians. Another night, she sees a vision of all the dead she had sent on the Christian road during the influenza epidemic, and Christ tells her to fetch even more. Pauline decides in chapter 8 that Christ is weaker than Satan and that she must be his champion and savior. At the end of that chapter, she marries him by becoming a nun.

In chapter 1 of *The Last Report on the Miracles at Little No Horse,* Agnes Dewitt, as the nun Cecelia, also considers herself the bride of Christ. After her sexual experience while playing the music of Chopin, she feels that she has been unfaithful, leaves the Fargo convent, and subsequently refuses to marry. When in the 1912 spring flood she washes ashore far north of Fargo (chapter 2), in her great need a radiantly kind man ministers to her, and she later realizes that it was Christ in human form. Having now met him in a man's body, she determines to love and follow him all her life. Six years later, during the influenza epidemic in chapter 7, Agnes sees his face again in the face of Mary Kashpaw.

Chuck Mauser. Jack Mauser's uncle on his German father's side in *Tales of Burning Love*. When young Jack runs away from Chuck's sister, Aunt Elizabeth, he apparently lives with Chuck on his farm near Argus (see "Best Western" [28]). In "Eleanor's Tale" [20], while a student at North Dakota State University, Jack visits Chuck's farm and helps him fix his machinery, and he is still staying there after college in "The Red Slip" [21]. In "The First Draw" [14] and "The Wandering Room" [26], we learn that when Chuck gets behind financially, Jack buys his quarter section of land west of Fargo. At first, Jack leases the land back to him for sunflower farming, but (apparently unknown to Chuck) Jack plans to turn it into a housing development as soon as he can get financing. By August 1992, **Chuck's wife** has left him. When Jack shows him the first large check of his development loan, Chuck is bitter about losing his land to development. Chuck and Jack apparently have an agreement that Chuck can harvest his sunflower crop before the development begins, but enraged by one of his ex-wives, in September Jack bulldozes Chuck's crop.

Two years later, after houses are built on the land but have not sold, in "Jack's House" [9] Chuck writes to Jack threatening to repossess and seed the land if Jack does not make his mortgage payments. Chuck attends Jack's supposed funeral in January 1995 ("Satin Heart" [12]). That same year, at the end of the novel Chuck leases his land back from Jack, again planting it in sunflowers ("Spring Morning" [41]). He also buys one of the houses in Jack's new subdivision, and his wife returns.

Circus performers. Performers who are part of the same circus as Anna Kuklenski in "Eleanor's Tale" [20] in *Tales of Burning Love*. **Ali-Khazar**'s act involves waltzing white Arabian horses; the **Lady of the Mists** makes herself appear and disappear; and the **Mysterious Bernie** folds himself into a painted cracker tin. See also **Flying Kuklenskis.**

Clarence Marek, Father. Argus priest in *The Master Butchers Singing Club*. In chapter 6, he is stumped when Eva Waldvogel asks him which of her two husbands she will spend eternity with. In chapter 9, he is outraged that someone has stolen altar candles.

Clarence Morrissey

Clarence Morrissey. Son of Bernadette Morrissey; older brother of Sophie and Philomena Morrissey. In chapter 4 of *Tracks,* we learn that Clarence is a big, handsome young man who has helped build a two-story house for his family on his uncle Napoleon Morrissey's farm. In the autumn of 1917, when Fleur casts a spell on Sophie, Clarence steals the statue of the Virgin to break the spell. That winter (chapter 5), Clarence avenges Eli Kashpaw's sexual liaison with Sophie by shaming Eli's mother, Margaret. Clarence and Boy Lazarre abduct Nanapush and Margaret and shave Margaret's head. In revenge, Nanapush and Nector Kashpaw set a snare for Clarence. He survives but is left with a twisted mouth.

There are several later references to this incident. Speaking with Margaret, Nanapush alludes to the snaring in chapter 9 of *Tracks.* In the early 1930s (chapter 9 of *Four Souls*), Nanapush recalls snaring Clarence and decides to use this method to kill his enemy Shesheeb, but he snares Margaret instead. Nector's reference to the Clarence incident makes Margaret realize that Nanapush had set her snare. It is also apparently Clarence to whom Marie Kashpaw is referring in 1983 as "the twisted-mouth" (*Love Medicine* "The Tomahawk Factory").

In chapter 7 of *Tracks,* Clarence marries a **Lazarre woman** (and Sophie, a Lazarre man). This joining of Morrisseys with Lazarres marks the beginning of the decline of the once-prosperous Morrissey family.

Clarence is one of the observers from the shore when Pauline Puyat goes to Matchimanito Lake to confront the devil in chapter 8 of *Tracks.* After Napoleon's body is found, Clarence claims in chapter 9 that his uncle has appeared to him in a (drunken) vision accusing Fleur of the murder.

Clarisse Strub. Apprentice mortician and friend of Delphine Watzka in *The Master Butchers Singing Club.* We learn from chapter 5 that Clarisse virtually grows up in the mortuary business, since her father, **Cornelius Strub,** and her uncle and aunt, Aurelius and Benta Strub, operate Strub's Funerary in Argus. Clarisse is apparently an only child with no cousins, since she is to inherit the family business. She has a natural aptitude for embalming, but her first love is theater. She and Delphine are active in theater through high school and beyond, including playing the part of two witches in *Macbeth.* For her part in *The Lady and the Tiger,* Clarisse makes a tight, shiny dress covered with iridescent red flapper beads (see pp. 159 and 189). In her teens, Clarisse contracts syphilis—perhaps from a corpse, since she is already helping with the embalming—and must undergo the terrible treatments. She and Delphine have dreams of escaping Argus after high school, but upon graduation, Clarisse's father and uncle want her in the business.

Clarisse is pretty, with curly black hair. She is multitalented, a refined cook and seamstress, and a smart dresser. But men who would normally flock to her are frightened away by her profession (see pp. 158 and 248), with one unfortunate exception. Sheriff Albert Hock is infatuated with Clarisse and has "chased" her for years (chapter 4). Clarisse despises Hock, partly because she sees the dangerously possessive nature of his supposed love. In chapter 11, Clarisse observes Hock's corpulent body, then realizes that this body had decided it owned her.

In early 1934 (late winter; see p. 100), Clarisse's father, Cornelius, dies. Her mother is already deceased (see chapter 5). We learn in chapter 4 that Cornelius had requested a party instead of a funeral. The party, at Roy Watzka's house, is recorded in chapters 7 and 11. Clarisse wears her red-beaded costume to give herself the courage to accept this loss. But Sheriff Hock corners her in Roy's pantry, almost rips the dress off of her, and puts his mouth on her. His violence breaks the beading threads on the dress and scatters the beads. (The same violence may knock jars of peaches off the pantry shelf, creating a gluelike mass on the pantry floor.) Enraged that Hock would so violate her time of grief, Clarisse slugs him.

The following summer, in chapter 5, when Delphine returns to Argus and discovers three rotting bodies (the Chavers family) in Roy's cellar, Clarisse comes with Aurelius and Benta to remove them. Clarisse is here referred to as an "apprentice mortuary assistant" (*MBSC,* 73), but now in her late twenties she is much more than an assistant. She tells Delphine about difficult clients she has handled—a drowning victim and a food poisoning (see chapters 5 and 7). A few days after their meeting at Roy's house, Clarisse visits Delphine at the butcher shop and tells her about Sheriff Hock's egregious behavior the night before. He had come to her house late and whispered a threat through her door. When Delphine jokes that they should "murther'm," Clarisse agrees—not altogether facetiously.

A year later, in the late summer of 1935, when Delphine's dear friend Eva Waldvogel dies in chapter 7, Clarisse, Benta, and Aurelius come for the body. After Eva's death, Clarisse and Delphine spend more time together. Also that summer, Delphine lashes out at Sheriff Hock, telling him to leave Clarisse alone, then worries that insulting Hock could be risky. She immediately goes to Clarisse to warn her that Sheriff Hock seems to be connecting the beads, Clarisse, and the bodies in Roy's cellar. Clarisse is outraged at Hock, but she asks Delphine to fetch the beaded dress from her closet. Delphine does so and buries it in Clarisse's garden. A glimpse into Hock's mind in chapter 8 reveals that Clarisse is correct in seeing his intentions as malicious and controlling.

More than a year later, on a snowy December evening two days before Christmas 1936 (chapter 11), Clarisse walks home and is shocked to see Sheriff Hock on her porch. He has obtained a warrant to search her house for evidence (the red beads) that could implicate her in the deaths of the Chavers family. Clarisse

Clarisse Strub

understands that he intends to use the threat of murder charges to blackmail her into accepting his suit. When she remembers how the dress had "dripped" beads after Hock tore it, she realizes that he will find beads in her bedroom. As Hock is riffling through her underwear, Clarisse goes downstairs, sharpens her favorite carving knife, and returns. When Hock shows her the bead he has found and lunges for her, Clarisse slices him open. He dies bleeding on her shoes.

Clarisse quickly makes her plans. She will take her money from the bank the next day and leave on the early train on Christmas morning. By Christmas Eve, she is packed and ready and has piled on the back porch for Step-and-a-Half the things she will not be taking with her. Cyprian Lazarre, Delphine's companion, shows up at Clarisse's house, spends the night, and leaves with her the next morning. As we learn in chapter 13, Clarisse does not tell Cyprian about Sheriff Hock until they are on their way to Minneapolis. They part there and no one hears from her again. When the town learns about the murder, most feel that Clarisse was simply defending herself. Delphine envisions Clarisse going south—to New Orleans, the Yucatan, or maybe even Brazil (chapter 13).

Cyprian Lazarre. Mixed-blood French-Ojibwe gymnast and performer in *The Master Butchers Singing Club.* Cyprian admires Louis Riel, the métis "martyr" whom he claims as an ancestor (chapter 5). There is no clear link between Cyprian and the Lazarres we meet in other Erdrich novels, but his family seems to carry the same stigma as the Lazarres of Little No Horse—they are a bunch of "no-goods," says Ojibwe Step-and-a-Half in chapter 9 (*MBSC,* 208). Chapter 4 tells us that his **mother and father** are drinkers (see also chapter 11), and his **uncles and aunts** are living lives he does not want to know about. Apparently his **grandparents** are decent folks, since they have left the others in disgust. By the present time of the novel, his **brothers** have moved up north into Cree country. Although his brothers and **cousins** are brown (chapter 5), Cyprian is light-skinned. Yet the handsome, classical lines of his face suggest his Ojibwe heritage.

During World War I, Cyprian joins the Marine Corps with a **cousin** and a **buddy** (chapter 2). Although Cyprian had recognized his homosexual feelings from his youth (chapter 5), in the war he falls in love for the first time, with a fellow soldier who is killed by a sniper's bullet (chapter 8). After suffering through the war, Cyprian realizes upon his return that, as an Ojibwe, he is not even a U.S. citizen.

In chapter 2, while working in the Argus theater community, the thirty-two-year-old Cyprian gets to know Delphine Watzka. In the spring of 1934, they decide to create their own traveling show. Their "finale" act, which Cyprian invents, has him doing gymnastics on chairs balanced on Delphine's stomach. They wear ordinary clothes in their act rather than costumes, to make their stunts even more

Cyprian Lazarre

surprising (chapter 7). Their road trip is for money, but also potentially for love. In their entire time together, Cyprian manages to make love to Delphine only twice, yet they very quickly come to love each other. Their first successful sexual encounter occurs on their travels, in Manitoba. Two days later, however, Delphine sees Cyprian making love to a man and realizes that this is his true passion.

After three months on the road, they return to Argus that summer. When they arrive at the house of Delphine's drunken father, Roy, the stench of the place is overwhelming. Cyprian helps Delphine shovel out the rotten mess that covers everything, but the next day they discover the smell's primary source—three rotting bodies in Roy's cellar. Cyprian loyally sticks by Delphine through the stress. Also, unlike Delphine's first impression of him, in chapter 5 he proves himself "handy" in a variety of ways—making their tent into a comfortable home and handling car maintenance. He also decides that summer to run liquor out of Canada. Delphine finally asks Cyprian about the man in Manitoba. He is uncomfortable with the question but tries to answer.

In the grueling heat wave in chapter 5, Delphine's friend Eva Waldvogel finally reveals the pain she has suffered for months. When Delphine drives her to the Mayo Clinic for emergency cancer surgery, Cyprian takes care of the butcher shop for a week so that Fidelis can join them. We learn in chapter 6, however, that he refuses the job Fidelis subsequently offers him. But Cyprian does visit the butcher shop occasionally. He also joins Fidelis's singing club and is present at the Waldvogels' July 4 gathering in 1935. Soon after Eva's death later that summer, when Markus runs away to Delphine's house, Cyprian teaches him urination tricks that help the boy overcome his bed-wetting. During this time, Cyprian makes love to Delphine for a second time. Over the following months (chapter 8), they both wonder if she is pregnant. (She is not.)

As summer turns to autumn (chapter 8), Cyprian continues to make his illegal whiskey runs, and the now-sober Roy goes with him from time to time. The evening after Fidelis kills the wild dogs with a rifle, Delphine tells Cyprian about the incident. The story makes him realize that Fidelis was a sniper in the war, and he wonders whether he killed any of Cyprian's war friends. Although the men normally do not talk about the war, one night Cyprian and Fidelis note each other's scars.

Another year passes, and in the autumn of 1936 (chapter 9), when Cyprian comes to pick Delphine up from the shop one evening, a "disagreeable feeling" grows between him and Fidelis, which escalates into open hostility. Ostensibly this hostility is about the war and ethnic issues, but when Delphine asks later what they were "fighting" about, Cyprian replies, "You" (*MBSC,* 210–211). One rainy November evening when Cyprian comes for Delphine, an actual fight breaks out

Cyprian Lazarre

between the men. But four panicked boys interrupt them with the news that Markus Waldvogel is buried alive in the hill they have been excavating. At the hill, it becomes clear that Cyprian is the one best equipped to rescue Markus. Negotiating the precarious passageway is for him like balancing. He uses what he has learned from his performances to control his mind and body, moving beyond fear. He reaches Markus and carefully pulls him out.

In chapter 11, on Christmas Eve of that year, Cyprian tries to create the perfect Christmas for Delphine. He cooks, decorates, and buys her a ruby ring in a little box. But Delphine is physically and emotionally exhausted. As she continues to react to his efforts with indifference, Cyprian grows increasingly angry. Believing that she really just wants to be with Fidelis, he picks up the ring box and leaves. He gets drunk, then drives to Clarisse Strub's house, gives her the ring, and stays the night there. The next morning, Christmas Day, Clarisse is catching an early train out of town, and Cyprian goes with her. We learn in chapter 13 that on their way to Minneapolis, Clarisse tells Cyprian the reason she is leaving—she has murdered the harassing Sheriff Hock. Cyprian leaves Clarisse and ultimately joins up with another gymnastic performer, Vilhus Gast. Cyprian takes Gast, who is a Jew, home to Cyprian's Ojibwe reservation.

Though now absent, Cyprian continues to play a role in Delphine and Fidelis's developing relationship. Fidelis feels indebted to Cyprian for saving Markus, so he doesn't want to wrong this man by taking his woman. Finally, convinced that Cyprian is not coming back, in chapter 13 Fidelis marries Delphine. Shortly thereafter, Cyprian returns to Argus with Vilhus, and they give a mesmerizing performance in the school gym, which Delphine, Markus, and many Argus townspeople attend. After the show, Cyprian and Vilhus leave, never to return.

After the United States enters World War II, the men's singing club looks for a non-German repertoire. One of the songs they practice is a métis waltz tune they had learned from Cyprian.

Cyprian's lover. In chapter 2 of *The Master Butchers Singing Club,* while the pair are traveling together in Manitoba, Delphine sees Cyprian involved in a sex act with a man wearing a suit (he is identified in chapter 4 as a hardware store owner).

D

Damien Modeste, Father (the first). The priest who visits Agnes DeWitt in chapter 1 of *The Last Report on the Miracles at Little No Horse.* He is a small, middle-aged man who, having left his comfortable parish in Illinois, is in the spring of 1912 on his way to become a missionary on a North Dakota Ojibwe reservation. Father Damien tells Agnes about his new mission, and seeing his nervousness, she teases him. As the priest makes his way along the Red River north to the reservation, he is drowned in the devastating March flood. In chapter 2, Agnes, who is also swept away by the flood, finds his body hanging from a branch, buries him, takes his clothing, assumes his identity, and continues north to become the priest for the Ojibwe at Little No Horse. See **Damien Modeste, Father.**

Damien Modeste, Father. Catholic priest on the reservation Little No Horse. Chapter 4 of *The Last Report on the Miracles at Little No Horse* recounts the young priest's arrival at the reservation in March 1912 to replace Father Hugo LaCombe, who has died of consumption that winter. (Chapter 1 of *Tracks* places this arrival in the spring of 1913.) Transported from the small train stop by Kashpaw, Father Damien moves into his predecessor's abandoned cabin. At the church, he meets Sister Hildegarde Anne, the other *nearly starved nuns,* and the vulturelike girl Pauline Puyat. At mass, the Eucharist becomes meat and blood that nourishes the partakers.

Soon after, Damien visits the remote cabin of Nanapush and Fleur Pillager, who have barely survived the winter (*Tracks* chapter 1; *Last Report* chapter 5). He and Nanapush then visit the Kashpaw household (chapter 6 of *Last Report*). Damien realizes with regret the harm that his arrival may bring to this family. His premonition is fulfilled that autumn when the newly baptized Kashpaw and his remaining wife, Quill, are killed in an accident on a feast day (chapter 7). (Significantly, this section of *Last Report* is entitled "The Deadly Conversions," p. 57.) The following winter, their daughter, Mary, is abused by Napoleon Morrissey, and that spring Father Damien brings her to stay at the convent. Over time, she becomes Damien's devoted caregiver.

Chapter 10 of *Last Report* tells us about a phenomenon Father Damien does not understand. His fingers are always moving, tapping out intricate, languagelike patterns. (See also chapters 1 and 4.) The priest suffers a memory loss, so he wonders if the movement indicates that he had once used sign language. What the reader knows and Damien has forgotten is that he was once a talented pianist. In 1913 Father Damien begins sending out a mission newsletter to a list of subscribers assembled by Father Hugo. In response, people send gifts to the reservation church. One day a battered piano arrives. When Father Damien touches a key, he is seized with panic. He has a powerful but inexplicable emotional response to the instrument. When he locks the keyboard lid, he feels safer.

Father Damien quickly becomes friends with Nanapush and Fleur. When Fleur's daughter, Lulu, is born in the spring of 1914, Father Damien comes and

Damien Modeste, Father

baptizes her. (See *Tracks* chapter 3 and *Last Report* chapter 10. In *Last Report,* he also baptizes a bear.) When Damien asks the father's name for the baptismal record, Nanapush says, "Nanapush." Because of his love for the child, Damien also adds his own name as father.

In the winter of 1917–1918, Nanapush makes confession to Father Damien, telling him that he is living with Margaret Kashpaw sans vows and that he has stolen wire from Damien's piano to snare Clarence Morrissey (*Tracks* chapter 5). Nanapush tells Lulu later ("The Island" in *Love Medicine*) that sometime during this period he loses his spirit to Father Damien in a card game. This account conflicts with Damien's attitude in *Last Report,* in which he views conversion as destructive (see especially p. 239). In chapter 7 of *Four Souls,* Father Damien seems more interested in helping the people with practical matters (like building a better outhouse) than he is in converting them.

In the winter of 1918–1919, Father Damien and Mary Kashpaw minister to the people during the deadly influenza epidemic in which more than two hundred die (*Last Report* chapter 7). That same winter (*Tracks* chapter 7), Damien brings a white doctor to help the frostbitten Lulu—help that Nanapush refuses. Damien also brings rations to the Kashpaw-Pillager family to relieve the winter's famine, along with a list of fees that threaten their land with foreclosure. As the families work to raise fee money, Damien contributes from his own pocket. That winter, the priest finds a reservation child frozen to death, a victim of its parents' alcoholism. He urges Nanapush to take a leadership position in tribal government to protect his people.

In the spring of 1919, Father Damien hears Pauline Puyat's confession that she had given birth to a child, which she claims was stillborn (*Last Report* chapter 7). Soon after, Damien tries unsuccessfully to fetch Pauline from her leaky boat on Matchimanito Lake (*Tracks* chapter 8). When Pauline is found in the church that night, naked, raving, and covered with muck, Damien assumes that her injuries and subsequent refusal to eat are a penance for the sin she had confessed. When she falls into a lengthy, rigid trance, the reservation people dub her a saint, though Damien thinks otherwise (*Last Report* chapter 7).

In late summer of that year (1919), the body of Napoleon Morrissey is found on Fleur's land (chapters 9 of *Last Report* and *Tracks*). In *Tracks,* tribal policeman Edgar Pukwan Junior handles, or mishandles, the investigation. As payback for Pukwan's meddling, Nanapush loudly "confesses" to Father Damien that he had seen Pukwan masturbate. In *Last Report,* however, Father Damien handles the investigation because Pukwan is too drunk to do so (see chapter 14). Damien reconstructs the crime by matching the neck-wounds on the corpse with the configuration of a barbed-wire rosary found in the bushes nearby. When interfamily strife breaks out at Napoleon's funeral, Father Damien decides to hold two separate masses for the enemy clans (*Last Report* chapter 9).

About that time, Father Damien learns that Nanapush's and Fleur's land has been sold to the lumber company (*Last Report* chapter 10). Stricken, Damien begins writing letters to every authority he can, to little avail. After Fleur leaves the reservation, in chapter 1 of *Four Souls* Father Damien and Nanapush piece together rumors and hunches into a story of the house to which Fleur is going and what she intends to do.

The following autumn, 1920 (chapter 11 of *Last Report*), Father Damien has his first encounter with the black dog. Damien strikes a bargain with the creature, trading his own life and soul for those of Lulu Nanapush. The dog says he will send a temptation to Damien, and shortly after, the church sends a young priest, Father Gregory Wekkle, for Damien to train. Damien is immediately attracted to him, and over the winter and spring of 1920–1921, the two carry on an intense affair.

After Gregory leaves, Damien becomes depressed and cannot sleep. He takes narcotics from the school infirmary and falls into a month-long sleep. Mary Kashpaw follows him on his dream travels and guides him back. Sometime later, probably the next spring, Damien goes into the woods carrying strychnine, intending suicide. But Nanapush arranges a sweat lodge to heal his spirit.

Other events that occur in Damien's life during this time appear in chapters 11 and 16 of *Last Report*. In the spring of 1921, Bernadette Morrissey confesses to Father Damien that she knew about her brother Napoleon's abuse of Mary Kashpaw. This news temporarily convinces Damien that Mary killed Napoleon (chapter 11). That October, Damien also begins planning the new church that had been Father Hugo's dream. In November, he writes the bishop in Minneapolis asking for information about Fleur. The bishop tells him of Fleur's marriage to John James Mauser, and Damien begins writing to her (chapter 16).

By the following spring (May 1922), Father Damien has begun building the new church (*Last Report* chapter 12). We learn in chapter 13 of *Four Souls* that its ceiling is decorated with stars that reflect Father Damien's hopes. By June, the church's piano, still locked and unplayed, is moved into the new building. One afternoon Damien unlocks the lid, sits down, and to his surprise begins to play. His audience is the snakes that live under the stone floor. This incident brings back to Damien's memory two long-forgotten facts—the fact that he is an accomplished pianist and the existence of a store of money. With this money, he buys a new piano and vestments and commissions a sculpture of the Madonna of the Serpents from a Winnipeg wood-carver. (This account of both the statue and Damien's piano playing are different from those in *Tracks*. In chapter 4 of *Tracks,* the church in

Damien Modeste, Father

1917 already owns a fine statue of the Virgin, and in chapter 5, Damien is already an ardent pianist in 1917–1918.) Damien later preaches to the snakes about the mystery of God's love.

In the early 1930s (for timing, see *Four Souls* chapters 11, 13, and 14) Father Damien wakes in the night thinking a powwow must be going on in the convent. It is Nanapush, drinking, singing, and dancing in the convent wine cellar (chapter 11).

Over the years, Damien continues to write to Fleur in Minneapolis and keep up with news about her (*Last Report* chapter 16). Finally, in the spring of 1933, Fleur returns to Little No Horse with a strange white boy. After she regains and settles on her land, Damien goes out to visit her. That same spring, Pauline Puyat, now Sister Leopolda, returns from Argus and comes to Father Damien for confession. This time she confesses what Damien has already realized—that she murdered Napoleon Morrissey. She refuses to turn herself in to the tribal police and apparently blackmails Damien into silence.

From Damien's subsequent musings, we learn the degree to which he now blends his Catholicism with Anishinaabe faith. He has been "converted by the good Nanapush" and forgives his parishioners "in the spirit of the ridiculous and wise Nanabozho" (*LR*, 276). Reservation rumor has it in "The Beads" in *Love Medicine* that Father Damien makes his confession to Fleur.

About a year later, Father Damien hears another important confession, as Marie Kashpaw recounts her physical abuse at the hands of Sister Leopolda (*Last Report* chapter 8). ("Saint Marie" in *Love Medicine* dates the abuse in the summer of 1934.) In the summer of 1940, Father Damien's caregiver, Mary Kashpaw, leaves for a time when she marries Fleur's son Awun (*Last Report* chapter 17). The following summer (chapter 18), Damien helps Nector tell old Nanapush the story of Moby Dick. When Nanapush dies that winter (1942), Damien attends his erratic funeral. Mary Kashpaw is released from a mental institution in about 1950 and returns to care for her beloved Father Damien (chapter 17).

In 1962 (*Last Report* chapter 19), Father Gregory Wekkle, dying of cancer, returns to Little No Horse. Damien takes him in and cares for him. After Gregory dies in a Fargo hospital, Father Damien encounters Kashpaw's former wife Mashkiigikwe in a nearby park. Damien grieves over her alcohol-wasted condition, a destruction set in motion by his own conversion of the Kashpaw family.

During his long tenure at Little No Horse, Father Damien is a record keeper (*Bingo Palace* chapter 3; prologue of *Last Report*). In 1994, a report about Sister Leopolda in these records catches the attention of an academic, Eleanor Schlick Mauser ("Night Prayer" [6] in *Tales of Burning Love*). Damien also writes letters to the pope, from the second night of his arrival until just before his death, letters to which he receives no reply. (See especially pp. 69 and 344 of *Last Report.*) In the wee morning hours of March 20, 1996, Father Damien, now over a hundred, begins what he dubs his "last report" to the pope (prologue and chapter 2 of *Last Report*). Later that morning, he meets Father Jude Miller, who has come as a papal emissary to interview Damien about Sister Leopolda. This mission has been inspired in part by the work of Eleanor Schlick Mauser the previous year.

Jude and Damien's conversations are recorded in multiple chapters of *The Last Report on the Miracles at Little No Horse,* beginning in chapter 3. Over successive days in March, Father Damien reveals to Jude much that is negative about Pauline/Leopolda: her bitter family legacy, her abuse of her daughter, Marie (chapter 8), her part in the deaths of Kashpaw and Quill and subsequent madness of their daughter, Mary, and her self-obsessed spirituality (chapter 14).

Damien wakes one night in chapter 20 to a second visitation by the black dog. This time he bests the creature and it disappears. The next day, Damien tells Jude about the dog, and the following morning (chapter 21), he finally reveals to Jude Pauline's murder of Napoleon. As Jude mulls over what he has learned about Leopolda, he realizes that he has been comparing Leopolda and Damien, and he wonders, "Am I writing the wrong Saint's Passion?" (*LR,* 341).

That summer, in chapter 22 Damien decides to row out to Spirit Island in Matchimanito Lake for the imminent death he foresees. He encounters the grieving Mary, who perceives his plans, a final time before leaving. On the island, he is aware of the presence of Ojibwe spirits. As he is dying, a strong hand clasps his and pulls him across. Mary comes a few days later and buries him in the deepest part of the lake.

The following year, 1997, in the epilogue to *The Last Report on the Miracles at Little No Horse,* the pope finally replies to Father Damien by fax. Jude has now moved to the reservation to work on his new project, researching Damien's potential sainthood. Damien's cabin has become a shrine, cared for by Mary Kashpaw. See also **Agnes DeWitt.**

Davan Eyke. Ne'er-do-well young man whose family lives on Revival Road in Stokes, New Hampshire, in part 1.1 of *The Painted Drum*. From childhood Davan is prone to mishaps. As a boy Davan cuts off his finger with his father's chainsaw. As a reckless teenager he breaks lawnmowers. And as a young man he drives his father's new car off the road into a clump of birch trees. Shortly after this incident, he leaves home and begins to work for sculptor Kurt Krahe. But when Davan kills one of Krahe's ravens, Krahe shoots an arrow at him, and Davan moves back home. About this time, he acquires a red Toyota.

When Davan begins seeing Krahe's college-age daughter, Kendra, he and Krahe

Davan Eyke

get into a fight in which Krahe kicks him and orders him to stay away. But Davan and Kendra ignore Krahe's prohibition. One spring day a police officer recognizes the Toyota as stolen, and in the ensuing chase, the car runs down an old man (John Jewett Tatro) and goes off a bridge, killing both Davan and Kendra. In part 1.3 the Assembly of God church holds a rousing funeral for Davan. But his mother is bitter over his death, partly blaming Krahe.

Dead man in woods. Body discovered by the seven-year-old Lulu Nanapush in the little clearing where she plays in "The Good Tears" in *Love Medicine*. (According to the dating in *Tracks,* Lulu would be five when she finds this body.) See also **Napoleon Morrissey.**

Deanna Whiteheart Beads. Daughter of Rozina Roy and Richard Whiteheart Beads; twin sister of Cally Whiteheart Beads in *The Antelope Wife*. According to chapters 11 and 18, Deanna's spirit name is Other Side of the Earth.

Deanna and Cally are probably born in the mid-1970s. When Rozin discovers that she is pregnant, she and Richard are separating (chapter 7), but she is overjoyed about the pregnancy and chooses to stay. Deanna is born before her sister and continues to take the lead through their childhood. The twins spend their early childhood on their parents' reservation (chapter 16), but when they are five, the family moves to Minneapolis (chapter 3).

Rozin adores her daughters. When she realizes in chapter 3 that she is falling in love with Frank Shawano, she weeps, fearing the effect her unwanted passion may have on the girls. One June afternoon in chapter 6, Richard takes Deanna and Cally to the city park where they see a woman who looks like their mother walking with a "deer man." When the girls' grandmothers come down from the reservation to babysit, they allow Deanna and Cally to dance in the yard naked because they are "part deer."

It is March in chapter 7, but a late heavy snow is falling. Deanna and Cally, now eleven, find their parents fighting when they come home from school. Deanna knows that something is badly wrong, but, typically maternal, she does not tell Cally so as not to upset her. When Deanna wakes in the night and sees her father leave the house, she sneaks out and climbs behind the backseat of the truck, whose engine is running. Richard had intended to commit suicide, but he accidentally locks himself out of the truck and changes his mind. As we learn in chapter 9, Richard finds Deanna in the truck the next morning, dead. Rozin buries Deanna on the reservation under a traditional grave house, where she regularly leaves offerings (chapter 17).

Deanna's death is a recurrent thread stitching together much of the remaining action of the novel. Blaming both Richard (chapter 16) and her own love for Frank (chapter 11) for the tragedy, in chapter 9 Rozin moves back to the reservation with Cally to live with her "mothers." Her grief over Deanna causes her to neglect Cally, who is allowed to run wild and becomes gravely ill.

Deanna's death has an even more devastating effect on Richard, who cannot face his guilt and becomes a drunken bum (chapters 10, 11, and 15). Richard's emotional emptiness ultimately causes him to commit suicide (chapter 16). Cally, too, misses her sister deeply, as we see in chapters 11 and 18.

After Richard's death, Deanna's spirit comes back briefly in chapter 17 to ask her mother if she is coming, too. Longing to hear her daughter's voice, Rozin begs her to stay and prepares a meal for her. When death beckons Rozin in her dreams, she decides to accept the invitation to join her daughter, until Frank intervenes and reconnects her with the living.

Death. When Kashpaw dies in 1912 predicting the death of two hundred Anishinaabeg from sickness, a figure representing death appears in the east—a gaunt, precipitous walker with a dog at his side (chapter 7 of *The Last Report on the Miracles at Little No Horse*). On the black dog's first visit to Father Damien in the fall of 1920 (chapter 11), Damien remembers this figure, which the dog calls its "master." See also **Black dog.**

Delphine Watzka Waldvogel. Companion of Cyprian Lazarre before becoming the second wife of Fidelis Waldvogel in *The Master Butchers Singing Club*. Delphine is introduced in chapter 2 as a "stocky Polish girl." She is "compelling" and "magnetic" (*MBSC,* 17), both in her personality and physically, with light golden brown eyes, a dimple, and small white teeth.

Delphine is born one October (chapter 16), probably in 1907 (see her age in chapter 14). She never knows her mother. When she is a toddler, one day, as Step-and-a-Half walks by, Delphine follows her and mistakenly calls her "Mama" (chapter 16). Delphine is reared by the town drunk, Roy Watzka, who tells her that her mother, Minnie, died when Delphine was a baby (chapter 2). Chapter 4 reveals that Roy never tells Delphine about her mother's life or how she died. All she has to connect her with a mother are Roy's blurred photos and a few objects in a cigar box. Her mother is the first of several women in Delphine's life who simply disappear through a "woman-shaped hole" (*MBSC,* 267; chapter 11). This loss and Roy's drunkenness are also the first of a series of events that establish a pattern in her perception—a sense of powerlessness to help others when awful things happen to them. Another such event is her best friend Clarisse Strub's affliction with syphilis when the girls are teens.

Delphine's devotion to performance begins in grade school (chapter 5). In high school, she and Clarisse are involved in local dramatic productions and dream of

Delphine Watzka Waldvogel

leaving Argus to become involved with real theaters in the city. Delphine is a clever student (chapter 4), demonstrated by her winning a state spelling contest as a teen. But she drops out of school early and goes to work. She tries to get some control over her life by driving Roy and his drinking buddies out of the house with an ax, but when Roy falls through thin ice and develops pneumonia, she must quit her job to nurse him.

In chapter 2, working in the Argus theater community, Delphine gets to know the Ojibwe gymnast and performer Cyprian Lazarre. In the spring of 1934, they decide to form a traveling act, for money and perhaps for love. They do make money, especially with the stunt in which Cyprian balances on Delphine's stomach, but they are less successful with their lovemaking. Even so, they soon establish a loving, if largely platonic, relationship. In Manitoba, they finally do make love, but two days later Delphine sees Cyprian making love to a man and recognizes that this is his true passion.

That summer (chapter 4), Delphine decides to go home. When they arrive at Roy's house, Delphine is overwhelmed by its stench, and Cyprian helps her shovel out the garbage and excrement. When they return the next day, the smell seems even stronger, and they discover its primary source: three rotting bodies in the cellar—the missing Chavers family, who had disappeared earlier that year. Sheriff Albert Hock comes to investigate.

At the butcher shop in chapter 5, Delphine meets Eva Waldvogel, who invites Delphine into her beautiful kitchen. Delphine confides in this new friend about the bodies she has found. Back at the house, morticians Clarisse Strub and her family come for the bodies. That night, Delphine finally asks Cyprian about his encounter with the man in Manitoba. The next day, Delphine returns to the butcher shop, where Eva gives her a job. Over the following days, Delphine meets the Waldvogels' regular customers and becomes acquainted with their sons, Franz, Markus, and twins Emil and Erich. Clarisse comes in one day complaining about would-be lover Sheriff Hock's behavior, and Delphine jokes that they should "murther'm" (*MBSC*, 92).

That summer, Cyprian begins making illegal liquor runs to Canada. When Markus overhears Delphine's conversation with Sheriff Hock about the Chaverses' deaths, he tells Delphine the Chavers child was named Ruthie. The next morning, Eva finally admits to Delphine that she is ill and needs the doctor. Dr. Heech discovers that Eva has advanced uterine cancer and directs Delphine to take her to the Mayo Clinic for emergency surgery.

Chapter 6 records events one year later, in the summer of 1935, as Delphine cares for the terminally ill Eva. One June afternoon, the women sit in Eva's lush, chaotic garden and muse together about death. Franz arranges for Pouty Mannheim to take Eva up flying. Afterward, Delphine gathers the boys to hear their mother talk about the experience.

By July, Eva's days have become nightmarish. On July 4, Delphine discovers that the morphine she has prepared for Eva is missing. She guesses (rightly) that Tante has stolen it and goes to Tante's house, but Tante has poured it down the drain. Because of the holiday, Delphine cannot find Dr. Heech or the druggist, so Eva spends hours in agony and is attempting suicide when, driving home in despair, Delphine comes across Roy, who has stolen morphine from the drugstore.

Delphine is the only one with Eva the night she dies (chapter 7). Delphine continues to help the family for a time and then leaves. Roy is sober, Cyprian is handy, and for a short time Delphine is at peace in her own home. Then Markus runs away to Delphine's house. Fidelis asks Delphine to return to help them, but she will do that only if Tante leaves. Delphine teaches Emil and Erich how to care for the chinchillas their mother had bought for them.

In chapter 7, Delphine and Cyprian make love a second time and subsequently wonder (chapter 8) if Delphine is pregnant. (She is not.) After Sheriff Hock asks Delphine about the red beads found on the door of the cellar where the Chaverses died, she goes to the mortuary to warn Clarisse (who had worn her beaded dress the night the Chaverses were trapped) and then buries the dress in Clarisse's flowerbed. Fidelis sends Tante away, and Delphine returns to the butcher shop.

Back at work that autumn (1935), Delphine's life again falls into a comfortable routine (chapter 8). One Friday night, however, a pack of wild dogs breaks in and kills the boys' chinchillas. Angry, Fidelis lures the dogs and shoots them with a rifle. The incident makes Cyprian realize that Fidelis was a German sniper in the war. The two men don't usually talk about the war, but one night they note each others' scars. Tante, upset at being dismissed by her brother, spreads rumors about Delphine.

Also that fall, Sheriff Hock arrests Roy for stealing the morphine. As Hock intends, Delphine at first thinks the arrest is connected with the death of the Chavers family. At the butcher shop, tension builds between Delphine and Fidelis, both of whom fear the sexual attraction they hide behind their strict formality. It is especially difficult for Delphine to thank Fidelis for paying Roy's bail.

Chapter 9 opens a year after Eva's death—the summer of 1936. One Saturday that year, Franz brings his sweetheart, Mazarine Shimek, to the butcher shop and introduces her to Delphine. Delphine knows the bad reputation of Mazarine's dirt-poor family, but decides that the girl herself is responsible and serious. Delphine sees a parallel between her potential relationship with Mazarine and her friendship with Eva. One morning in the butcher shop, Step-and-a-Half vaguely warns Delphine that the Waldvogel boys are "digging their own graves" (*MBSC,* 208).

Delphine Watzka Waldvogel

As chapter 9 continues, one evening that fall (1936) when Cyprian comes to pick up Delphine, a sudden tension develops between him and Fidelis. Delphine defuses the crisis and later asks Cyprian what they were fighting about, to which he replies, "You." One cold November night after three days of rain, the two men begin to fight in earnest but are interrupted by four panicked boys bringing urgent news that Markus is buried in a collapsed hill. Delphine fetches lanterns and a potential rescue party, but ultimately she must simply wait with Fidelis outside the hill while the more agile Cyprian rescues the boy.

In chapter 10, Delphine nurses Markus through his subsequent illness. When the healing woman (the **Braucher**) comes, Markus acts offended, gets out of bed, and goes to school. Franz later tells Delphine that Markus thought the woman was measuring him for a coffin. On Christmas Eve (chapter 11), Cyprian tries to create a perfect Christmas, but when Delphine—physically and emotionally exhausted— responds indifferently, he leaves in anger. The next morning, Christmas Day, Delphine walks to Clarisse's house with a present for her friend. When she goes inside, she sees the now-empty ring box Cyprian had tried to give her the night before and, outside, their car. A day or so later, Roy tells her that Sheriff Hock has been murdered and that Clarisse is gone. Delphine's reaction is not horror but loneliness. Yet another woman close to her has disappeared from her life.

Chapter 12 is set in some February between that December and the beginning of World War II. Fidelis and Delphine drive Tante and the three youngest boys to Chicago, in preparation for their trip to Germany. While Fidelis and Tante handle travel arrangements, Delphine takes the boys to the circus. She visits the Delver of Minds, who has an uncanny knowledge of Delphine's situation. In a rare moment alone with Fidelis, Delphine tries to convince him not to send the boys away. On departure morning, Markus falls seriously ill and cannot go with the others. On the way back to Argus, Fidelis and Delphine try unsuccessfully to settle issues about their own future.

In chapter 13, Delphine learns that Roy has started drinking again. As she is job-hunting one day in March, she chases down the naked, drunken Roy and calls in Doctor Heech. Delphine gets a job at the courthouse and falls into a boring but peaceful routine. This quiet existence is interrupted by a visit one night from Fidelis, who essentially proposes to her. Delphine begins working afternoons at the Waldvogels', where the tension and uncertainty between her and Fidelis remain intense for months. They finally set a wedding date and announce their plans to Franz and Markus. When they marry, probably that autumn, Franz leaves to join the air corps. Cyprian comes to Argus with his new performance partner, Vilhus Gast. They do one show in Argus (which Delphine and Markus attend) and then leave.

As Roy nears death, Delphine insists that he tell her about her mother. He tells only the story of Minnie's experiences as an Ojibwe child at Wounded Knee. But he also reveals, to Delphine's horror, that he had knowingly locked Porky Chavers in the cellar. After Roy's death, Delphine tries to tell Fidelis that her father was a murderer.

After the United States enters the war (chapter 14), Delphine grieves when Markus decides to enlist in the army. Their relationship is now so close that he calls her "Mom." Delphine is thirty-five when Markus leaves for boot camp. In her restlessness, she takes walks at bedtime, often visiting the cemetery. In the spring of 1944, Franz returns home on leave, and Delphine realizes that he and Mazarine have become lovers. Delphine is relieved when Markus writes that he failed his vision test and will be working a desk job. When he comes home, Markus tells Fidelis and Delphine that one of the twins is in a POW camp in northeastern Minnesota. Delphine will not go with the men to visit him, fearing the bitter changes their meeting will reveal. When Delphine realizes that Mazarine is pregnant, she buys her a wedding ring to deflect the town gossip. In August of the following year, 1945, Delphine reads the newspaper account of the atom bomb and feels that the boys "will be safe now" (*MBSC*, 370). But only Markus returns safely. Emil is dead, Erich returns to Germany, and Franz is injured in a freak accident. Delphine accompanies Mazarine on her first visit to the hospital.

In 1954 (chapter 15), Delphine and Fidelis visit his hometown of Ludwigsruhe to see his family and attend a memorial service. The experience is bewildering for Delphine, who hallucinates while the butchers sing. Delphine hears a knocking one day that she realizes is Eva calling for Fidelis. On their return trip, Fidelis collapses and dies on the floor of the New York customs area.

Chapter 16 reveals the musings of Step-and-a-Half, now an old woman, in the mid-1950s. Through her memories, readers gain new information about Delphine's parentage and birth. "Minnie," we learn, is largely fictional, Roy's nickname for Step-and-a-Half herself, who is not Delphine's mother. Delphine's natural parents are Mr. and Mrs. Shimek, Mazarine's good-for-nothing mother and father. Forty-some years before the chapter's present, Step-and-a-Half had rescued the newborn Delphine from the outhouse and left her with Roy Watzka to rear. Now in her late forties, Delphine runs a plant shop with Mazarine, who, unbeknown to either of them, is her sister, the one woman in her life who does not leave.

Delver of Minds, the. Sideshow attraction whom Delphine Watzka visits while she is in Chicago with the Waldvogels in chapter 12 of *The Master Butchers Singing Club*. The Delver has a young face, white hair, and powerful hands. Without asking

Delver of Minds, the

any questions, she has an uncanny knowledge of Delphine's life: the reason she is in Chicago, that she is in love with a widower, that an "ant" (aunt) is planning to remove the boys, and so on. The Delver gives Delphine advice about the boys and the man.

Demeter Hewes Gheen. High-society mother of Placide and Polly Elizabeth Gheen in *Four Souls*. We learn in chapter 2 that Mrs. Gheen is obsessed with the minutest details of propriety. She thus takes pride in the carefully executed details of Placide's house. But Placide's husband, John James Mauser, mocks Demeter's opinions as "one long swoon of platitudes" (*FS*, 17).

Mrs. Gheen poses for at least one of Placide's character portraits. She also has a talent for organizing social outings (chapter 4). Although Mrs. Gheen is usually in control of situations, in chapter 2 Polly Elizabeth feels that she failed properly to monitor Mauser's illness. By the novel's present time, Mrs. Gheen is deceased.

Destroismaisons family. Devout Catholic family in chapter 7 of *The Last Report on the Miracles at Little No Horse*. The Destroismaisons are respected, have a neat, well-furnished house, and are proud of their **handsome boy** and **intelligent girl**. At the Feast of the Virgin in 1912, before the procession begins, Father Damien sits drinking tea with **Alexandrine** and **Michael** at their cooking fire. In the procession, Michael carries the canopy for the host. During the influenza epidemic in 1918, the family falls gravely ill. When Father Damien and Mary Kashpaw come to help, they watch as the girl dies, then her brother, and then their mother. When Michael seeks to drown himself, Mary stops him. But he merely stares at death for two weeks and goes to sleep forever.

Devil. Sightings of the devil by reservation residents are recorded in chapter 16 of *The Last Report on the Miracles at Little No Horse*. He possesses the body of a cow that gives black milk and mumbles a curse. A man in elegant dress saunters through the woods seducing women on their way to church. See also **Satan** and **Black dog.**

Diablo. Pomeranian dog of Polly Elizabeth Gheen in *Four Souls*. In her loneliness and longing for a child in chapter 4, Polly Elizabeth buys the dog in order to have a companion who needs her. But after a short time, he becomes just one more tyrant in her life. In chapter 6, she thinks of how the dog is now indifferent to her, caring only for food. She refers to his contempt again in chapter 10. As times get hard, however, by the 1930s (chapter 12), the dog seems to realize that his survival requires affection, so he lies at her feet and wags his tail.

Doctors. In *The Beet Queen*, **Fritzie Kozka's doctor** tells her in chapter 4 that her lungs need dry warmth and that she should not be exposed to even one more Dakota winter. A **married doctor** in chapter 5 strings Sita Kozka along for three years until she realizes he will never leave his wife. The *doctor who assists Karl Adare* in chapter 6, after Karl injures his back, orders a plank to keep his spine straight. In chapter 14, *Wallace Pfef's doctor* tells him he is suffering from nervous exhaustion and recommends a muscle relaxant and a vacation.

In *Tracks* chapter 4, **Dutch James's doctor** cares for him after Dutch nearly freezes to death, amputating piece after piece of Dutch's rotting body. The *white doctor* who comes to examine Lulu Nanapush's frostbitten feet in chapter 7 leaves in anger when Nanapush refuses to let him amputate.

In *Tales of Burning Love,* Jack Mauser summons a *doctor* in "The Red Slip" [21] when he fears that Eleanor Schlick is having a miscarriage. (She is not pregnant.) Some years later, *doctors* periodically check on Eleanor in the hospital after she collapses of exhaustion and starvation in "Night Prayer" [6]. *Doctor Boiseart* attends Marlis Mauser during her pregnancy and the birth of her son in "The Waiting Room" [31]. He and Candice Pantamounty have a violent disagreement about how to treat Marlis during delivery. An *emergency room crew* treats Marlis, Candice, and Dot Mauser when they are brought in by a snowmobile rescue squad in "The Disappearance" [36]. A *hospital doctor* reassures Celestine James in "February Thaw" [40] when Dot seems to be sleeping too much after the blizzard ordeal. A *Filipino doctor* examines Jack at the Argus hospital after a stone statue nearly crushes him in "The Stone Virgin" [44].

When Cally Roy becomes gravely ill in chapter 9 of *The Antelope Wife,* the *doctor at the IHS* (Indian Health Service) orders an I.V. for her.

In *Four Souls* chapter 2, a **number of doctors** try to solve the riddle of John James Mauser's postwar illness, without success, though one of them prescribes opium to control his seizures. We learn in chapter 4 that the *doctor prior to Dr. Fulmer* treats Mauser for gonorrhea. Another **unnamed doctor** sees Fleur in chapter 6, when she threatens miscarriage, but he dismissively remarks that he does not treat servants and Indians. In chapter 8, Mauser takes their son to *several doctors,* who at first say that the child is normal, even advanced. But they later pronounce him a hopeless idiot.

In part 3.7 of *The Painted Drum,* an **IHS doctor** at the hospital checks Ira's ill toddler Apitchi and orders a chest X-ray. When Apitchi's fever brings on a seizure, *two doctors* come to the room to stabilize him. One of these doctors, a woman, speaks to Ira.

See also **Fulmer, Dr.; Heech, Doctor (old); Heech, Doctor (young); Nurses; Orderlies;** and **Psychiatrists and therapists.**

Dog people. See **Almost Soup, Black dog, Diablo, Hottentot, Original Dog, Pepperboy, Schatzie, Shesheeb's dog, Sorrow, Sorrow's mother,** and **Windigo Dog.**

Doosh

Doosh. Blood sister to Ziigwan'aage in part 2.3 of *The Painted Drum*. Doosh, who is somewhat slow and vacant, is the only one in Ziigwan'aage's family who treats Anaquot with any sympathy, so Anaquot buys small gifts for her when they go to town. Doosh urges Ziigwan'aage to send Niibin'aage to the Carlisle Indian School.

Doris and Raymond Shaawano. Twin siblings of Bernard Shaawano, four years younger, in *The Painted Drum*. In part 2.2, when the twins are six, *their mother* dies and their father begins to drink heavily and beat them. Under Bernard's guidance, the children learn to evade and exploit their drunken father. When they are nine and Bernard thirteen, the twins are both frightened and hopeful when Bernard stands his ground and fights their father. After that fight, their father lives his last years in sobriety and relative happiness.

The twins marry a brother and sister and live in the Cities. They and Bernard remain close, and when they are together, they compare memories of the hard times they shared as children.

Dot Adare Nanapush Mauser. Daughter of Celestine James and Karl Adare; wife of Gerry Nanapush and mother of Shawn Nanapush; fifth wife of Jack Mauser.

Dot is the product of a brief affair between Celestine and Karl that ends the day Celestine realizes that she is pregnant (chapter 7 of *The Beet Queen*). Stranded in a snowstorm on the night of January 18, 1954, in chapter 9 Celestine gives birth at Wallace Pfef's house, assisted by Wallace. Celestine names the baby girl Wallacette Darlene in his honor, but the baby's Aunt Mary nicknames her Dot. Celestine marries Karl in Rapid City but returns to Argus without him (chapter 15).

Throughout Dot's childhood, Celestine and Mary compete for her affections (chapter 10), Celestine the disciplinarian and Mary indulgent. After being disciplined in her first-grade class, Dot lies to Mary about the "naughty box," causing Mary to make a fool of herself with the teacher. Karl sends Dot an electric wheelchair the following summer, which Celestine insists she give to her paralyzed uncle, Russell Kashpaw. Dot misbehaves on that outing and Fleur Pillager disciplines her.

Dot runs away once to Wallace's house (chapter 12). When Dot is ten (1964), in chapter 11 Mary moves in with them temporarily, a circumstance that further undermines Celestine's authority. That winter, Dot gets the part of Joseph in the school's Christmas play. Chapters 11 and 12 record the incidents on the ill-fated night of the play: Dot humiliates herself at the performance, and later Wallace turns her away from his door. Dot will not speak to Wallace for weeks. In January, however (chapter 12), he gives a party for Dot's eleventh birthday. Although the adults view the party as a disaster, Dot loves it and forgives him.

Dot Adare Nanapush Mauser

Dot is a rebellious fourteen-year-old when she meets her father for the first time (chapter 12). When she is eighteen, in chapter 14 Wallace plans a Beet Festival so that Dot can be honored as Beet Queen. Chapters 13–16 relate the preparations for the festival, which takes place in July 1972. Dot is initially excited about her expected coronation but is mortified when she learns that Wallace has rigged the vote for her to win and that everyone knows. In revenge, she dunks Wallace in the dunking booth (chapters 14 and 16). With her family watching, in chapters 15 and 16 Dot climbs aboard a skywriting plane as it takes off. When she returns an hour later, her mother is still waiting for her on the grandstand. Dot realizes Celestine's love for her and, by the day's end, feels close to her.

We learn in "A Wedge of Shade" [3] in *Tales of Burning Love* that Dot has just enrolled at the University of Minnesota when she goes to hear the prisoner/escapee Gerry Nanapush speak publicly. Their relationship begins one night after one of his speeches. According to "Scales" in *Love Medicine,* Gerry impregnates Dot during a prison visit in the winter of 1979–1980. During her pregnancy, Dot works with Albertine Johnson at a construction site weigh station, while Gerry is in and out of prison. He is home when their daughter, Shawn, is born in October but leaves immediately afterward to escape the police. Gerry is recaptured and returned to prison, so Dot must rear Shawn alone. "Crossing the Water" in *Love Medicine* indicates that in 1984 Dot and Shawn are in Canada and that Gerry, newly escaped, is on his way to see them.

In *Tales of Burning Love,* in May 1994 Dot goes to work as a bookkeeper for Mauser and Mauser construction company in Fargo ("Caryl Moon" [8]). After becoming romantically involved with one of Jack Mauser's employees, Caryl Moon, she alters records in Moon's favor, and Jack fires her. Furious, Dot plays chicken with Moon, who is driving a Mauser gravel truck. In the incident the truck is disabled and Jack's red Cadillac is demolished, but Jack and Dot leave the accident scene together.

We learn in "Hot June Morning" [2] that Dot and Jack marry after knowing each other only a month. After their first weekend, they go to Argus to see her mother. In "A Wedge of Shade" [3], Dot tells Celestine that she intends neither to divorce Gerry nor to tell him about the new husband. (This statement is at variance with the reference to Gerry and Dot's divorce in chapter 21 of *The Bingo Palace.*) When Jack arrives at Celestine's house, he is immediately arrested for financial misconduct. Dot and Celestine go tell Aunt Mary about Jack, and when they return, Jack is there, out on bail.

Six weeks later, in August, Dot answers a phone call for Jack from Eleanor Mauser, an ex-wife Dot knows nothing about, who wants a ride from the Argus hospital ("Night Prayer" [6]). In "The Meadowlark" [7] Dot and Jack pick Eleanor

Dot Adare Nanapush Mauser

up from the hospital, and on their return to Fargo Dot learns that Jack has had four previous wives and a child. Wounded by Jack's revelations on this trip, Dot and Eleanor develop a camaraderie. The following evening, in "Caryl Moon" [8], Dot tells Eleanor how her relationship with Jack began. Dot begins paperwork to end both of her marriages, although she is still living with Jack a month later.

Before the year's end, Dot leaves Jack four times, the final time on New Year's Eve ("Jack's House" [9]). She and Shawn are living in an apartment, whose location she will not reveal to Jack. She warns him that something bad will happen, a prophecy that seems fulfilled when his house burns down ("The Garage" [15]). In "Memoria" [10] and "Satin Heart" [12], Dot attends Jack's supposed funeral, where she watches his history unfold as his former wives interact. After the funeral, Dot is at the West Fargo steakhouse-bar-casino with the other wives in "The B & B" [16] when a massive Indian "woman" enters, whom Dot recognizes as Gerry. Dot buys "her" a pizza and "she" follows Dot out of the room.

In "The Hitchhiker" [18], all the wives—Dot, Eleanor, Candice Pantamounty, and Marlis Cook—get into Jack's red Explorer, and Dot drives toward Fargo as a blizzard strikes. As they leave West Fargo, they pick up a snow-covered hitchhiker, whom Dot knows to be Gerry and who goes to sleep in the space behind the backseat. On the way to Fargo, the Explorer becomes stuck in a snowdrift. In "Secrets and Sugar Babies" [19], Dot sets the rules for the women's storytelling that night. Through the chapters in part 3 of *Tales of Burning Love*, Dot listens as Eleanor, Candice, and Marlis tell their stories, but Dot herself does not tell a tale. She instead lives out her tale of burning love, for in "The Tale of the Unknown Passenger" [34] she makes love with the hitchhiking Gerry while the other women sleep.

Eventually, a snowmobile rescue squad picks up the occupants of the car in "The Disappearance" [36] and "Two Front-Page Articles" [37]. By the time they arrive at the hospital, Gerry has disappeared. In "February Thaw" [40], Dot discards the divorce papers she had begun for her marriage to Gerry, and when Jack telephones, she tells him that he should go back to Eleanor. Later, taking a walk, Dot is overcome with longing for Gerry, lies on the ground, and weeps. As she walks back to the butcher shop, she considers going into business with her aunt and mother.

Dot Adare's classmates. Children at Saint Catherine's school in Argus. The children in Dot's *first-grade class* are intimidated by her aggressiveness in chapter 10 of *The Beet Queen*. Dot knocks out the tooth of one *first-grade girl,* and the *girl's mother* phones Dot's mother, Celestine James.

Dot's relationship with her classmates has not changed much by the time she is in fourth grade (chapter 11). Dot has a crush on the ***boy who plays the front end of the donkey*** in the Christmas play. When he does not cooperate with her during the performance, she smacks him with her mallet. A ***fat blond hysterical woman,*** apparently the boy's mother, runs from the audience to rescue him. The incident is referred to again in chapter 12. The ***three boys and one girl*** who are invited to Dot's eleventh-birthday party in chapter 12 are said to be Dot's only friends.

Dove, the. Nanapush's wife with finicky tastes, apparently the first of his three wives. Also referred to by her Indian name, Omiimii, she is mentioned in chapters 3 and 9 of *Tracks*. One morning years later, in chapter 13 of *Four Souls,* Nanapush dreams about his family, including Omiimii.

Dutch James. Second husband of Regina Puyat Kashpaw James and father of Celestine James. Chapter 3 of *Tracks* refers to him as a Dutchman. In chapter 2, he lives in Argus and works at Pete Kozka's butcher shop. On a delivery to the reservation, he meets Regina, whose Kashpaw husband has moved to Montana. Dutch apparently takes Regina and her son Russell back to Argus to live with him. In the spring of 1912, Regina's niece Pauline Puyat also comes to stay with them and work in the butcher shop. When Fleur Pillager comes to work at the butcher shop in June 1913, she, Dutch, and two of his coworkers play poker in the evenings. Resenting Fleur's persistent winning, one August night Dutch and his coworkers attack her. When a tornado strikes the next day—presumably Fleur's revenge—all three men take shelter in the butcher shop's meat locker, and Pauline locks them in. They are not found for several days. Dutch is the only one who survives, but in chapter 4, he loses parts of his arms and legs to gangrene. As Regina cares for him, they begin to love each another. By winter, Dutch has somewhat recovered, and he and Regina marry. Chapters 4, 6, and 8 indicate that Pauline is haunted by what she has done to Dutch.

According to chapter 2 of *The Beet Queen,* Dutch and Regina's daughter, Celestine, is born a month after the wedding. *The Beet Queen* also relates two other details at variance with the *Tracks* account—that after the wedding, Regina brings down from the reservation "three other children" whom Dutch knew nothing about (Russell among them) and that Dutch dies by freezing solid in the Kozkas' meat locker.

In chapter 6 of *Tracks,* Dutch, now dead and still missing pieces of his limbs, is one of the men who gambles with Fleur in Pauline's death vision.

Dympna Evangelica, Sister. Nun for several decades at the Sacred Heart Convent at Little No Horse. Dympna tells Father Damien that when Pauline Puyat is in her trance in the spring of 1919, the nuns hear arguing voices and

Dympna Evangelica, Sister

demonic growls behind her closed door (chapter 21 of *The Last Report on the Miracles at Little No Horse*). The following year, after the nuns drink soup touched by the black dog in chapter 11, they have voluptuous nightmares. Sister Dympna is one of those who urgently confess to Father Damien.

In "Saint Marie" in *Love Medicine,* Dympna witnesses the supposedly miraculous stigmata in Marie Lazarre's hand in 1934. In 1940, it is Dympna who calls for Awun to haul wood to the convent in *Last Report* chapter 17, a visit that leads to Mary Kashpaw's disastrous marriage to him. When Marie returns to the convent with her daughter Zelda in 1957 ("Flesh and Blood" in *Love Medicine*), Sister Dympna is the doorkeeper but does not recognize Marie.

In his 1996 interview with Father Damien (chapter 8 of *Last Report*), Father Jude refers to Sister Dympna's witnessing the stigmata that Leopolda bestowed on her young novice back in 1934. Knowing the truth of Marie's story, Damien scoffs at the idea of Dympna as a reliable witness. See also **Nuns at Sacred Heart Convent at Little No Horse.**

E

Edgar Pukwan. Tribal police officer who reluctantly helps Nanapush rescue Fleur Pillager in the spring of 1913 (chapter 1 of *Tracks;* the date would be 1912 in *The Last Report on the Miracles at Little No Horse*). Afraid of the consumption that has killed Fleur's parents, Pukwan will not touch her and tries to burn the Pillager house. He soon dies—possibly from consumption, although in chapter 8 his son, Edgar Pukwan Junior, blames a Pillager curse.

Edgar Pukwan Junior. Tribal police officer; son of Edgar Pukwan. Edgar is required by regulation to bury the dead, so after the spring thaw in 1913 he helps Nanapush bury the bodies of the five Pillagers who have died the previous winter (chapter 1 of *Tracks*). In the winter of 1917–1918 (chapter 5), Pukwan is off in the war (World War I). When he returns in chapter 7, he brings the influenza virus with him. Chapters 7, 8, and 9 indicate Pukwan's hatred of the Pillagers. Like the Lazarres and Morrisseys, he profits from his alliance with the government and apparently plays a part in foreclosing on Pillager land.

When Napoleon Morrissey's body is found in the late summer of 1919, *Tracks* chapter 9 indicates that Edgar Pukwan Junior conducts the so-called investigation—spying on the Kashpaws and Pillagers and listening beside the confessional. Nanapush gets revenge by publicly "confessing" Pukwan's masturbation and by defeating him in an election for tribal chairman. In the *Last Report* account, however, in chapter 14 Pukwan is drunk when Napoleon's body is found, so Father Damien conducts the investigation. See also **Pukwan family.**

Eleanor Schlick Mauser. Second wife of Jack Mauser in *Tales of Burning Love*. We learn in "Night Prayer" [6] and "The Meadowlark" [7] that Eleanor's appearance is dramatic, with black hair, strong eyebrows, large green eyes, and full lips. She has her mother's poise and energy.

The only child of Lawrence and Anna Schlick, Eleanor at first has a peacefully happy childhood ("White Musk" [4]). In "Eleanor's Tale" [20], her one-time trapeze-artist mother, Anna, rescues the six-year-old Eleanor from their burning house. A year or two later, one cold November night Eleanor and her mother save the life of young firefighter Jack Mauser after he has become encased in ice. When her father returns home and finds them asleep beside Jack, he abandons them in his jealousy, and they are reduced to poverty.

In "The Red Slip" [21], Eleanor, now a teenager, encounters Jack in a department store and takes revenge by grinding his hand into broken glass. She then decides to seduce him, but her efforts have the unexpected consequence of her falling in love with this former enemy.

Eleanor and Jack begin an on-and-off relationship. During this time, Jack goes to work in the oil fields of western North Dakota for a year (apparently 1980–1981). That fall, the now college-aged Eleanor falsely announces that she is pregnant by Jack, which precipitates her parents' reunion. She tries to end her relationship with Jack, but instead they go to Florida and marry. The marriage is a series of fights until Eleanor goes to London for a year as an exchange student. Some years after their divorce, in "Hot June Morning" [2] Jack recalls Eleanor as a professional Catholic and an intellectual—dysfunctional, dramatic, and unpredictable. Yet, as we learn in "Trust in the Known" [5], they continue to see each other and according to "Night Prayer" [6] even make love a few times.

Eleanor acquires two M.A. degrees and an arrest record ("Night Prayer"). In the fall of 1993 she is a college professor in Minneapolis, teaching a seminar on the "New Celibacy" ("White Musk" [4]). That October, Eleanor seduces one of her male undergraduate students, whose name she cannot remember ("Kim, Tim, Vim, or something like that" [*TBL,* 31]). When he brings sexual harassment charges against her, she loses her job and decides to visit the subject of her latest research project, Sister Leopolda, at a convent in Argus. (We learn in chapter 3 of *The Last Report on the Miracles at Little No Horse* that Eleanor, not named in this novel, writes a good deal about Leopolda from an academic perspective.)

In 1994, Eleanor is in her early thirties. She stays at the Argus convent for some time, where she helps care for Leopolda and finds the quiet life restorative ("Night

Eleanor Schlick Mauser

Prayer" [6]). One day, she receives a memo from Jack asking her to meet him in the garden at midnight, with no day specified. Two days later, on a hot June night, Eleanor sees Jack lowering himself over the convent wall. When Sister Leopolda enters the garden, Eleanor disguises Jack as a statue of the Virgin. As a storm gathers, Leopolda and Eleanor talk until the old nun appears to die at the feet of the "statue." Later, Jack comes to Eleanor's room in the convent, where they make love as the storm breaks. Following this encounter, Eleanor realizes that she has fallen back in love with Jack. She loses sleep, is unable to eat, and finally collapses in nervous exhaustion and is taken to the Argus hospital. In August, Eleanor calls for Jack to come pick her up.

Jack and his latest wife, Dot, come to the hospital in "The Meadowlark" [7]. On the trip back to Fargo, Eleanor and Dot are wounded to learn that Jack has a baby boy by one of his other wives. The women bond, and the following evening, Dot tells Eleanor the story of how her own relationship with Jack began ("Caryl Moon" [8]).

By December, Eleanor has moved back to Minneapolis. Jack thinks about her in "Jack's House" [9], "The Garage" [14], and "The Owl" [17]. After Jack's supposed death by fire, Eleanor is distraught. "Memoria" [10] and "Satin Heart" [12] depict the visitation room at Lawrence Schlick's funeral home on the day of Jack's funeral, January 5, 1995. Eleanor gets into an argument with Candice Pantamounty over how to dispose of Jack's remains because she secretly intends to be buried beside him.

After the funeral, Eleanor goes with the other wives to the steakhouse-bar-casino where Marlis Cook, Jack's fourth wife and mother of his child, is dealing blackjack ("The B & B" [16]). That evening, all of the wives get into Jack's red Explorer to return to Fargo, with Dot driving, just as a blizzard strikes. They become stuck in a snowbank beneath an overpass ("The Hitchhiker" [18]). In "Secrets and Sugar Babies" [19], the stranded women begin to argue about Jack, with Eleanor tending to defend him. Eleanor proposes that each woman tell her story to stay awake through the night. Eleanor's is the first of these "tales of burning love" ("Eleanor's Story" [20] and "The Red Slip" [21]).

Candice and Marlis tell their tales next. A little before 6 a.m., Eleanor criticizes Candice and insults Marlis ("Rotating Wild" [32]). Enraged, Marlis suggests that it is Eleanor's turn to clean the snow from the tailpipe. The women form a human chain, but Marlis lets go of Eleanor, who flies away into the storm. Sister Leopolda appears to her out of the darkness in "A Conversation" [33], and her instructions lead Eleanor to safety in the airport terminal. Eleanor alerts authorities to the plight of the other women, who are rescued in "The Disappearance" [36] and "Two Front-Page Articles" [37].

In "February Thaw" [40], Dot tells Jack that he should go back to Eleanor. That April, Jack sees Eleanor (and other women he has loved) in the face of the statue of the Virgin as it falls on him in "The Stone Virgin" [44].

In the following months, Eleanor rents an old farmhouse at the edge of the reservation, deciding to make her research on Leopolda her life's work ("A Last Chapter" [46]). In August, Eleanor's mother and father die ("A Light from the West" [43]), and as she dies, Anna recalls her daughter's newborn face. One lush, late-August night, Jack comes to Eleanor's farmhouse, and they make love.

Elena. Chook's daughter in *The Antelope Wife*. Since Chook and Janice seem to come as a couple to Frank Shawano and Rozina Roy's wedding, Janice is possibly Elena's mother. Elena is six years old when she comes with her father to the family Christmas dinner in chapter 18. By that time, Chook and his wife are divorced.

Eli Kashpaw. Second youngest of twelve children born to Kashpaw and Margaret. Eli is probably born in 1898. When Father Damien visits the Kashpaw household in March 1912, chapter 6 of *The Last Report on the Miracles at Little No Horse* indicates that Eli no longer lives there.

"The World's Greatest Fishermen" in *Love Medicine* reveals that the government allots Indian land sometime after Kashpaw's death. Eli's and Nector's allotments are adjacent to Margaret's. Although Margaret allows the government to put Nector in school, she hides Eli, so he learns the woods and the old Indian ways. According to chapter 10 of *The Beet Queen,* when Regina Puyat Kashpaw dies after moving to Argus, Eli leaves the reservation for the first time ever to attend her funeral.

In chapter 3 of *Tracks,* Eli is a shy fifteen-year-old when in the fall of 1913 he is tracking a wounded doe and comes upon Fleur Pillager in her clearing at Matchimanito Lake. Captivated, he goes to Nanapush for help. When he returns to her, armed with advice and gifts from Nanapush, they become lovers. Margaret is unhappy with Eli's choice of her daughter-in-law and tries unsuccessfully to get him to return home. The following spring (1914), Fleur gives birth to a daughter, Lulu Nanapush, but it is not clear whether Lulu is Eli's child or the product of a possible rape in Argus. (For a discussion of Lulu's paternity, see **Fleur Pillager** and **Lulu Nanapush Morrissey Lamartine.**)

According to chapter 4 of *Tracks,* after Lulu's birth, Margaret spends much of her time with Eli and Fleur at Matchimanito, and Pauline Puyat occasionally visits. The summer of 1917, Eli realizes that Pauline is sexually attracted to him and rejects her. In revenge, while Eli is working the hay harvest at the Morrissey farm, Pauline bewitches him into a torrid seduction of fourteen-year-old Sophie Morrissey. Aware of the infidelity, Fleur rejects him. As Eli recounts in chapter 5, on moonlit nights he watches her walk into the icy Matchimanito Lake and,

Eli Kashpaw

after a time, walk back out. Suspecting that she is pregnant with the lake creature's child, he goes to live with Nanapush. During that famine winter, the nineteen-year-old Eli, guided by Nanapush's spirit, shoots a moose. Later that winter, Eli gives Fleur the scarf of fine white cloth that becomes her trademark, and they reconcile.

During the following famine winter, 1918–1919 (chapters 6 and 7), Nanapush and Margaret stay with Eli and Fleur, who is pregnant with Eli's child. Fleur goes into premature labor, the baby dies, and Eli buries it in a shoebox by tying it with his own hair high in a tree. Eli can find no game, so the family nearly starves, saved only because Margaret and later Eli go to town for government rations. When they learn of the danger of foreclosure on Kashpaw and Pillager land, Eli helps the family raise money for land fees.

The following spring (1919), Eli is one of the observers on the shore when Pauline goes out onto Matchimanito Lake to meet the devil (chapter 8). Late that summer (chapter 9), Fleur learns that her land has been sold because Eli's brother Nector did not pay the fees on it. Eli tries to convince her to move onto Kashpaw land with him. Instead, she weights herself with stones and walks into the lake. Eli saves her, but he is frightened when she lays a curse on Nector. Ironically, in an effort to earn money to repurchase a piece of Pillager land, Eli goes to work for the very lumber company that is logging it. Nanapush will recall later, in chapter 7 of *Four Souls,* that Eli simultaneously adores and fears Fleur.

Fleur leaves the reservation in 1919. When she returns in 1933 (chapter 14 of *Four Souls*), Margaret wishes that love had worked out between Fleur and Eli, a reversal of her earlier attitude. When Nector returns from boarding school and various wanderings, in "The Plunge of the Brave" in *Love Medicine* Eli is again living with their mother at the old Kashpaw place. Eli and Nector hunt geese that Nector sells in "Wild Geese" (1934).

Fourteen years later (1948), in "The Beads" in *Love Medicine,* Eli is living in a mud-chinked shack on the far end of Kashpaw land. It is rumored that he still goes to visit Fleur. Eli establishes a rapport with the troubled nine-year-old June Morrissey, whom Nector and Marie have taken in, and June comes to live with him in the woods. As Eli recalls in "Crown of Thorns," June sleeps on a cot beside his stove, and he hates to send her off on the government school bus on cold dark mornings. In "The World's Greatest Fishermen," Albertine Johnson recalls Eli's affection for "his little girl" June. Even after June moves out, Eli keeps a photograph of her in his cabin along with an old pencil drawing she made in high school (chapter 10 of *The Beet Queen*). According to "The Beads," Eli has a way with children, and in chapter 19 of *The Bingo Palace,* Albertine recalls her Uncle Eli's amusing them with string designs like cat's cradle and chicken foot.

In 1953 (*Beet Queen* chapters 7 and 8), Russell Kashpaw comes to stay with Eli. The following winter, Eli leaves the reservation for the second time ever in chapter 10 to sign Russell out of the hospital after his stroke. In the summer of 1961 (chapter 10), Russell's half sister, Celestine James, comes to Eli's with her daughter, Dot Adare, to bring Russell a wheelchair. In 1972, Eli watches as a hospital orderly dresses Russell in his military uniform for the Beet Parade (chapter 13).

June remembers Eli's warm kitchen in "The World's Greatest Fishermen" as she walks to her death in an Easter snowstorm in 1981. Two months later Eli comes with Gordie Kashpaw, his nephew and June's former husband, to a family gathering at the old Kashpaw place. Early one morning after June's death, in "Crown of Thorns" Gordie comes to Eli's house to beg a beer. Afterward, Eli sits and remembers June as a child living with him.

Elsa Lamartine. Twin Cities wife of Beverly Lamartine in "Lulu's Boys" in *Love Medicine.* She is a natural blond who hides from her family the fact that Beverly is an Indian. Although she is rigid and unaffectionate with him, Beverly adores her. On a visit to the reservation in "The Good Tears," Beverly also marries Lulu Lamartine. When Lulu learns about this other wife, she sends him back to the city to divorce Elsa, accompanied by her twelve-year-old son, Gerry. Beverly apparently has Gerry thrown into detention and does not return to the reservation.

Elsie Travers. Daughter of the Pillager girl Niibin'aage and a teacher at Carlisle Indian School; mother of Faye and Netta Travers in *The Painted Drum.* Elsie is born on her mother's reservation, probably around 1920, but she grows up in her father's hometown of Stokes, New Hampshire (part 1.1).

In about the late 1940s (part 1.1) Elsie begins her own business handling estates, specializing particularly in Native American antiquities (part 2.1). Through this business, she meets philosophy professor Travers, whom she marries (part 1.4). Elsie has her daughters in her thirties (part 1.2). Once the family has enough money to live comfortably, Elsie makes a near fortune trading in rugs, an activity that brings her joy (part 1.4).

The early years of Elsie's marriage are pleasant, as she and Travers share an enjoyment of the natural world (1.4). But the relationship is increasingly characterized by conflict, and the two become absorbed in their own worlds, leaving the girls virtually without parents. The day Netta dies in a fall from an apple tree, Elsie is gone. We learn in part 4 that she is having an affair. Travers dies six months later (part 1.2).

After her husband's death, Elsie gets rid of all his things (1.4) and simply continues her own life, living in the same house and operating her business. After a stint at a London university, Faye joins her mother in the estate business. By the

Elsie Travers

novel's present time, they have been partners for almost twenty years (part 1.2). The two women have a peaceful relationship, based on familiar routines and a profound privacy (see parts 1.1 and 1.4).

Shortly after the death of the daughter of Kurt Krahe (Faye's lover), however, when Faye is upset about Kurt's mowing their yard in part 1.3, Elsie sides with him. She carries the matter further by agreeing with Kurt that he prune the ruined apple orchard, even though Faye is adamantly opposed.

One evening when Faye is gone, Elsie finds in her room the Ojibwe drum Faye had discovered in the Tatro estate. That night, Elsie confronts her about the theft, but by the next morning, she agrees with Faye that they should return the drum to its rightful owners. She recalls some of the old people from her home reservation who would have knowledge of the drum.

Early that fall, Elsie and Faye take the drum home to the Ojibwe reservation (part 2.1). They meet with Bernard Shaawano and others whose lives are connected with the drum, and Bernard relates to them stories of their Pillager forebears and the drum's history.

A year later, in September (part 4), Faye speaks to Elsie about the possibility of change in their lives. For the first time in all these years, the women talk openly about what happened the day Netta died. Shortly thereafter, Elsie and Faye receive a letter from Bernard telling the good the drum has accomplished since its return.

Elward Strong Ribs. Second husband of Irene Toose (Shawnee Ray Toose's mother), mentioned in chapters 2 and 10 of *The Bingo Palace.*

Emil and Erich Waldvogel. Twin sons of Fidelis and Eva Waldvogel in *The Master Butchers Singing Club,* born in Argus in 1929; brothers to Markus and Franz. In the summer of 1934 when the twins are five (chapter 5), they are "bull strong" and simple, focused on playing with toy guns and soldiers, and eating.

The next summer (1935) in the last days before Eva dies (chapter 7), the twins and Markus are largely on their own, staying outside all day. The twins are more aloof than their brothers in their response to Eva's death and afterward are even more on their own. After Markus runs away to Delphine Watzka's house, Delphine comes and shows the twins how to take care of Eva's chinchillas, motivating them by explaining that the money from their sale will allow the boys to buy more toy soldiers. Yet in chapter 8, wild dogs kill the chinchillas. When Fidelis lures and shoots the dogs, the boys pile the carcasses for burning. We see a glimpse of their disorderly life one morning that autumn when the exhausted Fidelis is trying to get all the boys off to school, and the twins keep going back to sleep and losing their clothes. We learn from chapter 9 that without Eva, they also lack the ordering routine of going to church.

The following summer (1936, chapter 9), when Markus discovers a man-made hill and decides to excavate, Emil and Erich join the effort. One November evening after three days of rain, the boys go out to repair the damage. About dark, the hill suddenly collapses, burying Markus. The twins and their friends run to the butcher shop for help, and Cyprian Lazarre is able to pull Markus to safety. That Christmas, when the Waldvogel family gets a crate of gifts from Germany in chapter 11, Emil and Erich receive whole regiments of toy soldiers.

Several mishaps over the next year or so help convince Fidelis to allow Tante to take Markus and the twins back to Germany. Besides the collapsed hill, in chapter 12 a neighbor boy makes dents in Emil's forehead with a BB gun, Erich falls off the roof more than once, and the boys construct a raft that is swept downriver by a spring flood. One February before World War II begins, Fidelis and Delphine drive Tante, Markus, and the twins to Chicago. When they are about to board the train to New York, Markus falls ill, so only Emil and Erich accompany Tante to Germany. We learn from chapter 14 that, once there, Erich becomes deeply attached to his grandfather.

A letter from Germany that spring informs Fidelis that the twins have started school and are in a government youth organization (chapter 13). Soon after his marriage to Delphine the following autumn, in a phone call with his family (chapter 14) Fidelis learns that the situation in Germany has deteriorated to the point that Emil and Erich cannot come home. By the end of chapter 13, the European war seems to have begun. Fidelis thinks that his American sons will have to fight Germany and rescue the twins. Before he leaves to join the U.S. Army, in chapter 14 Markus keeps Emil and Erich's collection of soldiers intact. Fidelis lies awake at night worrying about the twins.

Fidelis's anxiety is justified. Desperate for soldiers, Germany begins enlisting children (chapter 14). Emil and Erich are in their early teens when they are taken from school and put into the army. Early on Emil steps on a mine and is instantly killed. Erich slogs through the wartime horror alone, until some *American GIs* capture him, and he is taken to a POW camp in northeast Minnesota. Markus gets news that one of the twins is in the camp, and he and Fidelis try to visit him. But Erich, who is thoroughly indoctrinated with German propaganda, refuses to acknowledge them, even when they call out questions about Emil.

We know from chapter 15 that at the end of the war Erich returns to Germany. In 1954, Fidelis and Delphine go to Germany to see Fidelis's family. They see Erich and *his wife,* but the chapter records no conversation between them. On this trip, Fidelis is ill. His heart had begun to fail ten years earlier, when Erich had rejected him and he had received the letter about Emil's death. Fidelis dies on the return trip.

Erich Waldvogel

Erich Waldvogel. See **Emil and Erich Waldvogel.**

Eugene Kashpaw. The youngest of Marie and Nector Kashpaw's five children in *Love Medicine*. His 1948 birth is recorded in "The Beads," after a difficult labor in which Marie almost dies. In 1957, Marie leaves Eugene and Patsy in their sister Aurelia's care in "Flesh and Blood" when she takes their other sister, Zelda, to visit Sister Leopolda.

Eva Kalb Waldvogel. First wife of Fidelis Waldvogel; mother of Franz, Markus, Emil, and Erich in *The Master Butchers Singing Club*. Eva grows up in a German town immediately across the river from Ludwigsruhe (chapter 1). *Her father,* whom she dearly loves, is named Markus (chapter 5). He is apparently dead by the novel's present time, since only *her mother* is mentioned in chapter 1. Eva has reddish gold hair and green Magyar eyes streaked with silver (chapter 5). We learn in chapter 1 that Eva is engaged to Johannes Grunberg, a German Jew who is a soldier in World War I. In the late days of the war, Eva becomes pregnant with Johannes's child. At the war's end, Johannes's best friend, Fidelis Waldvogel, brings Eva the news of Johannes's death. Eva agrees to marry Fidelis as Johannes had wished. By the time of the wedding, she is big with child, but the priest is understanding. As Fidelis recalls years later (chapters 8 and 12), he and Eva know from their first night that they were meant to love each other.

When Eva has her child the following year (1919), Fidelis takes the boy, Franz, as his own. Fidelis immigrates to America in 1922 (chapter 1), opens his own butcher shop, and is eventually able to bring Eva and Franz to join him in Argus (chapter 3). Eva is appalled at the desolation of this prairie town but is determined to make a good life there. Three more boys are born to Eva and Fidelis: Markus in 1925 and twins Emil and Erich in 1929 (chapter 5). By the early 1930s, just as she had promised herself, Eva has managed to create a comfortable, pleasant home. Her rich-looking bathroom and warm, gleaming kitchen bespeak her ability to do much with little. Something of a domestic genius, Eva also keeps the butcher shop clean and the business running smoothly. Eva's domestic order is undermined when a rivalry between her husband and the other Argus butcher, Pete Kozka, turns sour, and Pete dumps rotting bones into her immaculate bed. Eva remains bitter toward the Kozkas and blames their dog for Fidelis's severely injured knee.

One summer day in 1934, Delphine Watzka, returning to Argus in chapter 4, sees Eva racing the fifteen-year-old Franz across a field by the butcher shop. Two days later, Delphine comes to the shop, and she and Eva meet (chapter 5). With her characteristic empathy for the outsider, Eva senses Delphine's trouble and invites her back to her lovely kitchen. Drawn by Eva's warmth, Delphine decides to tell her about the three bodies she has found in Roy Watzka's (Delphine's father's) cellar. When Delphine returns the next day, Eva offers her a job. As Delphine begins work, she continues to see examples of Eva's respect for outsiders, as well as her determination to triumph over any circumstance, a determination fueled by her devotion to "Old World Quality." During these first few weeks that Delphine works at the Waldvogels', Eva teaches her everything she needs to know about how to handle the household and the store (chapter 7).

As the summer's heat grows more intense in chapter 5, Eva suffers with the heat and the daily effort. One morning, she tells Delphine, "I am not so good," and asks to be taken to the doctor. Dr. Heech discovers that Eva has advanced uterine cancer. He gives her morphine for the pain and sends her to the Mayo Clinic for emergency surgery.

In chapter 6, after her surgery, Eva has horrible radium treatments at the hospital, but the cancer spreads, and Dr. Heech fruitlessly treats the new tumor in his office. By the following summer, 1935, there is nothing more doctors can do except control her pain. She will die before autumn. Yet early that summer, Eva still has some good days.

On one such afternoon in June, Eva and Delphine sit in her lush, chaotic garden and muse together about death. Erdrich highlights our sense of Eva's fading life through her step-by-step description of afternoon becoming evening then fading into night. During these June weeks, Franz, infatuated with airplanes, shares his excitement with his mother and decides that he and Pouty Mannheim must take her up flying. When Franz carries her to the plane, Eva thinks of his father and wonders what will happen when she, Johannes, and Fidelis are all in heaven together. The flight heightens both Eva's pain and her joy, and when she returns she shares with her boys her vision that life and death are all part of a design. On one of Eva's last good days, she takes the delivery truck and gets chinchillas from a neighboring farm for her boys to raise.

By July 4, 1935, Eva's days have become nightmarish. Fidelis is hosting a holiday gathering that day, and Eva listens from the little room by the kitchen where she now has her bed. As Eva's pain rises, Delphine goes to get her morphine—and discovers it missing. While Delphine and Fidelis look for Dr. Heech and the druggist, Eva spends hours in agony. When Delphine finally returns with morphine, Eva has a knife and is attempting to kill herself.

During Eva's sleepless nights, Fidelis at times sings to her for comfort (chapter 7). Eva has one more birthday, to which Tante (Fidelis's sister) and her Lutheran friends come, essentially to gloat over Catholic Eva's suffering. The night Eva dies, only Delphine is with her. Delphine wakes to hear a knocking—in her bed, Eva is running in place, mimicking the race with Franz just a year before, and her fists are hitting the headboard. She asks that only Delphine handle her body, tells her

Eva Kalb Waldvogel

once again about Franz's natural father, and asks her to write Eva's **Mutti**. Delphine finally sees the silver streak in Eva's eyes go dark. We glimpse Eva's funeral through the eyes of both Fidelis and Markus. As he throws the first clods on her coffin, Fidelis is overwhelmed with a sense of "some beautiful immensity passing . . . away from him forever" (*MBSC*, 195, chapter 8). Markus recalls in chapter 9 that he cannot release his fistful of dirt until Franz empties it for him. Although Fidelis never speaks about Eva after her death and her things quickly disappear from the house, in Markus's thoughts, his mother grows ever more powerful.

In fact, Eva's influence remains strong in all the lives she has touched. In chapter 7, her death turns Roy Watzka sober for the first time in his adult life. Delphine sees as a gift from Eva the comfort and order that emerge in her own house. In a dream in chapter 8, Fidelis sees Eva in Ludwigsruhe. The next autumn (1936, chapter 9), when Markus is buried in the collapsed hill, the clinging earth feels like his mother's wrapping him in a blanket as a small child, and when he is ill afterward, Delphine feeds him Eva's heavy dumpling soup (chapter 11). Even after she marries Fidelis, Delphine visits Eva's grave and sits under the pine tree she had planted there (chapter 14). When Franz's plane is shot down during the war sometime in the early 1940s, Eva seems to come to him bodily. In 1954 (chapter 15), when Delphine hears a knocking sound in her dream, she realizes it is Eva asking for Fidelis. A few years later, the now-old Step-and-a-Half thinks back over her life in chapter 16 and remembers her sorrow at Eva's death.

Everett "Kit" Tatro. See **Kit Tatro.**

Eyke, Mr. Father of Davan Eyke in part 1.1 of *The Painted Drum*. Eyke is a sporadically employed mechanic, looked down upon by his more intellectual neighbors on Revival Road. When Davan takes his father's new, bought-on-credit car without permission and damages it, Eyke does not forgive the offense, and Davan leaves home. The destructive tension between the two is manifest in the fact that Davan uses his father's things—chainsaw, crossbow, car—to destructive ends.

Eyke, Mrs. Mother of Davan Eyke in *The Painted Drum*. We learn in part 1.1 that Mrs. Eyke, like her husband, is a blue-collar worker. She drives a gas truck and then a school bus. When her neighbor Faye Travers sees her after Davan's death in part 1.3, Mrs. Eyke is bitter—toward her Assembly of God church, which apparently has not been supportive, and toward Kurt Krahe (and even Faye, as Krahe's lover), whom she blames in part for her son's death.

Eyke dog. Dog of the Eyke family on Revival Road in *The Painted Drum*. A mix of German shepherd and husky, in part 1.1 the dog is kept for years on a short chain attached to a tree, exposed to all weathers and never released. Narrator Faye Travers makes of the dog a symbol for human entrapment and, in foreshadowing, comments on how dearly the neighbors will pay for their apathy to its plight.

One day the tree, killed by the chain's rubbing and the dog's excrement, falls over, and the dog escapes, dragging its chain. It turns wild and eats a cocker spaniel and a veal calf. When it meets the school bus one day with a hungry look, the state police are called in. One of these officers spots Davan Eyke's stolen car, and in the ensuing chase, Davan and Kendra Krahe are killed. The following year (part 4), on a walk in the woods, Faye sees the dog's corpse, caught by its chain between two boulders.

F

Fanny Migwans. See **Under the Ground.**

Fantan. The manservant of John James Mauser in *Four Souls.* We learn from chapter 8 that Fantan is a New Orleans card shark and ladies' man who flees his gambling debts by enlisting in World War I. He and Mauser become friends in the European trenches. One day, playing cards for a lucky sardine can, Mauser is holding the can when an incoming shell hits it instead of him. It explodes up through Fantan's chin and severs his tongue. Feeling that Fantan has saved his life, Mauser brings him home to Minneapolis. Chapter 3 says that although Fantan is "tongueless," he talks in his sleep (*FS,* 26). (Other references to his speech and lack of speech appear in chapters 2 and 8.)

Mauser becomes chronically ill after his war year, so in chapters 2 and 4, Fantan cares for him, changing linens from his night sweats, protecting him during his convulsions, and helping with his treatments. Mauser's sister-in-law, Polly Elizabeth Gheen, strongly dislikes Fantan, disapproving of his meddling and his handling of Mauser's medication (chapter 2). When Fleur Pillager joins the Mauser household staff in 1919 or 1920, Fantan's life becomes easier. She takes care of the mountains of nighttime linens (chapter 4) and is ultimately responsible for Polly Elizabeth and Placide's being driven from the house, which delights Fantan (chapter 6). As Fleur gets to know the movements of each member of the household, she observes Fantan's gait as "sly" (chapter 3).

In the early 1930s (chapter 8), Polly Elizabeth's and Fantan's attitudes toward each other change when Mauser tells her about Fantan's saving his life. By the time the Mauser household dissolves in the spring of 1933, in chapter 12 Fantan and Polly Elizabeth have fallen in love and married. After they finish closing up

Fantan

the Mauser house, they plan to run a trading store on Fleur's home reservation. Fantan will play cards with the wily Fleur as often as possible.

Father of Fargo baby. Man who leaves his car with the motor running outside the train station in Fargo, with his baby in the backseat, in chapter 24 of *The Bingo Palace*. When Gerry Nanapush and Lipsha Morrissey steal the car, the distraught father jumps onto the trunk, but soon rolls off. This story is told from an alternate point of view in "Funeral Day" [23] in *Tales of Burning Love*.

Faye Travers. Daughter of Elsie Travers; great-granddaughter of the Pillager man Simon Jack; finder of the drum in *The Painted Drum*. We get a composite picture of Faye from parts 1.2, 2.1, and 4. She is thoroughly westernized, rational, and lawyerlike in her manner, while her one-quarter Ojibwe blood shows in her eyes with their Chippewa slant. She also has Pillager hands, with long fingers. In part 1.4, Faye suggests her function as one of the novel's two historical narrators: "my purpose in life is to pay attention and to remember" (*PD*, 79).

Faye is probably born in the early 1950s. (By the novel's present time, set in the early 2000s, she has already had her fiftieth birthday, part 1.3.) We learn in part 1.4 that Faye and her younger sister, Netta, are born to half-Ojibwe Elsie and New England professor Travers. Although their father provides intellectual stimulation for the girls, and their mother provides a comfortable income from her estate business, it is a home full of tensions. As their parents become increasingly preoccupied with their own affairs, Faye and Netta spend more and more time in the apple orchard. One summer evening at dusk, Travers comes out and urges them to jump from the tree into his arms. When Faye slips and falls, her father steps aside and lets her hit the ground. Seeing this, Netta steps from her high branch and falls to her death. Faye's account suggests that, true to form, her father lies about the incident, representing it as Faye's fault.

As a young adult, Faye goes through a period of drug abuse, gets hepatitis, goes to a university in London, drifts though miscellaneous jobs and interests, and finally becomes her mother's partner in the estate business (part 1.1). This business, which involves them in a variety of places and lives and specializes in Native American antiquities, is a good fit for Faye. In part 1.2, by the novel's present time Faye has worked with her mother for almost two decades. They catalog, evaluate, and sell the estates of the deceased, tasks whose investigative and often solitary nature Faye relishes. Faye and Elsie have a peaceful relationship based on familiar routines, a regard for each other's privacy that approaches reticence, and a common love for art and nature.

Faye and Elsie live on Revival Road in the small New Hampshire community of Stokes (part 1.1). Faye has for some years carried on a surreptitious affair with one of their neighbors, widower and sculptor Kurt Krahe. She has given him a key to her back door, and he comes to visit her by night. The relationship is rather dysfunctional, each wearing a facade of arrogance, self-reliance, indifference, or scorn to gain power over the other.

One winter day in part 1.1, the inept Davan Eyke comes to Faye's door. He has driven his father's new car off the road. Faye tries to pull it out of the trees, but is unsuccessful. One late winter when Kurt's college-age daughter Kendra (whom Faye dislikes) is home visiting, Davan begins seeing her. When Faye brings Kurt's mail to him one day, she witnesses his fight with the boy about Kendra and advises him not to interfere. Faye records the disastrous car chase a few days later that takes the lives of Davan, Kendra, and an old man named John Jewett Tatro. After Kendra's death, Kurt becomes needier in his relationship with Faye.

In March of that year (part 1.2), Faye goes to the Tatro house to handle the estate of the old man killed by Davan's car. She knows that a Tatro ancestor, Jewett Parker Tatro, was once an Indian agent on Elsie's reservation, so she hopes to find a collection of Native artifacts. When she asks the Tatro niece Sarah about such artifacts, Sarah leads her to the attic, where Faye discovers a variety of valuable objects—moccasins, ceremonial clothes, bags, and a drum. Although Sarah is indifferent to these pieces, Faye is drawn to the drum, and when the niece leaves, Faye, not fully understanding her own motives, steals it.

That night at dinner as Faye describes the drum to her mother (without saying that she took it), Elsie explains its significance and interprets its ornamentation. After Elsie retires for the night, Faye takes the drum up to her room, where she lies in bed listening.

As Faye comforts Kurt after Kendra's death (part 1.3), she comes to feel that he is trying to control her, an impression deepened when she sees him mowing her yard. Afterward, she finds Kurt and Elsie engaged in a conversation that troubles her more than the yard mowing. Kurt wants to prune the apple orchard so that it will bloom again that spring, but because of the circumstances of Netta's death, Faye wants the orchard to remain ruined.

One evening, Faye and Kurt go to the Sweet Mansion for dinner, where they discuss their slipping relationship and Faye urges Kurt not to prune the orchard. That night, Elsie has discovered the drum and confronts Faye about its theft. But by morning Elsie begins recalling the old people from her home reservation and comes to agree with Faye that the drum should be taken home. The following day, despite Faye's expressed objection, Kurt prunes the orchard.

By May the apple trees are blooming, flipping the "switch" of Faye's memory to a time when the trees bloomed every year and her sister was alive. One moonlit night, in her memory she sees her sister climbing and smells the odor of blossoms.

Faye Travers

The next morning, Faye has Kit Tatro change the back door lock so Kurt cannot enter.

That summer (part 1.4), Faye handles the sale of the Tatro collection but still has the drum. Netta is visiting her dreams. One August day as Faye is picking blackberries, she hears a helicopter. Later, police officer Lonny Germaine shows up with his pistol drawn, looking for the grower of a marijuana crop in the woods. As the summer ends, all the memories surrounding Netta's death flood Faye's mind.

In early fall of that year (part 2.1), Elsie and Faye return the drum to the reservation. At a gathering at the house of Judge and Germaine Nanapush, Bernard Shaawano relates the stories of Elsie and Faye's Pillager forebears and the making and loss of the drum.

About a year later, in mid-September (part 4), Elsie and Faye are sitting on their back screened porch listening to the coyotes one night when Kurt enters and, not seeing them, is about to try the back door when Faye speaks. He begins a polite conversation as if nothing had happened between them. But when Elsie goes in, Kurt asks Faye why she turned him away. She does not explain, only says that she had to. He does not attempt to follow her into the house.

The next morning, Faye challenges Elsie with their need to break out of their stagnant routine. She also speaks Netta's name. When Faye relates the true details of Netta's death, Elsie truthfully answers Faye's question of where she was that day: "I was with someone" (*PD,* 264). Faye and Elsie receive a letter from Bernard Shaawano, telling them about an incident the previous winter in which the drum saved the lives of three children and about its present usefulness.

After a long walk through the woods that fall, Faye sits in the orchard and tastes its fallen fruit. Kurt phones to tell her about the vandalism of his studio, and that night their relationship begins again—this time with Faye going to his house. The novel ends almost two years after it began with a parallel scene—Faye visiting her sister's grave.

Faye Travers's grandmother. See **Niibin'aage.**

Fidelis Waldvogel. Master butcher and German émigré to North Dakota in *The Master Butchers Singing Club.* As a young man in Ludwigsruhe, Germany (chapter 1), Fidelis knows that he will become one of a long line of master butchers. His Metzgermeister's diploma and guild papers attest to the painstaking preparation and precision of his profession. As a singer, a Waldvogel (Forestbird) with a clear tenor voice, he is part of yet another family tradition. Fidelis is powerfully built, fair with reddish hair, high cheekbones, straight nose, and shapely mouth.

During World War I, Fidelis's natural stillness is key to his survival and the basis of his skill as a sniper. Life in the trenches is terrible, marked by filth, lice, and frostbite. Except for his friend Johannes Grunberg (see chapters 7 and 13), the other soldiers hate Fidelis, since his precision as a sniper makes them particular targets. At the war's end, Johannes dies on the way home. He makes Fidelis promise to tell his fiancée, Eva Kalb, about his death and to marry her.

Fidelis walks home, arriving in Ludwigsruhe in late November 1918. His sister, Maria Theresa, picks lice from his hair, and *his father* brings him fresh clothes. In the luxury of his bed, Fidelis goes to sleep to the sound of *his mother*'s weeping and sleeps for thirty-eight hours. When he wakes two mornings later, he dresses and puts on *his grandfather*'s boar's-head cuff links. He then goes to Eva's house in the town across the river to give her his bad news. When she falls against him, he realizes that she is pregnant. He also tells her of Johannes's wish that they should marry. By the time of the wedding, she is big with child. From the first night of their marriage, Fidelis falls deeply and unexpectedly in love. (See also chapters 8 and 12.) When Franz is born to Eva the following year, Fidelis's love includes the child's "defenseless beauty" (*MBSC*, 9).

Fidelis immigrates to the United States to make a better life for his family, arriving in New York in 1922 with his knives and his father's sausages—his ticket west. He hopes to go to Seattle, but money from the sausages runs out in Argus, North Dakota, a town of "appalling flatness" (*MBSC*, 12). In chapter 3, Fidelis immediately finds work as a butcher. Using money from his family (chapter 8), he buys a farmstead and opens his own shop. Through exhausting work and frugality, Fidelis gathers the money to bring Eva and Franz (and later his sister, Tante) to join him. Over the next few years, three more boys are born to Fidelis and Eva: Markus in 1925 and twins Emil and Erich in 1929 (chapter 5).

Chapter 3 gives insights into the kind of butcher Fidelis is, both frugal and open-handed. He is hardworking, painstaking, and frugal, but unlike Pete Kozka, he does not hoard the scraps he cannot sell. He and Eva give castoffs to hungry people, and in some cases, to dogs. By the early 1930s, Fidelis and Kozka's rivalry turns hostile because of Fidelis's overplayed joke with Pete's dog, Hottentot. One summer morning, a sow Fidelis is about to slaughter, enraged by Hottentot's barking, attacks Fidelis and tears up his knee. When Fidelis is at Dr. Heech's, Pete comes to his empty house and, as revenge for Fidelis's tricks, dumps rotting bones into Eva's immaculate bed. Shortly after his visit to Dr. Heech (the two men sing together), Fidelis decides to start a men's singing club. The gathering serves to reconcile the two butchers, since Pete wants to be part of the group.

Chapter 5 gives us miscellaneous glimpses of Fidelis in the butcher shop in the summer of 1934. His boys, though fairly wild much of the time, are subdued and obedient around their father, who plans to train them all as butchers. (Chapter 7 tells us that Fidelis keeps a bull pizzle to discipline his boys but seldom uses it.) One

Fidelis Waldvogel

day during a heat wave, Fidelis comes home from making deliveries to terrible news. Delphine has left him a note saying that Eva collapsed that morning, Dr. Heech said she has cancer, and Delphine has taken her to the Mayo Clinic for emergency surgery. Fidelis gets Delphine's companion, Cyprian Lazarre, to run the shop for a week so he can be with Eva in Minnesota (see chapter 6).

We learn in chapter 6 that after Eva becomes ill, Fidelis works virtually around the clock to pay her medical bills. By the following summer, 1935, all treatments have failed, and Eva is dying. One day in June while Fidelis is out on deliveries, Franz arranges for Pouty Mannheim to take Eva up in his airplane. They all know that Fidelis would not approve, so apparently no one tells him. On July 4, Fidelis closes the shop early and hosts a gathering of friends, at which he engages in a seemingly puerile stunt. With a loop attached to Sheriff Hock's belt, Fidelis picks up the large man with his teeth. Delphine, watching, realizes that he is doing this for Eva, frustrated that his great strength is powerless against her illness. That helplessness is reinforced moments later when Delphine tells him that Eva's morphine has been stolen. For hours, with Eva in agony, Delphine and Fidelis search in vain for the doctor and the pharmacist. Roy Watzka finally provides the morphine by stealing it from the drugstore. Fidelis makes arrangements with the pharmacist to pay for the new medicine (chapter 8).

Fidelis stays up some nights and sings to his dying wife (chapter 7). Eva dies late that summer. At her funeral, Fidelis has "the sense of some beautiful immensity passing . . . away from him forever" (*MBSC,* 195). At first Tante stays with Fidelis and the boys, but after several days, Fidelis returns from making deliveries to find that Markus has run away. When Fidelis goes to Delphine's to fetch him, he asks her to come back to the shop, but she will not come unless Tante leaves. A few days later, Fidelis tells her that Tante is gone and begs her to come help them.

That autumn (1935), a pack of wild dogs kills the boys' chinchillas (chapter 8). Enraged, Fidelis lures the dogs with scraps, then shoots each one with a rifle. Hearing this story makes Cyprian realize that Fidelis was a sniper during the war. The replies of Fidelis's parents to Tante's letters makes him miss them and **his brother.** That fall when the butcher shop is frantically busy for several days, Fidelis's sleep-deprived efforts to get the boys off to school one morning illustrate how difficult it is for him to cope without Eva.

When Delphine goes back to work for Fidelis, the tension between them becomes unbearable because of their attraction to each other, so they keep up a facade of rigid formality. When Fidelis pays her father's bail, Delphine tells him pointedly that she wants to deflect the town's rumors about them.

One autumn night in 1936 (chapter 9), hostility arises between Cyprian and Fidelis. Later, as Fidelis puzzles over the reason, he realizes that what the men are fighting about is Delphine. The boys come home late each night that fall, covered with dirt, but Fidelis doesn't see them till they are cleaned up and thus fails to notice their behavior. One cold, wet night that November, Cyprian and Fidelis begin to fight in earnest, but they are interrupted by the panicked twins, who tell them that Markus is buried in a collapsed hill. When the men run to the scene, at first Fidelis tunnels in to his son, with Cyprian following, but Cyprian convinces him that Fidelis's size makes the effort dangerous to them all. Thus, it is Cyprian who carefully pulls Markus to safety. Chapter 11 reveals that after the hill incident, Fidelis is more open to Tante's idea of her taking the younger boys to Germany. That Christmas, Fidelis's family in Germany sends a crate of gifts to the American Waldvogels.

Chapter 12 is not dated, but its events occur during a February sometime between that Christmas and the beginning of World War II. In this chapter, Fidelis and Delphine take Tante and the three youngest boys to Chicago in preparation for their travel to Germany. In a brief moment alone, Delphine tries to convince Fidelis not to send the boys to Germany, but he feels that he cannot change their plans now. Yet when Markus becomes ill and cannot go, Tante and the twins leave without him. In Chicago and again on the drive back home, Fidelis and Delphine talk about Cyprian (who left in December 1936) and about their own future, but they fail to resolve anything.

One night that spring, Fidelis walks to Delphine's house (chapter 13). He makes small talk at first, but then says what he came to say, that he has given Cyprian enough time. His gaze of adoration tells Delphine that he is proposing. Delphine begins to work at the butcher shop again, but nothing is resolved between them, and over the next months the two live in a state of extreme agitation. They finally set a date for their marriage and tell Franz and Markus about their plans. It is probably autumn of that same year when Fidelis and Delphine marry. Franz leaves for the air corps, and shortly after the wedding, Fidelis gets a phone call from Germany informing him that the twins will not be able to come home (see chapter 14). Cyprian and his new gymnastics partner come to Argus briefly, give a performance, and then leave. There is no record of Fidelis's reaction to this visit.

After Roy Watzka's death, Delphine tries to tell Fidelis that her father was a murderer, but he cannot hear her (chapter 13). Instead, her words trigger a flood of memories of men he himself had killed. Once World War II begins, Fidelis's singing club, conscious of anti–German sentiment, practices non–German songs. Fidelis now sees Germans as the enemy and thinks that Franz and Markus will have to fight to rescue their brothers.

In chapter 14, the United States has entered the war. It is probably 1942 when Markus goes into the army. Sales at the butcher shop are up, but continual shortages

Fidelis Waldvogel

hamper business. Fidelis is often awake at night, thinking of Emil and Erich. As a bedtime routine to help himself sleep, he drinks a highball and soaks his feet in Epsom salt while he reads the paper. One night when Delphine returns from a walk, she rubs his tender, frostbite-damaged feet, and they go to their room to make love.

A year or so later, when Markus is home on leave, he tells Fidelis that one of the twins is in a POW camp in northern Minnesota. They make the trip and spot Erich, but he refuses to acknowledge them. We learn from chapter 15 that Fidelis's heart starts failing when Erich walks past him, preferring a prison to his father. When they read about the atomic bomb that August (1945), Fidelis believes that his sons will now be safe. But only Markus returns safely. Franz is severely injured in a freak accident, and in chapter 15, we learn that he comes home "only to fade from life in bewildered anger" (*MBSC,* 377). Another blow for Fidelis is the letter telling of Emil's death, and after the war, Erich returns to Germany.

Chapter 15 records that in 1954 Fidelis and Delphine visit his hometown to see family and attend a memorial service. At the ceremony, they sit with Erich and *his new bride* on one side and Fidelis's brother and *sister-in-law* and their *two grown children* on the other. Although he manages to sing with the other master butchers at the ceremony, Fidelis is ill with liver and heart disease. On their return, he collapses and dies at the customs gate in New York. As Step-and-a-Half reminisces in chapter 16, she recalls Fidelis and his suitcase—it came with him in 1922 full of knives and sausages, and returned to Germany with his sons.

Fishbone. One of Kashpaw's four wives in 1912 in *The Last Report on the Miracles at Little No Horse.* We learn in chapter 5 that Fishbone is a distant relative of Nanapush. Chapter 6 depicts her as a young woman, the quietest and gravest of the women in the Kashpaw household. Softer and plainer than the others, even very pregnant she moves with grace and is gentle in her care of the children. She is present when Nanapush and young Father Damien come to visit that March. His family disturbed by the new priest's arrival, Kashpaw feels pressure to get rid of some of his wives, but he thinks of how much he loves Fishbone and how vulnerable she is. That spring, Fishbone's baby is stillborn, she falls ill, and her older child crawls into a fire and is burned.

At some point, Father Damien baptizes Fishbone with the name Marie, but other than that we do not learn her fate. In chapter 7, two of her and Kashpaw's children are living in Mashkiigikwe's cabin in 1918, where they all fall ill with influenza. Mashkiigikwe barely survives, but we are not told about the children.

Fleur Pillager. Medicine woman; wife of Eli Kashpaw and mother of Lulu Nanapush; wife of John James Mauser and mother of John James Mauser II. See **Pillager family** for variations in the story of her parentage.

In the *Tracks* version of Fleur's childhood, in chapter 1, she lives with her father (Pillager), mother (Boss Woman), and three younger siblings, two girls and a boy (Chokecherry Girl, Small Bird, and He Is Lifted By Wind), in a cabin on the far side of Matchimanito Lake. According to chapter 2, once as a child and then as a fifteen-year-old, Fleur seems to drown in the lake, but in each case she sends her rescuers on death's road in her place. "Love Medicine" (in *Love Medicine*) mentions a rumor about Fleur that when she is a girl the lake spirit, Misshepeshu, grabs her and has "its way with her" (*LM,* 236). Fleur is seventeen in chapter 1, when her parents and siblings die in the consumption epidemic of 1912–1913. (Chapter 5 of *The Last Report on the Miracles at Little No Horse* gives the date as 1911–1912.)

In the version of Fleur's family and infancy in *The Painted Drum,* her Pillager father (Simon Jack) is the lover rather than the husband of her mother (Anaquot), and she has no full siblings. In part 2.2, Fleur is born while Anaquot is still married to Shaawano, moves across to the Pillager side of the lake when she is a few months old, and in 2.3 grows up in the Pillager cabin with no father present, two "mothers" (Anaquot and Ziigwan'aage), and three older half-siblings, two boys and a girl (Niibin'aage). (See **Anaquot** for details.) Part 2.5 echoes the *Tracks* account of the death of Fleur's family in an epidemic but with several variations.

In chapter 1 of *Tracks,* toward the end of this winter, Nanapush rescues Fleur and brings her to his cabin, though they themselves barely survive. A visit that spring by the new priest, Father Damien, is the turning point in their survival. (See also chapter 5 of *Last Report*.) Later that spring, Fleur returns to her family's cabin and lives there alone (*Tracks* chapter 1). When surveyors and government fee collectors come, Fleur eludes them.

Fleur goes to Argus the following June (1913; *Tracks* chapter 2) and works in Pete and Fritzie Kozka's butcher shop. In the evenings, she plays poker with three of her fellow employees, Lily Veddar, Tor Grunewald, and Dutch James. One night in August, angered by her steady winning, the men attack Fleur in the smokehouse. The next day, Fleur apparently takes her revenge. A tornado destroys the butcher shop, and her three assailants freeze when they take refuge in the meat locker.

That fall (chapter 3), Fleur walks back to the reservation. With her Argus earnings and winnings, she pays the fees on all her Pillager land allotments. Local gossip speculates that she returns pregnant, but within a month, Eli Kashpaw becomes her lover, which "muddie[s] the water" (*Tr,* 39) for the gossips. When Lulu is born the following spring (1914), Fleur almost dies in childbirth, but she is assisted by Eli's mother, Margaret Kashpaw, and, in the *Tracks* account, by a drunken bear.

Like the reservation gossips, Erdrich's readers also cannot be certain of Lulu's paternity. The only knowledge we have of the attack in the Argus smokehouse

Fleur Pillager

comes from Pauline (recorded in *Tracks* chapters 2 and 3). Even Pauline admits that she did not see what happened that night, and more important, Pauline is a notorious liar. Of Pauline's story, Fleur comments, "the Puyat lies" (*Tr*, 38). Nevertheless, there is some evidence that Fleur may be pregnant before becoming Eli's lover. When she returns to the reservation in chapter 3, Nanapush notices that her dress is strained across the front, and Eli describes Fleur at their first meeting as having "no curve" and being ravenously hungry. By the time Margaret sees her and judges that she is pregnant, Fleur and Eli are already lovers. When Lulu is born in the spring of 1914, Nanapush thinks that Eli may be her father, but he adds, "who knew for certain . . . ?" (*Tr*, 61). (See also **Lulu Nanapush Morrissey Lamartine.**)

After Lulu's birth, Fleur and Eli refuse to move to the Kashpaw place, so Margaret often stays with them on Pillager land. Pauline also visits occasionally, jealous of Fleur and Eli's passion. In the autumn of 1917, after Pauline bewitches Eli into a sexual liaison with Sophie Morrissey in *Tracks* chapter 4, Fleur gets revenge by casting a spell over Sophie, and she rejects Eli.

In *Tracks* chapter 5, Eli returns to Fleur's cabin, though she will still not let him touch her. Eli comes to believe that Fleur is pregnant with the lake creature's child and goes to live with Nanapush. In that famine winter (1917–1918), Eli leaves meat at Fleur's door, though she mocks him. After Clarence Morrissey and Boy Lazarre attack Margaret and shave her head, Fleur shaves her own head in an act of solidarity with her mother-in-law, and her curse contributes to Boy Lazarre's death. To cover her bald head, Eli gives Fleur the scarf of fine-woven white cloth that will become her trademark. Fleur finally accepts Eli back, and the hungry people ice fishing on Matchimanito hear their love cries.

The following winter, 1918–1919, brings even worse famine. In *Tracks* chapter 6, Fleur, pregnant with Eli's child, is gaunt. She, Eli, Lulu, Nanapush, and Margaret are all living together, sharing their meager supply of food. When Fleur goes into labor prematurely, only Pauline and Lulu are present. Lulu goes through the snow to Margaret's for help (resulting in severely frostbitten feet), but Pauline fails to help. When the child is born, the enraged Fleur throws a knife at Pauline. According to Pauline's subsequent vision, Fleur walks down death's road and gambles for the lives of her children. She loses the life of the baby but wins Lulu's.

As the winter drags on in chapter 7, the family almost starves, saved only by the arrival of government rations. When Father Damien explains that they may all lose their land, Fleur scoffs. Yet after the loss of her child, Fleur's power wanes, and she becomes overly protective of Lulu. In the spring of 1919, Nanapush and Moses Pillager conduct a healing ceremony for her, interrupted by Pauline. That same spring, when Pauline takes a boat out onto Matchimanito in *Tracks* chapter

8 to confront the devil, Fleur is watching from the shore dressed in black. The body of Napoleon Morrissey is found late that summer, and Fleur is blamed for his murder (*Tracks* chapters 8 and 9; *Last Report* chapter 9).

The ultimate challenge to Fleur's power comes that same late summer of 1919 (*Tracks* chapter 9) as loggers move onto her land. When she learns that Nector and Margaret have failed to pay the Pillager land fees and that her land has been sold to the Turcot lumber company, Fleur loads herself down with stones and walks into the lake. Eli saves her from her third drowning, but she responds that Nector will take her place this time. The primary object of Fleur's vengeance, however, is the man who stole her land, John James Mauser (chapter 10 of *Last Report*). Staying beside the lake long into the night, Fleur plots how to destroy this man and regain her land.

In order to carry out her plan, as we learn from "The Island" in *Love Medicine*, *Tracks* chapter 9, and *Last Report* chapter 15, Fleur decides she must first send Lulu to the government school where she feels the child will be safe. She puts Lulu on the school bus in August 1919 (*Last Report* chapter 15 says September) and returns for a few weeks to her land. In *Tracks* chapter 9, as the loggers move in to take the last of the great oak trees around Fleur's cabin, they encounter the medicine woman's last stand. Using her cunning and power, she brings the trees crashing down on men, horses, and wagons. She then buckles herself into the traces of her cart and leaves the reservation.

We know from Lulu's story in chapter 15 of *Last Report* that when she is first sent to school, she longs for her mother. But after she tries to run away the next summer and is caught and punished, she has a change of heart and begins her near lifelong hatred of Fleur. (For variations in this story, see **Lulu Nanapush Morrissey Lamartine.**)

Chapter 1 of *Four Souls* picks up where *Tracks* ends, in the autumn of 1919. After leaving Matchimanito, Fleur follows the track of her trees east to Minneapolis. She takes as her secret name the name of her mother, Four Souls, a name that highlights Fleur's own ability to survive her own death. (For her arrival date in Minneapolis, see the discussion of the *Four Souls* chronology in the "Geography, Genealogy, and Chronology" section of this book.) At the Mauser mansion, Mauser's sister-in-law, Polly Elizabeth Gheen, hires Fleur as the laundress. Shortly after Fleur's arrival, the chronically ill Mauser has a seizure, and Fleur revives him and begins to heal him in secret (chapters 2 and 3). She wants him healthy before destroying him (see also chapter 7).

In chapter 3, when Fleur discovers that Mauser stays awake all night, she lurks in the hall outside his door, awaiting an opportunity for revenge. One night she falls asleep there, and Mauser sees her. Close to a year after Fleur's arrival, she decides that it is time to kill her enemy (chapter 5). She wakes him with a knife at his throat, but he dissuades her by promising to marry her, to give her everything he owns, and to do whatever she wants. In chapter 6, Mauser dismisses his wife and marries Fleur. In November 1921, in *Last Report* chapter 16 Father Damien writes to the Minneapolis bishop asking about Fleur and learns from him about her marriage and her appearance in Minneapolis society.

But we learn from chapters 6 and 7 of *Four Souls* that shortly after her marriage, Fleur unintentionally becomes pregnant. (For more about this marriage, see **John James Mauser.**) She must take to bed to avoid miscarriage. During this period of confinement, Polly Elizabeth begins visiting and caring for her, giving her whiskey to stop early contractions, beginning an addiction that lasts for years. After Fleur's boy is born, she begins to pity Mauser and is no longer able to hate him (chapter 10).

Although Fleur, Polly Elizabeth, and Mauser dote on the boy, he is physically flaccid and mentally absent (chapter 8). Yet he develops one skill: under Fleur's tutelage, he becomes an expert poker player. Fleur never names the child (see chapters 16 in *Four Souls* and *Last Report*), and he is usually called simply "the boy." (The name John James Mauser II is only for the chimookomaan records [chapter 8].)

When the boy is about two, in 1923 or very early 1924, Fleur begins to visit Lulu's school in *Four Souls* chapter 8 to try to fetch her, but Lulu refuses to go with her. (See also chapter 15 of *Last Report*. Nanapush brings Lulu back to the reservation in the spring of 1924 [*Tracks* chapter 9].)

Chapters 8 and 10 of *Four Souls* record events from the early 1930s (dated by *Last Report*). Mauser's financial empire is failing. Fleur demands that he give her his car and a deed to her land, and insists that she take their son with her to the reservation. By the spring of 1933, Mauser flees his creditors, and Fleur returns to the reservation with his car, her clothes, and the boy (*Four Souls* chapter 12). (For the date of Fleur's return, see chapter 16 of *Last Report*.) The events of this return appear in differing versions in *The Bingo Palace* chapter 12 and *Four Souls* chapters 14 and 15. In both accounts, however, Fleur regains her land from its current owner, Jewett Parker Tatro, through a poker game, and in both, it is the boy who plays the winning hands.

The following morning, in *Four Souls* chapter 16, Fleur and the boy go to Margaret's cabin. As always, Lulu (who is living with her grandparents) avoids Fleur. After Nanapush and the boy leave, Margaret bathes Fleur and tells her what she must do to heal. Fleur, she insists, must go on an eight-day fast on a rock beside Matchimanito Lake, aided only by Margaret and her medicine dress. If Fleur survives the eight days, the medicine dress will give her a new name. After this ordeal, Fleur returns to her land on Matchimanito, finally at peace with humans and spirits (*Four Souls* "End of the Story").

When Fleur first appeared in the 1986 *The Beet Queen,* Erdrich was just beginning to form her story. Thus, not surprisingly, the brief outline of Fleur's story in this early novel is quite different from the account of the same period of time (1920 to 1930s) cited above from *Last Report* and *Four Souls.* In chapter 2 of *The Beet Queen,* Fleur is a peddler in 1932 when she rescues the fourteen-year-old Karl Adare. In the two later novels, however, in this year, Fleur is a member of elite Minneapolis society.

There are other events in Fleur's life that are cited only in earlier novels, which are not necessarily inconsistent with the later, more developed story. Among these are Fleur's helping with the birth of Marie Kashpaw's last boy in the winter of 1948 ("The Beads" in *Love Medicine*); her helping Eli care for Russell Kashpaw from the late 1950s to the 1970s (*Beet Queen* chapters 10 and 13); and her presence at the naming ceremony of Albertine Johnson in the 1980s (*Bingo Palace* chapter 3).

After her final return to the reservation in 1933, Fleur continues to live at Matchimanito. Nanapush tries to convince Lulu to forgive her mother, his conversations with her recorded in the odd-numbered chapters of *Tracks.* In 1940, Fleur's son, apparently still unnamed but now referred to as Awun (the Mist), leaves her home to marry Mary Kashpaw (*Last Report* chapter 17).

In Fleur's old age, she is referred to variously as Old Lady Pillager, the Old Lady (Mindemoya), or just the Pillager ("Love Medicine" in *Love Medicine;* chapters 11 and 14 of *Bingo Palace*). She continues to be respected and feared as a powerful medicine woman. In the *Painted Drum* version of Fleur's story, in part 2.3, as an old woman, she tells Bernard Shaawano (son of her half-brother) the story of her arrival as an infant in the cabin of Simon Jack.

The final events of Fleur's life are recorded in *The Bingo Palace.* In chapter 1, reservation gossip suggests that Fleur is putting off dying until she can pass on her power to her great-grandson, Lipsha Morrissey. Lipsha is aware of fearful stories about Fleur (see "Love Medicine" in *Love Medicine* and chapters 5, 11, and 14 of *Bingo Palace*), but when he needs a love medicine, he gathers the courage to meet her. When Fleur comes into town on her "feast day" in chapter 11 of *Bingo Palace,* Lipsha goes home with her. As darkness settles, Fleur changes into a bear and speaks to him in the old language (chapter 22) about love (chapter 14) and the enduring value of the land (chapter 13). Fleur may also appear to Lipsha as the skunk he encounters at Matchimanito Lake in chapter 17 and again in his room in chapter 20. Fleur also appears to another grandson, Lyman Lamartine (chapters 13 and 20).

In chapter 27 of *Bingo Palace,* when the authorities come to Matchimanito in

Fleur Pillager

deep winter with signed papers to confiscate Fleur's property, they find her gone. They envision her setting out across the frozen lake to the island where the souls of the Pillagers wait for her. This journey is Fleur's death walk. Having sent others in her place on death's road, she now takes the place of "the boy"—probably her great-grandson, Lipsha. Some people, however, still hear her laugh, see her bear tracks, and are sure that the Pillager continues to walk the woods of Matchimanito Lake.

The reservation events of 1996 in *The Last Report on the Miracles at Little No Horse* cause some of its inhabitants to recall memories of Fleur. In his interviews in March with Father Jude, Father Damien often refers to Fleur. Thus, Jude decides to interview Lulu about her, and in chapter 15, Lulu recalls the story of Fleur's sending her to the government school. The following June, as Father Damien prepares to go to the Pillager island on Matchimanito to die in chapter 22, he looks forward to seeing Fleur there. Once there, he calls out to Nanapush and Fleur and feels Fleur approach. As he dies, one of these two old friends grasps his hand, and he is "pulled across" (*LR*, 350).

Fleur Pillager's boy. The son of John James Mauser and Fleur Pillager, born in Minneapolis. The boy is given a name for chimookomaan (white) records—John James Mauser II—but chapters 16 in *Four Souls* and *The Last Report on the Miracles at Little No Horse* indicate that Fleur herself does not name him. He thus has "no name for his spirit" (*FS*, 200). As a result, as a child, no one calls him by name. Fleur calls him only "my son," while others refer to him as "the boy." Only in adulthood is he called by his Mauser name. Nevertheless, for the sake of coherence, we include the boy's entire story under **John James Mauser II.**

Flying Kuklenskis. Family of trapeze artists who adopt the Montana runaway Anna in "Eleanor's Tale" [20] in *Tales of Burning Love.* Anna later marries young Harry Kuklenski. The *"original" Flying Kuklenski,* Harry's uncle, was the Polish man who started the circus trapeze act. He is now buried at a circus cemetery in Milwaukee. *Old master Kuklenski* is apparently the leader of the troop at the time Anna joins them. The family has a history of fatal accidents. Old master Kuklenski dropped his *daughter,* presumably to her death. His *son* (who may or may not be Harry) has also dropped his *wife,* also presumably to her death, since she is referred to as his "former" wife. See also **Anna Kuklenski Schlick, Baby Kuklenski girl, Harry Kuklenski,** and **Kuklenski brothers.**

Four Soul. In *The Bingo Palace,* a healer and the grandmother of Fleur Pillager. In chapter 3, the records of Father Damien identify Four Soul as being among the Ojibwe in the first decade of migration west to the reservation. It is her name that Albertine Johnson receives in a ceremony run by Xavier Albert Toose and attended by Fleur. The name of this healer is appropriate for Albertine since she is hoping to become a doctor. In chapter 27, Four Soul is one of the dead Pillagers who welcome Fleur on her death walk to the island in Matchimanito Lake. For the ambiguity concerning this name, see **Four Souls.**

Four Souls. A name of Fleur Pillager's mother according to *Four Souls.* In chapter 5, when twelve-year-old Anaquot, daughter of Under the Ground, survives a fever in the 1870s, she is given the spirit name Four Souls. She later gives birth to a daughter named Red Cradle, a son, and Fleur. See **Anaquot** for the rest of her story.

A comparison of this record of Fleur's mother with that in other novels reveals some ambiguity. Chapter 1 of *Tracks* gives Fleur's mother as Ogimaakwe (Boss Woman), whose other children are named Chokecherry Girl, Small Bird, and He Is Lifted By Wind. (Red Cradle is not mentioned.) Ogimaakwe's husband and the father of these children is Pillager. In chapter 16 of *Four Souls,* Margaret tells us that Ogimaakwe, Anaquot, and Four Souls are all names for the same person. Yet according to *The Bingo Palace,* Four Soul (spelled in the singular) is Fleur's grandmother rather than her mother (chapter 27), and in old records of the Pillager family, Ogimaakwe and Four Soul are listed as two separate people (chapter 3). (See also **Four Soul** and, for other variations in the structure of Fleur's family, **Pillager family.**)

In chapter 1 of *Four Souls,* Fleur takes on this secret name of her mother to help in her quest for revenge against John James Mauser in Minneapolis. In chapter 5, Nanapush tells us something of the significance of this name and its dangerous power. It is still one of the names Fleur wears in "End of the Story."

Frank Shawano. Son of Shawano the ogitchida and Regina; brother of Puffy, Klaus, and Cecille Shawano; second husband of Rozina Roy in *The Antelope Wife.* Since Frank is the only child named in the 1945 portrait of his family in chapter 13, he may be the oldest. In this chapter, a German prisoner of war named Klaus, whom Frank's father has kidnapped, offers to bake a cake in an attempt to save his life. The outcome is a heavenly confection that marks Frank for life. He becomes a baker whose quest is the exact reproduction of the blitzkuchen.

In the late 1970s or early 1980s (chapter 3), Rozina Roy Whiteheart Beads wanders into Frank's bakery in Minneapolis. The two rather quickly fall in love. Frank is big, strong, handsome, gentle, and quick to grin and joke (chapters 3 and 11). On one of their walks, they consummate their love—in the rain, in a piece of woods near a playground. Once, when Rozin's husband, Richard Whiteheart Beads, and her twin daughters, Cally and Deanna, see the lovers walking in the

Frank Shawano

city park, Frank appears to Cally like the "deer man" in the Shawano family story her grandmothers tell (chapter 6). Frank also comes to their house, bringing the girls sugar cookies cut in fancy shapes. But after one of Frank's visits, Richard finds evidence of the affair, confronts Rozin, and forces her to break off the relationship.

Six years after his and Rozin's initial meeting, in chapter 7 Frank is diagnosed with cancer and given little chance of surviving. He goes to old-time healing ceremonies but has also finalized his will. One snowy March morning, Rozin announces to Richard that she is leaving, taking the girls, and going to be with Frank. But Frank's life changes again when Deanna dies that night in her father's botched suicide attempt. Rozin feels that their love has killed Deanna, so she goes home to the reservation, leaving Frank to endure his cancer treatments alone.

Seven years later, Frank has recovered from his cancer, but as Cally notes in chapter 11, the radiation treatments have destroyed his "funny bone" along with his tumor. Meanwhile, his brother Klaus has become a street drunk, and Frank has taken in Klaus's "wife," Sweetheart Calico. Frank's younger sister, Cecille, is also living in the rooms above his bakery when the eighteen-year-old Cally moves back to Minneapolis and stays with them. Both Rozin and Frank wish to know how the other is doing but are afraid to talk to one another. Frank's frustrated passion for Rozin is now invested in his search for the recipe of the blitzkuchen.

About two years after Cally's arrival, Rozin moves back to Minneapolis. One August evening, Frank shows up at the food co-op where she works and asks her to go out with him. She rebuffs him, but he keeps calling until she agrees to go to the state fair with him at the end of the month. There, an out-of-control Gravitron ride is a turning point for the couple. They begin having long talks on the phone as they are pulled back together by the "gravity" of their mutual attraction.

Frank proposes to Rozin beside a cliff in the state park. Their wedding is in the autumn (apparently the year following Rozin's move to the city) on the site of Frank's proposal. As a horde of family members busy themselves preparing for the reception, Frank is working on the wedding cake, his latest effort to achieve the perfect blitzkuchen. When Richard Whiteheart Beads interrupts the cliffside ceremony, Frank grabs him by the throat, wanting to push him over the cliff. Richard shows up again at the reception with a letter for Rozin saying that he has poisoned the cake. After Richard admits that this is a lie, Frank cuts, eats, and serves his masterpiece. His quest, he discovers, has been achieved—this cake is the true blitzkuchen, and the guests experience both its gustatory and its spiritual effects. The missing ingredient had been fear.

That night, Richard comes to Frank and Rozin's hotel room and fatally shoots himself outside their door. In chapter 17, the grieving Rozin isolates herself in her mothers' apartment and will not eat. She will not let Frank in nor speak to him. When, after ten days, Frank finally gets in, Rozin warns him that she is now seeing ghosts and tells him to leave, but he stays and cares for her.

Frank's patient love seems to heal Rozin. In chapter 18, they are living in the apartment over the bakery, and that Christmas, a few family members join them. The assembly sits at a table lovingly made by Frank himself, decorated with a candelabra he has given Rozin. Dessert is an elaborate twelve-layer cake Frank had toiled over the night before. The couple's profound affection for one another is obvious to their guests.

The next autumn, a year after the "kamikaze" wedding, Frank and Rozin each worry over the best way to celebrate their upcoming anniversary. Frank recalls Rozin's mentioning a big party, with all of last year's wedding guests invited, while Rozin knows that Frank would prefer a private celebration, untraditional and sexy. Putting each other's wishes ahead of their own, both make their plans. These plans collide into an ending that catches everyone by surprise.

Franz Waldvogel. In *The Master Butchers Singing Club,* the eldest son of Eva Kalb Waldvogel by her fiancé Johannes Grunberg, who dies before Franz's birth. In chapter 1, Fidelis Waldvogel marries the pregnant Eva and takes Franz as his own son, telling the boy nothing of his true paternity (chapter 7). In 1922, when Franz is three, Fidelis goes to America to carve out a decent life for his family. Within a year or two, Fidelis brings Eva and Franz to join him in Argus, North Dakota (chapter 3). As he grows, Franz helps Fidelis in his butchery business. One summer morning when Franz is in his early teens, he is helping Fidelis drive a sow into the killing chute when the sow charges Fidelis and injures his knee. Franz manages to thwart her third charge so that Fidelis can kill her.

As Delphine Watzka drives into Argus in the summer of 1934 (chapter 4), she sees Eva and the fifteen-year-old Franz laughingly engaged in a footrace across a field. He is described in chapter 5 as cheerful and always polite, with a slight German accent, strong with a wiry frame, graceful in all sports, and a town hero. He has three brothers: Markus, who is nine that summer, and twins Emil and Erich, who are five. By the following summer, 1935, the sixteen-year-old Franz is able to take care of customers on his own (chapter 6). During this summer he becomes enamored of airplanes and flying. As he talks with his terminally ill mother about flying, he decides that flier Pouty Mannheim must take her up. When Mannheim comes for them, Franz carries his mother to the plane. On July 4, Eva's morphine is stolen, and by the time more morphine arrives, Franz and Markus are holding onto their mother to keep her from killing herself.

The night Eva dies later that summer, in chapter 7 Fidelis and the boys are grieving beside her body as they wait for the morticians. When Delphine touches

Franz Waldvogel

Franz a roar of grief emerges—from him, perhaps from them all. At Eva's funeral, when Markus is unable to let go of the clump of dirt he is to throw into the grave, Franz pries open his fingers and shakes the dirt into the hole (chapter 9).

Sometime that spring or summer, Franz and Mazarine Shimek become sweethearts. Chapter 8 shows a glimpse of them that autumn (1935), riding her bike and kissing under a pine tree whose drooping branches hide them. In chapter 9, one Saturday in the summer or fall of the following year (1936), Franz brings Mazarine to the butcher shop and introduces her to Delphine. Delphine sees that Mazarine loves Franz, and because of Franz's tenderness with his mother, she knows that his feelings for this first love will run deep. That fall, the banker's daughter Betty Zumbrugge pays particular attention to football hero Franz, but he still has eyes only for Mazarine. One wet evening in November, in their pine needle–covered rendezvous, Mazarine's touching arouses Franz. When Franz gets home that night, he finds the place deserted and knows something is wrong. Thinking of the pleasure he has been taking with Mazarine while his family is in trouble makes him ashamed.

In chapter 10, Franz's shame keeps him from talking to Mazarine, and he begins to allow Betty Zumbrugge to give him rides. One day they pass Mazarine on the road, and she and Franz see each other. During the Christmas holidays, after a disastrous date with Betty, Franz gets out of the car and walks six miles through the bitter cold to the Shimek house, but Mazarine refuses to accept him back (chapter 11).

In chapter 12, one February sometime after that Christmas, Fidelis and Delphine take Tante and the three youngest boys to Chicago in preparation for their travel to Germany, while Franz stays in Argus to take care of the butcher shop. A few days later, when Delphine goes to check on Markus (who fell ill and did not go to Germany), in chapter 13 she points out to Franz several things that are going undone at the shop. When Fidelis and Delphine decide to marry and set a wedding date, they announce their plans to Franz and Markus. Franz feigns indifference, but the real reason for his unhappiness is that after his rejection by Mazarine, he realizes how much he loves her. He assuages his loss by learning to fly Pouty Mannheim's plane. When Fidelis and Delphine marry (probably that fall), Franz leaves to join the air corps.

We learn in chapter 14 that although Franz is a pilot in World War II, flying does not protect him from the horrors of war. He sees his fellow pilot friends **Schumacher** and **Tom Simms** die, and twice his own plane is downed. The second time, the apparently bodily presence of his mother comforts him. When Franz returns to Argus on leave in the spring of 1944, he goes to see Mazarine as soon as he arrives. The two become lovers, and before Franz leaves, Mazarine is pregnant.

He writes her regularly and sends her an engagement diamond. When Mazarine is seven months pregnant, Franz sends a long letter suggesting that the war is almost over. Apparently Delphine has told Franz who his father was, because he and Mazarine name their baby boy Johannes (see chapter 15). The next spring, Franz writes that the European war has ended, but Franz does not return safely home. After the war's end, he suffers a severe head injury in a freak accident at an airfield. Readers are not given the whole story, just a glimpse, full of foreboding, of Mazarine's first visit to the hospital and the comment in chapter 15 that "Franz had come home only to fade from life in bewildered anger" (*MBSC*, 377).

By the mid-1950s (chapter 16), Mazarine is supporting herself by running a plant shop with Delphine.

Fritzie Kozka. Wife of Pete Kozka and mother of Sita Kozka. Pete and Fritzie operate Kozka's Meats in Argus. Fritzie is described in chapter 2 of *Tracks* as a string-thin blond chain-smoker. When Fleur Pillager comes to work at the butcher shop in the summer of 1913, Fritzie lets her live on the shop property, teaches her to cut meat, and gives her a black umbrella. While Fritzie and Pete are gone to Minnesota in August, their shop is destroyed by a tornado. When they return, Fleur is gone, and they find their three male employees—Lily Veddar, Tor Grunewald, and Dutch James—frozen inside the meat locker. Only Dutch survives.

We learn in chapter 3 of *The Master Butchers Singing Club* that during the 1920s and early 1930s, Fritzie and Pete raise purebred chow dogs. The progenitor of the line is named Hottentot. By the early 1930s, the rivalry between Pete and the other Argus butcher, Fidelis Waldvogel, turns hostile when Fidelis allows Hottentot to drag home reeking bones and offal from his shop. At Fritzie's prodding, Pete retaliates by dumping some of the rotting mess in the Waldvogels' bed. When Fidelis continues to let Hottentot drag home rotting pieces of animals, the Kozkas build a pen for the dog, to no effect. Eventually Hottentot turns wild, and the Kozkas raise German shepherds instead (chapters 5 and 7).

In "The Branch" and chapter 1 of *The Beet Queen*, in 1932 Fritzie and Pete take in the eleven-year-old Mary Adare, one of the children abandoned by their mother, Fritzie's sister, Adelaide Adare. Fritzie puts ads in the newspaper in Minneapolis, where Mary's baby brother had been kidnapped, offering a reward for information leading to his recovery. In chapter 3, Fritzie shows Mary a postcard from Adelaide asking about the children, a postcard to which Mary responds. When Mary is eighteen (about 1939), in chapter 4 Fritzie suffers a nearly fatal pulmonary hemorrhage and finally stops smoking. Over the following months, the wiry Fritzie softens, gaining weight and color. Months later, she and Pete move to Arizona for her health, and they leave the butcher shop to Mary.

Fritzie Kozka

After Fritzie and Pete leave, in chapter 5 (1950) the adoptive mother of Mary's now-grown baby brother attempts to contact Fritzie, but Fritzie never receives the letter. The suntanned Fritzie and Pete attend Sita's wedding to Jimmy Bohl. When Sita continues to be childless, her mother asks if she is violating the church's injunction against birth control (chapter 13). Fritzie is also mentioned briefly in chapters 10 and 11.

Years later, in 1995, in "A Wedge of Shade" [3] in *Tales of Burning Love,* Mary recalls Fritzie and Pete's leaving the butcher shop to her, though she does not mention them by name.

Fulmer, Dr. Specialist in male diseases who attends to John James Mauser in *Four Souls.* When Mauser is well enough from his post–World War I ailment to exercise some independence, in chapter 4 he summons Dr. Fulmer, who comes from Chicago to Minneapolis for a daylong house call. At first Dr. Fulmer suspects gonorrhea, but after hearing about Mauser and his wife's practice of Karezza (intercourse without emission) he decides that the dammed-up sperm has collected in Mauser's brain, causing his illness. The following day, he administers leeches to Mauser's temples. A few years later, in chapter 10 Dr. Fulmer also blames Mauser's former practice of Karezza for the apparent retardation of his son.

G

Geeshik. See **Kakageeshikok.**

Geezhig. Son of Lucille Lazarre and older brother of June Morrissey in *The Bingo Palace.* His name means "day." In chapter 6, Geezhig warns June to leave the house when Lucille's boyfriend, **Leonard,** arrives. Geezhig himself has apparently left by the time Leonard rapes June.

George Many Women. One of the guides in chapter 1 of *Tracks* who help government surveyors divide up tribal lands. In chapter 2, he witnesses the fifteen-year-old Fleur Pillager's survival from her second drowning and hears her hiss, "You take my place." The fearful Many Women stays away from the water, but he ultimately drowns in a bathtub. Many Women is among the group of men in Pauline's death vision in chapter 6 whose deaths Fleur is presumed to have caused. See also **Jean Hat.**

Geraldine Nanapush. Wife of Nanapush's nephew, Judge Nanapush, in part 2.1 of *The Painted Drum.* Geraldine and her husband live in a prefab house on the site of Nanapush's old shack. She has a particular interest in assembling tribal history.

When Elsie and Faye Travers return the painted drum to the reservation, it comes to the Nanapush house, where the couple hosts a small gathering of reservation people with connections to the drum. Geraldine plies the New England women with questions and hears Bernard's stories about the Pillager family and the drum.

Gerry Nanapush. Son of Lulu Nanapush and Moses Pillager. Gerry is not the oldest child of Lulu and Moses. Their *first son* seems to have been born in about 1935 or 1936, while Gerry is born in 1945 ("Scales," "Wild Geese," and "The Island" in *Love Medicine*). Chapter 16 in *The Last Report on the Miracles at Little No Horse* gives us a glimpse of Gerry as a baby.

In "Lulu's Boys" in *Love Medicine,* we learn that Lulu's three oldest boys bear her maiden name, Nanapush. One of these Nanapush brothers is in junior college when Gerry is twelve. When Lulu marries Beverly Lamartine in "The Good Tears" and then discovers that he has another wife, she sends the twelve-year-old Gerry back to Minneapolis with him to make sure that Beverly divorces the other wife. While he is there, Gerry is thrown into detention, an event Lulu blames on Beverly.

According to "Crossing the Water" in *Love Medicine,* when Gerry is just out of high school he has an affair with June Morrissey Kashpaw, which produces a son, Lipsha, born in 1965. About the time June's pregnancy begins to show, Gerry leaves. Shortly thereafter, possibly in 1964 or 1965, Gerry kicks a *cowboy* in the groin in a drunken fight, as recorded in "Scales." The cowboy presses charges, and Gerry is sentenced to three years in prison. He prolongs his sentence indefinitely, however, by continuing to escape, boasting that no prison can hold a Chippewa (see also "The Bridge").

Gerry's escapes turn him into a Chippewa hero ("Lulu's Boys" and "Crossing the Water" in *Love Medicine*). Whenever he is out of prison, Gerry is involved in a series of speaking engagements ("A Wedge of Shade" [3] in *Tales of Burning Love*). One of his supporters is Dot Adare, a student at the University of Minnesota. Their relationship begins one night at a Howard Johnson's in Grand Forks after one of his speeches.

Early in 1980, Gerry impregnates Dot on her visit to the state prison ("Scales" in *Love Medicine*). He escapes at least twice that next year to be with her. One cold autumn day, Gerry shows up at Dot's job and stays with her until she goes into labor. At the hospital, just after Dot gives birth to their daughter, Shawn, two officers arrive, but Gerry eludes them and escapes. Dot later hears that Gerry has been recaptured and also that he is said to have killed a state trooper and has been taken to a maximum-security prison in Marion, Illinois.

In "The World's Greatest Fishermen" in *Love Medicine* (1981), Gerry's son,

Gerry Nanapush

Lipsha Morrissey, wishes he knew his father. In "Crossing the Water" (1984), Lulu tells him who his father is, and Lipsha leaves home to look for Gerry. While being transferred from Marion to North Dakota, Gerry escapes. He goes to the Twin Cities apartment of King Kashpaw, June Kashpaw's legitimate son, to even an old score—King had betrayed Gerry in prison. Gerry finds Lipsha there, and he, Lipsha, and King play a game of five-card stud for the car King had bought with June's insurance money. Lipsha wins the car. When the police arrive, Gerry disappears. As Lipsha is driving "June's" car toward home, he discovers that Gerry has stowed away in the trunk. Lipsha drives Gerry to the Canadian border, where he disappears into the woods, on his way to see his wife and daughter.

In chapter 1 of *The Bingo Palace,* Gerry has recently been recaptured. In chapter 21, in his prison cell, he longs for Dot, his children, and June. (According to this chapter, Gerry and Dot are divorced, and he is aware that she has remarried. But in "A Wedge of Shade" [3], "Caryl Moon" [8], and "February Thaw" [40] in *Tales of Burning Love,* Dot remarries without divorcing Gerry.) Because of a tribal request initiated by Lulu, Gerry is transported to a Minnesota prison, and when the small aircraft transporting him is caught in a January storm and goes down, Gerry escapes. (The year appears to be in the late 1980s in *The Bingo Palace* but is 1995 in *Tales of Burning Love.*)

Gerry calls Lipsha from Fargo in chapter 22 of *The Bingo Palace,* but Lipsha does not fully understand his instructions in the old language. The two finally find each other the following night in a Fargo alley, but they are without transportation. In chapter 24, they steal a white car and are astonished when a man chases them and attempts to hang onto the trunk. Only later do they discover a baby in the backseat. Caught in a blizzard as they head north, Gerry and Lipsha follow in the wake of a snowplow. When they see June's ghost driving her blue Firebird, Gerry follows her off the highway, gets into her car, and drives away with her into the storm. That night in chapter 25, federal marshals come to Lulu's apartment to question her about the escape, but she merely confuses and misleads them. The following day, radio news indicates that the escape car has been found, but not Gerry Nanapush (chapter 26).

Two chapters in *Tales of Burning Love,* "Funeral Day" [23] and "Blizzard Night" [35], recount the story of Gerry and Lipsha's escape from the point of view of the man hanging onto the car, the baby's father, Jack Mauser, who is also Dot's new husband. Jack is also driving the snowplow that Gerry and Lipsha follow.

Tales of Burning Love also narrates these incidents from Dot's point of view. The radio bulletin announcing Gerry's January 5 plane crash is recorded in "Radio Bulletin" [11], and at Jack's supposed funeral, Lyman Lamartine gives Dot the news of Gerry's escape ("Satin Heart" [12]) and tells her she can find him at the B & B.

Dot is at "The B & B" [16] in West Fargo that afternoon when a massive Indian woman enters, covered with ice. The "woman" is Gerry ("The Tale of the Unknown Passenger" [34]). Apparently June's ghost has driven him back to town. Dot buys Gerry a large pizza and leaves the room for half an hour to talk to him. They apparently devise a plan for Dot to pick him up later in the car.

As Jack's ex-wives head back to Fargo in his Explorer with Dot driving ("The Hitchhiker" [18]), a half mile from the B & B they pick up a large, blanket-wrapped hitchhiker, who we later learn is Gerry. He immediately goes to sleep in the space behind the backseat. (For more detail, see **Hitchhiker.**) About midnight, the vehicle becomes stranded in a snowbank. Several hours later, in "The Tale of the Unknown Passenger" [34], Gerry revives Dot, who has been overcome by carbon monoxide, and while the other passengers sleep, Gerry and Dot make love. Dot gives Gerry a key to her apartment. When the passengers are rescued in "The Disappearance" [36], Gerry slips away.

At 7:40 that morning, in "Smile of the Wolf" [38] Gerry lets himself into Dot's apartment to spend a few minutes with their daughter, Shawn. Later, when marshals break down the door, Gerry has escaped, apparently on the neighbor's snowmobile. While Dot is in the hospital recovering from her blizzard ordeal ("February Thaw" [40]), her mother assures her that Gerry is all right. As she takes a walk the next month, Dot is overcome with longing for him.

Gerry's other woman. Woman on whose "mercy" Gerry is cast after June leaves him, referred to in chapter 1 of *The Bingo Palace*. It is not clear whether the reference is to June's original leaving of Gerry to return to her husband in 1964–1965, or to her death in 1981. If the latter, then this woman would probably be Dot Adare, who gives birth to Gerry's daughter in 1980. If the former, there are no hints about her identity.

Girl who lived with the antelope. Ancestor of Sweetheart Calico, according to chapter 2 of *The Antelope Wife*. Jimmy Badger tells the story of this long-ago girl who, along with her human daughters, ran with the antelope in summer and stayed at camp in winter. (The old man's use of the word "human" may suggest that she had other, nonhuman children as well.) His story is congruous with both the story of Matilda Roy in chapter 1 and that of Blue Prairie Woman (as Apijigo Bakaday) in chapter 6.

Gitchi-nookomis. See **Medicine Dress.**

Gordie Kashpaw. Eldest child of Nector Kashpaw and Marie Lazarre Kashpaw; husband of June Morrissey; father of King Howard Kashpaw in *Love Medicine*. Gordie is born about 1935 (see "Saint Marie" and "Resurrection"). As recorded in "The Beads" and "The World's Greatest Fishermen," Gordie is jealous when

Gordie Kashpaw

his nine-year-old cousin June comes to live with his family in 1948. He and his sister Aurelia try to hang June, but their mother and older sister Zelda stop them. Yet, as Gordie recalls in "Crown of Thorns," he and June grow close. In "Flesh and Blood," for example (1957), Gordie and June go hunting together.

Gordie and June eventually run away to South Dakota and marry, but the marriage is troubled from the outset. Gordie recalls their awkward honeymoon in "Resurrection" and his physical abuse of June in "Crown of Thorns." June's comment about this abuse appears in "The World's Greatest Fishermen." Gordie and June have one son, King Howard Kashpaw. "Crossing the Water" recounts June's brief affair with Gerry Nanapush, after which she returns to Gordie. When June gives birth to Gerry's son, Lipsha, in about 1965, Gordie cannot handle rearing another man's child, so June abandons the boy. According to "The World's Greatest Fishermen," June eventually divorces Gordie, but he continues to love her.

June dies in early spring of 1981, and a month later Gordie begins to drink heavily ("Crown of Thorns"). Two months after her death, in "The World's Greatest Fishermen," Gordie arrives drunk at a family gathering. King, his wife, and their baby are there in a new Firebird that King has bought with June's insurance money. When King, also drunk, begins smashing "June's" car, Gordie runs out to stop him and holds him as King sobs.

One night, in "Crown of Thorns," the distraught Gordie calls out June's name, and she responds, first appearing outside the window and then breaking the glass and entering the house. He flees to his car and drives to town for more wine. After he runs into a deer and then beats it to death, he believes that it is June he has killed. He confesses the supposed murder to a nun at the Sacred Heart Convent and is subsequently picked up by police and hospital orderlies. According to "Love Medicine," he spends some time in the Bismarck hospitals. After his father, Nector, dies and Marie moves back into the family house, in "Resurrection" Gordie comes to the house begging her for whiskey. When she refuses, in desperation he drinks a can of Lysol. That night, sometime after midnight, Marie senses that Gordie is "chasing [his] own death" (*LM,* 275) and, as his heart quits, he catches it. Lulu Lamartine refers to his death in "Crossing the Water."

Grandma making soup. Grandmother who almost cooks the dog Almost Soup in chapter 8 of *The Antelope Wife*. Two other *grandmas* argue about whether he should be cooked or given to Cally Whiteheart Beads, and a *grandpa* insists he be given to Cally.

Grandma Mary. See **Mary (II) Shawano.**

Grandma Zosie. See **Zosie (II) Shawano Roy.**

Gravitron operator. Young man, apparently high on drugs, who dangerously accelerates the Gravitron at the state fair while Rozina Roy and Frank Shawano are riding in chapter 14 of *The Antelope Wife*. Many of the ***Gravitron riders*** get sick. One ***woman*** breaks the window of the control booth, and the ***people watching*** bring the ride under control.

Gregory Wekkle, Father. Priest who becomes Father Damien's lover in *The Last Report on the Miracles at Little No Horse*. In chapter 11, the bishop of Fargo, Bishop DuPre, sends Father Gregory to Little No Horse in the autumn of 1920 for Father Damien to train for ministry on an Indian reservation. Gregory is a tall, energetic, friendly young man who enjoys carpentry work. Gregory and Damien (née Agnes DeWitt) are from the beginning physically attracted to one another. At first their beds are separated by a wall of books, but the night the books fall, they begin a passionate love affair. The relationship grows through the winter and into the spring. It is Gregory who gives Mary Kashpaw the nickname "Mary Stamper," since she stamps down a path in the snow for him. That autumn (1921), Gregory receives a letter reassigning him to another location. He begs Agnes/Damien to leave with him and marry him, but Damien refuses.

After he leaves, Gregory sends Damien letters, which Damien does not answer. We learn about the emotional cost of this relationship first from Damien's point of view, as he becomes ill and even suicidal with grief. He eventually heals, though there are times when thoughts of Gregory bring a "crippling sickness of emotion" (*LR,* 260).

We learn in chapter 19 that the affair and separation take an even greater toll on Father Gregory. He has been living in Indianapolis when—forty years later—he returns to the reservation in the summer of 1962 to see Father Damien before he dies. Over the years, Gregory has damaged his liver with alcohol and is now dying of liver cancer. Damien nurses Gregory through this final illness and accompanies him to the Fargo hospital where he dies.

In March 1996 (chapter 20), when the black dog visits Father Damien, it taunts him with its victory over Gregory Wekkle. That summer (chapter 22), Damien recalls Gregory in his final musings before his own death.

Gus Newhall. Argus town bootlegger in *The Master Butchers Singing Club*. We learn from chapters 3, 5, and 8 that Gus is a fat man who is a member of Fidelis Waldvogel's singing club and is a good customer at the butcher shop. During his bootlegging days, chapter 16 tells us, scrap-picker Step-and-a-Half always finds bottles in his trash bin. By the fall of 1935, when Gus hits Tante Waldvogel with his car, he is now selling patent medicines instead of bootlegging (chapter 8). ***Apple Newhall,*** who serves Roy Watzka his meals in jail that fall, is probably kin to Gus.

Gus Newhall

One evening in the fall of 1936 (chapter 9), Fidelis tells Cyprian Lazarre a story about Gus going bear hunting and deafening *his Indian guide* by shooting close to his head. Fidelis later realizes that Cyprian is himself Indian and that the Gus Newhall story had offended him, so he tries (unsuccessfully) to smooth over the offense. When Markus Waldvogel becomes ill that same fall, the *Braucher* who comes to heal him in chapter 10 is the wife of Gus's cousin. At a singing club meeting after the German war begins (chapter 13), Gus makes off-color remarks about Germans.

H

Hadji. Foreman at the construction site where Albertine Johnson and Dot Adare work in the summer and fall of 1980 in "Scales" in *Love Medicine*. Erdrich thanks her own foreman, also named Hadji, in the acknowledgments section in *Tales of Burning Love.*

Harry Kuklenski. First husband of Anna Kuklenski Schlick and father of Anna's stillborn baby in *Tales of Burning Love.* "Eleanor's Tale" [20] tells us that Harry is one of the Flying Kuklenskis, a family of Polish acrobats that takes in the runaway Anna and trains her to be part of their show. During a performance in Fargo, lightning strikes the circus tent, and Harry falls to his death. He is buried in a circus cemetery in Milwaukee, alongside his uncle, the original Kuklenski. His pregnant wife survives the accident, but their baby is stillborn six weeks after Harry's death. Years later, as Anna is dying of congestive heart failure in "A Light from the West" [43], she feels Harry's hand grab hers.

Hat family. Reservation family that appears to profit from its cooperation with the government. In chapter 7 of *Tracks,* the Hats are one of the few families who have been able to pay their allotment fees and thus retain their land. See also **Jean Hat** and **Two Hat.**

Heech, Doctor (old). Argus town physician in *The Master Butchers Singing Club.* Doctor Heech has curly silver hair and is a singer. When Clarisse Strub is in high school in the 1920s, Doctor Heech privately treats her for syphilis (chapter 5). In the early 1930s, when Pete Kozka's dog, Hottentot, rips open Pete's arm in chapter 3, Doctor Heech sews it up and advises Pete to shoot the dog. Shortly thereafter, a sow Fidelis Waldvogel is butchering destroys his knee (also Hottentot's fault), and Doctor Heech elaborately pieces it back together and designs a brace for it. While he works, the two men sing. This incident gives Fidelis the idea of starting a men's singing club, of which Doctor Heech becomes a charter member. Heech is also one of Fidelis's regular customers at the butcher shop (chapter 5).

When Eva Waldvogel collapses in the summer of 1934 (chapter 5), Doctor Heech discovers that she has advanced cancer. Grieving at his own helplessness, he scolds her for not coming to him sooner. He calls the Mayo Clinic in Minnesota and has Delphine Watzka take Eva there for emergency surgery. We learn from chapter 7 that after her surgery and treatment at Mayo, Eva's cancer spreads, so Doctor Heech continues her terrible (and he fears hopeless) treatments in his office. All he can really do for her is to control her pain, so he teaches Delphine how to mix and administer Eva's morphine. Doctor Heech is not present at the Waldvogels' gathering on July 4, 1935, so when Eva's morphine is stolen, Fidelis and Delphine spend hours fruitlessly searching for him.

After Markus is buried in a collapsed hill in November 1936, Doctor Heech sets the complicated break in Markus's arm (chapter 10) but doesn't know what is causing the boy's illness. In chapter 13, Doctor Heech goes by to see the now-invalid Roy Watzka, who has resumed his drinking. Heech castigates Roy for the damage he has done to his liver and prescribes two things—absolute rest and little sips of alcohol, controlled by Delphine, to taper him off.

Heech, Doctor (young). A dentist, son of old Doctor Heech, and a regular customer of Fidelis Waldvogel in chapter 5 of *The Master Butchers Singing Club*. Because he is a vegetarian, he is suspected of being a Communist.

Hegelstead. President of the First National Bank of Fargo. He makes a huge housing development loan to contractor and one-time friend Jack Mauser in *Tales of Burning Love*. In "The First Draw" [14], Hegelstead releases a check for Jack's first draw on the loan. Two years later, in "Jack's House" [9] Hegelstead calls Jack the day after Christmas to warn him he must make a payment on his overdue loan by the first of January. Four days after Jack's apparent death, in "The Owl" [17] Hegelstead pays Jack a brief, secret visit and warns that the bank will foreclose the next day. Jack suggests that the only way Hegelstead can recover the bank's money is to finance Jack again in a big project with Lyman Lamartine. We learn in "Mauser and Mauser" [39] that Hegelstead does call Lyman and makes a financing deal in order recoup the bank's losses.

He Is Lifted By Wind. Brother of Fleur Pillager in the *Tracks* account of the family. Also known by his Indian name, Ombaashi, he dies of consumption in chapter 1 and is mentioned again in chapter 9.

Henri Laventure. Ancestor of Rozina Roy named in chapter 3 of *The Antelope Wife*. He is the bastard son of a **bastard daughter** of a **French marquis.** Henri steals

Henri Laventure

gold coins from a ***bishop*** and then escapes to Canada. Somewhere in "the north," possibly Canada, he marries ***six Ojibwa women,*** the oldest of whom is the sister of the windigo Shesheeb.

Henry Lamartine Junior. Son of Beverly Lamartine and Lulu Nanapush Lamartine, born in 1950 or 1951. He is named after Henry Lamartine, Beverly's brother and Lulu's deceased husband, because he is conceived the night of Henry's wake ("Lulu's Boys" in *Love Medicine*). Beverly, whom Henry Junior knows as Uncle Hat, lives in Minneapolis, but he returns to the reservation when Henry Junior is seven to take the boy back to the city with him. Instead, Beverly falls in love with Lulu again and returns to the city without his son.

Of his eight half siblings, Henry Junior is closest to his younger brother, Lyman, a relationship described in "The Red Convertible" in *Love Medicine* and chapter 14 of *The Bingo Palace*. Henry is a talented grass dancer, and he and Lyman travel the powwow circuit together. When Henry is about eighteen, he enlists in the Marines, but before he enters the service, he and the sixteen-year-old Lyman have a gloriously carefree summer (apparently 1969), driving their red Oldsmobile convertible all over the northern Midwest and even to Alaska. When they return home, Henry goes off to training camp and shortly after Christmas is sent to Vietnam. (His first overseas letter arrives in 1970.)

Henry Junior spends nine months in combat and about six months as a prisoner of war, released after the evacuation (*Love Medicine* "A Bridge"). Three weeks after his return to the States, in the spring of 1973, in Fargo Henry encounters the fifteen-year-old Albertine Johnson from his home reservation. They have sexual relations that night, although Henry knows she is a minor. In the motel, Henry has flashbacks of a bayoneted ***Vietnamese woman*** whose eyes had the same Chippewa slant as Albertine's, and he shrieks and lashes out when Albertine touches him in his sleep.

Henry Junior returns home in "The Red Convertible," changed from a once easy-going youth to a withdrawn, tense shell of a man. Lyman batters their car, hoping that repairing it will bring Henry out of his shell. The strategy seems to work, and in the spring in 1974, Henry and Lyman drive to the Red River. But after drinking and fighting with his brother on the riverbank, Henry jumps into the river and drowns. Lyman tries unsuccessfully to rescue him, then sends "Henry's" car into the river after him. Lyman is deeply affected by Henry's death, as recounted in "The Good Tears" and "The Tomahawk Factory." Henry Junior is mentioned briefly by Albertine and Marie Kashpaw in "Scales" and "Love Medicine."

In *The Bingo Palace,* Lyman keeps Henry Junior's memory alive by dancing the traditional grass dance in Henry's costume (chapters 2, 14, and 18). Lyman briefly sees Henry's face in a vision in chapter 13, and in chapter 18, during a religious fast, Lyman has a visionary conversation with Henry. He finally accepts his brother's death and decides to retire Henry's old dance costume.

Henry Lamartine (Senior). Second husband of Lulu Nanapush Morrissey; brother of Beverly Lamartine in *Love Medicine*. We learn in "Lulu's Boys" that Henry has an **older brother, Slick,** who dies in boot camp, that Henry and Beverly serve in the military together, and that they both fall in love with Lulu. After playing a game of strip poker with the two brothers, Lulu decides to marry Henry. That marriage is for "fondness," and Henry builds a house for Lulu and her children ("The Good Tears"). Henry dies in 1950 in a car and train wreck, an event that is recounted from a variety of points of view in "Lulu's Boys," "Flesh and Blood," and "The Good Tears" (with a passing reference in "The Plunge of the Brave"). Although Lulu represents Henry's death as an accident, others see it as a suicide whose cause is Lulu's promiscuousness.

Hildegarde Anne, Sister. Mother superior of the Sacred Heart Convent on the Little No Horse reservation from at least the 1910s to the 1940s. She is referred to by this name in *The Last Report on the Miracles at Little No Horse* and *Four Souls,* and simply as Superior in *Tracks.* When Father Damien first arrives at Little No Horse in March 1912, in chapter 4 of *Last Report,* Sister Hildegarde Anne is one of the *six starving nuns* for whom he says mass. Afterward, she gives him information about his predecessor and about problems among the reservation people. As Damien prepares to visit Nanapush and Fleur in the bush, Sister Hildegarde sketches a map for him (chapter 5).

The following spring (1913, chapter 7 of *Last Report*), Sister Hildegarde insists to Father Damien that Mary Kashpaw is mad. Later that year (chapter 10), Hildegarde is delighted at the arrival of a piano given to the Little No Horse church and wants a new statue of the Virgin to complement it.

During the influenza epidemic in the winter of 1918–1919 (chapter 7), Pauline saves Sister Hildegarde, who subsequently rejects Damien's suggestion that they send the girl away. *Tracks* chapter 6 records that by this winter Pauline has moved into the convent and declared her intention of becoming a nun. "Superior" (as Hildegarde is called in *Tracks*) considers Pauline a saintly novice and is pleased when Pauline says (falsely) that she has no Indian blood.

Hildegarde of *Last Report,* however, is less sanguine about Pauline's character. According to chapter 7 (see also chapter 8), one cold spring night in 1919 when Pauline is found in the church, naked, filthy, and raving, Sister Hildegarde treats the infection in Pauline's wounded hands and keeps the girl alive with a feeding tube, but when the reservation populace begins treating Pauline as a saint, Hildegarde

Hildegarde Anne, Sister

becomes disgusted with the girl's self-indulgent martyrdom. We learn from chapter 8 that Hildegarde takes notes on these incidents (which Father Jude reads in 1996).

The *Tracks* account of the injury to Pauline's hands is different from that in *Last Report* (see **Pauline Puyat**), though in both cases the Superior cares for Pauline in her illness. Also different in the two novels is the part the Superior plays in Pauline's vows. In *Tracks* chapter 8, Pauline takes the vows at Sacred Heart in 1919, receiving her new name from Superior's hand. Superior then sends her to teach in Argus. In *Last Report,* however, Sister Hildegarde does not participate in this ceremony; Pauline becomes a nun after moving to Argus (see chapter 16).

In a chronology used only in *Last Report* chapter 9, in 1919 Sister Hildegarde teaches Nector Kashpaw penmanship, which helps secure him a job working with tribal records. That same summer, having been distracted by the epidemic, Hildegarde is taken by surprise in chapter 10 when the landholdings of Nanapush and Fleur are seized. When in chapter 11 Father Gregory Wekkle comes to stay with Damien in the fall of 1920, Hildegarde lends him a bed, and when the priests visit parishioners in the deep snow that winter, Damien knows that Sister Hildegarde will worry if they camp out overnight. After Gregory leaves in late 1921, Hildegarde finds Damien in a trance. Over the next month, she notes with approval Mary Kashpaw's zealous care for him and sees that Mary herself is in a kind of trance. (This chapter also notes that Hildegarde is the only one of the nuns who does not think the silent Mary is dangerous.)

When the piano is moved into the new church in June 1922 and Damien finally plays it in chapter 12, Sister Hildegarde comes to listen but is frightened away by the snakes. That fall when the new statue of the Virgin arrives, Hildegarde is repelled but Damien refuses to return it.

One night in the early 1930s, in *Four Souls* chapter 11 Nanapush steals from the convent cellar a keg of communion wine made by Sister Hildegarde. When he returns to steal another the following night, Hildegarde locks him into the cellar till the tribal police come for him. After her return from Argus in the spring of 1933, Pauline—now Sister Leopolda—asks Hildegarde's permission to wear a potato sack, and Hildegarde sends her to Father Damien (*Last Report* chapter 16).

In the fall of 1941, after Nanapush's strange adventure with the moose in *Last Report* chapter 18, Sister Hildegarde removes fishhooks from his buttocks and makes a sarcastic remark about his sexuality.

Hitchhiker. Large, strange, almost spectral figure who materializes out of the storm as Jack Mauser's four living "widows" leave the B & B the night of Jack's funeral, in "The Hitchhiker" [18] in *Tales of Burning Love*. It is not clear at first whether the figure is a man or woman. Dot picks the person up and lets her or him ride in the small space behind the backseat in the Ford Explorer, where the hitchhiker falls asleep ("Secrets and Sugar Babies" [19]). This passenger is also mentioned in "The Red Slip" [21] and "Surviving Sleep" [24]. In "The Tale of the Unknown Passenger" [34], the stranger turns out to be both the pizza-eating Indian "woman" who blew into the B & B (see **Massive Indian woman**) and the escaped prisoner, Gerry Nanapush. He makes love to Dot in the car while the others are asleep. She had apparently known his identity all along and had planned the pickup. Later, when the passengers are rescued by a snowmobile squad, in "The Disappearance" [36] the hitchhiker (Gerry) "falls off" in order to evade authorities, and Dot protects him by claiming that the missing person is her mother.

Hmong grandmas. Old women whom Cally Roy hears talking in their native language as they work in their gardens the morning after she has accompanied Sweetheart Calico to the outskirts of the city in chapter 18 of *The Antelope Wife*. Seeing their connectedness with each other and the earth reminds Cally of her own disconnectedness resulting from the loss of her indis.

Hock, Sheriff. See **Albert Hock, Sheriff.**

Honey. Ira's cousin; nurse at the Indian Health Service hospital in part 3.7 of *The Painted Drum*. Honey tells Shawnee that she should not blame her mother for their terrible experience. Her interference irritates Shawnee, who sees that Honey likes to visit them because it makes her feel even more satisfied with her own family. Shawnee turns Honey off by clicking her "mute button."

Hottentot. A brown champion chow dog, the progenitor of a line of purebred chow chows raised by Pete and Fritzie Kozka in *The Master Butchers Singing Club*. Hottentot's two breeding mates are Nancy and Ziguenerin, the latter named for her passion for music. Introduced in chapter 3 as a greedy, suspicious, and evil-minded stud, in the early 1930s Hottentot exacerbates the rivalry between the two Argus butchers by dragging home reeking bones and offal Fidelis Waldvogel gives him just to annoy Pete. Pete's revenge, in return, alienates Eva. When Pete tries to take an oozing boar's skull from Hottentot, the dog rips open his arm, and his barking goads a sow in Fidelis's slaughter yard into tearing up Fidelis's knee. By 1934 (chapter 5), the Kozkas have given up chow breeding. Hottentot now runs wild, and all his offspring bite their owners. By 1935 (chapter 7) Hottentot is the head of a pack of wild dogs, which in chapter 8 kill the Waldvogel boys' chinchillas. When Fidelis lures and kills the dogs, Hottentot is apparently the big brown one he shoots first.

Hugo LaCombe, Father. Reservation priest at Little No Horse before Father Damien. We learn in chapter 8 of *The Last Report on the Miracles at Little No Horse* that in his youth Father Hugo sleeps in a coffin and that his reservation flock reveres

Hugo LaCombe, Father

him for bringing luck to their buffalo hunts. When he accompanies them on one of their final hunts, LaCombe observes the conflict within the Puyat family and that between the Ojibwe and the Bwaanug they meet. He intervenes in the latter to avoid bloodshed. After the slaughter of the buffalo, LaCombe also witnesses the bizarre behavior of the surviving animals. He records these events in letters that Father Damien finds and uses in his own histories.

There are a number of projects recorded in chapter 10 that Father Hugo begins and is not able to finish before his death: an Ojibwe grammar and dictionary, plans for a new church, and preparation for a printed letter to be sent out to subscribers in the Fargo diocese and beyond. We learn from chapter 1 that Father Hugo also sends a letter to (the original) Father Damien about the great need for his help at Little No Horse.

Chapter 1 of *Last Report* tells us that Father Hugo dies of the sweating fever in the winter of 1911–1912. (*Tracks* chapter 1 gives differing details and date.) The nuns believe that they could have saved Hugo, but not wanting to endanger them, he barred himself into his cabin (*Last Report* chapter 4). When Father Damien arrives at the reservation the following March, he sleeps in the older priest's deathbed.

In 1913 (chapter 10), Father Damien picks up Father Hugo's project of a letter to send to subscribers. (The piano comes in response to this letter.) He also carries to completion Father Hugo's plans to build a new church on a flat slab of rock that rises abruptly into a cliff.

I

Ida. Woman who sponsors the big memorial powwow in Montana that Shawnee Ray Toose nearly wins in chapter 16 of *The Bingo Palace*. In chapter 10, Zelda claims to know Ida and says that Ida will not pay the promised prize money, but this prediction seems to be mistaken. (There are a number of similarities between Erdrich's Ida and the Ida of Michael Dorris's *A Yellow Raft in Blue Water*.)

Ignatius Lazarre. Father of Lucille Lazarre and purported father of Marie Lazarre. (Events in *Tracks* show that Marie actually has a different parentage.) Marie refers to Ignatius as her father in "The Beads" in *Love Medicine* and calls him a "sack of brew" in "Flesh and Blood."

Ira. Mother of Shawnee, Alice, and Apitchi in *The Painted Drum*. Ira is probably born around the mid-1970s (she is in her late twenties in the novel's present time, sometime after 2000, in part 3.2). Her mother, Alice, has long been dead (3.7). Her father, whose name is not given, has died within the last few years (2.3, 3.7). Ira is thin and pretty, with wavy black hair and small up-slanted features (3.2).

As a young woman, Ira lives in the Cities with her husband and children, but after her husband leaves them, her father brings them back to the reservation and helps them in a variety of ways (see 3.4 and 3.7; see also **Ira's father**). When he dies, Ira becomes virtually destitute (see 3.1 and 3.2).

The present-time story of Ira and her children begins in parts 3.1 and 3.2. Shawnee is nine, Alice six, and Apitchi a toddler. In the bitterest cold of winter, Ira cooks a last pan of oatmeal for the children and leaves them in the house while she hitchhikes to town to get heating oil and food. She manages to arrange for heating oil to be delivered, but she has no money, and the children have been hungry for several days. By evening, now willing to sell herself sexually for food, she is in a bar talking to John String. He buys groceries for her and asks his brother Morris to drive her home, twenty miles into the bush.

In part 3.4, Morris's behavior on the drive makes Ira uncomfortable, but she learns something about his history and illness. When they arrive at Ira's house, it is burned to the ground, and the children are gone. Ira guesses (part 3.6) that they have walked the three miles through the woods to Bernard Shaawano's house, so she and Morris follow. At Bernard's, an ambulance has already come for the hypothermic children.

The children are kept several days in the Indian Health Service hospital in part 3.7. Shawnee and Alice are mostly all right, but Apitchi develops pneumonia. Social worker Seraphine String interviews Ira about her leaving the children alone for so long. Ira realizes that Shawnee is angry with her and is afraid that she herself might blurt out an accusation about Shawnee's burning down the house. In the hospital, as Ira talks with Morris, who has apparently sacrificed what vision he had left to help Ira, her feelings toward him warm. When she asks Bernard if they may stay with him for a while, he agrees and tells Ira again the story about old Shaawano's drum leading Shawnee to his house. He also tells her that it is time to take the drum out of retirement. It called to Shawnee, and now Apitchi needs its power. He brings the drum up to Apitchi's room, and the following morning returns to sing a healing ceremony.

As we learn from a letter Bernard writes the following September to Elsie and Faye Travers, who had brought the drum home, the tribal government has come through for Ira and her children and built them a new house (part 4).

Ira's father. The man who talked to wolves in *The Painted Drum*. In despair as a young man in part 2.3, he goes out to be with the wolves, hoping to learn how

Ira's father

not to kill himself. He stays on the ice for three days and on the fourth finally sees the wolves. For several hours they play and watch him, then go away. But one wolf returns several times, and the young man realizes that they can communicate with their minds. The man asks how the wolves can live with so much sorrow, and the wolf answers, "We live because we live" (*PD,* 120). They accept what comes without regret or fear. So the man rejects his idea of suicide and becomes a sun dancer.

This wolf man is an Ojibwe traditional. According to parts 3.2 and 3.4, he hunts and traps all year, builds his house with his own hands, and shoots a bear for the rug on its floor. In part 3.7, we learn that he is a religious man and spirit namer. He gives Morris String the name "ma'iingan" (wolf) for protection during the war. The wolf man also has a sacred pipe, and he teaches Morris some of the songs used with old Shaawano's ceremonial drum.

We also learn in part 3.7 that the wolf man marries a woman named Alice, and they have a daughter, Ira. Alice dies when Ira is still young. When Ira marries and has three children, Shawnee, Alice, and Apitchi, her father gives spirit names to at least the older two. Ira's family lives in the Cities, but when her husband leaves them, her father brings them back to his cabin on the reservation and gives them all of his pension and social security money. He also takes care of the children so Ira can work (see 3.4).

Just a few years before the present time of the novel, this man, now old, is hospitalized for a few weeks before dying at home (2.3, 3.7). (One gauge of how recently he has died is the present age of his youngest grandchild. Ira is at least pregnant with the toddler Apitchi when her father brings them back to the reservation.) While the old man is hospitalized, his friend Bernard Shaawano sits with him at night and hears his story of the wolves. Some years later, his grandchildren are in the same Indian Health Service hospital after a house fire. Ira grieves that all her father's things are burned up, until she remembers that his ceremonial pipe is hidden in the woods.

Erdrich gives us a multitude of hints about this character but never tells us who he is. This is the pattern she had used with the character of Jack Mauser's mother in *Tales of Burning Love,* only dropping hints there but not revealing her identity until a later novel. Since Erdrich similarly arouses our curiosity in *The Painted Drum,* the reader wonders if a later novel will reveal the identity of Ira's father. As a traditional associated with the drum and a sacred pipe, is he related to the Ruse family, who protected the drum wood and smoked the pipe with it? to old Shaawano, who made the drum? or to the String family, who kept its songs?

Irene Toose. Mother of Shawnee Ray, Mary Fred, and Tammy Toose. After her first husband (Toose) dies, in chapter 2 of *The Bingo Palace* she marries

Elward Strong Ribs and moves with him to Minot, leaving her daughters on the reservation—Shawnee Ray still in high school and pregnant. In chapter 10, Shawnee Ray misses her mother, who now puts her new husband's needs before those of her daughters.

Isabel Kashpaw. Daughter of Regina Puyat and a Kashpaw man; older sister of Russell Kashpaw in *The Beet Queen*. In chapter 2 of *The Beet Queen,* Regina marries Dutch James, gives birth to his daughter, Celestine, and then brings three other children whom Dutch knows nothing about to Argus from the reservation. Only two of these three children are named in this chapter, Isabel and Russell. Their last name is Kashpaw, and *Tracks* chapter 2 indicates that Regina's Kashpaw husband (thus Isabel's father) goes to Montana before Regina moves to Argus. See **Montana Kashpaw.** (For the possible identity of the third sibling and variations in the family structure, see **Puyat family.**)

Chapter 2 of *The Beet Queen* reveals that Regina dies when Isabel's half sister, Celestine, is still small, and Isabel rears the child. She is a lenient guardian, letting Celestine do as she pleases. In chapter 7, we learn that Isabel marries a Sioux man, moves to South Dakota, and dies violently in some way. Russell goes to South Dakota but is unable to learn anything about her family or her death. In chapter 13, Isabel's ghost seems to beckon Russell onto the death road while he is taking part in the Beet Parade.

Izear Lazarre. Marries Sophie Morrissey in chapter 7 of *Tracks*. He has already been married, is rumored to have killed his first wife, and brings his six unruly children to the new marriage. When he moves into Bernadette's house with his children, Bernadette moves to town, leaving the house to him, Sophie, Clarence, and Clarence's new *Lazarre wife.*

J

Jackie and Ruby. Rozina Roy's two oldest cousins, sisters who are close in age in *The Antelope Wife*. They help with the preparations for Rozin's wedding in chapter 16. They may also be the cousins who put Rozin into the shower after Richard Whiteheart Beads's suicide.

Jack Mauser. Highway and housing contractor; husband successively to June Morrissey Kashpaw, Eleanor Schlick, Candice Pantamounty, Marlis Cook, and Dot Adare Nanapush. Virtually his entire story appears in *Tales of Burning Love,* but *The Last Report on the Miracles at Little No Horse* records his birth, apparently in 1941 (see chapter 15 of *Last Report*). The account in *Tales,* however, suggests a

Jack Mauser

later birth date. According to "Easter Snow" [1] in *Tales,* Jack is in his early thirties in 1981, which would put his birth date around 1950 or just before. Jack's legal name is John J. Mauser ("Jack's House" [9] in *Tales*). He is described in "Candice's Tale" [25] as a big man, tough and muscular, and "Marlis's Tale" [27] tells us that he is rugged, with brown hair and dark eyes.

The little we know about Jack's forebears from *Tales of Burning Love* is revealed through hints found in the following chapters: "A Wedge of Shade" [3]; "The First Draw" [14]; "The Owl" [17]; "The Red Slip" [21]; and "Mauser and Mauser" [39]. This novel tells us only that *his ancestors* are an assortment of big-shot and little-shot people, including North Dakota dirt farmers, Indians, and a railroad executive. Jack is part German through his father, who is identified in this novel only as the "big Mauser" and the son of "the original John Mauser." His mother, Mary Stamper, is an Indian, her family a mixture of several tribes. She is from the reservation, and Jack himself is an enrolled member of the Ojibwe nation. When Jack remembers his mother's face, it reminds him of the face of Sister Leopolda, who is a Puyat. When he whispers his mother's name to Celestine in "A Wedge of Shade" [3], she responds that she is a Kashpaw, so she and Jack are probably kin (actually, she is a Puyat). When he sees Lipsha Morrissey, who has a Pillager father, Jack thinks that he may be a cousin. The owners of the land where Lyman Lamartine intends to build his new casino—one of whom is a Pillager—are said to be Jack's relatives. Jack's specific connections with these reservation families, however, are not made clear in *Tales.*

The Last Report on the Miracles at Little No Horse, published five years after *Tales,* gives more information about Jack's parentage, filling in gaps created by the tantalizing hints in *Tales* and revealing previously unknown connections between Jack and some of Erdrich's familiar reservation characters. To begin tracing these links, see **Jack Mauser's father** and **Mary Stamper.**

We learn a little about Jack's childhood through his memories, especially memories of his mother, a strong but gentle woman, who, he recalls in "Blizzard Night" [28] in *Tales,* would break a path to school for him through the snow. But Jack's primary memories of his mother are painful. Every autumn she would experience catatonic spells in which she relived the early loss of her parents. In "The Owl" [17], Jack remembers his father's leaving him at age six at his Aunt Elizabeth's house to take Jack's mother to the hospital for shock treatments. Jack's aunt is strict and stingy, and he is miserable living with her. He waits for his parents to come back for him, but apparently they never do, since in "Best Western" [28] Jack seems to be living with his aunt during some of his grade school years. He finally runs away from her to live with her brother, his Uncle Chuck Mauser, on a farm near Argus. According to *Last Report* chapter 9, in 1950 when Jack is nine, his mother is released from the hospital and goes back to the reservation without him. After Jack is grown, he never sees her again ("The Owl" [17] in *Tales*).

In high school, Jack comes into his own as a football hero, lead tenor in the choir, and ladies' man ("Hot June Morning" [2], "Candice's Tale" [25], and "Best Western" [28]). One of the girls he dates is Candice Pantamounty. After graduation, he goes to North Dakota State University in Fargo, where he studies engineering ("Eleanor's Tale" [20]). While in college, he works as a part-time fireman in Fargo. Fighting a fire one bitterly cold November night (probably 1970), after being sprayed with water he nearly freezes to death. Anna Schlick, the wife of the fire chief, takes him home and thaws him out by giving him a warm bath and then crawling into bed with him. When her husband, Lawrence, finds them in bed together, in a fit of jealousy he disowns Anna and their daughter, Eleanor.

Eleanor Schlick resents Jack for his part in ruining her idyllic childhood. In "The Red Slip" [21], the teenage Eleanor sees Jack in a store and punishes him by stomping his hand into broken glass. Several weeks later, however, she calls him. On their first date, she loses her virginity to him in his Silverado pickup, the start of an on-and-off relationship. In one of his absences from her, Jack goes out to western North Dakota for a year (1980–1981) to work in the oil fields.

In the spring of 1981 ("Easter Snow" [1]), Jack is working a temporary job as a mud engineer (see **Mud engineer**). On Holy Saturday, he comes to Williston with a toothache, where he meets June Morrissey Kashpaw in a bar. Jack realizes that she is from his mother's home reservation and tries to hide his identity from her, telling her his name is Andy. After making the rounds to several bars, Jack marries June in a bar. He tries unsuccessfully to consummate the marriage in his pickup just outside of town. June wanders off, and although Jack tries to follow, when she leaves the road, he abandons her. She walks into a gathering snowstorm and freezes to death. (This scene is a replay from Jack's point of view of the opening scene of *Love Medicine*, in "The World's Greatest Fishermen.") Jack is troubled by guilt and seems to spend the rest of his life seeking to replace June with other wives.

When Jack returns to Fargo, Eleanor observes that he drinks too much and says strange things ("The Red Slip" [21]). That fall (pp. 238 and 244), she tells her parents that she is pregnant by Jack (a lie). She tries to break up with him, but he talks her into going to Florida, where they marry. The marriage is fraught with conflict until Eleanor leaves for a year in London. Over the years, through Jack's successive marriages, he and Eleanor continue to stay in contact ("White Musk" [4] and "Trust in the Known" [5]). According to "Night Prayer" [6], they even make love on a few occasions.

Jack starts his own construction company, Mauser and Mauser, based in Fargo

Jack Mauser

("The First Draw" [14]). His first big job is to build an economy motel ("Candice's Tale" [25]). Jack meets Candice Pantamounty at the town dump, where he has gone to shoot his dog. Candice, now a dentist, offers to fix his teeth in exchange for the dog, and Jack agrees. He and Candice date and eventually marry. In "A Wandering Room" [26], they go deer hunting together, after which he accidentally causes the death of her dog, Pepperboy, an event that contributes to the disintegration of their troubled marriage. Thus, the dog that brings them together ultimately helps drive them apart. We are not told how long Jack and Candice are married, but this is the longest of his five marriages ("Jack's House" [9]).

Sometime during this period, Jack buys land west of Fargo from his uncle, Chuck Mauser, and begins trying to get a line of credit to build a subdivision on it ("The First Draw" [14]). These efforts culminate in 1992 when Jack gets a huge loan from the bank for his housing development, the Crest, just as his construction business is about to begin a big highway project near Argus.

Two significant personal events also take place in the summer of 1992: Jack and Candice divorce, and Jack meets Marlis Cook. Jack's first encounter with Marlis occurs when he gives her mouth-to-mouth resuscitation after an accident, as recounted in "Marlis's Tale" [27]. She tries to sue him for her subsequent nerve damage, but he cures her. A few weeks later, Jack receives the first installment check of his development loan ("The First Draw" [14]). As he eats lunch and celebrates at a bar, Marlis walks in.

There are variations in the two accounts of what happens next. Marlis's account, which appears in "Marlis's Tale" [27] and "Best Western" [28], is more detailed. According to Marlis, as she and Jack drink together in the bar, he shows her his loan check and tells her he has just gotten divorced. After an afternoon and evening of drinking, they go to a motel, where he accidentally knocks himself unconscious and Marlis steals his check. When he comes to, she threatens him with statutory rape charges. The next day (day 2), she blackmails Jack into buying her a new wardrobe. After another evening of drinking, in "Best Western" [28] Marlis drives Jack to South Dakota where they are married by a justice of the peace early the next morning (day 3). They return to Fargo later that day, and while Jack sleeps off his drunk, Marlis secretly deposits the loan check into her own bank account. They spend the next month in Eugene, hiding out from Jack's creditors.

Jack's account of this same period, which consists of two brief paragraphs in "The First Draw" [14], is vague, perhaps reflecting his drunkenness. Some of the times and events in his account differ from Marlis's version. Yet the overall temporal structures of the accounts correspond. "The First Draw" reveals that it is August when Jack meets Marlis in the bar and September when he returns to Fargo, dates that agree with Marlis's reference to a month's absence from the city. Back in Fargo, when Jack finds his car, Candice is in the front seat. She drives him to work and takes his car keys. Enraged, Jack jumps on a bulldozer and strips one of his uncle's sunflower fields.

Over the next two years, while Jack oversees construction on the Argus interstate access and his new subdivision, he and Marlis also go on the road as a musical duo, Jack singing, Marlis playing the piano. In the winter of 1993–1994 (probably after Christmas), Jack realizes at a gig in Minneapolis–St. Paul that Marlis has stolen his loan check, and they begin to fight. On the way to their next engagement, Marlis tells him that she is pregnant. Not believing her, he becomes abusive. Marlis gets even in a motel room in Billings, Montana, tying him up and subjecting him to some of the pain of being a woman. When their baby is born (in or before June 1994, "Night Prayer" [6]), Marlis names him John Jr. after his father, and in "The Owl" [17] Jack holds his son.

Jack's new employee Dot Adare Nanapush first catches his eye in the spring of 1994 as she charges across his construction yard ("Hot June Morning" [2]). Dot's accounting skills temporarily save Jack's failing business. Nevertheless, Jack fires Dot for falsifying records in favor of Caryl Moon, an employee who is Dot's short-term boyfriend ("Caryl Moon" [8]). Shortly thereafter, Moon turns his dump truck over on Jack's prized Cadillac. Jack locks Caryl inside the overturned truck and rides away with Dot—the start of their stormy relationship.

Jack marries Dot (his fifth wife) that June, after knowing her for only a month. In "Hot June Morning" [2], Jack comes to Argus to meet Dot's mother, Celestine James, but in "A Wedge of Shade" [3] he is arrested by Officer Lovchik as soon as he arrives at Celestine's house. Within the first week of his marriage to Dot, in "Trust in the Known" [5] Jack makes plans to see Eleanor, who is staying in the Argus convent. In "Night Prayer" [6], while hiding in the convent garden he overhears Sister Leopolda predict that he will be crushed by a woman, and he inadvertently contributes to her death. Afterward, Jack and Eleanor make love in her convent room. A few weeks later, in August, Eleanor calls Jack's house, wanting a ride from the Argus hospital. In "The Meadowlark" [7], Dot accompanies Jack to Argus to pick her up. On their trip back to Fargo, Dot learns that she herself is Jack's fifth wife, and both she and Eleanor are hurt to learn that he has a son.

Over the next few months, Dot leaves Jack four times, the final time on New Year's Eve. That night ("Jack's House" [9]), Jack gets drunk and thinks about each of his five wives. His new house catches fire, neither smoke alarm nor sprinkler system works, and the house becomes an inferno. He leaves some "evidence" to indicate that he has burned to death, and at about midnight he breaks out of a basement window naked. His ruse nearly works. Many of Jack's creditors believe that he is dead.

Jack Mauser

Caryl Moon gives the naked Jack a ride in "Caryl Moon" [13] and then beats him unconscious. Jack then drags his nearly frozen body to his company's garage, where he slowly recovers ("The Garage" [15] and "The Owl" [17]). Tipped off by Caryl Moon, Jack's banker, Hegelstead, comes to the garage and confronts Jack about his unpaid loans. Jack suggests that the only way Hegelstead can recover the bank's money is to lend Jack more money for Lyman Lamartine's big casino project. We learn in "Mauser and Mauser" [39] that, after a phone conversation with Lyman, Hegelstead accepts this suggestion.

Others, however, including Jack's wives, still think that he is dead. Eleanor's father, funeral director Lawrence Schlick, hosts Jack's funeral on January 5, 1995 ("Memoria" [10] and "Satin Heart" [12]). Planning to head north from Fargo (perhaps even into Canada ("The Owl" [17]), Jack decides in "Funeral Day" [23] to "borrow" Candice's car while she is attending his funeral. He also wants to see his infant son, John Jr. After a battle of wits and force with the baby's nanny, the formidable Tillie Kroshus, Jack steals Candice's white Honda, reluctantly kidnaps his son, and drives to the train station. When the car and baby are stolen by Gerry Nanapush, Jack unsuccessfully attempts to hold onto the car. (This scene is related from the point of view of Gerry's passenger, Lipsha Morrissey, in chapter 24 of *The Bingo Palace,* although there is a discrepancy between the accounts' descriptions of the man holding onto the car.)

In "Blizzard Night" [35] in *Tales,* Jack goes back to his garage, starts up his snowplow, and heads north in an effort to recover his son. Out on the interstate, he sees the headlights of a car behind him, driving in the wake of the snowplow. (One aspect of this story is difficult to explain. Jack, in a lumbering snowplow, is now in front of the car driven by Gerry, which had left Fargo first and is driving fast. Compare this *Tales* chapter with *Bingo Palace* chapter 14.) When the car's headlights disappear, Jack begins to wonder if his son might be in that car, and he turns back to search for it. With the help of June Morrissey's ghost, just before dawn the following day (January 6) Jack finally locates the white car, drags Lipsha Morrissey to the cab of the snowplow and continues driving north, only then discovering that John Jr. is zipped safely inside Lipsha's jacket. That morning, in "Mauser and Mauser" [39] Jack, Lipsha, and the baby drive onto the reservation. The following day (January 7), Jack makes a deal with Lyman Lamartine to be the contractor for Lyman's tribal casino.

In "Spring Morning" [41] that same year, Candice and Marlis buy a house in Jack's new development. One Saturday in March, Jack visits his son at the house and makes love to Marlis. In "Spring Afternoon" [42], Jack goes to Candice's office to have a tooth repaired.

In April, while Jack's construction crew is moving a new statue to the Argus convent in "The Stone Virgin" [44], Caryl Moon drops the statue on Jack. This incident seems to be a fulfillment of Sister Leopolda's prophecy that Jack will be crushed by a woman, but miraculously, he survives virtually unhurt. This near-death accident with the statue is referred to briefly in chapter 8 of *The Last Report on the Miracles at Little No Horse* without giving Jack's name. In "A Last Chapter" [46], Jack visits Eleanor and they make love—this time, with a difference. Having survived fire and ice, Jack is a reborn man.

Jack Mauser's father. German man referred to in "The Owl" [17] in *Tales of Burning Love* only as "the big Mauser." In this chapter, Jack recalls the time his father leaves him, at age six, with Aunt Elizabeth. "Candice's Tale" [25] mentions that Jack inherited his taste for sweets from his father. In the later novels *The Last Report on the Miracles at Little No Horse* and *Four Souls,* we learn much more about this person. See **John James Mauser II.**

Jack Mauser's grandfather. Referred to in *Tales of Burning Love* only as Jack's "big white German grandfather" ("The First Draw" [14]) and "the original John Mauser" ("The Owl" [17]). This obliquely mentioned grandfather becomes a significant character in Erdrich's later novels *The Last Report on the Miracles at Little No Horse* and *Four Souls.* See **John James Mauser.**

Janice. One of the family members who, together with Chook, is supposed to bring turkey to Rozina Roy and Frank Shawano's wedding in chapter 16 of *The Antelope Wife.* See also **Chook's wife.**

Jean Hat. Guide who helps government surveyors divide tribal lands in chapter 1 of *Tracks.* In chapter 2, Hat and **an unnamed man** rescue Fleur Pillager as a child from her first drowning. Hat is later run over by his own surveyor's cart and thereby takes her place on death's road. The other man simply wanders off and disappears. In chapter 3, Hat's ghost is seen emerging from the bushes where he died, one of several uncanny occurrences marking Fleur's return to the reservation in 1913. In Pauline Puyat's death vision in chapter 6, he is among the group of men whose deaths Fleur is presumed to have caused. See also **George Many Women, Hat family,** and **Two Hat.**

Jewelers. A *Fargo jeweler* cleans and repairs Adelaide Adare's garnet necklace, which Sita Kozka has redeemed from a Minneapolis pawn shop, in chapter 5 of *The Beet Queen.* Sita is wearing the gleaming necklace when she dies (chapter 13). Years later, a *Fargo jeweler* sells Jack Mauser the expensive wedding ring that he gives to Dot. He shows up at Jack's funeral in "Satin Heart" [12] in *Tales of Burning Love,* demanding the ring back, since Jack had made only three payments on it.

Jewelers

The ring Cyprian Lazarre buys for Delphine Watzka for Christmas in 1936, in chapter 9 of *The Master Butchers Singing Club,* is the **Argus jeweler**'s favorite.

Jewett Parker Tatro. Indian agent for the Little No Horse reservation. Tatro is apparently the agent, or one of the agents, described in *Tracks* as being responsible for the Indians' losing much of their land. See **Agent.** In chapter 10 of *The Last Report on the Miracles at Little No Horse,* Tatro is one of the many people to whom Father Damien writes when Nanapush's and Fleur Pillager's lands are taken in 1919. The futility of this effort is evident in chapter 1 of *Four Souls,* where John James Mauser bribes Tatro to help him acquire Fleur's land. (See also chapter 7.)

The story of Tatro's own acquisition and loss of Fleur's land is told in chapter 12 of *The Bingo Palace* and then again in more (and altered) detail in chapter 15 of *Four Souls.* After retiring as Indian agent, Tatro stays on at the reservation. When Mauser also loses Fleur's land to taxes, Tatro buys it from the state. As owner of the Wild Goose bar, Tatro also acquires the heirlooms of desperate Indians and hangs them from the wall of his bar. Both novels' accounts tell us that Tatro makes plans to move back to New England, but *Four Souls* says that he stays because the pain imbedded in his wrongful possessions holds him. One example of such pain is the shame experienced by a Shaawano man in *The Painted Drum,* who in his drunkenness sells Tatro the tribe's sacred drum made by his father (see parts 2.1, 2.5, and 4).

When Fleur returns to the reservation in 1933 with her white suit, white boy, and white Pierce-Arrow, she begins frequenting the perpetual poker game at the Wild Goose (*Four Souls* chapter 15; *The Bingo Palace* chapter 12, has a different version). Tatro covets the car. One night Fleur's drinking and losing reels Tatro in, and he puts up his ill-gotten land to win the car. Fleur turns her place in the game over to the strange boy, who wins every hand. The next morning, in chapter 16 of *Four Souls,* Margaret, Nanapush, and Fleur talk about Tatro's folly and the "surprised malice" on his face.

We learn from *The Painted Drum* part 4 that shortly after this poker game, Tatro returns to his home in Stokes, New Hampshire, with his Ojibwe treasures, including the Shaawano drum. Decades later, after the death of his grandsons, estate dealer Faye Travers, herself a Pillager descendant, finds these artifacts in the Tatro attic, steals the drum, and returns it to the reservation (parts 1.2 and 2.1).

Jimmy Badger. Old medicine man to whom Klaus Shawano goes for advice at the Elmo, Montana, powwow in chapter 2 of *The Antelope Wife.* (He is probably the same as the **old man singing the stick game song** in that chapter.) Jimmy Badger is leaning on **his grandson** as he leaves the gambling tent, where he has won. He gives Klaus advice on catching antelope, but he warns him to stay away from the four antelope women, whose ancestry he relates to Klaus. After Klaus has kidnapped one of the women, the old man tells him to bring her back. Years later, in chapter 20, Klaus recalls Jimmy Badger's words: *"Bring her back to us, you fool"* (*AW,* 226).

Jimmy Bohl. Owner of several businesses in Argus and first husband of Sita Kozka. Jimmy begins dating Sita in chapter 5 of *The Beet Queen* after she breaks off her three-year relationship with a married doctor. When he proposes to her, Sita—a fashion model at the time—is not excited by the prospect of marriage to this unromantic steakhouse owner, but she eventually marries him. In chapter 7, Sita constantly criticizes Jimmy for the way he runs the Poopdeck Restaurant. He responds by overeating and gaining weight. When they divorce, Jimmy retains all of his businesses except the restaurant, giving the restaurant and the house to Sita. In chapters 8 and 13, we learn more about the house, which Jimmy builds as a kind of showplace, the largest home in Blue Mound. Jimmy is also mentioned in chapter 10.

Jimmy Bohl's brothers and cousins. The cousins and one brother kidnap Jimmy's bride, Sita Kozka, after their wedding and drop her off in front of a reservation bar in chapter 5 of *The Beet Queen.* The brothers are mentioned in chapter 13 as regularly getting drunk in Jimmy's recreation-room basement.

Johannes Grunberg. A German Jew; best friend of Fidelis Waldvogel during World War I and fiancé of Eva Kalb in *The Master Butchers Singing Club.* Johannes's story is told twice, very briefly in chapter 1 and in a little more detail in chapter 12. Johannes and Fidelis suffer through the agonies of the trench war together. Whereas most of Fidelis's trench mates hate him because his skill as a sniper puts them in danger, Johannes remains his faithful friend (chapter 13). Johannes twice saves Fidelis's life. Near the end of the war, when Johannes is home with Eva, she becomes pregnant. After he returns to the front, he suffers an abdominal injury. On their way home in the war's final days, Johannes and Fidelis take refuge from the guns and the freezing weather along with other fleeing soldiers in the ruins of an elegant house. As Johannes is dying to the "chimes" of breaking glass, he elicits a promise from Fidelis—to give Eva the news of his death and to marry her. He gives Fidelis a locket with Eva's picture in it and asks his friend to sing to him as he dies.

As soon as Fidelis returns home in November 1918 (chapter 1), he keeps his promise to Johannes—he gives Eva the news and later marries her. When Johannes's son is born to Eva the following year, they name him Franz, and Fidelis takes him as his own son. Sixteen years later, in chapter 6, when Eva is dying of cancer, Franz plans an airplane ride for her. As he carries her to the plane, Eva thinks of Johannes,

Johannes Grunberg

who died when he was not much older than Franz is now. Just before Eva dies that summer, in chapter 7 she tells her friend Delphine (for the fourth time) that Johannes was Franz's father but that the boy does not know this. Apparently, at some point Delphine gives Franz this information, since he and Mazarine name their own son Johannes (chapter 15). In chapter 12, on their return from Chicago, Fidelis tells Delphine the story of his marriage to Eva, beginning with Johannes's story. On that trip, after singing Markus to sleep, Fidelis hums a tune to himself, a simple song he and Johannes had sung at times of drunken forgetfulness.

Johannes Waldvogel. Infant son of Franz Waldvogel and Mazarine Shimek in chapter 15 of *The Master Butchers Singing Club,* apparently named after his paternal grandfather, Johannes Grunberg.

John James Mauser. Wealthy entrepreneur whose name becomes a symbol for white plunder of Indian land. According to chapter 6 of *The Last Report on the Miracle at Little No Horse,* Mauser is the descendant of "eastern mill barons and shrewd New York socialites" (*LR*, 106). He builds a fortune as a young man— through land speculation, the railroad, the lumber business, mining, and especially the acquisition of tax-forfeited Indian land (see also *Four Souls* chapter 4). Mauser's personal story is told in *Four Souls.* In chapter 8, he recalls that in his younger days he did "terrible things," yet he seems to have been rewarded with both luck and nine lives, as he evades death again and again. (He shares this trait with the woman he later marries, Fleur Pillager, and with their grandson, Jack Mauser.) There is irony in Mauser's plunder of northern Indian country, since what draws him there is the purity and spaciousness that he destroys (chapter 10), and he has a high respect for the intelligence of the people he plunders (chapter 2). One of the underhanded ways Mauser acquires Native land is by marrying a succession of Ojibwe girls, logging their land, and then leaving (chapter 3). He also offers the Ojibwe people papers to sign that they mistakenly assume are treaties (*Last Report* chapter 6).

Mauser is already acquiring land on Little No Horse reservation as early as 1912 (chapter 6 of *Last Report*). He is also co-owner of the Turcot lumber company, which is itself actively acquiring Ojibwe land (chapter 9).

Chapters 1 and 4 of *Four Souls* describe Mauser's marriage to Placide Gheen, whom he marries for her money. He lies to her family that he is the son of minor British royalty and a German industrialist (chapter 2). The two make a handsome couple, but when Mauser tries to make love to Placide, he discovers that she is frigid. Chapters 1 and 2 tell of the house Mauser builds for her (largely with her money) and the abuse of land, animals, and humans in its building. (See **Workers who build Mauser's house.**)

John James Mauser

Early in the marriage, Mauser serves a year in the trenches of World War I (chapter 2 of *Four Souls*). One day his friend Fantan is wounded by a sardine can struck by a bullet intended for Mauser (chapter 8). In gratitude, Mauser brings Fantan home to Minneapolis, determined not to part with him. After his war year, Mauser becomes chronically ill. In chapters 2 and 3, he suffers from profuse night sweats, chronic neuralgic pain, periodic convulsions, and a weakness that confines him to a wheelchair. A number of doctors try without success to understand this illness. It worsens over time, and Placide's sister, Polly Elizabeth, speculates that it is a result of gas attacks during the war. This explanation is reinforced in chapter 8 by Mauser's account of an attack after which his lungs are "shot" (*FS*, 97).

In the summer of 1919 (*Last Report* chapter 10), Mauser's Turcot lumber company buys Fleur Pillager's land, which has been confiscated for nonpayment of fees. Mauser himself does not come to the reservation (indeed, he is probably too ill to do so), but instead profits from the work of the land commissioner and tax collector. Mauser's company immediately sends loggers to strip it, taking the great oaks he covets for his house. When Fleur learns what he has done, she plots to destroy him and regain her land, and she begins her journey east to Minneapolis.

When Fleur arrives one snow-frosted day in 1919 or 1920, Placide's sister Polly Elizabeth hires her as the laundress. (For dating issues, see the discussion of the *Four Souls* chronology in the "Geography, Genealogy, and Chronology" section of this book.) Chapters 2 and 3 reveal that shortly after Fleur's arrival, Mauser has one of his convulsions, and Fleur restores him. When they are alone, Mauser speaks to her in the Anishinaabe language. Fleur begins to heal Mauser with traditional remedies and tapers him off his medicine. One night, hearing snores outside his door, he looks into the hall and sees Fleur, crumpled against the wall, fast asleep. He is caught by her beauty. Polly Elizabeth notices the way he now looks at Fleur and in chapter 4 warns Placide.

In chapter 4, Mauser calls in a doctor who specializes in male diseases. After Dr. Fulmer interviews Placide about her and her husband's practice of Karezza, sexual intercourse without emission, he decides that Mauser's illness is the result of this practice and begins an elaborate series of treatments.

One night, close to a year after Fleur's arrival, in chapter 5 Mauser is feigning sleep when Fleur slips into his room, puts a knife to his throat, and whispers that she has come to kill him. Mauser arouses her curiosity by saying that his spirit was meant to serve her, and he causes her to change her mind by promising to marry her, give her everything he owns, and become her animal, to do with as she pleases. Musing about his attraction to Fleur (chapter 10), Mauser says that he could not bear not to have her near because of something in her, "something that I went up north to have and only ended up destroying" (*FS*, 129). In chapter

John James Mauser

6, Mauser divorces Placide and marries Fleur. (We know from chapter 16 of *Last Report* that by November 1921 they are already married.)

Chapters 6 and 7 of *Four Souls* and chapter 16 of *Last Report* give us glimpses of the new couple's married life. They appear at gatherings of the highest level of Minneapolis society, where Fleur is received with "ironic curiosity" (*LR,* 259). Mauser also takes Fleur traveling and to concerts and museums. In a newspaper photo of the couple, Fleur's friends can see the hold she has on Mauser. Nanapush comments later that Mauser both "adored" and "feared" Fleur (*FS,* 72). Yet over time, he disturbs Fleur's peace as well. She seems overwhelmed by the extravagance of her circumstances, especially the exotic food. Mauser also seems to get the best of her in bed, so that she unintentionally becomes pregnant soon after the marriage and is confined to her bed. Mauser, however, is happy. He has always wanted an heir (*Four Souls* chapter 4). Thus, although Fleur has in some ways defeated him, in others he seems in control.

When the boy is born in chapter 6 of *Four Souls,* Mauser is fervently attached to him. But as the child grows, he becomes a fresh source of sorrow (chapter 8). At age two, he still does not speak, so Mauser begins taking him to various doctors. At first doctors say that the boy is normal or even advanced. But as his behavior becomes more erratic, they declare him an idiot. Dr. Fulmer blames the boy's condition on Mauser's earlier practice of Karezza (chapter 10).

Convinced that the child's condition is a punishment for his own evils, Mauser becomes a fervent Catholic (chapter 8). During the Depression, he suffers another kind of loss—his investments begin to fail, and he is forced to sell his ill-gotten land. Even his household is falling apart. His housekeeper is stealing, and Fleur pays no attention to household affairs (chapter 10). During these years, Fleur makes her demands—Mauser's car and the deed to her land, and that she will return to the reservation with his son. Mauser accedes to Fleur's demands, though he knows he will be unable to restore her land. (We learn in chapter 15 that he himself loses the land to unpaid taxes.)

In the spring of 1933, Mauser flees his creditors, and Fleur leaves for the reservation with his car and his son (*Four Souls* chapter 12; dated by *Last Report* chapter 16).

John James Mauser II. The son of John James Mauser and Fleur Pillager, born in Minneapolis. Erdrich uses this name for the boy only once, in chapter 8 of *Four Souls.* Throughout his childhood and teen years, this is only a name for the chimookomaan (white) records. His mother, who fails to give him a true spirit name, simply calls him "my son." Others refer to him in childhood as just "the boy."

Chapters 6 and 7 of *Four Souls* tell us that when Fleur's pregnancy is at risk, she is given whiskey to stop early contractions, and she becomes addicted. When the boy is born in 1921 or 1922, he is alcohol dependent and can be soothed only by a drop of whiskey. He subsequently ingests alcohol as he nurses his imbibing mother. The boy is fair and blue-eyed like his German forebears. His mother and father and Polly Elizabeth (Mauser's former sister-in-law) all dote on him.

When the boy is two, in chapter 8 he refuses to wean himself, and he is not yet talking. At first doctors say he is normal, but when he begins having spells of mental vacancy, they declare him an idiot. Even so, he is adept in math and under Fleur's tutelage becomes a skilled poker player. There are various explanations for the child's mental affliction. In chapter 8 of *Four Souls,* his father believes that the boy's disorder is a punishment on Mauser himself for his own evil past. In chapter 10, Dr. Fulmer considers it the result of Mauser's earlier practice of Karezza. In chapter 16 of *The Last Report on the Miracles at Little No Horse,* the people on Fleur's reservation say that the boy's strangeness is the result of Fleur's failure to follow necessary Ojibwe practices, including her failure to name him. Erdrich's readers may also wonder if his pre- and postnatal exposure to alcohol has contributed to his problems. Over the following years, in chapter 10 of *Four Souls* the boy's size increases at a bewildering rate as he develops unnatural hungers, especially for sweets. His vacant spells continue.

After Mauser's financial world crumbles, in the spring of 1933 Fleur takes his car and the boy and returns to the reservation. The primary accounts of this return appear in chapter 12 of *The Bingo Palace* and chapters 14 and 15 of *Four Souls* (also see *Last Report* chapter 16). Although the two accounts differ in several ways, there are certain details about the boy that Erdrich includes in both versions. In both, the boy is strikingly pale, he has an inordinate appetite for sweets, his hands are agile and swift, and it is he who wins back Fleur's land in the poker game with Jewett Parker Tatro. The morning after the poker game, Fleur and the boy go to Margaret's house (*Four Souls* chapter 16). When Margaret tells Nanapush to take the boy fishing, the child resists until Margaret's threat shocks him into obedience.

Fleur's son next appears in chapter 17 of *Last Report.* The year is 1940, so he is eighteen or nineteen. His neighbors now call him Awun (the Mist) because of his silence and elusiveness. Awun is huge and physically strong but his spirit remains hollow. Fleur has told him nothing of who he is, so he broods on his identity. He is said to be a "great weak thin[g]" looking for a "stronger counterpart" (*LR,* 277) as he wanders the reservation hiring out at various farms.

One morning in July 1940, Awun's work takes him to the convent, where he sees the physically powerful Mary Kashpaw chopping wood. Although he is much younger than she, he is smitten. That night he abducts Mary, dragging the sleigh

John James Mauser II

in which she sleeps out across the reservation sloughs. Mary wakes in fear and cuts the lines with her axe, thus freeing herself, but after brooding for an hour, she follows him. They make love that night, beginning "work on a tiny baby boy" (*LR,* 282).

This baby boy is not named in *Last Report,* but a comparison with *Tales of Burning Love* reveals that Awun and Mary's son is Jack Mauser, the protagonist of *Tales.* (See **Mary Stamper.**) We also know from *Tales* that Awun and Mary continue to live on the reservation after the boy's birth, since in "Mauser and Mauser" [39] Jack has childhood memories of the place.

Within a few years, however, the youth called Awun makes connections with his Mauser relatives in "The Owl" [17] in *Tales of Burning Love* and begins using his Mauser name. He is called "the big Mauser." When Mary begins having spells of rigid silence each autumn, he takes her to a hospital for treatment and leaves their six-year-old son with a Mauser relative, Aunt Elizabeth. When Mary is released from the hospital in 1950 (about three years later), she returns to the reservation without her husband and son. We hear no more of John James Mauser II.

John Jewett Tatro. Grandson of Indian agent Jewett Parker Tatro in *The Painted Drum.* John and his younger brother, **Burden Tatro,** are bachelors, last inheritors of their grandfather's estate in Stokes, New Hampshire. They are misers and hoarders, presiding over decades of accumulated objects they never use.

Burden dies first, and then late one winter in the early twenty-first century, John is killed by Davan Eyke's speeding Toyota (part 1.1). In part 1.2, the brothers' niece, Sarah, calls on the Travers estate business to evaluate and sell the contents of the house. Faye Travers finds in the attic a collection of valuable Ojibwe artifacts acquired by their grandfather on a North Dakota reservation. She oversees the sale of these items, except for a painted drum, which she steals and returns to its home (parts 1.2, 1.4, and 2.1).

John Mauser. See **Jack Mauser, John James Mauser, John James Mauser II,** and **John Mauser Jr.**

John Mauser Jr. Son of Jack and Marlis Mauser in *Tales of Burning Love.* He is referred to as "John Joseph Mauser" in "The Owl" [17] and as "John James Mauser Jr." in "Two Front-Page Articles" [37]. (His father's legal name is "John J. Mauser" [*TBL,* 115].)

In "Best Western" [28] Marlis realizes that she is pregnant with this baby near Christmastime, 1993. When she tells Jack about the pregnancy, he responds abusively. She considers having an abortion. When Candice Pantamounty learns that Marlis is pregnant, however, she wants to take care of Marlis and adopt the baby ("Baptism River" [29]). After the baby's birth, which has occurred by June 1994 ("Night Prayer" [6]), Marlis and Candice become lovers and thus his resident parents ("The Waiting Room" [31]). Over Candice's objection, Marlis names the baby after Jack, and in "The Owl" [17] Jack holds his son.

The following January (1995), John Jr. shows up in the care of his nanny at his father's supposed funeral in "Memoria" [10] and "Satin Heart" [12]. In "Funeral Day" [23], Jack comes to see his son but, in the process of taking Candice's car, ends up kidnapping the boy. Almost immediately after, Gerry Nanapush, newly escaped from prison, steals the car for a getaway vehicle, not knowing that the baby is in the backseat. Jack pursues the escape car in "Blizzard Night" [35] and several hours later rescues the baby, zipped inside the jacket of a nearly frozen young man, Lipsha Morrissey. (This story is told from Lipsha's point of view in chapter 24 of *The Bingo Palace;* see **Baby stolen in Fargo.**) Jack drives with Lipsha and John Jr. north to the reservation, where he phones the worried Marlis and Candice in "Mauser and Mauser" [39]. As he lies on the motel bed beside his son, Jack thinks about the name of his construction company, "Mauser and Mauser."

John Jr. is still nursing in March 1995, when Jack visits Marlis in "Spring Morning" [41].

John String. Son of Chook String and brother of Morris String in *The Painted Drum.* In the novel's present time, the early twenty-first century (parts 2.1 and 3.2), John is a handsome man in his early thirties. Though he has a job at the electric plant and lives in a prefab house, he is a traditional from a family of traditionals. He wears his hair long and is married to a healer, Seraphine, whom he met at a ceremony. Early one autumn, when two women from the East return the painted drum to the reservation in part 2.1, John is part of the small gathering that meets with them.

One bitterly cold night that winter, in parts 3.2 and 3.4 John meets the young woman Ira in a bar, buys food for her children, and has his brother Morris drive her home twenty miles into the bush. Later, at the hospital, Ira relates to Seraphine her encounter with John, and Morris phones him to say that he intends to marry Ira (part 3.7).

Johnny Mercier, Sheriff. See **Slow Johnny Mercier.**

Josette. See **Small Bird.**

Josette Bizhieu. Reservation gossip in *The Bingo Palace.* In chapter 12, Josette speaks to an owl at the church doorway. Both the owl and the mysterious deaths of *Josette's mother and niece* appear to be connected with the survival powers of the four-souled Fleur Pillager. Years later (probably the 1980s), now a resident at

Josette Bizhieu

the Senior Citizens, Josette spies on Fleur's descendants. She sees Lulu Lamartine mail a copy of Gerry Nanapush's Wanted poster to Lipsha Morrissey in chapter 1; she watches Lipsha try to heal Russell Kashpaw in chapter 7; and she is the reporting busybody when Lulu is arrested at the Senior Citizens in chapter 25. See also **Bizhieu family** and **Zozed Bizhieu.**

Jude Miller (Father). Son of Adelaide Adare and Mr. Ober; younger brother of Mary and Karl Adare; adoptive son of Martin and Catherine Miller; Catholic priest.

Jude is conceived shortly before Mr. Ober's death in chapter 1 of *The Beet Queen.* When he is born in Minneapolis in 1932, the destitute Adelaide refuses to name him and a month later abandons him and his siblings at the Saint Jerome's Orphans' Picnic. He is abducted by a young man who, we learn in chapter 2, is named Martin Miller. Martin steals the baby to replace the newborn he and his wife, Catherine, have just lost. Catherine clips out ads that the baby's aunt, Fritzie Kozka, has placed in the newspaper offering a reward for his return. The Millers, however, keep the baby and name him Jude.

Sixteen years later (chapter 4), Karl sees Jude—now a chubby, redheaded seminarian—at the Orphans' Picnic and recognizes him by his resemblance to Adelaide. Two years later, when Jude is about to be ordained as a deacon, Catherine writes to the Kozkas to reveal his whereabouts, but only his cousin, Sita Kozka, sees the letter (chapter 5). Sita attends Jude's ordination ceremony in Minneapolis, February 18, 1950, but she neither meets him nor tells his biological family his whereabouts. She writes Catherine Miller in reply but does not mail the letter. Thus Jude continues to be unaware that he is adopted.

In chapter 14 (July 1972), when Jude is forty and a priest, his ailing mother shows him the letter from Sita, which has finally arrived. Drawn by its contents, Jude goes to Argus, arriving on the day of the Beet Festival. He is in the grandstand when his niece, Dot Adare, is named Beet Queen, though he and his family members do not recognize one another.

In the summer of 1994, Father Jude is visiting Our Lady of the Wheat Priory in Argus when Sister Leopolda disappears in "Night Prayer" [6] in *Tales of Burning Love.* He at first supports the scientific explanation that she has been vaporized by a lightning strike, attempting to quell rumors of a miraculous assumption. By the following year, however, in "A Letter to the Bishop" [45], Jude appears to consider miraculous certain events surrounding the convent's new stone statue of the Virgin, and he suggests that the bishop investigate the history of Sister Leopolda, presumably to consider her for sainthood.

In 1996, the Church commissions Father Jude to conduct this investigation.

Jude Miller (Father)

Jude comes to the reservation in late March (chapter 3 of *The Last Report on the Miracles at Little No Horse*) to interview the ancient Father Damien as an eyewitness to Sister Leopolda's life. Their conversations over the ensuing days take on the nature of a debate—Father Jude citing miracles attributed to the nun and Father Damien insisting that the key issue is character. To illustrate his point, in chapter 8 Damien tells Jude a story about Pauline Puyat's (Leopolda's) family. When Damien tells him about Leopolda's abuse of Marie Lazarre, Jude tries unsuccessfully to interview Marie.

A week or so later (chapter 14), Father Jude meets Lulu Lamartine and is hypnotized. When he speaks at her culture class the following day, she is decked out in a red and silver jingle dress. Within the week, Jude realizes that, for the first time ever in his sixty-four years, he is in love. What makes this emotion even more remarkable is that his wished-for lady is eighty-two. (He thinks she is younger.) Jude interviews Lulu about her mother, Fleur Pillager, and at the end of the interview Lulu reveals that she is aware of Jude's attraction to her (chapter 15). In chapter 21, she takes him to the Sweetheart Bingo Bash.

A motif running through Father Jude's story in *Last Report* is his obsession with food. (See chapters 3, 8, and 20.) We also see that, despite his determination to use miracles to prove Leopolda's sainthood, Jude is consistently unwilling to believe in the unseen. In chapter 20, Erdrich weaves together these two attachments to the physical—Jude's physical hunger and his philosophical materialism. He is unwilling to believe in Father Damien's black spirit dog, and when Damien states his need to believe in the spiritual world, the frustrated Jude immediately thinks about his poor breakfast. When Damien states his desire for God to appear to him, Jude craves a hot roast beef sandwich. Then when Jude begins a disappointed reverie about Damien's "superstition" (*LR,* 315), he quickly leaves to seek a good meal.

Father Jude finds his stay at Little No Horse thoroughly unsettling. Father Damien's startling lack of orthodoxy (see especially chapter 14) raises uncertainties and doubts in Jude's mind, and his attraction to Lulu is terrifying. Jude's ministry in Argus had been predictable, and he longs to finish his work on the reservation and return to that "comfortable routine" (*LR,* 315). But he is failing at the task of gathering the information he needs. Thus, in hopes of completing his task, Jude decides to try again to interview Marie Kashpaw. This time Marie talks to him, and he learns the shocking truth that his candidate for sainthood was Marie's mother, who abandoned her.

Finally, the next day (chapter 21), Father Damien delivers the fatal blow to Jude's hopes for Leopolda's sainthood—he informs Jude that Leopolda was a murderer. Father Jude wonders what secret Leopolda knew about Damien that had made him withhold this information. When Jude finds Lulu's birth certificate, he decides

Jude Miller (Father)

(erroneously) that Damien is her father. That night, alone in the Little No Horse rectory, Jude faces the absurdity of his efforts—"Why this deep thirst to make a saint of this appalling woman?" (*LR,* 340). He then realizes that it is Father Damien, not Sister Leopolda, who is the potential saint.

Father Damien dies that summer. According to the epilogue of *Last Report,* Jude is present at the reservation convent in 1997 when a fax arrives to Father Damien from the pope—a reply at last to Damien's eighty-four years of unanswered correspondence. Jude has now moved permanently to Little No Horse to do further research on the possible sainthood, not of Sister Leopolda, but of Father Damien.

Judge Nanapush. Nephew of old Nanapush in *The Painted Drum.* We learn in part 2.1 that the family of this Nanapush nephew moves to Canada, then returns to the reservation for a powwow and stays. Old Nanapush apparently never learns of the existence of this nephew, who at the novel's present time lives with his wife, Geraldine, in a prefab house on the site of old Nanapush's cabin. One autumn in the early twenty-first century, when two women from the East return a sacred drum to the reservation, they bring it to the Nanapush house, where there is a small gathering of people connected to the drum. When the New England women tell of finding it in the estate of Jewett Parker Tatro, the judge recalls documents mentioning the old Indian agent's name.

June Morrissey Kashpaw. Daughter of Lucille Lazarre and Morrissey I; wife of Gordie Kashpaw and mother of King Kashpaw; lover of Gerry Nanapush and mother of Lipsha Morrissey.

As the daughter of an alcoholic mother, June suffers a childhood litany of abuse and abandonment. In chapter 6 of *The Bingo Palace,* Lucille's boyfriend **Leonard** rapes June. At various times June is found freezing in an outhouse, in a ditch, or on the convent steps (chapter 4). In 1948 ("The Beads" in *Love Medicine*), June is alone with her mother in the woods when Lucille dies. The nine-year-old June lives on pine sap and grass until she is found by her drunken Morrissey father and an old drunk Lazarre woman, who is apparently Lucille's mother. The two drunks bring her to Marie Kashpaw (Lucille's adoptive sister) to rear. Two of Marie's children, Gordie and Aurelia, try to hang June, apparently at June's instigation. June is furious when Marie rescues her, and she elects to go to live with Eli Kashpaw.

"Crown of Thorns" in *Love Medicine* and chapter 10 in *The Beet Queen* depict the period in which June lives with Eli as the one peaceful time in her turbulent life. She sleeps on a cot beside Eli's stove, and he teaches her to trap, hunt, and hide from game wardens. When June is in high school, she makes a pencil drawing of a deer, which Eli keeps in his cabin, along with her photograph.

June Morrissey Kashpaw

Even while she is living with Eli, June and Gordie are like a brother and sister ("Crown of Thorns"). She goes hunting with Gordie and his friend, for example, in "Flesh and Blood." As teenagers June and Gordie run away to South Dakota and marry ("Resurrection"), but it is an unhappy marriage. "Crown of Thorns" and "The World's Greatest Fishermen" refer to Gordie's abuse of June. They have one son, King Howard Kashpaw, who inherits his father's abusiveness.

On one of her absences from Gordie, June has a brief affair with the teenage Gerry Nanapush ("Crossing the Water"). June and Gerry's son, Lipsha Morrissey, is born about 1965. June does not want to keep Lipsha, but what she does with the baby is an open question. Either she brings Lipsha to Marie to rear (as suggested in "The World's Greatest Fishermen" and "Crossing the Water" in *Love Medicine* and in chapters 5 and 11 of *The Bingo Palace*), or she tries to drown him in a slough (as suggested in "Love Medicine" in *Love Medicine* and chapters 5, 11, and 20 of *The Bingo Palace*). June eventually divorces Gordie, leaves the reservation, and tries a number of occupations. By 1981, though not an outright prostitute, she sleeps with various men who give her money ("The World's Greatest Fishermen").

In 1981, June is in Williston, North Dakota, worn, broke, and hungry ("The World's Greatest Fishermen" in *Love Medicine* and "Easter Snow" [1] in *Tales of Burning Love*). She has bought a bus ticket to return to the reservation, but as she waits for the noon bus, an oil-field mud engineer named Jack Mauser, who tells her his name is Andy, beckons her into the Rigger Bar. They make the rounds to several bars, and that evening they get married on a whim in a quasi-legal ceremony. Desperate for someone to rescue her, June tells Jack that he is "the one" and has to be different from the others. After Jack tries unsuccessfully to consummate their marriage in his pickup just outside of town, June gets out and starts walking back to town. She then changes her mind and sets out for "home" in a gathering snowstorm, recalling the warmth of her Uncle Eli's kitchen. At first Jack follows her, but when she heads off over a fence, he goes back to town. The next morning, Jack and the police find her frozen body leaning against a fence post.

Although on the surface June does little more than die in the opening stories of *Love Medicine* and *Tales of Burning Love,* her spirit unifies several of Erdrich's early novels. She continues to haunt other characters, both figuratively—in their memories and thoughts—and literally, as a ghost. "The World's Greatest Fishermen" recounts various reactions to her death: Albertine Johnson's warm memories, Zelda Kashpaw's jealousy, Gordie's loneliness, and her son King's guilt. Even the blue Firebird that King buys with her insurance money is infused with her spirit.

June particularly haunts her husbands. A month after her death, June's ex-husband Gordie begins to drink. On one of his drunken binges in "Crown of

June Morrissey Kashpaw

Thorns," he sees June look in through the bathroom window. Later, after he hits a deer with his car and then clubs it to death, the deer seems to transform into June. He confesses this "murder," and the police and hospital orderlies come take him away. After Gordie gets out of the hospital in "Resurrection," he drinks a can of Lysol and dies. In *Tales of Burning Love,* Jack Mauser is also haunted by memories of June (see "Blizzard Night" [35]). He wonders, in "Jack's House" [9] and "The Garage" [15], if the manifold problems in his life are retribution for his having abandoned June to die in the snow.

June's ghost is kinder to her lover Gerry and their son, Lipsha. Although she is remembered by reservation gossips in chapter 1 of *The Bingo Palace* as having left her son to die and his father to the mercy of another woman, she does not really abandon them. Lipsha recalls in chapter 14 that his mother visits him in the Northern Lights (probably a reference to the Northern Lights incident in "The World's Greatest Fishermen" in *Love Medicine*). After Lipsha learns the identity of his parents in "Crossing the Water," he joins the newly escaped Gerry at King's apartment in the Twin Cities, where the three play poker for "June's" Firebird. As the game begins, Lipsha senses "the ghost of a woman" there with them. Lipsha wins, and June's car helps Gerry escape to Canada. After dropping his father off, Lipsha heads back west and "bring[s] her home" (*LM,* 367). June's ghost visits Lipsha in chapter 5 of *The Bingo Palace,* asking for her car. In a ghostly car trade, June takes the blue Firebird and gives Lipsha the bingo tickets with which he wins a fancy van (chapter 7). Driving around in his new van, Lipsha sees June in the Firebird.

Nor does June abandon Jack or take revenge. In fact, her activities on the blizzard night of January 5–6, 1995, connect Gerry, Lipsha, and Jack in an uncanny web of salvation and redemption. As recorded in chapter 24 of *The Bingo Palace* and "Blizzard Night" [35] in *Tales of Burning Love,* the re-escaped Gerry is driving north through the blizzard in a stolen white car, with Lipsha beside him and Jack's baby boy in the backseat, when June begins driving alongside in her blue Firebird. Both cars are following Jack, who is driving a snowplow, searching for his son. Jack does not know who is in the white car, but he recognizes June in his rearview mirror. Gerry follows June's car off the road and, leaving Lipsha in the white car, drives away with her in the Firebird. June apparently takes Gerry to West Fargo, since he shows up there later that evening in "The B & B" [16] in *Tales.* Meanwhile, Jack turns back to see what has become of the white car. When he himself becomes lost in the blizzard, June's ghost appears, wearing a wedding dress. She guides him to the white car, where he rescues her son Lipsha and his son, John Jr.

June is mentioned three more times in *Tales of Burning Love,* first by Lyman in "Mauser and Mauser" [39]. Then Jack sees June in the face of the statue in "The

Stone Virgin" [44], and in "A Last Chapter" [46] he compares the pain of her freezing to death with the pain of his own coming back to life.

Kakageeshikok (Geeshik). Shy, wise woman on the reservation in the early twentieth century in part 2.4 of *The Painted Drum*. Kakageeshikok's name means "eternal sky." She never marries and seldom speaks, but becomes knowledgeable and wise by quietly listening outside the circle when the old people talk. Shaawano goes to Geeshik (sky) for advice after the spirit of his daughter instructs him to make the painted drum. When he relates his story, Geeshik says he must do everything his daughter tells him. As her kinsman Albert Ruse helps Shaawano with the drum, Albert reports what happens to Kakageeshikok.

Karl Adare. Son of Adelaide Adare and Mr. Ober; brother of Mary Adare and Jude Miller; father of Dot Adare by Celestine James in *The Beet Queen*. Karl is born about 1918. We learn in chapter 1 that until he is fourteen, Karl lives with his mother and sister in Prairie Lake, where Mr. Ober, who is not married to Adelaide, visits them regularly (chapter 1). Karl has black hair (chapter 8), is described as spindly and sensitive, and seems to be his mother's favorite. After Mr. Ober's death in 1932, the destitute family moves to Minneapolis, where Adelaide gives birth to another boy. After their mother abandons them at the Saint Jerome's Orphans' Picnic and a stranger kidnaps the baby, Karl and Mary take a freight train to Argus where their aunt and uncle, Pete and Fritzie Kozka, live.

In "The Branch," Karl is frightened by a dog in Argus and runs back to the boxcar without Mary. In chapter 1, a tramp named *Giles Saint Ambrose* lets the ravenous Karl eat his food and has a sexual encounter with the boy. Later, the depressed Karl runs out the door of the moving boxcar. We learn in chapter 3 that Karl's leap from the train shatters his feet and that he subsequently develops pneumonia. Fleur Pillager cares for him and then transports him to the reservation convent. The nuns send him back to Minneapolis, where he stays at Saint Jerome's orphanage a year. Meanwhile, in Argus, Mary thinks she sees Karl's face in the shattered ice in chapter 2.

Karl returns to the Orphans' Picnic in about 1948 (chapter 4), where he sees his younger brother, who is now about sixteen. Karl recognizes him because he looks like Adelaide, but he does not identify himself. In 1952 (chapter 6), Karl is selling an air seeder at the Minneapolis Crop and Livestock Convention when he meets Wallace Pfef, a business promoter from Argus. Karl invites Wallace to his

Karl Adare

hotel room, where they have sexual relations and Karl injures his back in a fall. Wallace attends to Karl in the hospital (chapter 9).

Chapters 7 and 9 record Karl's return to Argus in 1953 to look for his sister. He first goes to the butcher shop, where he has a sexual encounter with Celestine James. He then goes to Wallace's house, where he stays for about two weeks. Selling knives door-to-door, one day Karl accidentally knocks on Celestine's door. Celestine lets him in and he stays, without letting Wallace know where he is. Karl lives with Celestine during their several-month-long affair. When Celestine becomes pregnant with Karl's baby, she sends him away. In chapter 8, Karl goes to his cousin Sita Tappe's house in Blue Mound, where Sita accuses him of stealing from her and Celestine. (Sita's accusations are false, but Karl apparently has stolen money from Wallace in chapter 12.)

Karl sees his infant daughter for the first time when he and Celestine get married in Rapid City, but Celestine and the baby return to Argus without him. He writes and sends Dot occasional odd gifts, items that he is selling at the time. The summer after Dot's first-grade year, Karl sends her an electric wheelchair (chapter 10). Karl does not see his family again until Dot is fourteen (1968), when he stops on his way through Argus. Their breakfast reunion in chapter 12 is tense.

Another four years have passed when, in chapters 14 and 15, Karl responds to Celestine's note about Dot's part in the Beet Festival. He quits his job in Texas and drives to Argus to attend the festival. There, he saves Wallace from drowning in the dunking tank and, along with Celestine, Mary, and Wallace, watches as Dot is proclaimed Beet Queen and flies off in a skywriting plane. An hour later, in chapter 16, his car is parked in front of Wallace's house.

Kashpaw. Original Kashpaw patriarch; father of many children by several wives. Kashpaw is also known as Resounding Sky (*The Bingo Palace* chapter 5). His father is Mirage (*The Last Report on the Miracles at Little No Horse* chapter 6), so he is half-brother to Nanapush. Chapter 3 of *Tracks* tells us that Kashpaw and Nanapush are partners in some youthful amorous pursuits (see also chapter 9). As a grown man, in *Last Report* chapter 6, Kashpaw is powerful, hunched, comic looking, and ugly, but he has keen eyes and a ready humor. Chapter 4 speaks of Kashpaw as "shrewd," a quality he bequeaths to his son Nector (see *Tracks* chapter 3). Kashpaw has a beautiful pipe, with a carved stem and rose-red bowl, which he smokes when he meditates (*Last Report* chapter 6). *The Bingo Palace* chapter 5 also reveals that this is the pipe smoked when the Ojibwe sign their treaty with the U.S. government.

Kashpaw's first wife is Margaret, who is strong, opinionated, and sharp-tongued. We learn in *Last Report* chapter 6 that she once bites Kashpaw so badly that he carries a scar. Yet he is pleased with her acid humor and bold inventiveness in lovemaking. She gives him twelve strong, intelligent children, of whom sons Eli and Nector are the youngest (see also *Love Medicine* "The World's Greatest Fishermen"). When smallpox sweeps through the tribe, *Last Report* chapter 4 tells us that Kashpaw contracts the illness but survives, while many of his family members die. Chapters 4 and 5 suggest that this circumstance is the basis for the complex but practical marital arrangement in his household in 1912. He now (chapter 6) has four wives: Margaret, Mashkiigikwe, Fishbone, and Quill. In addition to his older children by Margaret, there are many younger children in his compound. There are several good hunters in the household, so his family is well fed and healthy—also well housed. His camp includes two houses, a traditional bark lodge and a cabin. According to *The Bingo Palace* chapter 9, following generations will continue to live in the log house Kashpaw builds, adding to it over the years.

In March 1912 (*Last Report* chapter 4), Kashpaw drives his wagon over the icy roads to pick up the new priest, Father Damien, from the train stop and bring him to the reservation. The two manage to communicate without a shared language, and Kashpaw provides the priest's first introduction to Ojibwe words. Kashpaw notices young Father Damien's womanish manner, and according to chapter 13, he and Nanapush talk about it.

Chapter 6 describes Nanapush and Damien's visit to the Kashpaw compound. As Nanapush tries to get the priest to condemn Kashpaw's polygamy, Kashpaw sees with amusement what Nanapush is up to—he wants one of Kashpaw's wives for himself. Father Damien, however, explains that he has no authority over the unchurched Kashpaw, and Kashpaw himself sees no reason to abandon the polygamous ways of his father. Nevertheless, Kashpaw knows that this arrangement violates white law and that change is inevitable. Yet he grieves over each wife as he thinks about parting with her. Over the next weeks, Kashpaw's family falls apart, and he promises Mashkiigikwe to keep her sister Quill as his one remaining wife. These events also push Kashpaw reluctantly toward the Catholic Church. He sends Nector to the church to investigate, and to ease her mental disturbance, he brings Quill to mass.

By the Feast of the Virgin (chapter 7), Kashpaw and Quill have been baptized, and the morose Kashpaw drives the wagon carrying the statue of the Virgin. Quill and their daughter, Mary, are riding with him. Pauline Puyat spooks the horses, and in the subsequent crash, Kashpaw and Quill are both fatally injured. As he is dying, Kashpaw predicts the deaths of two hundred Anishinaabeg from a sickness that will come from the east (a prediction fulfilled in the influenza epidemic of 1918–1919). As Kashpaw and Quill die, their daughter, Mary, holds their hands. The exact season of Kashpaw's death is ambiguous. *Tales of Burning Love* "The Owl" [17] suggests autumn, and *Last Report* chapter 4 summer. The

Kashpaw

following spring (1913), Kashpaw and Quill appear to Father Damien in a dream (*Last Report* chapter 7), revealing that the man in the family keeping the orphaned Mary hurts her and that they hold Damien responsible.

When Nanapush goes to live with Margaret at the Kashpaw place in 1919, *Tracks* chapter 9 reports that he envisions meeting with Kashpaw in the land of the dead, where they will sort out their shared women. In *Last Report* chapter 18, when Nanapush comes back to life briefly at his own funeral, he tells the assembled mourners that he had visited the spirit world and greeted Kashpaw there.

Kashpaw boy and girl. Two unnamed children of Nector and Marie Kashpaw who die of a fever the same year, sometime before 1948. They are mentioned by Nector in "The Plunge of the Brave," by Marie in "The Beads," and by Lulu in "The Good Tears" in *Love Medicine*. Their loss is one reason Marie takes in the nine-year-old June Morrissey. If she had lived, Marie's daughter would have been almost the same age as June, who was born about 1939. The boy was probably older, since Nector refers to them as "a boy and a girl baby" (*LM*, 126).

Kashpaw family. See **Aurelia Kashpaw, Eli Kashpaw, Eugene Kashpaw, Gordie Kashpaw, Isabel Kashpaw, June Morrissey Kashpaw, Kashpaw, Kashpaw boy and girl, King Howard Kashpaw, King Howard Kash-paw Junior, Lynette Kashpaw, Margaret (Rushes Bear) Kashpaw, Marie Lazarre Kashpaw, Mary Kashpaw, Montana Kashpaw, Nector Kashpaw, Patsy Kashpaw, Regina Puyat Kashpaw James, Russell Kashpaw,** and **Zelda Kashpaw Johnson Bjornson.**

Kendra Krahe. Daughter of Kurt Krahe in *The Painted Drum*. In part 1.1, when Kendra is in junior high school, *her mother* dies in an automobile accident, and the girl goes through a stormy few years. Kendra is described as "self-absorbed and petulant" (*PD*, 11) and as having little real talent. Her former teachers are surprised when she gains acceptance to prestigious Sarah Lawrence College, but her father thinks she is extraordinary. When Kendra is home on a visit late one winter in the early 2000s and a ne'er-do-well neighbor youth, Davan Eyke, begins seeing her, her father is livid. He gets into a fight with the boy, kicks him, and orders him to stay away. But Davan and Kendra ignore Krahe's prohibitions. One spring day, chased by a police car, Davan loses control of his Toyota on a bridge, and both he and Kendra drown in the river. Krahe is devastated by her loss. Her *aunt* (Krahe's sister) and several of her *drooping friends* attend her memorial service (part 1.3). Krahe, a sculptor, makes her gravestone, a simple concave circle in white marble (part 4).

Kim, Tim, Vim. Undergraduate student in Eleanor Mauser's college seminar whom she seduces in "White Musk" [4] in *Tales of Burning Love*. Eleanor is not sure what his name is, but thinks it ends in "-im." When she gives him a B minus for the course, he brings charges of sexual harassment against her. He tells **his parents** the details of the seduction, and **his mother** spends two hours with the **college president,** who forces Eleanor to resign. Afterward, a **group of students** from the seminar claim to have been brainwashed. A **reporter** calls Eleanor to ask about her resignation. Jack Mauser saves a newspaper article about the incident ("Jack's House" [9]).

King Howard Kashpaw. Son of June Morrissey and Gordie Kashpaw in *Love Medicine.* "The World's Greatest Fishermen" and "Crown of Thorns" reveal King's parents' troubled marriage. His father sometimes hits his mother, and June periodically leaves them. When she divorces Gordie, June plans to establish herself and send for King, but she never manages to do so. King's troubled childhood produces an abusive, violent personality. As he is growing up, he often mocks and beats up his younger "cousin," Lipsha Morrissey, and once even tries to shoot him. (Lipsha is actually King's half brother, June's illegitimate son, a fact that Lipsha at first does not know but King apparently does.) We learn in "Crossing the Water" that when Lipsha is ten, he surprises King by punching him in the face.

In 1981, in "The World's Greatest Fishermen," King is living in the Twin Cities with his wife, Lynette, and infant son, King Junior. When June dies that Easter, King buys a blue Firebird with her life insurance money. Two months after her death, King drives the car to a family gathering at the old Kashpaw place. No one will ride in the car because it is June's. That evening, King becomes drunk, beats up the car, verbally abuses Lynette, and even tries to drown her. Observing him, Albertine makes the connection between his violence and Gordie's. She believes that, underneath his bully front, King is afraid.

In "Crossing the Water" we see other facets of King's cowardly personality. He claims, falsely, to have served as a Marine in Vietnam, where he supposedly used the code name "Apple" and his **Kentucky buddy,** the name "Banana." Actually, he has served time in the Stillwater prison, where he betrayed Gerry Nanapush to the authorities. Gerry quips ironically that King is indeed an "apple"—that is, red (Indian) on the outside and white on the inside. In 1984, Gerry, who is newly escaped, and Lipsha, who has just learned that he is Gerry's son, show up at King's apartment in the Twin Cities. The three men play poker for "June's car," which Lipsha wins. At his wife's urging, King surrenders the car, keys, and registration to Lipsha.

King Howard Kashpaw Junior. Son of King and Lynette Kashpaw in *Love Medicine.* King Junior is a baby when his parents bring him to a family gathering in 1981 in "The World's Greatest Fishermen."

In the final story, "Crossing the Water" (1984), King Junior is an intelligent

King Howard Kashpaw Junior

kindergartner who has taught himself to read and is moved up to first grade. He tells *his teacher* that he prefers to be called Howard instead of King. In this story, we see King and Lynette's family violence from their son's point of view. Howard despises his father and recalls a time when the police came for him and handcuffed him. Thus, when the police come to their apartment looking for Gerry Nanapush, Howard—assuming they are looking for his father—runs to the door to let them in.

Kit Tatro. Unconventional neighbor of Elsie and Faye Travers in *The Painted Drum*. Kit (real name, Everett) lives on Revival Road in Stokes, New Hampshire, in gypsylike disorder with a succession of *stoop-shouldered girlfriends.* Kit is convinced he is Native American and in part 1.3 is continually searching for his tribal identity. One early spring, when Faye Travers wants to induce Kit to mow her yard, she reveals to him that her mother Elsie is half Ojibwe. When he comes to mow, Faye also has him change the lock on her back door. In September of the following year (part 4), Kit tells Elsie and Faye about visiting a shaman to uncover his tribal heritage and about his subsequent experience in highway traffic that convinces him he is Ho-chunk.

Klaus, original German. Young German prisoner of war whom Shawano the ogitchida kidnaps in chapter 13 of *The Antelope Wife*. Klaus saves himself by baking the delicious and magical blitzkuchen. Afterward, he is adopted into the clan; Shawano's newborn son is named for him; and Shawano's older son Frank will spend his life trying to reproduce the blitzkuchen. Klaus is also mentioned, though not by name, in chapter 11.

Klaus Shawano. Son of Shawano the ogitchida and Regina; brother of Frank, Puffy, and Cecille Shawano; lover of Sweetheart Calico in *The Antelope Wife*. He narrates chapters 2, 4, 13, and 15.

Klaus is younger than Frank and at least one other sibling (see chapter 13). Shortly before his birth in about 1945, when his mother eats the magical blitz-kuchen baked by the young German prisoner of war, the unborn Klaus hears her speak to him, calling him by name. He is named Klaus after that German baker. We learn in chapter 12 that he gains a hard-won GED certificate and perhaps a college degree.

Klaus begins telling his story in chapter 2, one year after his fateful trip to Elmo, Montana. Before that trip, he is apparently content with his life as a sanitation engineer in Minneapolis, and on weekends he works the western powwow circuit as a trader (chapters 2 and 11). He describes himself as an ordinary man, a bit too broad, but proud of his long, dark, curly hair. (He mentions his "Buffalo Soldier" blood in chapter 2.) At the powwow in Elmo, however, he sees four "antelope" women and asks old Jimmy Badger for antelope medicine. Klaus takes Jimmy's advice about how to attract an antelope, but ignores the old man's insistence that he leave the women alone. After capturing their attention with a piece of sweetheart calico cloth, Klaus invites the daughters to nap in his tent, then kidnaps their mother.

When the woman, whom Klaus calls Ninimoshe ("my sweetheart"), realizes in Bismarck, North Dakota, that she is caught, she fights Klaus, breaking her teeth on the edge of the bathtub. Klaus carries her back to Minneapolis, where he guards her possessively. He thinks that she is trying to kill him with sex and calls Jimmy Badger, but he disregards Jimmy's demand that Klaus return her. Throughout his narration, Klaus makes excuses for his possessive behavior, placing the blame on the woman herself. Both Klaus and his family refer to the antelope woman as his "wife," but this may simply represent another of Klaus's rationalizations, representing as wife a woman who is in fact his captive. In the city, people most often call Klaus's woman Sweetheart Calico.

The sequence of the next several incidents in Klaus's life is left vague. According to chapter 3, Sweetheart Calico drives Klaus crazy, so that he disappears for four years, leaving her behind in the city. According to chapter 11, they both disappear for four years, and when Klaus returns, he has turned into a street bum.

The events of chapter 4 fall somewhere between Klaus's first bringing Sweetheart Calico to Minneapolis and his return some years later as a bum. Sweetheart Calico has already left him and returned several times, and Klaus now wears a buzz cut. He is part of a Native-owned trash collection business managed by Richard Whiteheart Beads. Richard gives Klaus a trip to Hawaii that Richard has won from the company. On the trip, however, Klaus and Sweetheart Calico are shadowed by *two big guys in suits,* who turn out to be government agents. Mistaking Klaus for Richard, they arrest him for Richard's illegal dumping practices. Ultimately Klaus loses everything—money, house, and Sweetheart Calico. Hints in chapters 4 and 10 suggest that Klaus may think Richard and Sweetheart Calico are lovers.

By chapter 10, both Klaus and Richard have made their descent into the gutter. They wander the city, drinking Listerine and cheap wine and accepting handouts. Klaus's physical and psychic misery is captured in the chapter's title, "Nibi"—water. His body is sick and dehydrated, and his spirit is "scorched" with longing. He dreams of his antelope wife, in the guise of the Blue Fairy, pouring out a glass of water in front of his eyes. As Klaus kneels and drinks the polluted water of the Mississippi, he watches the image of his Blue Fairy–antelope wife beneath the surface.

In chapter 11, Klaus and Richard wander into the bakery of Klaus's brother Frank. Klaus, speechless with thirst, passes out. When he wakes, still begging for

Klaus Shawano

"nibi," Sweetheart Calico mercifully gives him a cup of water. While Frank is on the phone trying to get his brother into detox, Klaus and Sweetheart Calico walk out the door with arms around each other.

Sweetheart Calico leaves, returns, and leaves again in chapter 12, sending Windigo Dog—a spirit of uncontrollable hunger—in her place. Windigo Dog tells Klaus a dirty dog joke, and in chapter 13, Klaus tells him the story of Klaus's German namesake. In chapter 15, Klaus and Richard are finally in a recovery program. Although Richard refuses to deal with his dishonesty, Klaus finally faces the fact that his excuses have been lies. Even so, he remains torn between his need to let go of Sweetheart Calico and his desire to cling.

At the preparations in chapter 16 for Frank's marriage to Rozina Roy, Klaus is four-months sober and struggling to stay away from the cold beer. Later, when Richard interrupts the cliffside wedding ceremony, Klaus and his brother Puffy restrain Frank from pushing Richard over the cliff. That afternoon, when Richard also disrupts the reception, Klaus hits him over the head with a frozen turkey.

Klaus's sobriety does not last. In chapter 20, he is again sleeping in the bushes at the park when a **young black man** mowing for the city runs over Klaus's head with a riding lawn mower. Klaus escapes with his life only because a stray dog (presumably Windigo Dog) bolts toward the lawn mower, is hit, and vanishes. When the windigo dog disappears, Klaus is finally able to master his own windigo cravings. Waking, he decides to stop drinking and to let his antelope wife go free. He carries out the latter decision in chapter 21. For a week he watches for Sweetheart Calico, and when she appears, he ties her wrist to his with a band of calico and walks through the city. When they reach the open spaces to the west, Klaus, fighting back his own longing, unties the cloth and watches as the antelope woman wearily makes her way west and disappears.

Kroshus, Mrs. See **Tillie Kroshus.**

Kuklenski brothers. Brothers of Harry Kuklenski. Anna Kuklenski sends her dead husband, Harry's body back to Milwaukee with them to be buried beside *his uncle,* in "Eleanor's Tale" [20] in *Tales of Burning Love.*

Kurt Krahe. Father of Kendra Krahe and lover of Faye Travers in *The Painted Drum.* We learn Krahe's background in part 1.1. At the present time of the novel, he is fifty-six. He is a sculptor who works with large pieces of native stone, an occupation facilitated by both his thick, strong body and his "sprightly" hands and feet (*PD,* 10). After some success in his career, he moves to the small community of Stokes, New Hampshire, where he is largely unproductive. Krahe's second wife has died some years back, and he idolizes their daughter, Kendra, now a university student. He has for some time had a rather secretive and dysfunctional affair with his neighbor Faye Travers. They do not go out together. Instead, he has a key to Faye's back door and comes to her at night. Both protect themselves from personal intimacy with facades of arrogance or invulnerability.

Neighbor youth Davan Eyke lives for a time in the cottage on Krahe's property and helps him handle the large stones for his sculptures. But when Davan kills one of the ravens nesting near the cottage, Krahe shoots an arrow at the boy and dismisses him. When Kendra is home visiting Krahe one late winter in the early 2000s, Davan begins seeing her. The infuriated Krahe kicks him and tells him to stay away. But soon after, when Kendra is riding in Davan's speeding car, both die in a watery crash, and Krahe is devastated with grief. We learn in part 4 that he sculpts Kendra's gravestone himself.

In part 1.3, Krahe becomes more vulnerable and needy in his relationship with Faye, but also more controlling. Early that spring, he takes it upon himself to cut Faye's grass, which she takes as a gesture of control. Even more disturbing to her is his proposal to prune the Travers apple orchard so that it will come back to life. When the two go out to dinner at the Sweet Mansion, Faye expresses her opposition to the plan, but Krahe goes ahead with the pruning. By May, the orchard is blooming again, reminding Faye of her sister's death, and one night that spring, when Krahe comes to her back door, he finds the lock changed. He does not know the reason, and Faye does not answer his phone calls (part 4).

One September night, a year and a half after he first finds the locked door, in part 4 Krahe enters Faye's screened back porch and is approaching the door when Faye, who is sitting on the shadowed porch with Elsie, speaks to him, and he sits down with them. We are not told, but it is probable that he has come and tried the door many times in the past year and a half. When Elsie goes in, Krahe urgently and accusingly questions Faye as to why she so abruptly abandoned him. She does not explain, only tells him that she had to, and when she goes in, he does not try to follow. Some days later, Krahe phones Faye to tell her that his studio has been vandalized. She comes over to survey the damage, and that night they renew their relationship, this time more openly.

Lake man. Man-monster-cat mentioned in chapter 8 of *The Antelope Wife*. See also **Misshepeshu**.

Lamartine family. See **Beverly "Hat" Lamartine, Elsa Lamartine, Henry**

Lamartine family

Lamartine Junior, Henry Lamartine (Senior), and **Lulu Nanapush Morrissey Lamartine.** Also wearing the Lamartine name is **Lyman Lamartine.**

Lawrence Schlick. Husband of Anna Kuklenski Schlick and father of Eleanor Schlick in *Tales of Burning Love.* In "The Meadowlark" [7], we learn that he is an undertaker and runs Schlick's Funeral Home.

"Eleanor's Tale" [20] tells the story of Lawrence's marriage to Anna Kuklenski. He meets Anna in the hospital after the trapeze accident that killed her first husband. They fall in love and marry. Lawrence, a leading Fargo businessman, provides for his family in grand style. They live in a turn-of-the-century mansion, and he dotes on his daughter, Eleanor, even building her a playhouse ("White Musk" [4]). After Anna saves six-year-old Eleanor from a house fire, the grateful Lawrence joins the fire department.

After putting out a terrible fire one frigid November night, however, Lawrence comes home to find his wife in bed with one of the young firemen, Jack Mauser. Although the circumstances are innocent, the impulsive Lawrence asks no questions. He immediately casts Anna and Eleanor out into a life of poverty.

We learn in "The Red Slip" [21] that in his distress, Lawrence's various businesses begin to fail until he is left with only his funeral business, which he moves into the mansion where he lives. He reconciles with Anna after Eleanor tells them she is pregnant with Jack Mauser's child and plans to marry him. Even so, his suspicions continue, and in "The Box" [22] (1983), he sneaks home two days early from a convention to see if Anna is sleeping with Jack. She is not.

In January 1995, Lawrence Schlick hosts Jack's funeral—at a financial loss—as told in "Memoria" [10] and "Satin Heart" [12]. Though Lawrence had considered him a rival and enemy in life, after Jack's (supposed) death, he is able to forgive him. He has painstakingly gathered what seem to be Jack's charred remains from the basement of his burned house. At closing time, Lawrence herds Jack's wives out the door in "The B & B" [16] but holds Eleanor for a moment before she leaves. Meanwhile, in "Funeral Day" [23], Jack imagines that Schlick is gloating over his death and wants some other undertaker to handle his real funeral.

In August of that year ("A Light from the West" [43]), Anna dies at home. The grieving Lawrence prepares her body for cremation and then crawls into the chamber to be cremated with her.

Lawrence Schlick's banker, lawyer, accountant, and realtor. Men who advise Lawrence the morning he finds his wife, Anna, in bed with Jack Mauser in "Eleanor's Tale" [20] in *Tales of Burning Love.* The realtor is Lawrence's cousin. The banker is probably the ***bank president*** who talks with Schlick about his financial losses in "The Red Slip" [21]. He may or may not be **Hegelstead.**

Lazarre family. See **Boy Lazarre, Boy Lazarre II, Cyprian Lazarre, Ignatius Lazarre, Izear Lazarre, Lucille Lazarre, Marie Lazarre Kashpaw,** and **Old drunk woman.** Also, Clarence Morrissey marries a *Lazarre woman.*

Leopolda, Sister. Nun and schoolteacher on the reservation and in Argus. *Tracks* and *The Last Report on the Miracles at Little No Horse* give differing accounts of Sister Leopolda's becoming a nun. At the end of chapter 8 of *Tracks,* she takes her orders at the Sacred Heart Convent on the reservation in 1919 and is subsequently assigned to teach arithmetic at Saint Catherine's school in Argus. Chapter 16 of *Last Report,* however, indicates that she takes her vows and the name Leopolda after moving to Argus. Chapter 2 of *The Beet Queen* records an experience Leopolda has in 1932 while teaching at Saint Catherine's. When Mary Adare cracks the ice in the schoolyard, causing the image of Christ to appear, Sister Leopolda takes photographs of the "miracle." Several nights later, Leopolda is found beside the icy image, scourging her arms with thistles.

After this incident, Leopolda returns to Sacred Heart, which, according to "Saint Marie" in *Love Medicine,* is a place where nuns are sent who do not fit in elsewhere. Dates in *Love Medicine, The Beet Queen,* and chapter 16 of *Last Report* indicate that Leopolda returns to the reservation in the spring of 1933. Shortly after, she confesses to Father Damien what the priest has long realized—that she is a murderer. She refuses to turn herself in to the authorities, and because of a secret she knows about Damien, she blackmails him into silence.

Leopolda appears in two *Love Medicine* stories told from Marie Lazarre Kashpaw's point of view. In "Saint Marie," Marie is one of Leopolda's students at the Sacred Heart convent school in 1934, and she depicts the nun as being obsessed with the devil. Leopolda's weapons against him include, for herself, fasting to the point of starvation and, for her pupils, terror and pain. Although Marie initially sides with the devil against Leopolda, one day the nun gets the best of them by hurling her metal-tipped oak pole through Satan's heart (an old black boot) and throwing Marie into the dark closet with it.

That summer, Marie comes to the convent as a novice, with Sister Leopolda as her sponsor. Leopolda professes love for Marie, but it is a twisted, violent love. She pins the child to the floor with her foot and pours a kettle of scalding water over her back to melt her "cold" heart and boil Satan out of her. After Marie kicks Leopolda into the oven, Leopolda stabs the girl through the hand and knocks her unconscious. Leopolda tells the other nuns that the child has had a vision and swooned, after which the miraculous stigmata appeared in her palm. Thus, when Marie regains consciousness, Leopolda must kneel beside her and accept her blessing. After Marie flees the convent, in chapter 20 of *Last Report* she lives for a

Leopolda, Sister

time in the woods, selling whiskey. One day Leopolda comes for her, holding out her hands, which are pierced like Marie's, trying to woo her back to the convent. But Marie leaves her standing in the yard.

Years later, in 1957, Sister Leopolda still lives at Sacred Heart and seems to be dying. In "Flesh and Blood," Marie takes her daughter Zelda to visit the nun. Leopolda has shriveled to a pile of sticks and is partially deranged, yet her mind is clear enough to know who Marie is and to remember their old enmity. The two trade insults and physically struggle. At the end of this struggle, Marie leaves the now-quiet old woman, certain that she will be dead by the next spring.

Leopolda, however, does not die in 1958. According to *Tales of Burning Love* ("Night Prayer" [6]), she is still alive in 1994, 108 years old. (This accounting conflicts with the chronology of *Tracks,* which suggests that in 1994 Leopolda would be 96 [see chapter 2].) In "White Musk" [4] in *Tales,* college professor Eleanor Mauser comes to the Our Lady of the Wheat Priory in Argus, probably in early 1994, to observe and interview the old nun. According to "Night Prayer" [6], Leopolda does not like her young interviewer. Yet when Leopolda goes out to pray in the convent garden one June night, she and Eleanor talk. Leopolda predicts that Eleanor's ex-husband, Jack Mauser (who is hiding there in the garden), will die screaming, crushed by a woman. After Leopolda utters her last words—"End this torment"—she appears to die in an ecstasy. Eleanor and Jack leave, lightning strikes Leopolda's metal walker, and the nun disappears, either vaporized by the lightning or, as some of the nuns believe, the object of a miraculous assumption.

The following January, in "A Conversation" [33], Leopolda appears to Eleanor, who is exposed at night in a subzero blizzard. In this appearance, they continue their conversation about love and desire, and Leopolda's instructions save Eleanor's life.

In "Jack's House" [9] and "The Garage" [15], Jack Mauser recalls Leopolda's prediction of his death, and in "The Stone Virgin" [44], her prophecy is partially fulfilled when a statue of the Virgin falls on him. His survival and other seeming miracles associated with Leopolda are the subject of Father Jude's "A Letter to the Bishop" [45], in which he suggests that the nun's history is worth investigating, apparently with a view to her possible beatification. That summer, Eleanor also muses on the old nun, recalling the obsessive nature of her desire and determining to make the study of Leopolda's possible sainthood her life's work.

The following spring, 1996, in chapter 3 of *The Last Report on the Miracles at Little No Horse,* the Church sends Father Jude to interview the now-ancient Father Damien about Leopolda's possible sainthood. Jude recalls some of her supposed miracles in chapter 8. Damien, however, considers Leopolda to be anything but a saint. As the priests' interviews continue over several days in March, Father Damien reveals a number of Leopolda's dark acts: her part in the deaths of Kashpaw and his wife Quill (chapter 8 and 14), her self-serving role of sacrificial victim (chapter 14), and her physical abuse of the young postulant Marie Lazarre (chapter 8). Damien also reveals to Jude the history of Leopolda's twisted family to illustrate the depth of her perversion (chapter 8). In addition to these interviews with Father Damien, Jude twice questions Marie herself about Leopolda (chapters 8 and 20).

Finally, in chapter 21 Damien reveals to Jude that Leopolda was a murderer. Alone in his room, Jude mulls over all these revelations and asks himself, "Why this deep thirst to make a saint of this appalling woman?" (*LR,* 340). By the following year, Father Jude has abandoned the project of Leopolda's beatification and is now researching the possible sainthood of Father Damien (epilogue of *Last Report*). See also **Pauline Puyat.**

Leo Pukwan. Third-generation tribal policeman who, along with Zelda Bjornson and the social worker Vicki Koob, in chapter 15 of *The Bingo Palace* seizes Redford Toose from the house of his aunts, Tammy and Mary Fred Toose. See also **Pukwan family.**

Lily Veddar. Employee at Pete Kozka's butcher shop in *Tracks.* In chapter 2, Lily plays cards with Tor Grunewald, Dutch James, and Fleur Pillager in the evenings after work. One hot night in August 1913, enraged at Fleur's winnings, Lily leads the men's attack on Fleur. The next day the three men take shelter from a tornado in the meat locker, and Pauline locks them in. When they are found several days later, Lily is frozen to death. He reappears in Pauline Puyat's death vision in chapter 6, again playing cards with Fleur.

Lipsha Morrissey. Son of June Morrissey and Gerry Nanapush. As we learn in "Crossing the Water" in *Love Medicine,* Lipsha is conceived in 1964 during a brief affair between June, who is married and already has a legitimate son, and Gerry, who is just out of high school. In "Crossing the Water," "Love Medicine," and chapter 5 of *The Bingo Palace,* we learn that when Lipsha is born, June does not want to keep him, but it is unclear what she does with him. One version of the story is that she brings baby Lipsha to Marie Kashpaw to rear. Another version is that she tries to drown him, and either Marie or her daughter Zelda rescues him. (See also chapters 11 and 20 of *The Bingo Palace.*)

In any case, Marie takes Lipsha in, but he grows up confused about his origins because she never tells him who his parents are. Some details of Lipsha's childhood appear in chapter 4 of *The Bingo Palace* and "The World's Greatest Fishermen," "Love Medicine," and "Crossing the Water" in *Love Medicine.* Lipsha is a withdrawn child who often clings to Marie. His supposed foster cousin (actually, his half

Lipsha Morrissey

brother), King Kashpaw, persistently mocks him and beats him up. Once, hunting gophers with Lipsha, King even takes a potshot at him. When Lipsha is ten, he surprises King by punching him in the face. Another cousin, Albertine Johnson, is like a sister to Lipsha, the only girl he ever trusts. Two months after June's death, as they watch the Northern Lights together in "The World's Greatest Fishermen," Albertine tries to tell Lipsha who his mother is, but he will not listen. Nevertheless, he recalls in chapter 14 of *The Bingo Palace* that he has been visited by his mother in the form of the Northern Lights.

We learn in "Love Medicine" that after his Grandma Marie and now feeble-minded Grandpa Nector move into the Senior Citizens, Lipsha often visits them. Partly because of the healing power in his hands, passed down to him from his Pillager ancestors, he is able to help Marie with Nector. Marie wants Lipsha to make a love medicine so that Nector will love her rather than his old flame, Lulu Lamartine. Lipsha eventually agrees but takes a shortcut, substituting frozen turkey hearts for the hearts of Canada geese, and his effort has tragic results. His Grandpa Nector chokes to death on one of the turkey hearts.

In 1983, Lipsha works briefly for his father's half brother, Lyman Lamartine ("The Tomahawk Factory"), and in 1984 he finally learns the story of his parentage from his paternal grandmother, Lulu Lamartine ("Crossing the Water"). Lipsha leaves the reservation and tries to find his father, who he feels will soon escape from prison. By chance or fate, they meet at King Kashpaw's apartment in the Twin Cities. Lipsha wins "June's car" (bought by King with June's insurance money) in a rigged poker game and then helps Gerry escape. As Lipsha visits with his father on their way to the Canadian border, he finally experiences a sense of belonging. At the end of this story, the last in *Love Medicine*, Lipsha drives June's car back home.

The reservation gossips who constitute the group narrator of *The Bingo Palace* chapter 1 also mention Lipsha's driving onto the reservation in the blue Firebird and his part in the tomahawk factory fiasco, although this narrative reverses the *Love Medicine* order of these events. This narration adds that, even though Lipsha finishes high school and scores high on college entrance exams, he does not go to college or get a steady job. After a series of temporary jobs, he ends up working in a sugar-beet factory in Fargo, where he is said to frequent the bars and rougher parts of town. When Lulu sends him a copy of his father's Wanted poster, however, he decides to return home.

Lipsha attends the winter powwow in chapter 2 of *The Bingo Palace* and is captivated by the beautiful Shawnee Ray Toose. Shawnee Ray, however, is semi-engaged to Lyman Lamartine and has a son, presumably Lyman's. Zelda Kashpaw is trying to promote the relationship between Lyman and Shawnee Ray. In chapter 4, Marie gives Nector's sacred pipe to Lipsha. When Lipsha tries to take Shawnee Ray to dinner at a restaurant in Canada, they are detained at the border for possession of drugs and Nector's pipe is confiscated. Lyman arrives in chapter 5 to work out the problem with the **border guards,** and he tries unsuccessfully to buy the pipe from Lipsha. He also gives Lipsha a job in his bingo hall. Their relationship is complicated by the fact that they are both in love with Shawnee Ray.

Also in chapter 5, Zelda tells Lipsha that his mother, June, had thrown him into a slough in a weighted gunnysack and that Zelda herself had dragged him out. (We learn in this chapter that Marie has at some point changed her version of the story, now claiming that Lipsha's mother sorrowfully gave him up to Marie.) Later that night, June's spirit visits Lipsha in the bingo hall bar, gives him a booklet of bingo tickets, and, as he discovers the next morning, takes "her" car, the blue Firebird. In chapter 7, Lipsha plays bingo in an attempt to win a fancy van. To finance his gambling, he starts charging for the use of his healing power, and his "touch" deserts him.

Also in chapter 7, Lipsha and Shawnee Ray make love for the first time in a motel room. When Lipsha buys condoms at a nearby gas station, he exchanges insults with Marty, the attendant. The next night, Lipsha wins the bingo van, using one of June's tickets. Driving around in the van, he sees June in the Firebird—their car trade is now complete. Later that night, Marty abducts Lipsha from a party, takes him to Russell Kashpaw's to be tattooed, and vandalizes the van.

When Lyman again asks to buy Nector's pipe in chapter 8, Lipsha offers to trade it in return for Lyman's stepping aside from his pursuit of Shawnee Ray. Lyman alters the deal. If Lipsha will just lend him the pipe, he will not tell Shawnee Ray about Lipsha's offer. By chapter 9, Lipsha is winning regularly at bingo, and Lyman persuades Lipsha to open a joint bank account with him. Although Shawnee Ray tells Lipsha to leave her alone, he goes to Zelda's house (where she is staying), and they make love a second time. Afterward, in chapter 10, Shawnee Ray uses money Lipsha has given her to escape from Zelda's control.

Desperate to secure Shawnee Ray's love, in chapter 11 Lipsha decides to ask his great-grandmother Fleur Pillager for a love medicine. When he accompanies the old woman to her house at the far end of Matchimanito Lake, she changes into a bear and speaks to him. Chapter 13 indicates that Fleur speaks of the enduring value of the land. We learn from chapters 14 and 22 that she speaks in the old language, which Lipsha does not usually understand, but that her thoughts enter his mind as pictures. When Fleur does not give him a love medicine, Lipsha decides to go on a spiritual quest, and he visits Lyman for advice. The two rivals undertake a vision quest led by Xavier Toose, Shawnee Ray's uncle, in chapter 17. Instead of the dramatic vision he expects, however, Lipsha encounters a skunk, who, like Fleur, lectures him on the importance of the land. In chapter 19, the skunk-reeking

Lipsha Morrissey

Lipsha gets a ride back to town with Albertine, who advises him to leave Shawnee Ray alone for a while. The following night, in chapter 20, Lipsha remembers being saved from drowning as an infant by the lake creature of Matchimanito, and he has a vision in which the skunk is spokesperson.

In January (*Bingo Palace* chapter 22), Lipsha has a dream about his father and then learns that Gerry has escaped. (In *The Bingo Palace,* the year appears to be in the late 1980s, although it is given as 1995 in *Tales of Burning Love.*) Gerry calls Lipsha from Fargo but his directions in the old language confuse Lipsha. When they finally meet, Lipsha's van will not start. In chapter 24 of *The Bingo Palace,* they steal a white car (which turns out to have a baby in the backseat) and, after evading the police, escape from Fargo. As they head north, they are caught in a blizzard but manage to fall in behind a snowplow.

When June appears driving the blue Firebird, Gerry goes with her. Left behind in the white car, Lipsha zips the baby into his jacket to protect him from the bitter cold. Lipsha is determined that he will not abandon this baby the way he and his mother were abandoned as children. In chapter 26, the radio news the next day says that "a hostage" has been found in good condition, and in chapter 27, Fleur takes the place of "the boy" in death, but the identities of this hostage and boy are ambiguous. Thus, as *The Bingo Palace* ends, Lipsha's fate remains uncertain. In "The Tale of the Unknown Passenger" [34] in *Tales of Burning Love,* Gerry and his wife, Dot Adare, worry about Lipsha and console themselves with the conviction that Lyman has gone out to find him.

In *Tales of Burning Love* "Funeral Day" [23] and "Blizzard Night" [35], the story of the car theft and subsequent storm is told from the point of view of the baby's father. Searching for the missing baby, the father is driving the snowplow that Gerry and Lipsha follow north on the interstate. (Although Gerry and Lipsha get a head start, they are delayed by traffic and have to evade police, so apparently by the time they reach the interstate, they are behind the snowplow.) *Tales of Burning Love* also resolves the ambiguity about Lipsha's survival. Near dawn after the night of the storm, the baby's father, Jack Mauser, finds the white car and drags Lipsha and the baby to safety. Jack notices Lipsha's Chippewa face and his one slightly crooked tooth, a feature Lipsha inherited from his mother, the woman who had also been Jack's first wife. Neither of the men is aware of the connection between them. As Jack drives on up to the reservation in "Mauser and Mauser" [39], the exhausted Lipsha sleeps with the baby still zipped against him.

Living lost. Assorted outlaws, drunks, addicts, fools, and artists—Anna Schlick's friends—whom Anna takes care of after she resumes her marriage with Lawrence Schlick. This collective term is used in "The Box" [22] in *Tales of Burning Love.*

Lonny Germaine. Young local police officer in *The Painted Drum*. One August day in part 1.4, Lonny comes to Elsie and Faye Travers's house with lights flashing, siren blaring, and pistol drawn. He is helping state troopers investigate a large marijuana patch in the woods behind the Travers house, and the troopers in a helicopter had misinterpreted Faye's blackberry picking earlier that day. Lonny leaves in confusion.

Louis Tappe. State health inspector who comes to Chez Sita to investigate the food poisoning in chapter 7 of *The Beet Queen*. He falls in love with Sita Kozka Bohl, now divorced from Jimmy Bohl. In chapter 8, Louis and Sita marry. He quits his job as health inspector and moves to Blue Mound to live in the big house that Sita has received as part of her divorce settlement. In his new job as county extension agent, he collects data about the local entomological pests and helpers. He also observes and takes notes on Sita's psychotic behavior. After long trying to manage Sita's psychotic episodes himself, when Sita pretends to be mute (chapter 10), Louis finally consults a psychiatrist, who admits her to the state mental hospital. After spending one night in the hospital, Sita is "cured."

Caring for Sita wears on Louis, and by the time they attend Dot Adare's eleventh-birthday party in chapter 12 (1965), he is suffering from angina and seems frail. Although Sita is largely withdrawn at the party, Louis seems to enjoy being with the children. We learn in chapter 13 that in the last years of his life, Louis stockpiles the tranquilizers to which Sita has become addicted. By 1972, Louis is dead and Sita's supply of pills is almost gone. She ends her life on the day of the Beet Festival by taking the last half bottle of Louis's legacy.

Lovchik. Ronald Lovchik is an Argus police officer in the 1950s to 1970s in *The Beet Queen*. In chapter 10, Ronald is described as a tall, sad, unassertive man who has a crush on Sita Kozka and brings her chocolates, until she marries Jimmy Bohl (c. 1950). He listens to Wallace Pfef talk about sugar beets in chapter 6 (1953). He is the officer in chapter 10 assigned to investigate the complaints made by Dot Adare's teacher, Mrs. Shumway, against Mary Adare in 1960. In chapter 13, Ronald stops Mary and Celestine James for speeding on the way to the 1972 Beet Parade and speaks to Sita, who sits between them on the front seat, not noticing that Sita is dead. He hopes to court Sita now that her husband Louis is dead, so he does not ticket them.

This may or may not be the same Lovchik who, in "Scales" in *Love Medicine,* tries several times unsuccessfully to arrest Gerry Nanapush in 1980. This Lovchik is referred to as a "local police" officer, although the setting of the story is not specified. There is also an officer Lovchik on the Argus police force in 1994 (Ronald's son?) in *Tales of Burning Love*. This Lovchik arrests Jack Mauser for

Lovchik

financial misconduct when Jack comes to Argus to meet his latest mother-in-law in "A Wedge of Shade" [3].

Lucifer. See **Satan.**

Lucille Lazarre. Mother of Geezhig and June Morrissey by a Morrissey man who does not marry her (Morrissey I); supposed sister of Marie Lazarre Kashpaw. Marie refers to Lucille as her sister and to Ignatius Lazarre as her—and thus presumably Lucille's—father in "The Beads" in *Love Medicine*. (The reader of *Tracks* knows that Lucille is not Marie's blood sister.) Marie declares Lucille to be the only Lazarre for whom she has any use. In chapter 6 of *The Bingo Palace*, Lucille is described as an alcoholic who has good days and bad days. One cold night, after her boyfriend *Leonard* shows up, Lucille ties the child June to the stove to keep her from running away, and later in the night Leonard rapes the child.

Lucille badly neglects June, who as a child is found abandoned on a number of occasions, freezing or starving, as recounted in chapter 4 of *The Bingo Palace* and "The Beads" in *Love Medicine*. Lucille dies in the woods, alone with the nine-year-old June. After her death, her drunk Morrissey "spouse" and an old drunk woman who is apparently her mother bring June to Marie for her to rear. Lucille is also referred to, though not by name, in "The World's Greatest Fishermen" in *Love Medicine*.

Lulu, daughter of Nanapush and White Beads. See **Red Cradle.**

Lulu Nanapush Morrissey Lamartine. Daughter of Fleur Pillager; mother of eight sons, including Gerry Nanapush, Henry Lamartine Junior, and Lyman Lamartine, and one daughter, Bonita.

Lulu's paternity is uncertain. She may have been conceived when Fleur was attacked by three men in an Argus smokehouse or during Fleur's subsequent relationship with Eli Kashpaw. Pauline Puyat even suggests that the child may have been fathered by the lake man, Misshepeshu (*Tracks* chapter 2). (For speculations about Fleur's pregnancy, see **Fleur Pillager.**) In trying to judge Lulu's parentage from her appearance, we have only the testimony of the unreliable Pauline; in chapter 2, she tells us that Lulu has green eyes and "skin the color of an old penny" (*Tr*, 31), suggesting either mixed blood or the lake creature as sire, but in chapter 4, she records that Lulu has "the Kashpaws' unmistakable nose" (*Tr*, 70). That Erdrich intends for Lulu's paternity to remain a mystery is evidenced by the fact that, years later, when her grandson Lipsha Morrissey asks who her father is, Lulu refuses to answer (*The Bingo Palace* chapter 11). Despite this uncertainty, after her birth everyone clearly accepts Lulu as Eli's child, even her grandmother Margaret Kashpaw, who earlier had been keen on proving the opposite. In chapter

Lulu Nanapush Morrissey Lamartine

9 of *Tracks,* for example, Nanapush, speaking to Lulu, refers to Eli as "your father" (*Tr,* 210).

The first eleven years of Lulu's life are recorded in *Tracks,* primarily from the point of view of her "grandfather," Nanapush. Lulu is born in the spring of 1914 after Fleur's dangerous labor (chapter 3). According to *Tracks,* the appearance of a bear in Fleur's cabin during her labor shocks her into giving birth. Nanapush names the child, giving her his own surname and the nickname (Lulu) of his deceased daughter. Chapter 10 of *The Last Report on the Miracles at Little No Horse* also records Lulu's birth, though the story of the bear is altered here. When Father Damien comes to baptize the newborn, he is enchanted by her and adds his own name to Nanapush's as father.

In *Tracks* chapter 4 Pauline records with envy the love and attention Fleur and the rest of the family lavish upon Lulu. When, in the winter of 1917–1918 (chapter 5), Nanapush and Margaret are attacked by Boy Lazarre and Clarence Morrissey, Lulu escapes and runs to Margaret's house. In the famine winter of 1918–1919 (chapter 6), the pregnant Fleur goes without food so that Lulu can eat. When Fleur goes into early labor, Lulu runs for help through the snow to Margaret's house. She almost freezes, but according to Pauline's death vision, Fleur wins Lulu's life in a card game in the land of the dead. In chapter 7, Nanapush cares for Lulu's severely frostbitten feet and refuses to let the white doctor amputate. Afterward, the anxious Fleur, whose premature baby has died, follows Lulu everywhere. The next spring (chapter 8), Lulu is among the group on the shore watching Pauline in the leaky boat on Matchimanito Lake.

According to her recollection in "The Good Tears" in *Love Medicine,* the summer that Lulu is seven, she finds a dead man by her "playhouse" in the woods. Chapters 8 and 9 of *Tracks* reveal the man to be Napoleon Morrissey. According to the accounts in chapters 9 of *Tracks* and *Last Report,* however, this incident takes place in 1919, when Lulu is five. Late that summer, Fleur learns that her land has been confiscated and sold and spends much of the night plotting how to get revenge and regain the land (*Last Report* chapter 10). As Fleur broods, Lulu creeps up, and the two play wildly and then embrace.

In light of what Fleur subsequently does, this scene is poignant, for her plan requires that she send Lulu to the government boarding school, an action that ultimately causes Lulu to hate her. Both "The Good Tears" in *Love Medicine* and chapter 15 of *Last Report* tell about Lulu's weeping on the bus to school. In all accounts of Lulu's experiences at school, she hates the place and rebels. But Erdrich's early novels *Love Medicine* and *Tracks* give us a different picture from that of the later *Last Report.* In the earlier versions, Lulu seems to continue to long for her mother the whole time she is at school and often tries to run away to find her

Lulu Nanapush Morrissey Lamartine

(*Love Medicine* "The Island"). When Lulu returns to the reservation in chapter 9 of *Tracks,* she still carries the marks of her rebellion—the ugly punishment dress and scabs on her knees from scrubbing sidewalks. Lulu's more detailed story in *Last Report* chapter 15, however, indicates that she tried to run away only once, in her first summer at school (1920). When she is caught and punished, she quickly comes to hate her mother, never tries to run away again, and is relieved immediately of her punishment dress and tasks. This *Last Report* account also tells that in Lulu's last year at school, Fleur, dressed like a white woman, comes six times to retrieve her, but Lulu refuses to go with her. (See also *Four Souls* chapter 8 and the **Fleur Pillager** entry.) Lulu especially resents the fact that her mother had been so caring all through her childhood, so that she was unprepared for this betrayal (*Last Report* chapter 15).

While Lulu is away, her other adult caretakers do what they can for her. In the autumn of 1920, a black dog who represents death and the devil appears to Father Damien in *Last Report* chapter 11, asking for Lulu. To spare her, Damien makes a deal with the dog—he will give his life and soul in exchange for Lulu's. Father Damien, Margaret, and especially Nanapush also work tirelessly to bring Lulu home (*Tracks* chapter 9). In the spring of 1924, they finally succeed. In *Last Report* chapter 16, Nector writes to Fleur in Minneapolis to tell her that Lulu is home, but Fleur does not respond.

After Lulu's return, there is hostility between her and Margaret ("The Island"). Later, however, Lulu apparently comes to revere Margaret as her grandmother and respects her commitment to holding onto the land ("The Good Tears"). One variation in Lulu's return story is in the place where she subsequently lives. In "The Island," she lives with Nanapush; Margaret often leaves them in a huff and returns to her own land. In chapters 15 and 16 of *Four Souls,* however, both Lulu and Nanapush are living with Margaret on her land.

In 1933, Fleur returns from Minneapolis to the reservation (see *The Bingo Palace* chapter 12, *Last Report* chapter 16, and *Four Souls* chapter 14), and Lulu continues to reject her (*Four Souls* chapters 15 and 16). Once Fleur is settled on her land, in *Last Report* chapter 16, she seeks out her daughter again, but Lulu will not relent. Now a young woman, she is as stubborn as her mother, even though both Nanapush and Father Damien try to persuade her to forgive Fleur (*Last Report* chapter 15). Father Damien also talks to Lulu in chapter 16 about the careless and bold way she flaunts her charms, fearing the kind of life this flaunting will bring her. He is not successful in changing her behavior with men, but he does convince her to become financially self-sufficient, and he sees that the one true romance of her life is her children.

Lulu's first love is Nector Kashpaw, Eli's younger brother, thus possibly her uncle ("Wild Geese" in *Love Medicine*). When Nector begins seeing Marie Lazarre, however, Lulu goes to the island home of her mother's kinsman, Moses Pillager ("The Island"). They become lovers, and in 1935 or 1936, Lulu gives birth to ***their son*** (his given name is not revealed). Moses is the father of at least one other of Lulu's sons, Gerry Nanapush (born about 1945), and possibly a third, since in "Lulu's Boys" her three oldest sons carry her maiden name and are thus probably born before her first marriage. (In *Last Report* chapter 16, there seem to be only two premarriage boys.)

Because Moses will not come live in town with her, Lulu decides to marry a Morrissey for spite (see "The Good Tears"). At this point, Nanapush takes her aside and tells her the stories about Fleur and the Kashpaw, Morrissey, and Lazarre families that are recorded in the odd-numbered chapters of *Tracks*. Nanapush's object in his lectures to Lulu is to make her understand Fleur's actions and to persuade her not to marry the Morrissey (see *Tracks* chapter 9). Lulu goes ahead with the marriage, though she later regrets it. According to *Last Report* chapter 16, by 1945 Lulu has left the Morrissey, pregnant with his child. (The continuation of Nanapush's *Tracks* history in the odd-numbered chapters of *Four Souls* may also be for Lulu's enlightenment, but he does not generally address her directly in this book.)

Lulu's second marriage is to Henry Lamartine (Senior), as recorded in "The Good Tears" and "Lulu's Boys" in *Love Medicine*. Henry dies in a car-train wreck in 1950, a probable suicide. When Henry's brother Beverly comes for the funeral, he and Lulu make love in a shed after the wake. Nine months later, Lulu gives birth to Beverly's child, her seventh son, whom she names Henry Lamartine Junior.

In 1952 Lulu and Nector begin a five-year affair, as related in "The Plunge of the Brave" and "The Good Tears." Lulu has a son with Nector—the youngest of ***her eight boys***—named Lyman Lamartine, born about 1953. (According to "Lulu's Boys," after her three Nanapush sons, the next oldest are Morrisseys, who are later renamed Lamartine, probably after Lulu marries Henry. Reservation gossips observe that Lulu's third group of sons, the younger Lamartine boys, look as if they have various fathers, which the reader knows to be the case.)

As recounted in "Lulu's Boys," "The Plunge of the Brave," and "The Good Tears," Beverly returns to the reservation from the Twin Cities in 1957 with the intention of taking Henry Junior back to the city. But he is once again attracted to Lulu, and they sleep together. While Beverly is staying with her, Lulu receives papers signed by Nector Kashpaw evicting her from her land. Furious, Lulu sics her dogs on Nector and marries Beverly. When she discovers that Beverly has another wife in the city, she sends him back to get a divorce, accompanied by her twelve-year-old son, Gerry.

Lulu Nanapush Morrissey Lamartine

After Beverly leaves, Nector goes to see Lulu to tell her he is leaving his wife for her, but instead he sets fire to her house ("The Plunge of the Brave," "Flesh and Blood," and "The Good Tears"). While rescuing her son Lyman from the burning house, Lulu loses her hair. (The incident is also referred to in chapters 5 and 14 of *The Bingo Palace*.) Lulu and her boys camp out on the site of the burned-out house for two months until the tribe builds her another house on better land.

In "The Good Tears," when Lulu is almost fifty, she gives birth to her last child, her only daughter, Bonita, fathered by an unnamed ***Mexican migrant farmworker.*** Bonita is apparently born in about 1963 ("The Red Convertible"). In "The Good Tears," "The Red Convertible," and "Scales," Lulu suffers a series of heartaches with her sons. Shortly after Gerry graduates from high school, he is arrested and imprisoned for assault. Although he continually escapes, he is never a free man again. Then Henry Junior, after returning from Vietnam with psychological problems, drowns in 1974, and his half brother Lyman is so distraught that he stays depressed and drunk for a year.

When Lulu is around sixty-five, she moves into the Senior Citizens, where she and Nector meet again ("The Good Tears" and "Love Medicine"). One day they embrace and kiss in the laundry room. When Nector dies in 1982, Lulu is in the hospital recovering from eye surgery. After her return to the Senior Citizens, her old rival Marie Kashpaw helps care for her. In "The Tomahawk Factory," the two women become political allies in support of traditional culture and in opposition to Lyman's efforts to create a souvenir factory. Yet over time, the tension between them revives, and one day in 1983 an argument between them erupts into a riot that destroys the factory. In "Crossing the Water" (1984), Lulu tells Lipsha that he is her grandson, the child of her son Gerry and June Morrissey. We also learn in this story that Lulu has a portion of the Pillagers' uncanny power, knowing things about people without being told.

The Bingo Palace continues the story of Lulu's relationship with Lipsha and Gerry. In chapter 1, Lipsha is living aimlessly in Fargo when Lulu mails him a copy of a Wanted poster of his father, apparently as a warning. Lulu keeps the original poster in a picture frame in her apartment (chapter 10). In chapter 7, Lulu is a regular patron of the bingo hall where Lipsha works, and he learns her businesslike approach to gambling. Lipsha goes to see Lulu briefly in chapter 11, when he is looking for Fleur. Lulu still does not talk about Fleur but says that she does not hate her mother, merely understands her. In chapter 21, Lulu's efforts are responsible for a tribal request that Gerry be transported to a Minnesota prison. When he escapes from the transport flight, rumors surface in chapter 22 about Lulu's part in the affair, and federal marshals question her in chapter 25. After she plays cat-and-mouse with the marshals for hours, they arrest her for possession of the stolen Wanted poster. As she leaves her apartment in handcuffs, dressed in traditional regalia, she dances and trills the old woman's victory yell.

The Last Report on the Miracles at Little No Horse shows that in 1996 Lulu's affection for the now-ancient Father Damien is still strong. In the prologue to this novel, Father Damien muses that Lulu is virtually his own daughter now. Whenever she comes to visit the old priest, her affection for him is obvious (see chapters 8, 14, and 21). It is also clear from the events of this year that Lulu, now eighty-two years old, has lost none of her verve and charm. In March, a somewhat younger priest, Father Jude, comes to the reservation to interview Father Damien. During his stay, Lulu comes by to see Damien, and Jude is caught by her piercing gaze (chapter 14). Lulu invites him to come speak to her culture class the next day, and within a week Jude realizes that he has fallen in love. When Father Jude interviews Lulu in chapter 15, she tells him about her rejection of her mother, apparently to warn him that if he hurts her, she will reject him as well. He later accompanies Lulu to the Sweetheart Bingo Bash (chapter 21). When Father Jude interviews Marie Kashpaw, she can tell from his expression that Lulu has caught him and says, "Don't blame yourself . . . you had no chance here, no chance at all" (*LR*, 325).

Lulu is mentioned two other times in *Last Report*. In chapter 21, Father Jude discovers her birth certificate and decides (mistakenly) that Father Damien is her biological father, and in chapter 22, as Father Damien goes to Spirit Island to die in June 1996, Lulu is one of the people he most hates to leave.

Lumber president. Man who, along with a *military captain* and the Indian agent, tries to convince the Ojibwe to sell their land for cash in chapter 3 of *Tracks*. He is probably president of the Turcot lumber company, which in chapters 5 and 9 is buying up and logging reservation land. See **Palmer Turcot.**

Lying Down Grass. Nanapush's first sexual partner, although not one of his three wives. Also known by her Indian name, Sanawashonekek, she is mentioned in chapters 3 and 9 of *Tracks*.

A woman with this name is also included in a long list of female acquaintances of Margaret Kashpaw's great-grandmother in *Four Souls* chapter 14. She is likely the same woman as the Lying Down Grass of *Tracks*.

Lyman Lamartine. Son of Nector Kashpaw and Lulu Lamartine; Lulu's youngest son. Lyman is conceived during Nector and Lulu's five-year affair, 1952–1957, while Lulu is between husbands and Nector is married to Marie (*Love Medicine* "The Good Tears"). He is born about 1953. Although Lulu will not tell Nector that Lyman is his child, Nector believes the boy looks like him ("The Plunge of

Lyman Lamartine

the Brave"), and in "The Good Tears" Lulu says he is "half Kashpaw." In 1957, when Nector sets fire to Lulu's house, young Lyman is alone in the house, sleeping ("The Good Tears"). Lulu rescues him and loses her hair in the fire.

From the time he is fourteen, Lyman is a smooth ladies' man (*The Bingo Palace* chapter 11). He is also a natural entrepreneur. From age fifteen, he owns and operates the Joliet Café (*Love Medicine* "The Red Convertible"). It is destroyed in a tornado, but he is financially savvy enough to have insured it.

Of his seven half brothers, Lyman is closest to Henry Junior, born about 1950 ("Lulu's Boys"). He describes their relationship in "The Red Convertible" in *Love Medicine* and in chapter 14 of *The Bingo Palace*. The summer Lyman is sixteen, he and Henry buy a red Oldsmobile convertible with the insurance money from the café and spend the summer driving all over the northern Midwest, and even to Alaska. When they get back home, Henry joins the Marines and, shortly after Christmas (1969), is sent to Vietnam. When Henry returns in 1973, Lyman tries to shake him out of his post-traumatic stress disorder by banging up the car so that Henry must repair it. The following spring (1974), Lyman and Henry drive the restored car to the Red River. Henry walks into the swift current and sinks, and, after an unsuccessful attempt to rescue him, Lyman sends the car in after him. When he returns home, Lyman tells his mother that there has been an accident and that the car went out of control and into the river ("The Good Tears").

In "The Tomahawk Factory," Lyman remains depressed and drunk for a year after Henry Junior's death, then becomes an ambitious administrator in the Bureau of Indian Affairs, eventually moving to Aberdeen. After Nector dies in 1982, Lyman asks Lulu about his father ("The Good Tears"), and he moves back to the reservation to run the tribal souvenir factory that Nector had started to build ("The Tomahawk Factory"). After an interfamily brawl destroys the factory in 1983, Lyman plans a future in Indian reservation gambling ("Lyman's Luck").

Lyman is an important character in *The Bingo Palace,* a book named after his latest business enterprise. In chapter 1, reservation gossip pegs him as a pleasant but scheming entrepreneur who, like his father, mixes the interests of the tribe with his own ambition. When we first see him in chapter 2, he is at a powwow doing a traditional dance in his half brother Henry's outfit. Lyman is now financially successful and is semi-engaged to a beautiful young woman, Shawnee Ray Toose, of whose small son, Redford, he is the reputed father. Shawnee Ray is living with Lyman's half sister, Zelda Kashpaw, who is promoting their marriage. Lyman's rival for Shawnee Ray's affection is Lipsha Morrissey, the son of another of Lyman's half brothers, Gerry Nanapush.

When Lipsha takes Shawnee Ray out for dinner in chapter 4 and gets into trouble with the Canadian border guards, the influential Lyman rescues him in chapter 5. When he sees that Lipsha has Nector's ceremonial pipe, Lyman offers to buy it, but Lipsha refuses to sell. Lyman hires Lipsha to be a watchman-janitor at the bingo hall and is irritated in chapter 7 when Lipsha wins his advertising lure, the bingo van. Lyman continues his efforts to buy Nector's pipe in chapter 8, and in chapter 9, Lyman manages to "borrow" the pipe by blackmailing Lipsha. Lyman then travels to an Indian Gaming Conference in Reno where, in an all-night gambling spree, he loses the tribe's money and pawns the pipe (chapter 8). He is later able to redeem the pipe (chapter 9).

Chapter 9 reveals that Lyman has a new moneymaking scheme—to build a larger facility, a casino, beside an undeveloped lake on a piece of reservation land that he believes will soon revert from individual ownership to ownership by the tribe. He talks the gullible Lipsha into going in with him on this project by opening a joint bank account with him. In chapter 22, Lipsha discovers that Lyman has withdrawn all of Lipsha's bingo winnings from this account. It becomes clear in chapters 17 and 20 that the lake property Lyman wants is none other than the Pillager land on Matchimanito. Lyman has a vision in chapter 13 in which Fleur repeats the words of Nanapush (recorded in chapter 3 of *Tracks*) regarding land as the only thing that lasts. Perhaps ironically, this message further encourages Lyman to acquire and develop Pillager land. It seems that Lyman is ultimately successful in seizing the land, for in the closing chapter of the novel, men come with signed papers to evict Fleur.

When Shawnee Ray leaves Redford briefly with her alcoholic sisters, Lyman get a court order to gain legal custody of the boy (chapter 14). The result of this court order is revealed in chapter 15, when authorities seize Redford by force from the Toose sisters. Lipsha is furious with Lyman about his intrusion into Shawnee Ray's life, and the two get into a food fight in the local Dairy Queen. Equally angry, in chapter 14 Shawnee Ray informs Lyman that he may not, in fact, be Redford's father. She adds that she will never marry him and warns him never to go to court again.

Lyman invites Lipsha to join him in a fast and vision quest under the direction of Xavier Toose (Shawnee Ray's uncle). Lyman's fast culminates in his solitary dancing in the woods and a visionary conversation with the dead Henry Junior (chapter 18). Afterward, Lyman sits in a circle with the other participants in the vision quest and tells them of his experience (chapters 17 and 20).

Lyman relinquishes the ceremonial pipe in chapter 23, returning it not to Lipsha but to Zelda as a way of conceding the failure of their alliance to control Shawnee Ray. From Shawnee Ray's thoughts in chapter 26, it is clear that Lyman has lost his battle with Lipsha for her affections.

In *Tales of Burning Love,* Lyman's efforts to realize his dream of a casino include

Lyman Lamartine

getting the part-Chippewa contractor Jack Mauser, a friend of one of Lyman's older brothers, involved in the project. In "Satin Heart" [12], he goes to Jack's supposed funeral convinced that Jack is not dead, and sometime that evening he apparently speaks with his half brother Gerry, who has recently escaped from prison. Lyman learns from Gerry that Lipsha is stranded in a snowbound car, and "The Tale of the Unknown Passenger" [34] suggests that Lyman goes out to try to rescue him.

In "The Owl" [17], Lyman calls Hegelstead, the Fargo banker who has made a now-defaulted loan to Jack. After a brief visit with Jack, Hegelstead calls Lyman back and makes a deal ("Mauser and Mauser" [39]): Lyman will pay off Jack's previous subcontractors, and Hegelstead will lend Jack (or Lyman) more money toward the construction of the casino. Besides the funding, Lyman wants Jack as chief contractor because he is an enrolled member of the tribe. Jack accepts Lyman's offer, and in "A Last Chapter" [46], Lyman is referred to as Jack's casino partner.

Lynette Kashpaw. King Howard Kashpaw's white wife; mother of King Howard Kashpaw Junior in *Love Medicine*. Lynette and King live in the Twin Cities. They come with their baby to a Kashpaw family gathering in 1981 ("The World's Greatest Fishermen"), two months after the death of King's mother, June Morrissey Kashpaw. They are driving a new blue Firebird purchased with June's insurance money. That evening, King threatens Lynette and tries to drown her. "Crossing the Water" gives a glimpse of Lynette and King's dysfunctional family from the point of view of their now school-aged son. When Gerry Nanapush visits their apartment in 1984, Lynette is afraid of Gerry and insists that King sign over the registration of June's car to him and June's son, Lipsha Morrissey.

M

Madonna of the Serpents. Statue of the Virgin commissioned by Father Damien in 1922. According to chapters 7 and 10 of *The Last Report on the Miracles at Little No Horse,* the statue of the Virgin at Little No Horse before this time is a poor, chipped thing, and Sister Hildegarde wants a "real" statue for the church. (This description is different from the account in *Tracks* chapter 4, which tells that the reservation already has a good statue before 1922.) In chapter 10 of *Last Report,* when Damien remembers money lying in a Fargo bank, he commissions the new statue from a ***Winnipeg wood-carver*** who uses a special plaster for his religious pieces. The seventy-five-year-old artist models the statue after his mistress, an ugly woman who nevertheless has kind, beautiful eyes. The Virgin is standing on a snake and a slivered moon (see chapter 16). When the statue arrives at the reservation, Sister Hildegarde wants to send it back. (There are similarities between this Virgin and the one described in *Tracks*. See **Statue of the Virgin on the reservation**.)

In chapter 16 of *Last Report,* Father Damien urges Lulu Nanapush to pray to the Virgin, here called Our Lady of the Serpents.

Man who talked to wolves. See **Ira's father.**

Man with frozen fingers. Recalled by Dot Mauser in "February Thaw" [40] in *Tales of Burning Love.* See **Xavier Albert Toose.**

Margaret (Rushes Bear) Kashpaw. Originally named Center of the Sky; oldest wife of the original Kashpaw and mother of twelve children, including Eli and Nector Kashpaw. Center of the Sky is raised as a traditional. In chapter 14 of *Four Souls,* we learn that **her mother** at first tried to live white but then abandoned the attempt. When Center of the Sky is a child, her mother hides her from the agents of the government school as long as possible—under the skirts of her great-grandmother, Medicine Dress. Especially through this grandmother, the child learns the countless names and stories in her matriarchal lineage, so that she feels deeply connected to her heritage. Thus when Center of the Sky becomes Margaret, goes to the government school, and converts to Catholicism, she does not abandon her Ojibwe name, language, and traditions.

Margaret first appears as an adult in chapter 6 of *The Last Report on the Miracles at Little No Horse,* when, in March 1912, Father Damien visits Kashpaw and his four wives. Margaret is his first and oldest wife and has borne him many strong children. A good Catholic, she is his only church-married wife. Her personality, though, is "pure vinegar" (*LR,* 93). *Last Report* chapter 9 describes her as a small woman, who nevertheless is physically strong and has a powerful voice. After Father Damien's visit, when Nanapush insists that Kashpaw should give up three wives, the family begins to disintegrate. When Margaret strikes Fishbone's child, Kashpaw strikes Margaret. In anger, Margaret visits Nanapush, who falls in love with her.

Later that year, Kashpaw and his remaining wife, Quill, are killed in an accident on a Catholic feast day (*Last Report* chapter 7). Sometime after his death, the government carves Ojibwe land into individual allotments. According to "The World's Greatest Fishermen" in *Love Medicine* and chapter 3 of *Tracks,* Margaret and her two youngest children, Eli and Nector, are allotted adjacent land on the reservation, while her ten grown children move away when they are allotted land in Montana. Since Nector is drawn to the town ways of the whites, Margaret is counting on Eli to stay and take care of her in old age. Thus, as chapter 3 of *Tracks* continues, when she learns about the fifteen-year-old Eli's relationship with

Margaret (Rushes Bear) Kashpaw

a pregnant Fleur Pillager in the fall of 1913, she is angry. She had wanted a more docile daughter-in-law.

Nevertheless, the following spring (1914), Margaret assists at the birth of Fleur's daughter, Lulu (who Margaret realizes may be her grandchild), saving Fleur's life. *Tracks* chapter 3 tells us that a bear enters Fleur's cabin while she is in labor, inducing the birth. After it leaves the cabin, Margaret marches straight up to it before realizing she has no gun. Because of this incident, she will later take the name "Rushes Bear" ("The Island" and "The Beads" in *Love Medicine*). In both the *Tracks* account and in *Last Report* chapter 10, without Fleur's knowledge, Margaret sends for Father Damien to baptize the infant. *Last Report* tells us that Margaret, in her own grumpy way, loves Father Damien.

When Eli refuses to return to his mother's home (*Tracks* chapter 4), Margaret and Nector often stay at Fleur's cabin. There, the Kashpaw and Pillager families join together into something of a clan, mixing Fleur's old religious ways with the Catholicism of Margaret, who often brings Lulu to mass.

In the autumn of 1917 (*Tracks* chapter 4), when Fleur casts a spell on Sophie Morrissey, Margaret tries to be kind to the girl. Even so, in the ensuing winter (chapter 5), she becomes the target of Clarence Morrissey's vengeance. One night, Clarence and Boy Lazarre tie up Nanapush and Margaret and shave her head. (This incident is also referred to in "The Tomahawk Factory" in *Love Medicine*, chapter 9 of *Last Report*, and chapter 14 of *Four Souls*.) When the men first grab Margaret, she utters a war cry and bites Lazarre's hand, a bite that results in blood poisoning and ultimately his death. When Fleur sees Margaret, she shaves her own head as a sign of solidarity with her mother-in-law. Nanapush avenges the insult to Margaret by snaring Clarence, and he buys her a large coal-black bonnet, which she wears daily, earning herself the nickname "Old Lady Coalbucket." His gallantry softens her feelings toward him, and by Ash Wednesday 1918, they are keeping company, although their relationship continues to be prickly. Father Damien suggests that they be church married, but Nanapush declines. This winter is a famine time. After Nanapush almost starves and Margaret comes and revives him, they both move to Fleur's cabin until spring.

In chapters 6 and 7 of *Tracks,* Margaret comes to Fleur's aid again after her second baby is born prematurely in the winter of 1918–1919. This is yet another famine winter, and the whole family is weak from starvation. But in chapter 7, Margaret walks to town, and she and Father Damien return with government rations. She also helps the family raise money to pay Kashpaw and Pillager land fees and in the spring accompanies Nector to town to pay the agent. But we learn in chapter 9 that because the fees are higher than expected, Margaret and

Margaret (Rushes Bear) Kashpaw

Nector—unbeknown to Nanapush and Fleur—use all of the money to pay the fees on Kashpaw land and do not pay them on Pillager land.

Also in the spring of 1919, Margaret is among the group on the shore of Matchimanito (*Tracks* chapter 8) who are watching Pauline in a leaky boat. Late that summer, the decomposed body of Napoleon Morrissey is found on Fleur's land. At his funeral in chapter 9 of *Last Report,* Margaret goads Bernadette Morrissey, which stirs up an interfamily riot between the Kashpaw family and the Lazarres and Morrisseys.

About the same time, Fleur learns of Margaret and Nector's betrayal (*Tracks* chapter 9). Although Fleur is angry with Nector and threatens revenge, she forgives Margaret because Margaret has twice saved her life. But Margaret takes the threat to Nector seriously. That fall she sends him to an off-reservation boarding school. (See also "The World's Greatest Fishermen" in *Love Medicine.*) Nanapush, his land and house forfeit, comes to live with Margaret. Once Fleur establishes herself in Minneapolis, she sends goods and supplies to the pair (*Last Report* chapter 16).

In chapter 9 of *Tracks,* after Fleur sends Lulu to the government school and she herself leaves the reservation, Margaret, Nanapush, and Father Damien go to work writing letters and filling out forms to bring Lulu home. It will be four years before they succeed. At school, Lulu thinks about her grandmother, and when she tries to run away home, she imagines seeing her (*Last Report* chapter 15). In 1924, when Lulu is finally able to return, Margaret and Nanapush go to meet her bus.

Tracks chapter 9, "The Island" in *Love Medicine,* and *Last Report* chapter 16, all make some reference to Lulu's homecoming. Chapters 15 and 16 of *Four Souls* indicate that, after her return, Lulu stays with Margaret and Nanapush on Margaret's land. In "The Island," however, she moves into Nanapush's cabin. Margaret objects to her intrusion and, in anger, begins spending more time on her own Kashpaw allotment, an hour's walk away. In her narrative in "The Island," Lulu considers Margaret mean—"She . . . didn't like me, never had"—and plots her downfall (*LM,* 69–70). Lulu's perception in this narrative contrasts to her *Last Report* narrative, cited above, and also with her perspective years later, after Margaret's death, in "The Good Tears" in *Love Medicine.* In this later chapter, Lulu recalls the stories Margaret told about the removal of the Ojibwe from their ancestral lands. Lulu attributes to Margaret's influence her own stubbornness about holding onto her land. Lulu's perspective in "The Island" is also at odds with the picture of Margaret as doting grandmother in several chapters of *Tracks.* Factors contributing to Lulu's perspective in "The Island" probably include her immaturity at the time and the fact that Margaret habitually hides a loving heart behind her defensive, prickly personality. In *Four Souls,* Margaret admits that, like Nanapush,

Margaret (Rushes Bear) Kashpaw

she has saved herself by talking, but with her, the words are "cutting and angry" (*FS,* 179).

Although Margaret has all of her life held onto her Ojibwe heritage and has especially fought to retain the land, in her older years, she is overcome by greed for chimookomaan (white) things. In chapter 7 of *Four Souls,* she becomes so enamored of the nuns' linoleum that she sells some of Nector's land allotment to buy the stuff for her own cabin.

Four Souls chapter 9 describes a conflict that arises between Margaret and Nanapush when Nanapush's old enemy Shesheeb moves in down the road. Margaret makes a habit of taking a shortcut through Shesheeb's property on her way to mass, and she deliberately inflames Nanapush's jealousy. Nanapush at first tries to use medicine on Shesheeb and even prepares a love potion for Margaret. When those efforts fail, he makes a snare to kill Shesheeb, but it is Margaret who is caught in the snare. As she thinks that she is dying, Margaret has a vision of her great-grandmother, Medicine Dress. In the vision, this grandmother gives Margaret the secret of her dress's power (no piece should ever be touched by a white) and instructs her to make a copy of the dress for herself. When Nanapush rescues Margaret, she tells him about the vision, and in chapter 11, she enlists his help in gathering materials for the dress.

Margaret and Nanapush have peace for a time, until Nector comes home from school and reveals Nanapush's snaring of Clarence Morrissey years earlier. (In contrast, *Tracks* chapter 9 suggests that Margaret had known all along about the snaring of Clarence.) This information makes her realize that Nanapush had set her snare. She punishes him by fueling his jealousy, but as she continues to make the dress in chapter 14, her heart softens toward him. The dress also brings back memories from fifty years of her life, including her relationship with old Medicine Dress and stories of her matriarchal lineage.

In chapter 11 of *Four Souls,* the evening the dress is finished, Nanapush comes home with a keg of wine stolen from the convent cellar. This is supposedly a gift for Margaret, but he has drunk most of it himself. Margaret dons the dress and dances, but the two get into an argument. When Nanapush puts on the dress and purports to show her how to dance correctly, Margaret leaves in anger. We learn from chapter 14 that she immediately walks to Shesheeb's place, knowing that she is just bluffing. After watching Shesheeb from a distance, she leaves.

Margaret doesn't come back home for two days. On the second evening, she returns to find a hole in both her linoleum and the roof and listens to Nanapush's far-fetched story about a falling star. Margaret sees through his ruse, but instead of rekindling her anger, she laughs.

Two other small incidents occur during this period of Margaret's life. In 1922,

Margaret (Rushes Bear) Kashpaw

after the new church is built and Father Damien buys new vestments in *Last Report* chapter 12, he commissions Margaret to bead the garments. She so covers them with beads that they are heavy like armor. Several years later, in chapter 16, after Lulu is home and has grown into a rather wild young woman, Father Damien asks Margaret to bring her to the church so he can talk to her. As they talk, Damien notes that Lulu has inherited Margaret's clear inner sight.

The day Fleur returns to the reservation in the spring of 1933, when she spots Margaret at the trader's store in chapter 14 of *Four Souls,* her eyes light and she smiles. When they meet later at Margaret's house, Margaret remembers Fleur's shaving her own head in solidarity with the shaven-headed Margaret, and her thoughts indicate how far her feelings for Fleur have progressed from her former antipathy: "I was eager to hold her close and wished as I always did that love had worked out between Fleur and Eli. . . . Fleur Pillager was the daughter of my spirit" (*FS,* 184). Even so, in chapter 15, Fleur refuses to stay with Margaret and Nanapush, because Lulu is living with them and refuses to see her mother. Margaret grieves when she sees how alcohol has affected Fleur. In chapter 16, the morning after Fleur wins back her land in a poker game, she comes to visit Margaret and Nanapush. Margaret sends Nanapush and the boy away, bathes Fleur, and tells her what she must do to renew her relationship with the Ojibwe spirits—she must fast for eight days and nights on a rock by Matchimanito. Margaret promises to assist Fleur, especially by giving her the medicine dress to help her through the ordeal. At the end of the eight days, Margaret says, Fleur will be given a new name. Margaret is qualified to direct this ceremony because she has purged herself of the influence of the whites through her vision and the making of the medicine dress.

Although *Four Souls* indicates that Nanapush lives in Margaret's cabin in the 1930s and that Nector returns home before 1933, *Love Medicine* gives a different version of these details. "The Wild Geese" suggests that Nector comes home in 1934, and "The Plunge of the Brave" says that he lives with Margaret and Eli in the old Kashpaw place. (This story doesn't mention Nanapush's presence, just as *Four Souls* doesn't mention Eli's.) In about 1935, Nector decides to marry Marie Lazarre. "The Island" records that Margaret is angry that her son is marrying a member of the family that had insulted her.

In the autumn of 1941 (chapter 18 of *Last Report*), Margaret spots a fat moose, and she and Nanapush try to kill it from a canoe. The hunt is a failure, and the moose drags Nanapush and his boat all over the reservation. The next day, Margaret finds them and kills the moose, but by now its meat is sour and stringy. Throughout that winter, Margaret punishes Nanapush for the moose fiasco by refusing to let him sleep with her and by feeding him undercooked beans. After the turn of the year, when Nanapush dies in digestive misery, Margaret regrets her

Margaret (Rushes Bear) Kashpaw

hard-heartedness and tries unsuccessfully to bring him back by making love to his corpse. But at his wake, Nanapush does come back from the dead—twice. After the second resurrection, their friends leave, and Margaret and Nanapush make love. By morning, Nanapush is permanently dead, but Margaret is at peace. She buries him as he had wished, in the traditional manner.

When she was writing *Love Medicine,* Erdrich had not yet developed this part of the story in her mind. Thus, her account of the end of Margaret and Nanapush's relationship in "The Beads" is different from the *Four Souls* account above. In the earlier story, Margaret leaves Nanapush, perhaps in the 1930s, and Fleur comes to care for him. (In 1948, Marie Kashpaw says this happened "Years ago" [*LM,* 98] and that Nanapush is still alive.) In this account, after leaving Nanapush, Margaret stays for a time with her children in Montana and then goes to her childhood home near Lake Superior. When she returns to the reservation in 1948, she moves in with Nector and Marie, who are now living in the Kashpaw house (see "The World's Greatest Fishermen" in *Love Medicine*). At first, she and Marie do not get along—Margaret demonstrates the same vinegar toward Marie that she has in all her other relationships. But after she helps Marie through the difficult birth of Marie's last child that winter, the two women bond. Margaret has finally found a home and a daughter who takes care of her until her death. Years later, after Nector's death, in "Resurrection" Marie has a dream about the past that includes Margaret, and afterward she thinks about the old Indian strengths that her mother-in-law had taught her.

Maria Theresa Waldvogel. See Tante (Maria Theresa) Waldvogel.

Marie Lazarre Kashpaw. Daughter of Pauline Puyat and Napoleon Morrissey; supposed youngest daughter of Ignatius Lazarre; wife of Nector Kashpaw. According to chapter 6 of *Tracks,* Marie is born in November 1918. The chronology in "Saint Marie" in *Love Medicine,* however, suggests a 1920 birth date, saying that Marie is "near age fourteen" in the summer of 1934 (*LM,* 43).

When Pauline discovers that she is pregnant in chapter 6 of *Tracks,* she tries to abort the child, but Bernadette Morrissey prevents her and later forcibly delivers Marie. Pauline abandons Marie at birth to join the reservation convent, and Bernadette takes care of the child. In chapter 7, when Bernadette's children Sophie and Clarence bring their Lazarre spouses into her house, Bernadette takes baby Marie and moves to town. The *Tracks* account indicates that Bernadette contracts consumption, and we learn in chapter 8 that as she grows weaker, the slovenly Sophie increasingly cares for the child. Marie grows up believing that she is a Lazarre, though her supposed Lazarre mother is probably not Sophie—Sophie's husband is Izear Lazarre and, according to "The Beads" in *Love Medicine,* Marie's supposed father is Ignatius. In this chapter (1948), the Lazarre woman she believes to be her mother is an old drunk.

In "Saint Marie" in *Love Medicine,* Marie recalls growing up in the bush. The only times she and the other children come to town are for school and for Sunday mass. At the Sacred Heart Convent school, Marie's teacher is Sister Leopolda, who makes it her mission to drive the devil from Marie. In 1934, when she is "near age fourteen," Marie goes up to the convent, hoping to become a "saint." Sister Leopolda is the novice Marie's sponsor. The day Marie arrives, Leopolda pours scalding water on her back and, after Marie kicks her into the oven, she stabs the girl's hand with a bread fork and knocks her out with a poker. When Marie regains consciousness, the sisters are kneeling at her bedside. Leopolda has told them that the wounds in Marie's hand are miraculous stigmata. (This incident is also referred to, without naming Marie, in "Night Prayer" [6] in *Tales of Burning Love* and chapter 8 of *The Last Report on the Miracles at Little No Horse.*)

Marie is leaving the convent, her head and wounded hand wrapped in torn bed linen, when Nector Kashpaw grabs her in "Wild Geese" in *Love Medicine.* As they grapple, the encounter becomes sexual, and Nector discovers in amazement that he, who is in love with the charming Lulu Nanapush, wants this "dirty Lazarre."

According to chapter 20 of *The Last Report on the Miracles at Little No Horse,* after her encounters with Leopolda and Nector, Marie does not go back to the Lazarres but lives in the woods for a time in the old shack once belonging to **Agongos,** selling diluted whiskey. She thinks about the strangeness of her relationship with Leopolda, how the nun, in her cruelty, loves Marie and how Marie hates Leopolda "with a deep longing" (*LR,* 318). One day Leopolda comes and begs Marie to return to the convent. As she stretches out her hands, Marie sees that the palms are pierced like her own. That day, for the first time ever, Marie drinks to numb her pain. Later, Sophie comes for whiskey, begins to talk about Marie's family, and tells her who her mother is—Sister Leopolda (née Pauline Puyat). Marie is astonished, but then, with her wounded hand burning, she laughs.

Also shortly after her experience at the convent, Marie confesses to Father Damien what happened to her there. In *Last Report* chapter 8, we hear pieces of that confession, which uses much of the same language as Marie's narrative in "Saint Marie."

Sometime over the next year, Marie and Nector marry. The story of their first two decades of marriage is told primarily in "The Beads" and "The Plunge of the Brave" in *Love Medicine.* The children begin to come quickly: Gordie in about 1935 (see "Resurrection"), Zelda in 1941 (see "The World's Greatest Fishermen" and "Flesh and Blood"), Aurelia and Patsy in unspecified years, and Eugene in the winter of 1948–1949 ("The Beads"). In "The Beads," we learn that Marie and

Marie Lazarre Kashpaw

Nector also lose two children, a boy and a baby girl, who die in the same year (the girl is born around 1939 or 1940). Marie makes up for this loss by taking in other children. In 1948, while she is still pregnant with Eugene, her adoptive sister Lucille Lazarre dies, and Marie takes in Lucille's daughter, June Morrissey. June is about nine, a little older than Marie's dead daughter would have been if she had lived. Later that year, June goes to live with Nector's brother Eli.

Also while Marie is pregnant with Eugene in "The Beads," Nector's mother, Margaret (Rushes Bear), comes to stay with them. Marie and Margaret have never liked each other, but when the baby is born that winter, Margaret, assisted by Fleur Pillager, helps Marie through her dangerous delivery. After that, the two women bond, and in Margaret, Marie at last finds the mother she never had. During this time, the family has little money. Nector is often gone or drunk, yet Marie is determined to make him into something big on the reservation. He eventually begins to support his family, serves as tribal chairman, and even goes to Washington. What Marie does not know is that in 1952 he also begins a five-year affair with Lulu Nanapush Lamartine.

One day in 1957, in "Flesh and Blood" Marie takes her daughter Zelda to visit old Sister Leopolda, who seems to be dying. The visit turns into a battle of insults and ultimately a physical struggle. When Marie and Zelda return home, Zelda finds a note from Nector under the sugar bowl, saying that he is leaving Marie for Lulu. While Zelda goes to bring Nector back, Marie washes the floor in her good dress, grieving. When Nector arrives home and is afraid to enter, Marie puts out her hand and pulls him in. She has repositioned his note, now under the salt can, and never mentions it. (Marie will be remembered in chapter 14 of *The Bingo Palace* as one of the few people who are able to stay calm through the vicissitudes of love.)

The last child Marie takes in to raise is June's abandoned son, Lipsha Morrissey, as we learn in *Love Medicine*'s "The World's Greatest Fishermen." Various versions of this adoption story are recorded in "Love Medicine" and "Crossing the Water" in *Love Medicine* and in chapter 5 of *The Bingo Palace*.

As Marie and Nector age, Nector becomes feeble-minded. Marie moves with him to the reservation's Senior Citizens, and Aurelia moves into their house on the Kashpaw allotment. Shortly after June's death in 1981, Marie and Nector join the rest of the family for supper at the old Kashpaw place in "The World's Greatest Fishermen." The following year, in "Love Medicine" Marie grieves that Nector, even with his failing mind, still loves Lulu, who also lives at the Senior Citizens. Marie asks Lipsha to make a love medicine to restore Nector's affection for her. Lipsha eventually agrees, but he uses a false medicine of turkey hearts. Marie chews and swallows her turkey heart, but Nector chokes on his and dies. Nector's spirit visits Marie, and Lipsha tells her that Nector visits because of his love for her, not because of Lipsha's medicine.

After Nector's death, Marie returns to the Kashpaw house in "Resurrection." While she is cooking and cleaning house, Gordie arrives—drunk, as he has remained since June's death. When Marie will not provide him with alcohol, Gordie drinks a can of Lysol and dies.

With Nector gone, Marie forms a friendship with her rival Lulu Lamartine. Marie nurses her after eye surgery in "The Good Tears," and the two women become allies in supporting traditional Indian ways in opposition to Lyman Lamartine's commercialism in "The Tomahawk Factory." The friendship disintegrates, however, and their feuding escalates into an interfamily brawl that destroys Lyman's souvenir factory. By the next year, Marie and Lulu have apparently become allies again, as recorded in "Crossing the Water." The contrast between the two women is mentioned in chapter 11 of *The Bingo Palace.*

When Lipsha is confused after learning the truth of his parentage from Lulu, in "Crossing the Water," Marie tries to help him by virtually inviting him to steal her money. (In this story and in chapter 4 of *The Bingo Palace,* Marie is once again living in her apartment at the Senior Citizens.) Lipsha recalls this act of generosity in chapter 9 of *The Bingo Palace.* In chapters 1 and 4 of *The Bingo Palace,* Marie continues to be an indulgent "grandma" to Lipsha even after he is grown, and in chapter 4, she gives him Nector's sacred ceremonial pipe. Marie is present in chapter 7 when Lipsha unsuccessfully attempts to use his "touch" to heal Russell Kashpaw and is mentioned briefly in chapters 10 and 11. She remains calm in chapter 25 when federal marshals come to the Senior Citizens asking questions about the escaped Gerry Nanapush.

When Father Jude from Argus comes to the reservation in 1996 to interview Father Damien about the possible sainthood of Sister Leopolda (now deceased), in *The Last Report on the Miracles at Little No Horse* chapter 8, he mentions to Damien the supposed miracle in which the nun bestowed stigmata on a young novice. Father Damien soundly corrects the younger man by telling him about Marie's confession shortly after the incident—how Leopolda had scalded, stabbed, and brained the girl. Damien urges Jude to believe Marie's account because of the good, solid life she has led. Marie, now almost eighty, is still living at the Senior Citizens, so Jude decides to interview her. On his first visit, Marie refuses to tell him anything about Leopolda, but when he returns a few days later (chapter 20), Marie tells him something of her story. Merely alluding to the convent incident, she tells about her time living in the woods, Leopolda's appearance there, and what she learned from Sophie—that Pauline had deliberately corrupted Sophie and that this woman, Pauline Leopolda Puyat, is Marie's mother. Learning that Leopolda abandoned and tortured her own daughter is one of the final elements rendering it impossible for Jude any longer to consider Leopolda a saint (see chapter 21).

Marie Lazarre's aunt. Remembered by Marie as taking "us children" to Sunday mass in "Saint Marie" in *Love Medicine*. The identities of this aunt and the *other children* are not specified, but since Marie was raised by Lazarres, the aunt is probably a Lazarre woman. She may be Sophie Morrissey Lazarre, since Sophie is beginning to care for the toddler Marie in chapter 8 of *Tracks* and, according to chapter 7, she marries a Lazarre and has numerous children and stepchildren.

Marie Lazarre's grandma. Remembered by Marie in "Saint Marie" in *Love Medicine* as the one person who knows as much about Satan as Sister Leopolda. The grandma, however, calls him by different names and is not afraid of him. Since Marie is mistaken about her parentage, this "grandma" is presumably a Lazarre rather than the mother of one of her birth parents. (Marie's comparison of this woman with Sister Leopolda takes on added significance for the reader of *Tracks* chapter 8.)

Markus Waldvogel. The second son of Eva Kalb Waldvogel, her first with husband Fidelis Waldvogel, in *The Master Butchers Singing Club*. Born in 1925, Markus is named after Eva's beloved father. He has an older half brother, Franz, and younger twin brothers, Emil and Erich. Of the four boys, Markus is the most like Eva and closest to her. Chapter 5 describes the nine-year-old Markus as having Eva's eyes, long hands, and red-gold hair. More reclusive and philosophical than the others, he dotes on his mother. His father, too, finds him gentler and easier to manage than his younger brothers (see chapters 7 and 8). In grade school, Markus and Ruthie Chavers are sweethearts, and he keeps in his pillow notes, small gifts, and a valentine from her (chapter 7). Ruthie and her parents mysteriously disappear early in 1934 (late winter), but Markus doesn't find out what happened to her until Delphine Watzka comes back to town that summer and finds the bodies of the Chavers family in Roy Watzka's locked cellar (see chapters 4 and 5). In chapter 5, Markus is checking his mother's business accounts a few days later when he overhears Delphine's conversation with Sheriff Hock about the bodies. He tells Delphine Ruthie's name, but at the beginning of their relationship, Markus is closed and reserved toward Delphine. That will change radically over time.

By the next summer, 1935, Eva is dying of cancer. In chapter 6, when Eva is in agony on July 4 because her morphine has been stolen, Markus and Franz try to hold her to keep her from killing herself. Sometime later, in chapter 7 the clacker in Markus's pillow (a gift from Ruthie) wakes him one night, and creeping down the hall, he sees his father sitting up with his mother, singing to her. On one of her last good days, Eva buys chinchillas for the boys to raise, and Markus takes primary responsibility for them. In Eva's final days, Markus and the twins are all but forgotten and spend the days roaming outside. Late that summer, the night Eva dies, Markus cries out and kisses her ankle.

As chapter 7 continues, Fidelis's sister, Tante, supposedly takes care of the family, but she is both incompetent and mean-spirited. She is especially hard on Markus. After Eva's death, he has begun wetting the bed, and Tante beats him. While Fidelis is off making deliveries, Markus runs away to Delphine's house. He has come to trust her since she took care of his dying mother. But he worries about the chinchillas, so Delphine teaches the twins to care for them. When Fidelis comes to fetch Markus, Delphine convinces him to let Markus stay longer. She has her companion, Cyprian Lazarre, teach the boy urinating tricks, which enable him to stop his bedwetting.

In chapter 8, the weather has turned cold and Markus is back at home. As the time for selling the adult chinchillas nears, he takes particular care of them. One Friday night, however, wild dogs kill them all, and Markus is heartbroken. He loses not only the money, but also a legacy from his mother.

A year after Eva's death, in the summer of 1936 (chapter 9), Markus discovers a hill of dirt and decides to excavate. He tells the twins, and through the summer and into the fall, the brothers, with friends Roman Shimek and **Grizzy Morris,** excavate a tunnel into a central "room" in the hill. In November, after three days of heavy rain, the boys miss warning signs that the hill is dangerous. After an evening of attempted repair, only Markus is still inside the hill when it collapses. Though Markus's arm is broken, he becomes comfortably unconscious in the tiny breathing space left in the blanketlike earth. He is thus unfrightened and unaware of his father's and Cyprian's frantic efforts to save him. When he has been pulled to safety, he wakes only briefly to see Delphine's face and feel her arms. In chapter 10, Markus falls ill from his burial in the damp earth. When the **Braucher** (healing woman) visits, however, Markus becomes angry, gets out of bed, eats, and goes to school, even though he still has a fever. He is offended because he thinks that she was measuring him for a coffin. Delphine waits several weeks until he is firmly among the living before rectifying his misunderstanding. We learn from chapter 14 that Markus's personality becomes even more studious after the hill incident and that Delphine essentially rears him as her own son.

That December, in chapter 11, Tante uses Markus's near-death to argue her plan to Fidelis—she wants to take the three youngest boys to Germany. That Christmas, a crate of gifts arrives from Germany, including boots, a warm hat, and a sweater for Markus. In chapter 12, one February after this Christmas (Markus is twelve

Markus Waldvogel

to fourteen years old), the Waldvogels plan to carry out Tante's idea of taking the younger boys to Germany. Both Markus and Delphine are grieving. They go to Chicago to complete the travel arrangements, but just before the travelers are to leave for New York, Markus becomes seriously ill, so Tante and the twins leave without him. When he is told that he is going home, even ill, Markus is filled with joy.

In chapter 13, after being back from Chicago for a few days, Delphine goes to check on Markus, who is still in bed, and feeds him the dumpling soup Eva always gave the boys when they were sick. Even a month later, Markus is still not back to full strength. After Fidelis proposes to Delphine, she starts working at the butcher shop again. Finally, months later, they set a wedding date and announce their plans to Markus and Franz. Although Franz feigns indifference, Markus is happy at the news. Soon after they marry that fall, Markus overhears Fidelis's phone conversation with his family in Germany and learns that Emil and Erich will not be able to come home. (Germany is on the brink of war.) At that point, he decides not to put the twins' toy soldiers away (see chapter 14). Also shortly after the wedding, Cyprian comes back through town. When he and his new partner give a gymnastic performance, Markus and Delphine attend, and Markus talks about it for weeks.

When the United States enters the war, in chapter 14 seventeen-year-old Markus manages to get into the army, despite his poor vision. As Delphine tries to dissuade him, Markus twice calls her "Mom." His last night at home, he arranges the twins' armies of toy soldiers. When he writes home that he has failed his vision test and has been given a desk job, Delphine is relieved. Home on leave (probably in 1944), Markus tells Delphine and Fidelis that one of the twins is in a POW camp in Minnesota. Fidelis and Markus drive to the camp. They see Erich, but he refuses even to look at them. On the way home, Markus encourages Fidelis to think positively about a more successful trip in the future.

But when the war ends, only Markus comes home safely. Emil has died, Erich returns to Germany, and Franz is seriously injured and "fade[s] from life" (*MBSC*, 377). In chapter 15, Fidelis and Delphine go to Germany in 1954 to visit. While they are there, Delphine writes to Markus that his father is ill. In her musings in the mid-1950s, Step-and-a-Half recalls Markus as the one unsealed from the hill of dirt (chapter 16).

Marlis Cook Mauser. Fourth wife of Jack Mauser and mother of John Mauser Jr. in *Tales of Burning Love*. In "Best Western" [28], Marlis says that she is Polish. Long before Marlis actually appears, the reader has formed impressions of this "most problematic" of Jack's wives. In "Jack's House" [9], Jack sees her as psychotic and manipulative. Eleanor Schlick Mauser refers to her as "that brain-dead Lolita" ("The Meadowlark" [7]). When Eleanor calls Marlis "Jack's slut" in "Satin Heart" [12], Candice Pantamounty defends her but admits that she is bipolar.

For her family background, see **Marlis Cook's father** and **Marlis Cook's mother.** In "Marlis's Tale" [27], we learn that she has a *brother* and a fifteen-year-old half sister. From the time she is twelve, Marlis wants to be a performer ("The B & B" [16]). Although she cannot sing, she takes piano lessons and devotes herself to transforming her originally plain appearance.

After leaving home, Marlis lives underneath the trailer house of her brother's ex-wife, *Lindsay,* although Lindsay's new husband, *Dane,* does not approve ("Marlis's Tale" [27]). She does not have a job, but lives off the settlements from two accidents. A third "accident" occurs in the summer of 1992 when Marlis grabs a live electrical cable in a store undergoing remodeling. Jack Mauser is there and resuscitates her, although imperfectly, so that she suffers nerve damage. She sues both the store and Jack, but Jack cures her.

A few weeks later (now August), Marlis runs into Jack in a bar, and tells him she is twenty-one. He shows her his huge loan check from the bank and reveals that he has just divorced. They get drunk and go to a motel, where Marlis steals the check. At the motel, she first claims to be twenty-five, then fifteen, and threatens to charge Jack with statutory rape if he does not buy her clothes and a car. The next day he buys her a whole new wardrobe.

That evening, in "Best Western" [28] Marlis takes Jack to her job at the Elkwood Lounge and gets him drunk again. That night she drives him to South Dakota, where they are married by a justice of the peace. Back in Fargo, she alters Jack's check and deposits it in her own bank account, showing the hesitant teller her marriage license as proof of identity. After they marry, Marlis and Jack hide out for a month in Eugene. Although Jack continues to oversee his construction projects near Fargo, Marlis convinces him to go on the road performing with her, he singing, she playing the piano.

Over the next two years, Marlis and Jack book gigs in hotels and nightclubs in various cities across the northern Midwest ("Best Western" [28]). In Detroit at Christmastime 1993, Marlis realizes that she is pregnant. Later that winter, Jack confronts her about the stolen check, and Marlis tells Jack about her pregnancy, to which he responds abusively. His anger and her pain and fear remind Marlis of her girlhood fear of her father. She gets revenge in the Best Western motel in Billings by tying Jack to the bed, subjecting him to some of the pain of being a woman, and then leaving.

In "Baptism River" [29], Marlis returns to Fargo. She gives half of Jack's money back to him, saving the rest to take care of the baby. Jack refuses to answer her

Marlis Cook Mauser

calls and letters. That spring (1994), Candice Pantamounty, one of Jack's previous wives, invites Marlis to take a trip with her. On the trip, Candice offers to help Marlis through the birth and then to adopt the baby. The woman in the adjacent motel room decides that Marlis and Candice are lovers, a notion the two find hilarious. The next morning, Marlis expresses her deepest misgivings about Candice's proposal—she fears that if she gives the baby up for adoption, it will hate her all its life. Candice guesses, perhaps correctly, that this is what Marlis's mother had done with her.

Although Marlis tells her to stay away, in "The Waiting Room" [31] Candice shows up at Marlis's late-term checkup, attends Lamaze classes with her, and helps her through labor. Weeks after the birth of John Mauser Jr. (which occurs sometime before June 1994, "Night Prayer" [6]), Marlis is still suffering from postpartum depression. Candice moves into her apartment to take care of her and the baby, and the women become lovers.

Marlis is determined to nurse the baby, promising Candice that she will not drink ("The B & B" [16]). For weeks she and Candice fight over custody. Marlis eventually gets a job dealing blackjack at the B & B in West Fargo, and Candice hires a nanny to help take care of the baby.

On the day of Jack's (supposed) funeral, January 5, 1995, Marlis is drinking and acting as if Jack is not dead. She is working at the B & B that afternoon when Jack's other wives come to the bar-casino after the funeral. Later that evening, the wives all leave together in a blizzard, and on the way to Fargo the car becomes stuck in a snowdrift ("The Hitchhiker" [18]). As the stranded women argue about Jack in "Secrets and Sugar Babies" [19], Marlis and Candice get into a fight and then make up.

The wives pass the time talking and telling their stories. In "Surviving Sleep" [24], Marlis expresses her naturalistic view of life, and in "Marlis's Tale" [27] and "The Best Western" [28], she tells about her relationship with Jack. Candice then picks up the thread of Marlis's story, recounting the development of her and Marlis's relationship. Marlis and Candice's memories in "The Waiting Room" [31] appear *not* to be told to the other women.

In "Rotating Wild" [32], Eleanor insults Marlis. Enraged, Marlis suggests that it is time to clean snow away from the tailpipe again and that it is Eleanor's turn. The women form a human chain, with Marlis holding Eleanor. When a strong gust of wind seizes her rival, Marlis lets go, allowing Eleanor to fly away into the storm. Overcome with fatigue and cold, in "The Tale of the Unknown Passenger" [34], Marlis and Candice sleep in each others' arms. "The Disappearance" [36] and "Two Front-Page Articles" [37] recount the wives' rescue by snowmobile. After being treated for frostbite at the hospital, Marlis and Candice are released.

While the women are at his funeral, in "Funeral Day" [23] Jack goes to Candice's house and kidnaps his son. When Jack phones Candice and Marlis in "Mauser and Mauser" [39], Marlis promises not to prosecute if Jack will bring the baby back immediately.

In "Spring Morning" [41], Marlis and Candice buy one of the houses in Jack's new subdivision. One Saturday morning in March, Jack is at the house visiting Marlis and their son while Candice is at her office. When John Jr. is asleep, Marlis seduces Jack. In "Spring Afternoon" [42], Marlis calls Candice at the office. The reader is not told, but suspects from what Candice later says to Jack, that Marlis tells her about the morning's lovemaking.

Marlis Cook's father. Man apparently responsible for much of Marlis's hatred and distrust of men that are revealed in her attitude toward Jack Mauser. In "Marlis's Tale" [27] in *Tales of Burning Love,* Marlis says that her father is rich, has kicked her out, and is a control freak. In "Best Western" [28], when Jack twists her arm, she remembers her father's impulsive temper and her own fearful hiding as she listened to him search for her.

Marlis Cook's half sister. Fifteen-year-old whose driver's permit Marlis shows to Jack Mauser, pretending it is her own in order to manipulate him with the threat of statutory rape charges, in "Marlis's Tale" [27] in *Tales of Burning Love.* The girl is possibly the daughter of Marlis's father by a second marriage, since Marlis says that her mother died young.

Marlis Cook's mother. Woman who died young, according to Marlis in "Marlis's Tale" [27] in *Tales of Burning Love.* But Marlis's riddles about her own origins—that she was made from "the clay her mother swallowed" and was "dragged in blue from a snowdrift"—may suggest a story not fully told. In "Baptism River" [29], Candice guesses that Marlis's mother gave her up at birth. The guess touches close enough to the truth to make Marlis weep, although it is possible that Marlis simply has experienced her mother's death as abandonment. In "Best Western" [28], we learn that the surname Marlis uses, Cook, had been her mother's maiden name.

Marshals. *Two marshals* are assigned to guard Gerry Nanapush as he is transported to a new prison facility in Minnesota in chapter 21 of *The Bingo Palace.* It appears that they die when their small plane crashes (see "Radio Bulletin" [11] in *Tales of Burning Love*). In chapter 25 of *Bingo Palace,* a ***group of marshals*** comes to Lulu Lamartine's apartment to question her about her son Gerry and to arrest her for stealing Gerry's Wanted poster. In "Smile of the Wolf" [38] in *Tales,* another ***group of marshals*** comes to Dot Nanapush Mauser's house to arrest Gerry, who has come to visit his daughter, Shawn, but escapes as they arrive. Two of the marshals stay

Marshals

and question Shawn. One of them, ***Ted,*** is tall and impatient; the other is short and has a soft voice.

Martin, Sister. See **Mary Martin de Porres, Sister.**

Martin Miller. Distraught father who, in chapter 1 of *The Beet Queen,* abducts the Adare baby from the Orphans' Picnic in Minneapolis in 1932. We learn in chapter 2 that he takes the child home to his wife, Catherine, to feed, because their ***own newborn son*** has just died. They decide to keep the Adare baby rather than return him to his family, thus becoming kidnappers. According to chapter 5, Martin dies in 1944, and in 1950 Catherine writes to the Kozkas, confessing the abduction.

Marty. Gas-station attendant wearing a T-shirt that says "Big Sky Country" with whom Lipsha Morrissey trades insults in chapter 7 of *The Bingo Palace.* Lipsha later encounters him at a party. Marty and his ***"Montana" friends*** pay Russell Kashpaw to tattoo a map of Montana on Lipsha's buttocks, and they vandalize Lipsha's new van. Lipsha tells Marty that he has a ***cousin named Marty,*** too.

Mary Adare. Daughter of Adelaide Adare and Mr. Ober; sister of Karl Adare and Jude Miller; niece of Pete and Fritzie Kozka. She is born about 1921.

In chapter 1 of *The Beet Queen,* until Mary is eleven, she lives with her mother and older brother Karl in Prairie Lake, where Mr. Ober visits them regularly. Unlike Karl, Mary enjoys Mr. Ober's visits, because he pays special attention to her, calling her "Schatze" (a German word for "treasure," a term of endearment). After Mr. Ober's death in 1932, the family, now destitute, moves to Minneapolis, where Adelaide gives birth to another boy. After their mother abandons them at the Saint Jerome's Orphans' Picnic and a stranger kidnaps the baby, Mary and Karl ride a freight train to Argus, where their aunt and uncle, Pete and Fritzie Kozka, live. Once in Argus, in "The Branch," Karl is frightened by a dog and runs back to the boxcar, but Mary runs to Kozka's Meats to find her family. Fritzie and Pete take her in, but her twelve-year-old cousin, Sita, is jealous of her.

Mary further alienates Sita in chapter 2 when she "steals" Sita's best friend, Celestine James, and when she is moved ahead a year into Sita and Celestine's seventh-grade class at Saint Catherine's school. After an ice storm the following March, Mary breaks the ice at the foot of the playground slide with her face. Mary thinks the pattern in the ice looks like Karl's face, but everyone else sees the face of Christ. Sister Leopolda takes photos of the image. (Years later, Mary's lost younger brother, who becomes Father Jude Miller, relates this incident as tentative evidence for Leopolda's sainthood in chapter 8 of *The Last Report on the Miracles at Little No Horse.* For the difference between the two novels' accounts of what happens to this ice portrait, compare *BQ,* 40, and *LR,* 142.)

In chapter 3 of *The Beet Queen,* Fritzie shows Mary a postcard from Adelaide asking about her children. Pretending to be Fritzie, Mary writes a card in reply, saying that all three of Adelaide's children "starved dead."

In chapter 4, Mary becomes infatuated with Russell Kashpaw, Celestine's Indian half brother, who has returned home wounded from "a war" (for dating of this incident, see **Russell Kashpaw**). But Russell has no interest in Mary. When Fritzie and Pete decide to move south for Fritzie's health in 1941, they leave the butcher shop to Mary. (We learn in chapter 10 that Mary changes the shop's name to The House of Meats.) The night before Sita leaves home, Mary is involved in a second "miracle"—Sita and Mary wake in the middle of the night to see Mary's hands glowing blue. In 1950 (chapter 5), Mary forwards a letter to Sita in Fargo, not knowing that it contains information about her missing baby brother.

Early in 1953, in chapter 7 Sita invites Mary to the formal-dress grand opening of her new restaurant, Chez Sita. But when Mary, Celestine, and Russell show up, they have to help in the kitchen because the chef is suffering from food poisoning. Not long afterward, Karl comes to Argus looking for Mary, but he stays in town several weeks before seeing her. Mary, who has never liked Karl, is upset when he has an affair with Celestine. Mary and Karl meet once for dinner but simply get into a fight. The night Celestine phones Mary to say that she is pregnant, Mary has a vision of Celestine's baby, a girl with red curls like Mary's baby brother and with the stubbornness of Mary herself. This chapter also reveals Mary's emerging interest in fortune-telling and signs, which seems to have developed from her earlier "miraculous" experiences.

After Celestine's daughter, Wallacette Darlene, is born in January 1954, Mary nicknames her Dot (chapter 9). Jealous of Celestine's relationship with Dot, Mary takes Dot's side whenever Celestine tries to discipline her (chapter 10). When Dot is in first grade, Mary believes her lie about the teacher's "naughty box" and makes a fool of herself when she confronts the teacher. Because of this incident, Celestine refuses to speak to Mary for months. That summer (1961), however, Mary joins Celestine and Dot when they take a wheelchair to the reservation for Russell, now paralyzed from a stroke.

After a fire at the butcher shop in 1964 (chapter 11), Mary moves in with Celestine and Dot through December. Her stay intensifies her and Celestine's conflict over Dot. It is Mary whom Dot tells when she is in love with the boy playing half of the donkey in the Christmas play, but it is Celestine to whom she turns after the humiliating evening. Because Dot's classmates are afraid of Mary, when Wallace Pfef throws an eleventh-birthday party for Dot in chapter 12 (1965), he attempts to subdue Mary by putting Everclear into her drinks. But the maneuver backfires as the drunken Mary turns the party into chaos.

In 1972 (chapter 13), when a brick is thrown through Mary's window, Mary,

Mary Adare

ever on the lookout for signs, predicts trouble. That night, Celestine dreams about Sita, and Mary's interpretation is that Sita is ill and is calling for Celestine. In response, Mary and Celestine go to Sita's house in Blue Mound, where Mary discovers Sita's hidden stash of pills. As Sita's health continues to deteriorate, Mary and Celestine's stay is prolonged. On the day of the Beet Festival (in July), when Mary and Celestine come to pick Sita up, they find her dead in the front yard. They do not know what to do with her, since the undertaker is with everyone else at the parade, so they take her with them to the festival. Mary is in the stands with Celestine, Karl, and Wallace in chapter 15, watching, stunned, as Dot flies off in a skywriting plane. Unknown to Mary, her "baby" brother, Jude Miller, now a priest, is also watching Dot's flight (chapter 14). Thus, for a brief moment, Mary is reunited with her brothers for the first time in forty years, again watching a red-haired Adare woman fly off in a plane. (Note: We learn in *The Last Report on the Miracles at Little No Horse* chapter 8 that Jude and Mary do at some point connect with one another, since he knows about the face of Christ appearing in the ice.)

Twelve years later, on a blistering June day in 1994 ("A Wedge of Shade" [3] in *Tales of Burning Love*), Dot returns to Argus to tell her mother and Aunt Mary about her marriage to Jack Mauser. Dot and Celestine find Mary keeping cool in the butcher shop meat locker. When Dot tells her about Jack's financial problems, Mary offers to teach him the meat and grocery business.

Early the next year, in "February Thaw" [40] Mary and Celestine take turns staying with Dot in the hospital while she recovers from hypothermia and exhaustion. When Dot comes to the butcher shop after her release from the hospital, Mary greets her in her usual matter-of-fact manner, but she is clearly relieved at Dot's recovery.

Mary Fred and Tammy Toose. Sisters of Shawnee Ray Toose. Mary Fred is mentioned as a factory worker in "The Tomahawk Factory" in *Love Medicine*. In chapters 2 and 10 of *The Bingo Palace,* we learn that Mary Fred and Tammy have a drinking problem. To get away from Zelda Kashpaw, in chapter 10 Shawnee Ray takes her son Redford and goes to stay with them for a time. We learn from chapter 14 that Shawnee Ray leaves Redford with her sisters while she attends a powwow and that Lyman Lamartine, the boy's presumed father, gets a court order to take custody of Redford. When Zelda, tribal policeman Leo Pukwan, and social worker *Vicki Koob* come for Redford in chapter 15, the Toose sisters try to turn them away. Mary Fred hides Redford and then attacks Pukwan with a large-buckled belt, but in the end Pukwan knocks her out and takes the child. (Shawnee Ray seems to be wearing that same belt in chapter 19.) In order to justify what she knows is a questionable action, while she is there, Koob takes notes on the squalor she sees in the house.

Mary Kashpaw. Daughter of Kashpaw and Quill; cook and housekeeper for Father Damien in *The Last Report on the Miracles at Little No Horse*. We do not know Mary's Ojibwe birth name, only that, according to chapter 6 of *Last Report,* in 1912 Quill gives her the Christian name Mary. As the Kashpaw family breaks up that year and Quill descends into madness, Mary tries to care for her, though Quill responds harshly. On a feast day in late summer or autumn, in chapter 7 of *Last Report* Mary is riding with her mother and father in the wagon that carries the statue of the Virgin. After Pauline Puyat spooks the horses, the runaway wagon crashes and Kashpaw and Quill are mortally wounded. Mary herself suffers painful injuries, yet she holds her parents' hands as they die. Mary is further traumatized when she goes to live with Bernadette Morrissey through the winter, because Bernadette's brother Napoleon molests her. By spring, Mary seems to be mad as she digs a succession of trenchlike graves. Realizing that Mary has been abused, Father Damien brings her to the convent.

As she matures, Mary grows large and powerful. She helps the nuns with their heavy work, especially chopping wood. She also becomes Father Damien's faithful caretaker, cooking (though not well), cleaning, making the fire, and so on. (See chapters 11 and 16.) As Father Damien says in chapter 3, his life becomes inextricably entwined with hers. During the influenza winter of 1918–1919 in chapter 7, as Father Damien makes his rounds to the sick and dying, Mary stamps down the snow, breaking a trail for him. One day as Mary walks before the priest, the downhearted Damien sees in Mary's face the face of Christ, the man with the horn spoon from chapter 2. Mary's trail-breaking becomes a touchstone of her service and two years later earns her a new name. In the early spring of 1921, Mary breaks a trail for Father Wekkle, and he jokingly calls her **Mary Stamper.** (See this entry, in which she performs the same service for her son.)

In chapter 11, that same spring Bernadette Morrissey confesses to Father Damien that she knew her brother had forced himself on the child Mary but did nothing. This information seems to confirm Damien's suspicion that it was Mary who murdered Napoleon. (He realizes later that she did not; see chapter 16.)

Mary demonstrates her deep connection with Father Damien to an even greater degree that autumn. In chapter 11, when Damien's grief at Father Gregory Wekkle's departure brings on physical pain and severe depression, he takes a large dose of narcotics and falls into a month-long sleep. During this period, Mary never leaves his side. When Damien grows no beard, Mary realizes that he is a woman,

Mary Kashpaw

and she pretends to shave him each morning to protect his secret. One day Sister Hildegarde finds Mary scrubbing the floor with great intensity and discovers that her mind is not present. Mary's spirit has followed that of Father Damien so that she can guide him safely home.

In chapter 12, when in the summer of 1922 Father Damien plays the piano for the snakes in the newly built church, Mary joins them and worships "as though with her kind" (*LR,* 220).

The events of July 1940 drastically change Mary's life. Chapter 17 relates that one July morning, Awun, son of Fleur Pillager and John James Mauser, brings wood to the convent, sees Mary chopping, and is smitten with her. (See **John James Mauser II** for Awun's story and his mental strangeness, which parallels the blankness and madness Mary sometimes suffers.) Mary notices the huge boy's attention sufficiently to be uneasy, so she sleeps that night with an ax in her sleigh bed. But Awun abducts the sleeping Mary, sleigh and all. She wakes in fear, seeing the powerful young man in the harness pulling her sleigh, so similar to the horses that had dragged her parents to their deaths. Mary cuts the lines with her ax, freeing herself. She then broods for an hour, torn between the pull of passion and her deep attachment to Father Damien. Finally, she follows Awun. When she catches up with him, they begin "work on a tiny baby boy" (*LR,* 282).

Last Report chapter 17 reveals only that Mary goes mad, the child is taken from her, and when she is finally released from confinement in 1950, she returns home empty-handed to Father Damien. But by comparing this story with *Tales of Burning Love,* we learn more about these ten years in Mary's life. In *Tales,* Mary is called by her nickname, Mary Stamper, and her son is Jack Mauser, the protagonist of this novel ("The Owl" [17]). They live on the reservation at first, apparently with Awun ("Mauser and Mauser" [39]), but Mary begins having spells of rigid silence each autumn in which she relives the death of her parents ("The Owl" [17]). When Jack is six (in 1947), Awun—now called "the big Mauser"—takes Mary for cold-water shock treatments and leaves the boy with a Mauser relative. Since we know from *Last Report* that Mary returns to the reservation in 1950, she is apparently institutionalized for three years. When chapter 17 of *Last Report* tells us that she returns home "brain shocked—bearing the nerve deadness of confinement" (*LR,* 282), the reader is reminded of Father Damien's perception during her childhood trench-digging that they could not put her in an asylum because that would destroy her (*Last Report* chapter 7).

Yet Mary Stamper Kashpaw survives this "disastrous marriage" (*LR,* 282), and in 1996 she is still caring for Father Damien. As she serves Damien and his visitor Father Jude in the spring of that year, we learn in chapters 3, 8, and 14 that her cooking (and coffee) is as horrifying as ever. That summer, in chapter 22, the

Mary (II) Shawano and Zosie (II) Shawano Roy

now-ancient Father Damien realizes that his death is near and decides to go to Spirit Island in Matchimanito Lake to die. The morning he decides to leave, he finds Mary standing in front of him with matches for his final journey. As always, she knows intuitively what he is thinking. Before he leaves, Mary kneels in grief and clasps his knees. A few days later, she rows to the island, where she finds Father Damien dead, and from a note pinned to his chest understands his wishes. She rows out with his body and buries him in the lake. By the next year, in the epilogue of *Last Report,* Father Damien's cabin has been made into a shrine, cared for by Mary Kashpaw.

Mary Martin de Porres, Sister. Nun at the Sacred Heart Convent from at least the 1960s through the 1980s. When Father Gregory Wekkle returns to the reservation in 1962, in chapter 19 of *The Last Report on the Miracles at Little No Horse,* Sister Mary Martin is the nun who gives the near-dead caller a drink of water. Playing her clarinet late one night in 1981, in "Crown of Thorns" in *Love Medicine,* she hears Gordie Kashpaw outside and through the open window takes his confession that he has killed his wife. When she goes out to investigate the death, she finds a dead doe in his car and breaks down weeping. Later, in the story "Love Medicine," she kindly but firmly refuses to bless Lipsha Morrissey's love charm of turkey hearts.

Mary (I) Shawano and Josephette (Zosie I) Shawano. Twin daughters of Blue Prairie Woman and Shawano the younger who, as infants, are given to their grandmother Midass to raise, according to chapters 1 and 3 of *The Antelope Wife.* One of these women marries an unspecified Shawano man and gives birth to twins, Mary (II) and Zosie (II) Shawano. This woman also receives a land allotment on the Shawanos' reservation (chapter 18).

Mary (II) Shawano and Zosie (II) Shawano Roy. Twin daughters of either Mary (I) or Zosie (I) Shawano; granddaughters of Blue Prairie Woman in *The Antelope Wife.* According to chapter 18, out of their family of six, the second Zosie and Mary are the sole survivors of a flu epidemic (possibly the epidemic of 1918–1919). They are living on a reservation "up north" from Minneapolis with their great-grandmother, Midass, when Augustus Roy II arrives (chapters 18 and 23). (For notes about the location of this reservation, see **Rozina [Rozin] Roy Whiteheart Beads Shawano.**) Augustus is smitten with the silent but sly Zosie and gives to Midass red whiteheart beads in exchange for her.

When Midass dies, Augustus and Zosie move in with Mary, producing a bizarre love triangle. Mary and Augustus meet in secret, but after Zosie learns about their trysts, the twins conspire to confuse him. In an effort to keep them straight,

Mary (II) Shawano and Zosie (II) Shawano Roy

Augustus marks Mary by burning her foot and Zosie by biting her ear. He later disappears without a trace. Rumor has it that the sisters, true to their windigo Shawano heritage, have eaten him. They are referred to as "murder suspects" in chapter 11. According to chapter 18, from their difficult experiences the sisters learn to relish hard luck, but the difficulties wear more heavily on Zosie than on Mary, who years later appears "unmarred" by her early experiences.

Pregnant with twins, Zosie sees Blue Prairie Woman in a dream, wearing northwest trader blue beads (chapter 18). Zosie gambles with the spirit of her grandmother, winning both her beads and her two names. Years later, she will give those names to her own granddaughters. (Since the beads later show up in the possession of Sweetheart Calico, Zosie may not win the actual beads, but a vision of their blueness.)

Zosie's twins, Rozina and Aurora, are apparently born in the 1940s or 1950s. She and Mary raise them together and, according to chapters 9 and 11, will not tell the girls which of them is their mother. When the girls are five, Aurora dies of diphtheria (chapter 3).

Rozin is still living on Mary and Zosie's reservation when she marries Richard Whiteheart Beads. According to chapter 11, both Zosie and Mary are "namers." Besides dreams and the wind, Mary acquires names from **little frog woman.** Thus, when Rozin's twin daughters, Deanna and Cally, are born, according to chapter 11, Zosie and Mary both participate in the naming ceremony. Rozin and her family move to Minneapolis when the girls are five. Mary and Zosie stay on the reservation, but they occasionally come down to babysit. Recounting one of these occasions in chapter 6, Cally recalls Grandma Zosie's telling her the story of their windigo forebear, Apijigo Bakaday, who married a deer man. When Deanna and Cally dance naked in the rain, Zosie says it's no wonder, since they are "part deer."

Either Zosie or Mary may be present when Cally saves the dog Almost Soup in chapter 8, because shortly afterward, he is transported to their reservation. He is at their house when Rozin and eleven-year-old Cally return to the reservation in chapter 9, following Deanna's death in March. When Cally becomes gravely ill during a February blizzard, Mary tries (at first unsuccessfully) to call an ambulance, and she forces the worried Rozin to rest. Zosie helps care for Cally, cuts wood for the fire, and shovels snow from the road so the ambulance can get through.

By the time Cally is eighteen, Mary and Zosie have moved to Minneapolis, which they call Mishimin Odaynang, Apple Town. They still spend most summers on the reservation, where they gather teas and bark (chapter 18), and in the fall, they harvest wild rice in a canoe (chapter 17). When Cally wants to move to Minneapolis in chapter 11, Rozin is unable to contact the grandmothers. After Cally comes to stay with Frank Shawano, Zosie and Mary continue to be elusive and Cally manages only one brief phone visit with one of them. One day, however, Zosie walks into Frank's bakery, and Cally gives her a piece of Frank's latest attempt at the blitzkuchen.

About two years later, in chapter 14 Rozin moves to Minneapolis to live with her mothers and go to night school. When Rozin marries Frank and Richard shoots himself after the wedding, Rozin isolates herself in her mothers' apartment in chapter 17. Zosie calls her from the hospital to say that Richard has died. Apparently Mary is not in Minneapolis for the wedding, since when Rozin continues to withdraw, Zosie goes up to the reservation to fetch Mary.

The following December, in chapter 18 Mary and Zosie join the family for Christmas dinner at Frank and Rozin's apartment. Since Zosie is self-conscious about her appearance, Cally compliments her looks. At the dinner table, the twins talk about morning sickness, difficult births, and their own funerals, to the discomfiture of their family. When Cecille Shawano challenges the sisters about the disappearance of Augustus Roy, the twins merely smile their "slightly windigo" smiles. After dinner, Zosie tells Cally about her dream of Blue Prairie Woman and the blue beads. In telling the story, she also reveals that she, not Mary, is Rozin's mother.

Mary Stamper. Mother of Jack Mauser. Mary is introduced in the novel *Tales of Burning Love,* which gives only hints about her life and identity: She is from the reservation, land that she calls "leftovers," which she nevertheless loves, as recorded in "Mauser and Mauser" [39]. Jack recalls spending at least part of his childhood there, and in "Jack's House" [9], he remembers some of his mother's Ojibwe language. "The Owl" [17] tells us that Mary is descended from some wandering people who join the Ojibwe but may be a mixture of Cree, Menominee, Winnebago, and even French. We also learn from this chapter that Mary's parents die when she is a child. Sometime after Jack is born, she begins to experience periods of rigid silence each autumn in which she relives their loss. When Jack is six years old, his father, "the big Mauser," leaves him with his German Aunt Elizabeth as Mauser takes Mary in for cold-water shock treatments for her catatonia.

Jack normally blocks out these painful memories, but after his near-death by fire ("The Owl" [17]), Jack has a vivid memory of his mother—her size, her strength and tenderness, as well as her mental disturbance. He remembers her staring at him for days with a hungry, wild expression, an expression similar to that of Sister Leopolda just before she dies in exaltation. Later, as he is lost in the storm in "Blizzard Night" [35], he also remembers how his mother used to break a path for him to school in the winter.

Mary Stamper

In "Easter Snow" [1] and "A Wedge of Shade" [3], Jack is reluctant to tell his mother's family name to June Morrissey and Celestine James, lest they be "wary" of him. Yet when Celestine learns his mother's name, she nods her acceptance and invites him in, since he is "a distant relative, after all" (*TBL,* 28).

Jack's "crazy mother" is also referred to in "The First Draw" [14]. In "The Stone Virgin" [44], Jack is not afraid when the statue of the Virgin falls on him, because in her face he sees that of his mother.

A later novel, the 2001 *The Last Report on the Miracles at Little No Horse,* reveals that "Mary Stamper" is actually a nickname for Mary Kashpaw (chapter 11), whose history is recorded in *Last Report.* For more of her story, and thus of Jack's ancestry, see **Mary Kashpaw.** (Note that the *Tales of Burning Love* description of Mary's ancestry of a wandering people of mixed tribes is at odds with the depiction of her parentage in *Last Report.*)

Mashkiigikwe. One of Kashpaw's wives; older sister of cowife Quill in *The Last Report on the Miracles at Little No Horse.* In chapter 6 (set in the spring of 1912), Mashkiigikwe is the most robust of the wives, a skilled hunter and as strong as a bear. She despises Christianity. It is Mashkiigikwe whom Nanapush wants to acquire when Kashpaw's family breaks up, though she scorns him. Mashkiigikwe cares for her weak-minded sister, Quill, and together with Margaret keeps Kashpaw's large family running smoothly, so there is always food, wood, and water. Thus, when Mashkiigikwe leaves, the family falls apart.

In the winter of 1918–1919, during the influenza epidemic in chapter 7, Mashkiigikwe is living in a cabin with two of Kashpaw's children by Fishbone. When Father Damien comes to check on them, they are all near death. But largely through the ministrations of Pauline Puyat, they survive.

We know nothing further of Mashkiigikwe's life until 1962, when Father Damien sees her in a park in Fargo. The once robust woman has now been physically and mentally devastated by alcohol. When she realizes who Father Damien is, she blames him for her condition. His conversion of the Kashpaw family, she accuses, marked the beginning of her ruin. More than thirty years later, in 1996, Father Damien calls to mind the young, strong Mashkiigikwe in his struggle with the demonic black dog (chapter 20).

Massive Indian woman. Mysterious large woman who enters the B & B restaurant and casino out of a January blizzard in "The B & B" [16] in *Tales of Burning Love.* Dot Mauser seems to know her and orders her coffee and a pizza. After the strange woman has finished eating, she follows Dot down the hallway. Half an hour later, Dot returns alone. "The Tale of the Unknown Passenger" [34] reveals this person's identity.

Matilda Roy. Firstborn daughter of Blue Prairie Woman; adopted daughter of Scranton Roy. Her story appears in chapters 1 and 6 of *The Antelope Wife.*

Matilda's mother has two husbands, first a deer man, then after his death a human, Shawano the younger. The narrative does not specify which of these husbands is Matilda's father. In chapter 6, the reference to Blue Prairie Woman's "winters" (plural) with Shawano appears before its reference to the infant Matilda, suggesting that Shawano is her father. But Matilda's reference to Scranton as "her human" and her later adoption by antelope people may suggest that the deer man is her father.

When the infant Matilda is still unnamed, a doe warns Blue Prairie Woman to leave. Blue Prairie Woman ties the baby's cradleboard to a dog, and as the U.S. Cavalry attacks, the dog runs onto the open prairie, a necklace of blue beads swaying from the cradleboard. One of the soldiers, Scranton Roy, follows it. By the time he is able to untie the child three days later, she is desperate with hunger. He calms her by letting her suck at his nipple. He eventually stops to build a sod house, and one morning as the baby is sucking, her faith is rewarded with milk. Scranton names his adopted daughter Matilda, after his mother.

When Matilda is six, she goes to school, wearing her blue beads. The young schoolteacher, Peace McKnight, becomes Matilda's friend and, soon, her stepmother. When Matilda sees her beloved father kiss Peace the first time, her confused feelings resolve into a new sense of self and freedom.

Peace becomes pregnant and then falls ill with a fever. Lying next to her one night, Matilda hears someone approach the house, then tap. Realizing that the woman who has come is her mother, she leaves Scranton a note and follows her. Matilda quickly falls ill with Peace's fever. As her mother cares for her, the two communicate in signs, and Blue Prairie Woman gives her child her own life-saving name, Other Side of the Earth. Matilda recovers, but her mother contracts the fever and dies within the day. Before dying, she kills and cooks the dog who accompanies them so that Matilda will have food. For two days Matilda sits and gazes west, singing her mother's dying song, until curious antelope come to investigate. Matilda is seven when she joins the antelope people, still wearing the blue beads.

Generations later, in chapter 2, when an old medicine man describes the forebear of Sweetheart Calico as a girl who lived with the antelope, he may be alluding to Matilda. The subsequent history of Matilda's blue beads is related in chapter 18.

Mauser family. See **Aunt Elizabeth, Candice Pantamounty Mauser, Chuck Mauser, Dot Adare Nanapush Mauser, Eleanor Schlick Mauser, Fleur**

Mauser family

Pillager, Jack Mauser, John James Mauser, John James Mauser II, John Mauser Jr., June Morrissey Kashpaw, Marlis Cook Mauser, and **Mary Stamper.**

Maynard Moon. Lawyer whose son, Caryl Moon, Jack Mauser reluctantly hires in "Caryl Moon" [8] in *Tales of Burning Love.* Maynard is mentioned again in "Jack's House" [9] as the personal representative for the estate of John J. Mauser, deceased. He is apparently one of the lawyers who attend Jack's funeral—see **Moon, Webb, and Cartenspeil.** In "The Stone Virgin" [44], Maynard again forces Jack to hire his son.

Mazarine Shimek. Sweetheart and wife of Franz Waldvogel in *The Master Butchers Singing Club.* A natural beauty characterizes both Mazarine's personality and her appearance (see chapters 8 and 14), despite the poverty and crudity in which she is reared. Her father is a roamer with a bad temper, her mother fat and lazy, and her brother, Roman, a hell-raiser (chapter 9). Franz and Mazarine become sweethearts sometime in 1935. In chapter 6, set in June of that year, Franz borrows her bicycle when he needs to go see Pouty Mannheim. We first glimpse the two together that fall, in chapter 8. They go places together on Mazarine's bike, Franz peddling and Mazarine balanced on the handlebars. They often stop on the way home at a secret place under a pine tree whose branches touch the ground, where they kiss and touch each other.

In chapter 9, the couple is still together the following year, 1936. One Saturday that summer, Franz brings Mazarine to the butcher shop where he introduces her to Delphine Watzka. (Mazarine had been there before, but Franz's father had completely ignored her.) Delphine sees that Mazarine loves Franz, and she is impressed with the girl's care and diligence in doing chores. When Delphine invites her back to the kitchen to eat, Mazarine is startled at the richness of the room. That fall, Mazarine is troubled by the attentions wealthy Betty Zumbrugge gives Franz, though Franz is not interested in Betty. One wet November afternoon, the pair is again playing love games in their hideout. Unknown to Mazarine, that night Franz has an experience that makes him ashamed of that time of pleasure together.

Thus, when Franz stops speaking to her in chapter 11, Mazarine has no explanation. One day when Betty Zumbrugge passes her on the road, Mazarine sees Franz in the car with her. One bitterly cold night in December, Franz comes unexpectedly to the Shimek house. Although Mazarine tries to turn him away, he comes in anyway to warm up. She refuses to accept him back, however, recalling her shame at his abandonment. On Christmas Day, Step-and-a-Half gathers several pieces of beautiful fabric and notions to give to Mazarine to make new clothes.

In the months after Mazarine's rejection of him, in chapter 13 Franz sees her in the new clothes he has never touched. He aches over his loss and stupidity, realizing how much he loves her. For respite, he turns his attention to learning to fly. After he joins the air corps, Delphine talks to Mazarine about him, telling her that they love each other, so Mazarine should write him.

After high school, Mazarine goes to a teacher training college in Moorhead and earns her grade school certification (chapter 14). When her brother, Roman, is wounded in the war in the fall of 1943, she returns to Argus, her mother takes permanently to bed, and Mazarine takes a temporary position teaching fourth grade. The following spring (1944), she receives a letter from Franz, saying that he is coming home on leave and wants to see her. When he comes, Mazarine wants to hear what has happened to him since they parted. Mazarine and Franz become lovers, and by the time he returns to his unit, she is pregnant.

When she learns that Mazarine is pregnant, Delphine buys her a wedding ring in Fargo. Franz writes to her regularly and sends a diamond engagement ring. The rings help deflect the gossip, but some people complain when Mazarine continues to teach up to her seventh month. Mazarine struggles with the emotional swings caused by her pregnancy and Franz's absence. Franz's letter the following spring (1945) tells her that the European war is over. By that fall, her baby boy, Johannes, has been born.

But Franz does not come home safely. He suffers a serious head injury in a freak accident at an airfield. Of his and Mazarine's subsequent story, we are given only a glimpse of her first visit to the hospital, heavy with foreboding, and the comment in chapter 15 that Franz comes home "only to fade from life in bewildered anger" (*MBSC,* 377). When Delphine writes to Markus (Franz's brother) from Germany in 1954, she sends a message to Mazarine and baby Johannes.

We get one more glimpse of Mazarine in chapter 16, set in the mid-1950s: Mazarine, who would now be in her thirties (Step-and-a-Half facetiously calls her an old woman), has gone into business with Delphine, who, as we learn in this chapter but remains unknown to the women, is her sister. They have renovated and now run a plant shop.

Medicine Dress. The great-grandmother (in Ojibwe, Gitchi-nookomis) of Margaret Kashpaw, mentioned in *Four Souls.* This woman is called Medicine Dress because of her powerful healing dress made by spirits (chapter 9). As a child, Margaret calls her Kookum, a childish shortening of Gitchi-nookomis. In chapter 14, Margaret recalls her great-grandmother as very old, blind, and unable to move from her wooden chair in the corner. When agents from the government school come, Margaret's mother hides her under Medicine Dress's skirt. Her Gitchi-nookomis tells Margaret about many women from her past, so that when she dies

Medicine Dress

and Margaret is taken to the white school, the girl is grounded in the old times, and the school cannot strip her of her heritage.

Decades later, when Margaret is strangling in Nanapush's snare in chapter 9, Medicine Dress appears to her in a vision, young and strong, wearing her powerful dress. She instructs Margaret to make a medicine dress of her own, following the rules Medicine Dress will give her. The power of the dress's desire to be made saves Margaret, and as she prepares it, she recalls her Gitchi-nookomis and the events of her own life. (See also chapter 11.)

Midass. Mother of Blue Prairie Woman in *The Antelope Wife*. According to chapter 3, Midass's full name is Midassbaupayikway, Ten Stripe Woman. The only knowledge we have of Midass prior to her becoming Blue Prairie Woman's mother comes from the genealogy sketched by her great-great-granddaughter, Rozina Roy, in chapter 3.

Midass's daughter Blue Prairie Woman is first known as Apijigo Bakaday, So Hungry, because of her insatiable appetite (chapter 6). People think the girl may be a windigo, but Midass insists that there is nothing wrong with her. It is Midass who passes down the story of her daughter's deer husband. In chapter 1, the U.S. Cavalry raids their village shortly after Blue Prairie Woman's first daughter is born. One of the soldiers, Scranton Roy, kills either Midass's mother or her mother-in-law. Blue Prairie Woman later has twin daughters, Mary (I) and Josephette (Zosie I), whom she leaves with Midass to raise so she can search for her firstborn. One of these daughters also has twins named Mary (II) and Zosie (II). After a flu epidemic wipes out the rest of Mary and Zosie's family, old Midass is left to raise these great-granddaughters as well.

In chapters 18 and 23, when the second Zosie and Mary are young women, Scranton Roy returns to the village, now situated on a reservation. He brings his grandson, Augustus (II), who falls in love with Zosie. The young man gives Midass red whiteheart beads in exchange for Zosie and promises to take care of her sister, Mary. Midass uses the beads to decorate a blanket, a gift for a pregnant woman (whose son will be known as Whiteheart Beads). Midass dies shortly after Zosie's marriage.

Mike String. A keeper of items and songs belonging to the Shaawano drum, mentioned in part 2.1 of *The Painted Drum*. Mike marries Chook, and they have two sons, Morris and John, and later *two more children. Mike's father* was a keeper of old Shaawano's drum, and after the drum leaves the reservation, Mike keeps its paraphernalia.

Mike dies suddenly of a heart attack and is buried on a ridge with the other traditionals. He instructs that the song scrolls be buried with him. Thus, when the drum returns, Chook phones Bernard Shaawano asking him to help her dig up Mike's grave to recover the songs.

Minnie. The name of the woman who Roy Watzka says is his deceased beloved and Delphine's mother in *The Master Butchers Singing Club.* Roy never gives a last name for Minnie. According to Roy's story in chapter 13, Minnie, who was of French-Cree-Ojibwe descent, was eight years old when she survived the massacre at Wounded Knee (1890), which makes her birth year around 1882.

According to chapter 2, Roy tells Delphine that Minnie died when Delphine was just three or four months old, but he tells her almost nothing about this woman. He has his blurred photographs of Minnie, and Delphine has only the objects in a wooden cigar box that she assumes had belonged to her mother (chapter 4).

When Roy is jailed briefly in 1935, he particularly misses Minnie's pictures and the afghan he says she knitted for him (chapter 8). As his health fails, Delphine decides that Roy must not die without revealing what he knows about Minnie. So he tells her for the first time the story of Minnie at Wounded Knee. Delphine wants to know more—what Minnie was like, whether she had loved Delphine— but Roy will give no more information (chapter 13). After Roy dies, he is buried with Minnie's pictures (chapter 16). In Ludwigsruhe, Germany, in 1954, while the master butchers are singing at a memorial ceremony, Delphine thinks of those pictures of her mother (chapter 15). The novel's ending reveals that Minnie is a mostly imaginary personage and is not Delphine's mother at all. See also **Step-and-a-Half.**

Mirage. Father of Nanapush and Kashpaw, whose Indian name is Kanatowakechin (*Tracks* chapter 9). When the northern Ojibwe are struck by disease in the early 1860s so that their numbers are decimated, an ***older wise woman*** tells them they must have many children (chapter 6 of *The Last Report on the Miracles at Little No Horse*). The man she herself chooses is Mirage, the strongest and handsomest of the men still living. Mirage also impregnates many of the other women and is revered for recreating the tribe. His procreative prowess is also referred to in chapters 11 and 14 of *Four Souls.* In chapter 9, Nanapush recalls that his father teaches him everything, including medicine lore. Mirage also tells this son (chapter 3 of *Tracks*) that the name Nanapush means trickery, living in the bush, and having a way with women.

Mirage is still alive in 1912 (*Last Report* chapter 6). When Nanapush sees the deceased members of his family in the fall of 1919 (*Tracks* chapter 9), he imagines himself again with his father, during one long-ago winter, eluding soldiers through the thick snow that covers the bodies of his mother and sister. In chapter 13 of *Last Report,* Nanapush dreams about his family, including Mirage.

Misshepeshu

Misshepeshu. Lake man (or monster) of Matchimanito Lake. He and his power are intimately connected with the Pillager clan. We learn in chapter 7 of *Tracks* that when the Pillagers settle on the reservation just after the turn of the century, Misshepeshu appears in the lake because of his connection with the Old Man, Fleur's father. To the Pillagers, he is benign, but others fear him. He is said to be waiting in hiding for the trespassing government surveyors in chapter 1, and in chapter 2, he may be involved in the deaths of two of their guides. Margaret Kashpaw is concerned that he might take her when she crosses the lake in a leaky boat in chapter 3. It is seen as a sign of their desperation that the starving people ice fish on Matchimanito one famine winter at the end of chapter 5. Mothers warn their daughters in chapter 2 that he is particularly desirous of daring young girls and that he takes on different forms to lure them to their death by drowning.

Pauline Puyat believes that Fleur Pillager may be a lover to the water man. After Fleur's first child (Lulu) is born, in chapter 4 Misshepeshu seems to grow more benign, and Pauline thinks the child's eyes and skin resemble the lake man's. Later, in chapter 5, even Fleur's husband Eli Kashpaw believes for a time that Fleur is pregnant with the lake man's child. In chapter 8, Pauline equates the lake man with Satan and believes that Fleur is his agent. Pauline believes that he appears to her and calls her to a confrontation, like Christ's temptation, in the "desert." She answers the call by going to Matchimanito, where she believes that she kills the monster. When dead, however, he turns into Napoleon Morrissey.

The lake man is mentioned once in *Love Medicine,* in the "Love Medicine" story, where his name is spelled "Missepeshu." Misshepeshu also appears, though not by name, in *The Bingo Palace.* When Lipsha Morrissey engages in a religious fast and quest close to Matchimanito in chapter 17, he thinks of the horned thing as an evil presence. In chapter 20, however, he realizes that it is the lake man who kept him alive as an infant at the bottom of the slough where his mother had thrown him in a weighted gunnysack. It is significant to this account of Lipsha's salvation that Lipsha is himself a Pillager and probably next in line to inherit the Pillager power—and presumably their special relationship with Misshepeshu.

In chapter 8 of *The Antelope Wife,* Almost Soup refers to the "man-monster-cat thing" in Ojibwe lakes whom humans seem obliged to placate, and Margaret Kashpaw guesses, in chapter 14 of *Four Souls,* that "the one in the lake" is jealous of Fleur.

Mission teacher. Man Anaquot and Ziigwan'aage meet at the reservation store who is recruiting students for Carlisle Indian School in part 2.3 of *The Painted Drum.* He is apparently the same person as the **Carlisle teacher from Stokes** who recruits and later marries Niibin'aage.

Montana Kashpaw. Husband of Regina Puyat Kashpaw and father of Russell and Isabel Kashpaw; apparently one of the older children of the original Kashpaw and Margaret who migrate to Montana when land allotments are made. The older Kashpaw children's migration is recorded in "The World's Greatest Fishermen" in *Love Medicine* and chapter 3 of *Tracks*. Chapter 2 of *Tracks*, set in 1912–1913, tells us that Regina's first marriage was to a Kashpaw man who is now living in Montana and that Russell is his son. *The Beet Queen* chapter 2 reveals that Isabel is Russell's sister.

The identity of the Montana Kashpaw is rendered somewhat ambiguous by the reference in *The Beet Queen* (chapters 7 and 10) to Eli (a younger son of Margaret and Kashpaw) as Russell's half brother. This would seem to suggest that Eli's father, the original Kashpaw, marries Regina, fathers Isabel and Russell, and then moves to Montana. But such a reading would not be consistent with the Kashpaw history recorded in *Tracks* chapter 3 and *The Last Report on the Miracles at Little No Horse* chapter 7, which indicate that the original Kashpaw dies in 1912 on the reservation and it is his older children who move to Montana. Thus, the *Beet Queen*'s "half brother" designation of Eli and Russell may simply be a general statement of kinship, or it may be one of several illustrations of the fact that when Erdrich wrote *The Beet Queen* in 1986, the stories of her characters and fictional families were not yet fully developed.

Moon, Webb, and Cartenspeil. Jack's representatives, who, along with virtually every other lawyer in the region, attend Jack's funeral in "Satin Heart" [12] in *Tales of Burning Love*. Jack owes each of these lawyers something. Although they each accept a chocolate from Dot Mauser, Jack's current wife, they do not want to appear appeased by this gesture and bury the candies among the palm and ficus tree roots in the visitation room. See also **Maynard Moon.**

Morris String. Son of Mike and Chook String; brother of John String in *The Painted Drum*. We learn in part 3.7 that Ira's father, the man who talked to wolves, gives Morris his spirit name, Wolf, for protection. Three people teach Morris songs used with old Shaawano's drum: his father, his namer (the wolf man), and Bernard Shaawano.

As a young man, Morris fights in the Gulf War and becomes ill, apparently from chemical weapons (part 2.1). His thyroid gland is affected, causing his eyes to bulge so that he cannot close them. He must use eye drops and avoid virtually all light. The Veterans Administration has sent him all over the world for treatment, but nothing has helped (3.4 and 3.7).

One deep winter night sometime after 2000, in part 3.4, John comes to Morris's house with the young woman Ira and asks Morris to drive her home, twenty miles

Morris String

into the bush, where she has left her children alone. Morris does so, but his overtly sexual behavior makes Ira uneasy. When they arrive at her house, they find it burned to the ground and the children gone. Morris walks with Ira the three miles through the woods to Bernard Shaawano's house, where they find the children (3.6), but Morris's exposure to the light reflected off the snow abrades his corneas, so he will probably lose his eyesight (part 3.7).

While Ira is staying in the hospital with her children (3.7), she comes to visit Morris in his room. He apologizes for his behavior in the truck. He has fallen in love with her and plans to ask her to marry him, wanting to provide for her and help her rear her children. He dreams of taking her to powwows with the drum.

Morrissey family. See **Bernadette Morrissey, Clarence Morrissey, Layla Morrissey, Lipsha Morrissey, Lulu Nanapush Morrissey Lamartine, Morrissey I, Morrissey II, Napoleon Morrissey, Philomena Morrissey, Sophie Morrissey,** and **Strict aunt in Grand Forks.** See also *Kyle Morrissey* in **Tomahawk factory workers.**

Morrissey I. Lucille Lazarre's companion and father of Lucille's daughter June Morrissey in *Love Medicine.* After Lucille's death, Morrissey and an old drunk woman, who is apparently Lucille's mother, bring the nine-year-old June to Marie Lazarre Kashpaw (Lucille's supposed sister) for her to rear ("The Beads"). Marie refers to him as "the whining no-good who had not church-married" her sister. After dropping off June, he is said (in "The World's Greatest Fishermen") to have run off to the Twin Cities. Lulu Lamartine refers to June's father in "Crossing the Water."

Morrissey II. Lulu Nanapush's first husband. In "The Good Tears" in *Love Medicine,* Lulu says that she married him for spite when her lover Moses Pillager would not come live with her in town. Nanapush's objections to the marriage are recorded in "The Island" in *Love Medicine* and in chapter 9 of *Tracks.* One of the purposes of the whole narration by Nanapush recorded in odd-numbered chapters of *Tracks* is to convince Lulu not to marry this Morrissey. She later admits that the marriage was a mistake, calling him "riffraff" in "The Good Tears." The children Lulu has while married to Morrissey she later renames Lamartine ("Lulu's Boys").

This Morrissey is mentioned in chapter 16 of *The Last Report on the Miracles at Little No Horse* in 1945 as the man Lulu has just left, but whose child she is carrying.

Moses Pillager. Cousin of Fleur Pillager; first lover of Lulu Nanapush; father of Gerry Nanapush. Margaret Kashpaw claims in "The Island" in *Love Medicine* that *Moses's grandfather* was windigo and ate his wife.

Chapters 1 and 3 of *Tracks* and "The Island" in *Love Medicine* tell of Moses's infancy and boyhood. Moses (not his original name) is still a nursing child during an early sickness that decimates the reservation tribe. Nanapush advises the child's mother, **Different Thumbs,** on how to fool death by pretending that Moses is already dead. This strategy protects him from the sickness but affects his mind. In the later consumption epidemic of 1912, Moses and his distant cousin Fleur appear to be the only Pillagers who survive. After that epidemic, Moses, still a boy, moves to the island on the far side of Matchimanito Lake, where he lives alone with his cats. When Fleur returns to the reservation with money in the fall of 1913, Moses helps her by going to town to buy supplies. Fleur's daughter, Lulu Nanapush, remembers his stalking through town as a wild boy and his sitting under the trees with Nanapush, talking in the old language about medicine ways.

Because of Moses's medicine knowledge, people on the reservation come to him for help. In chapter 4 of *Tracks,* he gives Pauline Puyat a love medicine; in chapter 6, he is said to provide pregnant girls with medicine to induce abortions; and in chapter 7, he helps Nanapush with a healing ceremony for Fleur. When Pauline rolls in mud and leaves in chapter 8, she compares herself to Moses. Moses seems to be Fleur's ally in her resistance to the Turcot lumber company in chapter 9, for rumor has it that he drowns two workers, and he is present when Fleur sabotages the company's equipment.

Some years later, Lulu comes to Moses's island in "The Island" in *Love Medicine.* When they become lovers, Moses tells her his real name. Lulu becomes pregnant and needs to leave the island, but Moses will not go with her. Their first son is probably born around 1935 or 1936. They have at least one other son, Gerry, who is born about 1945. Because Moses will not follow her to town, in "The Good Tears," Lulu marries Morrissey II for spite. We learn (in "The Red Convertible") that Moses is jealous of Lulu's later husbands and that he considers drowning to be the worst death for a Chippewa ("The Good Tears").

Chapter 14 of *The Bingo Palace* relates that Moses dies of desire on his island. Afterward, his windigo love-howl still rings across the lake, and in chapter 17, he is said to haunt the island with the howls of cats. He is mentioned in chapter 27 as Fleur makes her death walk across the frozen lake. In 1996 (chapter 22 of *The Last Report on the Miracles at Little No Horse*), as Father Damien prepares to go to the island to die, he thinks of Fleur going there to join Moses and her other relatives. When Mary Kashpaw follows the priest a few days later, she notices Moses's cave.

Moses also lives on in the traits he has passed down to his son. According to "The Good Tears" and "Crossing the Water" in *Love Medicine* and chapter 1 of *The Bingo Palace,* Gerry inherits his ability to escape and his Pillager grin from Moses, who, in "Crossing the Water," is referred to as Old Man Pillager.

Mud engineer. Oil field worker killed by a pressurized hose, whom June Kashpaw recalls hearing about in "The World's Greatest Fishermen" in *Love Medicine*. A mud engineer is the person at a drilling rig who is responsible for testing and correcting the composition of the "mud," a viscous fluid used in drilling oil wells. Another character working as a mud engineer is **Andy,** or **Jack Mauser.**

N

Nanabozho. Ojibwe trickster spirit, subject of Ojibwe stories. As he compares Christian and Indian gods in the story "Love Medicine" in *Love Medicine,* Lipsha Morrissey thinks of the tricky Nanabozho. Mirage alludes to the trickster in chapter 3 of *Tracks* when he tells Nanapush the meaning of his name. Chapter 16 of *The Last Report on the Miracles at Little No Horse* tells us that Father Damien absolves his parishioners in the spirit of the "ridiculous and wise" Nanabozho. In chapter 18, Nanapush's moose-hunting adventure in the fall of 1941 is an enactment of a Nanabozho story, and the old man's attempt to best his mythic namesake gets him into trouble. See also **Wenabojo.**

Nanapush. Ojibwe traditional and holdout; adoptive father of both Fleur Pillager and her daughter, Lulu Nanapush. Nanapush is born about 1862 (he is about fifty in December 1912 in *Tracks* chapter 1). We learn about Nanapush's early life from his memories in *Tracks* and *Four Souls*. (He is the narrator of odd-numbered chapters in both novels.) In chapter 5 of *Four Souls,* Nanapush, as a boy, and his uncle witness Under the Ground's healing of her daughter, Anaquot. In chapter 9 of *Tracks* he recalls fleeing from soldiers with his father and seeing the snow cover the bodies of his mother and sister. In chapter 9 of *Four Souls,* he remembers his favorite sister. The winter she was fifteen and Nanapush sixteen, the strange, ducklike Shesheeb comes to court her. They marry, but Shesheeb is cruel to her, and the next winter he apparently kills and eats her.

Nanapush's story as a young man continues in chapter 3 of *Tracks*. He receives the beginnings of a Jesuit education, enough to speak good English, read, and write (see also *Four Souls* chapter 5). He also acts as a guide to white hunters and, for a time (*Tracks* chapter 5), as a government interpreter. In chapter 6 of *Tracks,* we hear the story of one white man's hunt that he guides, after which the surviving animals grow strange and trample one another. (This is almost identical to a story in chapter 8 of *The Last Report on the Miracles at Little No Horse,* except that *Last Report* describes an Ojibwe hunt.)

Through these experiences, Nanapush gains a sophisticated knowledge of white ways. Yet he is deeply rooted in traditional Ojibwe culture, a holdout who will not sell or barter his land. His father tells him (in *Tracks* chapter 3) that his name means trickery, living in the bush, and having a way with women. As a young man, Nanapush is able to keep three wives satisfied. He and Kashpaw are friends and are notable for their amorous pursuits (even, according to chapter 9, sharing some women between them). Nanapush is also friends with the Pillager clan. He visits their home on Matchimanito Lake and, in the early days of sickness (prior to 1912), helps protect a Pillager child by giving him a false name, Moses.

Chapter 1 of *Tracks* tells of the consumption epidemic in the winter of 1912 that decimates the tribe and wipes out the last of Nanapush's family, including his three wives, a daughter, and a son (also mentioned in chapter 9). Nanapush especially mourns his third wife, White Beads, and their daughter, Red Cradle, nicknamed Lulu (chapter 3). Nanapush himself, fifty at the time, is taken ill but survives by telling a ceaseless story so that death cannot get a word in edgewise. In *The Last Report on the Miracles at Little No Horse* chapter 4, Sister Hildegarde Anne says that Nanapush is "too tricky to die" (*LR,* 73). In *Tracks* chapter 1, Nanapush rescues the seventeen-year-old Fleur Pillager, whose parents and three siblings have died in the epidemic. He nurses her back to life, then returns and buries her family. Even so, Nanapush and Fleur themselves barely survive the winter.

Chapter 1 of *Tracks* and chapter 5 of *Last Report* record the turning point in Nanapush's and Fleur's survival—a visit in March by the new priest, Father Damien. (This is 1913 in *Tracks,* 1912 in *Last Report.*) The starving pair revive enough to make tea for their guest and to catch, cook, and eat a porcupine. Nanapush's wry sense of humor also revives, and he tells Father Damien a story about Nanabozho's conversion of the wolves. That evening, Nanapush takes the priest to visit the camp of his friend Kashpaw in hopes that the presence of the priest will help him get one of Kashpaw's wives.

During this visit (*Last Report* chapter 6), Nanapush justifies his own numerous former wives with the story of his father, Mirage. As Kashpaw's family breaks apart in the following days, Margaret goes to see Nanapush, and he falls in love with her. At a feast day that fall (in chapter 7), when the newly baptized Kashpaw and his remaining wife, Quill, are fatally injured, Nanapush sits with his dying friend and sings him into the next world.

After consumption, the next threats Nanapush must confront are government agents and lumber companies. In chapter 3 of *Tracks* he refuses to sell or lease his allotment, arguing that land is the only thing that lasts. In the fall of 1913, after Fleur returns to the reservation from Argus, Eli Kashpaw gets Nanapush's advice on how to win her love. When the pregnant Fleur is ready to deliver the following spring (1914), Nanapush gives Margaret a boat ride across the lake to

Nanapush

assist Fleur with the birth. When Father Damien comes the next day to baptize the newborn girl, Nanapush both names her—giving her the nickname of his deceased daughter, Lulu—and falsely gives his name as her father (see also *Last Report* chapter 10). This is the only time during these early years that Nanapush allows his name to be written down.

We learn in chapter 4 of *Tracks* that after Lulu's birth, Nanapush is often a visitor at Matchimanito, as is Pauline Puyat. Nanapush notices Pauline's emerging sexuality, teases her, and points her out to Napoleon Morrissey. In the fall of 1917 (chapter 5), after a lovers' quarrel with Fleur, Eli moves in with Nanapush. The two men share the famine of that winter, relieved for a time by Eli's shooting a moose, guided by Nanapush's spirit.

That same winter, 1917–1918, Clarence Morrissey and Boy Lazarre capture Nanapush and Margaret and shave Margaret's head. Nanapush avenges her humiliation by snaring Clarence. By Ash Wednesday 1918, Nanapush and Margaret are keeping company. Nanapush declines Father Damien's suggestion that they be church married, but he does make confession to the priest, not only about Margaret, but also about snaring Clarence with a wire from Damien's piano. The snow and famine continue, and at one point Nanapush nearly starves before Margaret comes to his cabin and revives him. They both move to Matchimanito until spring. When Pauline, now a religious fanatic, visits the Pillager cabin in chapter 6, Nanapush, whom she refers to as "the fiend," mocks and torments her.

The following winter (1918–1919), Nanapush and Margaret are at Margaret's house (in *Tracks* chapter 7) when Nanapush finds Lulu outside, half frozen. Lulu has come for help for her mother, who has gone into premature labor with Eli's child. While Margaret goes to Fleur, Nanapush nurses Lulu's frozen feet, refusing to allow a white doctor to amputate. One day in late winter, Nanapush and Nector go to the Morrisseys' farm and force Clarence to give them part of a butchered cow. The Pillager-Kashpaw-Nanapush family again almost starves. Then, along with the government rations that save them, comes the news that they are in danger of losing their land allotments because of nonpayment of land fees. The combined family raises money for fees on Kashpaw and Pillager land, but Nanapush has already lost his home to the hated Lazarres. Father Damien encourages Nanapush to take a leadership position in the tribe to help his people, and he reluctantly agrees to do so. To counteract her depression over the loss of her premature baby, Nanapush and Moses Pillager conduct a healing ceremony for Fleur.

The following spring (1919, *Tracks* chapter 8), Nanapush tries to rescue Pauline Puyat from his leaky boat on Matchimanito Lake. Late that summer (*Tracks* chapter 9), Nanapush learns that Margaret and Nector paid the fees only on Kashpaw and not Pillager land. After this betrayal, although Nanapush continues to live with Margaret, he does not love her so well as before.

Nanapush

That fall (1919), just before Fleur leaves the reservation (in chapter 9 of *Tracks*), Nanapush sees the deceased members of his family among the trees around Fleur's cabin. He then witnesses her dramatic, tree-felling revenge on the lumber company. Shortly before her departure, Fleur sends Lulu to the government boarding school. During her time away, Lulu thinks of her "Grandpa" Nanapush several times (*Last Report* chapter 15). Meanwhile, Nanapush is working to bring Lulu home (*Tracks* chapter 9), though he has to become a bureaucrat to succeed, becoming buried in a blizzard of paperwork.

In his conversations with Father Damien in chapter 1 of *Four Souls,* Nanapush pieces together Fleur's Minneapolis story from rumor and speculation. He has insight into Fleur's actions in the city, he says in chapter 3, because the two have in common the "self-contempt of the survivor" (*FS,* 21). Once she is established in Minneapolis, Fleur sends goods and supplies to Nanapush and Margaret (*Last Report* chapter 16).

Last Report and *Four Souls* recount miscellaneous events in Nanapush's life during the period while Fleur is away. In the summer of 1920, he gives Nector and his cousins advice on how to deflect blame for their "borrowing" of a Model T (*Last Report* chapter 9). In *Four Souls* chapter 7, Nanapush becomes angry with Margaret for selling some of Nector's land to buy linoleum for her cabin.

Last Report also records incidents during the early 1920s in which Nanapush's friendship with Father Damien deepens. In the spring of 1922, Nanapush oversees a sweat lodge ceremony to heal the depressed and suicidal priest (chapter 11). Over the next year or so, the two have many meaningful conversations—about snakes, music, and time (chapter 12). The not-entirely-trustworthy Nanapush also recounts to the priest several versions of the story of Pauline Puyat's family (chapter 8). In 1923, three years after Father Damien's encounter with the demonic black dog, the two discuss various kinds of devils, and then play chess. Nanapush wins the match by distracting Damien with an emotionally loaded question (chapter 13). Although in *Tracks,* Nanapush makes two tongue-in-cheek "confessions" to Father Damien, Damien will remember in *Last Report* chapter 20 that Nanapush never really confesses a sin. Instead, Damien considers Nanapush his confessor and priest. Rather than converting Nanapush, Damien says in chapter 16 of *Last Report* that he himself has been converted by the old traditional.

Chapter 9 of *Tracks* and "The Island" in *Love Medicine* record Lulu's return to the reservation in 1924. Nanapush takes her in to live with him and Margaret, although Margaret objects. Lulu says in chapter 15 of *Last Report* that Nanapush immediately begins to urge her to forgive and accept her mother. (She refuses.) Nanapush tells Lulu (in "The Island") that Father Damien had won his soul in a card game (an account at odds with the *Last Report* picture of Damien's attitude toward conversion, cited above). When Lulu is a young woman and is determined

Nanapush

to go to Moses Pillager on his island in Matchimanito Lake (in "The Island"), Nanapush gives her advice on how to deal with Moses.

There are differences among the various accounts of where Nanapush is living during this time. We know from chapters 7 and 9 of *Tracks* that in 1919 he loses his property—a pack of Lazarres moves into his house—and he goes to live with Margaret on Kashpaw land. The reservation-set chapters of *Four Souls* also indicate that Nanapush is living with Margaret on her land in the 1920s and early 1930s. Yet when Lulu comes home (1924) in "The Island," he appears to be living on his own property, since whenever Margaret is angry with him, she leaves and goes to the Kashpaw allotment, an hour's walk away. In chapter 9 of *Last Report,* there is a probable clue to solving this seeming discrepancy. On their way home from Matchimanito Lake in 1920, Nector and his cousins stop off at "the place where Nanapush kept his shack when he wasn't living with Margaret" (*LR,* 177). Apparently, although Nanapush is generally living with Margaret, he has either recovered his old cabin or acquired another somewhere in the bush.

In what is probably the early 1930s, Nanapush's old enemy Shesheeb moves into a house down the road from Margaret's cabin. The ensuing events are recorded in several chapters of *Four Souls.* In chapter 9, Nanapush remembers Shesheeb's apparent murder of Nanapush's sister and becomes convinced that the "black duck" wants to steal Margaret's affection. After two unsuccessful attempts to use dark medicine, Nanapush makes a snare to kill his enemy. When Margaret is caught in the snare, Nanapush rescues her, but in chapter 11, she realizes that he is the snarer. She punishes him by inflaming his jealousy. In chapter 11, Nanapush steals wine from the convent, he and Margaret argue, and he dons her medicine dress. When Margaret leaves in disgust, Nanapush goes to steal more wine and is caught, and the next day he goes to jail and then to a council meeting, still wearing the dress. On his way to the meeting, he bares his bottom in a photo with a disrespectful *family of white tourists.* The next morning, in chapter 13, Nanapush captures a blowfly (which he thinks is Shesheeb) and buries it with his excrement, cutting out a piece of Margaret's linoleum in the process. He makes up a wild story about a falling star crashing through the roof and the floor to cover up his misdeed. Margaret finally returns home that evening, and though she sees through his ruse, she laughs and forgives him.

In 1933, Fleur returns to the reservation with a white boy, as recorded in *The Bingo Palace* chapter 12, *The Last Report on the Miracles at Little No Horse* chapter 16, and *Four Souls* chapters 14 and 15. There are several differences between the accounts of this return in *The Bingo Palace* and *Four Souls,* including the part Nanapush plays in these events. In *The Bingo Palace,* Fleur stays at Nanapush's house, and the poker game takes place in his yard. In *Four Souls* chapter 15, she will not stay with Margaret and Nanapush because Lulu is living there and refuses to see her. Instead, in this novel, Nanapush sees Fleur in town each day, at first at the agency office and then at the nightly poker game in Tatro's bar. Nanapush does not take part in the game in *Four Souls,* but on the climactic night, he and Fleur exchange words, and he understands what she is planning. The next morning, after winning back her land, in chapter 16 of *Four Souls* Fleur comes to visit Margaret and Nanapush. Nanapush takes Fleur's boy fishing so that Margaret can care for Fleur and talk to her alone.

We know from *Four Souls* chapter 1 that after her return, Fleur tells Nanapush about her years in Minneapolis. Nanapush also continues to reason with Lulu about her relationship with her mother. The chapters he narrates in *Tracks* are a record of those conversations. When as a young woman Lulu is considering marrying a Morrissey man, Nanapush tells her tales of family and tribal history, not only to persuade her not to marry a Morrissey (*Tracks* chapter 7) but also to help her understand Fleur's seeming abandonment (chapter 9). Nanapush's narration in *Four Souls* is a continuation of his *Tracks* narrative, taking the story of Fleur from 1919 to 1933. In this novel, however, for the most part, he does not directly address Lulu. There is one exception: when he adds the word "n'dawnis" to his narrative in chapter 11 (*FS,* 140), he is undoubtedly addressing Lulu.

In the early fall of 1941, Nanapush and Margaret go on an ill-fated moose hunt (*Last Report* chapter 18). When his shot at the lassoed moose misses, the moose drags him and his boat all over the reservation. With fishhooks in his buttocks, Nanapush cannot escape, and the moose does not stop until the next day. Margaret finally kills the moose, whose meat is now stringy and sour. That winter (1941– 1942), she punishes Nanapush by serving him undercooked beans so often that he dies of windy indigestion. At his wake, he comes back from the dead twice, the second time for one last session of lovemaking with Margaret, then dies for good. Three years later, in 1945 (*Last Report* chapter 16), Lulu is living in Nanapush's old house with her firstborn and her baby, Gerry.

A comparison of the account of Nanapush's death in *Last Report,* published in 2001, with the story "The Beads" in the 1993 *Love Medicine* reveals another example of how Erdrich's master story changes over time. According to "The Beads," Nanapush is still alive in 1948, cared for by Fleur on Pillager land.

A reference to Nanapush's death in the 2005 *The Painted Drum* also gives a different twist from the *Last Report* story. In part 1.3 of *Painted Drum,* Elsie Travers recalls that Nanapush dies of old age (not poorly cooked beans). But characteristic of the Nanapush of the other novels, she also recalls a portrait taken near his death in which he is making an obscene gesture.

Characters in *The Bingo Palace* and *The Last Report on the Miracles at Little No*

Nanapush

Horse remember Nanapush long after his death. In chapter 11 of *The Bingo Palace,* Lipsha Morrissey recalls stories of Nanapush as the healing doctor witch who was adoptive father to the now-old medicine woman Fleur. In Lyman Lamartine's vision in chapter 13, Fleur repeats Nanapush's words (from chapter 3 of *Tracks*) regarding land being the only thing that lasts. Gerry Nanapush hears Old Man Nanapush telling stories during a fevered vision in his solitary prison cell in chapter 21. On her death walk in chapter 27, Fleur sees Nanapush as a young man with clever hands, ceaselessly talking. In chapter 22 of *Last Report,* shortly before his own death in the summer of 1996, Father Damien hopes he will see Nanapush on Spirit Island and that they will sing together. On the island, Damien calls to Nanapush and Fleur, and as he is dying, he feels a hand grasp his and pull him across.

Sometime after the turn of the twenty-first century, in part 2.1 of *The Painted Drum* a surviving nephew whom Nanapush apparently knew nothing about, Judge Nanapush, is living with his wife in a prefab house on the site of old Nanapush's shack, which had caved in one winter.

Nanapush family. Nanapush is thought to be the last surviving member of his family. For information about his father and *his mother,* see **Mirage.** His mother and *one sister* die in the winter just before the family begins its forced migration westward. For the sister to whom Nanapush is closest, see **Nanapush's sister.** The deceased members of his immediate family include three wives (see **Dove, the; Unexpected, the;** and **White Beads**) and two children (see **Red Cradle** and **Standing in a Stone**). His adoptive granddaughter, **Lulu Nanapush Morrissey Lamartine,** and three of her sons, including **Gerry Nanapush,** wear the Nanapush name but are not blood kin. See also **Geraldine Nanapush, Judge Nanapush, Nanapush's uncle,** and, in **Tomahawk factory workers,** *Billy Nanapush.*

Nanapush's sister. Nanapush's much-loved sister, one year younger than he. Nanapush describes her in chapter 9 of *Four Souls* as laughing and curious, a sweet blossom with a "tender inner life" and a "beautifully wound" mind (*FS,* 105–6). The winter she is fifteen (about 1878), the greedy, sly Shesheeb comes to court her, but after they marry, Shesheeb is abusive. He strikes her face with a burning stick, and the next winter—a starvation winter—he apparently goes windigo and kills and eats her. When Shesheeb returns to the reservation in the early 1930s, Nanapush remembers his hatred and plans to kill Shesheeb in revenge.

Nanapush's uncle. A healer who, as an old man in the 1860s or 1870s, attends to the ill twelve-year-old girl Anaquot in chapter 5 of *Four Souls.* His young nephew

Nanapush accompanies him. Although the uncle sings and drums for three days and nights, he is unable to help Anaquot, who is saved by the efforts of her mother, Under the Ground.

Napoleon Morrissey. Brother of Bernadette Morrissey; lover of Pauline Puyat; father of Marie Lazarre. A note about Napoleon's surname—since Bernadette's children Clarence and Sophie use the name Morrissey (chapters 5 and 7 of *Tracks*), this would appear to be Bernadette's married name, so the reader wonders why her brother wears the same name. There are several possible explanations. Napoleon may be Bernadette's brother-in-law, he may have taken the surname of his sister's family, or Bernadette and her children may use her maiden name.

After the death of Mary Kashpaw's parents in the autumn of 1912, while Mary is staying with the Morrisseys that winter in chapter 7 of *The Last Report on the Miracles at Little No Horse,* Napoleon forces himself on her. Mary becomes violent whenever Napoleon is near, and when Father Damien realizes what has happened, he brings her to live at the convent.

In December 1913, Napoleon and Bernadette come to Argus and take Pauline Puyat back to the reservation to live with them (*Tracks* chapter 4). After several months, Napoleon and Pauline begin an ongoing sexual relationship. In chapter 6, when Bernadette learns that Pauline is pregnant by Napoleon, she banishes him to the barn. After giving birth to Napoleon's daughter in November 1918, Pauline abandons the baby, leaving her with Bernadette.

Early in 1919 (*Tracks* chapter 7), when his niece Sophie and nephew Clarence bring their Lazarre spouses to the house and Bernadette leaves, Napoleon begins to drink steadily. One night that spring, wandering drunk beside Matchimanito Lake, in chapter 8, Napoleon encounters the naked Pauline. Taking Napoleon to be the devil, Pauline chokes him to death with her rosary and then drags his body into the woods behind Fleur Pillager's cabin. We learn in chapter 9 of *Last Report* that this rosary is made of barbed wire.

Fleur's young daughter, Lulu Nanapush, discovers a man's body in the woods in "The Good Tears" in *Love Medicine,* and this man is revealed in chapter 9 of *Tracks* to be Napoleon. After Fleur has lost her land to the lumber company late that summer, surveyors find Napoleon's decayed body, and Fleur is suspected of causing his death. The drunken Clarence even claims to have a "vision" in which Napoleon's ghost accuses her. There is a variation of the story in *Last Report* chapter 9. Here, Napoleon's body is apparently found before Fleur's land is taken.

According to chapters 9, 14, and 16 of *Last Report,* Father Damien is the one who investigates Napoleon's murder. By examining the corpse, Damien sees that Napoleon was strangled, and when one of his helpers finds the barbed-wire rosary,

Napoleon Morrissey

he realizes that it is the murder weapon. (In chapter 9 of *Tracks,* it is Edgar Pukwan Junior who supposedly "investigates" the murder.)

At Napoleon's funeral, in *Last Report* chapter 9 Margaret Kashpaw initiates an interfamily conflict with her sarcastic remarks about Napoleon's evil ways. But unlike what the other Morrisseys assume, the reason these comments agitate Bernadette is that they remind her of what she knows too well—that Napoleon was utterly corrupt and that she is glad he is dead.

In 1934, Sophie Morrissey tells Marie Lazarre that Sophie's uncle Napoleon was Marie's "deydey" (*Last Report* chapter 20, but see "Saint Marie" in *Love Medicine* for the date).

Years later, in 1996, Father Jude Miller comes to the reservation in *The Last Report on the Miracles at Little No Horse* to interview the centenarian Father Damien about Pauline/Leopolda. Damien is trying to convince Jude that Sister Leopolda was not a saint without revealing everything he knows. The first time Damien raises the subject of Napoleon's murder, in chapter 14, he stops himself. A few days later, however, in chapter 21, Damien relates the whole story, the truth that utterly disqualifies Leopolda from sainthood—that she had murdered Napoleon.

Nector Kashpaw. Youngest son of Kashpaw (Resounding Sky) and Margaret (Rushes Bear); husband of Marie Lazarre Kashpaw. Chapter 5 of *Tracks* indicates that Nector is born in 1908. Our earliest glimpse of Nector is as a smartly dressed child in chapter 6 of *The Last Report on the Miracles at Little No Horse* when Father Damien comes to visit the Kashpaw family in March 1912. Kashpaw sends him to Father Damien's church to see if Damien's god is any good, and Nector becomes an altar boy.

Nector's father dies the following autumn (chapter 7 of *Last Report*). In "The World's Greatest Fishermen" in *Love Medicine,* we learn that when reservation land is allotted and Margaret's older children move away, Nector and his brother Eli receive allotments adjacent to their mother's. Nector has a natural aptitude for book learning and, like his father, for business and politics (*Tracks* chapter 3). Although as a child he imitates Eli, Nector is quite different from his woodsman brother. When Eli's wife, Fleur Pillager, gives birth to Lulu in the spring of 1914, Margaret sends Nector to fetch Father Damien to baptize her (*Last Report* chapter 10; see also *Tracks* chapter 3). Nector and his mother subsequently stay for long periods at Fleur's cabin (*Tracks* chapters 4, 5, and 6).

After Clarence Morrissey and Boy Lazarre shame Margaret in the winter of 1917–1918 (chapter 5), the nine-year-old Nector helps Nanapush make a snare for Clarence in revenge. Nector shows his awareness of tribal land issues both in this chapter, as he asks Nanapush questions, and in chapter 7, where he is the first in his family to understand the danger of unpaid land fees. That spring (1919) Nector and Margaret take the money the family has raised to the Indian agent, but there are hints that something is amiss. Chapter 9 reveals the problem. Nector and Margaret have used the money—intended for both Kashpaw and Pillager fees—entirely to pay Kashpaw land and late-payment fees. Since Pillager fees are not paid, the agent sells Fleur's land to the lumber company. Later that summer, when Fleur learns what has happened, she tries to drown herself in the lake, Eli rescues her, and she curses Nector. To protect him, Margaret sends Nector off to a government boarding school. He and Lulu, whom Fleur is also trying to protect, leave the reservation together.

At this point, there is a significant variation in Nector's story. Almost all of the accounts of Nector's years at school conform to the *Tracks* (chapter 9) chronology, above—that is, he leaves in late summer or autumn of 1919 and returns several years later. There is, however, one chapter that gives a different chronology and set of incidents. Chapter 9 of *Last Report* indicates that Nector comes *home* from school about the same time as Napoleon Morrissey's funeral, which is in the late summer of 1919—the same time that most accounts have him *leaving* the reservation. The following narrative will first give this alternate account of his story, and then will return to Erdrich's primary version of Nector's time away from the reservation.

According to *Last Report* chapter 9, when Nector returns home in late 1919, he again serves as altar boy for Father Damien, in both his own family's mass and the early one attended by their enemies. Bernadette Morrissey makes the mistake of underestimating Nector when she takes him on as an assistant in the agency office. Behind a facade of insignificance and neutrality, Nector hides a keen, aggressive intellect and a conviction that only the land matters. He recopies the tattered land records and destroys the originals, giving him control over the tribe's history.

This chapter also records an incident in Nector's life the following spring or summer. One day in 1920, Nector goes on a joyride with three Kashpaw cousins and a friend in a Model T Ford stealthily borrowed from **Makoons's uncle.** When they encounter a group of young Lazarres at Matchimanito Lake, the Lazarres manage to tie them to the car and push the car into the lake. Thanks to the skills of **Clay Onesides,** the Kashpaws break free and swim. **Adik Lazarre** follows them, but **Rockhead** knocks him out and drowns him. The other Kashpaw cousin and friend in this incident are **Johnny Onesides** and **Makoons.** Other Lazarres are **Eugene,** the **Half-Twin, Mercy Lazarre, Fred,** and **Virgil.** Nanapush helps the Kashpaw boys escape blame for taking the car.

Except for this variation, references to Nector's school years have him leaving the reservation in late summer or early autumn of 1919, on the same wagon or bus as Lulu (see *Tracks* chapter 9, *Love Medicine* "The Plunge of the Brave," and *Last*

Nector Kashpaw

Report chapter 15). In this primary version of Nector's youth, he is away from home for a number of years. Chapter 9 of *Tracks* reveals that, after finishing eighth grade, Nector travels south to Oklahoma. "The Plunge of the Brave" in *Love Medicine* indicates that he goes to high school in Flandreau, where he plays football and reads *Moby-Dick*. After Flandreau, he plays a bit part in a movie, works a year in the wheat belt, and poses virtually nude for a painting in Kansas. His experiences with the larger world persuade Nector to return to the reservation. While he is away, Margaret sells part of his allotment to buy linoleum for her cabin (*Four Souls* chapter 7).

Even in this primary version of Nector's story, the date of his return varies from novel to novel. In "The Wild Geese" in *Love Medicine,* Nector refers to the summer of 1934 as "the summer I am out of school" (*LM,* 61). His account in "The Plunge of the Brave" suggests a similar date. He says that he and Lulu (who returns in 1924 [*Tracks* chapter 9]) grow up apart, and when he returns home years later, she is already there and is an attractive young woman. In *Four Souls* chapter 11, Nector's return also seems to be in the early 1930s, but it is before Fleur's 1933 return. In contrast, *Last Report* chapter 16 indicates that Nector comes home before Lulu, since he writes to Fleur in Minneapolis to tell her that Lulu has returned.

When Nector arrives home (in chapter 11 of *Four Souls*), Nanapush teases him about his womanizing, and Nector remembers aloud the time he helped Nanapush snare Clarence Morrissey. This comment makes Margaret realize that Nanapush had set the snare that almost killed her. Nector lives with his mother and brother ("The Plunge of the Brave"), hunting geese with Eli and selling them for spending money ("The Wild Geese"). He soon falls in love with Lulu and plans to marry her.

One summer evening in 1934, however, in "The Wild Geese" Nector's plans are derailed by his confrontation with Marie Lazarre, who is descending the hill from the reservation convent. Thinking that Marie has stolen linens from the convent, Nector tries to grab her. As they scuffle, the encounter becomes sexual.

The remainder of Nector's life is chronicled in several *Love Medicine* stories. When Nector's relationship with Marie becomes known in "The Island," Margaret is dismayed that Nector is going to marry a Lazarre, a family she considers trash. "The Beads" and "The Plunge of the Brave" depict the next seventeen years of Nector's life as dominated by babies and work, and ordered by Marie's firm, controlling hand. Nector tries to be a drunk, but Marie wants him to be someone big on the reservation, so she throws away his bottles and drags him home from bars. When Marie gives birth to their last child, almost dying in childbirth, Margaret turns her affection from Nector, of whom she is ashamed, to Marie, whose stoicism she has come to admire. Over time, however, Nector becomes a stable provider for his family and chairman of the tribe.

After seventeen years of marriage, however, in "The Plunge of the Brave," Nector reflects upon his life and again wants Lulu. In July 1952, delivering commodity butter on the hottest day of the year, Nector and Lulu begin an affair that lasts for five years. During those years, Lulu gives birth to Nector's son, Lyman, and Nector works with the tribal council to get federal funding for a development project on the reservation, a factory. Nector becomes increasingly torn and exhausted by his double life. Matters come to a head in 1957 when Beverly Lamartine comes to court Lulu and Nector has to sign eviction papers forcing her off her land to make room for the factory. After Lulu receives the eviction notice, she sics her dogs on Nector when he comes to visit that night, and she marries Beverly ("The Good Tears").

In this crisis, Nector decides to leave Marie. One August afternoon, he leaves a letter for Marie on their kitchen table and goes to Lulu's house. While waiting for Lulu to return home, however, he starts a fire that burns down her house. (Nector's account in "The Plunge of the Brave" makes the house burning sound accidental, but Lulu's account in "The Good Tears" and Zelda's recollection in chapter 23 of *The Bingo Palace* suggests a more direct connection between the fire and his "burning" passion for Lulu.) In "Flesh and Blood," Zelda finds Nector's letter to Marie and comes to fetch him home. When he arrives at his house, uncertain whether he can enter, Marie reaches out and pulls him in.

Nector is apparently still looked upon as the family patriarch in 1973, since Henry Lamartine Junior asks the runaway Albertine Johnson in "The Bridge" whether her grandfather Kashpaw knows where she is. By 1981, however ("The World's Greatest Fishermen"), Nector has become feeble-minded. His doctor attributes Nector's condition to diabetes, but in "Love Medicine," Nector's adopted grandson Lipsha Morrissey suggests that the old man's mental absence is willed. As Albertine indicates in "The World's Greatest Fishermen," his loss of memory may be a protection from the past.

In "Love Medicine," Nector, now living with Marie at the Senior Citizens in town, again hankers after Lulu, who also lives at the center. One day, Lipsha finds them embracing in the laundry room and decides to honor Marie's request that he make a love medicine to keep Nector's heart fixed on his wife. Lipsha's love medicine goes awry, however, when Nector chokes to death on the raw turkey heart Lipsha provides. All the scattered family members assemble for Nector's funeral. Afterward, Marie senses the continuing presence of his spirit. Nector's spirit also visits Lulu, who is in the hospital at the time of his funeral ("The

Nector Kashpaw

Good Tears"). When Marie moves back into the old Kashpaw place for a time in "Resurrection," she remembers her years with Nector in that house.

Nector's spirit lives on in other ways as well. His son Lyman Lamartine inherits Nector's aptitude for business and politics. In "The Tomahawk Factory," Lyman carries forward Nector's project of a tribal souvenir factory, then hatches a grander scheme in "Lyman's Luck" of a bingo hall and a casino. By the opening of *The Bingo Palace*, Lyman is a successful bingo hall operator, and in chapter 1, the reservation folk compare his ambition and scheming to that of Nector. Lyman acknowledges his similarity to his father in chapter 13.

Lipsha also remembers his "Grandpa" Nector in chapters 11, 14, and 17 of *The Bingo Palace*. In chapter 4, as Marie gives Nector's ceremonial pipe to Lipsha, they remember the way Nector used to pray with the pipe—calmly, in the old language, eyes unfocused into the distance. We are told in chapter 5 that Nector had inherited this pipe from his own father, Resounding Sky. (Nector's pipe is also mentioned in chapters 8, 9, and 23.)

Zelda is haunted by a more troubling memory of her father. In chapters 5 and 23 of *The Bingo Palace*, she recalls watching Nector burn the house of his lover, which she sees as an example of the dangers of love.

In 1996 (chapter 20 of *Last Report*), Marie mentions Nector to Father Jude, who is visiting the reservation. She says that she never told Nector the true identity of her parents (Pauline Puyat and Napoleon Morrissey). The only things he knew about her were what she chose to reveal.

Netta Travers. Daughter of Elsie and Professor Travers; younger sister of Faye Travers in *The Painted Drum*. Netta is apparently born in the 1950s, a little over two years after Faye. Netta is quite different from Faye (part 1.4). She looks more like her father and has some of his combative personality. Whereas Faye is quiet, neat, and careful of detail, Netta has a strong sense of self and is bold, impatient, and at times cruel. One night when Netta is six, the sisters catch fireflies. Faye releases hers but Netta smashes hers into her body, amused that she glows in the dark. Faye recalls Netta's childish thoughtlessness (1.3), but she also recalls that her little sister would crawl into bed with her and that she was a good sister "who loved me so much that she sacrificed herself for me" (*PD*, 73).

During a time when their father is obsessed with publishers' rejection slips and their mother is preoccupied and often gone, Netta and Faye spend their days in the apple orchard. One evening their father comes out and, finding them in a tree, challenges them to jump to him. When she sees Faye fall and their father step aside and let her hit the ground, Netta willfully steps from her high branch and falls to her death.

Faye's grief over her sister's death still affects her painfully in her fifties (part 1.3), and she regularly visits Netta's grave (parts 1.1 and 4). Close to fifty years later, Faye finally tells Elsie what really happened that day, and Elsie confesses that the reason she was gone when Netta stepped from the tree was that she was having an affair (part 4).

Nettie Testor, Mrs. Housekeeper in the mansion of John James Mauser in *Four Souls*. Under the oversight of her mistress's sister, Polly Elizabeth Gheen, Mrs. Testor seems to be in charge of all the mechanics of the household, as well as the other household servants. When Fleur Pillager becomes the laundress in chapter 2, Mrs. Testor shows her how to use the machines. Chapter 4 describes Polly Elizabeth as "directing Mrs. Testor" about household matters. Tester is offended when, during Dr. Fulmer's visit, Fleur orders hot water from her.

When Mauser divorces Placide and sends her and Polly Elizabeth away (chapter 6), Mrs. Testor sobs—but she chooses to stay. Soon, Polly Elizabeth begins to visit Mrs. Testor every week. They have tea and Mrs. Testor gives her the household news. One day, she reveals that Fleur is not out, but upstairs in bed—pregnant. She later tells Polly Elizabeth that Fleur is in danger of miscarriage.

In chapter 8, even after Mauser's finances begin to fail, Mrs. Testor still spends large amounts on meat for the household, and in chapter 10, we learn that, with the rest of the family distracted, she is stealing. By the time Polly Elizabeth and Fantan are preparing the house for bankruptcy auction in chapter 12, Mrs. Testor seems to be gone.

Niibin'aage. Middle child and only daughter of Ziigwan'aage and Simon Jack; mother of Elsie Travers in *The Painted Drum*. In part 2.3, Niibin'aage is living in the Pillager cabin on Matchimanito Lake with her parents and an older and a younger brother. One winter when Niibin'aage is school-aged, the woman Anaquot and her infant daughter arrive at the cabin. Sensing her mother's hostility toward the woman, Niibin'aage hates her. Anaquot's narrative describes the girl with such words as "hard," "greedy," "cold," "frozen," and "snake-eyed" (*PD*, 123, 140–42, 145).

The following spring (2.3), a young white teacher-recruiter for the Carlisle Indian School in Pennsylvania is in the trader's store when Ziigwan'aage goes to town with her sister Doosh and Anaquot. Doosh urges Ziigwan'aage to send Niibin'aage to the school, and Anaquot hints at the same. We learn in part 1.2 that when Niibin'aage is ten, she does go to Carlisle, recruited by the young teacher. She learns both practical and academic skills, and because she is there, she escapes the epidemic that takes the lives of her family (parts 2.1 and 2.5). Niibin'aage later marries the young teacher, and since he is from New Hampshire,

Niibin'aage

she stays in the East. They return to the reservation for a time when Niibin'aage inherits land, and their daughter, Elsie, is born there. They then move back to Stokes, New Hampshire, where her husband works in a rich family's game park. Elsie's daughter Faye recalls her grandmother in 1.2 with words quite similar to Anaquot's impression years before. She was a "cold little woman," Faye recalls, an "anti-Grandma" who felt neither love nor any human emotion (*PD,* 30). (See also **Carlisle teacher from Stokes.**)

Nuns at convent in Fargo. Several sister-nuns to Sister Cecilia are mentioned in chapter 1 of *The Last Report on the Miracles at Little No Horse* as being overly moved by her piano playing, so the **Mother Superior** hides much of Cecilia's sheet music. These same nuns take care of Cecilia when, as Agnes DeWitt Vogel, she is wounded twice when she is taken hostage by a bank robber.

Nuns at Our Lady of the Wheat Priory. Nuns at the Argus convent where Sister Leopolda is living in 1994 in *Tales of Burning Love.* Mentioned briefly in "Night Prayer" [6], they reappear as background characters in "The Stone Virgin" [44]. The full name of the convent is given in "A Letter to the Bishop" [45].

In "White Musk" [4], Eleanor Mauser asks the **Mother Superior** for permission to stay at the convent while she is doing research on Leopolda. In "Night Prayer" [6], the Mother Superior gets Jack Mauser's highway construction workers to remove a cracked wooden statue of the Virgin. In "The Stone Virgin" [44], she persuades the road crew to help again, this time to transport the new stone statue to the convent. See **Adelphine, Sister,** and **Leopolda, Sister.**

Nuns at Sacred Heart Convent at Little No Horse. Sisters at the convent on the hill overlooking the reservation township. The day after his arrival at Little No Horse in March 1912, in chapter 4 of *The Last Report on the Miracles at Little No Horse* Father Damien serves mass to its *six starving nuns* (including the Superior, Sister Hildegarde Anne). In 1918–1919, Pauline Puyat lives with these nuns as a novice (chapters 6 and 8 of *Tracks*). According to the *Tracks* version of her story, Pauline takes her vows there in the spring of 1919.

In 1932, Fleur Pillager leaves Karl Adare with these nuns after nursing him back to health in chapter 3 of *The Beet Queen.* They later send him to Saint Jerome's orphanage in Minneapolis. Two years later (1934), these sisters serve as mild and sane foils to the Satan-obsessed Sister Leopolda in "Saint Marie" in *Love Medicine.* They kneel beside the fourteen-year-old Marie Lazarre, who is lying on the Mother Superior's couch after the stigmata-like wound appears in her hand. Among those present on this occasion are **Sister Bonaventure, Sister Cecilia Saint-Claire,** and the **two French nuns** "with hands like paddles." These two call

Marie "Star of the Sea" and, ironically, feel that she has unusual humility of spirit (*LM*, 54).

In chapter 5 of *The Bingo Palace,* the sisters on the hill are depicted as praying for the drunks who patronize Lyman Lamartine's bingo hall in the 1980s. During Father Jude's visit in 1996, the sisters, including **Sister Mauvis,** search Father Damien's house when he appears to be drunk. They find no alcohol.

See also **Adelphine, Sister; Anne, Sister Saint; Dympna Evangelica, Sister; Hildegarde Anne, Sister; Leopolda, Sister;** and **Mary Martin de Porres, Sister.**

Nuns at Saint Catherine's school in Argus. Teachers who in 1932 witness Mary Adare's "miracle" in chapter 2 of *The Beet Queen. Sister Hugo* helps Mary to the infirmary after the mishap. Almost thirty years later, the nuns at this school have to deal with Mary's niece, Dot Adare. They are said not to know what to do with Dot in chapter 11, and in chapter 12, they have to stop the school Christmas play when Dot knocks down another child. In chapter 10, Dot learns that *Sister Seraphica* will be her second grade teacher. See also **Leopolda, Sister.**

Nuns at Saint Jerome's orphanage. Nuns who apparently take care of Karl Adare after he is sent to the orphanage from Sacred Heart Convent in chapter 3 of *The Beet Queen.* Several of the nuns are present at the Orphans' Picnic on the day Karl returns to visit in chapter 4, among them *Sister Ivalo, Sister Mary Thomas, Sister Ursula,* and *Sister George.*

Nuns at Sobieski. Teachers at a Catholic school that Marlis Cook attends before she comes to Fargo, as recorded in "Marlis's Tale" [27] in *Tales of Burning Love.* They are referred to in "Best Western" [28] as having taught Marlis the basics of piano playing.

Nurses. The *morning nurse* during Karl Adare's stay in the hospital in Minneapolis becomes a friend to Wallace Pfef in chapter 9 of *The Beet Queen,* and Wallace continues to correspond with her. The *nurse in the state mental hospital* in chapter 10 has strict instructions not to read Sita Tappe's lips or her notes.

The *nurse in the Argus hospital* who leads Jack and Dot Mauser to Eleanor Mauser's room, in "The Meadowlark" [7] in *Tales of Burning Love,* criticizes Jack for bringing wine into the hospital, but she seems relieved to have him come to take "Mrs. Mauser" home. In "Best Western" [28], Marlis Cook Mauser recalls the *school nurse* (who seems also to be a counselor) who had said that Marlis was obsessed with men. When as a young woman Marlis is pregnant, in "The Waiting Room" [31], a *nurse* escorts her in to see the Lamaze instructor. *Maternity nurses* attend the birth of her baby. The *nurse in the Fargo hospital* is grumpy with Dot,

Nurses

in "February Thaw" [40], when Dot is recovering after nearly freezing to death in the blizzard. A ***nurse in the Argus hospital*** cleans Jack Mauser's cuts and bandages him after a falling statue nearly crushes him in "The Stone Virgin" [44].

When Cally Roy becomes gravely ill in chapter 9 of *The Antelope Wife*, **nurses at the IHS** (Indian Health Service) help care for her. A number of **IHS nurses** also help Ira's children in part 3.7 of *The Painted Drum,* when they are in the hospital with hypothermia.

O

Ober, Mr. Lover of Adelaide Adare; father of Karl and Mary Adare and Jude Miller in *The Beet Queen*. In chapter 1, Mr. Ober is described as a tall man with a neat black beard. He is possibly German, since his term of endearment for his daughter is "Schatze," a German word that means "treasure" or "sweetheart." He owns a large Minnesota wheat farm and has a wife, but he keeps a separate household in Prairie Lake with Adelaide. He dies in 1932, smothered in a grain-loading accident. Suicide is suspected, since he has borrowed heavily against his land during the Great Depression. His death leaves the pregnant Adelaide and her children homeless and destitute.

Ogimaakwe. In *Tracks* chapters 1 and 9, the Indian name of Fleur Pillager's mother, Boss Woman. In *The Bingo Palace,* her name appears in chapter 3 and she herself in chapter 27. In *Four Souls* chapter 16, Ogimaakwe is said to be the same person as Anaquot or Four Souls. See also **Boss Woman** and **Four Souls.**

Ojibwe villagers. People in the ancestral Shawano village somewhere south of their original Canadian homeland (chapter 3) in *The Antelope Wife*. In chapter 6, some of these villagers call Apijigo Bakaday a windigo because she is continually eating. After the death of Apijigo Bakaday's deer husband, the people rename her Blue Prairie Woman, and her women relatives accept her into their number. When the U.S. Cavalry attacks in chapter 1, old men, women, children, and a few warriors are present in the village, which loses its store of food in the raid and thus suffers famine through the next winter. In the spring, the elders hold a feast for the survivors, and they find a new name for Blue Prairie Woman. Sometime later, in chapter 23, remaining villagers are confined to the reservation "up north," where the granddaughters and great-granddaughters of Blue Prairie Woman grow up. (For notes about the possible location of this reservation, see **Rozina [Rozin] Roy Whiteheart Beads Shawano.**)

Old drunk woman. Purported mother of Marie Lazarre; mother of Lucille Lazarre and wife of Ignatius Lazarre. She shows up at Marie's door in 1948 with Lucille's daughter, June, and June's father, Morrissey I, in "The Beads" in *Love Medicine*.

Since Sophie Morrissey Lazarre seems to be the one taking care of Marie in infancy (chapter 8 of *Tracks*), we might conjecture that this drunk woman is Sophie. A problem with this reading is that Sophie's husband in chapter 7 of *Tracks* is Izear Lazarre, while in "The Beads," Marie's presumed father is Ignatius.

Old Lady Blue. Nosy woman in *Love Medicine* who needles Marie Kashpaw in "The Beads" about Marie's husband's drinking and his brother Eli's too-frequent visits to Marie's house. In "Crossing the Water," Marie fights with her at the mission bundle sale for a Stetson hat.

Old Lady Pillager. Name Lipsha Morrissey uses for Fleur Pillager in the "Love Medicine" story in *Love Medicine* and in chapters 11 and 14 of *The Bingo Palace*. See **Fleur Pillager**.

Old Man Pillager. Name used to refer to Fleur Pillager's father in chapter 9 of *Tracks* and to Moses Pillager in "Crossing the Water" in *Love Medicine*. Fleur's father is also called Old Pillager in chapter 2 of *Tracks* and the Old Man in chapter 7. See **Moses Pillager** and **Pillager**.

Old Swedish widow and her daughter. Referred to in "Satin Heart" [12] in *Tales of Burning Love*. The widow owns a basement apartment where, as a young man, Jack Mauser eats cookies. It is not clear whether he is just visiting or whether he lives there as a tenant. Jack proposes to the daughter. Years later, the daughter, now a tax lawyer, attends Jack's funeral.

Old woman killed by Scranton Roy. See **Blue Prairie Woman's grandmother I**.

Omar, The Great. Airplane stunt pilot and sometime bootlegger in *The Beet Queen*. In chapter 1, Omar is performing stunts at the Orphans' Picnic in Minneapolis in 1932 when he takes Adelaide Adare for a ride. She flies off with him, abandoning her children. In chapter 3, Adelaide's son Karl imagines, mistakenly, that Omar has abducted her against her will. Also in this chapter we learn that Omar and Adelaide are living in Florida and that Omar believes she has left a life of comfort to be with him. Omar has a serious accident with Adelaide as his passenger, but they both survive. Jealous of her children, Omar leaves beside her hospital bed a postcard that Mary has sent from Argus, falsely announcing that Adelaide's children have died of starvation.

Omar, The Great

In chapter 11, Omar and Adelaide are apparently still in Florida, where they operate a "birdorama." One morning, Omar hears glass breaking in the house and sees that Adelaide has had one of her periodic fits of rage and is standing with her feet bloody in the broken glass.

Omiimii. See **Dove, the.**

Onesides family. Reservation family whose members appear several times in *The Last Report on the Miracles at Little No Horse.* During the influenza epidemic in the winter of 1918–1919, in chapter 7 **one member** of the Onesides family dies. When Pauline Puyat is in her tetanus trance the following spring, **Danton Onesides** asks to see her. When his request is denied, he asks for threads of this saint's death blanket. Brothers **Johnny and Clay Onesides** are among the group of Nector's cousins who take a Model T joyride in 1920 and encounter a group of Lazarres at Matchimanito Lake. When the Lazarres try to drown the Kashpaw group, Clay, who is good with ropes, manages to untie himself and the others so they can swim free.

When a moose is dragging Nanapush and his boat around the reservation in the fall of 1941, **Mr. Onesides** hears a gun blast and looks up to see Nanapush's boat bump up and down. He runs for his rifle but is not able to shoot the moose and free Nanapush (chapter 18).

Orderlies. *Orderlies* come to the hotel in Minneapolis to take Karl Adare to the hospital after he has injured his back in chapter 6 of *The Beet Queen.* The young **orderly in the psychiatric hospital** where Sita Kozka Tappe is staying in chapter 10 takes her to the phone so she can call her husband Louis and report that she is "cured" of her speech impediment. An **orderly from the American Legion** helps to dress Russell Kashpaw for the Beet Parade in chapter 13.

Original Dog. Mythic female ancestor to whom Almost Soup attributes much of his survival wit in chapter 8 of *The Antelope Wife.* Original Dog was companion to Wenabojo, trickster creator of humans.

Other Side of the Earth. Name given to Blue Prairie Woman when she seems to be dying of grief after the disappearance of her first child, in chapter 1 of *The Antelope Wife.* When Blue Prairie Woman finds her lost daughter (Matilda Roy) and the girl falls ill, the mother gives her this life-restoring name.

According to chapter 18, Zosie Shawano Roy acquires the name from Blue Prairie Woman in a dream and later gives it to her granddaughter, Deanna Whiteheart Beads. Cally Roy also alludes to this name in chapter 18 when she says that Sweetheart Calico has been to the "other side of the earth," where she has seen Blue Prairie Woman.

Ozhawashkwamashkodeykway. Ojibwe word for Blue Prairie Woman, found in chapter 1 of *The Antelope Wife.* According to chapter 11, this is also Cally Roy's spirit name, given to her by her Grandma Zosie, who won it from the original Blue Prairie Woman. See **Blue Prairie Woman** and **Cally Whiteheart Beads Roy.**

Palmer Turcot. Co-owner of the Turcot lumber company that acquires and logs Ojibwe land. Chapter 9 of *The Last Report on the Miracles at Little No Horse* reveals that the co-owner with Turcot is John James Mauser. The story of this company's acquisition and logging of Fleur Pillager's land is told in *Tracks* chapters 5 and 9, and *Last Report* chapter 10. When the government confiscates Fleur's Matchimanito property for unpaid taxes in the summer of 1919, the company immediately purchases the land and begins to log. The Pillagers take their revenge. In *Tracks* chapter 9, Moses Pillager is said to drown two of Turcot's workers, and Fleur fells the giant trees around her cabin to crush crew, horses, and equipment. Father Damien notes in *Last Report* chapter 10, however, that although not all of the *Turcot employees* survive, enough of them do to strip the land and send the best of the oaks to Minneapolis for Mauser's house.

Patsy Kashpaw. Second youngest of Marie and Nector Kashpaw's five children. Their sister Aurelia takes care of Patsy and Eugene in "Flesh and Blood" (1957), when Marie takes their other sister Zelda to visit Sister Leopolda. Patsy is nearby as Marie reads the letter from Nector that says he is leaving her.

Pauline Puyat. A métis on Little No Horse reservation who is fanatically pious and becomes a nun. Pauline is the narrator of the even-numbered chapters in *Tracks,* though the increasingly bizarre nature of her accounts causes the reader to doubt her credibility. Descriptions of Pauline's family change from novel to novel. See **Puyat family.**

There are two differing accounts of Pauline's early story, one in *The Last Report on the Miracles at Little No Horse,* in which she is living on the reservation in March 1912 and the following autumn, the other in *Tracks,* in which she moves to Argus in the spring of 1912 and stays through December 1913. Some temporal confusion arises from the different dates these two novels give for the consumption epidemic that takes the lives of so many reservation families: 1912–1913 in *Tracks* and 1911–1912 in *Last Report.* But even allowing for this difference, Pauline's absence in the *Tracks* account would prevent her from being present on the reservation during the events in her life recorded in the *Last Report* account.

Pauline Puyat

Pauline's earliest appearance in *Last Report* is in March 1912, when she is the only layperson present at Father Damien's first mass on the reservation (chapter 4). Father Damien notes Pauline's gaunt appearance and bizarre behavior. Sister Hildegarde Anne hesitates in her comment about the girl, saying only that she is "most devout, but . . ." (*LR,* 69). That autumn, at the Feast of the Virgin (chapter 7), Pauline flings herself in the path of the wagon carrying the Virgin statue, spooking the horses, perhaps deliberately (see chapter 14). Kashpaw and his wife Quill are fatally injured in the ensuing crash, making their daughter, Mary, an orphan.

According to *Tracks,* however, Pauline leaves the reservation in the spring of 1912 and thus would have been gone by the time Kashpaw and Quill die the following autumn. Even if we adjust the dates, in *Last Report* Kashpaw and Quill die the autumn after the consumption epidemic, and in *Tracks* Pauline is still in Argus at that time.

Pauline moves to the largely white town of Argus because she wants to be like her Canadian grandfather and her light-skinned mother (*Tracks* chapter 2). While there, she lives with her father's sister, Regina Puyat Kashpaw; takes care of Regina's son, Russell; and helps at the butcher shop where Regina's companion, Dutch James, works. After many reservation Indians die of consumption that winter, Pauline is not able to learn whether her parents and sisters have died or have moved north to avoid the sickness. The following June (1913), Fleur Pillager arrives in Argus and begins working at the butcher shop. The fifteen-year-old Pauline watches each night as Fleur wins money in poker games with the three butcher shop employees. When Pauline and Russell witness the men's attack on Fleur one hot August night, Pauline does not try to stop them. The next morning, a tornado—which Pauline believes Fleur has called up in revenge—wrecks the town, particularly the butcher shop. Fleur's attackers take shelter in the meat locker, and Pauline locks them in. After several days, the townspeople find the men inside, frozen. Only Dutch survives, so frostbitten that he loses parts of his body to gangrene.

Chapters 3 and 4 of *Tracks* tell of Pauline's return to the reservation, first from Nanapush's point of view and then, in more detail, from her own. Pauline wants to leave Argus because of her nightmares about the three frozen men, intensified by watching Dutch rot piece by piece. That December (1913), Bernadette Morrissey comes to town and agrees to take her home. Pauline lives with Bernadette, her brother Napoleon, son Clarence, and two daughters Sophie and Philomena, and she assists Bernadette as she sits with the dying and prepares the bodies of the dead. When **Mary Pepewas** dies, there is a suggestion that Pauline could have saved the girl, but does not. Afterward, Pauline believes that she herself mutates into a scavenger bird, and the next morning she is found asleep in a high tree. Margaret Kashpaw induces her to tell about the Argus activities of Fleur, who has returned to the reservation with money and is perhaps pregnant, but Fleur claims that Pauline's account is a lie. When Fleur's baby, Lulu, is about to be born in the spring of 1914, Pauline fetches Margaret to help and, just before the birth, shoots at a drunken bear.

As Pauline continues to visit Fleur's cabin over the next two years, Fleur and Eli Kashpaw's overt sexuality convinces Pauline that she needs a husband. She agrees to a rendezvous with Napoleon in an abandoned house, but they do not consummate this first sexual encounter, and Napoleon leaves the reservation for a time. A year later, in late summer of 1917, Pauline flirts with Eli, who rejects her. In revenge, Pauline uses a love medicine to make Eli have relations with the fourteen-year-old Sophie, whose body Pauline enters. (In a perhaps-Freudian slip, after recounting this incident, Pauline refers to herself as "Pauline Kashpaw.") In retaliation, Fleur casts a spell on Sophie. When that spell is broken by the statue of the Blessed Virgin, Pauline believes that she is sole witness to a miracle—the statue's weeping. By the close of chapter 4, Pauline has become Napoleon's lover. Her revenge against Eli is complete by chapter 5, when Fleur rejects him because of his escapade with Sophie.

In chapter 6, Pauline has decided to become a nun, but she is pregnant with Napoleon's child. She tries to abort the baby and even in labor tries to keep from giving birth, so that Bernadette must forcibly deliver the child. According to *Tracks,* the birth is in November 1918. (The "Saint Marie" story in *Love Medicine* suggests a different birth date. See **Marie Lazarre Kashpaw.**)

Bernadette keeps the baby girl, Marie, and Pauline enters the convent, devoting herself to her twin missions of converting the Ojibwe and assisting the ill and dying. The two are connected. One night in the deep cold of that winter (1918–1919), Pauline believes that Christ appears to her. Sitting on the convent stove, he tells her to confront the Ojibwe devil (the lake creature Misshepeshu) and fetch more Indian souls for him (*Tracks* chapter 6). When Pauline helps Father Damien minister to the victims of the Spanish influenza epidemic that winter (*Last Report* chapter 7), Damien suspects that she baptizes their "defenseless bodies" (*LR,* 122). Yet he also observes that the crises of illness and death bring out an uncharacteristic kindness in her.

During this same winter, Pauline continues to visit Fleur's cabin, where Fleur (pregnant again), Eli, Lulu, Nanapush, Margaret, and Nector are all living (*Tracks* chapter 6). Nanapush teases Pauline for another aspect of her fanatical spirituality— her unusually severe penances. One day when Pauline comes, Fleur strips off her filthy clothes and gently washes her. Yet when Pauline later finds Fleur, alone

Pauline Puyat

with Lulu, beginning to miscarry, this usually skillful caretaker for the sick bungles and fails to stop the premature birth. Five-year-old Lulu goes out into the bitter cold to summon help, and the enraged Fleur throws a knife at Pauline. Pauline's death vision follows. In it, she sees Fleur gamble with the dead for the lives of her baby and Lulu. Fleur loses the baby's life but wins Lulu's. When Margaret arrives at the cabin, she blames Pauline for the baby's death and spits on her. When Pauline returns to the convent the next morning, she breaks the ice in the kitchen buckets with her bare hands, deliberately scraping them raw (one of several Pauline "stigmata" incidents).

There are also two different versions of the events in Pauline's life in the spring of 1919. In the *Tracks* account, which Erdrich wrote first, in chapter 7 Pauline interferes with a healing ceremony Nanapush is conducting for Fleur and, in the process, burns her hands badly in boiling water. She returns to the convent in chapter 8, where Superior cares for her. In her ensuing fever, Pauline sees a figure who she decides is Lucifer and who calls her to meet him "in the desert" (*Tr*, 193). A second vision that night clarifies the first. She is to go to Matchimanito and confront the lake creature.

When her hands have healed, in chapter 8 Pauline goes to Matchimanito one "calm blue spring afternoon" (*Tr*, 197) and steals Nanapush's leaky boat. She anchors the boat in the middle of the lake, planning to stay forty days, or until she is able to confront and kill the lake devil. Pauline rejects the shouts of people on the shore and Nanapush's attempt to save her, but finally the anchor rope breaks and the boat drifts toward the shore. Now alone, she strips off all of her clothes, armed only with her rosary to confront the demon. On the shore, the lake monster appears, they grapple, and she chokes him to death. Once dead, however, the demon changes into the body of Napoleon Morrissey, which Pauline drags into the woods behind Fleur's house. Realizing that she is still naked, she rolls in slough mud, leaves, and feathers, and returns to the convent in the early morning hours (chapter 8).

The Last Report on the Miracles at Little No Horse, written thirteen years after *Tracks,* gives another version of events in the spring of 1919 (chapter 7). There is no account here of Pauline's injuring her hands in boiling water, and this novel tells of a confession she makes to Father Damien that is unrecorded in *Tracks* (that is, about her pregnancy and the birth of a child she claims was stillborn). A short time after this confession, on "an extremely cold spring night" (*LR,* 146), Sister Hildegarde finds Pauline in the church, naked, covered with muck, and raving. This is the day, it is later revealed, on which Pauline has killed Napoleon. By the time Father Damien learns about her condition and her strict fast and visits her, her heavily bandaged hands are rigid claws that reek of infection. Over the next few days, her whole body becomes rigid. The reservation populace believes Pauline is in a visionary trance. Considering her a saint, they bring petitions to the convent. Actually, Pauline has tetanus, contracted from the barbs on the rosary with which she had strangled Napoleon (see chapter 21).

A comparison of these two accounts of Pauline's supposed stigmata—the brief, uncomplicated story of the burned hands in *Tracks* and the much more complex and integrated story of the barbed-wire rosary and tetanus in *Last Report*—suggests a phenomenon characteristic of Erdrich's writing, the growth and development of her story over time, reflected in variations from novel to novel.

Another event in Pauline's life that is recorded differently in *Tracks* and *Last Report* is her taking her vows as a nun and acquiring a new name. In chapter 8 of *Tracks,* Pauline takes her vows "here at the church" (*Tr,* 204), that is, on the reservation, and she receives her nun's name from Superior's hand. This ceremony occurs shortly after Napoleon's murder, thus in 1919. After her initiation, she is sent to teach school in Argus. In contrast, chapter 16 of *Last Report* tells us that Pauline takes her vows while she is in Argus. She does not wear her new name on the reservation until she returns in the spring of 1933.

For the remainder of Pauline's story, see **Leopolda, Sister.**

Pausch, Sheriff. Summoned by the paranoid Sita Tappe to arrest her cousin Karl Adare for stealing her jewelry in chapter 8 of *The Beet Queen.* The sheriff comes, frisks Karl, but finds no evidence of theft. Pausch is a former botany teacher and a friend of Sita's biologist husband, Louis Tappe.

Peace McKnight. Wife of Scranton Roy; mother and grandmother respectively of Augustus Roy I and II in chapter 1 of *The Antelope Wife.* Peace is a sturdily built but graceful Scot from Aberdeen (in east-central Dakota territory) who moves onto the Great Plains to teach school after **her father**'s business fails. Her **few pupils** are unpromising until the six-year-old Matilda Roy arrives. Peace becomes friends with Matilda and moves in with the child and her adoptive father, Scranton Roy. She and Scranton soon become a couple. But Peace is put off by the discomfort of her husband's bed and sleeps with the poultry instead. Finding herself pregnant, she further rejects her husband sexually, especially after she becomes ill with a fever. During this illness, the seven-year-old Matilda disappears in the night, leaving a note that she has gone with her mother. After three agonizing days in labor during a blizzard, Peace dies after giving birth to the son she has already named Augustus.

Pembina woman. Woman wearing the necklace of northwest trader blue beads whom Zosie Shawano sees as a child, according to chapter 18 of *The Antelope Wife.* Later, when Zosie is pregnant, she sees the Pembina woman again in a dream, still

Pembina woman

wearing the beads. Zosie gambles with her and wins both her beads and her two names. The dream woman is Zosie's grandmother, Blue Prairie Woman.

The fact that the woman with blue beads is described as Pembina possibly suggests that the reservation "up north" (chapters 6 and 8) where Blue Prairie Woman's descendants live may be in the Pembina region, that is, far northeastern North Dakota.

Pepperboy. Candice Pantamounty's dog in *Tales of Burning Love*. According to "Candice's Tale" [25], this rakish stray dog shows up at Jack Mauser's construction site. Jack tries to tame him, but the dog bites him, so Jack takes him to the Fargo city dump to shoot. Candice intervenes and adopts the dog, whom she names Pepperboy. Candice and Pepperboy become devoted to each other, and when Candice and Jack marry, he becomes a source of conflict. Following a hunting trip in "The Wandering Room" [26], unaware that Pepperboy has jumped out of the back of his pickup, Jack accidentally drags him to his death. Kneeling beside the dog as he dies, Candice sees the end of her marriage.

Pete Kozka. Husband of Fritzie Kozka and father of Sita Kozka; owner of Kozka Meats in Argus. Pete is described in chapter 3 of *The Master Butchers Singing Club* as good-natured but humorless. He is also frugal to the point of miserliness. He has trouble keeping help because he is cheap with his pay. He also hoards and sells scraps rather than giving them away. In chapter 2 of *Tracks*, Pete's butcher shop employees are Lily Veddar, Tor Grunewald, Dutch James, Pauline Puyat, Pauline's young cousin Russell Kashpaw, and—in the summer of 1913—Fleur Pillager. Pete occasionally plays cards with his male employees after closing, rubbing his good-luck talisman, the lens of a cow's eye. When Fleur comes to work for Pete, she joins the card games. Pete is gone to Minnesota when his employees attack Fleur and the butcher shop is demolished by a tornado.

In 1922, Pete hires German immigrant and master butcher Fidelis Waldvogel (chapter 3 of *The Master Butchers Singing Club*). His business improves because of Fidelis's sausage making. Pete knows from the beginning that Fidelis will be opening his own butcher shop, so their rivalry is initially friendly. But by the early 1930s, hostility develops over Pete's champion breeder chow dog, Hottentot. As a joke, Fidelis sends Hottentot home with hideous, even rotting, remains. One day, Pete tries to take a boar's skull from the dog, and Hottentot rips open his arm. Deciding to pay Fidelis back, Pete takes a rotten mess of bones to the Waldvogel house. Finding them gone and assuming that Fidelis can afford to take the day off, the jealous Pete dumps the bones in the Waldvogels' bed. This action earns Eva Waldvogel's undying ire but fails to end Fidelis's joke. When Fidelis starts a men's singing club, however, Pete longs to join, swallows his anger, and shows up at the meeting one night. We learn in chapter 5 that Pete and Fritzie finally give up raising chows. When they give the Waldvogels a puppy as a token of reconciliation, it is a German shepherd.

In 1932, the abandoned child Mary Adare, Fritzie's niece, comes to stay with the Kozkas (chapter 1 of *The Beet Queen*). Pete and Fritzie are kind to Mary, and Pete gives her his lucky cow's lens, which angers his daughter, Sita. Several years later, in chapter 13 of *The Master Butchers Singing Club* Pete attends a gymnastic show in which the performers call on him to test the sharpness of a saw. As World War II begins and the singing club looks for non-German songs, Pete contributes what he says is the Polish national anthem ("Roll Out the Barrel").

After Fritzie collapses with a pulmonary hemorrhage, she and Pete move south for her health in about 1941, leaving the butcher shop to Mary (*Beet Queen* chapter 4). About ten years later, the suntanned Pete and Fritzie attend Sita's wedding to Jimmy Bohl in chapter 5. Pete's junk collection still remains in the backyards of the butcher shop in chapter 7. By the 1960s (chapter 11), because of the new supermarkets, the butcher shop is not doing as well as it had when Pete ran it. Shortly before her death in 1972, in chapter 13 Sita thinks about how much her father would have loved to have had a grandchild.

Years later, in 1995 ("A Wedge of Shade" [3] in *Tales of Burning Love*), Mary recalls Pete and Fritzie's leaving the butcher shop to her, although she does not mention them by name.

Philomena Morrissey. Youngest child of Bernadette Morrissey and sister of Clarence and Sophie Morrissey. According to Pauline Puyat, in chapter 4 of *Tracks* Philomena is sweet and fat, but she is apparently not as messy as Sophie. Both girls have dainty French ways, the product of their mother's education in Quebec. When Pauline comes to stay, she sleeps with the sisters and kicks them in her nightmare-ridden sleep. In chapter 6, Philomena grows thinner and is seen dancing wildly with Sophie. Bernadette leaves home with Philomena in chapter 7, when Sophie and Clarence both marry Lazarres and bring them to the house.

Pillager. Father of Fleur Pillager. In *Tracks,* he is called Old Pillager (chapter 1), the Old Man (chapter 7), and Old Man Pillager (chapter 9). In *The Bingo Palace,* Pillager's mother is apparently Four Soul, since chapter 27 names her as Fleur's grandmother and chapter 3 lists her as a Pillager. (See **Four Soul** and **Four Souls** for variations in this account.) Chapter 7 of *Tracks* tells us that the water spirit Misshepeshu first appears in Matchimanito Lake when the family arrives because Pillager has a special connection with him. The lake man is a source of the family's medicine power, which Pillager apparently inherits from his mother and passes on to his eldest daughter, Fleur.

Pillager

According to *Tracks* chapter 1, Pillager dies in the consumption epidemic of 1912–1913, along with all of his family except the seventeen-year-old Fleur. They are buried when the snow recedes, but their spirits continue to haunt the land around Matchimanito. (In *The Last Report on the Miracles at Little No Horse,* these events take place in the winter of 1911–1912.) Pillager is one of the spirits who appear to Nanapush in Fleur's clearing in *Tracks* chapter 9. In *The Bingo Palace* chapter 27, he is among the spirits who wait for Fleur on the island in Matchimanito as she makes her death walk across the frozen lake. (For variations in the story of Fleur's parentage, see **Pillager family.**)

Pillager family. This is one of two of Erdrich's fictional families whose structure varies significantly from novel to novel. (The other is the **Puyat family.**) The first portrait of Fleur Pillager's family of origin appears in *Tracks,* a quite different family structure is drawn in *The Painted Drum,* and the brief sketch in *Four Souls* serves as something of a transition between the two.

In *Tracks,* Fleur's father is called simply **Pillager.** He is best known for his special relationship with the lake creature Misshepeshu, who, according to chapter 7, appears in Matchimanito Lake when Pillager arrives from the east and who is the source of Pillager medicine power. Fleur's mother in this novel is Pillager's wife **Boss Woman** (Ogimaakwe), and her younger siblings (two sisters and one brother) are **Chokecherry Girl, Small Bird,** and **He Is Lifted By Wind** (also apparently children of Pillager and Boss Woman). According to chapter 1, all these Pillagers except Fleur die together in a consumption epidemic in the winter of 1912–1913. Nanapush finds their bodies in the cabin on the far shore of Matchimanito Lake.

Four Souls gives us a somewhat different picture of Fleur's parentage. Chapter 5 says that the woman **Anaquot,** who takes the spirit name Four Souls, is Fleur's mother. (For ambiguity about this spirit name, see **Four Soul** and **Four Souls.**) In this *Four Souls* account, Anaquot is married to Shaawano, has a daughter named Red Cradle and a son, runs off with a Pillager man, and becomes Fleur's mother. Although this picture may startle the reader of *Tracks,* it is not impossible to reconcile the two portraits. Perhaps, readers of *Tracks* and *Four Souls* may reason, Anaquot has the first two children while living with Shaawano, then after running off with the Pillager man, she gives birth to Fleur and three more Pillager children and lives with them until the family dies in the consumption epidemic. Seen in this way, the *Tracks* and *Four Souls* accounts would be two parts of the same story.

The Painted Drum, however, makes this reading impossible. While the account of Fleur's family in *The Painted Drum* is consistent with that in *Four Souls,* it cannot be reconciled with the portrait in *Tracks.* The alteration of this family structure from *Tracks* to *The Painted Drum* is another example of Erdrich's evolving master narrative. Fleur's father in *The Painted Drum,* the Pillager man **Simon Jack,** has a different character from the reader's impression of Pillager in *Tracks.* More significantly, the facts of these two accounts of the family do not match. In *The Painted Drum,* Fleur has no siblings born to her mother and father. She grows up in a household with two women, Anaquot and Simon Jack's wife, **Ziigwan'aage;** no father (see part 2.5); and three half-siblings, *two boys* and a girl named **Niibin'aage,** all of whom are older than Fleur. Also, though Anaquot, Ziigwan'aage, and the two boys die together in an epidemic, in this novel Fleur's female half-sibling has gone to Carlisle Indian School and survives. (In *Tracks,* both of Fleur's sisters are among the bodies Nanapush finds by Matchimanito.) Furthermore, in *The Painted Drum,* Fleur's Pillager father does not die in the epidemic with the rest of the family. He dies sometime earlier, killed by the spirit of Anaquot's first daughter (a Shaawano) who indwells a ceremonial drum. Although Margaret Kashpaw says in *Four Souls* chapter 16 that Anaquot and Ogimaakwe are different names for the same woman, certainly the Pillager man and Fleur's two sisters and one brother described in *Tracks* do not exist in *The Painted Drum.*

Certain characteristics of the Pillager family are recorded in both versions. Most notable is the Pillagers' power for healing or harm (see *Love Medicine* "Love Medicine"; *Tracks* chapters 1, 2, 3, 5, and 9; *The Bingo Palace* chapter 11; and *The Painted Drum* parts 2.3 and 2.5). Pillagers are also known for their long, clever fingers (see *Love Medicine* "Crossings the Water"; *Tracks* chapter 2; *Bingo Palace* chapter 12; *Four Souls* chapter 15; and *Painted Drum* part 2.1). Other Pillager traits recorded in earlier novels that are neither mentioned nor contradicted in *The Painted Drum* are their penetrating gaze and wolf grin. They are members of the bear clan (*Tracks* chapter 2). (See also **Ziigwan'aage's relatives.**)

Other members of Fleur's family include her children, **Lulu Nanapush Morrissey Lamartine, Baby Pillager,** and **John James Mauser II;** her grandsons, **Gerry Nanapush, Lyman Lamartine,** and **Jack Mauser;** and her great-grandson, **Lipsha Morrissey. Blue Prairie Woman** is apparently some kind of aunt to Fleur (see Margaret Kashpaw's comment in chapter 16 of *Four Souls* about the woman who killed the dog Sorrow). Other Pillagers include **Moses Pillager, Moses Pillager's grandfather,** and **Pillager woman.** Four other Pillagers are listed in Father Damien's records of the Pillager clan (*Bingo Palace* chapter 3): ***Comes from Above, Strikes the Water, Unknown Cloud,*** and ***Red Cradle*** (this may refer to **Red Cradle II,** who is not actually a Pillager).

Pillager woman. One Shawano man stops with this woman as his clan is migrating from the north (probably Canada) to the south (probably the Dakotas) in chapter 3 of *The Antelope Wife.* It is not clear whether there is a connection

Pillager woman

between this Pillager woman who marries a Shawano and Four Souls, who is said in chapter 5 of *Four Souls* to have been "the bad wife of Shaawano" (different spelling) before she runs away with a Pillager man (*FS*, 57). See also **Four Souls** and **Shawano family.**

Pilot. Man who pilots the small airplane transporting Gerry Nanapush to a prison facility in Minnesota in chapter 21 of *The Bingo Palace*. "Radio Bulletin" [11] in *Tales of Burning Love* indicates that two men are confirmed dead in the accident, but since there are also two federal marshals aboard, we do not know if the pilot survives.

Placide Armstrong Gheen Mauser. First wife of John James Mauser in *Four Souls*. Most of Placide's early story appears in chapters 1, 2, and 4. She is born into the wealthy Minneapolis Gheen family. As girls, Placide and her sister, Polly Elizabeth, attend *Miss Katherine Hammond*'s school, where they learn refined manners and where Placide finds her vocation, painting. Placide's obsessively proper mother is apparently also an influence on her. (See **Demeter Hewes Gheen.**) Placide is known as a beauty who attracts men (despite her long front teeth), tall and slim, with a mass of curly, dark golden hair. She is scatterbrained, however, and has a fragile beauty that will fade quickly after she loses her youth. Her gait is a "dreamy slide" and her sleep, "petulant tossing" (*FS*, 25, 26).

While Placide is still a young woman, she meets the young John James Mauser, who is himself handsome and wealthy and who claims to be the son of minor British royalty and a German industrialist (a lie). They marry sometime before World War I. As the two come together sexually for the first time, Mauser discovers that Placide is stiff, cold, and frightened. Mauser wants a son, but Placide wants no children. In fact, she insists that they practice Karezza, a nonejaculatory form of sexual intercourse, because she is terrified of pregnancy. Although they are a fine-looking couple, we learn from chapter 8 that when Mauser goes off to the war, he is fleeing Placide. He returns ill a year later.

After Mauser's return, he completes an opulent house on a Minneapolis hill. We learn in chapter 1 that it is made out of both the finest materials and the agony of abused animals and people. Placide knows the human cost of the house but is unbothered, feeling it is her fate. During its building, a lynx is shot, and Mauser has a muff made out of its fur for Placide.

Chapter 2 depicts Placide as removed and isolated, attending only to her painting in the little tower studio at the top of the house. When her husband has seizures, she keeps painting and allows others to care for him. (Chapter 6 reveals that during this time she is also having an affair with her painting teacher.) Placide conscripts Polly Elizabeth as her model, insisting on hours of her sister's time and discomfort.

Fleur Pillager's arrival at the Mauser house in about 1920, where she becomes the laundress, begins to work radical changes in Placide's life. First, in chapter 3, the Ojibwe woman heals Placide's husband, making him more independent. In chapter 4, the newly assertive Mauser calls in a specialist, Dr. Fulmer, who interviews Placide about her husband's illness, an interview Placide finds distressing. Dr. Fulmer's diagnosis blames the illness on the practice of Karezza, thus on Placide herself.

Fleur's presence ultimately costs Placide her marriage. Within the first few months, Polly Elizabeth warns her sister that Mauser has eyes for Fleur, but Placide ridicules the idea. Besides, she likes the laundress's ironing and doesn't want to send her away (chapter 4). A year after her arrival, however, in chapter 6, Fleur has gained control of Mauser and of the house. Mauser divorces Placide and marries Fleur. Nevertheless, in their new home in St. Paul, Polly Elizabeth is able to keep Placide's life running smoothly.

Two more changes are in store for Placide. When Fleur and Mauser's child is born the following year, Polly Elizabeth leaves Placide and moves back into the Mauser house (chapter 6). Then, some ten years later, in 1933, the total collapse of Mauser's financial empire in chapter 12 seems to leave Placide with no resources. Polly Elizabeth marries, but Erdrich does not tell us what happens to Placide.

Placide and Polly Elizabeth's mother. See **Demeter Hewes Gheen.**

Placide's painting instructor. Man from the university who gives Placide Mauser painting instruction in *Four Souls.* In chapter 2, the instructor comes twice a week, and they seclude themselves for hours in her studio high in the Mauser house. We learn in chapter 6 that Placide and her teacher are having an affair using the practice of Karezza.

Polly Elizabeth Gheen. Sister of Placide Gheen and sister-in-law of John James Mauser in *Four Souls.* Polly Elizabeth narrates the first six even-numbered chapters of the novel. Chapter 4 gives us background information about her. Unlike her beautiful sister, Polly Elizabeth's face is "bleak and martial" (*FS,* 32). Although she will do anything for Placide, she often resents playing second fiddle to her self-centered sister. Polly Elizabeth has a soft heart for children and grieves that she has been unable to marry and that her sister is unwilling to have children. After her mother dies, she seems to miss the social outings Mrs. Gheen would organize.

While the Mauser mansion is being built in the late 1910s, in chapter 1 Polly Elizabeth serves as a self-appointed decorating assistant to the architect, whom she unsuccessfully attempts to attract sexually. In chapter 2, she is in charge of the household and its staff and is often drafted into service as Placide's model. After

Polly Elizabeth Gheen

Mauser returns ill from his year in the trenches of World War I, the household workload multiplies because of his night sweats. Thus, when Fleur Pillager arrives looking for work in 1919 or 1920, Polly Elizabeth hires her as a laundress. When Mauser has a seizure after Fleur arrives, Polly Elizabeth, who is normally in charge of his care, is shocked when Fleur takes over. Polly Elizabeth subsequently ties him to his bed, and Mauser manages to clamp her thumb between his teeth. Again, Fleur handles the situation.

Besides Fleur's quiet assertiveness, her beauty disturbs Polly Elizabeth as well, and in chapter 4, she regrets the smartness of Fleur's uniform. Polly Elizabeth warns Placide that Mauser, whom Fleur has now virtually cured, has eyes for the laundress, an idea Placide mocks. Lonely for a child in the house, Polly Elizabeth buys a Pomeranian dog to have some creature who needs her. (We learn in chapters 6 and 10, however, that even the dog, named Diablo, treats her with contempt.) As Mauser gains strength and independence, he calls in a specialist, Dr. Fulmer, and Polly Elizabeth eavesdrops on his very personal conversation with Placide. She is unwilling to help with Fulmer's treatment of Mauser, because it involves soaking her brother-in-law's feet, the task of a servant.

In chapter 6, a year after Fleur's arrival, Mauser divorces Placide to marry Fleur, though he provides a generous settlement for the sisters. When Fleur stops appearing in public, Polly Elizabeth begins visiting Nettie Testor, the Mausers' housekeeper, and learns that Fleur is pregnant and not doing well. The prospect of a baby draws her repeatedly back to the Mauser house, where she takes over Fleur's care, giving her whiskey to stop premature contractions. When the baby boy is born, Polly Elizabeth moves back into the house to help with his care. She loves him as if he were her own.

Polly Elizabeth's joy is marred, however, when in chapter 8 the boy goes vacant-minded, and she realizes there is something wrong. Mauser begins to open himself to Polly Elizabeth, telling her personal things about his life, including the incident in the war when Fantan (now his manservant) saved his life. Polly Elizabeth, who has despised Fantan, changes her view of him.

By the early 1930s (chapter 10), Polly Elizabeth sees that the household is falling into chaos and that Mrs. Tester is stealing. As the boy grows enormous and ever more strange, she is furious with God for so wronging a child. One day at the lake, the women encounter Mauser's architect and his fiancée. When the couple tries to humiliate Polly Elizabeth, Fleur intervenes. When she learns that Fleur is planning to return to the reservation, Polly Elizabeth vows to go with her.

In the spring of 1933, chapter 12, Mauser has fled his creditors, Fleur and the boy have returned to the reservation, and Polly Elizabeth and Fantan, now married, are preparing Mauser's household for auction. They plan to run a trading store on the reservation to be close to Fleur and the boy. Polly Elizabeth's life has completely changed, and she declares herself that rare thing, a happy woman.

Pope. The prologue to *The Last Report on the Miracles at Little No Horse* reveals that Father Damien writes lengthy documents, which he calls reports, to every pope during his long tenure as reservation priest from 1912 to 1996. These popes include Pius X, Benedict XV, Pius XI, Pius XII, John XXIII, Paul VI, and the pope during Damien's last days [John Paul II]. Parts of these letters appear in various chapters of *Last Report.*

In chapter 4, the second night after Damien's arrival at Little No Horse in March 1912, he begins his first report, about his experience at his first reservation mass earlier that day. A few days later, in chapter 6, Damien writes a second letter, asking the pope two questions: how should he treat cases of "irregular connection" (such as Kashpaw's multiple wives), and how far can he enter the political situation to protect the people? Another letter to the pope is recorded in chapter 11, which Father Damien writes the morning after he is visited by the black dog (autumn of 1920). Still another appears in chapter 13, apparently written in 1923 after Nanapush reveals that he knows Damien's secret. Chapter 10 includes just the beginning of a letter in which Damien begs the pope to send him an answer.

The night of March 19–20, 1996, Father Damien begins what he calls his "last report" (prologue and chapter 2). The letter seeks to document certain events relating to the possible blessedness of Sister Leopolda Puyat and to confess Damien's own life as an imposter. The letter relates Agnes DeWitt's early life, her taking the identity of the original Damien Modeste, and the beginning of her ministry to the Ojibwe. The letter continues in chapter 3, as Damien hopes the pope will understand his motives for assuming Modeste's identity and lists seven good things he has accomplished. When Father Jude arrives the next afternoon, in his confusion Damien thrusts two pages of this letter into Jude's hands and then snatches them back. Late that night, Damien pens another, briefer letter complaining about Jude's inadequacy as a papal emissary (chapter 4).

Although Father Damien had called his March 1996 letter his last report to the pope, he jots one final, short missive in chapter 22 that closes with "Don't bother with a reply" (*LR,* 344). In the epilogue, after Damien's death, a message arrives on the Little No Horse convent's new fax machine in 1997. It is from the pope, addressed to Father Damien. The pontiff has received a fragment of Damien's 1996 letter and requests that Damien send the Vatican copies of his papers. He closes by praising the priest's love, faith, and good works.

Portland "Porky" Chavers. Bank employee who dies in Roy Watzka's cellar in *The Master Butchers Singing Club.* Porky's nickname, although something of a short

Portland "Porky" Chavers

for Portland, may derive from the fact that he wears a porkpie hat (see chapter 4). Clarisse Strub, a relative of Chavers, tells her friend Delphine awful things about Porky, but we don't learn their nature. In the early 1930s (chapter 3), Porky becomes a member of Fidelis Waldvogel's singing club. His voice is quite similar to Roy's, so they sometimes duel instead of harmonizing. We learn in chapter 13 that it offends Roy for Chavers to puff his chest, inch forward, and sing "over" him.

In early 1934, in late winter (see chapter 5 for the time), Chavers, his wife, **Doris,** and daughter, Ruthie, attend the funeral party of kinsman Cornelius Strub at Roy's house. The events of that night are recorded in chapters 4 and 13. During the party, Roy sends Porky to the cellar for ginger beer. Unknown to Roy, Doris and Ruthie go down with him. Roy yells down at him, "Hey, Chavers, you can come up again after you quit singing over me in practice!" (*MBSC,* 328). Roy later ambiguously recalls that he "maybe" shut the cellar hatch. Roy wanders off drunk during the party and is then away on a drinking binge for more than three weeks. Thus, though the Chaverses call for help, there is no one to hear them. After the party, the Chavers dog comes to Roy's cellar and will not leave. Just before his death, Roy admits that when he returned to get liquor from his cellar weeks later, he found the three bodies but told no one. In chapter 7, after Clarisse finds out what had happened to the family, she specifically grieves for Doris and Ruthie, but she never mentions Porky.

Pouty Mannheim. Airplane enthusiast in *The Master Butchers Singing Club.* According to chapter 5, Pouty is a regular customer at the Waldvogel butcher shop, along with his confused girlfriend, **Myrna.** He is chubby and has rich-boy airs. But the scrap-picker Step-and-a-Half predicts that he will fail in business because of his profligacy—when he gets a hole in one sock, he throws away the other (chapter 16).

In chapter 6, Pouty is fascinated with flight, buys a war-surplus Jenny, and spends all his free time with the plane. When he lands in the field by the Waldvogels' house, Franz Waldvogel explores the plane and watches it take off. Franz convinces Mannheim to take his dying mother, Eva, up for a flight. Pouty imagines that the adventure might heal her. On the eve of World War II, Pouty teaches Franz how to fly (chapter 13).

Priests and preachers. In *Love Medicine,* one of Nector Kashpaw's high school teachers, a **priest in Flandreau,** teaches him *Moby-Dick* all four years ("The Plunge of the Brave"). The **priest at the Sacred Heart Convent** in 1982 refuses to bless Lipsha Morrissey's turkey hearts in "Love Medicine." (His name is not given, but he may be Father Damien.)

In chapter 2 of *The Beet Queen,* the **priest at Saint Catherine's school** proclaims the face in the ice on the school playground to be an image of Christ. He may be the same as the *priest who baptizes Dot Adare* in chapter 9. *Father Mullen* and *Father Bonaventure* are priests at Saint Jerome's orphanage in Minneapolis who are present when Karl Adare returns to the Orphans' Picnic in chapter 4. Father Mullen had apparently called Karl the devil while Karl was living at Saint Jerome's. Catherine Miller's spiritual advisor, *Father Flo,* counsels her in chapter 5 to write a letter to the family of Jude Miller, the baby she and her husband had abducted eighteen years earlier.

In chapter 1 of *Tracks,* when Fleur Pillager comes to Argus in 1913, the *priest in Argus* lives in a residence attached to the church. In chapter 2, the priest or someone at his residence secures a job for Fleur at Pete Kozka's butcher shop.

When Jack Mauser marries June Morrissey in a Williston bar in 1981 ("Easter Snow" [1] in *Tales of Burning Love*), a drunken, card-carrying **reverend** performs the ceremony. A **reservation priest** is referred to in "Night Prayer" [6] as having documented a stigmata miracle at which Sister Leopolda was present. The incident is probably Marie Lazarre's "miracle" (related in "Saint Marie" in *Love Medicine*), and the priest is probably Father Damien.

At the request of Klaus Shawano, the *Father at the recovery lodge* tries unsuccessfully to calm the sobbing Richard Whiteheart Beads in chapter 15 of *The Antelope Wife.* When Richard tries to leap from a cliff at Rozin and Frank's wedding in chapter 16, the female **Reverend** performing the ceremony grabs his ankles.

Chapter 13 of *The Last Report on the Miracles at Little No Horse* describes eighteenth-century Jesuit *Father Jolicoeur* as the man who teaches the Ojibwe to play chess. An unnamed *young priest* is mentioned in chapter 19 as living in the new rectory and as having taken over, by 1962, many of Father Damien's duties. The prologue mentions **Fathers Dennis and Gothilde** as being younger priestly colleagues of the aging Father Damien in 1996. In each of these cases, reservation people prefer to confess to Father Damien.

In chapter 1 of *The Master Butchers Singing Club,* in 1918, the *priest who marries Fidelis Waldvogel and Eva Kalb* in Ludwigsruhe, Germany, blesses them, understanding the circumstances of her pregnancy. According to Roy Watzka's story in chapter 13, when young Minnie walks away from the Wounded Knee massacre, she follows the others' tracks to the mission of *Father Jutz.*

See also **Damien Modeste, Father; Hugo LaCombe, Father; Jude Miller;** and **Clarence Marek, Father.** Also see **Bishops.**

Psychiatrists and therapists. The *psychiatrist treating Sita Tappe* is convinced that Sita is faking her speech impediment and puts her into a psychiatric hospital (chapter 10 of *The Beet Queen*). After one night there, Sita is "cured." **Doctor Hakula** is the therapist in *Tales of Burning Love* who, after Candice Pantamounty's

Psychiatrists and therapists

hysterectomy, helps her to deal with her psychological and addiction problems in "Candice's Tale" [25]. Some years later, in "The Waiting Room" [31], Candice arranges for a *psychiatrist to treat Marlis Mauser* for postpartum depression. *Dr. Fry,* whose card Rozina Whitcheart Beads holds in chapter 7 of *The Antelope Wife,* is probably a psychiatrist.

Puffy Shawano. Brother of Frank, Klaus, and Cecille Shawano in *The Antelope Wife.* The reference to his mother's "children" (plural) prior to Klaus's birth (chapter 13) suggests that Puffy is older than Klaus. (Frank is the only child named in this chapter.)

According to chapter 16, Puffy is a tribal judge. When Frank marries Rozina Roy, Puffy provides some of the meat that is cooked for the reception. As the family makes preparations, Puffy watches the four-months-sober alcoholic Klaus struggle to stay away from the cold beer. Later, when Richard Whiteheart Beads interrupts the cliffside ceremony, Puffy and Klaus restrain Frank from pushing him over the cliff. That afternoon, after Klaus hits Richard with a frozen turkey, judge Puffy remarks that a frozen turkey would make a perfect murder weapon.

Pukwan family. See **Edgar Pukwan, Edgar Pukwan Junior,** and **Leo Pukwan.** In the early 1930s (chapter 11 of *Four Souls*), some unnamed *Pukwans* arrest Nanapush, who has been locked in the Sacred Heart Convent wine cellar all night. The Pukwans mock Nanapush because he is wearing Margaret's dress, but they let him out in time to make a speech at the day's council meeting. See also *Felix Pukwan* in **Tomahawk factory workers.**

Puyat family. This is one of two of Erdrich's fictional families whose structure varies significantly from novel to novel. (The other is the **Pillager family.**) There is a hint of the Puyat family structure in *The Beet Queen;* a fairly clearly drawn family in *Tracks,* which seems to differ from the structure suggested in *The Beet Queen;* and a more elaborate, and quite different, picture in *The Last Report on the Miracles at Little No Horse.*

In chapter 2 of *The Beet Queen,* Regina Puyat is said to have three Kashpaw children before she marries Dutch James and has his child. This chapter names only two of these children, Isabel and Russell. Chapter 10, however, suggests that the third child is Pauline. As children, Isabel, Pauline, and Russell explore the reservation together. The suggestion here that Regina's third child is Pauline is strengthened by the fact that in the short story "Fleur," published the same year as *The Beet Queen* (1986), Pauline is the daughter of the woman Dutch brings down from the reservation to Argus—Regina.

In *Tracks,* however, it is Pauline's father who is the Puyat, not her mother.

(Regina is Pauline's aunt.) Chapters 2 and 3 tell us that, except for Pauline, the Puyats are quiet and shy. *Pauline's father* does not want her to become "white," but *her mother* is half-white, the daughter of a *Canadian man.* Pauline has *sisters* who are darker-skinned than she. In chapter 2, Pauline's parents and sisters disappear during the consumption epidemic in the winter of 1912–1913 while Pauline is living in Argus. She doesn't learn whether they die or go north to escape the sickness. Pauline misses her mother and sisters and dreams that they are buried high in the trees. She sees her mother and father in her death vision in chapter 6.

The far more detailed account of Pauline's family in chapter 8 of *The Last Report on the Miracles at Little No Horse,* however, takes a quite different shape. This Puyat family is opposite to the quiet and shy Puyats of *Tracks,* in which Pauline's excess is an aberration. *Last Report* represents Pauline as the product of a hate-filled, psychotic family. She is descended from seven generations each of *bitter French peasants* and *enemy-harassed Ojibwe.*

In *Last Report,* Pauline's Puyat parent is again her mother, whose name is also Pauline (*Pauline I*). As in *Tracks,* Pauline's maternal grandfather is a *French Canadian man,* and in this novel her maternal grandmother is an Ojibwe from the Crane clan *(Crane clan girl).* The hatred of these grandparents for each other is clear from the chapter 8 narrative, which relates the ways in which, on a buffalo hunt, each spouse tries to get the other killed. There is also hostility between Pauline I and her mother, a hostility so intense the daughter ultimately kills the mother. Pauline I has two children of her own. First is the boy Shesheeb, who is fathered by a pureblood Ojibwe and on whom Pauline I dotes. Then, twenty years later, the girl Pauline (who becomes Sister Leopolda) is born, fathered by a *Polish aristocrat* passing through from Canada. (Notice the difference between this version of Pauline/Leopolda's father and her Puyat father in *Tracks,* who is Native American.) To this child Pauline I passes down her own heritage of mother-daughter hatred. It is a heritage the younger Pauline will act out even after she becomes Sister Leopolda. In this *Last Report* version of the Puyat family, Pauline/Leopolda has no sisters. See **Pauline Puyat; Leopolda, Sister;** and **Shesheeb II.**

Quill. One of Kashpaw's four wives in 1912; younger sister of cowife Mashkiig-ikwe; mother of Mary Kashpaw in *The Last Report on the Miracles at Little No Horse.* After Father Damien comes to the reservation in March 1912 and religious pressure causes Kashpaw's family to break up in chapter 6, Kashpaw promises Mashkiigikwe

Quill

that he will keep Quill as his one wife. Mashkiigikwe is concerned about Quill because of her mental pain and instability. Yet when Mashkiigikwe leaves, Quill completely loses her bearings. The **matchimindemoyenh** (evil old woman) *spirit* that has haunted her from time to time now drives her to play cruel tricks on her family. Father Damien is now the only person able to calm Quill, so Kashpaw begins bringing her to mass. Sometime in the following weeks or months after these incidents, Father Damien baptizes Quill with the Christian name Marie.

During a feast-day procession in late summer or autumn of that year, in chapter 7 Kashpaw, Quill, and Mary are in the wagon that is carrying the statue of the Virgin. When Pauline Puyat spooks the horses, they bolt, and Kashpaw and Quill are both mortally injured in the crash. As they are dying, they prophesy. Remarkably, Quill is rational as she speaks, urging the warring reservation families to make peace. The next spring, Quill and Kashpaw appear to Father Damien in a dream and tell him to fetch Mary from the family she is staying with, because the man is hurting her.

Years later, in 1996 (chapter 8), Father Damien tells Father Jude Miller that, ironically, Pauline had cured Quill's madness. She had caused the accident that brought on Quill's dying lucidity. In chapter 14, Father Damien emphasizes Pauline's guilt in Quill's death.

R

Raymond Shaawano. See **Doris and Raymond Shaawano.**

Red Cradle. Daughter of Nanapush and White Beads, nicknamed Lulu, who dies as a young child. According to chapter 3 of *Tracks,* her Indian name is Moskatikinaugun. Of all his dead family members, Nanapush grieves most for Red Cradle and her mother. A few years later, Nanapush gives Fleur Pillager's first child Red Cradle's nickname, Lulu. Red Cradle is also referred to in chapter 9 of *Tracks.* One morning years later, in chapter 13 of *Four Souls,* Nanapush dreams about his family, including "comical" Red Cradle licking maple sugar.

Red Cradle II. Earlier daughter of Four Souls (Anaquot), Fleur Pillager's mother, in chapter 5 of *Four Souls.* This passage suggests that Red Cradle has a different father from Fleur, apparently the Shaawano man who is Four Souls' husband, but gives no other information about her. She may be the same Red Cradle as the one listed as a Pillager in reservation records in chapter 3 of *The Bingo Palace,* even though the Red Cradle of *Four Souls* is apparently not a Pillager by birth.

The Painted Drum gives readers information about Anaquot's daughter by Shaawano but never gives her name. Nevertheless, this Shaawano daughter is likely the same person as the Red Cradle of *Four Souls*. See **Shaawano girl.**

Redford Toose. Son of Shawnee Ray Toose and (possibly) Lyman Lamartine in *The Bingo Palace*. Redford is mentioned in chapter 1, and we first see him at a powwow in chapter 2. He seems to be a toddler at the time. Chapter 10 shows him just beginning to talk, and in chapter 15, he is old enough to understand where his mother is and why she is away. Redford and his mother live with Lyman's half sister, Zelda Kashpaw, who plays the part of a controlling grandmother.

When Lipsha visits Shawnee Ray at Zelda's house in chapter 9, Redford is with Zelda at church. In chapter 14, Shawnee Ray leaves Redford with her sisters, Mary Fred and Tammy, when she goes to a Montana powwow. While staying with his aunts, in chapter 15 Redford dreams that a huge metal crushing "thing" is coming for them. He wakes as a tribal policeman, social worker, and Zelda arrive to take him back to Zelda's house. They have a court order granting Lyman custody.

Redford and his mother are again living with Zelda in chapter 14. Redford has always been subject to nightmares (chapter 9), but after his abduction from the Toose house, they apparently increase in intensity (chapter 23). He also becomes more timid and reluctant to leave his mother (see chapter 19). Lyman thinks of Redford as the heir to his acquisitive talents in chapter 13, but in chapter 17, Shawnee Ray warns Lyman never to try to get custody of Redford again. She says that she had other boyfriends at the time of his conception, so Lyman cannot be sure that he is the father. Using her powwow winnings and money from Lipsha, Shawnee Ray finally escapes from Zelda's house with Redford. In chapter 26, Redford and his mother are living in drafty housing at the university where she is enrolled.

Regina (in *The Antelope Wife*). Companion to Shawano the ogitchida and mother of Frank, Puffy, Klaus, and Cecille Shawano. According to chapter 13, Regina refuses to marry her children's father or to take his windigo family name. Regina may have some African American ancestry. (It is not clear whether Klaus is speaking of his maternal or paternal heritage in his chapter 2 reference to his "Buffalo Soldier" blood.)

When, shortly after his return from World War II, Shawano the ogitchida kidnaps a young German POW, Regina is far along in her pregnancy with Klaus. Frank and at least one other of her children are with her in the kitchen as she watches the German cook the blitzkuchen. When she eats the magical cake, she communicates with the unborn Klaus.

In chapter 16, Frank, now a middle-aged man, recalls the smells associated

Regina (in *The Antelope Wife*)

with his mother and loves Rozina Roy in part because her scent reminds him of Regina.

Regina Puyat Kashpaw James. Mother of Russell and Isabel Kashpaw by a Montana Kashpaw, and of Celestine James by Dutch James in *The Beet Queen;* aunt of Pauline Puyat in *Tracks.* Chapter 2 of *Tracks* relates that Regina is the sister of Puyat, Pauline's father, and that the Puyats are mixed-blood. Chapter 7 of *The Beet Queen* indicates that one trait of Regina's family is that their teeth look fierce when they grin (a trait shared with the Pillager clan). Chapter 2 of *Tracks* indicates that Regina marries a Kashpaw who later goes to live in Montana. (For details about this man's identity, see **Montana Kashpaw.**)

Chapter 2 of *Tracks* also tells that Regina meets the white man Dutch James on the reservation and that she and Russell go to live with him in Argus. In 1912, Regina takes in her niece Pauline. In the summer of 1913 (*Tracks* chapter 4), Dutch nearly freezes to death in the butcher shop's meat locker, where he has taken refuge during a tornado. Oddly, Regina apparently does not notice that he is missing until he has been trapped in the locker for several days. When he is found, however, Regina cares for him as his limbs rot away with gangrene, and for the first time they seem actually to love each other. By the time cold weather comes, he is more or less healed, and he and Regina marry. After Pauline returns to the reservation, she claims in chapters 2 and 4 that she leaves Argus because Regina beats her, but in chapter 3, Nanapush says that Regina sends Pauline away because the girl begins to act strange.

Chapter 2 of *The Beet Queen,* however, records these incidents differently. According to this chapter, after her marriage to Dutch, Regina brings down from the reservation three other children that Dutch "hadn't known about" (*BQ*, 30–31), including Russell and Isabel. *Tracks* indicates that Russell is already living with Regina in Argus before she and Dutch marry and makes no mention of Isabel. There is also some confusion about the identity of the third child. (Concerning this confusion and other differences between the *Beet Queen* and *Tracks* accounts, see **Puyat family.**)

Chapter 2 of *The Beet Queen* relates that Regina dies when Celestine is still young and, according to chapter 10, that Eli Kashpaw and Fleur Pillager come down to Argus for her funeral.

Reservation girl. Girl whose hands bleed, a stigmata manifestation mentioned in "Night Prayer" [6] in *Tales of Burning Love.* The same girl and incident are referred to in chapter 8 of *The Last Report on the Miracles at Little No Horse.* See **Marie Lazarre Kashpaw.**

Resounding Sky. See **Kashpaw.**

Richard Whiteheart Beads. First husband of Rozina Roy and father of Deanna and Cally Whiteheart Beads in *The Antelope Wife.* According to chapter 23, Richard's surname comes from the original Whiteheart Beads, who was named for a bead-embroidered blanket given to his mother by Midass, great-great-grandmother of Richard's wife, Rozina.

We learn in chapter 16 that as a young man Richard has a promising future in tribal politics. He marries Rozina Roy on an Ojibwe reservation somewhere "up north" of Minneapolis. According to chapter 7, Richard is an idealistic student and is proud of marrying a girl with Roy blood. (Chapters 1, 18, and 23 reveal that the Roy ancestors were educated men and women.) According to chapter 16, however, Richard's obsessive love maddens Rozin, and she tries to leave three times. Twice, he persuades her to stay. The third time, she stays because she is pregnant with twins. Richard apparently suggests an abortion, since he later recalls Rozin's insistence, *"No abortion"* (chapter 7). Their twin daughters, Deanna and Cally, are probably born in the mid-1970s.

By the time the girls are five, Rozin insists that the family leave the reservation because Richard's job has become too dangerous and political (chapter 7). They move to Minneapolis in chapter 3, where Rozin teaches school and Richard pursues his scheme of large-scale garbage disposal on reservation land. While Richard is busy meeting with environmental engineers, however, Rozin is falling in love with a different sort of man, the baker Frank Shawano.

In chapter 4, Richard appears entirely successful. He is a leading player in the nation's first Native-owned waste-disposal business, and he has won the company's top prize of a paid vacation to Hawaii. Over the next months and years, however, the problems created by his obsessions will destroy his life, both professionally and personally, and he will often plan suicide (chapter 7). The exact sequence of his business and family crises is left vague, but the events are as follows.

In business, the obsessively ambitious Richard illegally dumps toxic waste and takes a payoff, which he uses to buy a lake cabin (chapter 18). At the company party in chapter 4, Richard gives his Hawaii trip to Klaus Shawano, along with his I.D. Klaus notes Richard's nervousness at the party but misinterprets it. Richard, apparently aware that he is in trouble, is setting Klaus up. On the trip, law enforcement officials assume that Klaus is Richard and arrest him for the company's dumping violations. But Richard does not entirely escape the consequences. Although he still seems to have a job in chapter 7, we learn in chapter 18 that he is prosecuted for his violations.

In his family, Richard's obsessive love and Rozin's affair with Frank work to undermine their relationship. One afternoon when Deanna and Cally are still small (chapter 6), Richard takes the girls to the city park, where they see a woman who looks like Rozin walking with an athletic-looking man. Richard insists that she is

Richard Whiteheart Beads

not Rozin, but his grave manner seems to belie his words. When Richard comes home one day, he senses that Frank has been there and later finds signs of Frank's presence. His confrontation with Rozin ends the affair, but in her grief, she grows to hate him.

Richard and Rozin's relationship reaches a crisis when their daughters are eleven. The snowy March morning in chapter 7 seems to be the beginning of an ordinary day. But when the girls go to school, Rozin stuns Richard with the announcement that Frank has terminal cancer and that she is leaving Richard to be with him. That evening after work, he fights with Rozin, both verbally and physically, but she is implacable. After drinking himself to sleep, he wakes in the night, determined to kill himself. But Richard's efforts to die of carbon monoxide poisoning in his pickup truck are foiled by his own bumbling. He changes his mind, but the next morning, as we learn in chapter 9, he discovers Deanna behind the truck's seat, dead.

Richard tries to care for Rozin in the early days of their grief, but she cannot forgive him (chapter 16). In chapter 9, Rozin takes Cally and moves back to the reservation to stay with her "mothers," Zosie Roy and Mary Shawano. Both Rozin and Cally reject Richard, changing their surname to Roy (chapters 14 and 11). Seven years later, the eighteen-year-old Cally still says that she never wants to see her father again.

By chapter 10, Richard has become a drunken bum—wandering the streets with Klaus, drinking Listerine and cheap wine, and accepting handouts from strangers. Seven years after Deanna's death, in chapter 11 Richard walks into Frank's bakery and seems to see her behind the counter (it is actually Cally). In horror, he staggers out the door and runs down the street. Richard and Klaus eventually join a recovery program, but according to chapter 15, Richard is more obnoxious sober than drunk. Instead of taking responsibility for Deanna's death, Richard weeps for imaginary pasts he has invented.

Richard's final crisis comes when Rozin decides to marry Frank in chapter 16, a wedding he attempts to disrupt in a variety of ways. He interrupts the ceremony with a suicide attempt and the reception with a claim that he has poisoned the cake. That night, he shoots himself in the head at the door of Rozin and Frank's hotel room. In chapter 17, he dies in the hospital.

Rozin is haunted by memories of Richard (chapter 17). For a time, his suicide gives rise to her own death wish, since she feels that his ghost is inescapable. Cally is also haunted by her father. During the Christmas dinner in chapter 18, as Cally listens to the family's conversation, she sees her father's bloody head and feels his tears in her hands.

Roland Zumbrugge. Argus town judge and brother of banker Chester Zumbrugge in *The Master Butchers Singing Club.* When Roy Watzka is in jail in the fall of 1935, in chapter 8 Zumbrugge sets the amount of his bail. Just before Christmas the following year, Sheriff Hock badgers the judge into giving him a warrant to search Clarisse Strub's house. Clarisse's thoughts that evening imply that Zumbrugge has an inappropriate influence over some of the town's lawyers.

Roman Shimek. Brother of Mazarine Shimek in *The Master Butchers Singing Club.* In chapter 9, Roman is one of the crew of boys that helps Markus Waldvogel excavate a man-made hill in 1936. To help in their work, Roman steals altar candles from the Catholic church. He is referred to as the worst boy in town and a hellraiser. That November, Roman is the last to leave the excavation before the hill collapses on Markus. He runs with the other boys to get help.

When in the fall of 1944 Roman is decorated for wounds he sustained in the war and has a difficult recovery, in chapter 14 Mazarine comes home from Moorhead. The next spring she recalls the summer smell of Roman's hair as a boy.

Ronald Lovchik. See **Lovchik.**

Rooming house residents. Assorted *veterans* and pensionless retired *farmhands* who live in the rooming house where Marlis Cook stays for a month, in "Marlis's Tale" [27] in *Tales of Burning Love.* Marlis is talking to the oldest of the residents, an *eighty-seven-year-old man,* when Jack Mauser comes to see her.

Rose Pentecost. Lulu Nanapush's friend at government school in chapter 15 of *The Last Report on the Miracles at Little No Horse.* Rose is a large girl from a family named by a priest in the last century. The autumn Lulu arrives at school (1919), the other girls throw her into a deep pit. Two days and nights later, Rose sneaks out of the breakfast line and pulls her out. As they become friends, Rose tells Lulu that gasoline is squeezed from dead bodies and you die if you breathe it. When the Indian children have a program at a local school, Rose performs the Lord's Prayer in sign language. Over the next few years, Rose and Lulu go everywhere together and learn to perform the Lord's Prayer and the Twenty-third Psalm in synchronized sign language. Rose's mother may be the *Mrs. Pentecost* who, with her daughter, sees the black dog on the way to mass in chapter 16. (See **Black dog.**)

Roy family. Family in *The Antelope Wife* that includes non-Indians **Augustus Roy I, Augustus Roy II, Peace McKnight,** and **Scranton Roy,** and Shawano Ojibwes **Aurora Roy, Cally Whiteheart Beads Roy, Deanna Whiteheart**

Roy family

Beads, Matilda Roy (by adoption), **Rozina (Rozin) Roy Whiteheart Beads Shawano,** and **Zosie (II) Shawano Roy.** In addition to these Ojibwe women, chapter 16 also refers to (apparently Ojibwe) *Roy men,* but their identity is not clarified. For the ancestry of this family, see also **Shawano family.**

Roy Watzka. Argus town drunk and adoptive father of Delphine Watzka in *The Master Butchers Singing Club.* Chapter 2 reveals that Roy begins his chronic drinking when Delphine is a small child. The story he tells her and the town is that he drinks from grief because of the death of his beloved Minnie, Delphine's mother. We learn in chapter 4 that he worships his blurred photos of Minnie but never tells Delphine anything about her mother. By the time Delphine is ten, Roy is drinking more out of physical need than any sense of loss. Virtually the only income they have is from *a farmer who leases Roy's small plot of land.* When Delphine drops out of high school and goes to work, Roy takes half her earnings for liquor. But when he brings *his drunken friends* to the house, she chases them out with an ax. That night Roy falls through thin ice and subsequently develops pneumonia, so Delphine must quit her job to nurse him. All her life, Roy uses his self-pity to manipulate Delphine. The years of drinking take a physical toll as well. In addition to severe liver damage, by his fifties Roy has a small, crooked frame and the fat red nose of a "sinister clown" (*MBSC,* 47; chapter 4). Nevertheless, the townsfolk don't despise Roy—he seems to love Delphine, and when sober, they note, he is hardworking (chapter 6).

In the early 1930s (chapter 3), Fidelis Waldvogel forms a men's singing club, which Roy joins. As long as he has his liquor, he can sing most any part. But Roy resents one of the other singers, Porky Chavers, whose voice is similar to his so they often duel instead of harmonizing. In the winter of early 1934 (see chapter 5 for date), Roy hosts a funeral party for his friend Cornelius Strub. Two accounts, in chapters 4 and 13, tell the story of that night. At the gathering, Roy tells Chavers to go down into his cellar for ginger beer and then shouts down to him, "Hey, Chavers, you can come up again after you quit singing over me in practice" (*MBSC,* 328). Roy wanders off during the party and then stays away on a weeks-long drunk. In Roy's first account of these events, he says that when the Chaverses are missing, he thinks they have gone to Arizona, and that when he returns to his house and hears noises from the cellar, he thinks they are his own drunken hallucinations. In truth, however, when Roy returns to get liquor from his cellar after his binge, he finds the Chaverses' bodies. But he tells no one and leaves the house for good.

That summer (1934), when Delphine and her companion, Cyprian Lazarre, return to Argus in chapter 4, they are overwhelmed by the stench in Roy's house.

When they find the three bodies in his cellar, Roy tells part of the story of the funeral party but claims that he had not known the Chaverses' whereabouts and certainly did not lock the cellar door. During a heat wave in chapter 5, the drunken Roy becomes covered with armyworms.

When Eva Waldvogel is dying of cancer the next summer (1935), in chapter 6 Roy comes to see her and tells tall tales to distract her. But Roy's greatest service to Eva occurs on July 4. When Eva's morphine is stolen, it is Roy who brings the agonized Eva relief by stealing morphine from the drugstore. We learn in chapter 8 that Fidelis immediately takes care of potential legal problems.

When Eva dies later that summer (chapter 7), moved by her death and haunted by the Chavers family, Roy enters an unprecedented period of sobriety. To everyone's amazement, he begins fixing up the house and taking care of Delphine. When Markus Waldvogel stays with them for a couple of weeks, Roy takes him fishing. That autumn (chapter 8), Roy is still sober. He even goes with Cyprian on some of his liquor runs to Canada without sampling the product. He also for the first time begins to make his payments to the bank on time. But that fall (1935), Sheriff Hock belatedly arrests him for the theft of the morphine. Although Roy has been to jail before, this time he is sober, so he is uncomfortable and ashamed. Over the next year, Roy, still sober, thins and weakens (chapter 9). Yet he works mornings at the butcher shop and afternoons helping Step-and-a-Half. Just after Christmas 1936, in chapter 11 Roy tells Delphine the news that her friend Clarisse Strub has murdered Sheriff Hock and then disappeared.

We learn from chapter 13 that sometime during the next year or so Roy begins drinking again on the sly. Step-and-a-Half knows this and kicks him out, but Delphine does not learn of his backsliding until after her trip to Chicago with the Waldvogels. One spring day, she spots her naked, drunken father on the street, chases and catches him, and takes him home. At Dr. Heech's instructions, she gives the now bedfast Roy little sips of whiskey to taper him off. When Cyprian passes through town, he visits with Roy. As Roy sleeps more and more, Delphine realizes that he is preparing to die and insists that he tell her something about her mother. He tells her only Minnie's story of Wounded Knee, then stops. But Roy has other things he needs to say. He finally reveals the truth about the night the Chavers family is shut into his cellar, revealing that "maybe" he sealed the cellar door (*MBSC*, 328). Soon after, a visiting nurse finds Roy dead. Many townsfolk attend his funeral. One evening a few days later, Delphine tries to tell Fidelis that her father was a murderer. Years later, in chapter 14 when Delphine takes evening walks, she goes through the cemetery and notices Roy's grave near the place she will be laid.

In chapter 16, readers finally learn the truth about Roy's relationship to

Roy Watzka

Delphine, who is not his biological daughter. She is born to the derelict Mrs. Shimek and as a newborn is rescued by Step-and-a-Half, whom Roy loves and has nicknamed "Minnie." Although she later regrets her choice, Step-and-a-Half takes the infant to Roy. The lost mother, Minnie, whom Delphine grows up longing to see, is merely a creation of Roy Watzka's imagination.

Rozina (Rozin) Roy Whiteheart Beads Shawano. Daughter of Zosie (II) Shawano Roy and Augustus Roy II; mother of Deanna and Cally Whiteheart Beads in *The Antelope Wife*. The Roy blood mixed with her Ojibwe ancestry gives Rozin her wavy hair and lightened skin (chapter 3). Chapter 14 records her Ojibwe name, Waubanikway (Dawn Woman). She is the narrator of chapter 3.

Rozin grows up on an Ojibwe reservation. Although its precise location is not revealed, the narrative does give a few hints. It is said to be "up north"—north of both Minneapolis (chapter 6) and the prairie country "out in Bwaanakeeng" (Dakota-land), where the dog Almost Soup is born (chapter 8). The dog's prairie birthplace may be near the region referred to in chapter 1 as the "vast carcass of the world west of the Otter Tail River," that is, the Wahpeton area in southeastern North Dakota. Also, the woman wearing Blue Prairie Woman's beads whom Zosie (II) sees as a child is referred to in chapter 18 as a "Pembina woman," indicating perhaps that Blue Prairie Woman's descendants live in the Pembina region, in far northeast North Dakota.

The marriage of Rozin's parents is ill fated (chapter 18), and by the time of her and Aurora's birth, their father has disappeared. The girls are probably born in the 1940s or 1950s. (By the end of the novel, which seems to be in the mid-1990s, Rozin has a twenty-two-year-old daughter.) Rozin's mother, Zosie, and Zosie's twin sister, Mary, together rear Rozin and Aurora, and they will not tell the girls which of them is their mother (chapters 9 and 11). When the girls are five, Aurora dies of diphtheria, and according to chapter 3, she must be pried from Rozin's arms.

Rozin seems still to be living on the reservation when she marries Richard Whiteheart Beads, who according to chapter 16 is a young tribal leader. We learn in chapters 7 and 16 that Rozin chafes at Richard's possessive love. (In chapters 3, 9, 16, and 17, as she looks back on her marriage and the subsequent catastrophes, she wishes that she had kept to the old-time ways and never become involved with Richard, although her anger is mixed with love.) From the first year of marriage, Rozin plots her escape, and she tries to leave three times. Twice Richard persuades her to stay. The third time she stays because she discovers, to her joy, that she is pregnant. Her twin girls, Deanna and Cally, are born probably in the mid-1970s.

When life on the reservation becomes too dangerous and political, Rozin insists

Rozina (Rozin) Roy Whiteheart Beads Shawano

that they leave. The family moves to Minneapolis in chapter 3, where Rozin teaches school and Richard pursues his scheme of creating a big-time garbage-disposal business. Shortly after they arrive, when the twins are five, Rozin sees Sweetheart Calico in front of Frank Shawano's bakery. Rozin enters the bakery and meets Frank, and they begin seeing one another. Because she loves Richard and the girls, Rozin grieves to find herself falling in love with Frank. They first consummate their relationship in a woods near a playground. One June afternoon, unknown to Rozin, Richard and the girls see her and Frank walk through the city park in chapter 6. To young Cally, her mother's companion appears as a deer man, like the deer husband of their forebear, Apijigo Bakaday.

Frank also comes to Rozin's house, bringing cookies. Richard eventually confronts Rozin about the affair, and it ends. But in her sadness, she grows to hate Richard. (The duration of Frank and Rozin's affair is uncertain. In chapter 7, Richard refers to the "years" she was Frank's lover.)

One snowy March day when the twins are eleven, in chapter 7 Rozin tells Richard that Frank is dying of cancer and that she is leaving Richard to be with him. The depressed Richard tries to commit suicide that night through carbon monoxide poisoning, but he fails. Deanna, who surreptitiously climbs into Richard's truck, dies instead.

Rozin is overwhelmed with grief. Richard tries to take care of her, but she cannot forgive him (chapter 16). Blaming both Richard and her own love for Frank, Rozin goes to live with her twin mothers on the reservation (chapter 9). Her grief for Deanna makes Rozin absent-minded and careless with Cally. After playing outside one sunny but freezing February day nearly a year after Deanna's death, Cally becomes gravely ill. Rozin, Zosie, and Mary nurse her for three days while a blizzard prevents their getting medical help, and Cally almost dies before the ambulance arrives. After Cally recovers, Rozin realizes that she can now read Rozin's mind. Rozin continues to brood over her anger and love for Richard and to worry about what he has become. As we learn in chapters 10 and 11, he has become a drunken bum.

When Cally is eighteen and determined to leave home, Rozin tries to contact her mothers, who have moved to Minneapolis (chapter 11). She is not able to reach them, so Cally goes to stay with cancer survivor Frank Shawano instead.

By the time Cally is twenty, in chapter 14 Rozin moves to the city to go to night school to become a lawyer. She stays with her mothers and works in a food co-op. She has taken back her maiden name, Roy, and also uses her Ojibwe name, Waubanikway. One August evening, Frank shows up at Rozin's checkout counter saying that he needs her. He continues to phone her until she agrees to go with him to the state fair. There, after a frightening ride on the Gravitron, Rozin allows

Rozina (Rozin) Roy Whiteheart Beads Shawano

herself to fall in love with Frank again. According to chapter 16, she is attracted by both his physical strength and their ability to be honest with one another.

Rozin and Frank's wedding, recorded in chapter 16, is in the autumn. Many family members come to Frank's bakery to help with the preparation, and an even larger family group goes out to the cliffside ceremony. Richard interrupts the ceremony with another botched suicide attempt and disrupts the reception with a letter claiming that he has poisoned the wedding cake—a lie, as he later admits. That evening, however, Richard shows up again—at Rozin and Frank's hotel room. He knocks on their door, puts a gun to his head, and although the naked Rozin rushes to stop him, shoots.

In chapter 17, Rozin withdraws to her mothers' apartment, where this new grief merges with the old. She hears Deanna's voice and prepares a meal for her daughter's ghost. For ten days, Rozin refuses company and food and struggles with dreams about Richard, Frank, and a windigo stranger who is a gateway to death. Finally Frank gets into the apartment, refuses to leave, and cares for her.

Afterward, Rozin and Frank are apparently able to begin a normal married life. The following December (chapter 18), the family gathers at their apartment for Christmas dinner. As Cally and other dinner guests observe, the new couple are deeply in love. The next autumn, in chapter 22 Frank and Rozin each try to think of a way to celebrate their upcoming anniversary. Frank would prefer something private; Rozin would like a big party. Putting the other ahead of self, however, Rozin devises a private sexy encounter and Frank makes elaborate plans for a surprise party. Their plans collide into an ending that catches everyone, including the reader, by surprise.

Rozin's cousins. Women who put Rozina Roy Shawano into the shower to wash off the blood after Richard Whiteheart Beads's suicide in chapter 16 of *The Antelope Wife.* They may be **Jackie and Ruby.**

Ruby. See **Jackie and Ruby.**

Rushes Bear. See **Margaret (Rushes Bear) Kashpaw.**

Russell Kashpaw. Son of Regina Puyat Kashpaw and a Montana Kashpaw; younger brother of Isabel Kashpaw and older half brother of Celestine James. As children, Russell, Isabel, and their cousin Pauline Puyat seek out Eli Kashpaw on the reservation to get to know him, as related in chapter 10 of *The Beet Queen.* (For ambiguity about the structure of Russell's family, see **Montana Kashpaw.**)

We learn in chapter 2 of *Tracks* that after Russell's father goes to Montana, he and his mother move to Argus to live with Dutch James. (Chapter 2 of *The*

Russell Kashpaw

Beet Queen gives a variant account of the timing of Russell's move to Argus.) As a boy, Russell helps out in the butcher shop where Dutch works, joined in 1912 by his cousin Pauline and in 1913 by Fleur Pillager. Although Pauline takes care of Russell, he prefers Fleur, whom he follows around the shop. One August night, he and Pauline see Dutch, Lily Veddar, and Tor Grunewald attack Fleur. Russell throws himself on Dutch in an attempt to stop the attack, but Dutch cuffs him off. When a tornado strikes the next day and the three men take refuge in the meat locker, Russell and Pauline lock them in, although Pauline acknowledges in chapter 4 that she, not Russell, is the one responsible. She recalls Russell's reaction to the incident in chapter 8. Tor and Lily freeze to death, and Dutch later loses parts of his limbs to gangrene.

After Dutch somewhat recovers, he marries Regina and becomes Russell's stepfather, although Russell never takes the James surname. According to chapter 2 of *The Beet Queen,* Russell's half sister Celestine is born a month later, and Regina and Dutch die when Celestine is still small.

About twenty years later (1932), in chapter 2 of *The Beet Queen* Russell is still living with Celestine and his older sister, Isabel, on Dutch James's homestead just outside Argus. When Sita Kozka and her cousin Mary Adare come to visit Celestine, Russell mocks them. But after Mary's "miracle," when the face of Christ seems to appear in the ice, Russell kneels beside the image and blesses himself.

In chapter 4, Russell goes off to war, and when he returns home a "second time," he has been wounded. The dating of this incident is problematic, because it appears in a chapter dated 1941, but Mary, who is narrating, says that Russell is back "from Korea." Russell's wounding and return could be a flash-forward to the Korean War, but aspects of the narration suggest otherwise. This chapter indicates that Fritzie and Pete move south for Fritzie's health in about 1941, and yet when Russell comes home wounded, Fritzie and Pete are still living in Argus. In addition, chapter 7, set in 1953, seems to refer to a later war and wounding when its narrator, Celestine, says that Russell has returned "from his latest war, Korea," with "even more wounds." After his chapter 4 return, he is handsomely scarred, gets a job, and seems in control of his life, whereas after his chapter 7 return, he is listless, limping, and almost animal-like in appearance. Celestine also says in chapter 7 that Russell had his earlier "more attractive" scars "when he came back from Germany." Perhaps in mentioning Korea in chapter 4, Mary gets her wars confused. Even so, the early dating remains problematic, since the United States did not enter World War II until the end of 1941.

In chapter 4, while Russell is recovering in a Virginia hospital, Mary sends him a get-well card, but he does not respond. When he returns to Argus, he is considered a hero and gets a job at the bank. Mary sees him, falls in love with his

Russell Kashpaw

scars, and asks Celestine to invite him to dinner. During dinner, Russell is mostly cold toward Mary, but he eventually lets her touch his scars.

In chapter 5, Russell is drinking in the bar that Sita Kozka Bohl enters after being kidnapped from her wedding dance (about 1950). When he returns home from Korea in 1952 or 1953 (chapter 7), there is talk of honoring him as North Dakota's most-decorated hero. Hearing that his sister Isabel has died violently, he goes to South Dakota to find out about her but is unable to learn anything. Back in Argus, the unemployed Russell mopes and drinks until Mary hires him to work on the butcher shop's equipment. He goes with Celestine and Mary to the grand opening of Sita's restaurant, Chez Sita, where he, Celestine, and Mary help in the restaurant's kitchen after the chef becomes ill. When Karl Adare moves in with Celestine, Russell disapproves, particularly when Celestine becomes pregnant. He leaves the house and goes to stay with Eli Kashpaw on the reservation.

That winter (1953–1954), in chapter 8 Russell has a stroke while ice fishing that leaves him largely paralyzed. (The account of his condition in chapter 10 makes clear that he cannot walk or dress himself, and his speech is seriously impaired.) Seven and a half years later, in chapter 10 Celestine makes her daughter, Dot Adare, give Russell the wheelchair Dot's father had sent her. Dot mentions other visits to her Uncle Russell and Eli in chapter 12, and in chapter 14, one of her various dreams of the future is to live with them on the reservation. In chapters 13, 15, and 16, Russell participates in the 1972 Beet Festival and is honored as the town's most-decorated hero. Just before the parade begins, Dot notices that Russell is thirsty and makes his attendants give him some water. During his ride on a parade float, Russell sees his sister Isabel on the old Chippewa road of death and thinks that he himself has died. He is jerked back into life when he laughs.

In these later chapters of *The Beet Queen* (1972), Russell appears to be unable even to pin on his medals, put on his hat, or ask for a drink of water. By the time of *The Bingo Palace,* however (sometime after 1984), although he is still wheelchair-bound and suffering from his multiple strokes and shrapnel wounds, his condition has obviously improved, since he is now a tattoo artist. In chapter 7, Lipsha Morrissey tries unsuccessfully to use his healing power to ease Russell's pain. Later, Lipsha is forcibly taken to Russell's tattoo parlor by some Montana men, but after the abductors leave, Russell is kind to him. We learn in chapter 17 that Russell works with Xavier Toose, apparently in religious ceremonies.

Ruthie Chavers. Daughter of Porky and Doris Chavers in *The Master Butchers Singing Club.* As schoolchildren Ruthie and Markus Waldvogel are sweethearts. We learn in chapter 6 that Ruthie gives Markus notes, a Valentine, and little gifts, including a clicker that looks like a cricket, all of which Markus keeps inside his pillow.

In early 1934, in late winter, Ruthie goes with her parents to a funeral party at Roy Watzka's house honoring their relative Cornelius Strub. (See chapters 4, 5, and 13.) When Roy sends Porky into the cellar to get ginger beer, Doris and Ruthie go with him. The cellar door becomes locked, no one hears their cries, and the Chaverses are trapped. After weeks perhaps, they eventually die. In chapter 4, Delphine Watzka comes home that summer and discovers the three bodies in her father's cellar. Markus Waldvogel overhears Delphine's conversation with the sheriff a few days later, in chapter 5, and tells her the name of the Chavers child. Delphine feels that since the child was a girl, she would have handled her fate better than a boy would have.

The next summer (1935) when Eva Waldvogel is near death, in chapter 6 Ruthie's clicker wakes Markus in the night so that he sees his father singing to his mother. As he goes back to sleep, he touches Ruthie's paper heart. Later that year, in chapter 7 Clarisse Strub expresses grief over Doris and Ruthie's deaths. Markus sometimes confides in Delphine while she is cooking, and in chapter 12, he tells her about Ruthie's giving him the valentine. Shortly before his death in chapter 13, Roy admits that he had "maybe" locked Chavers into the cellar but says he did not know that Doris and Ruthie were with him. In 1942, the night after Markus leaves for Ft. Snelling to join the army, Delphine dreams about Ruthie and her family.

S

Sal Birdy. Argus pharmacist in *The Master Butchers Singing Club.* We learn from chapter 3 that the drugstore serves customers at a counter and wood-paneled booths, from which they can see the street. During the heat wave in the summer of 1934, when the noise of mosquitoes wakes Delphine Watzka and Cyprian Lazarre in their tent in chapter 5, Sal is probably the pharmacist from whom they buy cotton wax for their ears. On July 4, 1935, when Eva Waldvogel's morphine is stolen in chapter 6, Delphine and Fidelis spend hours looking for the doctor and Sal to replace it. Roy Watzka is the one who provides the needed medicine—by breaking into Sal's drugstore and stealing it. We learn from chapter 8 that Fidelis works out arrangements with Sal to make monthly payments on the new medicine. The following autumn, as an excuse for arresting Roy, Sheriff Hock makes up a

Sal Birdy

lie that Sal had turned in the theft to the state commission before learning the circumstances. By the start of World War II, in chapter 13, Sal is meeting with the singing club.

Sarah Tatro. Niece of John and Burden Tatro in *The Painted Drum*. After the death of her uncles, in part 1.2 Sarah calls in the Travers estate business to appraise and sell their property. An RN with an open, pleasant personality, Sarah has no interest in keeping the accumulation of two centuries of misers. When Faye Travers comes to begin the appraisal, Sarah shows her the fawn-skin doll she used to play with and the attic full of Ojibwe artifacts. She is surprised when Faye tells her these objects are valuable, but she has no other interest in them and leaves the house while Faye does the inventory.

Satan. Variously called Lucifer, the Dark One, and the devil (or Devil). See also **Devil.** In chapters 6 and 8 of *Tracks,* Pauline Puyat believes that Satan appears to her. According to these chapters and chapter 2, she believes that the lake creature Misshepeshu is one of his manifestations, that Fleur Pillager and Nanapush are his agents, and that it is Satan (as the lake creature) whom she kills on the lake shore. She also seems to think that Satan is the father of her child, Marie, and—in the form of Misshepeshu—of Fleur's child, Lulu.

As Sister Leopolda, Pauline continues her battle with Satan in "Saint Marie" in *Love Medicine*. Marie, however, affirms in "Saint Marie" and "Flesh and Blood" that the devil is in Sister Leopolda and loves her best. Marie does not believe he has touched the abandoned child June Morrissey in "The Beads."

Schatzie. The white female German shepherd that the Kozkas give to the Waldvogels as a token of reconciliation in *The Master Butchers Singing Club.* In chapter 5, even as a puppy with boundless energy, Schatzie has remarkable dignity and intelligence. She and Eva immediately form a bond. She is the one animal the Waldvogels do not treat as a utilitarian commodity. Throughout the novel, Schatzie is protective of her people. At first she follows the boys on their errands and outdoor wanderings, but in chapter 7, after Eva becomes ill, Schatzie stays with her, guarding her and waiting to take her across to the other side. In chapter 8, after Eva dies, Schatzie sleeps guard outside the boys' door. She now looks at Delphine with the same recognition and intelligence she had formerly directed toward Eva. The night after Fidelis kills the wild dogs, as Delphine turns the sleeping boys over to Schatzie's watch, in the long gaze they exchange Delphine realizes that it is Eva staring back at her. Schatzie has only one or two annoying habits: she sometimes hides the boys' boots (chapter 8), and she digs up former dogs' bones in Eva's garden and does not rebury them (chapter 6). One night in 1942 (chapter

14), when Delphine and Fidelis retire for the night, the now old, arthritic, and half-blind Schatzie checks the shop before lying down outside their door.

Scranton Roy. Adoptive father of Matilda Roy; father of Augustus Roy I and grandfather of Augustus Roy II in *The Antelope Wife.*

In chapter 1, Scranton Teodorus Roy is born in a small Pennsylvania community to a **Quaker father** and **poet mother.** As a young man, he is stung by the scorn of a **traveling drama troupe woman,** follows her west, and enlists in the U.S. Cavalry at St. Paul, Minnesota. Farther west, his company attacks an Ojibwe village. Surprised by his sudden hatred, Scranton kills two children and an old woman. He sees a dog fleeing into the open spaces west of the Otter Tail River (Dakota territory) with a baby tied to its back, and he follows them. After three days, Scranton is finally able to approach the dog and remove the child, a girl. He can find nothing to feed her and ultimately stops her crying by putting her to his nipple. The three continue farther into the wilderness, Scranton stops and builds a sod house, and one morning as the child is sucking, milk floods Scranton's nipples and she is fed. He names her Matilda, after his mother.

An educated man, Scranton apparently teaches Matilda to write. When she is six, she becomes fast friends with the young schoolteacher, Peace McKnight. At Matilda's request, Scranton lets Peace stay at the house, and shortly thereafter they marry. Peace becomes pregnant and later falls ill with a fever. While she is ill, Scranton experiences another loss. One morning, there is no Matilda in the bed beside Peace, only a note indicating that the seven-year-old has gone with her mother, who came for her in the night. Peace dies after giving birth to their son, Augustus. Scranton revives the unbreathing child and puts him to his breast. This son may die shortly after his own son (also named Augustus) is born, because in chapter 23 Scranton raises Augustus II alone.

Many years later, Scranton falls ill and is visited by the spirit of the old woman he had killed. After a hundred days of fever and seizures, he offers to find the woman's village and try to make amends. Taking his grandson, Scranton makes his way east with supplies and finds the remnant of villagers, now on a reservation. Here, Scranton experiences yet another loss. Augustus falls in love with a young Ojibwe woman, Zosie Shawano, the great-great-granddaughter of the woman Scranton killed. Sometime after his marriage to Zosie, Augustus disappears without a trace.

Senior Citizens, residents of the. Nosy neighbors of Marie Kashpaw and Lulu Lamartine. Lulu is their favorite topic of gossip, and Josette Bizhieu is their chief informant. They seem to be the "we" narrating chapters 1 and 25 of *The Bingo Palace,* in which Lulu steals the Wanted poster of her son Gerry Nanapush and, after refusing to cooperate with the marshals looking for Gerry, is arrested for that theft. As the marshals lead Lulu away, these residents join in Lulu's old-lady trill, a victory yell.

Seraphine String. Traditional medicine woman; wife of John String in *The Painted Drum*. Seraphine is raised traditionally by her grandparents, but when they die, she is sent to the white boarding school, where a matron punishes her for speaking Ojibwe by tearing her lips with a heavy needle, leaving a lifelong scar (part 3.7). We learn in part 3.2 that Seraphine is beautiful despite her scar, that she learns the old-time medicines, and that she meets her future husband at a ceremony. In the present time of the story, she and John have children and she is a social worker. One winter in the early twenty-first century, in part 3.7 she interviews the woman Ira and two of her children in the IHS hospital about the incidents of the last two days, in which Ira leaves the children alone in the bitter cold, the house burns down, and the children become hypothermic trying to reach safety.

Shaawano family. A family central to *The Painted Drum*. We are not given particular links between these Shaawanos and the Shawanos (different spelling) of *The Antelope Wife*, but both families come from a people whose name means "south" and dates back to the early times when the people moved to (or lived in) the south (that is, south of Canada) (see *Painted Drum* part 1.3). *The Painted Drum* Shaawanos include **Bernard Shaawano, Doris and Raymond Shaawano, Shaawano girl, Shaawano husband,** and **Shaawano son.**

Shaawano girl. Daughter of Anaquot and her Shaawano husband in *The Painted Drum*. We learn in parts 2.3 and 2.4 that this is the person whom both Shaawano and Anaquot love most. One autumn (part 2.2), after Anaquot gives birth to a baby girl (Fleur) fathered by her Pillager lover, her nine-year-old Shaawano daughter cares for both baby and mother to the point of exhaustion. The following winter, when Shaawano sends Anaquot to her lover, Anaquot insists on taking their daughter with her. As the girl's five-year-old brother chases the speeding sled, he sees shadows rushing out of the woods. Worried by the boy's account, Shaawano follows and finds his daughter's shawl and bones, torn by wolves.

Two interpretations of the girl's death are put forward. Shaawano thinks, and tells his son, that Anaquot threw her to the wolves. But years later, when this son has his own son, the child (Bernard) suggests to his father that because of her love for her family, the girl willingly sacrificed herself to save them. According to part 2.5, Shaawano places the girl's bones in the hollow of a birch clump in the woods near his house.

After Anaquot arrives at the Pillager cabin in part 2.3, her Shaawano daughter's spirit repeatedly speaks to her, warning her and telling her how to protect herself from the revenge of the Pillager's wife, Ziigwan'aage. It is probably also the girl's spirit whose hand Anaquot feels and whose tracks appear in the snow when Anaquot enters the house. Later, when Ziigwan'aage kills a wolf, the girl's spirit tells her mother that this is the wolf who ate her heart.

In part 2.4, the girl's spirit also speaks to her Shaawano father, telling him to make the drum the people have been preparing for generations. When Albert Ruse helps Shaawano with the task, the girl appears in a dream to thank him. It is also apparently his daughter's spirit who sends Shaawano the signs in part 2.5 showing him how to ornament the drum, and she later instructs him to put her (that is, her bones) inside. The girl also teaches Shaawano some of the songs to be used with the drum (part 3.7).

The girl's spirit living in the drum brings both good and ill. In part 2.5, the drum strengthens the people and holds them together. Yet when Simon Jack, Anaquot's Pillager lover, comes into the drum circle, the girl's spirit overpowers him and causes him to dance to his death. Because of this destruction, Shaawano judges that the drum should not be used for forty years. Many decades later, in part 3.5 the drum leads three children, lost in the snow, to safety. The Shaawano girl's spirit thus saves a "sister" (*PD,* 251). (See also parts 3.6 and 3.7.) After this incident, Shaawano's grandson, Bernard, puts the drum back into regular use (part 4).

In part 2.1 of *The Painted Drum,* Bernard says that his aunt's name is never spoken, apparently because of the manner of her death. This unspoken name, however, may be Red Cradle, referred to in *Four Souls* chapter 5 as a daughter of Anaquot prior to Fleur, apparently fathered by her Shaawano husband.

Shaawano husband. Husband of Anaquot; father of two children, a girl and a boy; maker of the painted drum. Anaquot's Shaawano husband and children are mentioned in chapter 5 of *Four Souls,* as is her unfaithfulness with a Pillager man. But the detailed account of Shaawano's story appears in *The Painted Drum.*

The daughter of Shaawano and Anaquot is nine and their son is five in part 2.2 of *The Painted Drum.* (See **Shaawano girl** and **Shaawano son.**) The previous year, Anaquot had become the lover of a Pillager man and in the autumn had given birth to the man's daughter. Although Anaquot remains at Shaawano's house, she is lovesick, so that winter Shaawano sends her to the Pillager camp and even allows her to take his beloved daughter. When a Pillager man arrives to fetch them, the Shaawano boy futilely chases the sled. Shaawano finds his son collapsed in the snow and brings him home. But the boy's story of "shadows" following the sled worries him, so Shaawano, who already has tuberculosis, goes out again and finds the bones of his daughter, eaten by wolves. He retrieves her bones and plaid shawl and, according to part 2.5, places the bones in the hollow of a birch clump.

The grief-stricken Shaawano begins wandering in part 2.4, leaving his young

Shaawano husband

son for weeks at a time. Upon each return, Shaawano falls ill and is visited by the ghosts of strangers, who judge and sneer at him. He is often cruel to his son, letting him go hungry and even ridiculing his grief.

One day, as Shaawano is remembering his daughter's death, her spirit appears in a dream and directs him to make the drum the people have been preparing for generations. Puzzled, Shaawano speaks with the retiring but wise Kakageeshikok, who instructs him to do exactly as his daughter says.

Shaawano does not begin the project at once. For nearly a year, he continues his furniture making, each day putting out tobacco for the spirits. Finally, in late spring of the following year, he sets out to find the cedar prepared for the drum. Knowing that its place is far across the lake, he asks a group of fishermen for a boat. One of them, Albert Ruse, tells him he may repair and keep Ruse's old birchbark canoe. With a week's hard work, Shaawano makes it good as new. When it is finished, Albert, whose grandfather had been a keeper of the wood, comes with his fifteen-year-old son, Chickie, to talk with Shaawano about preparations for the drum.

That same spring, Shaawano, Albert, and Chickie go out to find the drum trees. After crossing the lake, they come to a clearing and pray with Albert's pipe for guidance. Seeing a wolf watching them from the woods, Shaawano divines the location of the trees, on a ledge at the bottom of a cliff. As he sits by the four great cedars, he sees across the lake the island where he and Anaquot had gone when they were first in love.

In part 2.5, Shaawano sets up camp beside the cedars and forms the body of the drum, hollowing it out with hot stones. As he paddles back home, spirit signs show him how it should be ornamented. Around the top will be four beaded figures: a girl, a hand, a running wolf, and a "cross" (the sign of the four directions) (see also part 1.2). A yellow line will glow across its head. Chickie shoots a moose for the drumheads, but before Shaawano lashes them on, his daughter speaks again, telling him to put her inside. When he goes to the place where her bones are resting, two long bones crawl from their nest. He strings them inside the drum, east to west, and trims the drum's skirts with the ribbons she had loved. The girl's presence is his secret, which he tells years later only to his grandson Bernard.

Once the drum is finished, people dream its songs, and it becomes a powerful force for good, uniting and healing the people. But one day, as Simon Jack (Anaquot's former Pillager lover) enters the drum circle, both the songs and the man begin to move in the wrong direction. Dancing backwards, faster and faster, the Pillager falls dead. Realizing that the girl in the drum killed the Pillager out of anger, Shaawano puts the drum away. It should be cared for but not used, he decides, for forty years.

Years later, Shaawano's son has a son, Bernard. Old Shaawano cares for him when his parents are drinking and tells him the story of the drum. But when Shaawano dies, the drum goes to his son, who is driven by his alcoholism to sell it to Indian agent Jewett Parker Tatro. Tatro eventually takes the drum and other Ojibwe artifacts back to his New Hampshire home. For the rest of the story of Shaawano's drum, see **Faye Travers** and **Bernard Shaawano.**

Shaawano son. Son of Anaquot and Shaawano; brother of the girl eaten by wolves; father of Bernard Shaawano in *The Painted Drum.* Erdrich never gives readers a name for this Shaawano son. The boy is five the winter Anaquot leaves with her two daughters (part 2.2). As he tries to jump into the wagon, his mother pries his hands loose. He runs after them until he collapses, and something in his spirit dies. Far ahead he sees dark shadows bounding from the trees.

The boy's father finds him in the snow and takes him home. But the child's description of the shadows moves Shaawano to go out again with his gun. For more than a year, the boy doesn't know what happened and wonders why his sister's torn shawl is in their house. He finally learns that wolves had eaten her, and he visualizes their mother throwing her to the beasts. We learn in part 2.4 that in his grief, the Shaawano father abandons the boy for weeks at a time and, when home, is cruel to him, so that the child's spirit is wounded beyond repair. Eventually another family takes him in and will not let Shaawano see him.

When this Shaawano son is a young man, already addicted to alcohol, in part 2.5 he sees much of his father's making of the drum. He eventually marries and has three children, Bernard and, later, twins Doris and Raymond (2.2). *His wife* always makes sure he is present at the drum ceremonies, and his father teaches him the songs and keeps him near the drum even when he is drunk, because of its healing influence (2.5). Sometimes when the younger Shaawano and his wife drink, old Shaawano keeps Bernard (2.4). After old Shaawano dies, his son inherits the drum (2.5).

When his wife dies in part 2.2, this son of the elder Shaawano begins to drink more heavily. In his drunkenness, he sells his father's drum to trader Jewett Parker Tatro (part 2.5), and he begins to beat his children. They learn to evade him and even to take advantage of his drunken stupors. But after three years of abuse, Bernard is sufficiently grown to fight his father. In the melee, Bernard gives him a thorough beating but then relents. As Bernard wipes the blood from his face with a ragged shawl, his father clasps the old shawl to his forehead and tells Bernard the story of his dead sister.

Finally, this wounded Shaawano man takes another woman and experiences several happy years (2.2). Now sober, he talks often to Bernard about the making

Shaawano son

of the drum and about its loss, which is his greatest shame (see parts 2.1, 2.5, and 4). On one of these occasions (2.2), Bernard gives his father a new, redeeming interpretation of his sister's death—that the girl, seeing the wolves and loving her family, willingly sacrificed herself so they could live.

Shawano, first. Referred to in the headnote to part 3 of *The Antelope Wife* as the great-grandson of Sounding Feather. He is presumably the same person as the original Shawano, below.

Shawano, original. Windigo man whom the long-ago Shawano brothers accept into their family in the north, in chapter 17 of *The Antelope Wife*. He is presumably the same person as the first Shawano, above. There is some evidence that this original Shawano may also be the Shesheeb of chapter 3: both are windigos, the clan begins to be called Shawano shortly after Shesheeb's capture, and the people are still living in the north in both accounts. (See also **Windigo stranger.**)

Shawano brothers. Shawano family members who long ago in the far north accept the "original" Shawano, a windigo, into their family, according to chapter 17 of *The Antelope Wife*.

Shawano family. Clan name of the "south-looking" people in *The Antelope Wife,* as well as surname of certain families within that clan. (The name means "south" or "people of the south.")

The *clan* name Shawano begins about the time of the windigo **Shesheeb I** and *Shesheeb's sister,* who marries the Frenchman **Henri Laventure** (chapter 3). Shesheeb may be the man referred to as "first Shawano" and "original Shawano." Shesheeb's people originally live in the north, probably Canada, but after Shesheeb is captured, they begin migrating south and are called "those people who had just left for the south," or "Shawano." One *Shawano man* stopped with a **Pillager woman.** "He was lost" (*AW,* 35). Virtually all of the Indian characters in *The Antelope Wife* are descendants of this south-looking people, including the **Roy family** and probably the **Whiteheart Beads family.** Forebears of this clan in the generations prior to Shesheeb include *Magid* and her lover, the *Ivory Coast slave;* Magid's father, *Everlasting;* and the great-grandmother of the first Shawano, **Sounding Feather.**

Several family units use the Shawano family surname:

(1) The **Shawano brothers,** who take in the original Shawano.

(2) **Shawano the younger,** who marries **Blue Prairie Woman.** Their descendants include **Mary (I) Shawano and Josephette (Zosie I) Shawano; Mary (II) Shawano and Zosie (II) Shawano Roy; Aurora Roy and Rozina (Rozin) Roy Whiteheart Beads Shawano;** and **Deanna Whiteheart**

Beads and **Cally Whiteheart Beads Roy.** Blue Prairie Woman's (and possibly Shawano the younger's) descendants also include **Matilda Roy** and perhaps, through Matilda, **Sweetheart Calico.**

(3) **Shawano father of Mary (II) and Zosie (II).**

(4) **Shawano the ogitchida** and his children, **Frank Shawano, Puffy Shawano, Klaus Shawano,** and **Cecille Shawano.**

The Shawano clan is fundamentally Ojibwe. But as Cally Roy says in chapter 11, it is like "mixed party nuts," characterized by a wide mixture of bloods, including African (chapters 2, 3, and 16), French (chapters 3 and 16), Irish (chapters 11 and 18), German, Cree, Winnebago, Lakota, and Brazilian (chapter 16). Shawano ancestry includes both windigos (chapters 1, 3, 6, 13, 17, and 18) and deer or antelope people (chapters 1 and 6; also chapter 2). Present-day members of the clan represent all walks of life, from professors and politicians to blue-collar workers and alcoholic bums (chapter 11).

Shawano father of Mary (II) and Zosie (II). According to chapter 11 of *The Antelope Wife,* this man is the cousin of Shawano the ogitchida, Klaus and Frank Shawano's father. Thus when Zosie's daughter Rozin marries Frank, she is marrying a kinsman.

Shawano the ogitchida. Father of Frank and Klaus Shawano and cousin of the Shawano father of Mary (II) and Zosie (II) (chapter 11 in *The Antelope Wife*). In chapter 13, Shawano is referred to as the ogitchida (warrior) because he fights on the German front in World War II. After returning home in 1945, Shawano discusses with *clansmen* who are meeting in the house of *his uncle* how to avenge the death of *his cousin.* That night he kidnaps the young German prisoner of war Klaus, who bakes the blitzkuchen and is subsequently adopted into the clan.

Shawano the younger. Second husband of Blue Prairie Woman in *The Antelope Wife.* After the deer husband of Apijigo Bakaday is killed and her name is changed to Blue Prairie Woman (chapter 6), she marries the human man Shawano, even though he is descended from windigos. The couple spends winters away from the village, on the traplines with *Shawano's father* and *brothers.* When the U.S. Cavalry attacks the village in chapter 1 (probably in autumn), Shawano the younger is away harvesting wild rice. When he returns, he and his wife become "windigo" (insatiable) lovers. On his next return after a winter of trapping, however, his pregnant wife is indifferent to him.

Shawnee. Ira's oldest child in *The Painted Drum.* She is named for the "Shawnee prophet" respected by Ira and her family. The nine-year-old Shawnee is an unusually responsible child, a second mother to her siblings, Alice and Apitchi.

Shawnee

In part 3.1, Shawnee is taking care of the cold, hungry children while their mother is gone to town for supplies. When the heating oil runs out, Shawnee rigs a makeshift stove and builds a fire. But in part 3.3, she wakes to find the house burning and drags their blankets outside. When the ashes of the house fire cool, Shawnee ties Apitchi to her back, and pulling Alice along behind her, sets out through three miles of dark, freezing woods to their neighbor Bernard Shaawano's house, determined to save their lives. By part 3.5, however, her mind is slipping from the cold, and they fall into a snow-filled ditch. Shawnee is roused and led on by the sound of a drum. We learn in 3.6 that it is Shaawano's drum. No one is playing it. The "little girl drum" is calling to Shawnee on its own (*PD*, 148, 251).

In the hospital (part 3.7), Shawnee longs for her mother to acknowledge what she has done—gone to the edge of life and returned with her brother and sister. Instead, she feels that Ira blames her for burning down the house. Later, however, when her mother smiles at her, Shawnee's anger melts. That night, she hears the drum and is filled with joy.

Bernard is the one who best recognizes Shawnee's courage and strength. In the hospital, he pats her shoulder and tells her she is a strong little girl, a good sister. We learn from his letter the following September (part 4) that the tribe has built Shawnee and her family a new house.

Shawnee prophet. Wise person respected by Ira's family in *The Painted Drum*. Ira quotes this person in a conversation with John String in a bar in part 3.2. Her eldest daughter is named for the prophet, as are several members of her family, including her **cousin** and **great-aunt**.

Shawnee Ray Toose. Daughter of Irene Toose; mother of Redford Toose; lover of Lyman Lamartine and Lipsha Morrissey in *The Bingo Palace*. Chapters 1 and 2 introduce Shawnee Ray. After her father dies in a threshing accident, her mother remarries and moves to Minot. The teenage Shawnee Ray becomes pregnant, presumably by Lyman, and remains on the reservation to finish high school, living with Lyman's half sister Zelda Kashpaw. Zelda is trying to promote a marriage between Shawnee Ray and Lyman. Shawnee Ray, however, has plans of her own. Chapters 7 and 9 reveal that she is going to the local junior college and has a dream of creating Chippewa-accented fashion designs and ultimately opening a boutique.

When Lipsha Morrissey returns to the reservation in chapter 2, he sees Shawnee Ray dancing at the powwow and immediately falls in love with her. In chapter 4, he finally gets the courage to ask her out. On their way to a restaurant in Canada, they are stopped at the border and mistakenly taken into custody for drug possession. Lyman arrives to clear up the misunderstanding. In chapter 7, Shawnee

Ray encounters Lipsha at the laundry. Some friends drop them off at a motel where they make love for the first time. Shawnee Ray borrows money from Lipsha to help her launch her fashion design enterprise.

The rivalry between Lipsha and Lyman for Shawnee Ray's love is intense, as is clear in chapters 8, 11, 13, and 14. The ceremonial pipe of Nector Kashpaw, Lipsha's foster father and Lyman's actual father, becomes a symbol of that rivalry. Shawnee Ray continues to be attracted to Lipsha but, in chapter 9, tells him to give her some time so she can get her bearings. Lipsha honors her request for a short time, but then drives to Zelda's house to see her. They argue, Lipsha begs for another chance, and they make love on Shawnee Ray's bedroom floor. In chapter 10, Shawnee Ray feels confused. She had pictured herself marrying a stable man like Lyman, but she is in love with the still-directionless Lipsha. With the aid of Lipsha's money, she decides to get away from Zelda for a while.

In her efforts to raise money for college, where she wants to study art, in chapter 14 Shawnee Ray enters a big powwow in Montana, leaving Redford with her sisters, Tammy and Mary Fred Toose. Lyman and Zelda do not approve of this arrangement, so Lyman files a court order for custody of Redford, and in chapter 15, Zelda and the authorities take him from his aunts by force. At the powwow in chapter 16, as Shawnee Ray prepares for the jingle dress dance, she reminisces about her father.

After placing second in the powwow, Shawnee Ray returns to Zelda's house in chapter 17. She violently rejects Lipsha's marriage proposal, but she is angriest with Lyman because of the court order. She tells Lyman that he may not be Redford's father and says that she will never marry him. When Zelda's daughter, Albertine Johnson, comes to visit, she takes Shawnee Ray's side against Zelda.

In chapter 22, Shawnee Ray regains custody of Redford, leaves the reservation, and enrolls at the university. That winter, in chapter 26 Shawnee Ray and Redford are living in poorly insulated university housing. The morning after a January blizzard, she and Redford play in the snow, and then, while he sleeps, she works on a ribbon shirt for Lipsha—interest on the money he has loaned her. As she sews the shirt, she thinks of Lipsha with an ache and considers buying two wedding bands. The scene is made poignant by a knowledge that the reader, but not Shawnee Ray, possesses: Lipsha is snowbound in the blizzard and, as the book ends, his fate is uncertain.

Shawn Nanapush. Daughter of Gerry Nanapush and Dot Adare. According to "Scales" in *Love Medicine,* Shawn is conceived in the visiting room of a state prison, where Gerry is doing time. Gerry escapes once while Dot is pregnant with Shawn. He is recaptured but escapes again in order to be present at Shawn's birth

Shawn Nanapush

in October 1980. Four years later, Dot and Shawn seem to be living in Canada, where the newly escaped Gerry is headed in "Crossing the Water" so that he can see them.

As a thirteen-year-old in *Tales of Burning Love,* Shawn is athletic and tomboyish and is a much kinder, easier child than Dot had been at the same age. The summer after Shawn's thirteenth birthday, Dot marries Jack Mauser without divorcing Gerry. From brief references in "A Wedge of Shade" [3] and "Trust in the Known" [5], as well as their teasing and amiable jousting in "The Meadowlark" [7], it is clear that Shawn and Jack like each other. Even after Dot leaves Jack and moves with Shawn into an apartment in "Jack's House" [9], he wants to see Shawn ("February Thaw" [40]). But Shawn's affection for Jack does not compare with the attachment and longing she feels for her own father, Gerry. We learn in "Funeral Day" [23] that she keeps a framed photograph of Gerry on her bureau.

In his prison cell, in chapter 21 of *The Bingo Palace* Gerry also longs to be with his daughter. When, newly escaped from prison, he visits her early one January morning in "Smile of the Wolf" [38] in *Tales of Burning Love,* Shawn is overcome with emotion. In her seeming small talk, she tells Gerry about her neighbor's snowmobile and where the key is hidden. When marshals break down the door looking for him, he has already escaped again, presumably on the snowmobile. When two of the marshals question her, Shawn denies that she has seen her father and pretends that she and her mother are afraid of him.

Shesheeb I. Court-convicted windigo brother of Henri Laventure's oldest wife in chapter 3 of *The Antelope Wife.* **Shesheeb's sister** is a forebear of Rozina Roy. Shesheeb is an Ojibwe whose people live in the north, but after he is caught they begin moving south. Since the clan begins to be called Shawano after Shesheeb's capture, he may be the man referred to as the "original Shawano" in chapter 17. Both are windigos, and in both stories the people are still living in the north.

Shesheeb II. Older half brother of Pauline Puyat. According to chapter 8 of *The Last Report on the Miracles at Little No Horse,* Shesheeb is the firstborn child of Pauline's mother (whose name is also Pauline). The genealogical chart on the novel's end sheet indicates that Shesheeb's pureblood Ojibwe father is named **Mikwomengwane.** (Pauline is born twenty years later to a different father.) Chapter 7 of *Last Report* indicates that Shesheeb becomes a feared medicine man.

We learn more about this Shesheeb in *Four Souls.* In chapter 9, Nanapush says that Shesheeb has been cruel from childhood. Shesheeb's aunt **Iron Sky,** with whom he lives, sends him out on several vision quest attempts, after which he becomes even crueler. He gets his name, meaning black duck, at the Nanapush camp when he burns his hands in boiling sap (similar to Pauline's experience in

Tracks chapter 7). He even grows to look like a duck, and his laugh is a quack. Shesheeb begins to court Nanapush's beloved sister the winter she is fifteen. After they marry, he strikes her with a burning stick, leaving a darkening mark on her face, and the following starvation winter he turns windigo and kills and eats her. (He is never convicted in a white man's court.)

Shesheeb's second wife is a Lazarre, so when he moves back to Little No Horse as an old man, he helps the Lazarre family, thus reinforcing his enmity with Nanapush. He moves into Iron Sky's house down the road from Margaret. As Margaret cuts across his land on her way to church, he tries to stop her with his talk. Nanapush becomes jealous, suspecting that Shesheeb is using his medicine to steal her affections. These feelings, in turn, remind him of his dead sister, and he decides to take revenge. He first tries to use his medicine on Shesheeb, without success, and then makes a love medicine for Margaret. But when Shesheeb's dog eats the love potion, Nanapush returns to his plan of killing Shesheeb, this time with a snare. Nanapush's trap, however, snares Margaret instead of Shesheeb.

In chapter 11, when Margaret realizes that Nanapush was the one who set the snare, she punishes him by fueling his jealousy with admiring remarks about Shesheeb. One night after a fight between them, Margaret leaves. Wearing Margaret's medicine dress, Nanapush follows, assuming that she is at Shesheeb's. Shesheeb's failing eyes take Nanapush to be a woman, and he uses a medicine tea to control him. But under the influence of Nanapush's love medicine, Shesheeb's dog breaks the spell by frantically making love to Shesheeb's shin.

The next day, in chapter 13, when a blowfly harasses him, Nanapush decides that it is Shesheeb and captures and buries it. We learn in chapter 14 that Margaret has, in fact, walked to Shesheeb's house the previous night, but she knows that she is bluffing. Spying the unattractive old man, she admits that she loves Nanapush.

This half brother of Pauline is not the same Shesheeb as the one in *The Antelope Wife,* though there may be a connection, since both are windigo.

Shesheeb II's dog. The dog that eats Nanapush's love powder in *Four Souls.* Shesheeb's gray mutt is the skinniest, saddest, most runty-looking dog on the reservation. In chapter 9, Nanapush makes a love medicine to give to Margaret but when he is not looking, the dog eats it. A few days later, affected by the love potion, the dog breaks the spell Shesheeb has cast on Nanapush by making love to his master's shin. Apparently the medicine is powerful, because in "End of the Story" Nanapush says that the dogs subsequently born on the reservation all look like Shesheeb's mutt—round-faced runts.

Shimek, Mr. Father of Mazarine Shimek in *The Master Butchers Singing Club.* The Shimek family is introduced in chapter 5 as among the poor who come to

Shimek, Mr.

Fidelis Waldvogel's butcher shop for scraps and generally do not pay. In chapter 9, Delphine Watzka recalls hearing that Mr. Shimek is a roamer with a bad temper. As we learn in chapter 16, ironically, Mr. Shimek's laziness helps save newborn Delphine's life. Because he did not dig the hole for their new outhouse deep enough that autumn, after Mrs. Shimek casts the infant into the hole, Step-and-a-Half is able to reach her and pull her out.

Shimek, Mrs. Mother of Mazarine Shimek in *The Master Butchers Singing Club.* Like her husband, Mrs. Shimek is poor and lazy. We learn in chapter 16 that when she is young and newly married, Mrs. Shimek is a large, bovine woman, vacuous and incurious. In about 1907, she gives birth in an outhouse to her first child, casts the infant into the outhouse hole, and staggers away. Step-and-a-Half rescues the baby and takes her to Roy Watzka, who names her Delphine and does not reveal her true parentage.

Almost thirty years later, in chapter 9, Mrs. Shimek has become pendulously fat despite having little food and is frequently laid up with sick headaches. She runs up a large bill at the Waldvogel butcher shop. That December, when Franz Waldvogel walks through the bitter cold to Mazarine's house in chapter 11, the slovenly and crude Mrs. Shimek comes to the door, but she shuts it in his face. When Mazarine opens the door, her mother yells for her to "shut the damn door" (*MBSC*, 242), and when she builds up the fire to warm Franz, Mrs. Shimek warns her not to use up all the wood.

In chapter 14, when the Shimek son, Roman, is wounded and comes home in the fall of 1943 and Mazarine returns from teachers' training college, Mrs. Shimek goes to bed and won't get up. Mazarine does some menial chores for her, but mostly ignores her peevish cries.

Shumway, Mrs. Dot Adare's first-grade teacher at Saint Catherine's school in Argus who is forced into the classroom toy box in chapter 10 of *The Beet Queen* by a raging woman she does not know. She calls the police, and Officer Ronald Lovchik discovers that Mary Adare is the culprit and that she had been motivated by Dot's lie. Mrs. Shumway is also present at the Christmas pageant in chapter 11.

Simon Jack. Husband of Ziigwan'aage; lover of Anaquot; father of Niibin'aage and Fleur Pillager in *The Painted Drum.* In part 2.4, Anaquot's Shaawano husband refers to Simon Jack as "that demon Pillager" (*PD*, 149). Simon Jack is a different version of Fleur's father than the man simply called "Pillager" in *Tracks.* (See **Pillager family** for the differing versions of this family.) Simon Jack's contradictory character is summed up in the words, "He had a strict mind and a somewhat foolish heart" (*PD*, 135). Like Pillager in *Tracks*, Simon Jack is respected and somewhat feared, and the center of his consciousness is Ojibwe spirituality (*Painted Drum* part 2.3). Yet his folly is clear in his relationship with Anaquot, which ultimately destroys him. Even so, his irrationally passionate nature, as well as his love for gambling, is characteristic of the Pillagers that readers have met in earlier Erdrich novels.

We learn in part 2.3 that Simon Jack's manner gives him a power over others, which plays a part in Anaquot's falling in love with him. Although he is married to Ziigwan'aage and has three children with her (including Niibin'aage), he tells Anaquot that he is no longer married and never mentions his children. One autumn, Anaquot gives birth to Simon Jack's daughter (2.2), later called Fleur. That winter, Ziigwan'aage intercepts a message sent by Anaquot's Shaawano husband, and while Simon Jack is out on the trapline, she sends her brother to fetch Anaquot. When Simon Jack returns, an uncle warns him of Anaquot's presence, so he is able to avoid reacting when he sees her.

Over the following days, the tension in the cabin grows acute. One night, Simon Jack tries to slip beneath Anaquot's blanket, but she refuses him. After that night, Ziigwan'aage's heart turns firmly away from her husband toward Anaquot, and Simon Jack sleeps alone. He notices that the women work together each evening at their beading, and he guesses aloud that they are beading a dance outfit for him.

As the years pass, in part 2.5 Ziigwan'aage and Anaquot increasingly rebel against Simon Jack, making him a laughingstock. They also continue to bead and rebead Simon Jack's dance costume. When it is finished, he puts it on and never takes it off, even to sleep or to do dirty tasks, so he begins to reek. People avoid him, and his women bar him from his own cabin. Ziigwan'aage even begins sharing a tent with a younger man. One summer afternoon, the stinking Simon Jack joins the other men in a ceremonial dance circle. Both the songs and the direction of his dancing begin to go backward and become faster and faster until Simon Jack falls dead in the circle. The spirit of Anaquot's Shaawano daughter, who lives in the drum, has taken her revenge. When the reservation women prepare Simon Jack for burial, they discover that the beads of his costume have stitched themselves to his flesh. He is buried on the path to the Pillager camp, so that his women walk over his body as they come and go.

We learn in part 2.1 that Elsie and Faye Travers of New Hampshire are descendants of Simon Jack through his daughter Niibin'aage.

Singing Club. Men's singing group in Argus in *The Master Butchers Singing Club.* After living in the United States several years, in the early 1930s Fidelis Waldvogel misses his German master butchers singing club, and his singing with Doctor

Singing Club

Heech prompts him to start a similar group in Argus (chapter 3). Meeting in his butcher shop, the original members include Porky Chavers, Chester Zumbrugge, Gus Newhall, Albert Hock, Doctor Heech, and sometimes Roy Watzka. Pete Kozka later joins, and, according to chapter 13, so do Cyprian Lazarre and Sal Birdy.

After the Chavers family disappears in early 1934, in chapter 4 the group wonders where they are. Singing club members come to the July 4, 1935, gathering at the Waldvogels' in chapter 6. They sing patriotic songs and watch Fidelis pick up Sheriff Hock with his teeth. When Markus Waldvogel is buried in a collapsed tunnel in November 1936 (chapter 9), the whole singing club gathers, though there is nothing they can do to help. As Roy relapses into alcoholism in the late 1930s, he talks to his singing cronies about his reasons for drinking (chapter 12). In chapter 13, when Cyprian comes back through Argus shortly thereafter, he inquires about the singing club members. Once the German war begins, the singing club feels that, because of anti-German sentiment, they should sing non-German songs. By then, three of their original members have died.

Sioux vet. Old war veteran who talks with Lipsha Morrissey in a border-town hotel in "Crossing the Water" in *Love Medicine.* He says he was at Iwo Jima with Ira Hayes. When he accidentally hits Lipsha in the head with an empty Old Grand Dad bottle, Lipsha has a vision that his father is about to escape from prison. Lipsha recalls the incident in chapter 14 of *The Bingo Palace,* although there he remembers the bottle as a wine bottle.

Sita Kozka Bohl Tappe. Daughter of Pete and Fritzie Kozka. Sita is introduced in chapters 1 and 2 of *The Beet Queen* (1932) as a twelve- or thirteen-year-old living in her parents' house, which is attached to their butcher shop in Argus. She is beautiful, although almost frail, and, as the Kozkas' only child, she is accustomed to having her own way. When her eleven-year-old cousin, Mary Adare, comes to live with them, Sita dislikes having to share her room, her parents, and, especially, her best friend, Celestine James. In chapter 4, Sita is in her early twenties and wants to move away from Argus. Two incidents precipitate her leaving: her parents' move to the Southwest for Fritzie's health and Mary's hands' mysteriously glowing in the dark one night. Sita moves to Fargo to work in the DeLendrecies department store, hoping to marry a well-off young professional.

Nine years later, in chapter 5, Sita is still living in Fargo and modeling for DeLendrecies. She has had a three-year affair with a married doctor and is now (1950) dating Jimmy Bohl, who operates a steakhouse in Argus. She receives a letter, addressed to her parents but forwarded to her, from Catherine Miller, the woman who had raised Mary Adare's kidnapped infant brother, now named Jude

Miller. Sita goes to Minneapolis for Jude's February 18 ordination as a deacon, but she has no contact with the Millers. While in Minneapolis, she redeems from a pawn shop the garnet necklace of her aunt, Mary's mother Adelaide. Back in Fargo, she writes to Mrs. Miller, but never mails the letter, and she marries Jimmy Bohl. As a cruel prank, Jimmy's brother and cousins abduct her from the wedding dance and deposit her near a bar on the Indian reservation.

The year 1953 is eventful for Sita. In chapter 7, she is operating the Poopdeck Restaurant in Argus with her husband, Jimmy. When they divorce, in the settlement, Sita gets their house and the restaurant, which she remodels and reopens as Chez Sita. The grand opening of Chez Sita is a near disaster, however, and business soon dwindles to nothing. Because of several cases of food poisoning, the state health inspector visits the restaurant, and he and Sita begin dating. We learn from accounts at the end of chapter 7 and the beginning of chapter 8 that Sita marries the health inspector, a man named Louis Tappe. She sells the restaurant, he sells his house and takes a job as county extension agent, and they move to the big house in Blue Mound that Jimmy Bohl had built. As chapter 8 opens, Sita is bordering on a nervous breakdown. When her cousin Karl Adare shows up in her garden, she imagines that he steals her jewelry and hallucinates that he sinks down into the earth. In chapter 9, Wallace Pfef blames Mary Adare for Sita's mental problems.

At some unspecified time, as recorded in chapter 10, Louis has Sita committed to a mental hospital. She has decided that she is unable to speak, and the psychiatrists and nurses insist that Louis must stop humoring her. After spending only one night as roommate to a self-proclaimed cannibal, Sita is "cured." The next morning she can speak.

In chapter 12, Wallace invites Louis and Sita to Dot's eleventh-birthday party in January 1965. Sita, still high-strung, has thinned and aged since her stay in the hospital, and her condition has been a strain on Louis. At the party, Sita is hit in the face by a flying birthday cake.

By 1972 (chapter 13), Sita's husband Louis is dead. One night, Celestine has a dream about Sita, which Mary interprets as meaning that Sita is ill and is asking for Celestine. The two women drive to Sita's house in Blue Mound. At first they find little evidence of Sita's illness, but then they discover the orange pills hidden in a canister of flour, painkillers or tranquilizers to which she has become addicted. Because Sita continues to grow weaker, Celestine and Mary stay for weeks, even though Sita does not want them there.

One night, Mary accidentally hits Sita in the head with a brick. After this incident, Sita loses the use of her left arm and continues to weaken, but she has less pain. She stays in the basement, sleeping on the pool table and hiding her few remaining pills in the toilet tank. On the morning of the Beet Festival, while Celestine and Mary are gone, Sita swallows the remaining half-bottle of pills, dresses carefully, fixes her hair and face, and puts on Adelaide's garnet necklace. When Celestine and Mary return to take her to the parade, Sita is standing in the front yard, propped up in the yew bushes, dead. Since the funeral home is closed for the parade, the two women load Sita's body into the passenger seat of the truck and take her with them to the fairgrounds. On the way, in a scene of macabre humor, Sita is greeted by her former suitor, Officer Lovchik, and is accidentally included in the Beet Parade. Celestine and Mary leave her body in the truck while they attend the festival.

Sita continues to outlive her own death in chapters 14 and 15. In response to her twenty-year-old letter to Catherine Miller, which Celestine had found and mailed in chapter 13, Jude Miller comes to Argus on the day of the Beet Festival (chapter 14). Then, in chapter 15, Karl Adare rests in the truck for a few minutes and speaks to Sita, not realizing that she is dead. After the Beet Queen ceremonies are over, in chapter 16, Mary takes Sita's body to the funeral parlor.

Skunk. Appears to Lipsha Morrissey twice in *The Bingo Palace.* When Lipsha goes on a vision quest beside Matchimanito Lake (chapter 17), one morning he wakes to find a large female skunk sleeping on top of him. When she opens her mouth, Lipsha sees her pointy teeth and hears the words, "This ain't real estate." She then smiles and sprays him. The next night in his bed, in chapter 20 Lipsha again sees the skunk, who repeats her admonition and sends him a vision of what it would mean to commercialize sacred Pillager land.

Several details seem to connect the skunk to Fleur Pillager: her proximity to Matchimanito, her respect for the land, her gender, and her toothy smile, reminiscent of the dangerous Pillager grin. Furthermore, Fleur is a channel for animal spirits. In chapter 11 of this novel, she takes the form and voice of a bear. In chapter 3 of *Tracks,* Nanapush hears all the Manitous of the woods speak through her—Turtle, Loon, Otter, and others.

Slow Johnny Mercier. Incompetent Fargo sheriff in chapter 1 of *The Last Report on the Miracles at Little No Horse.* Slow Johnny is clumsy, physically and mentally slow, and hard of hearing. When he and *his deputy* respond to the Actor's bank robbery in 1911, Slow Johnny shoots the hostage, Agnes DeWitt, in the hip. He has difficulty getting a car to pursue the robbers both because he is such a bad driver and because everyone fears he will get Agnes killed. This is close to what happens. When Johnny and the deputy reach the Actor's mired car, they keep approaching even though the Actor is holding a gun to Agnes's head. Johnny's actions cause Agnes's severe injury and Berndt Vogel's death. Johnny and his deputy apparently capture the other two robbers and bring Agnes back to Fargo. *His posse* later finds the dead Actor and Berndt.

Small Bird. Sister of Fleur Pillager. Also known as Bineshii and Josette, she dies of consumption in chapter 1 of *Tracks.* She is mentioned again in chapter 9 of *Tracks* and chapter 3 of *The Bingo Palace.*

Sophie Morrissey. Middle child of Bernadette Morrissey; sister of Clarence and Philomena Morrissey. If we use dates from both *Tracks* and *The Last Report on the Miracles at Little No Horse,* it would appear that Sophie is already a drunk by age nine. In chapter 4 of *Tracks,* she is fourteen in 1917, and in chapter 7 of *Last Report,* she is part of a group of *seven drunks* in 1912. In *Tracks* chapter 4, however, Pauline Puyat describes the teenage Sophie as tall and beautiful, though lazy and slovenly. Both she and her younger sister have dainty French ways, the product apparently of their mother's education in Quebec. When Pauline comes to stay with the Morrisseys, she kicks the sisters in her nightmare-ridden sleep. In revenge for Eli Kashpaw's rejection of her, during hay cutting in 1917, Pauline uses a love medicine to bewitch Sophie and Eli into making love while Pauline's spirit enters Sophie's body. Bernadette beats Sophie and tries to send her away from the reservation, but she escapes and goes to Fleur Pillager's house. There Fleur casts a spell on her that roots her to the ground, rigid, for two days. Sophie's brother, Clarence, steals the statue of the Virgin to break the spell. The following winter, in chapter 5 Clarence avenges Eli's liaison with his sister by shaving the head of Eli's mother, Margaret Kashpaw.

Sophie grows thinner and wilder in chapter 6 and is seen dancing with Philomena. In 1919 (chapter 7), she marries Izear Lazarre, who already has six children by a previous wife, whom he is rumored to have killed. Sophie's new family, along with Clarence and his Lazarre wife, move into Bernadette's house. Disgusted with their behavior, Bernadette takes Philomena and the foster child Marie (Sophie's first cousin) and moves to town, after which the once-prosperous Morrissey household quickly deteriorates into a slum. Sophie is soon pregnant with the first of her many children. As Bernadette grows weak from consumption, in chapter 8 the slovenly Sophie Lazarre is increasingly the caretaker of Marie, who grows up thinking she is a Lazarre. (This caretaking raises the question of whether Sophie is either the **Old drunk woman** in "The Beads" in *Love Medicine,* whom Marie refers to as her mother, or **Marie Lazarre's aunt** in "Saint Marie.")

Fourteen years later, in 1934 (chapter 20 of *The Last Report on the Miracles at Little No Horse*), Marie is living in the woods selling whiskey, and Sophie is one of her regular customers. One day when Marie makes a delivery, Sophie begins talking about Marie's parents and finally tells Marie that her mother is Sister Leopolda.

Sorrow

Sorrow. Female dog who as a puppy nurses at Blue Prairie Woman's breasts in chapter 1 of *The Antelope Wife*. She is a puppy of the bitch who carries Blue Prairie Woman's baby (Matilda Roy) on her back (chapter 6). Sorrow follows Blue Prairie Woman in her search for this lost child and becomes the food that enables Matilda to survive. One of her descendants is Almost Soup, the dog saved in chapter 8 by Cally Roy, Blue Prairie Woman's great-great-granddaughter.

Margaret Kashpaw mentions Sorrow in chapter 16 of *Four Souls*. She says that one of Fleur Pillager's names is also "Sorrow," and she refers to the fact that the woman who slaughtered the dog is Fleur's aunt.

Sorrow's mother. Bitch who carries the infant Matilda Roy into the open spaces west of the Otter Tail River in chapter 1 of *The Antelope Wife*. When she flees the village, the bitch is young and swift and, according to chapter 6, has *six fat puppies.* Of these puppies, only Sorrow survives. One of the soldiers attacking the village, Scranton Roy, follows the fleeing dog. After three days he is able to lure her with food and remove the baby from her back. The bitch follows Scranton to the place where he settles on the Great Plains. By the time Matilda is six, this Indian dog may be dead, because a *hound* has taken her place.

Sorven, Mrs. Orlen. Friend of Tante Waldvogel in *The Master Butchers Singing Club.* Mrs. Sorven is apparently one of the *pious Lutheran ladies* in chapter 6 who, with Tante, hover over the dying Eva Waldvogel like vultures and "cluck" over the morphine she takes. Mrs. Sorven specifically tells Tante that Eva is addicted— Tante's excuse for stealing Eva's medicine in July 1935. When Delphine Watzka is chasing her drunken, naked father, Roy, in the street one March morning a few years later, he nearly runs down Mrs. Sorven near the Lutheran church (chapter 13).

Sounding Feather. Great-grandmother of first Shawano in *The Antelope Wife*. In the headnote to part 3, Sounding Feather dyes feathers in a mixture of copper and her own urine. The final color is affected by her treatment of *her mother, her child, her sisters,* and *her husband,* and she is frightened by the purity of the blue created after she has done wrong.

Standing in a Stone. Son of Nanapush and White Beads, mentioned in chapter 9 of *Tracks*. His Indian name is Asainekanipawit, and he is also known as Thomas. He dies as a child, along with his sister, Red Cradle.

Stan Mahng. Young Indian who commits suicide over a lost love. After his *girlfriend* leaves him, marries *another man,* and has *Stan's baby,* Stan visits them and holds his son. Then he goes to Matchimanito Lake, cuts a hole in the ice, ties stones to his feet, and slips through the hole into the freezing lake. Lipsha Morrissey recalls Stan when he is himself despairing over his unrequited love for Shawnee Ray Toose in chapter 14 of *The Bingo Palace.* Stan may have been a kinsman of Fleur Pillager or Xavier Toose, because we are told that his cousin's house was on Matchimanito Lake.

State health inspector. See **Louis Tappe.**

State trooper. Man Gerry Nanapush is said to have killed on the Pine Ridge reservation in "Scales" in *Love Medicine.* In "Crossing the Water," while Gerry's son, Lipsha Morrissey, is driving him to Canada after his 1984 escape, Lipsha asks him whether he really killed the trooper. Gerry apparently replies, but Lipsha refuses to tell readers his answer.

Statue of the Virgin at Argus. Near-human Italian stone statue given to Our Lady of the Wheat Priory in *Tales of Burning Love,* which, in "The Stone Virgin" [44], falls on Jack Mauser, nearly crushing him. An *anonymous benefactor* donates the money for the statue (this donor is also mentioned in "A Letter to the Bishop" [45]). An *Italian stonecutter* rough-cuts the statue, and an *Italian sculptor* fine-carves it. The *sculptor's wife* had recently lost a baby, their long-awaited *son,* and he carves the statue with an expression of repressed passion and wild grief.

Although not a character in the usual sense, the stone Virgin does appear to kiss Jack, to have an independent will, and later to sweat blood. Jack recognizes in her face all the women he has ever loved, and he believes that the accident fulfills Sister Leopolda's prophecy in "Night Prayer" [6] that he would be crushed by a woman, who would "snap his bones" and "throttle him with her kiss." The Virgin is gracious, however, for Jack is miraculously unharmed. The miracles surrounding the statue are detailed by Father Jude Miller in "A Letter to the Bishop" [45].

Statue of the Virgin on the reservation. Statue that seems to come to life in 1917 and weep frozen tears in chapter 4 of *Tracks.* Only Pauline Puyat sees the tears. Pauline refers to the statue as "the treasure of the mission," made of finest French plaster. The Virgin is stepping past the moon and standing on a serpent. She is full-figured, with a large nose, full lips, and, like the snake under her feet, eyes full of curiosity. See also **Madonna of the Serpents.**

Step-and-a-Half. Ojibwe woman who makes her living as a scrap picker—a collector of castoffs—in *The Master Butchers Singing Club.* A member of a northern French-Cree-Ojibwe tribe, her childhood experiences are recorded in chapters 13 and 16. She is apparently born in 1882, since she is eight in the winter of 1890 when she and her father go south to learn the ghost dance from the Lakotas. The

Step-and-a-Half

freezing and starving band they join meets its end in the massacre at Wounded Knee, where the child's father is killed. She follows the tracks of others who are fleeing till she reaches a mission and is saved. As an adult, she takes on her profession of wandering, always walking to escape the memories of murdered children and mothers. She takes the name Step-and-a-Half because of her long stride (see chapter 5), which can eat up twenty to thirty miles of North Dakota roads in a day.

We learn from chapter 16 that on her journeys she comes to Argus, where she stays a few weeks in the barn of farmer Roy Watzka, who falls in love with her and nicknames her Minnie. One night, passing the nearby Shimek place, Step-and-a-Half discovers Mrs. Shimek's newborn baby cast into the outhouse hole. She rescues the child and takes her to Roy's house, where they clean her and feed her. Eventually Step-and-a-Half goes back to her walking and Roy rears the child, whom he names Delphine. His fictitious story of Minnie, supposedly the child's dead mother, is modeled after Step-and-a-Half. Though Step-and-a-Half leaves Argus, she is drawn back again and again because of Delphine, and she eventually stays. When Delphine is a toddler, she calls out "Mama" to the passing woman and hits her for saying that her mother is dead. Delphine recalls Step-and-a-Half's giving her candy or a coin (chapter 5). After Step-and-a-Half settles in Argus, she lives in a cabin (chapter 9), and she gets to know the townspeople from the type of castoffs they leave on their back porches (chapter 16).

Our first direct glimpse of Step-and-a-Half, in chapter 5, is in the summer of 1934 when Delphine waits on her at the Waldvogel butcher shop, where Step-and-a-Half is a regular but nonpaying customer. She is rangy and string-bean shaped, has bright black eyes and a face that could be beautiful except for its lines of bitterness. Delphine guesses that she is in her thirties, but Step-and-a-Half by now would be about fifty-two. Knowing nothing of Step-and-a-Half's intervention twenty-some years before, Delphine is somewhat rude to her at first but then begins to reflect the respect with which Eva Waldvogel treats her.

After Eva dies in the summer of 1935 (chapter 7), Step-and-a-Half gives Delphine a fancy, tasseled lamp. (Delphine still enjoys it some years later in chapter 13.) One day that fall (chapter 8), when Step-and-a-Half comes to the butcher shop, Fidelis has used the scraps meant for her. Delphine tries to give her a steak, but Step-and-a-Half is resentful, feeling she must now pay for the meat. About the same time, Roy begins working with Step-and-a-Half (chapter 9). One day when she comes to the butcher shop, she warns Delphine vaguely that the Waldvogel boys are in danger. She also tells Delphine to beware of Cyprian (Delphine's companion), since he is a no-good Lazarre.

Sometime in 1936 (chapter 11), Step-and-a-Half opens a shop called Notions, which sells fabrics and miscellany. A very pregnant **Mrs. Knutson** works as shop-keeper. Step-and-a-Half is said to have leased the store and the room above with the stashes of money she is rumored to have buried at various places along her traveling route. One December day, Tante Waldvogel comes into the shop to ask for a job. She is horrified at the idea of working for someone she feels is a low-class woman, but Step-and-a-Half decides to hire her anyway, if she will learn to use the sewing machine.

Sometime that fall, Step-and-a-Half finds a red beaded dress on Clarisse Strub's back porch (chapter 11), and at dawn on Christmas morning, there is a whole trove of castoffs at Clarisse's house, including a fine carving knife. After breakfast, Step-and-a-Half gathers from her shop several pieces of fine fabric to give to Mazarine Shimek. A year or so later, after some of the Waldvogels move back to Germany, in chapter 13 Delphine comes to Notions looking for a job. Step-and-a-Half tells Delphine that Roy is drinking again and that she has kicked him out.

Years later, in probably the mid-1950s (chapter 16), Step-and-a-Half is an old woman (probably midseventies) who is able to do little walking and spends much of her time remembering and musing. She recalls her experience as a child at Wounded Knee, her saving the newborn Delphine forty-some years before, and the various scraps she has found on the back porches of Argus. She is pleased that Delphine and her (unbeknown to them) sister, Mazarine, now operate a plant shop together.

String family. A family that ministers to the drum in *The Painted Drum*. See **Chook String, John String, Mike String,** and **Morris String.**

Superior. Mother superior of the Sacred Heart Convent at Erdrich's fictional reservation in *Tracks*. See **Hildegarde Anne, Sister.**

Susy. Hitchhiking girl whom Henry Junior and Lyman Lamartine take home to Chicken, Alaska, during their long summer trip in "The Red Convertible" in *Love Medicine.* Her family befriends the brothers, who stay with them a while before returning home.

Swede Johnson. First husband of Zelda Kashpaw; father of Albertine Johnson. As recounted in "The World's Greatest Fishermen" in *Love Medicine,* he impregnates and then marries Zelda, joins the Army, goes AWOL from boot camp, and disappears. Albertine knows him only by his pictures. Eli recalls feeding him and Zelda skunk for dinner. Swede is also mentioned in chapter 3 of *The Bingo Palace.*

Sweetheart Calico. Present-day "antelope wife" of the novel *The Antelope Wife;* lover of Klaus Shawano. We are not told her true name. Klaus calls her Ninimoshe,

Sweetheart Calico

which means "my sweetheart" and is used to refer to a cross-cousin of the opposite sex, that is, a different-clan cousin whom one can marry. (In chapter 15, however, Klaus guesses that he and Sweetheart Calico may be from the same clan, possibly suggesting that their relationship is taboo.) Klaus's family in Minneapolis sometimes calls her Auntie Klaus, but most often they call her Sweetheart Calico, for the cloth Klaus uses to lure and bind her (chapter 11).

Sweetheart Calico may be descended from the Shawano deer-antelope women Blue Prairie Woman and Matilda Roy. Jimmy Badger's story in chapter 2 about Sweetheart Calico's ancestor, the girl who lived with the antelope, is congruous with the stories of both Matilda Roy in chapter 1 and Blue Prairie Woman (as Apijigo Bakaday) in chapter 6. This association is strengthened toward the end of the novel when we learn in chapter 18 that Sweetheart Calico is the possessor of Blue Prairie Woman's necklace of blue beads, which Matilda is wearing when she joins the antelope herd. Sweetheart Calico remembers running beside **her mother** in chapter 5. In chapter 21, she recalls being knocked into a horse pasture by a speeding car at age nine.

Klaus first encounters Sweetheart Calico and her three daughters in chapter 2 at a powwow in Elmo, Montana, where he has a trader's booth. Several details in the initial description of these women suggest their connection with the antelope people: their doeskin clothing, their effortless movement, and the mother's feathers from the red-tailed hawk, the bird that follows the antelope. Klaus attracts their attention by flicking a piece of sweetheart calico cloth. He then tricks the girls into taking a nap, gives the mother a soporific tea, and when she falls asleep, kidnaps her. When they stop in Bismarck, North Dakota, she realizes that he has trapped her. She fights to get free and breaks her teeth on the edge of the bathtub, but Klaus takes her home to Minneapolis. At night, he sometimes ties her to himself with a strip of sweetheart calico cloth. Although he appears not to believe Jimmy Badger's account of her ancestry, Klaus does think of Sweetheart Calico as his antelope woman (see chapters 2, 4, 10, 15, and 21).

In Minneapolis, Sweetheart Calico watches television, eats junk food, drinks, and (according to Klaus) tries to kill him with sex (chapter 2). What she does not do is talk. Klaus's narratives record her thoughts, but these are his subjective interpretations. (See especially chapter 4.)

According to chapter 5, Sweetheart Calico keeps trying to escape the city but is unable to do so. Chapter 11 notes that she walks sometimes for days, then returns with a pitiful, baffled look and sleeps for a week. Although she leaves Klaus again and again, she keeps coming back. His need, like the calico cloth, has tied her to a stake in the Minnesota soil (chapter 5); in his eyes she sees only an "ungated fence" (chapter 19); and she feels that she is "drowning" in him (chapter 18).

Sweetheart Calico

Our knowledge of Sweetheart Calico's life in the city is sketchy, and the chronology is unclear. In chapter 3, Rozina Roy sees her begging for money and eating a pastry in front of the bakery belonging to Klaus's brother Frank Shawano. At one point, Rozin tells us, Klaus disappears for four years, leaving Sweetheart Calico behind for his family to take care of. In chapter 11, Cally Roy says that Klaus and Sweetheart Calico both disappear for four years and that when Klaus returns, he has become a drunk and a bum. Thirteen years after the day Rozin sees her begging in front of Frank's bakery, Sweetheart Calico is living in rooms above the shop with Frank and his sister, Cecille.

Sometime between Sweetheart Calico's arrival in Minneapolis and Klaus's final return as a bum, while she is still living with him off and on, the two take a trip to Hawaii in chapter 4, using tickets given to them by Richard Whiteheart Beads. But on this ill-fated trip, the couple is shadowed by two government agents, who ultimately arrest Klaus. This incident is apparently the beginning of the end of their relationship, since a year later Klaus insists that Richard is responsible for his losing Sweetheart Calico. (Klaus seems to hint in chapters 4 and 10 that he thinks Sweetheart Calico and Richard are lovers.)

Another incident that takes place sometime before Sweetheart Calico moves in with Frank and Cecille, probably after the Hawaii trip, is alluded to in chapter 5. There is apparently an explosion where she is staying, and she is thrown through the window into the snow, covered with a melted plastic shower curtain. Street people take her to a shelter and clothe her.

When the eighteen-year-old Cally Roy moves to Minneapolis in chapter 11, Sweetheart Calico is living in the rooms above the bakery. Cally is unnerved by the silent "Auntie Klaus," with her fixed stare and jagged grin. Sweetheart Calico, however, seems to see Cally as a possible mode of escape. She wants the younger woman to join her on her multiday wanderings, which Cally will not do. One day Klaus, now a street bum, walks into the bakery, speechless with thirst. Sweetheart Calico, in a kind of "savage mercy," brings him a cup of water. Afterward, they walk out the door with arms around each other. If the accounts in chapters 11 and 12 are in chronological order, then Sweetheart Calico leaves Klaus after the cup-of-water incident, returns, and leaves again.

When Frank and Rozina Roy marry in chapter 16, both Sweetheart Calico and Klaus attend the wedding. When Richard Whiteheart Beads interrupts the cliffside ceremony and tries to leap from the cliff, Sweetheart Calico helps the Reverend hold onto his legs, smiling her dreamy, jagged-tooth smile.

The following Christmas (chapter 18), Sweetheart Calico does not seem to be still living at Frank's, but she is present at the family gathering. After dinner, she is in the kitchen as Cally washes dishes. Another suggestion of the relationship between

Sweetheart Calico

Sweetheart Calico and Cally's great-great-grandmother, Blue Prairie Woman, is Cally's comment that Sweetheart Calico has been to "the other side of the earth" (one of Blue Prairie Woman's names) where she has seen Blue Prairie Woman.

When Cally's grandmother, Zosie Shawano Roy, joins them in the kitchen, Zosie tells the story of Blue Prairie Woman's necklace of northwest trader blue beads and reveals that Sweetheart Calico is their owner. If Cally wants them, she must trade with the antelope woman. To Cally's astonishment, Sweetheart Calico draws the string of beads from her mouth, where she has been hiding them. These beads are the reason Sweetheart Calico has never spoken. Now, more than fifteen years after being kidnapped, she speaks, offering Cally her terms for trade—the beads in exchange for her freedom. At last Cally agrees to accompany Auntie Klaus on her long ramble through the city, walking north beyond the river. On their walk and through the night, Sweetheart Calico releases her pent-up words. When Cally wakes before the first light, the antelope woman is gone.

Sweetheart Calico's first sensations of freedom are recorded in chapter 19, but her full freedom requires that Klaus choose to release her. In chapter 20, he decides to do so, and in chapter 21, he carries out his decision. When Klaus sees her, Sweetheart Calico is not full of antelope life, but walks hesitantly, her once-vivid eyes and hair (see chapter 2) now lifeless. He ties their hands together with the old strip of sweetheart calico cloth. They walk north and then west. Where they sleep that night, they see the skeleton of a dog chained to a shed, a mirror of Sweetheart Calico's life-defeating captivity. The next morning they reach the vast open spaces west of the city. When Klaus unties the strip of cloth and tells her to go, she does not bound off, as he expects, but wearily makes her way west. Once or twice she attempts to run—leaps and falls—until finally she disappears at the horizon.

Sweetheart Calico's daughters. Polite, demure women who dance with their mother at the Elmo, Montana, powwow in chapter 2 of *The Antelope Wife*. Each girl ties up her hair differently as she dances. The trader Klaus Shawano tricks the girls into taking a nap so that he can kidnap their mother. Sweetheart Calico makes numerous long-distance calls to Montana from Minneapolis, apparently trying to find them. She dreams about them in chapter 5.

According to Jimmy Badger in chapter 2, the women are descended from a girl who lived with the antelope, and they seem to have special powers. After their mother's abduction, they are angry, causing the tribe's luck to change for the worse. Much later, the alcoholic Klaus sees a vision of them (chapter 10). Richard Whiteheart Beads warns Klaus that the daughters will "get" him for destroying their mother (chapter 15).

Sweetheart Calico's sisters. In the alcoholic Klaus Shawano's vision in chapter 10 of *The Antelope Wife,* the twenty-six sisters are antelope women, galloping with Sweetheart Calico and her daughters.

T

Tammy Toose. See **Mary Fred and Tammy Toose.**

Tante (Maria Theresa) Waldvogel. Sister of Fidelis Waldvogel in *The Master Butchers Singing Club.* Tante is one of Erdrich's least sympathetic characters. Glimpses of her character are found in multiple chapters (see especially 5, 6, 7, 8, and 12). She is depicted as spoiled and arrogant, keenly sensitive to her status. Her sense of superiority renders her cold and critical, even cruel. Yet she has little to be proud of, with virtually no useful skills, and except for her slim, pretty feet, she has an unattractive, severe appearance. Like certain others of Erdrich's unsympathetic characters, Tante is narrow, self-righteous, and intense in her religion. She is both stingy and greedy, as seen especially in her attitude toward food. Although she does a few helpful things for her family, she does them without a real spirit of generosity.

We first meet Tante (Maria Theresa) in Germany in 1918 (chapter 1), when she picks lice from Fidelis's hair upon his return from the war. Chapter 8 reveals that after Fidelis immigrates to the United States in 1922, he works eighteen-hour days to save the money to bring Eva and Franz, and then Tante, to join him in Argus. The tiny house Tante buys is next door to the Lutheran church, where she prays each Sunday that the dreadful Catholic her brother has married will give up her idolatry (chapter 6). In chapter 5, Tante lends Fidelis five hundred dollars to buy equipment for his butcher shop. He pays her back, but ever after she takes as her due anything she wants from the shop. Sometime in the early 1930s, on a trip to Canada, Tante smuggles whiskey back through customs to avoid paying taxes on it. When Delphine begins working at the butcher shop in the summer of 1934, from the beginning Tante treats her with contempt.

After Eva becomes terminally ill that summer, in chapter 6 Tante and a group of *pious Lutheran ladies* come every few afternoons, like "turkey vultures" (*MBSC,* 122), to pray over this heathen Catholic. When Eva becomes too weak to chase them off, Delphine learns she can get them to leave Eva alone by having food available in the kitchen. Tante and her friends become convinced that Eva is addicted to her morphine, so Tante steals the medicine and pours it down her

Tante (Maria Theresa) Waldvogel

drain. On July 4, 1935, an enraged Delphine shows up at Tante's door and throws things out of her fridge, looking for the medicine. When she sees the empty vial by the sink, she forces Tante to stay with the agonized Eva while Delphine looks for the doctor. At first, Tante is delighted to be put in charge, but by the time Delphine returns, after hearing Eva's wailing for hours, Tante is white with shock. Later that summer, Tante comes to Eva's last birthday in chapter 7 for the usual reason—the cake. While there, she asks Delphine how much extra Fidelis pays her to take care of Eva, and Delphine calls her a "hypocrite sow" (*MBSC,* 134).

After Eva dies, Tante distributes Eva's clothes to the needy but takes her figurines and jewelry for herself (see chapter 13). With Eva (and eventually Delphine) gone, Tante supposedly cares for the family (chapter 7), but she is totally inept. She cannot cook and is unable to keep up with the laundry, and worse, she beats Markus because he has begun wetting the bed. When Fidelis goes out on deliveries, Markus runs away to Delphine's house. The next morning, Tante comes to fetch him and is angry when Delphine lies that she hasn't seen him. When Fidelis comes for Markus, Delphine sees his dirty, rumpled clothes and realizes how bad things have become with Tante in charge. But she refuses to return to work unless Fidelis tells Tante to leave. When he comes back a few days later, he has sent Tante away and begs Delphine to return.

In chapter 8, Tante is angry over her dismissal by her brother, realizing that it has diminished her standing in Argus. She gathers information about Delphine and bad-mouths her in town gossip, to Fidelis, and in letters home. She has fantasies of returning to Ludwigsruhe but realizes that for status's sake, she must return with the boys, as their caretaker, not alone. Another status option would be to make money. The bookkeeping she does for Fidelis and two other businesses earns little, so she pawns her grandmother's cameo, buys a metallic suit, and begins to hunt a job. She has no success and is further demoralized when, wearing her shiny suit, she is struck by a car. When Sheriff Hock comes to the shop to tell Delphine he has arrested her father, Tante overhears—more fuel for her gossip. She also spreads rumors about Delphine and Fidelis.

The summer after Eva dies (1936, chapter 9) the younger Waldvogel boys are unsupervised and virtually without taming influences in their lives. When Tante lobbies Fidelis to take them to the Lutheran church, he turns a deaf ear. But by that December, chapter 11, after Markus's dangerous experience in the collapsed hill, Fidelis is more receptive to another of her campaigns—that she should take the boys to Germany. Tante also continues to job hunt. She finally swallows her pride and takes a job in Step-and-a-Half's shop, Notions, where she learns to use a Singer sewing machine. That Christmas, when Fidelis mentions wanting to visit home, Tante stresses the value of such a move for the boys.

One February between this Christmas and the beginning of World War II, in chapter 12 the Waldvogels prepare for Tante and the three youngest boys to go to Ludwigsruhe for a year or two. Fidelis and Delphine drive them to Chicago, where they will take the train to New York. The food items Tante and Delphine take on the trip illustrate the contrast between Tante's stinginess and Delphine's nurturing generosity, as do the women's differing reactions to the idea of lunch the next day. Tante and Delphine's two nights together in a hotel room are difficult for Delphine. When the travelers are ready to leave for New York, Markus becomes ill, so Tante and the twins go without him. Later that year, in chapter 14 Tante writes Fidelis from Germany telling him that the twins are involved in a government youth group.

In chapter 15, when Fidelis and Delphine go to Ludwigsruhe in 1954, at the memorial ceremony, Delphine sits beside Tante, who ignores her. Delphine notices that Tante still has her elegant feet clad with fine shoes.

Tatro family. See **Jewett Parker Tatro, John Jewett Tatro, Kit Tatro,** and **Sarah Tatro.** John Tatro's brother is *Burden Tatro* (*The Painted Drum* part 1.2). Also, in an earlier generation, a road in Stokes, New Hampshire, is named for *Colonel John Tipton Tatro* (part 1.3).

Tensid Bien. Elderly customer of the Waldvogel butchery in *The Master Butchers Singing Club*. Introduced in chapter 5, Tensid is stone broke but courtly and immaculate. He buys meager supplies in the butcher shop and browses at length (and samples) the Sunshine cookies. In chapter 13, Tensid helps Delphine Watzka land a clerical job at the courthouse.

Testor, Mrs. See **Nettie Testor, Mrs.**

Thomas Nanapush. See **Standing in a Stone.**

Three fires people. Term used to refer to Rozina Roy's distant ancestors in chapter 3 of *The Antelope Wife*. (Three Fires was the name of a confederation of three Algonquian tribes, including the Ojibwe.)

Tillie Kroshus. Nanny of John Mauser Jr., infant son of Jack Mauser and Marlis Cook Mauser, hired by Candice Pantamounty in *Tales of Burning Love*. Mrs. Kroshus shows up first in "Memoria" [10], taking care of the baby at Jack's funeral. After the funeral, in "The B & B" [16], she takes John Jr. home to Candice's house. There, in "Funeral Day" [23], she has to deal with a stranger at the door who claims to be Jack's brother and asks to see the baby and to borrow Candice's car. (The "brother" is actually Jack.) Mrs. Kroshus tries unsuccessfully to outsmart him and escape with the baby, but Jack ties her up and steals the car with John Jr. strapped inside. The incident is retold in "Two Front-Page Articles" [37], in which Mrs. Kroshus accuses Jack of faking his own death.

Tillie Kroshus

Titus. Bartender in Lyman Lamartine's bingo hall. He brings Lipsha Morrissey a hamburger in chapter 8 of *The Bingo Palace* and warns him to be alert in dealing with Lyman. He is also mentioned as Lipsha's friend and coworker in chapters 14, 20, and 22.

Tomahawk factory workers. Reservation inhabitants employed in Lyman Lamartine's tribal business, Anishinabe Enterprises, in "The Tomahawk Factory" in *Love Medicine*. These workers are members of various reservation families and include **Norris Buny, Agnes Deer, Eno Grassman, Bertha Ironcloud, Kyle Morrissey, Billy Nanapush,** and **Felix Pukwan.** See also **Lipsha Morrissey, Lulu Nanapush Morrissey Lamartine, Marie Lazarre Kashpaw,** and **Mary Fred Toose.**

When these workers' employment is threatened because of low-volume sales of their products, an interfamily brawl precipitates a riot in which the workers destroy the factory.

Tom B. Peske. Pilot hired by Wallace Pfef in chapter 14 of *The Beet Queen* to skywrite "Queen Wallacette" at the Beet Queen coronation. Dot Adare herself (that is, Wallacette) is an unexpected passenger on the flight, as recorded in chapters 15 and 16.

Toose. First husband of Irene Toose and father of Shawnee Ray, Mary Fred, and Tammy Toose. We learn in chapter 15 of *The Bingo Palace* that he dies in a threshing accident. It is clear from his daughters' memories of him that they loved and miss him. In chapter 15, the tribal police officer tries to weaken Mary Fred by speaking of her dead father. Before the jingle dance competition of an important powwow in chapter 16, Shawnee Ray remembers that her father helped her learn the steps to this dance and, when she was eight or nine, helped her access the grace of the butterfly.

Toose family. See **Irene Toose, Mary Fred and Tammy Toose, Redford Toose, Shawnee Ray Toose, Toose,** and **Xavier Albert Toose.**

Tor Grunewald. Employee at Pete Kozka's butcher shop in *Tracks*. In chapter 2, Tor plays cards with Lily Veddar, Dutch James, and Fleur Pillager in the evenings after work. One hot night in August 1913, enraged at Fleur's winnings, Tor and the others attack her. The next day the three men take shelter from a tornado in the meat locker, and Pauline locks them in. When they are found several days later, Tor has frozen to death. He reappears in Pauline Puyat's death vision in chapter 6, again playing cards with Fleur.

Travers, Professor. Husband of Elsie Travers and father of Faye and Netta in *The Painted Drum*. Travers meets Elsie when she is handling his mother's estate (part

1.4). After they marry, they buy a new house in Stokes, New Hampshire (1.2), and Travers commutes thirty miles to the university where he teaches.

Travers is described in part 1.4 as graceful and scholarly in appearance, with a puffed mass of hair. He is an underpaid philosophy professor who prides himself on being an intellectual, but whose dissatisfaction with his lack of achievement renders him petty and contentious. A controller and a liar, he deliberately sets family members against one another. When the book he has worked on for years collects editors' rejection slips, he withdraws even further from his wife and children.

One summer evening when Elsie is away (Faye is at least nine), Travers leaves his study and goes out to fetch his daughters from the apple orchard. When they taunt him and refuse to come, he tries to coax them to jump from the tree for him to catch. But when Faye slips and falls, he steps aside and allows her to hit the ground. Netta sees this cruelty and deliberately steps from her high branch, falling to her death. Travers apparently lies about the incident, implying that Faye is responsible for Netta's death. We learn in part 1.2 that Travers dies six months later. We are given no cause of death.

Twins, beading. Mythical twins in the headnotes to parts 1 and 2 of *The Antelope Wife,* also alluded to in chapter 23, who sew the pattern of the world, one working with light beads, the other with dark. Each tries to add one more bead than her sister, thereby upsetting the balance of the world. In the headnote to part 4, the *second twin* gambles everything for ruby-red whiteheart beads. When *her children* swallow the beads, she pursues them with a knife.

The beading of Zosie Roy, Mary Shawano, and Rozina Roy in chapters 9 and 18 mirrors the pattern-creation of the mythic twins.

Two Hat. Man under whose window a fox barks. The incident is referred to in chapter 12 of *The Bingo Palace* as possible evidence of the occult doings of Fleur Pillager. The context seems to associate the fox's barking with Fleur's designation of people to take her place on death's road. Jean Hat, possibly related to Two Hat, had been one of the first to take Fleur's place. See also **Hat family** and **Jean Hat.**

U

Under the Ground. Healer and mother of Anaquot in chapter 5 of *Four Souls.* As a child, her name is Fanny Migwans. She is born on the great red Ojibwe island, daughter of a long line of women healers. When Fanny is still a young girl, her mother dies of the "welted sickness." So Fanny decides to pursue death by having herself buried alive for four days, connected to the world only by a breathing straw.

Under the Ground

From this experience she gains great knowledge and healing power and takes the name Anamaiiakiikwe—Under the Ground woman.

In midlife, Under the Ground has a daughter by an **Odawa man** whom she loves. She names the laughing child Anaquot (Cloud). At age eleven, Anaquot falls sick from an unfamiliar disease. Traditional healing seems to cure her, but the next winter she falls ill again and is close to death. Healing fails until Under the Ground slashes her own arms to the bone and then throws out one of the girl's souls. The soul returns to Anaquot, who is subsequently known as Four Souls. (See **Four Souls**.)

Unexpected, the. Nanapush's second wife, mentioned in chapters 3 and 9 of *Tracks*. Her sexual desires are said to live up to her name. Her Indian name is Zezikaaikwe.

V

Veteran. See **Sioux vet.** See other war veterans by their given names, such as **Henry Lamartine Junior** and **Russell Kashpaw**.

Vilhus Gast. The Snake Man, Cyprian Lazarre's balancing-act partner in chapter 13 of *The Master Butchers Singing Club*. Sometime after Cyprian leaves Argus with Clarisse Strub in December 1935 and then parts from her in Minneapolis, he hooks up with Vilhus, a Jew from Lithuania. Vilhus is interested in the fact that Cyprian is an Indian, so Cyprian takes him home for a visit on the Ojibwe reservation. The performing pair travels with the lyceum series and comes to Argus shortly before the beginning of World War II. Their show features Vilhus's python and hairy spiders, one of which is named Mighty Tom, and a spoof of Adolf Hitler. Cyprian and Vilhus leave after the performance and do not return.

W

Waldvogel family. German immigrant family in *The Master Butchers Singing Club*. See **Delphine Watzka Waldvogel, Emil and Erich Waldvogel, Eva Waldvogel, Fidelis Waldvogel, Franz Waldvogel, Johannes Waldvogel, Markus Waldvogel, Mazarine Shimek,** and **Tante (Maria Theresa) Waldvogel**.

Waldvogel, Mrs. Sita Tappe's elderly roommate in the state mental hospital who believes herself to be a cannibal in chapter 10 of *The Beet Queen*. Mrs. Waldvogel shows Sita photographs of her family—including **her son,** a **baby,** and someone named **Markie**—and implies that she has eaten one of them. There is no indication that this woman is kin to the Waldvogels of *The Master Butchers Singing Club.*

Wallace Pfef. Argus community leader in *The Beet Queen.* In chapter 9, we learn his full name, Wallace Horst Pfef, and something of his family background and his involvement in the Argus community. To deflect curiosity about the fact that he has never married, Wallace keeps in his living room a picture of a girl he doesn't know, telling the townsfolk that she is his *"poor dead sweetheart."* (She is also referred to obliquely in chapter 6.) In 1952, Wallace attends the Crop and Livestock Convention in Minneapolis (chapters 6 and 9), where he learns about the sugar beet as a successful cash crop. While there, he meets Karl Adare and has his first homosexual experience. After Karl injures his back, Wallace visits him in the hospital. On his way home, Wallace stops beside the road and converses with Ronald Lovchik about his vision of Argus's future wealth from the sugar beet industry.

As chapter 9 continues, over the next year Wallace tries to forget about Karl, although frequenting the butcher shop of Karl's sister, Mary, makes this more difficult. On one of these visits to the butcher shop, Wallace gives Mary and Celestine James invitations to the opening of the restaurant Chez Sita (chapter 7). One spring evening in 1953, Karl phones Wallace and then shows up at Wallace's house the next night. They live together for two weeks, and then Karl suddenly disappears. Following a stray dog one evening about a week later, Wallace finds Karl sitting in his underwear in Celestine's backyard. (This dog is mentioned in chapter 13 as later belonging to Wallace.) The following January (1954), stranded in a blizzard, Celestine gives birth to Karl's baby in Wallace's living room. Grateful for his help, Celestine names the baby girl Wallacette, although everyone except Wallace calls her by her nickname, Dot.

As Dot grows up, chapters 9 and 12 record that she and Wallace are close. Once, when she runs away from home, she goes to Wallace's house. In 1964, she invites him to come see her in the school Christmas play and borrows his old bathrobe for her costume. During the performance, dressed in the bathrobe that Karl once wore, Dot is transformed in Wallace's eyes into Karl himself. Thus, when she comes to his house after the ill-fated play, he refuses to let her in. After this incident, Wallace feels guilty, and Dot will hardly speak to him. Finally, when he gives her a party in January for her eleventh birthday, they are friends again.

As a rebellious teenager in chapter 14, Dot at times shares her feelings with Wallace, and he tries to help her. When she is eighteen, he dreams up the idea that Argus should hold a Beet Festival that will include coronation of a Beet Queen—

Wallace Pfef

namely Dot. Wallace throws himself completely into the yearlong preparations, and to ensure Dot's triumph, he rigs the vote. By the day of the festival (chapters 14, 15, and 16), Wallace is near collapse. After Dot overhears people gossiping about Wallace's vote-rigging, she takes revenge by dunking him in the dunking tank. Wallace, Karl, Celestine, and Mary watch from the grandstand as Dot runs away from the Beet Queen coronation and flies off in the skywriting plane. That evening Karl's car is parked in front of Wallace's house.

Wallacette Darlene Adare. See **Dot Adare Nanapush Mauser.**

Wekkle, Father Gregory. See **Gregory Wekkle, Father.**

Wenabojo. Trickster spirit who creates humans. According to chapter 8 of *The Antelope Wife,* Original Dog is Wenabojo's companion. See also **Nanabozho.**

White Beads. Third and most-loved wife of Nanapush, mentioned in chapters 3, 5, and 9 of *Tracks.* Her Indian name is Wapepenasik. They have a daughter, Red Cradle, and a son, Standing in a Stone. By the winter of 1912, White Beads and her children have died, leaving Nanapush with no immediate family. In chapter 3, Nanapush gives Eli Kashpaw some of White Beads's personal belongings for Eli to use as a love gift to Fleur Pillager, and in chapter 5, he tells Eli to fall to his knees and clutch Fleur's skirt, as he himself used to do to soften the heart of White Beads.

Whiteheart Beads family. According to chapter 23 of *The Antelope Wife,* this family name originates because of a blanket decorated with red whiteheart beads that Midass gives to a ***pregnant woman.*** The woman's son so loves the decoration that he is called ***Whiteheart Beads.*** The ***Whiteheart Beads ancestors*** are also referred to in chapter 16. This family may be part of the Shawano clan, since the original Whiteheart Beads lives in the same village as the Shawanos.

See **Cally Whiteheart Beads Roy, Deanna Whiteheart Beads, Richard Whiteheart Beads,** and **Rozina (Rozin) Roy Whiteheart Beads Shawano.**

Windigo Dog. Dog or dog spirit that visits the drunken Klaus Shawano after Sweetheart Calico leaves him in *The Antelope Wife.* In chapter 12, Windigo Dog tells Klaus a dirty dog joke about a ***Ho Chunk Winnebago dog,*** a ***Sioux dog,*** and an ***Ojibwa dog.*** In return, Klaus tells him the story of the original Klaus (chapter 13). In chapter 20, Windigo Dog tells Klaus an anti-Indian story about ***three dogcatchers*** and their ***trucks full of dogs.*** (Lyman Lamartine tells Lipsha Morrissey another version of this story in chapter 9 of *The Bingo Palace.*) Windigo Dog verbally abuses Klaus, but at least once also gives him advice (chapter 15). He is probably the ***stray dog*** who sacrifices himself to save Klaus's life in chapter 20.

There may be a connection between Klaus's Windigo Dog and Cally Roy's dog, Almost Soup. "Windigo Dog" is the subtitle of Almost Soup's chapter 8; both dogs are white; and both are ultimately willing to sacrifice themselves for their humans. Nevertheless, there are important differences. Although he narrates two chapters, Almost Soup is a real dog who stays on the reservation when Cally comes to the city. Klaus's Windigo Dog lives in Minneapolis and seems more metaphysical than physical. He is the "bad spirit of hunger" that overpowers Klaus in Sweetheart Calico's absence (chapter 12). As such, he mirrors Klaus's insatiable, destructive passion. When Windigo Dog disappears in chapter 20, Klaus is finally able to master his windigo cravings.

Windigo stranger. Man in Rozina Roy's dream who invites her to pass to the next life through his icy body in chapter 17 of *The Antelope Wife*. (In the myths, Windigo is a bad ice spirit, possessed of an insatiable, often cannibalistic, hunger. Erdrich at times uses this figure to represent any excessive, possessive passion.) See also **Shawano, original.**

Workers who build Mauser's house. Common people whose pain and death produce Mauser's showplace house in chapter 1 of *Four Souls*. Unhappy *Italians* quarry the brownstone from a tree-stripped, holy Ojibwe island. *Young women at Indian missions* use native talents to create lace for the windows. In a famine autumn, a *destitute family* sells a crystal of pyrite. Starving *Norwegians* and *Sammi* mine iron on the Mesabi Range. *Sweating men* set stone, bevel glass, and lay floors. *Coughing women* sew linens in a basement. It is a house made of *crushed hands, collapsed horses,* and *unpaid masons and drivers.*

X

Xavier Albert Toose. Uncle of Shawnee Ray, Mary Fred, and Tammy Toose in *The Bingo Palace*. Xavier is referred to as Shawnee Ray's uncle in chapter 4, apparently her father's brother. According to the "tale of burning love" recounted by Zelda Kashpaw in chapter 5, as a young man, the handsome Xavier courts Zelda for a year. She consistently refuses him, because she wants a city life and Xavier is an old-time Indian devoted to the traditional religious ceremonies. One winter night, he says he will wait outside until she admits that she loves him. As a result of his freezing vigil, he loses the fingers on one hand. (Without naming Xavier, Dot Mauser recalls this incident in "February Thaw" [40] in *Tales of Burning Love*.) Although Zelda marries two other men, both white, Xavier is the only man she ever loves. Chapter 3 indicates that she names her daughter, Albertine, after Xavier,

Xavier Albert Toose

and in chapter 19, Albertine confronts Zelda with the fact that she has never gotten over him.

In chapter 10, Xavier continues his devotion to traditional Ojibwe ways and passes his knowledge on to his nieces. Shawnee Ray has learned from him the Chippewa way to make moccasins. He has studied the old-time medicine and is conducting sweat lodge ceremonies with Mary Fred to cure her alcoholism. It is Xavier to whom Lipsha Morrissey and Lyman Lamartine turn when they want to do a vision quest in chapter 14, and in chapter 17, Xavier guides them through the attendant ceremonies. One night, thirty years after her rejection of Xavier, in chapter 23 Zelda realizes that she has never stopped loving him. When she goes to see him the next day, without any exchange of words, he understands and escorts her into his house.

Z

Zelda Kashpaw Johnson Bjornson. Eldest daughter of Nector and Marie Kashpaw. According to Nector, in "The World's Greatest Fishermen" in *Love Medicine,* Zelda is born September 14, 1941. In 1948 ("The Beads"), Zelda prevents her sister and brother, Aurelia and Gordie, from hanging their cousin, June Morrissey. That same year, when their grandmother Margaret (Rushes Bear) comes to stay with the family, she bedevils the children and pulls Zelda's hair. In "Flesh and Blood" (1957), Marie takes sixteen-year-old Zelda to show off to Sister Leopolda, Marie's former teacher and adversary. Upon returning from that visit, Zelda finds Nector's letter saying that he is leaving Marie. She hands the letter to her mother, goes after her father—who has just set fire to Lulu Lamartine's house—and brings him home. Zelda's coming to fetch her father is told from Nector's point of view in "The Plunge of the Brave." As Zelda grows up, she is haunted by the memory of her father's burning his lover's house, an incident she views as evidence of the dangers of love. As a result, according to chapters 1, 5, and 23 of *The Bingo Palace,* she closes her heart to love.

While Zelda is still a young woman, the handsome Xavier Toose courts her, as recounted in chapter 5 of *The Bingo Palace.* Zelda loves him, but he is a traditional Indian and she wants a city life with a white man. Thus she rejects him, even though he freezes his fingers courting her. (This incident seems to occur not long after Nector's burning of Lulu's house, since chapter 23 of *The Bingo Palace* places both incidents thirty years in the past.) After rejecting Xavier, Zelda is said in chapter 14 to lose her "love-luck." At one point, she aspires to become a nun, but

Zelda Kashpaw Johnson Bjornson

instead she allows herself to become pregnant by a white man, Swede Johnson, whom she then marries, as recounted in "The World's Greatest Fishermen" in *Love Medicine.* But before their daughter is born in 1958, Swede goes AWOL from boot camp and is never seen again. According to chapter 3 of *The Bingo Palace,* Zelda names the child Albertine after Xavier, whose middle name is Albert.

"The World's Greatest Fishermen" indicates that after her daughter is born, Zelda moves into a trailer near Marie and Nector and works as a bookkeeper. She blames Albertine for her lost opportunities, and Albertine repays her by being a difficult child, even running away as a teenager. (See also "A Bridge" and chapter 19 of *The Bingo Palace.*) In 1981, Zelda has a new white husband, Bjornson, who has a wheat farm on the edge of the reservation, and her daughter is a responsible young woman in nursing school. But Zelda and Albertine still do not get along. Zelda's conversations with Aurelia in "The World's Greatest Fishermen" and with Lipsha Morrissey in "Love Medicine" also reveal that she is as controlling and critical with other members of the family as she is with her daughter.

In *The Bingo Palace,* Bjornson is never mentioned, Zelda once again uses her Kashpaw name, and according to chapters 4 and 9, she is living at the old Kashpaw house. She has taken in Shawnee Ray Toose and her son, Redford, and is attempting to control their lives. Her ultimate goal is for Shawnee Ray to marry Lyman Lamartine (Zelda's half brother). She is thus an obstacle to Lipsha's courtship of Shawnee Ray (chapters 9 and 19). There are hints in chapters 11 and 14 that Zelda is not above manipulating tribal records to achieve her goals: she seems to have written in Lyman as Redford's father, and she may be hindering Lipsha's efforts to become enrolled. To get her to lighten up on Shawnee Ray, in chapter 5 Lipsha slips gin into her tonic water at the bingo parlor. Stimulated by the gin, Zelda tells Lipsha about Xavier and about her rescue of Lipsha as an infant.

In chapter 10, Zelda tries unsuccessfully to keep Shawnee Ray from going to stay with her sisters, Tammy and Mary Fred Toose. When Shawnee Ray is away at a powwow in chapter 15, Zelda goes with a social worker and tribal police officer to take Redford from the Toose sisters. Shawnee Ray returns to Zelda's house in chapter 17, but in chapter 19, she decides to leave for good. Albertine confronts Zelda about her attempts to control Shawnee Ray and strikes a nerve when she asks Zelda about Xavier.

One afternoon after Shawnee Ray leaves, in chapter 23 Zelda finds her father's ceremonial pipe in her kitchen, a token from Lyman conceding that their pact has failed. That night, believing that she is having a heart attack, Zelda thinks back over her life. She regrets her lifelong rejection of passion and realizes that she has always loved Xavier. With the realization comes a kind of repentance. The next

Zelda Kashpaw Johnson Bjornson

day, she goes to see Xavier, thinking they will only smoke the pipe together. But when Xavier accepts her into his house, the pipe stays in the car—it appears that they have become lovers at last.

Zelda Kashpaw's brothers. See **Eugene Kashpaw** and **Gordie Kashpaw**. They are also mentioned without names in chapter 5 of *The Bingo Palace*.

Ziigwan'aage. Wife of the Pillager man Simon Jack in *The Painted Drum*. In part 2.3, Ziigwan'aage has three children with Simon Jack: an *older boy;* a daughter, Niibin'aage; and a *toddler boy.* She learns of her husband's affair with Anaquot from other women. She does not at first hold him responsible but hates his lover for this distraction from her efforts to keep her children alive and well.

In the winter after the birth of Simon Jack and Anaquot's baby, Ziigwan'aage intercepts a message sent by Anaquot's Shaawano husband, and when Simon Jack is out on the trapline, she has her brother fetch Anaquot across the frozen lake. When Anaquot and the baby arrive, Ziigwan'aage welcomes her with no hint of enmity. After drugging Anaquot into a deep sleep, Ziigwan'aage, who has extensive knowledge of medicines, puts a drug beneath the baby's tongue that will transfer to Anaquot when she nurses the child. When Anaquot realizes who Ziigwan'aage is and that she plans to kill Anaquot and the baby, she confronts Ziigwan'aage openly: "you don't have to poison my baby" (*PD*, 133). After Anaquot points out that the two women would not be enemies were it not for Simon Jack, explaining that he never told her about a wife and children, Ziigwan'aage's loyalties begin to shift.

After Simon Jack returns, Ziigwan'aage again considers killing Anaquot, but when Anaquot refuses his advances one night, her resolve confirms the women's bond and their alliance against the man. They begin beading his elaborate dance costume and by spring have become virtual sisters. That spring, Ziigwan'aage meets the young recruiter from Carlisle Indian School.

We learn from part 2.5 that Ziigwan'aage and Anaquot utterly rebel against Simon Jack. They defy his every request, barring him from his own cabin, and Ziigwan'aage even begins sharing the tent of a *younger man.* They also work on his beaded outfit over several winters, and once he puts it on, he never takes it off, so that he begins to stink. One early summer, when the spirit of Anaquot's Shaawano daughter kills Simon Jack, the women who prepare his body discover the horrible power of Ziigwan'aage's beading—the beads have stitched themselves to Simon Jack's flesh and must be cut from his body. Simon Jack is buried on the path to the Pillager cabin, so Ziigwan'aage and Anaquot walk over him as they come and go.

Sometime later, during an epidemic, Ziigwan'aage dies, along with her children and Anaquot. The only family members spared are Anaquot's daughter Fleur and Ziigwan'aage's daughter Niibin'aage, who has gone east to the Carlisle Indian School.

Ziigwan'aage's relatives. Family that surrounds Ziigwan'aage in part 2.3 of *The Painted Drum*. The whole family comes to Ziigwan'aage's cabin at least twice after Anaquot's arrival, once while Anaquot is in a drugged sleep and again the following evening. After Ziigwan'aage decides to adopt Anaquot instead of killing her, the family coldly accepts her.

Included in this group are three of **Simon Jack's sisters, grandmothers and a great-grandfather of Ziigwan'aage's children,** and Doosh. Although the group includes both Ziigwan'aage's and Simon Jack's relatives, they are referred to collectively as being of the band of "Pillagers" (*PD,* 138). They are described as having severe, handsome faces, wavy hair, and restless hands.

Zosie (I) Shawano. See **Mary (I) Shawano and Josephette (Zosie I) Shawano.**

Zosie (II) Shawano Roy. See **Mary (II) Shawano and Zosie (II) Shawano Roy.**

Zozed Bizhieu. Reservation everywoman and gossip from the 1910s to the 1940s. Chapter 9 of *The Last Report on the Miracles at Little No Horse* comments that "Mrs. Bizhieu was impressed with anything" and thus is "unreliable" (*LR,* 172, 178).

As the influenza epidemic devastates the reservation in the winter of 1918, in chapter 7 of *Last Report,* Zozed reports seeing a **man horribly disfigured** by the illness who falls dead at her feet. While Pauline Puyat is in her trance the following spring, Zozed asks Sister Hildegarde to place a red stick by her bed, representing some request for the "saint." During the winter Father Gregory is on the reservation (1920), in chapter 11 he and Father Damien go out on snowshoes to visit Zozed and **her troublesome daughter.**

Sometime in the early 1930s, Zozed takes a photo of Nanapush with a family of tourists in chapter 11 of *Four Souls.* Nanapush is wearing Margaret's medicine dress, and just as Zozed snaps the picture, he lifts the skirts and does a dance. In the fall of 1941, when a moose drags Nanapush all around the reservation (*Last Report* chapter 18), Zozed hears him cursing as he passes her house and thinks it is the devil. See also **Josette Bizhieu and Bizhieu family.**

Miscellaneous Minor Characters

Minor characters who do not appear in the alphabetized dictionary are given in **boldface** below. We have divided this portion of the dictionary by novel and have placed the characters into something of a running narrative to help readers see how they fit into the larger story. As would be expected, novels set largely in towns and cities have more of such "extras" than those set primarily on the reservation.

LOVE MEDICINE

In "The Island," Nanapush tells Lulu Nanapush about Moses Pillager's history, including the fact that he stole his cats from an **old Frenchwoman.** Lulu takes Moses some nickels she has earned scrubbing floors for a **teacher in town** and her smile, which she says has won barley sugar from the **trader.** After Nector leaves school, an **old rich woman** in Kansas pays him to model, almost nude, for a painting in "The Plunge of the Brave."

In "The Beads," the nosy woman **LaRue** implies that Eli Kashpaw is not a fit caretaker for the child June Morrissey. On the day Marie Kashpaw goes to visit Sister Leopolda in 1957, in "Flesh and Blood," she and Aurelia are watching the **baby** of a **young girl** who lives across the road. Meanwhile, Aurelia's brother Gordie is out hunting with a **boy down the road.** When Marie finds Nector's letter saying that he is leaving her, she recalls **Mary Bonne,** who found her husband in bed with a **La Chien woman** and cut them both.

In "The Bridge," an **airport guard** searches Henry Lamartine Junior on his way home from Vietnam in 1973, after Henry's shrapnel sets off the metal detector. On the streets of Fargo, the fifteen-year-old runaway Albertine Johnson sees an **Oriental man,** a **woman in a tiger-skin shirt,** and **two Indian men** dragging a **dazed woman.** A **night clerk** signs Albertine and Henry Junior into the Fargo hotel where they sleep together. After Henry Junior's death the following year in "The Red Convertible," his brother Lyman's friend **Ray** helps Lyman conceal Henry's picture.

When Gerry Nanapush's pregnant wife, Dot, is working with Albertine at a construction weigh station in 1980 ("Scales"), truck driver **Ed Rafferty** teases them. **Police Officer Harris** comes to the hospital with Officer Lovchik to try to arrest Gerry when Dot is having her baby.

Away at nursing school in 1981, Albertine hears the vacuum cleaner of her **white landlady** while thinking about her aunt, June Morrissey ("The World's Greatest Fishermen"). Albertine recalls the time that June, studying to be a beautician, deliberately burned green the hair of **an unruly customer.** A month after June's death, liquor dealer **Royce** reluctantly delivers wine on credit to Gordie Kashpaw in "Crown of Thorns." On Gordie's drunken drive later that night, he passes the settlement of the **Fortiers.**

In "Love Medicine," **Mary MacDonald** pays Lipsha Morrissey to treat her arthritis with his "touch."

While Marie Kashpaw is working at the old Kashpaw house after Nector's death ("Resurrection), **Old Man LaGrisaille** brings her ripe corn to can. Dreaming about the old days, Marie recalls the desperate **Skinners** who used to live up the trail from them and who would eat her cast-out potato peelings. When Gordie comes to the house, he remembers that on their honeymoon, he and June stayed in an unfurnished cabin in **Johnson**'s rundown, closed resort.

Lulu recalls in "The Good Tears" that she was having coffee with her neighbor **Florentine** when she realized her house was on fire. In protest of "The Tomahawk Factory," Lulu occupies the office of Lyman's boss, Bureau of Indian Affairs superintendent **Edgar "Dizzy" Lightninghoop.**

In "Crossing the Water," Lipsha tells about several incidents demonstrating Lulu's powers. Without being told, she knows that the **Defender girl** is pregnant, that **Old Man Bunachi** has a large Social Security credit, and that **Germaine**'s commodity flour is wormy. (The story of **Wristwatch** in "Love Medicine" also suggests her uncanny powers.) As Lipsha begins his journey to find his dad, a **clerk at the Rudolph Hotel** in a border town asks him to leave the lobby because he is drinking. In Minneapolis, King Kashpaw tells Lipsha that some **Winnebago prisoners** spread false rumors that he had betrayed Gerry's confidences in prison.

THE BEET QUEEN

In chapter 1, at the 1932 Orphans' Picnic in Minneapolis, there are **nuns** and **vendors** selling items and a **crowd** watching the aeronaut Omar. In the boxcar leaving Argus, Karl Adare encounters the bum **Giles Saint Ambrose,** with whom Karl has his first sexual experience. In chapter 2, an Argus **newspaper photographer** takes Mary Adare's picture after her playground accident causing the face of Christ to appear in the ice. **Farmers** from around Argus drive for miles to see the miracle.

After the peddler Fleur Pillager rescues Karl in chapter 3, he observes the variety of **customers** who buy her wares. One **man with lumps on his neck** invites them to sleep in his dead wife's parlor. In chapters 2 and 4, **Canute** is one of the butchers at Kozka's Meats. The **shop's customers** in chapter 4 include Germans, Poles, and Scandinavians.

In chapter 5 (1950), Sita Kozka is living in Fargo and attends a charm school run by **Dorothy Ludlow.** The **postman** brings to her apartment one day a letter containing the news that Mary Adare's lost baby brother, now eighteen and named Jude Miller, is about to be ordained a deacon. Sita recalls hearing her mother, Fritzie, and **Fritzie's friends** talk about the child's disappearance (see also chapter 13). When she goes to Minneapolis for the ordination, an **elevator operator** offers to take her up to the top floor of the Foshay Building (she does not go), and a **shopgirl** in a department store helps her with a dress. At Jude's ordination, a **bishop** presides and an **aged nun** plays the organ. Afterward, a **cab driver** takes Sita to a pawnshop, where a **young pawnbroker named John** sells her the garnet necklace her aunt, Adelaide Adare, had pawned to the young man's father, **John Senior,** in 1932.

Also in chapter 5, following Sita's wedding to Jimmy Bohl, Jimmy is dancing with the **waitresses from the Poopdeck Restaurant** while his brother and cousins kidnap Sita. When the kidnappers drop Sita off on the reservation, **seven old men and two loud women** are drinking at the Indian bar as she blows in.

When Sita transforms the Poopdeck into Chez Sita in chapter 7, her fancy **chef and his helpers** come down with food poisoning just before the restaurant's grand opening. The **waiters and waitresses,** young people from Argus, must cope with the fiasco. Despite the crisis, the **customers** leave satisfied. The **hostess** that evening, a simpering woman in a prom dress, takes Sita's family to their table.

In chapter 6, a **waitress in the hotel bar** serves Karl Adare and Wallace Pfef a drink when they are in Minneapolis for the Crop and Livestock Convention. A **bellhop** brings dinner to Karl's room after he and Wallace make love.

During one bitter winter, recorded in chapter 10, an **old man** freezes beneath his clothesline, his arms full of clothes. The Argus **postmaster and postmistress,** a nosy husband-and-wife team, spread gossip about

Karl Adare's mail and packages to his daughter Dot. When Eli Kashpaw comes to the hospital to fetch Russell Kashpaw after his stroke, **Eli's cousin** is working at the desk. At the end of this chapter, Sita is disgusted by the crudeness and poor grooming of her fellow **patients in the state mental hospital.**

The **Birdorama customers** in Florida are subdued by Adelaide Adare's snapping voice and eyes in chapter 11. In chapter 12, Wallace Pfef visits with the **school principal** after the disastrous Christmas pageant at Saint Catherine's school. In the same chapter, the **waitress at the Flickertail** serves breakfast to Karl Adare, Celestine James, and Dot Adare at their first family gathering in fourteen years. In chapter 13, Celestine jokes about **Tol Bayer,** who had all the symptoms of an alcoholic but didn't drink. When Celestine and Mary visit Sita, we learn that Sita has given away Mary's sewing machine to the disreputable **Grinne family.** When Sita dies, Mary and Celestine cannot find the undertaker, **Langenwalter,** because he is at the Beet Parade.

We learn in chapters 14 and 15 that while Karl is working for **Elmo**'s Landscape Systems in Texas, their **contractors** are either amused or disturbed by his singing. When **one of the managers** of the business sneers at Karl for bragging about his daughter, he quits and returns to Argus to see Dot crowned as Beet Queen.

Numerous people are involved with the July 1972 Argus Beet Festival that closes the novel (chapters 13, 14, 15, and 16). Argus **chamber of commerce members, club presidents,** and **other town leaders** endorse Wallace's idea of having such a festival, although a drought makes some want to cancel it. People quote the Fargo weatherman **Dewey Berquist** about the drought. Even so, many townspeople pitch in to help. A **former contestant for Miss North Dakota** teaches Dot and the other **Beet Queen princesses** how to wave and smile from their parade float. **National guardsmen** organize the **Beet Parade participants,** which include a group of **senior citizens. Members of the American Legion** salute military veteran Russell Kashpaw, who is riding on their float, and one **Legionnaire** gives Russell a drink of water. In chapter 16, Dot says that her three friends driving the cars pulling Beet Parade floats, **P. J., Eddie,** and **Boomer,** are "half buzzed" at parade time. The **mayor, police chief, sheriff,** and **members of the town council** each take a turn in the dunking booth. **Arnie Dotzenrud** is the ticket taker at the festival. An **emcee** on a bullhorn urges people to the grandstand for the Beet Queen coronation. As the mayor presides over the ceremony, the **Legion post commander** stands by. Others from the state who are asked to participate in the festival include the **governor and his wife, nine high school marching bands, rock bands, polka bands,** a **motorcycle-riding team, car show drivers,** and **tractor drivers.**

Huge **crowds** attend the festival (chapters 13–16). One **shrill woman** watching the parade says that Russell Kashpaw looks stuffed (chapter 13). Dot and her court overhear a **group of spectators** discussing Dot's rigged election as Beet Queen (chapter 16), and the other princesses are resentful and mock her. When Jude Miller arrives in Argus the day of the festival, he talks to the **train conductor** and asks the **ticket agent** for information (chapter 14).

TRACKS

When Eli Kashpaw wants to win the love of Fleur Pillager, Nanapush tells him in chapter 3 that **old lady Aintapi** sells love medicines. **Mary Pepewas** contracts consumption in chapter 4 and her brother, the fat little **Pepewas boy,** is sent to fetch Bernadette Morrissey. In the same chapter, **DuCharme,** who runs the trading store, notices Sophie Morrissey's beauty and gives her free candy. After Sophie's sexual encounter with Eli, Bernadette tries to send her to a **strict aunt in Grand Forks.**

Nanapush recalls in chapter 5 having advised Ojibwe landholder **Rift-In-A-Cloud** not to put his thumbprint on a treaty. That winter, a **trader** buys mink furs from Eli, who uses the money to buy supplies for his family. In chapter 7, Father Damien finds a **child** who has been neglected by **drunken parents** frozen to death. The Kashpaws and Pillagers sell cranberry bark that winter to the **Pinkham's dealer** (presumably for Lydia E. Pinkham's tonic) to raise money to pay the families' land fees.

THE BINGO PALACE

In the opening scene of the novel (chapter 1), reservation postmaster **Day Twin Horse** tries to watch Lulu Nanapush as she steals a Wanted poster of her son Gerry.

Patrons of the bingo palace mentioned by Lipsha Morrissey in chapter 5 include people from all walks of life. Two **bingo callers** are working the night Lipsha wins the bingo van in chapter 7. In chapter 20, Lipsha imagines the **bingo caller, dealer,** and **customers** at the new casino Lyman Lamartine plans to build.

In chapter 7, Lipsha and Shawnee Ray Toose get a ride to Hoopdance with some **friends,** who let the couple off at the motel where they make love for the first time.

At a casino in Reno, Nevada, where Lyman Lamartine attends the Indian

Gaming Conference in chapter 8, he notices **trim hostesses** smelling of chlorine from the swimming pool and **two elderly women** playing the slot machine. A **room–service waiter** brings a large order to Lyman's hotel room, but instead of eating, he returns to the casino, where he plays blackjack with **other players.** The **dealer** tries to get rid of him when he is winning. An **elderly man** accidentally knocks Lyman's chips to the floor, temporarily interrupting his gambling spree. When Lyman begins losing and runs out of money, a **pawnshop clerk** gives him a hundred dollars for Nector Kashpaw's ceremonial pipe.

The day Mindemoya (Fleur Pillager) comes to town in chapter 11, **Layla Morrissey** questions her cousin Lipsha about her. This chapter also recalls **Flying Nice,** one of several people Fleur has forced to take her place on death's road. Chapter 12 is Fleur's narrative of her last return to the reservation, in which the **Migwans girls** look longingly at the candy Fleur buys for the white boy with her.

In chapter 14, Lipsha recalls several people who have done drastic things because of love, including Stan Mahng, **Stacy Cuthbert,** and **Martha May Davis.** When Lipsha and Lyman Lamartine begin to fight at the Dairy Queen, the other **Dairy Queen customers** get involved in the melee.

Just before Shawnee Ray dances in the final round of the Montana powwow in chapter 16, she watches the **other dancers** and a **boy spraying water** to settle the dust. She recalls the story of the **Mille Lacs man** who was given the Ojibwe jingle dress by **women** who appeared to him in a dream.

At the religious ceremony that Xavier Toose leads for Lipsha and Lyman in chapter 17, muscled, tattooed **Joe** is the fire-tender.

While Lipsha is playing games in **Art's** Arcade in Fargo in chapter 22, waiting for his father, **other arcade patrons** come in. Some of them watch Lipsha play his last game, and when he stops, **one kid** takes over the game. In the Fargo public library, Lipsha is still looking for Gerry when he is approached by a **librarian** asking if he can help Lipsha. When Lipsha steals a stuffed toucan in chapter 24, the **manager of Metro Drug** begins to chase him, followed by a **policewoman** and a **crowd.** When Lipsha and Gerry steal a car, a few miles out of town, a **smoky** (highway patrol officer) takes up the pursuit until the stuffed toucan breaks loose and crashes through his windshield.

When federal marshals come to the Senior Citizens in chapter 25, resident **Maurice Morris** sees them enter Lulu Lamartine's apartment.

By the time the marshals arrest Lulu, **newspaper photographers** from all over North Dakota are on hand to record the event, along with **local tribal officials and police** to question the marshals' jurisdiction.

TALES OF BURNING LOVE

In the backstory of the novel, **two circus watchers** die in the lightning storm that takes the life of Harry Kuklenski, Anna Schlick's first husband ("Eleanor's Tale" [20]). Other **men** put out the tent fire with their jackets. A **rescuer** breaks Anna's arm and knocks her unconscious in his attempts to help her, and she is taken to a hospital operated by **Franciscans.** After her second husband, Lawrence Schlick, divorces her, **her landlord** offers her ways to pay her rent without money. Years later, when Lawrence is looking for Anna in a poor part of Fargo ("The Red Slip" [21]), he is approached by an eager **missionary** and a **drunk man** asking for a quarter.

In 1981 ("Easter Snow" [1]), Jack Mauser is in Williston. He calls a dental office and talks with an offensively perky **receptionist.** That night when he marries June Morrissey in a bar, Jack's buddy and sometimes roommate acts as **best man,** while the bar patrons serve as **witnesses.** The next morning local and state **police officers** help Jack find June's body.

When Anna Schlick's teenage daughter, Eleanor, grinds Jack's hand in broken glass in a department store in "The Red Slip" [21], a **store clerk** and **several customers** stare at them, and the **manager** tries to pull her away. After they begin dating, Eleanor gives to Jack a photograph of herself lying on a couch in a red satin slip, taken by a **girlfriend.** Eleanor tells her parents she is going to visit a **girlfriend in Minneapolis,** but she actually goes to Florida and marries Jack. At their Florida hotel, a **room–service waiter** brings them breakfast.

As a young woman, Candice Pantamounty has a **friend in Baltimore** who helps her join a class-action lawsuit against the makers of the Dalkon shield ("Candice's Tale" [25]). When Jack goes to Candice's dental office, her hygienist **Andrea** X-rays his teeth. On Jack and Candice's first date, a **solid–hipped waitress** flips Jack the finger. Months later, a **car driver** in "The Wandering Room" [26] signals to Jack that he is dragging a dog with his pickup truck. The dog, Candice's Pepperboy, dies.

Before Marlis Cook meets Jack, a **man opening his car door** accidentally clips her ("Marlis's Tale" [27]), and she lives for a time on the money from the out-of-court settlement. In August 1992, the **waitress at the Library** bar brings Jack a hamburger and five beers the day he celebrates getting the first check of his huge bank loan in "The First Draw" [14]. He meets Marlis in the bar. That night, the **host at the Treetop** restaurant seats Jack and Marlis by a window, and they sing along with the **piano player**'s popular old songs. That night in the motel, Jack finds a picture of an unidentified **elderly woman** in Marlis's wallet. Two days later, a female **justice of the peace** sleepily performs Jack and Marlis's early-morning marriage ceremony in "Best Western" [28].

Also in "Best Western" [28], while Marlis and Jack are staying at the Garden Court in Eugene, Jack notices a group of **young people with orchestra instruments.** Jack admires one of them, a **long-legged blond girl** with a violin. On the way to Billings, Montana, just after Jack wrenches Marlis's arm at a highway rest stop, she catches the eye of a **woman walking a dog.** An **elderly woman at a gas station** stares at them as they fight. The woman is shocked when Marlis offers a condom to an **old rancher.** That spring, in "Baptism River" [29], the **desk clerk at the Mariner Motel** in Minnesota where Candice and Marlis are staying also doubles as its **café waitress.** The **partying woman** in the room next to theirs invites them to her solitary birthday celebration. In "The Waiting Room" [31], a **Lamaze instructor** teaches the pregnant Marlis natural childbirth techniques. After the baby's birth, when Marlis walks in her sleep, Candice recalls that **her grandmother** had warned her not to wake sleepwalkers.

In June 1994, the **farmer** who lives next to Celestine James in Argus has just sold his field for a subdivision, probably to Jack Mauser ("A Wedge of Shade" [3]). Employees of Jack's construction company are mentioned several times in the novel. A **truck driver** drops Jack off in Argus in "Hot June Morning" [2] to meet the mother of his new wife, Dot Adare Nanapush. As Dot and her mother wait for Jack to show up in "A Wedge of Shade" [3], his **construction workers** are busy in the background. A few days later in "Night Prayer" [6], the Mother Superior at Our Lady of the Wheat Priory asks the **foreman** of Jack's **construction crew** to remove the old wooden statue of the Virgin Mary. This crew also appears in "The First Draw" [14] and "The Stone Virgin" [44].

When Dot begins paperwork that fall to divorce both Jack and Gerry Nanapush in "Caryl Moon" [8], her **lawyer** thinks she is crazy. As Jack's house is burning down in December 1994 ("Jack's House" [9]), he recalls that his **insurance agent** had tried to sell him additional coverage, but he had declined to buy. The **guests at Jack's funeral** a few days later (January 1995; "Satin Heart" [12]) include assorted farmers, businessmen, and police officers. During his funeral, Jack steals Candice's car, inadvertently kidnapping his son ("Funeral Day" [23]). When Jack rushes into the Fargo train station, the **Stationmaster,** a former employee of Jack's, does not recognize him.

When Jack's wives go to the B & B in West Fargo after his funeral ("The B & B" [16]), other customers include a group of **blackjack players,** one of whom, a morose **man in a tractor hat,** speaks to several of the wives. The **blackjack dealers** are all blond women. That evening, in "The Hitchhiker" [18] the **TV weatherman** comments that the developing storm is a "lollapalooza." Earlier, neither he nor various **other weather prognosticators** (local farmers and state meteorologists) had predicted the storm. There had once been a rumor, however, among the present generation's **Scandinavian and German grandmothers,** that the end of the world would come in the middle of a terrible winter and that the doom would begin in January. The **manager of the B & B** cooks a pizza for the massive Indian woman who sweeps into his restaurant out of the blizzard ("The B & B" [16]). He and the **cocktail waitress** argue over whether they should serve this woman.

An **airport watchman** and a **rental car agent** discover the nearly frozen Eleanor Mauser in the airport terminal in "A Conversation" [33]. The watchman is mentioned again, in "Two Front-Page Articles" [37], as having alerted the Fargo police and fire departments to the plight of Jack Mauser's other wives in a snowbound car. In "The Disappearance" [36], a **snowmobile rescue squad** rescues the three wives and a hitchhiker. One of the rescuers is distraught because he lets the fourth "woman" fall off his snowmobile. The missing passenger, Gerry Nanapush, visits his daughter, Shawn, in "Smile of the Wolf" [38]. Shawn tells him about a **neighbor woman** who has a cat named Uncle Louie and, more importantly, about the snowmobile of neighbors **Mr. and Mrs. Morton,** which becomes Gerry's escape vehicle.

The next month, while Dot is walking Mary Adare's dog in "February Thaw" [40], she sees a **man with a dog.** The longing of Mary's dog for the other animal parallels Dot's own longing for Gerry.

In "The Stone Virgin" [44], a **delivery truck driver** brings the stone statue to the Argus convent. After Jack is nearly crushed by the falling statue, a **store clerk** brings five hundred dollars' worth of new clothes to him in the Argus hospital. Following his release from the hospital, Jack tells a local **newspaper reporter** that he had "recognized her" (that is, the statue). In "A Letter to the Bishop" [45], Jude Miller writes about the **janitorial workers** who clean Jack's blood from the statue. The blood, however, reappears, and the **manager of the janitorial company,** a Lutheran, says that it seems "as though the stone itself were sweating blood."

THE ANTELOPE WIFE

Just after World War II, Shawano the ogitchida captures the German prisoner of war Klaus (chapter 13). Among those who come to see the man at Shawano's house are **Asinigwesance (Asin),** a formerly judicious old man who insists that they execute Klaus; the ogitchida's brother **Pugweyan,** who reasons with Asinigwesance; and **Bootch,** who suggests they allow the prisoner to cook the blitzkuchen.

Years later, when Klaus Shawano is at the Elmo powwow in chapter 2, the neighbors next to his trading store are a **family from Saskatoon.** When he goes to see old Jimmy Badger about catching an antelope, the **gamblers** whom the old man has beaten are folding their chairs and grumbling. Back in Minneapolis, Klaus is jealous when **men in bars** approach his antelope wife, Sweetheart Calico. The **old women** say that any man who follows an antelope woman, as Klaus has, is lost forever.

When Rozina Roy and Frank Shawano make love the first time in chapter 3, they can hear **children** on the playground nearby.

In chapter 4, Klaus tries to change his and Sweetheart Calico's seating for their flight to Hawaii, but the **airport check-in person** says that she cannot help them. Back in Minneapolis, when Sweetheart Calico is thrown through a window by an explosion in chapter 5, the **street people** get clothes for her, including the silk blouse of a **rich lady.**

In chapter 8, when Cally Roy visits **relatives** in Bwaanakeeng, the child **Melvin** goes to fetch the white puppy for a grandmother to make into soup. Cally is playing with a **boy cousin** when she rescues the dog (Almost Soup). In his narration, Almost Soup mentions several humans who die by drowning, so that dogs are offered as a sacrifice to the lake spirit. These drowned humans include **Fatty Simon, Agnes Anderson, Alberta Meyer,** the **Speigelrein girls,** old **Kagewah,** and **Morris Shawano,** the track star who disappears from **his dad**'s boat.

As the alcoholic Klaus wanders the streets with Richard Whiteheart Beads in chapter 10, several people give them money: a **Korean or Mexican woman, two men,** and a **group of people,** all exiting an art museum, and later a **woman leaving an antique store.** When Klaus tries to drink from the lawn sprinklers, the **museum guard** and a **large woman** tell them to leave. A **grocery store security guard** and a **liquor store clerk** also will not give him a drink of water. Seeing images of the

Blue Fairy in his mind, Klaus recalls watching *Pinocchio* eight or ten times with different **nieces and nephews, their friends,** and **relatives of their friends.**

According to chapter 11, there is a photo of **Cally's one-time boyfriend** taped to the wall of her room on the reservation. After she moves back to Minneapolis at age eighteen, she works in Frank Shawano's bakery, and **passersby** glance in at the display of breads and cakes. The **kung fu clients** from Cecille Shawano's studio next door come in for pastries. When looking for Cally's Minneapolis grandmothers, Cally and Cecille knock on a door answered by a **dark-eyed young woman,** perhaps from Ethiopia.

In chapter 15, Klaus and Richard check into a recovery lodge, where they live with **three other recovering alcoholics.** One day when all of his clothes are dirty, Klaus wears his **counselor**'s pants.

Rozin and Frank's **wedding guests** in chapter 16 include a diverse assortment of Shawano and Roy family members, one of whom is Frank's cousin **Darrell.** Cecille Shawano tries to tell the other guests the story about **her neighbor,** the neighbor's family member **Kerry,** and the missing dishes. After Richard Whiteheart Beads tries to leap from the cliff at the ceremony, **ambulance technicians** take him away. **Police** come to the reception to investigate Richard's letter claiming to have poisoned the cake, and a **police sergeant** dusts the letter for fingerprints. That night, **medics** remove Richard from Rozin and Frank's hotel after he shoots himself in the head.

At the Christmas dinner in chapter 18, Zosie Roy and Mary Shawano tell a story about a **woman in labor for two weeks.** The woman survives but **her baby** dies. Later, Sweetheart Calico tells about seeing a vision of the economic oppression of **children in China** and **young virgins.**

THE LAST REPORT ON THE
MIRACLES AT LITTLE NO HORSE

Among the first whites to visit the Ojibwe (chapter 13) are **a trader** who, to save himself, pretends not to know how to play chess and **another trader** who has played all his life. On one of the last buffalo hunts in the nineteenth century (chapter 8), a **band of Ojibwes** encounters a band of their mortal enemies, the **Bwaanug** (Dakotas). To defuse the hostility, the parties agree to a race to the death between Pauline Puyat's grandmother and a **Bwaan woman,** and another between Pauline's grandfather and a **Bwaan winkte,** a woman-man. After the massive slaughter of buffalo, one **old hunter** weeps when the surviving buffalo trample their dead.

In chapter 1, Berndt Vogel has a **hired man** on his farm who, after the arrival of Agnes DeWitt in 1910, sleeps in the barn with Berndt. The following spring, eighteen **bank customers,** including Agnes, witness a bank robbery. Two tellers are there that day—**a florid red-headed woman** and a **young dark-haired bristling man** who is shot and killed by Arnold "the Actor" Anderson. Some months after the Actor kills Berndt, in her distraction Agnes is naked when the **neighbor children** come to buy eggs.

In chapter 6, in the spring of 1912, the members of Kashpaw's large family include, besides the named characters, **two young men** who are older sons of Margaret, **two children** who run out naked into the frigid air, and several other **round, healthy children.** Later in the chapter, **Fishbone's baby** is stillborn, and **her boy** is burned when he crawls into the fire. On the feast day the following autumn (chapter 7), Mary Kashpaw's **female cousin** sits with her in the wagon carrying the statue of the Virgin. During the 1918–1919 influenza epidemic, some **two hundred Ojibwe** die. Among those spared are the **Waboose** family and the **Parisiens.**

A **circle of men** takes part in the investigation of the death of Napoleon Morrissey in chapter 9. Only one is named, **George Aisance,** who finds the murder weapon (see also chapter 16). Worried about what the Lazarres may do to them in chapter 9, Nector thinks of the young prizefighter **Paguk,** who ended up stupid and drooling. In 1920 (chapter 11), the **trader's wife** hands Father Damien a letter announcing that a young priest is coming for Father Damien to train.

According to her chapter 15 narrative of boarding school, Lulu misses the **Yellowboy girls** and the **Anongs** from home. People at the school include the janitor **Mr. Eaglestaff,** the matron **Mrs. Houle,** and the unnamed **principal.**

Among the reservation folk who witness the spectacle of old Nanapush's being dragged overland in his boat in chapter 18 (1941) is a **family digging cattail roots.** At Nanapush's funeral that winter **"everyone"** (reservation populace) shows up. When Father Gregory Wekkle returns to the reservation in 1962 (chapter 19), **Mrs. Bluelegs** and other **ladies at the Senior Citizens** watch with interest.

When Father Jude comes to the reservation in 1996 to research the possible sainthood of Sister Leopolda (chapter 3), he tells Father Damien about people who have experienced miraculous cures associated with the nun. A **man who suffered from hemorrhoids** was miraculously cured by eating honey from flowers touched by Leopolda's ashes. A **cardiac**

surgeon reported a **young girl with a heart virus** who was healed. In chapter 20, Father Jude tells Father Damien that he was drunk the previous night, but Damien reminds him of the early saint **Portrartus,** who appeared drunk without consuming alcohol. In their chapter 20 interview, Marie Kashpaw tells Father Jude that as a young bootlegger she lived in the former cabin of **Agongos.** She also mentions **Call the Day,** a whiskey customer to whose house she takes Sophie Morrissey.

THE MASTER BUTCHERS SINGING CLUB

When Delphine Watzka is a child, her father's primary income is from the **farmer who leases Roy's land** (chapter 3). Two local misfortunes recorded in chapter 4 contribute to Delphine's fatalistic worldview: a **child struck blind** and **Mrs. Vashon,** the mother of nine who tries to hang herself after her husband leaves. After dropping out of high school, among the jobs Delphine holds is one at the **Ogg** Dairy.

In chapter 1, a **neighbor well known to Fidelis Waldvogel's parents** shows off a square piece of bread from the United States, which a **crowd of people** admires and which induces Fidelis to move to America. In the New York train station in 1922, a **sharp-mouthed girl** at a ticket window writes down for Fidelis the rail fare to Seattle and her own phone number. Fidelis gets money for his ticket by selling sausages to **passersby in the station.** A **kind waitress** in the station diner gives him extra bread with his stew. The next day an **impatient elderly gentleman** sells him a ticket.

In chapter 2, Delphine and Cyprian Lazarre meet while doing town theater in Argus with the **congenial town troupe.** As they go on the road in the spring of 1934, a **landlady** and a **cluster of people** on the street of a Minnesota town react to seeing the naked Cyprian practicing his balancing act in their rented room. The **café owner** supplements their large breakfast with extra sugar and a leftover pancake. Delphine and Cyprian join up with a **vaudeville group and traveling circus from Illinois** in the town of Shotwell, North Dakota, where they carouse with **three other couples** in a bar. When Delphine becomes bored, she goes outside and talks to a **farmer,** whom she invites to their show. While she is gone, Cyprian and the others leave, except for one **mean, ugly girl,** so Delphine leaves, too.

The **Mecklenbergs'** prize sow mauls Fidelis's knee in chapter 3. The chapter mentions several tragedies that capture the town's attention from time to time: the **smothered child,** the **pregnant woman who kills her baby,** the **shot-and-killed young man,** the **raped girl** who is institutionalized and the **rapist** who disappears after evading conviction, the **boy killed in a thresher,** and the **favorite schoolteacher** who commits suicide.

In chapter 5, two days after arriving in Argus, Delphine sees the **sheriff's boy-deputy** and **a couple of curious neighbors** in front of her father, Roy's house, watching the removal of three bodies. A few days later, Clarisse Strub comes to the butcher shop from the funeral of a **thirty-four-year-old drowning victim** whose body, Clarisse says, looks better than the **drowned boy** she had seen in Fargo. In addition to several major characters, others mentioned in chapter 5 as regular customers at Fidelis's butcher shop are **Scat Wilcomb, Mercedes Fox,** and the dentist, young Doctor Heech. There are also the **family of Dakota Sioux** who trade wild meats or berries for flour and tea, and other moneyless people who come for scraps and bones, including **Simpy Benson** and **fathers who are out of work** during the Depression. During that summer's heat wave, Roy Watzka sleeps by the river with **two drinking buddies.** Fidelis is out looking at stock with a **farmer** when Eva collapses, and Dr. Heech phones **a surgeon** at the Mayo Clinic.

In chapter 7, by the time of Eva's death in 1935, arrangements have been made with a **fur dealer** to buy the Waldvogel boys' chinchillas (see also chapter 8). When Delphine stops by the mortuary, Clarisse speaks of the **guy from South Dakota** who stood her up on a date because of her profession. The client Clarisse is working on that day, **Mr. Pletherton,** died of food poisoning and is thus a difficult case. Delphine recalls Aurelius Strub's humorous remark about the **boy who went through the corn picker.**

When Delphine returns to work at the butcher shop that fall (chapter 8), she improves business by dealing with an **ambitious wholesaler** working out of the Twin Cities. When Cyprian realizes that Fidelis had been a sniper in the war, he wonders whether he was the one who killed Cyprian's lover or his friend **Syszinski,** or blew off the hand of **Malaterre.** During this time, Tante does bookkeeping for Fidelis's shop, **Krohn**'s hardware store, and **Olson**'s café but makes little money. After she sells her cameo and buys a suit, she applies for work at the bank, looking around at **all the bank tellers and clerks.** One evening, Sheriff Hock thinks about **Governor Langer**'s order for banks to cease foreclosures, an order the Argus banker ignores. Clarisse is preparing **the body of a child** the next time Delphine visits.

In chapter 9, during the Depression years, Step-and-a-Half knows the

banker's cook and other wealthy households where she can collect quality castoffs. Markus Waldvogel has a **tunneling crew** helping with his excavation in 1936, of which only he, the twins, **Grizzy Morris,** and Roman Shimek stay with the job. In chapter 11, late in the year, Step-and-a-Half sells the beaded dress from Clarisse's back porch to a **woman traveling through town** with **her husband,** who deals in scrap metals. Tante considers approaching the **owner of the pool hall** for a job, but changes her mind. For Christmas, Cyprian buys a fat goose from a **Bohemian farmer.**

In chapter 12, when Tante and the younger boys are about to leave for Germany, Delphine and the boys see an assortment of circus sideshows in Chicago. Besides the Delver of Minds (see entry), these include a **woman called the needle,** the **fat lady, Seal-O, Mr. Tiger, Girl Wonder Calculator,** a **strong man,** a **person with half-a-person growing out of its belly,** and an **exotic four-breasted mermaid.**

After returning to Argus in chapter 13, when Delphine chases the streaking Roy, a **woman with a toddler** sees him. The **gym teacher** helps Delphine catch Roy, while **children and teachers** watch from the school windows. At the courthouse, where Delphine gets a job, there is a **secretary** who ignores her. When Cyprian comes through town after Delphine's marriage, Roy mentions the barber, **Oly Myhra,** who is old and may be retiring. The story Roy tells Delphine of Minnie's experience at Wounded Knee brings in a host of characters: **Crazy Horse,** a **ragtag band of Minneconjou Lakotas, Sitting Bull,** a **camp of Hunkpapa Lakota, Chief Hump, remnants of ghost dance believers,** the **Seventh Cavalry** under **Major Samuel M. Whitside,** old chief **Big Foot,** a **woman with a baby tied to her, women holding their babies in the air,** a **soldier on horseback chasing down a stumbling boy,** and a **dead girl stripped naked.** After Roy dies, when Delphine tells Fidelis that her father was a murderer, the faces of men he had killed in the war flash before him, including a **blond man who resembled Pouty Mannheim.** As World War II begins, the **Schmidts** change their name to Smith and the **Buchers** to Book.

In chapter 14, the **two American GIs** who capture Erich are surprised to hear him beg for his life in English. At Erich's POW camp in Minnesota, an **American soldier,** one of **six guards,** asks a **military officer** to unchain the **prisoners of war** when they arrive at the camp. One **supervising soldier** censors the German prisoners' camp newspaper. A **former prison guard from the Midwest** gives Markus a lead on his brother's POW status. When Markus and Fidelis arrive at the camp, they encounter a **lone guard.** On their way home, a **gas station attendant** and **bartender** serve them. In August 1945, as she is reading about the atomic bomb in the newspaper, Delphine sees another article about a man named **Rzeazutko** who kills his wife and himself while they are dancing at the homecoming party that **Mr. and Mrs. Michael Wojcik** hold for **their son Edwin.** In chapter 15, at the 1954 war memorial dedication in Ludwigsruhe, Germany, Fidelis sings with a **group of master butchers,** and Delphine breathes in the gardenia smell on **some woman**'s bosom.

In chapter 16, Step-and-a-Half knows people by their trash, so she knows about the **Bouchards'** habit of throwing plates when they fight, and the candy wrappers in the Mannheim trash bespeak the candy-eating obsession of **Pouty Mannheim's mother,** who loses her teeth to the habit. As Step-and-a-Half remembers her experiences at Wounded Knee, she recalls a **toddler who tries to be invisible** and a surviving **baby with an American flag cap.**

FOUR SOULS

Several minor characters appear in the novel's stories from the 1800s. In chapter 5, Fleur's ancestor Under the Ground heals a badly burned boy, **LaFortier's son,** by taking the fire into her hands and taming it. After she heals her own daughter (thereafter called Four Souls) by throwing out a soul, the soul enters a white raccoon. But when an **old man** traps the raccoon, he finds it hollow. Fours Souls's daughter Fleur gets her French name from a **trapper's wife.** Chapter 16 refers to the woman who names Fleur as a **French trader's wife.**

In chapter 14, Margaret mentions the names of several of her own ancestor women, such as **Standing Strong, Fish Bones, Different Thunder, Yellow Straps, Sky Coming Down,** and **Lightning Proof,** and her great-grandmother's female friends, such as **Steps Over Truth, I Hear, Glittering, Standing Across, Playing Around, Ice, Shining One Side, Opposite the Sky, Rabbit, Prairie Chicken, Daylight, She Tramp, Cross Lightning, Setting Wind, Gentle Woman Standing, Stop the Day, Log, Cloud Touching Bottom, Wind, Musical Cloud, Dressed in Stone,** Lying Down Grass, **She Black of Heart, She Knows the Bear** (later christened Marie), **Sloping Cloud** (Jeanne), **Taking Care of the Day** (Catherine), and **Yellow Day Woman** (another Catherine).

Chapter 1 tells that the Indian child **Wujiew** (Mountain) is born, long before the city of Minneapolis exists, on the mountain where John James Mauser will one day build his mansion. In chapter 3, we learn that as a young man Mauser marries a series of **Ojibwe girls.** Once he has logged their land, he moves on, leaving the women and **their children** behind. Chapter 8 mentions two trench-mates of Mauser and Fantan during World War I, **Bert Chiswick** and **Mr. Dragon.**

The Mausers' laundress, an **Irish woman,** quits her job the day before Fleur arrives at the Mauser house in chapter 2. When Mauser has a seizure and sinks his teeth into Polly Elizabeth's finger in chapter 3, **Mauser's huge cook** sits on him and pinches his nose shut. After Fleur marries Mauser, at a social occasion in chapter 6 **Virgil Hill** calls Fleur a squaw and then senses that she may attack him with a carving knife. In chapter 12, the now-married Polly Elizabeth and Fantan plan to take over the trading store on the reservation from an **old Lebanese man.**

In chapter 7, Nanapush thinks about government officials like the **Allotment Agent,** who facilitates the Ojibwes' selling their land, and the **Farmer in Charge,** who teaches them to destroy it. When Margaret sells some of Nector's allotment, Nanapush sees **three white workers** clearing the property. One Sunday in chapter 9, while Nanapush is impatiently waiting for Margaret to return from mass, **George Bizhiew, Short Little Sweetheart,** and **Mrs. Cardinal** pass his cabin. In the poker game at Tatro's Wild Goose bar in chapter 15, one of the onlookers is a **Kashpaw man** who accuses Tatro of taking advantage of Fleur.

THE PAINTED DRUM

In the early twentieth century, Chickie Ruse is watching for the moose he kills for Shaawano in part 2.5 because he recalls **his great-aunt**'s telling **his great-uncle** that big flies are a sign of moose.

Toward the end of the first winter in the novel's present, in part 1.1 a **"dog posse"** of state and local police and volunteers searches for the escaped Eyke dog. **One officer** spots Davan Eyke's stolen car. As the speeding Davan drives off a bridge, an **early fisherman** feels the car's shadow pass over him. Later, a **woman witness** describes the accident. Four **wet-suited divers** work for several days to recover Davan's and Kendra Krahe's bodies from the river.

In part 1.3, Kurt Krahe and Faye Travers have dinner at the Sweet Mansion, built in the nineteenth century by mill owner **Henry Sweet. Thousands of young women** went to early graves working for him. **Sweet's children** sold the estate to a **developer,** who restored the mansion as a restaurant. The following August (part 1.4), as Faye picks blackberries, she walks over the land of an **absentee landlord** and a **neighbor with a horse farm** and sees **men in a helicopter.**

That autumn on the reservation (part 2.1), among the people who make excuses to deflect Chook String's request for help are **Mary Sunday,** who says that her stove blew up, and **Teddy Eagle,** who says that he has yellow fever. In the deep cold of the following winter (part 3.7), Ira speaks with **Itchy Boyer** at the Indian Agency about getting heating oil and food vouchers. When she returns home and finds her nearly frozen children at Bernard Shaawano's house, two **EMTs** are with the ambulance that has come for them (part 3.6).

Sometime that summer in New Hampshire (part 4), Kit Tatro consults a **shaman** to help him discover what kind of Indian he is.

Glossary of Ojibwe Words, Phrases, and Sentences

Louise Erdrich has increasingly inserted Ojibwe words, phrases, and even full sentences into her novels. The purpose of this section of our book is to provide her readers with a glossary of Ojibwe expressions that appear in the ten novels published through 2005.[1]

One of the reasons for Erdrich's increasing use of Ojibwemowin (the Ojibwe word for the language) in her writing is her own growing personal knowledge of the language. Ojibwemowin is very much a second language for Erdrich, who is modest about her ability to use it: "It's not simple. It's intellectually complex, and it's so far beyond what I could ever hope to achieve in understanding." She later elaborated, "My love for the language far exceeds my ability to speak it. . . . I just keep trying."[2]

Erdrich uses her character Agnes/Damien in *The Last Report on the Miracles at Little No Horse* to describe the gradual process by which she herself has acquired facility with the language. As priest to the reservation people, Father Damien makes a concerted effort to learn "the formidable language

---

1. We gratefully acknowledge the assistance of two women who generously helped with this project. First, Marlene Robinson Stately, whose Ojibwe name is Anangokwe, or "Star Woman," translated some of the Ojibwe words, phrases, and sentences in this document. She is a native first speaker enrolled with the Minnesota Chippewa Tribe's Leech Lake Band of Ojibwe. Second, Louise Erdrich herself kindly looked over early drafts of this glossary and corrected, in private correspondence, some of our errors and misunderstandings. She asks us to express here her gratitude to Marlene Stately and acknowledges as well the help of her friend and teacher, Jim Clark (Naawigiisis, or "Center of the Day"), a native speaker of Ojibwe. An earlier version of this glossary appeared in *American Indian Culture and Research Journal* 27, no. 3 (2003): 53–70. We are grateful for permission to reprint that material, which appears here with corrections and added material from *Four Souls, The Painted Drum*, and the glossary at the end of *The Game of Silence*. Note that the two articles in our bibliography by David Treuer, an Ojibwe from the Leech Lake reservation in northern Minnesota, question Erdrich's use of Ojibwe language in *The Antelope Wife* and *Love Medicine*.

2. From "Louise Erdrich," an interview with Mark Anthony Rolo published in the *Progressive*, April 2002, 40 (the full interview includes pages 36–40); Louise Erdrich, private correspondence in the fall of 2003.

of my people" (*LR,* 49). As a result, Ojibwemowin becomes integral to his thinking: "early on, Ojibwe words and phrases had crept into Damien's waking speech and now sometimes he lapsed into the tongue" (*LR,* 51). Agnes increasingly understands the language of nature and music as she nears death, and she compares this understanding with the way she had come to understand Ojibwemowin: "The constant murmur of the pines, her beloved music, now became comprehensible to her in the same way that flows of Ojibwe language first began to make sense—a word here, a word there, a few connections, then the shape of ideas" (*LR,* 348).

In much the same way, Erdrich's own "concerted effort" to learn the language has influenced her development as a writer: "Slowly the language has crept into my writing, replacing a word here, a concept there, beginning to carry weight."[3] Although sometimes Erdrich's use of these scattered Ojibwe words and phrases is comic, as in the conversation of the mischievous Nanapush, more often it represents serious, straightforward communication. She seems to want to lend an air of native realism to her writing and to educate her readers to the fact that Ojibwemowin is a living language still.

ERDRICH'S USE OF OJIBWE LANGUAGE

The use of native languages in books by American Indian authors has attracted little commentary. One notable exception is Elizabeth Cook-Lynn, who writes about the way literary agents and book editors have sometimes tried to coerce American Indian writers into being more fully accessible to mainstream (that is, Euro-American) readers. She quotes an editor's query on a submitted manuscript: "How and why is it that you use an Indian language word or phrase at certain places in your narrative, and don't you think you should have a glossary at the end of the manuscript?"[4]

---

3. Louise Erdrich, "Two Languages in Mind, Just One in the Heart," was originally published in the *New York Times,* May 22, 2000, E 1–2, but is conveniently reprinted in *North Dakota Quarterly* (American Indian Issue) 67 (fall 2000): 213–16. The quotation is taken from p. 216. This sentence is repeated, with slight changes, in Erdrich's afterword to Jim Clark's *Naawigiizis: The Memories of Center of the Moon,* ed. Louise Erdrich (Minneapolis: Birchbark Books, 2002), 115.

4. From "The American Indian Fiction Writers: Cosmopolitanism, Nationalism, the Third World, and First Nation Sovereignty," first published in Elizabeth Cook-Lynn's *Why I Can't Read Wallace Stegner and Other Essays: A Tribal Voice* (Madison: University of Wisconsin Press, 1996). We quote from p. 24 of the essay as reprinted in *Nothing but the Truth,* ed. John L. Purdy and James Ruppert (Upper Saddle River, N.J.: Prentice-Hall, 2001).

Erdrich has increasingly used "an Indian language word or phrase" in her fiction. Although she had virtually no Ojibwe words in the first and shorter 1984 edition of *Love Medicine,* in the expanded 1993 edition she has many. Most of the Ojibwemowin is in the new chapters, but she sometimes adds a word, like Eli's use of an Ojibwe word to describe himself: " 'I'm an old man,' Eli said in a flat, soft voice. *'Ekewaynzee'* " (*LM,* 33). It may be that her commercial success as a novelist has given her the authority to embed more and more Ojibwe language into her fiction. Naturally, in her novels with an Ojibwe setting and traditional Ojibwe characters, she uses more Ojibwemowin than in other novels. There are no Ojibwe words or phrases in *The Beet Queen,* which is not surprising, since most of its characters are white. There are few Ojibwe expressions in *Tales of Burning Love* and *The Master Butchers Singing Club,* which are also cast primarily with white characters. The Erdrich novel that makes the greatest use of Ojibwe words and phrases is *The Last Report on the Miracles at Little No Horse,* a later novel set largely on the reservation. *The Antelope Wife, Four Souls,* and *The Painted Drum* also make considerable use of Ojibwemowin.

In these novels Erdrich often refers to Ojibwe as "the old language." In *Love Medicine,* for example, Lulu Nanapush, who spent her formative years at a boarding school speaking only English, tells about Moses Pillager's talking with Nanapush: "One summer long ago, when I was a little girl, he came to Nanapush and the two sat beneath the arbor, talking only in the old language" (*LM,* 73). Much later, as a young woman, Lulu visits Moses on his cat-crawling island and sleeps with him. She wakes up beside Moses to discover that he is talking in a language that she scarcely recognizes: "I woke to find him speaking in the old language, using words that few remember, forgotten, lost to people who live in town or dress in clothes" (*LM,* 81).

When Fleur is attacked in the town of Argus in *Tracks,* she cries out for help "in the old language" (*Tr,* 26). In chapter 6 of *Tracks,* Pauline tries to obey the call of Jesus by urinating only twice a day, but the mischievous Nanapush gives her delicious tea to drink and then torments her with talk of water: "In the old language there are a hundred ways to describe water and he used them all—its direction, color, source and volume" (*Tr,* 149). He asks her why Jesus never calls her to "relieve yourself." Pauline tells us that he "said this last to me in the old language, and the words were strong and vulgar" (*Tr,* 147). We do not know precisely what words Nanapush said to Pauline in the old language, but we can perhaps assume that at least one of the words he used for "relieve yourself" was a form of *zaukumowin,* the Ojibwe word for "female pissing."[5]

Erdrich refers to the Ojibwe language similarly in *The Bingo Palace.* Gerry Nanapush, fearing that Lipsha's telephone is tapped, speaks to Lipsha "in the old-time language" about where to meet him in Fargo. The fact that Lipsha has not made a concerted effort to learn the old language becomes a barrier to communication with his father. Gerry's life is at risk, but Lipsha does not know where to meet him: "My father is either playing Star Wars games at Art's Arcade, or he is holed up at the Fargo library, or he is hiding curled up in the lodge dumpster of the Sons of Norway" (*BP,* 223).

One of the few uses of the old language in *Tales of Burning Love* comes when the drunken Jack Mauser is alone in his new house, hounded by bad marriages and angry creditors. The scene, despite its near-tragic dimensions, is also broadly comic: "Mauser lifted the bottle again and then lay back carefully in the king-size pillows. *Booshkay neen,* he said. *Booshkay neen.* Where had that come from? Some book? His mother? Sometimes Ojibwa words snared his tongue. Sometimes German" (*TBL,* 102). Although Erdrich gives no hint in the text what *booshkay neen* means, a dictionary of the Ojibwe language shows that a near form, *booshke giniin* means "it's up to you, it's your decision."[6] The appositeness of the phrase becomes clear a little later in that chapter when Jack makes, quite on his own, a joyously drunken decision to let his new house burn down and collect the insurance. If the phrase is his mother's, then her advice is ironical at best: "And then, at that moment, he decided what to do. Or rather, what not to do. He decided not to move" (*TBL,* 109). Part of his decision is to make it look as if he has burned to death in the fire, and then to escape naked into the freezing night. The decision, of course, is less rational than he thinks it is, but it is his decision. Without some knowledge of Ojibwe, we would have no way of knowing what *booshkay neen* means.

In *The Antelope Wife,* Cally Roy says that "Grandma Mary, then Zosie, made a long talk in our old language" (*AW,* 102). We can guess from the context what some of the Ojibwe words in this novel mean, but not all of them. One key word, *daashkikaa,* spoken by the old dying woman whom

5. We take this word from Basil Johnston's *Ojibway Language Lexicon for Beginners,* published in 1978 in Ottawa, Canada, "under the authority of the Hon. J. Hugh Faulkner, Minister of Indian and Northern Affairs Canada." This lexicon is out of print and is not readily available.

6. John D. Nichols and Earl Nyholm, *A Concise Dictionary of Minnesota Ojibwe* (Minneapolis: University of Minnesota Press, 1995), 39. This book is a revision and expansion of the authors' *Ojibwewi-Ikidowinan: An Ojibwe Word Resource Book,* published in 1979.

Scranton Roy has just bayoneted on page 4, is not defined until just a few pages from the end of the novel as meaning "cracked apart" (*AW*, 213). Other Ojibwe language is defined in only the most general terms. We find this conversation, for example, about the quality of a moose dinner:

> "This moose is tough!"
> "Dahgo chimookoman makazin!"
> "Magizha gaytay mooz."
> "The old are the tenderest, though, really they are!"
> "Magizha oshkay." (*AW*, 171)

A "translation" of sorts is given afterwards, but it does not reproduce the precise meaning of the Ojibwe sentences:

> Cecille understood enough Ojibwa to know that they were talking about meat and hunting, though she didn't understand that the grandmas thought the meat was tough as a whiteman's shoe, probably from an old skinny bull, poached midwinter, stored until it burned from cold, given by Puffy to Chook because he wanted to make room in his freezer. (*AW*, 172)

Perhaps part of Erdrich's private joke, to be shared only with readers who know a little Ojibwe, is that only part of this "translation" is actually said in the Ojibwemowin quoted in the conversation. (The three Ojibwe sentences are translated at the end of the glossary, below.)

For some of her Ojibwe language, Erdrich gives even less help. She sometimes includes several sentences that readers are left to guess at. This is especially true in *The Last Report on the Miracles at Little No Horse*, which contains several extended passages in the old language for which Erdrich gives only general hints at meaning. For such sentences, perhaps the general meaning is all that we really need, and the context usually provides that.[7] In any case, we have included these sentences at the end of the glossary, along with suggested translations we have worked out.

Some of Erdrich's Ojibwe words do not appear in any of the dictionaries that are readily available, at least not with her spelling. Any use of an Ojibwe-English dictionary is rendered difficult by certain features of the language. Ojibwemowin was originally only a spoken, not a written language. Thus,

---

7. Erdrich notes in private correspondence that "I wanted the work to wash over a reader and to me it is fine if a reader understands in a general way. Also, I thought it might spur readers to look into Ojibwemowin."

it has no alphabet of its own, and there is no standard English-letter spelling for many Ojibwe sounds. The orthography is further complicated by differences in dialect. Because of these factors, among Ojibwe dictionaries, *p* can be substituted for *b, d* for *t, k* for *g, z* for *s, j* for *tch, a* for *aa, ii* for *ee,* and so on. Some of these variations are regional, with, for example, Canadian forms differing from forms in the United States, but some are just different ways of "hearing" the words. Furthermore, the word forms shift with grammatical function, so that dictionaries cannot always give reliable word equivalents. The result, of course, is a certain readerly frustration.

Erdrich may not want non-Ojibwe speakers to understand the meaning of some of these sentences, or at least may not care if they do not understand them precisely. She may want to keep some phrases as private messages for those few readers, most of them Ojibwe themselves, who can understand the old language. Or she may want to encourage her readers to struggle to learn at least the rudiments of the language, and so help to keep that language alive.

Nevertheless, we feel that there is a place for a glossary like this one, since readers who make no effort to understand Erdrich's Ojibwe passages miss something. In the *"booshkay neen"* example above, unless they consult a glossary, readers have no way of knowing what message Jack's memory wants to give him. Another example of the importance of access to an Ojibwe glossary comes at the end of *The Antelope Wife,* where Klaus Shawano sends Sweetheart Calico, his antelope wife, back to her people. His parting words to her are in Ojibwe: "Ninimoshe," he tells her, "Gewhen, gewhen!" (*AW,* 229). If we do not know that *ninimoshe* means "my sweetheart" or "my love," we miss the combined affection and grief with which Klaus sends her off. And if we do not know that *gewhen* means "go home," we fail to understand both her destination and the connection of this novel with other novels that end with a character's returning home. We think particularly of the ending of *Love Medicine,* where Lipsha finally decides that it is right to "cross the water, and bring her home" (*LM,* 367). The referent for "her" is June, who at the end of the first movement in the novel walked over the snow "like water and came home" (*LM,* 7). The *gewhen* lets readers know that for Erdrich, June and Sweetheart Calico are both women whose only way to survive, even in death, is to return home.[8]

8. "Coming home" is as important a theme in the novels of Native American writers as "leaving home" is to the fiction of white novelists. Although for many white protagonists their ability to break their ties with their familial past and strike out confidently on their own is a sign

Without a translation, most readers would miss that important connection. In providing this glossary we also hope to stimulate among Erdrich's many non-Indian readers an interest in studying her revered old language.[9]

SOURCES

The glossary below is in no sense a full Ojibwe-English dictionary. Rather, it gives only those Ojibwe words, phrases, and sentences that Erdrich uses in her novels, spelled as she spells them (sometimes inconsistently). Often the context of a certain word, phrase, or sentence provides or implies the meaning, but not always or fully. Especially where the context is uncertain, we have looked in one or more of the available Ojibwe-English dictionaries, although, as mentioned above, due to the use of prefixes, inflectional markers, and variable spellings, we are not always able to find her words there.

One example of the difficulty of looking up Ojibwe words is the command *neshke,* meaning "look, behold," which is variously spelled *neshke, nashke,* and *neshkey.* It is necessary, at times, to be aware of such variations in order to locate a word. Yet such awareness can also cause readers to guess incorrectly. The two words in Erdrich's phrase *kitchi manitiminin (LR,* 96), for example, do not appear in the Nichols and Nyholm dictionary, though the look-alike word *gichi-manidoo,* meaning Great Spirit, does. It seems reasonable to guess that this is also the meaning of Erdrich's similar phrase, but *kitchi manitiminin* turns out to mean, instead, "have big sexual intercourse."

In this glossary, we translate only Ojibwe words, not words in other languages, such as the German *blitzkuchen* in *The Antelope Wife* or the various words that appear on the last page of *The Master Butchers Singing*

---

of growth, for many Indian protagonists, who have lost touch with their family or reservation community, a sign of growth is that they return to the homeplace. For further discussion of the difference in attitude to home, see William Bervis, "Native American Novels: Homing In," in Brian Swan and Arnold Krupat, eds., *Recovering the Word: Essays on Native American Literature* (Berkeley and Los Angeles: University of California Press, 1987), 580–620.

9. In the glossary we make no effort to try to show how the words, phrases, or sentences would have been pronounced. Readers interested in the basics of Ojibwe pronunciation might want to gain access to the following course in Ojibwe, which consists of four cassettes and two booklets. The booklet *Everyday Ojibwe* covers commands and common expressions, while *Ojibwe Word Lists* includes separate lesson units on time, weather, feelings, household items, actions, food, clothing, and other topics of daily living. The four tapes (spoken by Rick Gresczyk [Gayakognaabo] and Margaret Sayers [Awasigilizhikok]) and the two undated booklets are available from Eagle Works, Box 580564, Minneapolis, MN 55458–0564.

Club. We include proper names only when Erdrich herself translates them or suggests English equivalents. We list main entries according to the spellings Erdrich uses, but we have indicated in the definitions some alternate spellings found in various dictionaries. When we are particularly unsure of the accuracy of our guesses at meaning, we use parenthetical question marks.

We list alphabetically each Ojibwe word and phrase that Erdrich uses in her novels published through 2005, excluding *The Birchbark House* and *The Game of Silence,* two novels for young readers. We give page citations from the novels, which are listed in the order of publication. Ojibwe sentences that Erdrich includes are grouped by novel at the end of the glossary. We generally capitalize only proper names, leaving other words in lowercase, even when Erdrich capitalizes them for syntactic reasons. Words and sentences used in Erdrich's acknowledgments are not included, since those usually offer private thanks to specific individuals. When available, we use definitions given or implied in Erdrich's novels. For meanings obtained from dictionaries, we indicate the source—one of six reference works listed below, with our abbreviation, in chronological order of original publication:

Baraga refers to Frederic Baraga's *A Dictionary of the Ojibway Language* (1878; reprint, St. Paul: Minnesota Historical Society Press, 1992). This two-part dictionary, comprising more than 700 pages, was the work of an early Christian missionary to the Ojibwe. Our page references are all to part 2, the Ojibwe-to-English half of the dictionary. Its entries reflect the state of the language on the southern shores of Lake Superior about 150 years ago. An introduction by John D. Nichols to the 1992 one-volume reprint gives biographical information about the Catholic priest who wrote the dictionary mostly for the use of other missionaries. Baraga may in some sense have been a model for one feature of Father Damien, who, in *The Last Report on the Miracles at Little No Horse,* is said to want "to finish an incomplete Ojibwe grammar and dictionary" (*LR,* 180).

Johnston refers to Basil Johnston's *Ojibway Language Lexicon for Beginners* (Ottawa: Ministry of Indian and Northern Affairs, Canada, 1978), which Erdrich acknowledges in the front matter of *Tracks:* "There are many dialects of Ojibway, or Anishinabe. I tried to conform to Basil Johnston's excellent *Ojibway Language Lexicon.*" Johnston is difficult to use for translation, since the words are grouped by kind rather than alphabetically. Nouns are separated from verbs, for example, and the nouns themselves are grouped by categories like geography, weather, anatomy, and so on. The dictionary was designed for teaching the language, not for translation.

Kegg refers to Maude Kegg's *Portage Lake: Memories of an Ojibwe Child-hood,* edited and transcribed by John D. Nichols (Edmonton: University of Alberta Press, 1991). This dual-language volume is graced by a useful glossary prepared by Nichols, itself prefaced by an equally useful discussion of the language (see pp. 187–272). There is evidence that Erdrich is familiar with this book. See especially, in connection with *The Last Report on the Miracles at Little No Horse,* Kegg's chapters on the steamboat (pp. 26–27) and the chase by a big black dog (pp. 96–101). The spelling of the words generally accords with that in the next item.

Nichols refers to *A Concise Dictionary of Minnesota Ojibwe,* by John D. Nichols and Earl Nyholm (Minneapolis: University of Minnesota Press, 1995). Earl Nyholm's Ojibwe name is Earl Otchingwanigan. Erdrich refers readers to this volume in her "Author's Note on the Ojibwa Language" in *The Birchbark House,* p. 240. It has apparently become her own most frequently used reference for matters of orthography and meaning, though she seems also to rely often on the advice of Ojibwe-speaking friends and teachers, whether or not their dialect, vocabulary, or spelling coincide with the Nichols and Nyholm dictionary. There is also a useful glossary at the end of Anton Treuer, ed., *Living Our Language: Ojibwe Tales and Oral Histories* (St. Paul: Minnesota Historical Society Press, 2001), based largely on Nichols and Nyholm. Erdrich says in private correspondence, "I think it is important to note that many Ojibwe do not accept the Nichols and Nyholm spellings and prefer phonetic spellings. Also that the double vowel spellings are an academic distinction I've adopted on the advice of speakers (Canadian) who teach at the University of Minnesota. But all spellings that convey meanings are 'correct.' "

Birchbark refers to Erdrich's own short "Glossary and Pronunciation Guide of Ojibwa Terms" that appears at the end of *The Birchbark House* (New York: Hyperion, 1999), pp. 241–44. This glossary is only four pages long, but it is particularly useful in that it provides Erdrich's own definitions of her Ojibwe words, and because it gives some indication of how to pronounce the words. Our glossary does not include words from *Birchbark House* unless they also appear in her other novels.

Silence refers to Erdrich's expanded but still short "Glossary and Pro-nunciation Guide of Ojibwe Terms" (pp. 251–56) that appears at the end of *The Game of Silence* (New York: HarperCollins, 2005), a sequel to *The Birchbark House.* Since Erdrich's children's novels are not included in this reader's guide, we include in the glossary only references to help us to define words used in her other novels. The glossary in *The Game of Silence* contains some sixty words not used in *The Birchbark House*. Some of the words she repeats there are spelled in alternative ways.

GLOSSARY OF ERDRICH'S OJIBWE WORDS AND PHRASES

A

aadizokaan(ag)—sacred myth(s), legend(s), or spirit(s). The **-ag** or **-ug** suffix usually marks the plural in Ojibwe. Nichols 16, spelled **aadizookaan**. *Birchbark* 241, spelled **adisokaan**, "a traditional story that often helps explain how to live as an Ojibwa." *LR* 95, 243, 285, 310, *FS* 114.

aaniin, ahnee—greetings, hello; how? why? *interrogative adverb.* See also **aneesh.** Kegg 223. Nichols 18. *Birchbark* 241, spelled **ahneen,** "a greeting, sometimes in the form of a question." *LM* 263, *LR* 79, 187, 245, *PD* 124.

aaniindi—where? Nichols 18. *LR* 241.

Agongos—Swedes or Scandinavians. See Nichols 5, where we learn that the term literally means "chipmunk." In her article reprinted in *North Dakota Quarterly* (see our note 3 above), Erdrich says (p. 215), "Agongosininiwag, the chipmunk people, are Scandinavians. I'm still trying to find out why." *AW* 215.

Ahabikwe—Ahab-woman (Nanapush calls Margaret this during the moose hunt, a combination of Captain Ahab of Melville's *Moby-Dick* and the Ojibwe word for "woman"). Nichols 64, **ikwe,** woman. *LR* 285.

ahau, ahua—attention-getting exclamation meaning "so!" "well!" or "listen up!" (?). Possibly related to Kegg 222, **aa,** *exclamation,* or 243, **haa, ha, haw,** or **haaw,** *exclamation,* so! well! *LR* 96, *PD* 182.

akik, akikoog—kettle(s). Nichols 7. *Silence* 251. *LR* 257.

akiwenzii—old man. Kegg 219. Nichols 7. *LM* 33, spelled **ekewaynze.** *FS* 116, 140.

amanisowin—fright, frightful dreams. Baraga 27, spelled **amanissowin,** "alarm, fright." Nichols 8, spelled **amaniso,** "to be alarmed." *PD* 111.

ambe—see **ombay.**

anama'ay—praying. Nichols 8, spelled **anami'aa,** "pray, be Christian." *LR* 182, "the Ojibwe word for praying . . . with its sense of a great motion upward."

Anamaiiakiikwe—Under the Ground. Nichols 8, spelled **anaamakamig,** and 64, **ikwe,** woman. *FS* 50.

anamibiigokoosh—hippopotamus (underwater pig). Nichols 9, spelled **anaami-biig,** "underwater," and 62, spelled **gookoosh,** "pig." Erdrich notes in private correspondence: "According to Jim Clark's uncle, who invented a name or knew one for every non-indigenous creature he saw in the zoo." *LR* 246.

Anaquot—Cloud. Nichols 17, spelled **aanakwad.** *FS* 51, 123, 203, etc.

ando—search out. *LR* 305.

aneesh—how? why? *interrogative adverb,* well now, you see. Kegg 223 and Nichols 18, spelled **aaniish.** *Tr* 47.

ani—going on. Baraga 283, under **ni, ani.** Kegg 219, **ani-,** "going away from, on the way." Nichols 9. *LR* 95.

anibishaabo—tea. Nichols 11, spelled **aniibiishaaboo.** *PD* 126.

animosh(ug)—dog(s). Kegg 219. Nichols 10, spelled **animosh(ag).** *AW* 75, 80, *FS* 180.

Anishinabe(g), Anishinaabe(g)—human, Indian, Ojibwe people, or their language. Johnston 6, spelled **Anishaubeg.** Kegg 219. Nichols 10. Defined by Father Damian in *LR* 208 as "the Spontaneous or Original People." *Tr* 1, 99, 110, 116, *AW* 48, 107, 137, *LR* 78, 81, 85, 96, etc., *MBSC* 77, *FS* 24, 74, 80, 154, 210, *PD* 108, 117, 120, 174, 175.

anishinabedok—men, male Ojibwe. The people the old woman addresses with this word in *Last Report* are told to have erections. *LR* 96.

Anishinaabekwe—Indian or Ojibwe woman. *LR* 150, 261, *FS* 23.

anokee—work. Nichols 11, spelled **anokii.** *AW* 104.

Apijigo Bakaday—So Hungry. Nichols 18, spelled **aapiji,** "very, quite," and 24, spelled **bakade,** "hungry." *AW* 56.

Apitchi—Robin. Nichols 110, spelled **opichi.** *PD* 189, etc., 228 ("named Apitchi for the robin"), etc.

Asainekanipawit—Standing in a Stone. *Tr* 220.

Asasaweminikwesens—Chokecherry Girl. Nichols 13, **asasawemin,** chokecherry, and 64, **ikwezens,** girl. *Tr* 7.

asemaa—tobacco. Nichols 13. *LR* 187.

asin(iig)—stone(s). Nichols 14. In her article reprinted in *North Dakota Quarterly* (see our note 3 above), Erdrich says (p. 215), "The word for stone, *asin,* is animate. Stones are called grandfathers and grandmothers and are extremely important in Ojibwe philosophy. Once I began to think of stones as animate, I started to wonder whether I was picking up a stone or it was putting itself into my hand." Erdrich notes in private correspondence that "in *Birchbark House* Omakayas uses stones as people." *Silence* 252. *LR* 257, *FS* 77.

audoomobiig—automobiles. See also **waasamoowidaabaanag.** Erdrich notes in private correspondence: "The word is in common use, clearly derived from the *chimookoman* word for car." *LR* 243.

awegonen—What? Nichols 118, **wegonen, awegonen.** *PD* 125.

awenen—who? Nichols 15. *FS* 44.

awiyaa—someone, anyone. Kegg 221, spelled **awiiya.** *LR* 95.

Awun—mist, fog. Johnston 9. Nichols 14, spelled **awan,** "be foggy, there is a fog." *LR* 277, 278, etc.

awus—scat, go away. Nichols 26. *FS* 111.

ayaan'na—have, own, does he or she have? Nichols 15, spelled **ayaan.** *LR* 133.

ayiih—exclamation of surprise or approval. *Birchbark* 241, spelled **ayah,** "yes." *LR* 222.

B

babaumawaebigowin—driven along by waves. Johnston 54. *LM* 102, 103.

bashkwegin—leather, hide. Nichols 26. *FS* 143, *PD* 126.

baubaukunaetae-geezis—April, patches of earth, developing sun. Johnston 22. *Tr* 192.

bayzhig, bezhig—one. Johnston 19, spelled **beshig.** Nichols 30. *AW* 1, *FS* 153, *PD* 132.

bebezhigongazhii—horse, one-nailed animal. Nichols 30, spelled **bebezhigooganzhii.** *LR* 359, 360.

beeskun k'papigeweyaun—put on this shirt. Johnston 36, 51, spelled **beeskoniyaewin** and **beesekoniyaewin,** "dressing, putting on clothing" and 20, **pupagewiyaun(un),** "shirt(s)." Nichols 20, spelled **babagiwayaan,** "shirt." *LM* 263.

be izah—come. Nichols 31, spelled **bi-izhaa.** *AW* 109.

bekaayan—wait, hold on. Nichols 30, spelled **bekaa.** Erdrich notes in private correspondence that it means "You, wait!" *LR* 167.

bezhig—see **bayzhig.**

bimautiziwaad—those who live the good life. Erdrich notes in private correspondence that it "refers to *bimaudiziwin*—the good life—a very complicated concept." *LR* 95.

bine—partridge. Nichols 33. *FS* 131.

Bineshii—Small Bird. *Silence* 252, spelled **binesi,** "thunderbird." *Tr* 7, *BP* 23.

bizindan, bizindamoog—listen, listen up. Nichols 34. Erdrich notes in private correspondence that it means "all of you be quiet." *LR* 85, 167, *FS* 116.

boogidiwin(an)—fart(s). Johnston, 72, "farting." Nichols 38, spelled **boogidi.** *LR* 291.

boonishin—leave me alone. Nichols 39, spelled **booni,** "leave . . . alone, quit." *LR* 284.

booshkay neen—it's up to you, it's your decision. Nichols 39, spelled **booshke** or **booshke giniin.** *TBL* 102.

booshoo, boozhoo—greetings, hello. According to Erdrich in *Birchbark* 242, "an Ojibwa greeting invoking the great teacher of the Ojibwa, Nanabozho." Nichols 39. The word is sometimes thought to be related to the French *bonjour,* but Erdrich insists in private correspondence that it "is *not* related to *bonjour.*" *LM* 246, *BP* 131, *AW* 109, 126, 228, *LR* 79, 91, etc., *PD* 224, 231.

Bungeenaboop—Almost Soup. Nichols 52, **gegaa,** "nearly, almost," and 90, **nabob,** "soup." *AW* 81.

Bwaan(ag)(ug)—Sioux or Dakota Indian(s). Kegg 230. *Birchbark* 242, "the Dakota or Lakota people, another Native tribe, whose reservations spread across the Great Plains." *LR* 96, 150–53, 360, *FS* 102.

Bwaanakeeng—Sioux country, land of the Dakotas. Nichols 39, **bwaan,** "Dakota (Sioux)," and 7, **aki** or **akiing,** "land . . . country." *AW* 75, 80.

Bwaaninini—Sioux man. See also **inini** (man). *LR* 360.

C

chi—big (sometimes used as a shortened form of **kitchi**). *LR* 95, *PD* 209, 244.

chimookoman(ag)(ug)—big knife, or white person(s). See also **mookamon.** Nichols 283, spelled **gichi-mookomaan.** *Birchbark,* 242, "word meaning 'big knife,' used to describe white people or non-Indians." *AW* 138, 142, 171, 206, *LR* 81, 92, 94, 95, 100, 120, 158, 186, 261, 283, *FS,* spelled **chimookomaan(ag),** 74, 79, 80, 117, 131, 155, 177, 200.

chimooks—white people (see previous item). *LR* 114.

ciga swa?—Do you have a cigarette? Derived from **zagaswaa,** to smoke tobacco. Nichols 121. *LM* 32.

D

daashkikaa—cracked apart, split. Nichols 43. *AW* 4, 196, 212, 213.

daga—please!, come on! Kegg 231. Nichols 40. *Silence* 252. *LR* 51, 252, 323.

dagasaa, dagasana—please now (see previous item). Erdrich notes in private correspondence that this form is an "extra polite" way to say "please." *LR* 96, *FS* 143.

dahgo—just like. Nichols 96, spelled **indigo,** "just like, as if." *AW* 171.

dewikwey—have a headache. Nichols 44. [Possibly related to Ojibwe sentence in *TBL* 53?]

Deydey—Father, Daddy. See also **n'deydey**. *Birchbark* 242, "Daddy." *PD* 176.

djessikid—magician, "tent-shaker." Cognate with **jeesekewinini** (see below). Erdrich notes in private correspondence that the term means "conjurer, illusionist." *LM* 74, *BP* 132.

dodem—clan. Nichols 66, spelled **indoodem**, "my totem, my clan." *AW* 135, *LR* 261, 262, *FS* 135.

E

ekewaynzee—see **akiwenzii**.

etaa—only. Kegg 235. Nichols 46, spelled **eta**. *LR* 95.

eyah—yes, verily. Nichols 46, spelled **eya'**. *Birchbark* 241, spelled **ayah**. *Silence* 252. *AW* 85, *LR* 88, 97.

ezhichigeyan—you are doing. Nichols 71, spelled **izhichigewin**, "way of doing things." *Silence* 252, "to be doing something." *LR* 187.

G

gaag—porcupine. Nichols 50. *LR* 85, 86.

Gakahbekong—Minneapolis, Place of the Falls. Nichols 48, spelled **Gakaabikaang**, Minneapolis, and spelled **gakaamikijiwan**, "be a waterfall." *AW* 25, 49, 84, 101, 106, 124, 219, *FS* 5, spelled **Gakaabikaang**.

gakina—all. Nichols 48. *LR* 95.

gakinago—all of it. Nichols 48, spelled **gakina gegoo**, "everything." *LR* 96.

gashkadino-giizis—November, the freezing moon. Johnston 22, **kushkudini-geezis**, "freezing sun." Nichols 49. *LR* 258.

gaween—no, not. Nichols 52, spelled **gaawiin**. *Birchbark* 242. *AW* 128.

gaween gego—it's nothing special. Nichols 52, spelled **gaawiin gegoo**, "nothing." *AW* 135.

gay, gey—and, also; as for. Kegg 237 and Nichols 50, spelled **gaye**. *LR* 95.

gaytay—old. Nichols 52, spelled **gete-**, "old, old-time." *AW* 171.

g'dai—your dog, animal. Nichols 168, **inday**, "my dog," and 52, **gi-**, *second-person prefix*. *FS* 46.

Geeshik, Geezhig—Day, Sky. Johnston 6, 7, 18. Nichols 60, spelled **giizhig**, "sky, heaven, day." See also **Kakageeshikok**. *BP* 57, *PD* 157, 158, etc.

gegaa—nearly, almost. Nichols 52. *PD* 210.

gegahwabamayaan—see you. Nichols 114, spelled **waabandan**, "see." Erdrich notes in private correspondence that it can mean "I'll see you." *LR* 133.

geget—surely. Nichols 52, "sure, indeed, certainly, really." *Silence* 252, "surely, or for emphasis, truly or really." *AW* 107, 224, *LR* 321, *FS* 200, 204.

geget igo—absolutely, unquestionably. *LR* 321, 322.

geget na—is that right? *BP* 131.

gego—don't! Nichols 52. *Silence* 252, "stop that." *AW* 88, *FS* 134, 193, *PD* 109.

genwaabiigigwed—giraffe. Nichols 52. *LR* 246.

gewhen, gewehn—go home. Nichols 60, spelled **giiwe**. *AW* 229, *MBSC* 385.

gey—see **gay**.

Gichi gami—Lake Superior. Nichols 53, spelled **gichigami**. *FS* 5.

gigaa, giigaa—you will. Nichols 52, **gi-**, *second-person prefix*. *LR* 81, 96.

giin—you. Nichols 58. *PD* 171.

gi-izhamin—you are going. Nichols 52, **gi-**, *second-person prefix*, and 71, **izhaa** and **izhaamagad**, "go to a certain place." *LR* 241.

ginebig(oog)—snake(s). Nichols 55. *LR* 220.

ginitum—it's your turn. Nichols 59, spelled **giinitam**, "your turn." *LR* 232.

gisina—cold (weather). Nichols 56, spelled **gisinaa**. *PD* 208.

gitchi-nookomis(iban)—great-grandmother. Nichols 53, spelled **gichi**, "big, great, very," and 102, **Nookomis**, "my grandmother." *FS* 178.

gitimishk—lazy, lazybones. Nichols 56, spelled **gitimishki**, "be habitually lazy, be a lazybones." *LR* 285, *FS* 170.

giwii—do you want to? Nichols 52, **gi-**, *second-person prefix*, and 118, **wii-**, "want to, will," *prefix*. *PD* 126.

gizhawenimin—I love you. Nichols 57, spelled **gizhaawenim**, "be jealous of." *Silence* 252. Erdrich notes in private correspondence that "it means loving in a kind way—the root is the word for kindness or compassion. The love-word **nizaagi-iin** has the double meaning of being jealous or stingy about keeping another person." *LR* 252.

Gizhe Manito—God, Great Spirit. Nichols 57, spelled **gizhe-manidoo**, "God (especially in Christian usage)." In her article reprinted in *North Dakota Quarterly* (see note 3 above), Erdrich says (p. 214), "What the Ojibwe call the Gizhe Mandidoo [is] the great and kind spirit residing in all that lives." Erdrich notes in private correspondence that it means "the kind-hearted god." *LR* 100, 315, *FS* 48, 72, 132.

H

hihn—too bad. *Birchbark* 242, spelled **hiyn**, "exclamation of sympathy or chagrin, meaning 'that's too bad.'" Erdrich notes in private correspondence that it is "an expression of regret." *LR* 133, 323.

howah—okay. *Birchbark* 242, "a sound of approval." *LR* 97, 174, 292.

I

idash—and, but. Kegg 243. Nichols 64. *LR* 95.

igo—very, especially. Nichols 64, also **go**, (61), *emphatic word*. *LR* 321, *PD* 171.

ii'iih—and so, well. From private correspondence with Erdrich. *LR* 94.

i'in—I, can I. Nichols 64, **in-**, *first-person prefix*. *LR* 81.

i'iwe—that. Nichols 64, spelled **i'iw,** also **i'iwedi,** "that over there." *LR* 95.

ikwe, ikweywug—woman, women. Kegg 243. Nichols 64. *BP* 6, *TBL* 53, (spelled **ikway**), *LR* 96.

ikwe-inini—a woman-man (perhaps suggesting a gay person or hermaphrodite), called **winkte** by the Bwaanag. *LR* 153.

ina, inah—indicates a question. Nichols 64, *"yes-no question word."* *AW* 109, *LR* 241, *PD* 126.

indah—I. Nichols 66, **ind-**, *first-person prefix*. *AW* 109.

indis—my umbilical cord, belly button. Nichols 66. *AW* 86, 101, 219, *LR* 261.

ingitizima—my parent. Nichols 67, spelled **ingitiziim.** *LR* 247.

in'gozis—my son. See also **n'gozis.** Nichols 67, spelled **ingozis.** *LR* 133.

inini(wag)—man (men). Kegg 245. Nichols 68. *LR* 96.

ishkodewaaboo, ishkode wabo—liquor, fire water. Nichols 69 (cf. Nichols 69, **ishkode,** "fire"). Kegg 245. *Silence* 253. *LR* 107, 322, *FS* 141, *PD* 112, 173.

ishkonigan—reservation, leftovers, desolate lands. Nichols 69, **ishkonan,** "reserve something, save something back," **ishkonigan,** "reservation," and **ishkwanjigan,** "leftover food." In private correspondence, Erdrich thanks Jim Clark for the word. *AW* 239, *LR* 360, *FS* 48, 200, 210.

ishkwaa anokii wug—Friday or Saturday (literally, "after work day"). Nichols 69, **ishkwaa,** "after," and 11, **anokii,** "work." *AW* 104.

ishte—how nice! *Birchbark* 242, "exclamation meaning how good, nice, pleasant." *Silence* 253, spelled **ishtay.** *AW* 138, *LR* 165, 287.

izah, izhah—go. Nichols 71, spelled **izhaa,** "go to a certain place." *AW* 109, *LR* 206.

izhadaa—let's go. *Silence* 253, spelled **izhadah.** *LR* 252.

izhinikaazo—to be named a certain way. Kegg 247, spelled **izhinikaade** and **izhinikaazh.** Nichols 72. *PD* 124 (spelled **izhinikaazoyan**), 204.

J

jeesekeewinini—medicine man, tent-shaker. Johnston 25, "a medicine man who communes with incorporeal beings to determine the cause of afflictions, physical or mental, may prescribe remedies, usually a member of the Midewewin, and one who has reached the third degree or order." Nichols 74, spelled **jiisakiiwinini,** "seer who uses a shaking tent." *Tr* 188.

jibay—ghost or spirit. Nichols 73, spelled **jiibay.** See also **odjib.** *LR* 187.

jiimaan(an)—canoe(s), boat(s). Nichols 74. *PD* 164.

K

Kakageeshikok—Eternal Sky. See also **Geeshik.** *PD* 157, 166.

Kanatowakechin—Mirage. *Tr* 220.

kaween onjidah—not on purpose. Nichols 52, spelled **gaawiin,** "no, not," and 109, **onjida,** "on purpose." *LM* 80.

kinnikinnick—bark-based tobacco, sometimes spelled **kinikinnick.** *Birchbark* 242, "type of smoking mixture made of the inner bark of dogwood or red willow, sometimes mixed with regular tobacco." *LM* 71, 341, *BP* 28, *AW* 57.

kitchi—big, abundant, grand. Johnston 125, 131. Nichols 53, spelled **gichi-,** "big, great, very." *LR* 96.

Kokoko, Ko ko ko—owl. Johnston 14, spelled **kookookoo(k).** *Tr* 67, 206, *BP* 196.

kookum—shortened or child's form of **gitchi-nookomis,** great-grandmother. *FS* 177.

M

maaj—leave, go. Nichols 80, spelled **maajaa.** *AW* 224.

magizha—maybe, perhaps. Nichols 80, spelled **maagizhaa.** *AW* 171, 213.

ma'iingan—wolf. Nichols 75. *PD* 204, 213, 219, 232.

majigoode—dress. Nichols 75. *Silence* 253. *LR* 242, *FS* 141.

majii—bad. Kegg 249 and Nichols 75, spelled **magi-** (prefix). *LR* 133.

makade-mashkikiwaaboo—black liquid medicine, coffee. Kegg 249. Nichols 75, 78. *LR* 108.

makak(oog), makuk—birchbark box or basket. Nichols 75. *Birchbark* 243, "a container of birchbark folded and often stitched together with basswood fiber. Ojibwa people use these containers today, especially for traditional feasts." *LM* 310, *AW* 18, 19, 135, 198, *LR* 104, *PD* 163, 165.

makazin(an), makizin(an)—footwear, moccasin(s). Kegg 249. Nichols 76. *Birchbark* 242, "footwear usually made of tanned moosehide or deerskin, often trimmed with beads and/or fur." *AW* 171, *LR* 152, 187, 242, 251, 264, 268, 287, 294, *FS* 2, 77, 165, 191, *PD* 123, 144, 182.

manaa—lust, sexual intercourse. See also **manitadaa** and **manitiminin**. *FS* 74, 132, 133, 148.

manidominenz, manidoominens(ag)—bead, "little spirit seed." Nichols 77. *AW* 91, *PD* 182.

manidoo(g), manitou(s), manito(s)—spirit(s), god(s). Johnston 25, "a god or spirit, an incorporeal being, used as a verb means to be godlike, spiritual, incorporeal, and medicinal." Kegg 250. Nichols 77. *Birchbark* 243, "spirits, beings who inhabit the Ojibwa world and often communicate in dreams." Marie (*LM* 87) refers to Manitous as "invisible ones who live in the woods." *LM* 77, 87, *Tr* 139, *BP* 7, *AW* 136, *LR* 315, 360, *FS* 100, 157, *PD* 110.

manidooens—little spirits. Nichols 77, spelled **manidoons**, "bug or insect." *LR* 315.

manitadaa—have sexual intercourse. See also **manaa**. *LR* 96.

manitiminin—have sexual intercourse. *LR* 96.

manitou-geezis—January, the strong spirit sun. Johnston 22. Nichols 77, spelled **manidoo-giizis**. *Tr* 96.

manitou-geezisohns—December, the little spirit sun. Johnston 22. Nichols 77, spelled **manidoo-giizisoons**. *Tr* 1.

manomin, manoomin—wild rice. See also **zashi manoomin**. Nichols 77. *Silence* 253, "the good seed." *AW* 138, *LR* 187, *PD* 163.

manominike-giizis—September, the wild rice sun. Johnston 22, spelled **mino-mini-geezis**. Nichols 78, spelled **manoominike-giizis**, "the month of ricing: September, August." *LR* 242.

mashkiig—swamp, slough. Baraga 223, spelled **mashkig**, "swamp, marsh." *LR* 201, 359.

mashkiki—medicine. Kegg 250. Nichols 78. *FS* 24.

mashkimood, mashkimodenz—bag or sack. See also **'skimood**. Nichols 78, spelled **mashkimod**. *AW* 133, 219.

Matchimanito—the bad spirit, the name of the large lake on Erdrich's fictional Ojibwe reservation. Nichols 75, **maji-**, "bad," and 77, **manidoo**, "god, spirit, manitou." *LM* 234, 236, etc., *Tr* 8, etc., *LR* 97, 242, 263, 343, etc., *FS* 9, 204.

matchimindemoyenh—evil old woman, witch. *LR* 104.

mazhiwe, mazhiweyt—have intercourse. Nichols 79. *LR* 95, 96.

meen-geezis—July, the blueberry sun. Johnston 22. *Tr* 62.

megwitch, miigwech, miigwetch—thank you. Johnston 132, spelled **meeg-waetch**. Nichols 89. *Birchbark* 242, spelled **megwetch**. *Silence* 254, spelled **meegwech**. *LM* 313, *AW* 120, *LR* 167, 174, 320, *PD* 209, 244.

mekadewikonayewinini—priest. Nichols 83. Erdrich notes in private correspondence that it means "black-robe man." *LR* 133.

mekinak—snapping turtle. Nichols 84, spelled **mikinaak.** *FS* 135.

Michif—mixed blood. *LR* 96.

Midassbaupayikway—Ten Stripe Woman. Nichols 83, **midasso,** "ten," and 64, **ikwe,** "woman." *AW* 35.

mii'e—(?) either "that's it, that's enough" (like **mi'iw** below) or "it is thus that, it is that" like Nichols 89, spelled **mii.** *LR* 95.

miigis—shells, pearls. Nichols 89. Erdrich notes in private correspondence that "these are extremely sacred items." *LR* 156, 301, *FS* 48.

miiwech, miigwetch—see **megwetch.**

mii nang—yes, for sure, certainly, of course. Nichols 89. *FS* 142, 171, 200, 204.

miishishin—give it to me. Nichols 89, spelled **miizh,** "give to," and 64, **in-,** *first-person prefix.* *LR* 323.

mi'iw—that's it, that's enough. Baraga 235. *LR* 175, *FS* 181, 189.

mindemoya, mindimooyenh—old woman. Kegg 253. Nichols 85. *BP* 123, 126, 127, 129, *LR* 286, etc., *FS* 150.

minikweken, minikwen—to drink. Nichols 85, spelled **minikwe.** *FS* 193, *PD* 126.

miniquen—a drink. See also **minikweken.** *LR* 305.

mino—good, nice. Nichols 85. *LR* 206.

mino ayaa—be well. Nichols 85, spelled **mino-ayaa.** *FS* 50.

minomini-geezis—September, the wild rice sun. Johnston 22. See also **mano-minike-giizis.** *Tr* 206.

minopogwud—tastes good. Nichols 86, spelled **minopogwad.** *LR* 292.

minwendam—be happy, glad. See also **niminwendam.** Kegg 254. Nichols 87. *LR* 81.

mi'sago'i—that's all, the story is over. Kegg 18, 46, 60, etc., spelled **mii sa go i'iw,** "That's it." *LR* 85, 96, 361.

Mishimin Odaynang—Apple Town (Minneapolis). Nichols 87, **mishiimin,** apple, and 112, **oodena,** town. See also **Gakahbekong.** *AW* 198.

mishkeegamin—cranberry. Nichols 162, **maskiigimin,** "lowbush cranberry." *Tr* 176.

miskomini-geezis—August, the raspberry sun. Johnston 22. *Tr* 10.

miskwa—red. Nichols 87, spelled **miskwaa.** *AW* 113.

miskwaabik—copper. Johnston 7, spelled **misqwaubik.** Nichols 87. *AW* 113 (spelled **miskwa wabic**), *FS* 6.

Missepeshu, Misshepeshu—the great lynx (refers to the lake or water monster in Matchimanito Lake). Johnston 24, spelled **mishi-bizheu,** "the great lynx—the enemy of Nanabush," and 31, spelled **mishibizheu(k),** "lion(s), the great lynx." Nichols 87, spelled **mishibizhii,** "lion, panther, underwater panther." *LM* 236, *Tr* 8, 175, etc.

Mizi zipi—Big River, Mississippi River. Nichols 54, spelled **gichi-ziibi.** *AW* 96.

mogate—go, leave. Erdrich notes in private correspondence that it is "a Wahpeto-nian 'load' term once used primarily by drunk teenagers rousing themselves to leave for another party." Used in the phrase, "Let's mogate" in *AW* 96.

mookamon—white person, white culture, literally "knife" (short for **chimoo-komaan,** "big knife," [i.e., white person]). Nichols 90, spelled **mookomaan,** "knife." *BP* (later editions) 6, 58, 140.

moowan—excrement. Nichols 89, under **moo.** *FS* 137, 167.

mooz—moose. Johnston 16, spelled **moozo.** Nichols 90. *AW* 171, *LR* 283, 284, *FS* 136.

Moskatikinaugun—Red Cradle. *Tr* 220.

N

na?—no? isn't that right? Nichols 90, *yes-no question word. FS* 23.

naanan—five. Nichols 94. *PD* 132.

naazh—go and get, take. Keeg 257. Nichols 95. *LR* 51.

Nadouissioux—Sioux or Dakota Indians. *Tr* 1.

namadabin—sit down. Kegg 256, spelled **namadabi.** Nichols 91. *PD* 123.

Nanabozho—trickster namesake of Nanapush. *Silence* 254, "the great teacher of the Ojibwe, who used his comical side to teach lessons, often through hilarious mistakes." Erdrich notes in private correspondence that it is "a variation of Wenebosho." *LM* 236, *LR* 63, 83–85, etc.

Nanakawepenesick—Different Thumbs. *LM* 74.

n'dawnis—my daughter. Johnston 29, spelled **daun(iss),** "daughter." Nichols 164, spelled **indaanis,** "my daughter." *Silence* 254. The prefix **n'** or **ni-** or **in-** indicates first-person pronoun or first-person possessive (Nichols 90, 95, 64). *LM* 69, 83, *AW* 85, *LR* 206, 252, *MBSC* 385, *FS* 140, 193, 194, 202, 204, *PD* 167.

n'deydey—my father. See also **Deydey.** Nichols 66, spelled **indeed,** also **-de-dey-.** *PD* 117, 167.

neej—two. Johnston 19, spelled **neezh.** Nichols 101, spelled **niizh.** *AW* 73.

neenawind—we, us. Johnston 121. *Tr* 138.

neewin, niiwin—four. Johnston 19. Nichols 101. *AW* 183, *PD* 132.

neshke—look, behold. Kegg 256 and Nichols 93, spelled **nashke.** *Birchbark* 243, spelled **neshkey.** *LR* 51, 95, 162, 244.

n'gah—my mother. Johnston 29. Nichols 66, spelled **inga.** *Silence* 254, spelled **n'gaa,** "old way of saying mother." *LR* 104, *FS* 53, 201.

n'gozis—my son. See also **ingozis.** Nichols 67, spelled **ingozis.** *FS* 196, 200.

n'gushi—I'm sorry. *LM* 102, 266.

n'gwunajiwi—my love. *BP* 104 (early editions; Ojibwe term cut from later editions).

nibaan—sleep. Nichols 95, spelled **nibaa,** "sleep," **nibaagan,** "bed." *LR* 206, *FS* 50 (spelled **niiban**).

nibi—water. Kegg 258. Nichols 96. *AW* 92, 124, *LR* 104.

niiji—my friend. Nichols 100, spelled **niijii.** *LR* 289, *PD* 203.

niimin—dance. Nichols 100. *FS* 146.

niin—I, me. Kegg 260. Nichols 100. *LR* 98.

niinag—my penis. See also **wiinag(ag).** Nichols 100. *FS* 135.

niiwin—see **neewin.**

niizh—two. Nichols 101. *FS* 153, *PD* 132.

nimanendam—I am sad. Nichols 82, spelled **maanendam,** "feel bad, feel depressed," with the **ni-** prefix designating the first person. *LR* 293.

niminwendam—I am happy, glad. See also **minwendam.** Kegg 258, where **ni-** indicates first person, and 254, where **minwendam** means "be glad, be happy." *LR* 133.

nimishoomis—my grandfather. Nichols 96. *LR* 303.

ninaandawenimaa—I want. Nichols 92, spelled **nandawendan,** "want, desire." *LR* 95.

nindebisinii—I have eaten plenty. Nichols 44, spelled **debisinii,** "eat enough, be full (after eating)." *LR* 292.

nindinawemaganidok—all my relatives, or everything that has existed in time. *LR* epigraph and 360–61 (where it is spelled **nindinawemagonidok**), *FS* 154.

ninimoshe—my sweetheart, my love, my cousin. Baraga 298. Nichols 100, spelled **niinimoshenh.** *AW* 22, 30, 229, *FS* 136, *PD* 210.

niswi—three. Johnston 19, spelled **nisswih.** Nichols 99. *AW* 99 (spelled **niswey**), *FS* 153, *PD* 132.

niwiiw—my wife. Nichols 99. *LR* 112, 292.

n'kawnis—my brother, my friend. Johnston 29, spelled **kawniss,** "brother, friend." *LM* 263.

n'mama—my mother. Nichols 96, spelled **n'maamaa.** *LR* 187.

n'missae—my oldest sister. Johnston 29, spelled **missaehn,** "eldest sister." *BP* 50.

nokomis—my grandmother. Nichols 102, spelled **nookomis.** *LR* 245.

n'tawnis—my brother-in-law. Johnston 29, spelled **neetawiss.** Nichols 101, spelled **niitaa,** "my (male's) brother-in-law." *LR* 112.

O

odaemin—strawberry. Nichols 104, spelled **ode'imin.** *AW* 135.

odjib—made of smoke, ghostly, without a body. See also **jibay.** *Tr* 35.

Ogimaakwe—Boss Woman. Nichols 108, "wife of chief or leader, woman leader." *Tr* 7, 220, *BP* 23, *FS* 203.

ogichidaa, ogitchida—soldier, ceremonial chief. Nichols 105. *Silence* 254, "male leader." *AW* 130, *PD* 123.

ogitchidaa-ikwe—strong woman, soldier woman, ceremonial headwoman. Kegg 262, where **ogichidaa** means "ritual attendant in a ceremony," and 243, where **ikwe** means "woman." Nichols 105, spelled **ogichidaakwe.** *Silence* 255, spelled **ogitchidakwe,** "female leader." *LR* 166, *FS* 142 (spelled **ogichidaa-ikwe**).

Ojibwemowin—the Ojibwe language. Nichols 105. *LR* 79, 164, 223, 258, 284, 290, *FS* 81, 179.

ojiid—his or her rectum. Nichols 68, spelled **injiid,** "my rectum." Erdrich notes in private correspondence that it "can also refer to the entire rear end." *LR* 291, *FS* 81, 166.

okij—pipestem. Nichols 106. *PD* 168.

Omakakayakeeng—frog land, Finland (Germany?). See Nichols 106, where **omakakii** is translated as frog, and *Birchbark* 5, where the protagonist's name **Omakayas** is translated as Little Frog. *AW* 132.

Omakakayininiwug—frog people, Finlanders (Germans?). *AW* 132.

Ombaashi—He Is Lifted By Wind. *Tr* 7, 220.

omaa, omah—here (see next item). Kegg 263. Nichols 106. *FS* 153, 166.

ombay, ombe—come here, let's go. Nichols 8, spelled **ambe,** "come on!, let's go!, attention!" *Silence* 255, "come here; let's go." Erdrich notes in private correspondence that **ombe omaa** can mean "come, or come here." *LR* 252, *FS* 153 (spelled **ombe omaa**), 166 (spelled **ombay omah**), *PD* 113 (spelled **ambe**).

Omiimii—Dove. *Tr* 45, 220, *FS* 163.

onaubin-geezis, onaabani-giizis—March, crust on the snow month. Johnston 22, spelled **onaubini-geezis.** *Tr* 32, *LR* 61.

onizhishin—be nice, pretty, lovely. Nichols 109. *FS* 77.

onji—from, because. Kegg 264 and Nichols 109, spelled **onji-** (a prefix), "from a certain place, for a certain reason." Nichols adds "because." *LR* 95.

opwaagaansz—cigarette (pipe). Kegg 264, spelled **opwaagan,** "pipe for smoking." Nichols 110, spelled **opwaagaans,** "cigarette." *LR* 51.

oshkay—new, young. Nichols 110, spelled **oshkayi'ii** and **oshki.** *AW* 13, 171.

owah—Oh! *Birchbark* 244, "exclamation of alarm or surprise, like 'Oh!' " *AW* 77, 130, 133, 171, 209.

Ozhawashkwamashkodeykway—Blue Prairie Woman. *AW* 12, 102.

ozhibi'igan(an)—written note(s). Nichols 111, spelled **ozhibii'iganan,** "something written." *LR* 357.

pagetinamahgehg—let them, allow them to. Nichols 23, spelled **bagidinamawaad.** *LR* 96.

pahtahneynahwug—many. Nichols 211, spelled **baataylinowag.** *LR* 95.

pakuks—skeletons of babies. *Birchbark* 244, "skeletons of children that fly through the air." *AW* 12, 13.

patakizoog—have erections. Erdrich notes in private correspondence that it is "the plural command form of 'stand it up.' " She adds that " 'patakizoog' was of course meant for Ojibwe speakers. I had lots of help with it." *LR* 95, 96.

pauguk beboon—skeleton winter. *Tr* 165.

payaetonookaedaed-geezis—the wood louse sun (November?). Not in Johnston's list of months on p. 22, but this chapter of *Tracks* refers to the armistice that ended World War I, which took place November 11, 1918. On p. 23, Johnston defines **payaetenookaedaed** as wood louse. *Tr* 131.

peendigaen, piindegen, piindigen—welcome, come in. Kegg 230, spelled **biindige,** "enter, go inside, come inside." Nichols 37, also spelled **biindige.** *Silence* 255, spelled **peendigen.** *BP* 28, 139, *LR* 183, *FS* 145, *PD* 102.

pikwayzhigun—bread (sliced), bannock. Johnston 26, spelled **piquaezhigun.** Nichols 25, spelled **bakwezhigan.** *AW* 56, *FS* 133 (spelled **pikwezhigan**).

puckoons—nuts. Baraga 183, spelled **pakan,** nut. Johnston 26, spelled **pagaun(uk),** nut(s). Nichols 22, spelled **bagaan,** nut, hazelnut. *PD* 178.

pukwe—hand-woven reed mats. *Silence* 255, "reed used in making mats." *LR* 103, 104.

sa—an intensifier. Kegg 265, "emphatic." Nichols 112. *Silence* 255, "part of **geget sa;** a polite addition to speech." *LR* 98.

saaah, sah, saaa—sound of disapproval or contempt, a kind of hiss. *LM* 98, *Tr* 47, *LR* 97, *FS* 136.

sana—and (?). It is part of the sentence **Niiban . . . mino ayaa sana** in *Four Souls* that is translated in the text as "Sleep and be well." **Nibaan** means "sleep," while **mino ayaa** means "be well" (see those entries above). *FS* 50.

Sanawashonekek—Lying Down Grass. *Tr* 220.

shabwii'ing—get through, survive. Nichols 124, spelled **zhaabsii,** "go through, pass through, survive." *LR* 95.

Shesheeb—Duck. Johnston 15, spelled **zheesheeb** and Nichols 127, spelled **zhiishiib.** Nanapush says in *Four Souls* that his enemy Shesheeb is "named for the black duck, greasy and sly." *FS* 99, 100, 101, etc.

shkendeban—erect penis. *LR* 293.

'skimood—bag. See also **mashkimood.** *AW* 134.

shkwebii, skwaybee—tipsy, drunk. *AW* 126, *LR* 111, 312, *FS* 143, 195, *PD* 113.

T

tahnee—there will be (?). *LR* 95.

tikinaagan, tikinagaan, tikinagan, tikinagun—cradle board. *Birchbark* 244, "a cradle board made of lightweight wood, with a footrest on one end and a bow-shaped frame at the other. A baby is wrapped snugly into the tikinagun with cloth, blankets, and skins. The tikinagun can be carried on the mother's back, leaned against a tree or a wall, or safely hung from a tree branch." Nichols 45, spelled **dikinaagan.** *AW* 3, 58, *LR* 184, 261, *FS* 100, *PD* 123, 127.

W

waabooyaan(an)—blanket(s). Kegg 266. Nichols 115. *LR* 164.

waasa—far off, distant. Nichols 116. *FS* 5.

waasamoowidaabaanag—automobiles, the wagons that move by themselves. See also **audoomobiig.** Nichols 116, **waasamoo,** "powered, electric," and 45, **ditibidaabaan(ag),** "wagon(s), truck(s)." *LR* 243.

waawaashkeshi—deer. Johnston 16, spelled **wawashkaesh.** Kegg 267. Nichols 117. *FS* 136.

Waubanikway—Dawn Woman. Nichols 114, spelled **waaban,** "dawn." *AW* 142.

we'ew(ug)—wife (wives). *AW* 134, 228.

weh'ehn—namesake. *AW* 172.

Wenabojo—trickster creator. Nichols 118, spelled **Wenabozho,** "character viewed as culture hero and trickster, also Nenabozho." *AW* 81.

weyass—meat. Johnston 26, spelled **weeyauss.** Nichols 121, spelled **wiiyass.** *Silence* 256. *AW* 14, 138, *FS* 3.

wiigwaas—birch bark. Nichols 119. *PD* 164 (spelled **wiigwassi,** used as a prefix).

wiigwaasi-jiimaan—birchbark canoe. See also **jiimaan(an).** Nichols 119, also **wiigwass,** birch tree, birch bark. *PD* 164.

wiinag(ag)—penis(es). Nichols 100, spelled **niinag,** "my penis." *LR* 93, 96, 153, *PD* 198.

wiisaakodewinini(wag)—half-breed(s), "half-burnt wood," person(s) of mixed ancestry, Métis. Nichols 120. *Birchbark* 244, spelled **wisikodewinini,** " 'half-burnt wood,' a descriptive word for mixed-blood (part white) Aninishabeg." *LR* 63, 96.

wiiw—wife. See also **we'ew(ug)** and **niwiiw** (Nichols 99, "my wife"). *LR* 285.

wika-iganan—house, building. Nichols 116, spelled **waakaa'igan.** *LR* 187.

windigo(og)—starvation winter beast(s). Johnston 24, spelled **weendigo,** "the glutton—the spirit of excess and paradoxically of moderation, excess in any form leads to self-destruction." Nichols 120, spelled **wiindigoo,** "winter cannibal monster." *Birchbark* 244, "a giant monster of Ojibwa teachings, often made of ice and associated with the starvation and danger of deep winter." *LM* 75, 318, *Tr* 3, 6, 31, *BP* 155, 224, 273, *AW* 35, 55, 57, 109, 212, etc., *LR* 93, 284, etc., *FS* 102, *PD* 198.

Wishkob—Sweet, Sweet One. Nichols 120, spelled **wiishkobi-,** "sweet." *LR* 64, 231.

Wujiew—Mountain. Nichols 113, spelled **wajiw.** *FS* 5.

Z

zagimeg—mosquitoes. Nichols 121. *FS* 205, *PD* 168.

zashi—slippery. Nichols 111, spelled **ozhaashaa.** *PD* 163.

zashi manoomin—slippery rice (oatmeal). Nichols 111, spelled **ozhaashaa,** slippery, and 77, **manoomin,** wild rice. *PD* 163.

Zezikaaikwe—Unexpected. *Tr* 220.

zhaaganaash(iwug), zhaaginaash, zhaginash—English language; white person(s) or culture. Nichols 124, "Englishman." *BP* (early editions) 6, 58, 140, *AW* 139, *LR* 64, *FS* 22, 74, 76, 115, *PD* 202.

zhaaganaash-akiing—English-speaking land (Canada?). Nichols 124, **zhaaganaash,** "Englishman," and 7, **aki** or **akiing,** "land . . . country." *LR* 83.

zhaaganaashimowin—the English language. *Silence* 256, spelled **zhaganashimowin,** "white man's language." *LR* 169.

zhaawanong—to the south. Nichols 125. *AW* 35 (spelled **Shawano**), *LR* 243, *PD* 69 (spelled **Shaawano**).

zhooniya, zhooniyaa—money. Nichols 128. *Silence* 256. *LR* 167, *FS* 206.

ziiginigewigamig—tavern, bar, or "pouring house." Nichols 129. *FS* 189.

Ziigwan'aage—Wolverine. Nichols 63, spelled **gwiingwa'aage**. *PD* 134 ("she was named for the spirit of the wolverine"), 135, etc.

FULL SENTENCES IN OJIBWE

Below are several sentences or combinations of sentences from five of Erdrich's novels. Generally, the individual words also appear in the glossary above. The sentences are arranged by page number within each novel.

TALES OF BURNING LOVE

Day wi kway ikway!—In a moment of emotional intensity, Sister Leopolda glares at Eleanor Mauser and flings these words at her (53).

We have not been able to decipher the meaning of this Ojibwe sentence. Only **ikway** (woman) is a word found in our Ojibwe vocabulary sources (spelled **ikwe**). Nor does Erdrich give explicit contextual hints to the meaning. For our readers who would like to work out the meaning for themselves, we suggest that you refer to two words from Nichols that we have included in this glossary: **ikwe** and **dewikwey**. (If "Day wi kway" in the quotation is equivalent to the Ojibwe word "dewikwey," we have the amusing possibility that Leopolda is telling Eleanor, "You're a headache, woman!" or "You give me a headache, woman!") You may also want to consider the meaning of the **-day** suffix in our entry for **g'dai** and the meaning of the **wii-** prefix in our entry for **giwii**.

THE ANTELOPE WIFE

Indah be izah inah?—Cally calls her grandmother and asks, "Shall I come over?" (109).

Dahgo chimookoman makazin!—One of the older women at Frank and Rozin's wedding dinner complains about the tough moose meat by saying, "Just like a white man's shoe!" Another replies, **Magizha gaytay mooz.** "Maybe it was an old moose." When one claims, in English, that the old ones are the tenderest, her colleague answers, **Magizha oshkay.** "Maybe it was a young one" (171).

THE LAST REPORT ON THE MIRACLES AT LITTLE NO HORSE

Neshke. Daga naazh opwaagaansz!—Father Damien says to Father Jude, "Look. Please get me a cigarette!" (51).

Gigaa minwendam i'in?—Father Damien says to Fleur, "May I make you feel good?" (or " . . . be happy?") (81).

Mii'e etaa i'iwe gay onji shabwii'ing, gakina awiyaa ninaandawenimaa chi mazhiweyt. Neshke idash tahnee pahtahneynahwug gey ani bi-mautiziwaad.—The strong older woman says to the surviving tribal members, "Here it is, because this is the only way to survive. I want you all to have lots of sex. And look, there will [then] be many who go on to live a good life" (95). She then adds, **Gakinago giigaa kitchi manitiminin. Ininiwag, dagasaa patakizoog! Ikweywug, pagetinamahgehg! Ahau, anishinabedok, patakizoog! Ahua! Manitadaa!** "All of you will have big intercourse. You men, please now, get those erections up! You women, allow them to do what needs to be done. So, men, erections! Well! Have sex!" (96).

Mekadewikonayewinini majii ayaan'na? Hihn! Niminwendam gegahwa-bamayaan, in'gozis.—Lulu teasingly asks Father Damien, "Is it the naughty priest we have here? Too bad. I'm glad to see you, my son" (133).

Aaniin ezhichigeyan, n'mama?—Lulu asks Fleur, "How are you doing, my mother?" (187).

Izhah, mino nibaan, n'dawnis.—Father Damien says to Mary Kashpaw, "Go get a good sleep, my daughter" (206).

Aaniindi gi-izhamin ina?—Lulu asks Fleur, "Where are you going?" (241).

Daga, daga, n'dawnis, ombe. Gizhawenimin. Izhadaa.—At the school, Fleur begs Lulu to accept her as her mother and come home with her, saying, "Please, please, my daughter, come on. I love you. Let's go" (252).

Ando miniquen!—Father Damien tells the drunken Mashkiigikwe, while giving her some money, "Go find yourself a drink" (305).

Hihn! Daga, miiishishin!—Sophie Morrissey says to Marie Kashpaw, "Hey! Please, give it [the bottle] to me!" (323).

FOUR SOULS

Niiban . . . mino ayaa sana.—The old people, hoping that Fanny Migwans (Fleur's grandmother Under the Ground) is not dead, say, "Sleep and be well" (50).

N'dawnis, gego minikweken!—In Tatro's bar during the poker game, Nanapush warns Fleur, "My daughter, don't drink!" (193).

THE PAINTED DRUM

Aaniin izhinikaazoyan?—Anaquot asks her host Ziigwan'aage, "What is your name?" (more literally, "How are you named?") (124).

Giin igo.—As they search for the sacred trees, Albert Ruse tells Old Shaawano, "You go" (171).

Giwii minikwen anibishaabo ina?—Ziigwan'aage asks her visitor Anaquot, "Do you want to drink tea?" (126).

Ma'iingan izhinikaazo.—John String tells Ira his brother Morris's Ojibwe name: "He is named wolf" (204).

Bibliography

Louise Erdrich has drawn a great deal of scholarly attention. This section is designed to list the most important interviews, bibliographic aids, and scholarly studies that have appeared in print. In the references below *American Indian Culture and Research Journal* is shortened to *AICRJ* and *Studies in American Indian Literatures* is shortened to *SAIL*.

BOOKS BY LOUISE ERDRICH

Imagination. Westerville, Ohio: Merrill, 1982.

Jacklight. New York: Holt, Rinehart & Winston, 1984.

Love Medicine. New York: Holt, Rinehart & Winston, 1984; New and Expanded Version, New York: Holt, 1993.

The Beet Queen. New York: Holt, 1986.

Tracks. New York: Holt, 1988.

Baptism of Desire. New York: Harper & Row, 1989.

The Crown of Columbus. By Louise Erdrich and Michael Dorris. New York: HarperCollins, 1991.

Route Two. By Louise Erdrich and Michael Dorris. Northridge, Calif.: Lord John, 1991.

The Bingo Palace. New York: HarperCollins, 1994.

The Blue Jay's Dance: A Birth Year. New York: HarperCollins, 1995.

Grandmother's Pigeon. New York: Hyperion, 1996.

Tales of Burning Love. New York: HarperCollins, 1996.

The Antelope Wife. New York: HarperCollins, 1998.

The Birchbark House. New York: Hyperion, 1999.

The Last Report on the Miracles at Little No Horse. New York: HarperCollins, 2001.

The Range Eternal. New York: Hyperion, 2002.

Books and Islands in Ojibwe Country. Washington, D.C.: National Geographic Directions, 2003.

The Master Butchers Singing Club. New York: HarperCollins, 2003.

Original Fire: Selected and New Poems. New York: HarperCollins, 2003.

Four Souls. New York: HarperCollins, 2004.

The Game of Silence. New York: HarperCollins, 2005.
The Painted Drum. New York: HarperCollins, 2005.

INTERVIEWS

Louise Erdrich has granted a large number of interviews, many of which have been transcribed and published. Some twenty-three of them, not listed separately here, have been gathered into the Chavkins' *Conversations with Louise Erdrich and Michael Dorris* volume listed below.

Berkley, Miriam. "Louise Erdrich." *Publisher's Weekly,* August 15, 1986, 58–59.
Bonetti, Kay. "An Interview with Louise Erdrich and Michael Dorris." *Missouri Review* 11, no. 2 (1988): 79–99. Reprinted in *Conversations with American Novelists: The Best Interviews from* The Missouri Review *and the American Audio Prose Library,* ed. Kay Bonetti, Greg Michalson, Speer Morgan, Jo Sapp, and Sam Stowers, 76–91. Columbia: University of Missouri Press, 1997.
Bruchac, Joseph. "Whatever Is Really Yours: An Interview with Louise Erdrich." In *Survival This Way: Interviews with American Indian Poets,* 73–86. Tucson: University of Arizona Press, 1987.
Chavkin, Allan, and Nancy Feyl Chavkin, eds. *Conversations with Louise Erdrich and Michael Dorris.* Jackson: University Press of Mississippi, 1994.
Coltelli, Laura. "Louise Erdrich and Michael Dorris." In *Winged Words: American Indian Writers Speak,* ed. Laura Coltelli, 41–52. Lincoln: University of Nebraska Press, 1990.
George, Jan. "Interview with Louise Erdrich." *North Dakota Quarterly* 53, no. 2 (1985): 240–46.
Hansen, Liane. "Interview: Louise Erdrich Talks about Her Latest Book, *The Last Report on the Miracles at Little No Horse.*" *Weekend Edition.* National Public Radio. Washington, D.C., July 8, 2001.
Kirch, Claire. "Marching to the Beat of Her Own Drum: Louise Erdrich on Living, Writing, and Bookselling." *Publisher's Weekly,* September 19, 2005, 38–39.
Neary, Lynn. "Interview: Louise Erdrich Discusses Her Latest Novel, *The Master Butchers Singing Club.*" *All Things Considered.* National Public Radio. Washington, D.C., February 12, 2003.
Olson, Karen. "The Complicated Life of Louise Erdrich." *Book,* May/June 2001, 32–35.
Pearlman, Mickey. "Louise Erdrich." In *Inter/view: Talks with America's Writing Women,* ed. Mickey Pearlman and Katherine Usher Henderson, 143–48. Lexington: University of Kentucky Press, 1989.

Rawson, Josie. "Interview: Louise Erdrich—Cross-Dressing the Divine." *Mother Jones,* May/June 2001, 102–4.

Rolo, Mark Anthony. "Louise Erdrich." *Progressive,* April 2002, 36–40.

White, Sharon, and Glenda Burnside. "On Native Ground: An Interview with Louise Erdrich and Michael Dorris." *Bloomsbury Review* 8, no. 4 (1988): 16–18.

Wong, Hertha D. "An Interview with Louise Erdrich and Michael Dorris." *North Dakota Quarterly* 25, no. 1 (1987): 196–218.

BIBLIOGRAPHIC AIDS

The scholarship on Erdrich's work has grown so fast that bibliographers, right from the start, have felt called upon to provide guidance for students and other scholars. Here are some of the most important bibliographical articles and books dealing with Erdrich's poetry and fiction.

Bataille, Gretchen M., and Kathleen M. Sands. *American Indian Women: A Guide to Research.* New York: Garland Publishing, 1991.

Beidler, Peter G. "Louise Erdrich." In *Native American Writers of the United States,* ed. Kenneth M. Roemer, 84–100. Vol. 175 of the *Dictionary of Literary Biography.* Detroit: Gale Research, 1997.

Brewington, Lillian, Normie Bullard, and R. W. Reising. "Writing in Love: An Annotated Bibliography of Critical Responses to the Poetry and Novels of Louise Erdrich and Michael Dorris." *AICRJ* 10, no. 4 (1986): 81–86.

Burdick, Debra A. "Louise Erdrich's *Love Medicine, The Beet Queen,* and *Tracks:* An Annotated Survey of Criticism through 1994." *AICRJ* 20, no. 3 (1996): 137–66.

Chavkin, Allan, and Nancy Feyl Chavkin. "Selected Bibliography." In *The Chippewa Landscape of Louise Erdrich,* ed. Allan Chavkin, 189–99. Tuscaloosa: University of Alabama Press, 1999.

"Louise Erdrich: A.S.A.I.L. Bibliography #9: Poems and Short Stories." *SAIL* 9, no. 1 (1985): 37–41.

Pearlman, Mickey. "A Bibliography of Writings by Louise Erdrich" and "A Bibliography of Writings about Louise Erdrich." In *American Women Writing Fiction: Memory, Identity, Family, Space,* ed. Mickey Pearlman, 108–12. Lexington: University Press of Kentucky, 1989.

Ruoff, A. LaVonne Brown. *American Indian Literatures: An Introduction, Bibliographic Review, and Selected Bibliography,* 84–88. New York: MLA, 1990.

Szanto, Laura Furlan. "An Annotated Secondary Bibliography of Louise Erdrich's Recent Fiction: *The Bingo Palace, Tales of Burning Love,* and *The Antelope Wife.*" *SAIL* 12, no. 2 (2000): 61–90.

CRITICISM

The scholarship on Erdrich's work is rich and complex. Almost all of it focuses on her fiction, particularly the novels set in and around her fictional Chippewa reservation in North Dakota. Her poetry and nonfiction have been all but ignored by scholars. With a few exceptions, the following list does not include reviews.

Ahokas, Pirjo. "Constructing Hybrid Ethnic Female Identities: Alice Walker's *Meridian* and Louise Erdrich's *Love Medicine.*" In *Literature on the Move: Comparing Diasporic Ethnicities in Europe and the Americas,* ed. Dominique Marçais, Mark Niemeyer, Bernard Vincent, and Cathy Waegner, 199–207. Heidelberg, Germany: Carl Winter Universitätsverlag, 2002.

————. "Narrative Strategies of Resistance in Louise Erdrich's *Love Medicine.*" In *Telling, Remembering, Interpreting, Guessing,* ed. Maria Vasenkari, Pasi Enges, and Anna-Leena Siikala, 188–94. Joensuu, Finland: Suomen Kansantietouden Tutkijain Seura, 2000.

————. "Transcending Binary Divisions: Constructing a Postmodern Female Urban Identity in Louise Erdrich's *The Antelope Wife* and Zadie Smith's *White Teeth.*" In *Sites of Ethnicity: Europe and the Americas,* ed. William Boelhower, Rocío G. Davis, and Carmen Birkle, 115–29. Heidelberg, Germany: Universitätsverlag Winter, 2004.

Ainsworth, Linda. ["Louise Erdrich's *Love Medicine.*"] *SAIL* 9, no. 1 (1985): 24–29. Reprinted in *Critical Perspectives on Native American Fiction,* ed. Richard F. Fleck, 274–76 [Ainsworth's name is omitted]. Washington, D.C.: Three Continents Press, 1993.

Aldridge, John W. "Medium without Message (Bobbie Ann Mason, Mary Robison, Louise Erdrich)." In *Talents and Technicians: Literary Chic and the New Assembly-Line Fiction,* 79–100. New York: Scribner's, 1992.

Angley, Patricia. "Fleur Pillager: Feminine, Mythic, and Natural Representations in Louise Erdrich's *Tracks.*" In *Constructions and Confrontations: Changing Representations of Women and Feminisms, East and West (Selected Essays),* ed. Cristina Bacchilega and Cornelia N. Moore, 159–69. Honolulu: University of Hawaii Press, 1996.

Armstrong, Jeanne. *"Tracks."* In *Demythologizing the Romance of Conquest,* 17–38. Westport, Conn.: Greenwood Press, 2000.

Babcock, Barbara. " 'A Tolerated Margin of Mess': The Trickster and His Tales Reconsidered." In *Critical Essays on Native American Literature,* ed. Andrew Wiget, 153–85. Boston: G. K. Hall, 1985.

Bak, Hans. "Circles Blaze in Ordinary Days: Louise Erdrich's *Jacklight.*" In *Native*

American Women in Literature and Culture, ed. Susan Castillo and Victor M. P. Da Rosa, 11–27. Porto, Portugal: Fernando Pessoa University Press, 1997.

———. "The Kaleidoscope of History: Michael Dorris and Louise Erdrich's *The Crown of Columbus* (with a Coda on Gerald Vizenor's *The Heirs of Columbus*)." In *Deferring a Dream: Literary Sub-versions of the American Columbiad,* ed. Gert Buelens and Ernst Rudin, 99–119. Basel, Switzerland: Birkhäuser Verlag, 1994.

———. "Toward a Native American 'Realism': The Amphibious Fiction of Louise Erdrich." In *Neo-realism in Contemporary American Fiction,* ed. Kristiaan Versluys, 145–70. Amsterdam: Rodopi, 1992.

Barak, Julie. "Blurs, Blends, Berdaches: Gender Mixing in the Novels of Louise Erdrich." *SAIL* 8, no. 3 (1996): 49–62.

———. "Un-becoming White: Identity Transformation in Louise Erdrich's *The Antelope Wife.*" *SAIL* 13, no. 4 (2001): 1–23.

Baringer, Sandra. " 'Captive Woman?': The Re-writing of Pocahontas in Three Contemporary Native American Novels." [On *The Bingo Palace.*] *SAIL* 11, no. 3 (1999): 42–63.

Barker, Debra K. S. "Tracking the Memories of the Heart: Teaching *Tales of Burning Love.*" In *Approaches to Teaching the Works of Louise Erdrich,* ed. Greg Sarris, Connie A. Jacobs, and James R. Giles, 118–29. New York: MLA, 2004.

Barnett, Marianne. "Dreamstuff: Erdrich's *Love Medicine.*" *North Dakota Quarterly* 56, no. 1 (1988): 82–93.

Barry, Nora Baker. "Fleur Pillager's Bear Identity in the Novels of Louise Erdrich." *SAIL* 12, no. 2 (2000): 24–37.

Barry, Nora, and Mary Prescott. "The Triumph of the Brave: *Love Medicine*'s Holistic Vision." *Critique: Studies in Contemporary Fiction* 30, no. 2 (1989): 123–38.

Barton, Gay. "Family as Character in Erdrich's Novels." In *Approaches to Teaching the Works of Louise Erdrich,* ed. Greg Sarris, Connie A. Jacobs, and James R. Giles, 77–82. New York: MLA, 2004.

Bataille, Gretchen M. "Louise Erdrich's *The Beet Queen:* Images of the Grotesque on the Northern Plains." In *Critical Perspectives on Native American Fiction,* ed. Richard F. Fleck, 277–85. Washington, D.C.: Three Continents Press, 1993.

Bauer, Margaret D. "When a Convent Seems the Only Viable Choice: Questionable Callings in Stories by Alice Dunbar-Nelson, Alice Walker, and Louise Erdrich." In *Critical Essays on Alice Walker,* ed. Ikenna Dieke, 45–54. Westport, Conn.: Greenwood, 1999.

Beidler, Peter G. " 'The Earth Itself Was Sobbing': Madness and the Environment in Novels by Leslie Marmon Silko and Louise Erdrich." *AICRJ* 26, no. 3 (2002): 113–24.

———. "The Facts of Fictional Magic: John Tanner as a Source for Louise Erdrich's *Tracks* and *The Birchbark House*." *AICRJ* 24, no. 4 (2000): 37–54.

———. "Gender and Christianity: Strategic Questions for Teaching *The Last Report on the Miracles at Little No Horse*." In *Approaches to Teaching the Works of Louise Erdrich,* ed. Greg Sarris, Connie A. Jacobs, and James R. Giles, 140–46. New York: MLA, 2004.

———. "'In the Old Language': A Glossary of Ojibwa Words, Phrases, and Sentences in Louise Erdrich's Novels." *AICRJ* 27, no. 3 (2003): 53–70.

———. "Louise Erdrich." In *Native American Writers of the United States,* ed. Kenneth M. Roemer, 84–100. Vol. 175 of the *Dictionary of Literary Biography.* Detroit: Gale Research, 1997.

———. "Louise Erdrich's Lulu Nanapush: A Modern-Day Wife of Bath?" *SAIL* 15, no. 1 (2003): 92–103.

———. "Study Guides to Eight Erdrich Novels." In *Approaches to Teaching the Works of Louise Erdrich,* ed. Greg Sarris, Connie A. Jacobs, and James R. Giles, 230–38. New York: MLA, 2004.

———. "Three Student Guides to Louise Erdrich's *Love Medicine*." *AICRJ* 16, no. 4 (1992): 167–73.

Beidler, Peter G., and Gay Barton. *A Reader's Guide to the Novels of Louise Erdrich.* Columbia: University of Missouri Press, 1999.

Bennett, Sahra. "*Love Medicine:* New and Expanded Version." *SAIL* 7, no. 1 (1995): 112–18.

Bensen, Robert. "Creatures of the Whirlwind: The Appropriation of American Indian Children and Louise Erdrich's 'American Horse' (1983)." *Cimarron Review* 121 (1997): 173–88.

Berninghausen, Tom. "'This Ain't Real Estate': Land and Culture in Louise Erdrich's Chippewa Tetralogy." In *Women, America, and Movement: Narratives of Relocation,* ed. Susan L. Roberson, 190–209. Columbia: University of Missouri Press, 1998.

Bird, Gloria. "Searching for Evidence of Colonialism at Work: A Reading of Louise Erdrich's *Tracks*." *Wicazo Sa Review* 8, no. 2 (1992): 40–47.

Bloom, Harold, ed. "Louise Erdrich." In *Native American Women Writers,* 24–37. Philadelphia: Chelsea House, 1998. [Contains excerpts from articles included in this bibliography by Schneider, Van Dyke, Cornell, Friedman, Peterson, Walsh and Braley, Pittman, and Purdy ("Building Bridges").]

Bowers, Sharon Manybeads. "Louise Erdrich as Nanapush." In *New Perspectives on Women and Comedy,* ed. Regina Barreca, 135–41. Philadelphia: Gordon and Breach, 1992.

Brady, Laura A. "Collaboration as Conversion: Literary Cases." *Essays in Literature* 19, no. 2 (1992): 298–311 [see especially 306–9].

Brehm, Victoria. "The Metamorphoses of an Ojibwa *Manido.*" *American Literature* 68, no. 4 (1996): 677–706.

Breinig, Helmbrecht. "(Hi)storytelling as Deconstruction and Seduction: The Columbus Novels of Stephen Marlowe and Michael Dorris/Louise Erdrich." In *Historiographic Metafiction in Modern American and Canadian Literature,* ed. Bernd Engler and Kurt Müller, 325–46. Paderborn, Germany: Ferdinand Schöningh, 1994.

Brogan, Kathleen. "Haunted by History: Louise Erdrich's *Tracks.*" *Prospects* 21 (1996): 169–92. Reprinted [with slight revision] as "Ghost Dancing: Cultural Translation in Louise Erdrich's *Tracks,*" in *Cultural Haunting: Ghosts and Ethnicity in Recent American Literature,* 30–60. Charlottesville: University Press of Virginia, 1998.

Brown, Alanna Kathleen. " 'Patterns and Waves Generation to Generation': *The Antelope Wife.*" In *Approaches to Teaching the Works of Louise Erdrich,* ed. Greg Sarris, Connie A. Jacobs, and James R. Giles, 88–94. New York: MLA, 2004.

Brown, Dee. ["Louise Erdrich's *Love Medicine.*"] *SAIL* 9, no. 1 (1985): 4–5. Reprinted in *Critical Perspectives on Native American Fiction,* ed. Richard F. Fleck, 264–65. Washington, D.C.: Three Continents Press, 1993.

Camp, Gregory S. "Working Out Their Own Salvation: The Allotment of Land in Severalty and the Turtle Mountain Chippewa Band." *American Indian Culture and Research Journal* 14, no. 2 (1990): 19–38.

Carr, Susan. "The Turtle Mountain/Yoknapatawpha Connection." *Bulletin of the West Virginia Association of College English Teachers* [West Virginia Institute of Technology] n.s. 16 (fall 1994): 18–25.

Castillo, Susan Perez. "The Construction of Gender and Ethnicity in the Poetry of Leslie Silko and Louise Erdrich." In vol. 2 of *The Force of Vision,* ed. Earl Miner and Haga Toru, 637–45. Tokyo: International Comparative Literature Association and University of Tokyo Press, 1995.

———. "The Construction of Gender and Ethnicity in the Texts of Leslie Silko and Louise Erdrich." *Yearbook of English Studies* 24 (1994): 228–36.

———. "Postmodernism, Native American Literature, and the Real: The Silko-Erdrich Controversy." *Massachusetts Review* 32, no. 2 (1991): 285–94.

———. "A Woman Constantly Surprised: The Construction of Self in Louise Erdrich's *The Blue Jay's Dance.*" *European Review of Native American Studies* 11, no. 1 (1997): 39–41.

———. "Women Aging into Power: Fictional Representations of Power and Authority in Louise Erdrich's Female Characters." *SAIL* 8, no. 4 (1996): 13–

20. Reprinted in *Native American Women in Literature and Culture,* ed. Susan Castillo and Victor M. P. Da Rosa, 29–36. Porto, Portugal: Fernando Pessoa University Press, 1997.

Castor, Laura. "Ecological Politics and Comic Redemption in Louise Erdrich's *The Antelope Wife.*" *Nordlit: Arbeidstidsskrift i litteratur* 15 (summer 2004): 121–34.

Catt, Catherine M. "Ancient Myth in Modern America: The Trickster in the Fiction of Louise Erdrich." *Platte Valley Review* 19, no. 1 (1991): 71–81.

Chavkin, Allan. "Vision and Revision in Louise Erdrich's *Love Medicine.*" In *The Chippewa Landscape of Louise Erdrich,* ed. Allan Chavkin, 84–116. Tuscaloosa: University of Alabama Press, 1999. Reprinted in *Louise Erdrich's* Love Medicine*: A Casebook,* ed. Hertha D. Sweet Wong, 211–19. New York: Oxford University Press, 2000.

Chavkin, Allan, ed. *The Chippewa Landscape of Louise Erdrich.* Tuscaloosa: University of Alabama Press, 1999.

Chick, Nancy L. "Does Power Travel in the Bloodlines? A Genealogical Red Herring." In *Approaches to Teaching the Works of Louise Erdrich,* ed. Greg Sarris, Connie A. Jacobs, and James R. Giles, 83–87. New York: MLA, 2004.

———. "Genealogical Charts." Appendix A of *Approaches to Teaching the Works of Louise Erdrich,* ed. Greg Sarris, Connie A. Jacobs, and James R. Giles, 211–22. New York: MLA, 2004.

Cid, Teresa. "Wanting America Back: *The Crown of Columbus* as a Tentative Epic in an Age of Multiculturalism." In *The Insular Dream: Obsession and Resistance,* ed. Kristiaan Versluys, 342–49. Amsterdam: VU University Press, 1995.

Clarke, Joni Adamson. "Why Bears Are Good to Think and Theory Doesn't Have to Be Murder: Transformation and Oral Tradition in Louise Erdrich's *Tracks.*" *SAIL* 4, no. 1 (1992): 28–48.

Cooperman, Jeannette Batz. *The Broom Closet: Secret Meanings of Domesticity in Postfeminist Novels by Louise Erdrich, Mary Gordon, Toni Morrison, Marge Piercy, Jane Smiley, and Amy Tan.* New York: Peter Lang, 1999.

Cornelia, Marie. "Shifting Boundaries: Reflections on Ethnic Identity in Louise Erdrich's *The Master Butchers Singing Club.*" *Glossen* 19 (2004). <http://www.dickinson.edu/glossen/heft19/cornelia.html>.

Cornell, Daniel. "Woman Looking: Revis(ion)ing Pauline's Subject Position in Louise Erdrich's *Tracks.*" *SAIL* 4, no. 1 (1992): 49–64.

Couser, G. Thomas. "Tracing the Trickster: Nanapush, Ojibwe Oral Tradition, and *Tracks.*" In *Approaches to Teaching the Works of Louise Erdrich,* ed. Greg Sarris, Connie A. Jacobs, and James R. Giles, 58–65. New York: MLA, 2004.

Cox, Jay. "Dangerous Definitions: Female Tricksters in Contemporary Native American Literature." *Wicazo Sa Review* 5, no. 2 (1989): 17–21.

Cox, Karen Castellucci. "Magic and Memory in the Contemporary Story Cycle: Gloria Naylor and Louise Erdrich." *College English* 60, no. 2 (1998): 150–72.

Crabtree, Claire. "Salvific Oneness and the Fragmented Self in Louise Erdrich's *Love Medicine.*" In *Contemporary Native American Cultural Issues,* ed. Thomas E. Schirer, 49–56. Sault Ste. Marie, Mich.: Lake Superior State University Press, 1988.

Cutchins, Dennis. "Sugar Cane and Sugar Beets: Two Tales of Burning Love." *SAIL* 12, no. 2 (2000): 1–12.

Czarnecki, Kristin. "Postcolonial Theory and the Undergraduate Classroom: Teaching 'The Red Convertible.'" *Pedagogy: Critical Approaches to Teaching Literature, Language, Composition, and Culture* 2, no. 1 (2002): 109–12.

Daniele, Daniela. "Transactions in a Native Land: Mixed-Blood Identity and Indian Legacy in Louise Erdrich's Writing." *RSA Journal* [*Revista de Studi Nord Americani,* Florence, Italy] 3 (1992): 43–58.

Davis, Rocío G. "Identity in Community in Ethnic Short Story Cycles: Amy Tan's *The Joy Luck Club,* Louise Erdrich's *Love Medicine,* Gloria Naylor's *The Women of Brewster Place.*" In *Ethnicity and the American Short Story,* ed. Julie Brown, 3–23. New York: Garland, 1997.

Däwes, Birgit. "Local Screenings, Transversal Meanings: Leslie Silko's *Ceremony* and Michael Dorris's/Louise Erdrich's *The Crown of Columbus* as Global Novels." *Amerikastudien/American Studies* 47, no. 2 (2002): 245–56.

Deans, Jill R. "'File It under "L" for Love Child': Adoptive Policies and Practices in the Erdrich Tetralogy." In *Imagining Adoption: Essays on Literature and Culture,* ed. Marianne Novy, 231–49. Ann Arbor: University of Michigan Press, 2001.

Delicka, Magdalena. "American Magic Realism: Crossing the Borders in Literatures of the Margins." [Concerning *Tracks.*] *Journal of American Studies of Turkey* 6 (1997): 25–33.

Desmond, John F. "Catholicism in Contemporary American Fiction." *America,* May 14, 1994, 7–11 [see especially 9].

Diana, Vanessa Holford. "Reading *The Beet Queen* from a Feminist Perspective." In *Approaches to Teaching the Works of Louise Erdrich,* ed. Greg Sarris, Connie A. Jacobs, and James R. Giles, 175–82. New York: MLA, 2004.

Downes, Margaret J. "Narrativity, Myth, and Metaphor: Louise Erdrich and Raymond Carver Talk about Love." *MELUS* 21, no. 2 (1996): 49–61.

Durante, Robert. "Beyond Ethnicity: Realism and Postmodernism in Louise Erdrich's Novels." In *The Dialectic of Self and Story: Reading and Storytelling in Contemporary American Fiction,* 53–70. New York: Routledge, 2001.

Dutta, Pratima. "Erdrich's 'The Red Convertible.'" *Explicator* 61, no. 2 (2003): 119–21.

Egerer, Claudia. "Exploring the (In)Between Spaces: Cultural Hybridity in Louise Erdrich's Fiction." In *Fictions of (In)Betweenness,* 53–93. Göteborg, Sweden: Acta Universitatis Gothoburgensis, 1997.

Erdrich, Louise. "Rose Nights, Summer Storms, Lists of Spiders, and Literary Mothers." In *Louise Erdrich's* Love Medicine*: A Casebook,* ed. Hertha D. Sweet Wong, 220–23. New York: Oxford University Press, 2000.

———. "Where I Ought to Be: A Writer's Sense of Place." In *Louise Erdrich's* Love Medicine*: A Casebook,* ed. Hertha D. Sweet Wong, 43–50. New York: Oxford University Press, 2000.

"Erdrich, Louise." In *Contemporary Authors,* new revision series, vol. 41, ed. Susan M. Trosky, 124–28. Detroit: Gale Research, 1994.

Faris, Wendy B. "Devastation and Replenishment: New World Narratives of Love and Nature." *Studies in the Humanities* 19, no. 2 (1992): 171–82.

Farrell, Susan. "Colonizing Columbus: Dorris and Erdrich's Postmodern Novel." *Critique: Studies in Contemporary Fiction* 40, no. 2 (1999): 121–35.

———. "Erdrich's *Love Medicine.*" *Explicator* 56, no. 2 (1998): 109–12.

Fast, Robin Riley. "Resistant History: Revisiting the Captivy [Captivity] Narrative in 'Captivity' and *Black Robe: Isaac Jogues.*" *AICRJ* 23, no. 1 (1999): 69–86.

Ferguson, Suzanne. "The Short Stories of Louise Erdrich's Novels." *Studies in Short Fiction* 33, no. 4 (1996): 541–55.

Flavin, James. "The Novel as Performance: Communication in Louise Erdrich's *Tracks.*" *SAIL* 3, no. 4 (1991): 1–12.

Flavin, Louise. "Gender Construction amid Family Dissolution in Louise Erdrich's *The Beet Queen.*" *SAIL* 7, no. 2 (1995): 17–24.

———. "Louise Erdrich's *Love Medicine:* Loving over Time and Distance." *Critique: Studies in Contemporary Fiction* 31, no. 1 (1989): 55–64.

Friedman, Susan Stanford. "Identity Politics, Syncretism, Catholicism, and Anishinabe Religion in Louise Erdrich's *Tracks.*" *Religion and Literature* 26, no. 1 (1994): 107–33.

Gallego, Maria del Mar. "The Borders of the Self: Identity and Community in Louise Erdrich's *Love Medicine* and Paule Marshall's *Praisesong for the Widow.*" In *Literature and Ethnicity in the Cultural Borderlands,* ed. Jesús Benito and Anna María Manzanas, 145–57. Amsterdam: Rodopi, 2002.

Gaughan, Sara K. "Old Age, Folk Belief, and Love in Stories by Ernest Gaines and Louise Erdrich." *Louisiana Folklore Miscellany* 10 (1995): 37–45.

Gish, Robert F. "Life into Death, Death into Life: Hunting as Metaphor and Motive in *Love Medicine.*" In *The Chippewa Landscape of Louise Erdrich,* ed. Allan Chavkin, 67–83. Tuscaloosa: University of Alabama Press, 1999.

Gleason, William. " 'Her Laugh an Ace': The Function of Humor in Louise Erdrich's *Love Medicine.*" *AICRJ* 11, no. 3 (1987): 51–73. Reprinted in *Louise*

Erdrich's Love Medicine: *A Casebook,* ed. Hertha D. Sweet Wong, 115–35. New York: Oxford University Press, 2000.

Griffin, Gwen, and P. Jane Hafen. "An Indigenous Approach to Teaching Erdrich's Works." In *Approaches to Teaching the Works of Louise Erdrich,* ed. Greg Sarris, Connie A. Jacobs, and James R. Giles, 95–101. New York: MLA, 2004.

Grödal, Hanne Tang. "Words, Words, Words." *Dolphin* 18 (1990): 21–26.

Gross, Lawrence W. "The Trickster and World Maintenance: An Anishinaabe Reading of Louise Erdrich's *Tracks.*" *SAIL* 17, no. 3 (2005): 48–66.

Gutwirth, Claudia. " 'Stop Making Sense': Trickster Variations in the Fiction of Louise Erdrich." In *Trickster Lives: Culture and Myth in American Fiction,* ed. Jeanne Campbell Reesman, 148–67. Athens: University of Georgia Press, 2001.

Hafen, P. Jane. *Reading Louise Erdrich's* Love Medicine. Boise, Idaho: Boise State University, 2003.

———. "Sacramental Language: Ritual in the Poetry of Louise Erdrich." *Great Plains Quarterly* 16, no. 3 (1996): 147–55.

———. " 'We Anishinaabeg Are the Keepers of the Names of the Earth': Louise Erdrich's Great Plains." *Great Plains Quarterly* 21, no. 4 (2001): 321–32.

Hall, Vanessa. "Review Essay." [On the first three novels.] *SAIL* 13, nos. 2–3 (2001): 67–77.

Hansen, Elaine Tuttle. "What If Your Mother Never Meant To? The Novels of Louise Erdrich and Michael Dorris." In *Mother without Child: Contemporary Fiction and the Crisis of Motherhood,* 115–57. Berkeley and Los Angeles: University of California Press, 1997.

Hanson, Elizabeth I. "Louise Erdrich: Making a World Anew." In *Forever There: Race and Gender in Contemporary Native American Fiction,* 79–104. New York: Peter Lang, 1989.

Hendrickson, Roberta Makashay. "Victims and Survivors: Native American Women Writers, Violence against Women, and Child Abuse." *SAIL* 8, no. 1 (1996): 13–24.

Hescher, Achim. "Remembering Lulu and Albertine: Intertextual Constellations in Louise Erdrich's *Love Medicine.*" *Amerikastudien/American Studies* 43, no. 2 (1998): 301–12.

Hessler, Michelle R. "Catholic Nuns and Ojibwa Shamans: Pauline and Fleur in Louise Erdrich's *Tracks.*" *Wicazo Sa Review* 11, no. 1 (1995): 40–45.

Holt, Debra C. "Transformation and Continuance: Native American Tradition in the Novels of Louise Erdrich." In *Entering the Nineties: The North American Experience,* ed. Thomas E. Schirer, 149–61. Sault Ste. Marie, Mich.: Lake Superior State University Press, 1991.

Hoover, Sharon. "Academic Conversation: Computers, Libraries, the Classroom, and *The Bingo Palace.*" In *Approaches to Teaching the Works of Louise Erdrich,* ed.

Greg Sarris, Connie A. Jacobs, and James R. Giles, 130–39. New York: MLA, 2004.

Horne, Dee. "A Postcolonial Reading of *Tracks*." In *Approaches to Teaching the Works of Louise Erdrich,* ed. Greg Sarris, Connie A. Jacobs, and James R. Giles, 191–200. New York: MLA, 2004.

Hornung, Alfred. "Ethnic Fiction and Survival Ethics: Toni Morrison, Louise Erdrich, David H. Hwang." In *Ethics and Aesthetics: The Moral Turn of Postmodernism,* ed. Gerhard Hoffmann and Alfred Hornung, 209–20. Heidelberg, Germany: Universitätsverlag C. Winter, 1996.

Houlihan, Patrick E. " 'This Ain't Real Estate': A Bakhtinian Approach to *The Bingo Palace*." In *Approaches to Teaching the Works of Louise Erdrich,* ed. Greg Sarris, Connie A. Jacobs, and James R. Giles, 201–10. New York: MLA, 2004.

Howard, Jane. "Louise Erdrich: A Dartmouth Chippewa Writes a Great Native American Novel." *Life,* April 18, 1985.

Huang, Hsinya. "Disease, Empire, and (Alter)Native Medicine in Louise Erdrich's *Tracks* and Winona LaDuke's *Last Standing Woman*." *Concentric: Literary and Cultural Studies* 30, no. 1 (2004): 37–64.

Hughes, Sheila Hassell. "Falls of Desire/Leaps of Faith: Religious Syncretism in Louise Erdrich's and Joy Harjo's 'Mixed-Blood' Poetry." *Religion and Literature* 33, no. 2 (2001): 59–83.

———. "Tongue-Tied: Rhetoric and Relation in Louise Erdrich's *Tracks*." *MELUS* 25, no. 3–4 (2000): 87–116.

Jacobs, Connie A. "A History of the Turtle Mountain Band of Chippewa Indians." In *Approaches to Teaching the Works of Louise Erdrich,* ed. Greg Sarris, Connie A. Jacobs, and James R. Giles, 23–31. New York: MLA, 2004.

———. "Important Dates in the History of the Turtle Mountain Band of Chippewa Indians." In *Approaches to Teaching the Works of Louise Erdrich,* ed. Greg Sarris, Connie A. Jacobs, and James R. Giles, 227–29. New York: MLA, 2004.

———. *The Novels of Louise Erdrich: Stories of Her People.* New York: Peter Lang, 2001.

Jaskoski, Helen. "From Time Immemorial: Native American Traditions in Contemporary Short Fiction." In *Since Flannery O'Connor: Essays on the Contemporary American Short Story,* ed. Loren Logsdon and Charles W. Mayer, 54–71. Macomb: Western Illinois University, 1987. Reprinted in *Louise Erdrich's Love Medicine: A Casebook,* ed. Hertha D. Sweet Wong, 27–34. New York: Oxford University Press, 2000.

Katanski, Amelia V. "Tracking Fleur: The Ojibwe Roots of Erdrich's Novels." In *Approaches to Teaching the Works of Louise Erdrich,* ed. Greg Sarris, Connie A. Jacobs, and James R. Giles, 66–76. New York: MLA, 2004.

Kellman, Steven G. "Cardiograms from the Heartland." [Concerning *The Master Butchers Singing Club.*] *Michigan Quarterly Review* 43, no. 3 (2004): 467–76.

Khader, Jamil. "Postcolonial Nativeness: Nomadism, Cultural Memory, and the Politics of Identity in Louise Erdrich's and Michael Dorris's *The Crown of Columbus.*" *ARIEL* 28, no. 2 (1997): 81–101.

Kleiner, Elaine, and Angela Vlaicu. "Revisioning Woman in America: A Study of Louise Erdrich's Novel *The Antelope Wife.*" *FEMSPEC: An Interdisciplinary Feminist Journal Dedicated to Critical and Creative Work in the Realms of Science Fiction, Fantasy, Magical Realism, Surrealism, Myth, Folklore, and Other Supernatural Genres* 2, no. 2 (2001): 56–65.

Kloppenburg, Michelle R. *Contemporary Trickster Tales: The Pillagers in Louise Erdrich's North Dakota Quartet and Their Stories of Survival.* Essen: Verlag Die Blaue Eule, 1999.

———. "The Face in the Slough: Lipsha's Quest for Identity in Louise Erdrich's *Love Medicine* and *The Bingo Palace.*" *European Review of Native American Studies* 11, no. 1 (1997): 27–34.

Kolmar, Wendy K. "'Dialectics of Connectedness': Supernatural Elements in Novels by Bambara, Cisneros, Grahn, and Erdrich." In *Haunting the House of Fiction: Feminist Perspectives on Ghost Stories by American Women,* ed. Lynette Carpenter and Wendy K. Kolmar, 236–49. Knoxville: University of Tennessee Press, 1991.

Kroeber, Karl. ["Louise Erdrich's *Love Medicine.*"] *SAIL* 9, no. 1 (1985): 1–4. Reprinted in *Critical Perspectives on Native American Fiction,* ed. Richard F. Fleck, 263–64. Washington, D.C.: Three Continents Press, 1993.

Lansky, Ellen. "Spirits and Salvation in Louise Erdrich's *Love Medicine.*" *Dionysos: The Literature and Addiction TriQuarterly* 5, no. 3 (1994): 39–44.

Larson, Sidner. "The Fragmentation of a Tribal People in Louise Erdrich's *Tracks.*" *AICRJ* 17, no. 2 (1993): 1–13.

———. "Louise Erdrich: Protecting and Celebrating Culture." In *Captured in the Middle: Tradition and Experience in Contemporary Native American Writing,* 78–103. Seattle: University of Washington Press, 2000.

Lee, A. Robert. "Ethnic Renaissance: Rudolfo Anaya, Louise Erdrich, and Maxine Hong Kingston." In *The New American Writing: Essays on American Literature since 1970,* ed. Graham Clarke, 139–64. New York: St. Martin's Press, 1990.

Le Guin, Ursula K. ["Louise Erdrich's *Love Medicine.*"] *SAIL* 9, no. 1 (1985): 5–6. Reprinted in *Critical Perspectives on Native American Fiction,* ed. Richard F. Fleck, 265. Washington, D.C.: Three Continents Press, 1993.

Lincoln, Kenneth. "'Bring Her Home': Louise Erdrich." In *Indi'n Humor: Bi-*

cultural Play in Native America, 205–53. New York: Oxford University Press, 1993.

———. Preface to *Native American Renaissance.* Berkeley and Los Angeles: University of California Press, 1985.

Linden, Mary Ann. "Breaking the Ice with Winter Stories: Using 'Short-Short' Stories to Introduce the Narrative Essay in First-Year Composition Classes." *Eureka Studies in Teaching Short Fiction* 4, no. 2 (2004): 102–6.

Lischke, Ute. " 'Blitzkuchen': An Exploration of Story-Telling in Louise Erdrich's *The Antelope Wife.*" In *Interdisciplinary and Cross-Cultural Narratives in North America,* ed. Mark Cronlund Anderson and Irene Maria F. Blayer, 61–72. New York: Peter Lang, 2005.

Lischke-McNab, Ute. "An Introduction to Louise Erdrich's *The Antelope Wife.*" In *Germans and Indians: Fantasies, Encounters, Projections,* ed. Colin G. Calloway, Gerd Gemünden, and Susanne Zantop, 281–86. Lincoln: University of Nebraska Press, 2002.

Little, Jonathan. "Beading the Multicultural World: Louise Erdrich's *The Antelope Wife* and the Sacred Metaphysic." *Contemporary Literature* 41, no. 1 (2000): 495–524.

"Louise Erdrich." In *Contemporary Literary Criticism,* vol. 54, ed. Daniel G. Marowski and Roger Matuz, 164–73. Detroit: Gale Research, 1989.

Ludlow, Jeannie. "Working (in) the In-Between: Poetry, Criticism, Interrogation, and Interruption." *SAIL* 6, no. 1 (1994): 24–42.

Lumsden, Paul. " 'And Here Is Where Events Loop around and Tangle': Tribal Perspectives in *Love Medicine.*" In *Approaches to Teaching the Works of Louise Erdrich,* ed. Greg Sarris, Connie A. Jacobs, and James R. Giles, 114–17. New York: MLA, 2004.

Lyons, Rosemary. *A Comparison of the Works of Antonine Maillet of the Acadian Tradition of New Brunswick, Canada, and Louise Erdrich of the Ojibwe of North America with the Poems of Longfellow.* Lewiston, N.Y.: Edwin Mellen Press, 2002.

Magalaner, Marvin. "Louise Erdrich: Of Cars, Time, and the River." In *American Women Writing Fiction: Memory, Identity, Family, Space,* ed. Mickey Pearlman, 95–108. Lexington: University Press of Kentucky, 1989.

Manley, Kathleen E. B. "Decreasing the Distance: Contemporary Native American Texts, Hypertext, and the Concept of Audience." *Southern Folklore* 51, no. 2 (1994): 121–35.

Maristuen-Rodakowski, Julie. "The Turtle Mountain Reservation in North Dakota: Its History as Depicted in Louise Erdrich's *Love Medicine* and *Beet Queen.*" *AICRJ* 12, no. 3 (1988): 33–48. Reprinted in *Louise Erdrich's* Love Medicine:

A Casebook, ed. Hertha D. Sweet Wong, 13–26. New York: Oxford University Press, 2000.

Martínez Falquina, Silvia. "Beyond Borders: Trickster Discourse in Louise Erdrich's Fiction." In *Beyond Borders: Re-defining Generic and Ontological Boundaries,* ed. Ramón Plo-Alastrué and María Jesús Martínez-Alfaro, 139–56. Heidelberg, Germany: Carl Winter Universitätsverlag, 2002.

———. "From the Monologic Eye to Healing Polyphonies: Dialogic Re/Vision in Native American Narratives." *Revista Alicantina de Estudios Ingleses* 16 (November 2003): 239–53.

Maszewska, Jadwiga. *Between Center and Margin: Contemporary Native American Women Novelists: Leslie Marmon Silko and Louise Erdrich.* Lódz, Poland: Wydawnictwo Uniwersytetu Lodzkiego, 2000.

———. "Functions of the Narrative Method in William Faulkner's *Absalom, Absalom!* and Louise Erdrich's *Tracks.*" In *Faulkner, His Contemporaries, and His Posterity,* ed. Waldemar Zacharasiewicz, 317–21. Tübingen, Germany: Francke, 1993.

Matchie, Thomas. "*The Antelope Wife:* Louise Erdrich's 'Cloud Chamber.' " *North Dakota Quarterly* 67, no. 2 (2000): 26–37.

———. "Building on the Myth: Recovering Native American Culture in Louise Erdrich's *The Bingo Palace.*" In *American Indian Studies: An Interdisciplinary Approach to Contemporary Issues,* ed. Dane Anthony Morrison, 299–312. New York: Peter Lang, 1997.

———. "Collaboration in the Works of Erdrich and Michael Dorris: A Study in the Process of Writing." In *Approaches to Teaching the Works of Louise Erdrich,* ed. Greg Sarris, Connie A. Jacobs, and James R. Giles, 147–57. New York: MLA, 2004.

———. "Exploring the Meaning of Discovery in *The Crown of Columbus.*" *North Dakota Quarterly* 59, no. 4 (1991): 243–50.

———. "Flannery O'Connor and Louise Erdrich: The Function of the Grotesque in Erdrich's *Tracks.*" In *Papers Presented to the Linguistic Circle of Manitoba and North Dakota: 1989–1993,* ed. Harold J. Smith and Gaby Divay, 67–78. Fargo: Center for Writers, North Dakota State University, 1996.

———. "Louise Erdrich's 'Scarlet Letter': Literary Continuity in *Tales of Burning Love.*" *North Dakota Quarterly* 63, no. 4 (fall 1996): 113–23.

———. "*Love Medicine:* A Female *Moby-Dick.*" *Midwest Quarterly* 30, no. 4 (1989): 478–91.

———. "*Miracles at Little No Horse:* Louise Erdrich's Answer to Sherman Alexie's *Reservation Blues.*" *North Dakota Quarterly* 70, no. 2 (2003): 151–62.

———. "*Tales of Burning Love:* Louise Erdrich's 'Scarlet Letter.' " In *Telling the*

Stories: Essays on American Indian Literatures and Cultures, ed. Elizabeth Hoffman Nelson and Malcolm A. Nelson, 153–68. New York: Peter Lang, 2001.

McCafferty, Kate. "Generative Adversity: Shapeshifting Pauline/Leopolda in *Tracks* and *Love Medicine.*" *American Indian Quarterly* 21, no. 4 (1997): 729–51.

McCay, Mary A. "Cooper's Indians, Erdrich's Native Americans." In *Global Perspectives on Teaching Literature: Shared Visions and Distinctive Visions,* ed. Sandra Ward Lott, Maureen S. G. Hawkins, and Norman McMillan, 152–67. Urbana, Ill.: National Council of Teachers of English, 1993.

———. "Louise Erdrich." In *American Women Writers: A Critical Reference Guide from Colonial Times to the Present,* vol. 5: supplement, ed. Carol Hurd Green and Mary Grimley Mason, 131–34. New York: Continuum, 1994.

McKenzie, James. "Lipsha's Good Road Home: The Revival of Chippewa Culture in *Love Medicine.*" *AICRJ* 10, no. 3 (1986): 53–63.

McKinney, Karen Janet. "False Miracles and Failed Vision in Louise Erdrich's *Love Medicine.*" *Critique: Studies in Contemporary Fiction* 40, no. 2 (1999): 152–60.

McNab, David T. "Of Beads and a Crystal Vase: An Exploration of Language into Darkness, of Michael Dorris's *The Broken Cord* and *Cloud Chamber.*" [Concerning Dorris's influence on Erdrich.] *West Virginia University Philological Papers* 47 (2001): 109–19.

———. "Of Bears and Birds: The Concept of History in Erdrich's Autobiographical Writings." In *Approaches to Teaching the Works of Louise Erdrich,* ed. Greg Sarris, Connie A. Jacobs, and James R. Giles, 32–41. New York: MLA, 2004.

———. "Story-Telling and Transformative Spaces in Louise Erdrich's *The Blue Jay's Dance, The Birchbark House,* and *The Last Report on the Miracles at Little No Horse.*" In *Interdisciplinary and Cross-Cultural Narratives in North America,* ed. Mark Cronlund Anderson and Irene Maria F. Blayer, 73–88. New York: Peter Lang, 2005.

———. " 'Time Is a Fish': The Spirit of Nanapush and the Power of Transformation in the Stories of Louise Erdrich." In *(Ad)dressing Our Words: Aboriginal Perspectives on Aboriginal Literatures,* ed. Armand Garnet Ruffo, 181–204. Penticton, B.C.: Theytus Books, 2001.

McWilliams, John. "Doubling the Last Survivor: *Tracks* and American Narratives of Lost Wilderness." In *Approaches to Teaching the Works of Louise Erdrich,* ed. Greg Sarris, Connie A. Jacobs, and James R. Giles, 158–69. New York: MLA, 2004.

Medeiros, Paulo. "Cannibalism and Starvation: The Parameters of Eating Disorders in Literature." In *Disorderly Eaters: Texts in Self-Empowerment,* ed. Lilian R. Furst and Peter W. Graham, 11–27. University Park: Pennsylvania State University Press, 1992.

Meisenhelder, Susan. "Race and Gender in Louise Erdrich's *The Beet Queen*." *ARIEL* 25, no. 1 (1994): 45–57.

Mermann-Jozwiak, Elisabeth. " 'His Grandfather Ate His Own Wife': Louise Erdrich's *Love Medicine* as a Contemporary Windigo Narrative." *North Dakota Quarterly* 64, no. 4 (1997): 44–54.

Mitchell, David. "A Bridge to the Past: Cultural Hegemony and the Native American Past in Louise Erdrich's *Love Medicine*." In *Entering the Nineties: The North American Experience,* ed. Thomas E. Schirer, 162–70. Sault Ste. Marie, Mich.: Lake Superior State University Press, 1991.

Mitchell, Jason P. "Louise Erdrich's *Love Medicine,* Cormac McCarthy's *Blood Meridian,* and the (De)Mythologizing of the American West." *Critique: Studies in Contemporary Fiction* 41, no. 3 (2000): 290–304.

Morace, Robert A. "From Sacred Hoops to Bingo Palaces: Louise Erdrich's Carnivalesque Fiction." In *The Chippewa Landscape of Louise Erdrich,* ed. Allan Chavkin, 36–66. Tuscaloosa: University of Alabama Press, 1999.

Moreau, Michole E. "Erdrich's *Love Medicine*." *Explicator* 61, no. 4 (2003): 248–50.

Moser, Irene. "Native American Imaginative Spaces." In *American Indian Studies: An Interdisciplinary Approach to Contemporary Issues,* ed. Dane Anthony Morrison, 285–97. New York: Peter Lang, 1997.

Nelson-Born, Katherine A. "Trace of a Woman: Narrative Voice and Decentered Power in the Fiction of Toni Morrison, Margaret Atwood, and Louise Erdrich." *LIT* 7, no. 1 (1996): 1–12.

Neubauer, Paul. "Re-charting the Route Columbus Traveled." [Concerning *The Crown of Columbus*.] In *The Sea and the American Imagination,* ed. Klaus Benesch, Jon-K Adams, and Kerstin Schmidt, 252–67. Tübingen, Germany: Stauffenburg, 2004.

Orban, Maria. "Religion and Gender in *The Last Report on the Miracles at Little No Horse. European Review of Native American Studies* 17, no. 2 (2003): 27–34.

Owens, Louis. "Acts of Recovery: The American Indian Novel in the Eighties." *Western American Literature* 22, no. 1 (1987): 53–57.

———. "Erdrich and Dorris's Mixed-bloods and Multiple Narratives." In *Other Destinies: Understanding the American Indian Novel,* 192–224. Norman: University of Oklahoma Press, 1992. Reprinted in *Louise Erdrich's* Love Medicine: *A Casebook,* ed. Hertha D. Sweet Wong, 53–66. New York: Oxford University Press, 2000.

Pasquaretta, Paul. "Sacred Chance: Gambling and the Contemporary Native American Indian Novel." *MELUS* 21, no. 2 (1996): 21–33.

Peiffer, Katrina Schimmoeller. "Louise Erdrich: Seeking the Best Medicine." In

Coyote at Large: Humor in American Nature Writing, 80–114. Salt Lake City: University of Utah Press, 2000.

Pellérin, Simone. "An Epitome of Erdrich's Art: 'The Names of Women.'" *European Review of Native American Studies* 11, no. 1 (1997): 35–38.

Peterson, Nancy J. *Against Amnesia: Contemporary Women Writers and the Crises of Historical Memory.* Philadelphia: University of Pennsylvania Press, 2001.

———. "History, Postmodernism, and Louise Erdrich's *Tracks.*" *PMLA* 109, no. 5 (1994): 982–94. Reprinted in *Contemporary American Women Writers: Gender, Class, Ethnicity,* ed. Lois Parkinson Zamora, 175–94. London: Longman, 1998.

———. "Indi'n Humor and Trickster Justice in *The Bingo Palace.*" In *The Chippewa Landscape of Louise Erdrich,* ed. Allan Chavkin, 161–81. Tuscaloosa: University of Alabama Press, 1999.

Pittman, Barbara L. "Cross-Cultural Reading and Generic Transformations: The Chronotope of the Road in Erdrich's *Love Medicine.*" *American Literature* 67, no. 4 (1995): 777–92.

Prince-Hughes, Tara. "Worlds in and out of Balance: Alternative Genders and Gayness in the *Almanac of the Dead* and *The Beet Queen.*" In *Literature and Homosexuality,* ed Michael J. Meyer, 1–21. Amsterdam: Rodopi, 2000.

Purdy, John [Lloyd]. "Against All Odds: Games of Chance in the Novels of Louise Erdrich." In *The Chippewa Landscape of Louise Erdrich,* ed. Allan Chavkin, 8–35. Tuscaloosa: University of Alabama Press, 1999.

———. "Betting on the Future: Gambling against Colonialism in the Novels of Louise Erdrich." In *Native American Women in Literature and Culture,* ed. Susan Castillo and Victor M. P. Da Rosa, 37–56. Porto, Portugal: Fernando Pessoa University Press, 1997.

———. "Building Bridges: Crossing the Waters to a *Love Medicine* (Louise Erdrich)." In *Teaching American Ethnic Literatures: Nineteen Essays,* ed. John R. Maitino and David R. Peck, 83–100. Albuquerque: University of New Mexico Press, 1996.

———. "Karen Louise Erdrich." In *Dictionary of Native American Literature,* ed. Andrew Wiget, 423–29. New York: Garland, 1994. Reprinted as *Handbook of Native American Literature.* New York: Garland, 1996.

Quennet, Fabienne C. *Where "Indians" Fear to Tread? A Postmodern Reading of Louise Erdrich's North Dakota Quartet.* Hamburg, Germany: Lit, 2001.

Rader, Dean. "Sites of Unification: Teaching Erdrich's Poetry." In *Approaches to Teaching the Works of Louise Erdrich,* ed. Greg Sarris, Connie A. Jacobs, and James R. Giles, 102–13. New York: MLA, 2004.

Rainwater, Catherine. *Dreams of Fiery Stars: The Transformations of Native American Fiction.* Philadelphia: University of Pennsylvania Press, 1999.

―――. "Ethnic Signs in Erdrich's *Tracks* and *The Bingo Palace*." In *The Chippewa Landscape of Louise Erdrich,* ed. Allan Chavkin, 144–60. Tuscaloosa: University of Alabama Press, 1999.

―――. "Reading between Worlds: Narrativity in the Fiction of Louise Erdrich." *American Literature* 62, no. 3 (1990): 405–22. Reprinted in *Louise Erdrich's* Love Medicine*: A Casebook,* ed. Hertha D. Sweet Wong, 163–78. New York: Oxford University Press, 2000.

Ratcliffe, Krista. "A Rhetoric of Classroom Denial: Resisting Resistance to Alcohol Questions while Teaching Louise Erdrich's *Love Medicine*." In *The Languages of Addiction,* ed. Jane Lilienfeld and Jeffrey Oxford, 105–21. New York: St. Martin's, 1999.

Rayson, Ann. "Shifting Identity in the Work of Louise Erdrich and Michael Dorris." *SAIL* 3, no. 4 (1991): 27–36.

Reid, E. Shelley. "The Stories We Tell: Louise Erdrich's Identity Narratives." *MELUS* 25, no. 3–4 (2000): 65–86.

Riley, Patricia. "There Is No Limit to This Dust: The Refusal of Sacrifice in Louise Erdrich's *Love Medicine*." *SAIL* 12, no. 2 (2000): 13–23.

Rosenburg, Ruth. "Louise Erdrich." In *American Novelists since World War II, Fourth Series,* ed. James R. Giles and Wanda H. Giles, 42–50. Vol. 152 of the *Dictionary of Literary Biography*. Detroit: Gale Research, 1995.

Rosenthal, Caroline. *Narrative Deconstructions of Gender in Works by Audrey Thomas, Daphne Marlatt, and Louise Erdrich*. Rochester, N.Y.: Camden House, 2003.

Ruffo, Armand Garnet. "Inside Looking Out: Reading *Tracks* from a Native Perspective." In *Looking at the Words of Our People: First Nations Analysis of Literature,* ed. Jeannette Armstrong, 161–76. Penticton, B.C.: Theytus Books, 1993.

Ruoff, A. LaVonne Brown. Afterword to *The Chippewa Landscape of Louise Erdrich,* ed. Allan Chavkin, 182–88. Tuscaloosa: University of Alabama Press, 1999.

Ruppert, James. "Celebrating Culture: *Love Medicine*." In *Mediation in Contemporary Native American Fiction,* 131–50. Norman: University of Oklahoma Press, 1995. [This chapter is a somewhat altered version of Ruppert's *NDQ* article, below.] Reprinted in *Louise Erdrich's* Love Medicine*: A Casebook,* ed. Hertha D. Sweet Wong, 67–84. New York: Oxford University Press, 2000.

―――. "Identity Indexes in *Love Medicine* and 'Jacklight.'" In *Approaches to Teaching the Works of Louise Erdrich,* ed. Greg Sarris, Connie A. Jacobs, and James R. Giles, 170–74. New York: MLA, 2004.

―――. "Mediation and Multiple Narrative in *Love Medicine*." *North Dakota Quarterly* 59, no. 4 (1991): 229–42.

Sanders, Scott R. ["Louise Erdrich's *Love Medicine*."] *SAIL* 9, no. 1 (1985): 6–11.

Reprinted in *Critical Perspectives on Native American Fiction,* ed. Richard F. Fleck, 265–68. Washington, D.C.: Three Continents Press, 1993.

Sands, Kathleen M. ["Louise Erdrich's *Love Medicine.*"] *SAIL* 9, no. 1 (1985): 12–24. Reprinted in *Critical Perspectives on Native American Fiction,* ed. Richard F. Fleck, 268–73. Washington, D.C.: Three Continents Press, 1993.

———. "*Love Medicine:* Voices and Margins." In *Louise Erdrich's* Love Medicine*: A Casebook,* ed. Hertha D. Sweet Wong, 35–42. New York: Oxford University Press, 2000.

Sarris, Greg. "Reading Louise Erdrich: *Love Medicine* as Home Medicine." In *Keeping Slug Woman Alive: A Holistic Approach to American Indian Texts,* 115–45. Berkeley and Los Angeles: University of California Press, 1993. Reprinted in *Louise Erdrich's* Love Medicine*: A Casebook,* ed. Hertha D. Sweet Wong, 179–210. New York: Oxford University Press, 2000.

Sarris, Greg, Connie A. Jacobs, and James R. Giles, eds. *Approaches to Teaching the Works of Louise Erdrich.* New York: MLA, 2004.

Sarvé-Gorham, Kristan. "Games of Chance: Gambling and Land Tenure in *Tracks, Love Medicine,* and *The Bingo Palace.*" *Western American Literature* 34, no. 3 (1999): 277–300.

———. "Power Lines: The Motif of Twins and the Medicine Women of *Tracks* and *Love Medicine.*" In *Having Our Way: Women Rewriting Tradition in Twentieth-Century America,* ed. Harriet Pollack, 167–90. *Bucknell Review* series vol. 39, no. 1. Lewisburg, Pa.: Bucknell University Press, 1995.

Scarberry-García, Susan. "Beneath Creaking Oaks: Spirits and Animals in *Tracks.*" In *Approaches to Teaching the Works of Louise Erdrich,* ed. Greg Sarris, Connie A. Jacobs, and James R. Giles, 42–50. New York: MLA, 2004.

Scheick, William J. "Narrative and Ethos in Erdrich's 'A Wedge of Shade.'" In *The Chippewa Landscape of Louise Erdrich,* ed. Allan Chavkin, 117–29. Tuscaloosa: University of Alabama Press, 1999.

———. "Structures of Belief/Narrative Structures: Mojtabai's *Ordinary Time* and Erdrich's *The Bingo Palace.*" *Texas Studies in Literature and Language* 37, no. 4 (1995): 363–75.

Schiavonne, Michelle. "Images of Marginalized Cultures: Intertextuality in Marshall, Morrison, and Erdrich." *Bulletin of the West Virginia Association of College English Teachers* [West Virginia Institute of Technology] n.s. 17 (fall 1995): 41–49.

Schneider, Lissa. "*Love Medicine:* A Metaphor for Forgiveness." *SAIL* 4, no. 1 (1992): 1–13.

Schultz, Lydia A. "Fragments and Ojibwe Stories: Narrative Strategies in Louise Erdrich's *Love Medicine.*" *College Literature* 18, no. 3 (1991): 80–95.

Schweninger, Lee. "A Skin of Lakeweed: An Ecofeminist Approach to Erdrich and Silko." In *Multicultural Literatures through Feminist/Poststructuralist Lenses,* ed. Barbara Frey Waxman, 37–56. Knoxville: University of Tennessee Press, 1993.

Scott, Steven D. *The Gamefulness of American Postmodernism: John Barth and Louise Erdrich.* New York: Peter Lang, 2000.

Secco, Anna. "The Search for Origins through Storytelling in Native American Literature: Momaday, Silko, Erdrich." *RSA Journal* [Florence, Italy] 3 (1992): 59–71.

Sergi, Jennifer. "Storytelling: Tradition and Preservation in Louise Erdrich's *Tracks.*" *World Literature Today* 66, no. 2 (1992): 279–82.

Shaddock, Jennifer. "Mixed Blood Women: The Dynamic of Women's Relations in the Novels of Louise Erdrich and Leslie Silko." In *Feminist Nightmares, Women at Odds: Feminism and the Problem of Sisterhood,* ed. Susan Ostrov Weisser and Jennifer Fleischner, 106–21. New York: New York University Press, 1994.

Shechner, Mark. "Until the Music Stops: Women Novelists in a Post-Feminist Age." *Salmagundi* 113 (1997): 220–38 [see especially 223–27].

Silberman, Robert. "Opening the Text: *Love Medicine* and the Return of the Native American Woman." In *Narrative Chance: Postmodern Discourse on Native American Indian Literatures,* ed. Gerald Vizenor, 101–20. Albuquerque: University of New Mexico Press, 1989. Reprint, Norman: University of Oklahoma Press, 1993. Reprinted in *Louise Erdrich's* Love Medicine*: A Casebook,* ed. Hertha D. Sweet Wong, 136–54. New York: Oxford University Press, 2000.

Silko, Leslie Marmon. "Here's an Odd Artifact for the Fairy-Tale Shelf." *SAIL* 10, no. 4 (1986): 178–84. Originally published in *Impact Magazine, Albuquerque Journal,* October 8, 1986, 10–11.

Silkü, Atilla. "Challenging Narratives: Cultural Mediation and Multivocal Storytelling in Louise Erdrich's *Love Medicine.*" *Interactions: Aegean Journal of English and American Studies* 13 (2003): 89–101.

Sims-Brandom, Lisa. "Smoked Jerky vs. Red Pottage: Native American Tradition and Christian Theology in Louise Erdrich's *The Bingo Palace.*" *Publications in the Arkansas Philological Association* 21, no. 2 (1995): 59–69.

Skow, John. "An Old Bear, Laughing Once Again: Louise Erdrich Examines the Cross-Cultural Muddle of the Indian Reservation." *Time Domestic* 143, no. 6 (1994): 1.

Slack, John S. "The Comic Savior: The Dominance of the Trickster in Louise Erdrich's *Love Medicine.*" *North Dakota Quarterly* 61, no. 3 (1993): 118–29.

Slethaug, Gordon E. "Centrifugal Writing, Multivocal Narration, Undecidability, and a Sense of the Past: Louise Erdrich's *Tracks.*" In *Postcolonialism and Cultural*

Resistance, ed. Jopi Nyman and John A. Stotesbury, 232–43. Joensuu, Finland: Faculty of Humanities, University of Joensuu, 1999.

Sloboda, Nicholas. "Beyond the Iconic Subject: Re-visioning Louise Erdrich's *Tracks.*" *SAIL* 8, no. 3 (1996): 63–79.

Smith, Jeanne Rosier. "Comic Liberators and Word-Healers: The Interwoven Trickster Narratives of Louise Erdrich." In *Writing Tricksters: Mythic Gambols in American Ethnic Literature,* 71–110. Berkeley and Los Angeles: University of California Press, 1997.

———. "Transpersonal Selfhood: The Boundaries of Identity in Louise Erdrich's *Love Medicine.*" *SAIL* 3, no. 4 (1991): 13–26.

Smith, Karen R. "Ethnic Irony and the Quest of Reading: Joyce, Erdrich, and Chivalry in the Introductory Literature Classroom." *Journal of the Midwest Modern Language Association* 35, no. 1 (2002): 68–83.

Stokes, Karah. "Sisters, Lovers, Magdalens, and Martyrs: Ojibwe Two-Sisters Stories in *Love Medicine.*" In *Approaches to Teaching the Works of Louise Erdrich,* ed. Greg Sarris, Connie A. Jacobs, and James R. Giles, 51–57. New York: MLA, 2004.

———. "What about the Sweetheart?: The 'Different Shape' of Anishinabe Two Sisters Stories in Louise Erdrich's *Love Medicine* and *Tales of Burning Love.*" *MELUS* 24, no. 2 (1999): 89–105.

Stookey, Lorena L. *Louise Erdrich: A Critical Companion.* Westport, Conn.: Greenwood Press, 1999.

Storhoff, Gary. "Family Systems in Louise Erdrich's *The Beet Queen.*" *Critique: Studies in Contemporary Fiction* 39, no. 4 (1998): 341–52.

Strandness, Jean. "When the Windigo Spirit Swept across the Plains . . . : Ojibway Perceptions of the Settlement of the Midwest." *Midamerica: The Yearbook of the Society for the Study of Midwestern Literature* 25 (1998): 36–49.

Stripes, James D. "The Problem(s) of (Anishinaabe) History in the Fiction of Louise Erdrich: Voices and Contexts." *Wicazo Sa Review* 7, no. 2 (1991): 26–33.

Sutton, Brian. "Erdrich's *Love Medicine.*" *Explicator* 57, no. 3 (1999): 187–89.

Tanrisal, Meldan. "Mother and Child Relationships in the Novels of Louise Erdrich." *American Studies International* 35, no. 3 (1997): 67–79.

Tharp, Julie. " 'Into the Birth House' with Louise Erdrich." In *This Giving Birth: Pregnancy and Childbirth in American Women's Writing,* ed. Julie Tharp and Susan MacCallum-Whitcomb, 125–40. Bowling Green, Ohio: Bowling Green State University Popular Press, 2000.

———. "Windigo Ways: Eating and Excess in Louise Erdrich's *The Antelope Wife.*" *AICRJ* 27, no. 4 (2004): 117–31.

———. "Women's Community and Survival in the Novels of Louise Erdrich."

In *Communication and Women's Friendships: Parallels and Intersections in Literature and Life,* ed. Janet Doubler Ward and JoAnna Stephens Mink, 165–80. Bowling Green, Ohio: Bowling Green State University Popular Press, 1993.

Thibaudeau-Pacouïl, Isabelle. "The Fragment, the Spiral, and the Network: The Progress of Interpretation in Louise Erdrich's 'American Horse.'" *Journal of the Short Story in English* 36 (spring 2001): 65–79.

Thomas, Trudelle. "Motherhood as Spiritual Crisis: Memoirs of Childbirth and Early Motherhood." [On *The Blue Jay's Dance.*] *A/B: Auto/Biography Studies* 14, no. 2 (1999): 273–91.

Towery, Margie. "Continuity and Connection: Characters in Louise Erdrich's Fiction." *AICRJ* 16, no. 4 (1992): 99–122.

Treuer, David. "Reading Culture." [On *The Antelope Wife* and Silko's *Ceremony.*] *SAIL* 14, no. 1 (2002): 51–64.

———. "Smartberries: Interpreting Erdrich's *Love Medicine.*" *AICRI* 29, no. 1 (2005): 21–36.

TuSmith, Bonnie. "Native American Writers." In *All My Relatives: Community in Contemporary Ethnic American Literatures,* 103–36 [see especially 129–32]. Ann Arbor: University of Michigan Press, 1993.

Van Dyke, Annette. "Of Vision Quests and Spirit Guardians: Female Power in the Novels of Louise Erdrich." In *The Chippewa Landscape of Louise Erdrich,* ed. Allan Chavkin, 130–43. Tuscaloosa: University of Alabama Press, 1999.

———. "Questions of the Spirit: Bloodlines in Louise Erdrich's Chippewa Landscape." *SAIL* 4, no. 1 (1992): 15–27.

Velie, Alan R. "American Indian Literature in the Nineties: The Emergence of the Middle-Class Protagonist." *World Literature Today* 66, no. 2 (1992): 264–68.

———. "Magical Realism and Ethnicity: The Fantastic in the Fiction of Louise Erdrich." In *Native American Women in Literature and Culture,* ed. Susan Castillo and Victor M. P. Da Rosa, 57–67. Porto, Portugal: Fernando Pessoa University Press, 1997.

———. "The Trickster Novel." In *Narrative Chance: Postmodern Discourse on Native American Indian Literatures,* ed. Gerald Vizenor, 121–39 [*Love Medicine* mentioned on 121–23]. Albuquerque: University of New Mexico Press, 1989. Reprint, Norman: University of Oklahoma Press, 1993.

Walker, Victoria. "A Note on Narrative Perspective in *Tracks.*" *SAIL* 3, no. 4 (1991): 37–40.

Walsh, Dennis. "Catholicism in Louise Erdrich's *Love Medicine* and *Tracks.*" *AICRJ* 25, no. 2 (2001): 107–27.

Walsh, Dennis M., and Ann Braley. "The Indianness of Louise Erdrich's *The Beet Queen:* Latency as Presence." *AICRJ* 18, no. 3 (1994): 1–17.

Wiget, Andrew. "Singing the Indian Blues: Louise Erdrich and the Love That Hurts So Good." *Puerto del Sol* 21, no. 2 (1986): 166–75.

Wilson, Norma C. "(Karen) Louise Erdrich." In *A Reader's Companion to the Short Story in English,* ed. Erin Fallon, R. C. Feddersen, James Kurtzleben, Maurice A. Lee, Susan Rochette-Crawley, 143–55. Westport, Conn.: Greenwood, 2001.

Winsbro, Bonnie. "Predator, Scavenger, and Trickster-Transformer: Survival and the Visionary Experience in Louise Erdrich's *Tracks.*" In *Supernatural Forces: Belief, Difference, and Power in Contemporary Works by Ethnic Women,* 52–81. Amherst: University of Massachusetts Press, 1993.

Winter, Kari J. "Gender as a Drag in *The Beet Queen.*" In *Approaches to Teaching the Works of Louise Erdrich,* ed. Greg Sarris, Connie A. Jacobs, and James R. Giles, 183–90. New York: MLA, 2004.

———. "The Politics and Erotics of Food in Louise Erdrich." *SAIL* 12, no. 4 (2000): 44–64.

———. "Refusing the 'Sovereign Territory' of Language: The Trickster Nanapush vs. a Storm of Government Papers." *Northwest Review* 35, no. 3 (1997): 115–24.

Wittmier, Melanie. "Erdrich's *The Last Report on the Miracles at Little No Horse.*" *Explicator* 60, no. 4 (2002): 241–43.

Wong, Hertha [Dawn]. "Adoptive Mothers and Thrown-Away Children in the Novels of Louise Erdrich." In *Narrating Mothers: Theorizing Maternal Subjectivities,* ed. Brenda O. Daly and Maureen T. Reddy, 174–92. Knoxville: University of Tennessee Press, 1991.

———. "Louise Erdrich's *Love Medicine:* Narrative Communities and the Short Story Sequence." In *Modern American Short Story Sequences: Composite Fictions and Fictive Communities,* ed. J. Gerald Kennedy, 170–93. New York: Cambridge University Press, 1995. Reprinted, as "Louise Erdrich's *Love Medicine:* Narrative Communities and the Short Story Cycle," in *Louise Erdrich's* Love Medicine: *A Casebook,* ed. Hertha D. Sweet Wong, 85–106. New York: Oxford University Press, 2000.

Wong, Hertha D. Sweet, ed. *Louise Erdrich's* Love Medicine: *A Casebook.* New York: Oxford University Press, 2000.

Woodward, Pauline G. "Chance in Louise Erdrich's *The Beet Queen:* New Ways to Find a Family." *ARIEL* 26, no. 2 (1995): 109–27.

Zeck, Jeanne-Marie. "Erdrich's *Love Medicine.*" *The Explicator* 54, no. 1 (1995): 58–60.

Index

38, 200; moving, 207, 278, 284; Sister
Leopolda's prophecy about, 216; stolen to
break spell, 93, 118, 331; stone, 37–38,
333; sweating blood, 361–62; weeping,
285; wooden, 360
Vision quests, 31, 219, 229, 324–25, 330,
348
Visions, 42, 247, 270, 363; of Christ, 116–17;
Clarence's, 118, 271; death, 106–7, 139,
170, 217, 286, 299, 342; dream, 45;
Klaus's, 339; Lipsha's, 328; Lyman's,
178–79; Margaret's, 60, 234, 257; Pauline's,
160, 191

Wahpeton, North Dakota, 13
Wake: at Roy's house, 54, 88–89, 119
Wars, 305; Cyprian in, 53, 120–21, 131,
366; effects of, 133, 140, 228, 261; effects
on Waldvogels, 157–58, 242, 257; Fidelis
in, 53, 131, 154–55, 193, 367; Gulf,
261; Henry Jr. in Vietnam, 21, 90, 228,
353; Little Crow's War, 39–40; Mauser
and, 195, 292, 294; Mauser and Fantan
in, 58–59, 151, 369; ogitchida and, 42,
321; Russell in, 23–24, 113, 311–12;
Waldvogel boys in, 55, 147, 168–69, 242,
367; wounds from, 23–24, 113, 121,
131, 261, 311–12. *See also* World Wars I
and II
Wealth, 28–29, 101, 114

Weddings: Fidelis and Delphine's, 132, 157;
Fidelis and Eva's, 148, 155; Frank and
Rozin's, 45, 108, 112, 115, 166, 212, 253,
304, 310, 337, 363; Jack's, 359–60; Sita's,
329, 355
Wheelchair, 24, 86, 136, 145, 206, 247, 312
Windigo Dog, 44, 212, 346–47
Windigo heritage (cannibalism), 252–53,
258, 262, 280; Shawano's, 96, 301, 320–21;
Shesheeb's, 264, 270, 324–25. *See also*
Cannibalism
Witchcraft: Fleur's curses, 106, 144, 273;
Fleur's spell on Sophie, 118, 160, 331;
Nanapush's, 268, 325; Pauline's spell on
Eli, 27, 143, 160, 285; Pillager curse, 140.
See also Love medicine
Wives, 34; beads traded for, 95; in blizzard,
110, 114, 142–43, 173, 361; and hitchhiker,
180–81; Jack's, 33–37, 109–11, 137–38,
141, 185, 187–89, 242–44, 359; Kashpaw's,
47, 158, 207, 231, 254, 299–300; multiple,
207, 295; Nanapush's, 139, 265, 346;
Simon Jack's conspiring, 92, 327, 350
Wolves, 318; attack by, 63, 92; Shaawano
daughter and, 100, 316–17, 319–20;
talking to, 65–66, 100, 183–84
World Wars I and II: in *Master Butchers*, 51,
53, 55, 154–55, 157–58, 367
Wounded Knee, 52, 55–56, 133, 258, 334,
368

About the Authors

Peter G. Beidler is Lucy G. Moses Distinguished Professor of English Emeritus at Lehigh University. He now lives in Seattle, Washington. Gay Barton is retired from the English faculty at Abilene Christian University in Abilene, Texas.